EARLY HISTORY OF JAMMU REGION

EARLY HISTORY OF JAMMU REGION

(Pre-historic to 6th Century A.D.)

(In Two Volumes)

(Volume -1)

Raj Kumar

Early History of Jammu Region : Pre-historic to 6th Century A.D.

Rs. 1800 (Set)

ISBN: 978-81-7835-768-3 (set)
ISBN: 978-81-7835-769-0 (Vol. 1)

Published in 2010 in India by
Kalpaz Publications
C-30, Satyawati Nagar,
Delhi-110052
E-mail: kalpaz@hotmail.com
Phone : 9212729499

Lasser Type Setting by: Rudra Computer Graphics, Delhi
Printed at : Young Art Press, Delhi - 92

Contents

List of Illustrations or List of Plates

Abbreviations

The following list of the standard abbreviations are used:-

A.P.	Archaeology of Punjab
A.H.I.	An Advance History of India
C.J.K.L.	Crafts of Jammu, Kashmir and Ladakh
Fig.	Figure
G.T.C.	A Glossary of the Tribes and Castes of the Punjab and North-West Frontier Provinces
H.S.I.	History of Science in India
I.H.C.	Indian History Congress
L.N.L.E.M.	Life Natural Library-Early Man
P.H.P	Pre-Historic Punjab
P.H.C	Punjab History Conference
P.L.J.R	Paintings and Lifestyles of the Jammu Region
R.T.	Raja tarangini
S.H.	Science in History
S.I.B.I.H.C	Selected Inscriptions Bearing on Indian History and Civilization
Tr.	Translation
V.I.	Vedic India
W.T.W.I.	The Wonder That Was India

Preface

This book entitled *'Early History of Jammu Region'* (Pre-historic to 6th Century A.D.) has been written in the interest of, to understand the basic concept of the '*History*' which is not away from the human history, it is always alive in the one form to another as a Supernatural Force which works for the humanity and its services like a *'Coolie'* or *Kulli* as a load-carrier of the whole world, but at the same time some fundamentalists forces having *'Brahminical Ideology'* either there is *Hindu, Sikh, Muslim* or anyother community, they have forgotten the *Father* who is a *'Creative Power'* since the earliest to the Pre-historic period of Indian History i.e., *'Baba Ravidas' 'Chamar by Caste'* having the part of the *'Natural History'* as stated by Pliny. Now, it is coming out in the forefront of the Indian Society in another form like Dr. Raj Kumar belongs to the same background i.e., *'Chamar'* as his *Jat* or caste. As this book entitled mentioned above, we have tried to explain that people of India belong to the Chamar category were not belong to an ordinary background, they had a big culture in the world since the time immomerial, but '*Brahminical Thinkers*', they have the criminal background because they do not believe to serve the society, they work for their own benefit, even they are not satisfy, because their living *mana* believe in the lust of power to dominate the innocent people of the *'Father'* having a simple background of the *'Nam'*. Now, the time has come to give a befitting reply with the stroke of a pen in their minds which have been polluted with the corruption, 'Power' and '*Status'* and forgotten the Father who took the trouble for 'Constituting the Law' as a force above the man i.e, 'Nam' who belonged to the '*Sudhra Family*' of the 'Scheduled

Caste Category' or 'Scheduled Tribe Category.' So far the contents of the book are concerned. They contain the facts and figure that without discoverying the '*Reality*', one cannot obtain the bliss of the *'Father'*, but modern historians like *ShriMalli, Irfan Habib,* etc. having their self-style tendency to see the *'Nature'* or *'God'*, which cannot be obtain in this way, but there is a natural bridges between the man and the God.There is an order in the physical world by the nature. Those who believe in the existence of God have no difficulty in answering the question putforth before death. There is simple answer the moral order of the Universal may be good or it may be bad, it ensures from Divine will. Man is bound to obey the God, who is maker and he must be obedient of God which maintains the moral order of the human life. But according to the Buddha the moral order rests on man and on nobody else. It is for this reason that the religion of the Buddha, Morality has been given to the place of God. Therefore, it is the duty of the man to maintain the moral order in this universe by obtaining the *Gurumantra* or *Madhumantra* as obtained by Mohammad Prophet from the Master of period of *Raj* or Vedic Family of the '*Nam*', wherefrom every religion of the world has been developed or originated. In the Brahminical literature this God is called by a variety of names *Guru, Prajapati, Ishwar, Allha, Brahma* or *Maha* Brahma. Those who believe in God describe him as a being who is *Omnipotent,* i.e., all powerful, *Omni-present,* i.e., he fills the whole universe, and *Omniscient* i.e. he knows everything. Therefore, *Guru* or *Nam* has the right in this universe to serve the society through *'Nam-Dana'* else is nothing. He is unknown and unseen. He is 'Creative Power' in the man itself, but it can not be realised without the meditation of the '*Nam*'. Dr. B.R Ambedkar has rightly expressed that "the centre of religion lay not in the relation of man to God. It lays in the relation between man to man. The purpose of religion is to teach man how he should behave towards man i.e. *'love'*. But Brahminical heroes having *'Sexual Love'* as a corruption to keep away from the moral order. How it is possible in the ' *Natural History* ', who loves with the moral values and to serve the society in positive manners. This attitude have been forgotten by the '*Brahminical Ideology*'. Therefore, from time to time, there was a movement in the history, which has been developed by Lord Buddha to Dr. B.R Ambedkar in different form sometimes by *Qutib-din-Aebik*, *Firoza Shah Tughalq, Akbar*, *Kabir, Nanak,* and many more in real form as a Divine Right on Earth. The books entitled '*History of the Chamar Dynasty*' and *'Encyclopaedia of Untouchables Ancient, Medieval and Modern'* are also have been based on the scientific history of the *Guru or Nam* and their background has been developed from the said text entitled. *'Early History of Jammu Region'* or based on

Bharatvarsha the story of the Great *Bharat,* once upon a time he was born in the region of Jammu and historians have been forgotten him in the form of 'Dr. Raj Kumar' who is working in the same pattern. Text deals with the bundle of facts related to this story to justify the readers that those works did not understand by the Brahmins of the society, it has been done by the *'Sudhra Family'* from the background of the *Ravidas, Valmiki, Ved Vyas, Kabir, Babar,* etc. which have been ignored by the Brahminical historians. They believe on the rite and ritual practise which left behind after the death of a Saint as their identity which were ignored during the life time by them. In this way, society was gripped by the 'Brahminical Ideology' on the basis of keeping educational manuscript in their own possession and became priest of the society and ignored the people on their occupation and called themselves we are the supreme of the society. Therefore, to teach a lesson of such a society, it is necessary to reveal the *mantra* of Guru *Ravidas,* who always defeated them, time and again, in this universe to regulate a 'New Society', on the basis of *Humanism* as a regular stream of life like Ravi and Chenab as his tributary places '*To Repeat The History Itself.*' There are rich sources of the *'Sudhra Family'* which help to compose a fresh book of the 'New Society' as composed by the said authors of the same background. To write down a true history, one must have to seek the blessing of 'Father' as a '*Nam*' on Earth and it is an historical fact that it is very difficult to the student of history to elaborate and to understand the historical values of life to compile the thesis. The natural process which kept by our forefather, we are again predicting the same values of life to regulate the life when there is a confusion created by the Brahmins in the society. It is our moral deputy since the time immorial to defuse the commotions of the life, to go for evolution from one culture to another in a very simple manner. Keeping in view, the above mentioned historical facts of the *'Nam'* or *'God',* one must have to go for the study of authenic history by adopting the real approach in the life i.e., *'Nam'* or *'Chamar'* or *'Kalma'.* Moreover, the area of Jammu Region was neglected by the modern historians that it is a backward and having no importance in history. But, it is lesson for those who neglected the importance of the areas having historically rich in culture and advancement in human history to '*Repeat the History of man itself,*' the future course of action in human life as '*Nam*' on earths.

Lastly, in the *'Introduction'* we have made an attempt to clarify the concept of the *Bharata* and *Mahabharata* i.e., belonged to very place of the Jammu region, where from the every event of history, was took place to called '*History Repeat itself*'. In the conclusion, we have given a brief survey of the historical facts in evolution form that in Jammu region one after the another

'Sudhra Dynasty' was established in Kashmir to control this area through the power of *'Nam'* as their *'Natural History'* which most of the historians deviated the historical facts in twisting manners, one after another event of history. Therefore, the '*History of Sudhra* is an '*Authenic History of the man*' and the 'History of Brahminical historians is 'Destructive One' and a problem creative.

Raj Kumar

Introduction

'Early History of Jammu Region,' since the *Rig-vedic* period, as has been, somewhat rashly dominated by the Brahminical thought for a period of number of years without any reasoning, but, on the contrary, *Sudhras* were advanced and complex one in this area, which had been developed[1] since the time of *Bahulochana* and *Jambulochana*[2]. *Bahulochana* attributed the existence of a fort known as *Bahu*, who was the son of a Raja *Agnigrabhah*[3] since the *Rigvedic* period. After his death his younger brother *Jambulochana* occupied the throne of Jammu for a very long period of the Indian history. (*See Plate I-A View of Bahu Fort-Jammu, Fig.1 Chapter I*).

The sub-continent of India, stretching from the Himalayas to the sea in English called *Samudra* in Sanskrit as a part of the *Sudhra* territory, is known to the Hindus as *Bharata-Varsha* or the land of *Bharata,* where *Bharat* was born, a King famous in *Puranic* tradition. It was said that he formed a part of a larger unit called *Jambu-dvipa,* which was considered to be the innermost of seven concentric island-continents which the earth, as conceived by Hindu *Cosmo* graphers, was supposed to have been divided the *Puranic* account of these insular continents contains a good deal of what is fanciful, but early Buddhist evidence suggests that *Jambu-dvipa,* was a territorial designation, was given to the area of the Jammu region as a nucleus name of this country, actually in use from the third century B.C. at the latest to begin with the Brahminical rule in India, and that was applied to the part of Asia, outside the China and Nepal, throughout which the process of the great Imperial family of the Mauryas made itself felt the name "India" was applied to the country by the Greeks[4] to the *Sudhra* rulers of this area. It corresponds to the "*Hi(n)du*" of the old Persian epigraphs already described in the previous study of the same author.

In this historiographical format India, i.e., *Bharata*, is timeless. The first man was born here. Its people were the authors of the first human civilization, the Vedic, which is the same as the *Indus-Saraswati*[5], of the Akhnoor. "The country that lies North of the ocean and South of the snowy mountains is called *Bharata*; there dwell the descendants of Bharata[6]." i.e., Jammu Region. In its centre, it was Mount Meru round which Sun, Moon and Stars revolved round Meru, there were four continents (*dvipa*), separated from the Central Peak of oceans and named according to the great trees which stood on their shores opposite to Meru. The Southern continent, on which human beings dwell, had a *Jambu* (rose-apple) as its distinctive tree, and it was therefore called *Jambudvipa* or the Region of the Jammu territory. Wherefrom the 'light' of the new events were took place as a change in human history. The Southern zone of this continent, separated from the rest by the Himalayas, was "the land of the sons of Bharata" (*Bharatavarsa*) or *India* as itself is meaning 'Light of the story' for the Civilizational Growth. *Bharatavarsa* alone was 9,000 *Yojanas* across, and the whole of *Jambudvipa* 33,000, or according to some sources 100,000 *Yojanas*[7]. The fundamental unity of India is emphasised by the name of *Bharatavarsha,* or the land of Bharatas, given to the whole country of the Indian Epics both *Mahabharata* and *Ramayana,* and the *Puranas*, and the designation *Bharata Santati*, or descendants of Bharata, applied to its people and mentioned the *Rigvedic* as *'Asikni'* two or three times in history of *India* as an Enligthing power of the *'Nam-History'*.

> *"Uttaram Yat Samudrasya*
> *Himadres chaiva dakshinam*
> *Varsham tad Bharatam nama*
> *Bharati Yatra Santatih."*
> (*Vishnu Purana*, II, 3.1[8]).

The geographical horizon knowledge of the early Aryans those might be used to live in India or in Jammu region, as we came to know from the study, was limited to the North-Western part of the Indian sub-continent discussed above i.e. *Saptasindhava,*[9] and the *'Word'* Bharata in this sense of a country is absent from the entire later Vedic period to begins with the 'Brahminical Ideology'. Only the theory of Mind not of the God. In the *Astadhyayi* of Panini (500 B.C.), we find a reference to *Pracya Bharata* in the sense of a territory (*Janapada*) which lay between *Udicya* (North) and *Pracya* (East[10]). It must have been a small region occupied by Bharat in the *Akhanda Bharat* or Bharata in the Hindutva Camp. The earliest reference to *Bharatavarsha* (Prakrit *Bharahavasa*) is found in the Inscription of *Kharavela* (first century B.C.[11]). Who lists it among the territories; he invaded the Jammu Kingdom, but it did not include Magadha, which is mentioned separatedly in the record of the ancient literature of *India*. The word may be refer here in a general way to Northern India exactly the Jammu Region, but its precise connotation has been in vague in Indian continents. Its huge geographical region is visualized by the use of the word in the *Mahabharata*, Ved Veyas (200 B.C to A.D. 300), which provides a good deal of knowledge about the geographical conditions of the sub-continent from the Deccan to the North. Among the five divisions of *Bharatvarsha* named, *Madhyadesa* (Panjab) finds frequently mentioned in the Ancient as well as in the Medieval Indian texts; in the *Amarakosa* (also known as the *Namalinganusasana),* a work of the fourth and the fifth centuries A.D., it is used synonymously with Bharata and *Aryavarta*[12] means the story of the Indian Aryans, the latter, according to the commentator of *Ksirasvamin* of the eleventh century A.D. being the same as Manu's holy land situated between the Himalayas and the Vindhyachal range[13]. But in Bana's *Kadambri* of the seventh century A.D. *Bharatavarsa* has been mentioned to have been ruled by *Tarapida,* who "set his seal on the four oceans" (*dattacatuhsamudramudrah*[14]); and at another place, Ujjaini is indicated as being outside the *Bharatavarsa*[15], which leaves its location far from clear the event of history far the time being. Similarly, in the *Nitivakyamrta* of *Somadeva* of the tenth century A.D. the word *Bharatiyas* cannot be taken into consideration to mean anything more than the inhabitants of *Bharata* i.e, *'Nam'* or '*Word'* or '*Chamar'*, which itself remains undefined[16]. It is the '*Inner Message*' or '*Inner Voice*' of the *Dalit* community. In the *Abhidhanantamani* of the Jain scholar Hemacandra of the twelfth century A.D. mentions that the land of Bharata is the land of *Karma* (*Karmabhumi*), as opposed by the *Phala* (*Phalabhumi*[17]) on the basis of *Karma* theory.

It was one of the geographical connotation that four *mahadipas* (*mahadvipas*) ruled by a *Cakkavatti* ruler of the *'Nam'*. It has been came to our knowledge that *Buddhas* and *Cakkavattis* were born only in the *Jambudvipa* area or only in the Jammu Region, whose people were more courageous, mindful and religious in nature than that of the inhabitants of *Uttarakuru*[18]. As per the description of the *Jambudvipa* of the Jammu region, *Uttarakuru* in the early Buddhist literature, they both appear to be identical in this region. However, juxtaposed with *Sihaladvipa* (*Simhaladvipa*= Sri Lanka). *Jambudvipa* as stands for India[19] or *Bharata.* Thus, the words of *Ashoka* as a *'Dalit King'* were used to mean the whole of his empire, which entirely covered the Indian sub-continent from Afghanistan to the Southern part of its peninsula[20]. In a sixth-century Inscription of *Toramana,* for instance, *Jambudvipa* occurs without any precise territorial connotation[21] i.e., Jammu. Similarly, the identification of *Jambudvipa* remains uncertain for the Brahaminical Ideology in the *Puranic Cosmological* scheme, because, they believed on the theory of minds not on the Cosmological Order is based on earth and thinks about the Heaven with the theory of Nature i.e., '*Nam*' or

'*Word*' or '*Chamar*' like Ravidas had the knowledge of this Universe. In this way or manners the earth is divided into four *Mahadvipas* as already mentioned above, *Jambudvipa* being larger than the others[22] territorial expansion from the very ancient period of the Indian history. In both these conceptions of the world, *Bharatavarsha* is at some places said to be the part of the Jammu Region and others two are also treated as an identical[23] part of the natural theory, not an artificial thought but a permanent thought of the Lord on this earth to moblise the world from one generation to another.

Study also reflects that since the time immemorial an Institute of learning was established there in Jammu Region, but historians of the modern time ignored this area. As it is well-known by the historians, an organisation called the 'Greater Indian Society' was found in Calcutta in 1926 with the objective of organising the study of history and culture of the Asian countries in which the ancient Indians supposed to establish a 'Great Colony of India', headed by Rabindranath Tagore. The scholars like P.C. Bagchi, Nalinaksha Datta and R.C. Majumdar (Susan Bayly), "Imagining 'Greater India' : French and Indian visions of colonialism in the Indic Mode[24]." In their perception *'Greater India'* included many Asian countries, especially *Burma, Java, Cambodia, Bali* and *Vietnam,* in which the ancient adventures will have to establish a colony of the great transmitted "high culture to a melange of unlettered primitives." Indeed, there were certain historical writer who know their comitment toward the Father for the establishment of a "Greater India[25]" on the basis of 'social justice' and 'equality' which Brahmins of the period could not provide to the *Sudhras* and the other Backward Classes.

According to the view of one scholar[26], the earliest use of the word 'Hindu' in a religious sense is found in the account of Hsuan Tsang, who tells us that the bright light of "holy men and sages, guiding the world as the shining moon,have made this country eminent and so it is called *in-tu*[27] (the Chinese name of India being *Indu*, Moon). But the religious affiliation, if any, of these "holy men and sages" remains unknown in this world, which hardly supports the view that Hsuan Tsang used the word *In-tu* (Hindu) in a specifically religious sense: indeed, the later Chinese pilgrim I-tsing questioned the veracity of the statement that it was a common name for the country[28].

In the study, problem demands a co-relation of the Vedic Age with the culture of the region. It involves the examination of the protohistorical date in relationship between the pre-Harappa and Early Harappa is noted from the settlements in the '*Sarasvati-Yamuna Basin*'. Several sites such as Siswal, *Mitathal, Banawali, Daulatpur, Mirzapur, Bhagwanpur, Balu, Kunal, Sugh, Hat Rakhigarhi,* etc. were excavated by the Archaeologists for obtaining cultural sequence and to solve the problem of the modern historians by establishing the evolution sequence of the cultural development in the following manners discussed as under:-

Period I - Pre- Harappan (Early Siswal) or Early Harappan Culture. C. 2600 B.C.

Period II - Harappan Culture (Urban) C. 2300 B.C.

Period II - Late Harappan and Post- Harappan Culture C. 1900 B.C.

Period IV - Painted Grey Ware Culture C.1100 B.C.

Period V - Northern Black Polished Ware Culture - C. 600 B.C.

The Vedic literature preceding the age of Buddha (C.600 B.C.)broadly falls into two period i.e. the Early Vedic and the Later Vedic period. The Early Vedic period corresponds with the early parts of the *Rig-veda,* which the Later Vedic period relates to the *Brahmins* and *Sutra* literature. The later Vedic period represents a more developed stage for the development of the Early Vedic Age.

The Early *Rig-vedic* period is characterised by a cattle keeping and barely cultivated tribal society dominated by war-lords; and the priestly class. The use of horse and charriots, copper artifacts, knowledge of silver and gold ornaments and the use of bows and arrows of the *'Nam'* marked in the life-style of the *Rig-vedic* Aryan elites. Their religion was polytheistic and community feasts were arranged on the occasions of sacrifices. The Later Vedic period was distinguished by settled agrarian society, rise of territorial states, cultivation of rice and wheat alongwith barley and cattle keeping. Technological change from one stage to another is noticed in the Introduction of *Iron Age.* The cultural growth is marked by the introduction of large scale sacrifices and the growth of monotheistic tendencies in the religion. But the end of the later Vedic period, they had almost reached the threshold of the second[29] phase of the Urban Civilization. Thus, the old *Avestan* is dated between C.1300 and 1000 B.C. and the *Rig-veda* has to be dated between C. 1500 and 1000 B.C. while the Indus Valley Civilization falls between the period of C.2500 B.C to 1900 B.C[30]. Thus, it is clear from the Archaeological Survey Report of India that the Vedic Age cannot be co-related with the *Indus Valley Civilization* or *Late Harappa or Post Harappa Culture*, because there was the advancement of the one culture to the another in different form as a civilizational growth in the human nature, one after the another race which leads towards the evolution in human objectivity.

As, we know that Panjab is the land of the Vedic Aryans about whom are Max Muller expressed 'on one on the earth can say for certain how old were the *Vedas*, 1000 B.C., 2000 B.C., 3000 B.C. or 5000 B.C., but the eminent Archaeologists of the World like Prof. B.B. Lal, Prof. G.L. Possehl, Prof. Mark Kenoyer, Prof. F.R. Allchin now feel that there is some likelihood that the Harappan Civilization and the Vedic Civilization were more or less contemporary going back to the 3rd millennium B.C. Even those remains of later phases of which are found at Harappa or the river of Ravi or *Iravati;* it is called the *Ravi-Hakra* Culture by the American excavators like Richard Meadow and the Pakistani Archaeologist like Rafique Mughal who excavated the site of Jalilpur near Harrapa on the Ravi or *Iroti.* There are several other sites also on the rivers like the *Indus* i.e., Akhnoor (Chenab), the Ravi and the Sutlej which take the antiquity of Dogra civilization in Punjab to the 4th to 5th millennium B.C.[31] Judging from the excavation of the Jammu Region at the site of Manda near Akhnoor, a double headed, metallic hair-pin fasioned on the Harappan pattern[32] to the female of the period.

However, this is also only a part of human history in Panjab, where the Aryan Civilization had to reside for a long period of the Indian History. Moreover, the hills of the Punjab region is, infact, the cradle of Primates who are supposed to be earliest stage of Ape-man of the remotest ancestors of humans. They are dated to 12 to 8 million years ago. The fossilized bones of several species of these Primates named *Ramapithecus, Sivapithecus,* etc., have been found in the Sivalika hills of the Jammu Region. It is significant to note that alongwith the fossilized bones of these Primates, these are the bones of animals of the contemporary period of the Indian society which are now completely extinct, the specimens of the said material are to be found in the Panjab University Museum Chandigarh[33].

In the study, we learn that the first *Ramapithecus* fossils (fragments of an upper jaw and some teeth) were discovered in 1932 A.D. in fossil deposits in the Sivalika hills of Northern India i.e., again in the area of Jammu Region. No significance, was attached to these fossils until 1960, when Elwyn Simon in 1972 A.D. of Yale University begin studying them and fit the jaw fragments together. Based on his observations of the shape of the jaw and of the dentition '*Word*' which he thought for the transitional of the Apesinto human form. Simon advanced the theory that *Ramapithecus* represented the first step in the evolutionary divergence of human form the common hominoid stock that produced modern Apes into humans form. Simon's theory was strongly supported by his student David Pilbeam, and it soon gained wide acceptance among anthroplogists to study the real history of the man which is based on scientific study that is *Chamar* or '*Nam*' of the '*Ravidas Culture*'. Our Supreme Father expects even more from the learned and the Brahmins. Every knowledgable person should imbibe this instruction of the Veds[34].

Notes & References

1. Zanaide-A-Ragozin; *Vedic India*; New Delhi, 1961; p.303 Henceforth referred as *V.I.* 1.

2. *Note*: Term *Babulochana* soothed of two words *Bahu+Lochana; Bahu* means repetition of the *'Nam'* during the time of meditation as the 'good deeds' while for the living man to satisfy him or her. (J.R. Puri & K.S Kak; *Sultan Bahu*; Punjab (India); 1998; p.17). The prefix *Bahu* means within the body and 'Hu' means 'God'. The name thus means 'united with God'. On the basis of *Bahu's* Persian book entitled *Aeen-ul-Faqr*, the author of *Manaqib-i-Sultan* writes, the name of *Bahu,* which with the addition of one dot under *Ba*, becomes *Ya, hu, Ya, hu* means 'O' i.e., called *'Infinite'* and is invocation through which Sufis as God for his mercy and grace. Term *Sufi* was used by the Aryan, a name signifying so much, if born by a person of a relative quality. Therefore, term, *'Jambu'* is associated with living *mana* or Mind Only, who has to qualify the 'Natural Law, i.e, '*Nam*' or '*Word*'. And, there is a common term between the two i.e. '*Lochana*' which is also composed of two words *Lo+ Chana* in both Dogri and Hindi, 'Lo' means 'Light' and '*Chana*' means *'Pati'*. Hence, 'Light' or 'Nam' is *Pati* (husband) of all. (Dr. Raj Kumar, *Paintings and Lifestyles of Jammu Region*. (From 17th to 19th century A.D.) Delhi; 2006; p.76. Hereafter discussed as P.L.J.R.
3. Term *Agnigrbhaha* which is composed of two words *Agni+grbhaha*; Agni has treasured up in the *Rig-veda* among the hundred of hymns, few indeed could be found that did not contain *Soma* allusion '*Word*' description, simile, epithet *man* to the absolutely literal and material nature of the original fire worship in Aryan India. And indeed, this is the view most explicitly expressed in this brief line. "*Agni* is Surya or Ravi, a source of light in the morning, Surya is Agni at night" will have been discussed in the first chapter (V.I. pp. 156, 161). *Grabhaha* means 'ego' which is destructive and 'Black Power' i.e., Brahmin, who used to believe (*Krishna grabhah*), who ruled over mind not on nature like *Sudhra*.
4. R.C. Majumdar, H.C. Raychaudhuri & K. Datta; *An Advanced History of India;* London; 1963 pp. 3-4. Henceforth referred as *A.H.I.*
5. D.N. Jha, *Looking for a Hindu Identity;* General Presidential Address; Indian History Congress, 66th Session, 28 to 30 January, 2006 Santiniketan; p.3
6. *A.H.I.*,p.7
7. A.L Basham; *The Wonder That Was India*; New Delhi, Reprint; 2003. pp.488-89. Hereafter discussed as *W.T.W.I.*
8. *A.H.I.*, p.7
9. *RV*, VIII, 24,27. In the *Rig-veda* term *Saptasindhava* was used by the Persian people for the people of India those used to live in the adjoining area of Indus. (*Vedic Index*, II, p.324).
10. *Astadhyayi*, IV. 2.113

11. D.C. Sarkar, *Selected Inscriptions Bearing on Indian History and Civilization;* Calcutta; 1965, I, no. 91, line No tenth. Hereafter described as *S.I.B.I.H.C.*
12. *Amarakosa,* II. 6,8, *The Namalinganusana: Amarakosa* of *Amarasimha* (with the commentary of Ksirasvamin) edited by Krishanji Govind Oka; Delhi; 1981; p.47).
13. *Manusmriti*, II. 22. According to the *Kausitaki Upanisad* (II. 13), *Aryavarta* was located near the *Kuruksetra* and on the east it is located near Allahabad.
14. V.S. Agrawal, *Kadambari: Ek Samskritik Adhyayan*; Varnasi; 1958. p. 188. *Kadambari,* edited and Tr. by M.R. Kale, Delhi; 1968; p.290.
15. *Ibid,* p.205; *Ibid*, p.311
16. *Nitivakyamrtam* of Somedeva Suri; *Prakiraka;* p.78.
17. IV. 12. *Abhidhana Cintamani,* edited with an Introduction by Nemichandra Sastri in Hindi Commentary *Maniprabha* by Haragovind Sastri; Varanasi, 1964, p.235.
18. G.P. Malalasekera; *Dictionary of Pali Proper Names,* II, p. 942, S.V. *Jambudivipa*
19. *Ibid, Mahavamsa,* V.13; *Culavamsa,* XXXVII. 216, 246.
20. *S.I.B.I.H.C,* p.1 line 2, no.2
21. *Ibid.* No. 56, line 9.
22. Pravin Chandra Jain and Darbari Lal Kothia, edits, *Jaina Purana Kosa* (in Hindi), Jain Vidya Samsthan, Srimahavirji; Rajasthan; 1993; p.9. note.1
23. D.C. Sircar; *Studies in the Geography of Ancient and Medieval India.* Delhi; 1960, pp.6& 8.
24. *Modern Asian Studies*; Vol.38, no.3, Calcutta; 2004. pp.703-44.
25. A. Bharati; *The Hindu Renaissance and Its Apolegetic Patterns,* Journal of Asian Studies, 29 (1970), p.276.
26. Arvind Sharma, *Hindu, Hindustan, Hinduism and Hindutva;* Numen, vol.49, 2002, pp.3-4.
27. *Si-yu-ki : Buddhist Records of the Western World.* Tr. by Samuel Beal, Delhi, 1969, p.69.
28. J. Takakusu, Tr; *A Record of Buddhist Religion as Practised in India And* the Malay *Archipelago* (A.D. 671-695) by I-tsing, Delhi, 1966, P.118.
29. Dr. Amar Singh; *Archaeology of the Vedic Age in Haryana;* Presidential Address in the PHC, 36th Session, March 18-20, 2004; Punjab University Patiala. pp.24-5.
30. *Ibid,* p.25
31. Dr. Arun Kesarwani; *Pre-Historic Punjab: A Reassessment (From the Dawn of Man to the First Urban Civilization):* Presidential Address, (Ancient Section) in the PHC 37th Session, March 18-20, 2005. PHC; pp.37-8.
32. P.L.J.R, Vol.II. p.470
33. Dr. Arun Kesarwani; Op.Cit, p.38
34. Pt. Shriram Sharma Acharya; *Divine Message of the Veds;* Mathura; Reprint, 2007, p.25

1

Pre-historic: Civilization of Jammu Region

Primitive Man of Jammu Region

Like Pre-historic man of Europe, Northern India was also experienced of the cold ages, which is known as the 'Second Intergalacial Period' of the Indian history from about 400,000 to 200,000 B.C. is still surviving in the Jammu region. There are the Palaeolithic pebble tools of the Sohan Culture so called from the little river of the Punjab[1], called as '*Ravi Culture*[2]' or '*Ravidas Cultural sites*'. It is interesting to note that the first human like Primate already mentioned, dated 9 to 12 million years before the '*Black Polish Culture*', i.e., the theory of mind called '*Brahminical Culture*', appeared for the first time in Punjab only during the period of historical culture in India or *Bharata.* In 1932, G.E. Lewis discovered the first historical origin of man in the *Siwalika* Hills of Punjab presently now in Pakistan a right upper jaw fragment of the human being which *analysis* by the various anthropologists that man's first ancestors of a single species which Lewis named it as *Ramapithecus, Punjabicus* in the human history. Thus : *Ramapithecus* was the first man, who became the hero of Hindu mythology, the incarnation of deity Vishnu, his work was only to collect the money from the historical traditions made by the philosophers not by the God. In the Greek word for '*Ape*' and '*Punjabicus*' is signified by the '*Pithecus*' in the part of the Indian history where from it was founded by the Archeaologists from time to time to construct an authentic history of the man with the references literally evidences of the areas as well as with numismatic study of the region. Later from the same collection lower jaw was identified by Lewis and named as '*Brahmapithecus*' having the similar story as Brahmins keep. While at the same time Elwyn Simons re-examined both the *lower* and *upper* jaw and found that they were fitted together as if of the same species. Thus, the name *Brahmapithecus* was dropped and *Ramapithecus* was retained forever in the life of human beings. A total of the some fifteen jaw fragments and more then forty teeth, represented perhaps twelve to twenty individual, were found by Professor Pfieffer in 1972[3]. In the Siwalika Hills of Northern India particularly in Jammu Region where they have been found in large numbers. The ages of the fossils (about 14 million years) fit well with the then prevailing notion that the ape-human split was took place at least 15million years ago. The first challenge to the theory of the human being was given by the "*Ravidas Culture*" in the late 1960's from biochemist Allan Wilson and Anthropologist Vincent Sarich, who at the University of California at Berkeley, had been compared the molecular Chemistry of albumins (blood proteins) among various animal species. They concluded that the ape-human divergence must have been occurred much later than the dates for the *Ramapithecus Culture,* similar to *Ravidas Culture,* and it is now thought that the final split was took place near about 6 to 8 million years ago[4]. In type, they resemble with the various tools widely distributed in all over the Old World, from England to Africa and China. In India no human remains have been found in association with the tools, but elsewhere such industries have been shown to be for the work of primitive anthropoid types in the area such as the *Pithecanthropus* of Java and China[5]. Thus, the first *Ramapithecus* fossils (fragments of an upper jaw and some teeth) were discovered in 1932 in fossile deposits again in the Siwalik Hills of the Northern India. No significance was attached to these fossils untile 1960, when Elwyn Simons (1972) of Yele University began study them for the historical knowledge of the human history and it has been found fit the jaw fragments together as God and man in human life. Based on his observation of the shape of the jaw and of the dentition of the small '*Word*' which he thought were transitional between those of apes and humans as '*Chamars*' of the world. Simon advanced in the theory of nature study that of *Ramapithecus* represented the first step in the evolutionary process in the human history which was divergented by Brahmins without logic and reasoning from the common hominoid stock[6] of the human race already mentioned above.

In the South, there existed another prehistoric stone industry, which is not conclusively dated, but it may have been the contemporary to that of the Sohan Valley. The men of this culture made cover tools, especially fine hand axes, formed by striking of flakes from a large pebble, and they evidently had much better command over their material than that of Sohan Valley men[7]. It is befitting to the history and culture of the Keral people with a special *focus* on

Malabar on this occasion. Malabar, the Northern part of Kerala (in some of the travelogues and other records of the Malabar, which depicted as the whole geo political area which later called Keralam) is a land of rich culture heritage of *"Untouchables"* or *Sudhras.* Spices, as for this land is concerned, had a descisive role in the shaping of political economy of the area which retains the culture of *Malabar*[8]. For the very ancient, Jammu and Kashmir is labouring under many disadvantages, with a large Muhammadan population absolutely illiterate in the context of labouring under poverty and very low economic conditions of living in "the villages and practically governed like Dumb driven cattle there is no touch between the government and the people, no suitable opportunity for representing grievances and the administrative machinery itself requires overhauling from top to bottom to bring them into the modern conditions of the efficiency which they have been forgotten in the very ancient period of the India history. It has at present little, or no sympathy with the people's wants and grievances. There is hardly any public opinion in the State both in Jammu and Kashmir. As regards the press it is practically non existence in the front of peoples '*Voice*', with the result the government is not benefited to that extent that it should be by the impact of healthy criticism.

In some parts of the world, however, the rhythm of the life has set its own pace and the gentle relationship between the people and nature has been maintained in the history of India 'A code of Gentoo Law' to rediscovered India. One such area is the State of Jammu and Kashmir, where the crafts reflect from the ancient period of the Indian history to modern man as a religious centre of the world resided to the uphill of the Panjab, in equal measure, its history and culture widely spread in whole of the world as a Buddhist of learning and was popularized in land scaping and the way of life[9] in life style as simple as saints of the period. Archaeological and historical evidence of the Neolithic settlements in Burzahom in Kashmir which were assigned to the period 2300 and 1500 B.C., indicate that these were the earliest inhabited areas of the valley. The Neolithic settlers made their pottery by hand in grey, dull red, brown, or buff with a burnished surface. The items consisted of dishes, bowls, funnel shape vases and globular pots and jars. Some pots have a mat-impressed designed which shows that grass mat, weaving was also carried out during the same period by the '*Sudhra Family*' of the working class. Tools such as mace heads and hand axes were made of stone and bone were prevalent during this period. In Jammu, evidence of primitive or *Mulnavasi* man is available from stone age tools and pottery unearthed at Akhnoor and *Ambaran*[10].

It is an established fact that from the time immemorial Kerala had contacts with the western countries through the coast relationship. Thus the reputation of the ancient Kerala was the land of spices brought the foreigners to this part of the country[11]. William Logan's[12] has rightly mentioned in his historiography of the *Malabar* that information of the areas based on geology, rivers, geography, fauna and flora, the people, and their economy a product of the innocent scholarship to reveal the traditional ancient history through the life of man. *Panchanam Mitra* makes a passing reference to the representations assigning them to the Early Neolithic on the basis of their comparability with the Mesolithic engraving at Ghatasitia in Chottanagpur. Thus, the people of Malabar raised their hands against such hegemonic forces from the very beginning of the Indian history. Kunjali, Marakkar, Syed Alavi, Syed Fazal. Pazhassi Raja, etc. epitomize the early phase of glorious anti -Colonial struggles not only in Malabar, but also in whole of the Indian territory. The National movement along with the peasant struggles in the South addressed various burning social issues to the Britishers colonists including question of land, feudal oppression, *Sati system, Purdha system, child marriage*, the question of caste and untouchability, education and more importantly, the absolute freedom of this land which Brahminical thought have been engraved with the power of money like Amitabh Bachchan, Big B, etc. Therefore, it is essential for the natural theories to give a solace to the poor people of the '*Father'*, the reason obviously cleared from the study of the primitive man's history.

It came to our knowledge that River Chenab has clear crystal very fast flowing water and spanning its bank like the fins of a whale as its debunchis from the hill down to the plains of the Akhnoor area of the '*Indus Valley Civilization*' or '*Indus Saraswati Civilization of Manda*'. Akhnoor is situated overlooking on the higher terrace of the Chenab River belonged to village Manda to third millennium B.C. The right bank of the Chenab River has the long history of the human beings more than 5000 years before this perod as per the Archaeological Survey Report of India is concerned. The left bank is plain and barren still has many of the Archaeological sites in her lap like *Malpur,* a Neolithic site (New Stone Age site) known as locally "*Pamdaran*" in the history Jammu Region. The Chenab originates from the Bara Lacha Pass in Himachal Pradesh at the height of 4891 meter above the sea level, has been considered as the source of the glacier fed perennial river. In the ancient time this river was called as *Asikni,* it has two sources one which flows down to South known as *Chandra* called *'Nam'* and that goes to North as *Bhaga.* About 26 km. further south from *Manali* (a tourist spot in Himachal Pradesh), a motarable road runs along with the river from *Khoskhas* to Tandi area. The *Chandra* and *Bhaga* meets at Tandi (2825 MSL) than called River *Chandrabhaga* at this point. It become Chenab, when it joins with the river Meru at Bhandera Kot 12 km from Kishtwar town. The river then travels to

Reasi, Salal, Mehara, Poonch, Atholi, Malhori, Peral, Ramban, Kautham, Indri Patan and *Mirpur, Khour, Kedha, Akhnoor, Rajouri, Nowshera, Sunderbani Jammu itself.*

All along the road the various offices and modern buildings in patches have encroached. The ancient fort of the Akhnoor town, now it became a picnic spot for the tourist as well. The Akhnoor fort has the glorious history of the ancient time as already discussed more than 5000 years back from this period. A proto-historic Archaeological site, a historic fort and a picturesquely located place is always away from the hustle and bustle of the Jammu City since the long period of Indian history, because, this area has the life cool pure and unpolluted due to certain historical facts, that it always provided pure water for the refreshing bath to the human history by changing the course from time to time. The high current of the river is dangerous for the good swimmer during the time of summer to across it. The river has served as the one of the famous trading ports in ancient times to cross it, i.e. *'Nam'* having a strong power to change the history as Gulab Singh *Barawala* in Hindi and *outcaste* called in English; was coronated over here and the history of Jammu and Kashmir was founded in the interest of human life. It might have been the ancient trading port and the source of transporting of pine wood and walnut peel used as teeth cleaner, which anchored before it could enter wooden logs and walnut peel which were transported through the force of water from the higher reaches to the low down as *Sudhar* did in their history. The border of the river which bound in conglomerate like the man made cementation which displays the geological formation about two Km, long after the river enters the plain on the outskirts of the Akhnoor near *Pambranvan* already mentioned above. The fast current of the River Chenab gives cold water in summer and extreme cold in winter. The colour of the water was changed[14] from time to time with the season as per the theory of nature i.e., sometimes, black, white, yellow, red, blue mixed with multi-contents of the earth and washed by the water from time to time with the pure water during the time of heavy flood to begins with the new history of the civilizational growth with the power of the *'Nam'* which is determined in the history of the human life. This is traditional history as recorded from the rivers and the streams as a source of the life in evolution by providing water of irrigation, drinking, washing of clothes, for the cooking of our meals, for the construction of houses even means of transport in ancient time. The two great rivers, i.e., Chenab and Ravi pass through the parts of the Jammu[15] region. This traditional story to form the history of the human being is also described in the *Puranas* and the *Brahminical* literature that flood supposedly occurred in many times in the life of man. As, we take the example of the *Puranas,* the descent of Manu's progeny to the Kings of the epic period *'Nams'* or *'Chamars'* were the Royal Heroes of the two great epics of India, i.e., *Ramayana* and *Mahabarata*[16].

Study also reflects that Early Harappan pottery found at Manda in *Akhnoor* in Jammu Region had added a new dimension in the history of India, because its pottery was became contemporaneous with the Indus Valley Civilization since the Harappan time as an Urban Civilization. The sequence of the pottery at Manda is similar to that found at Rupar, Bara and Banavail. These are represented by the dish –on-stand, beakers, bowls, jars and other proto types of Harappan pottery[17]. Earthernware is still very much in demand for human use particularly in rural areas of the Jammu region. Low priced and colourful day objects are used to store water, set curd, and cook vegetables and meat. A tiny rice bowl, *kenz* with a stand and high edges is designed so that children can beed themselves conveniently without spilling the grains of river [18].

Moreover, primitive historical pottery is represented by thin to thick red ware from sites of *Mabh* and *Pambarwan* in Akhnoor and Rajouri in Jammu Region. The manufacture of this type of pottery at Jammu is highlighted by the discovery of Archaeologists about the beautiful terracotta heads found at the Buddhist monastery at Akhnoor[19] near *Ambaran. (See Plate II Ambaran-A Buddhist Bastion Fig. 2).* Now the terracottas found besides, Lord Buddha's head, torso of bodies and pieces of drapery belonging to Lord Buddha figures or figures of monks and laymen and women propusely decorated by various parts of the decorative designs on the walls of the Buddhist monastry and Stupa at this place. These terracotta's are closely related to the terracottas of unearthed at *UshKura* (ancient *Haviskapura*) near Baramulla in Kashmir Valley and at Taxila in Pakistan[20]. There was a definite change in pottery making with the arrival of the Mughals, clues of which certain object were found on the banks of the river Chenab.

The potter has always been an integral part of the rural economy and still plays an active role in the large scale in the area of the Jammu State which are not urbanized at that time. While mind pots for staring water continue to be widely used in every village home, even aristocratic urban homes in Jammu use large earthern storage jars called *matha* lightly decorated and fired at high temperatures in simple backyard kilns, these vessels last almost a lifetime and are used for storing wheat, rice, sugar and pulses. They stand one metre tall and around 0.75 metre wide *Koll*, earthern grain containers with folk motifs and decorated pots and *Surahis* prominently display the Jammu potter's ingenuity in handlimg clay with perfect manners as an artist do. In this rural areas, mud pots were used both for cooking and storage. Standing almost 80 cms. high the storage *maths* contain wheat, rice and corn, were decorated by woman flok of the areas particularly, if they are given at present or received on auspicious occasions[21] to improve worth of the man in woman form. They are still slave under the theory of mind or *mana.* (*See Plate II. Akhnoor- A Historical Township. Fig. 3, and Declining Scene of Forest in Jammu and Kashmir State, Fig. 4*), a concept of deterioration of the eco-system of the areas.

In the study, it indicates that like pottery, stonewares provide indestructiable historical evidence of the human settlements not in the Jammu Region, but it was also have the evidence in various parts of India like Kashmir, Ladakh, etc. For example, the Neolithic people of Kashmir fashioned various stone tools which were unique in the context of the stone craft of India. Master stone carvers made delicate stone chisels for carpentry and potter's works, complex tools including the adze, axe, ring stone, grinder, as well as other tools to shape pristine cornelian heads of various shapes for jewellery. An outstanding stone panel from 1700 B.C. with engravings by detrous stone carvers (*naqas*) reveals the full drama of a Neolithic hunt. The carver faithfully depicts the interdependence of the elements of nature i.e., *'Nam'* or *'Chamar'*, animals and human beings represented by two suns,a *Hangul,* i.e., *'Nam'* and dog a *Brahmana* and a male and female [22]. Study demonstrates that traditional potter does not use a wheel in moulding the objects of the pot by hand, but a technique was used to make the pot through *matha,* which reflects the evolution of culture in complex form, because the natural simplicity of the surrounding is reflecting in the manner of his work as an artist by nature from the historical mind i.e., God and man. No doubt, stones have been frequently used in Ladakh at different occasion referred above to carve the human figure on rock faces or as votive offerings at cross-roads and other conspicuous places of the time. One can not miss the fine stone of carving *Maitreya* as per the Archaeologists Survey of India is concerned, the future Buddha, 12 metres high on a monolithic rock at Mulbeck or the Dyani Buddhas at Shey has been founded at this place. This portrayal of Buddhist manifestatious in stone is not an isolated phenomenon and indicates an early stone tradition during the time of '*Ravidas Culture*' mentioned above, it dependes on the maturity of the master carvers during the ancient period of our study. The long *Mani* walls all over Ladakh, capped with thousands of inscribed stones in variegated colours and shapes have engaged stone carvers for centuries. Carving turquoise for the ceremonial Ladakhi head dress, caps and other items from precious stones to the ordinary stones shaping the various ornaments which keep the traditional stone carver busy working at a height of over 3,500 metres above the sea level[23].

Paleolithic Man

The Earliest Stone Age tools, which the human beings made and used of the Paleolithic period are reported from the *Sivalika* Hills and *Chakapalwal* in Jammu [24] Region, Potwar Plateau of Rawalpini and other Districts of the Western Punjab. The stone choppers tools of the Early Man in a definite geological context in the Sohan Valley were first found by D. N. Wadia then by the late Colonel Tod and Helmut *de Terra* between 1922 to 1932. Definite presence of man is first noticed in the Boulder Conglomerate which forms the topmost surface in the *Indus*, the Sohan and other rivers. This was formed during the second galacial [25] period of the Indian history. The earliest human burials have been recorded from the Upper Paleolithic Cultural phase in *Bhimbetka* in Madhya Pradesh and some are found in Mirzapur District in U.P.

Long Stone Age tools or coppers were reported in East Punjab from the Sirsa Valley, the Beas and the Banganga Valley and the Ghagger Valley. Olaf Pruffer discovered Nalagarh in 1951 which is located on the river Sirsa, a tributary of the Sutlej in the foothills of the Shimla Valley. It is not very far from Ropar and from the Bhakhra Nangal Project, in District Hoshiarpur. Later D. Sen[26] noticed three terraces at the height of 70 feet, 40 feet and 10 feet respectively which yielded tools made of light coloured quartzite and consist of pebbles tools and flake tools of the Jammu Region which resemble the Early Sohan Valley of North-West of Punjab. However, highly advanced tools (scrapers and awls) not characteristic of the Early Sohan Valley have been found in this area like Jammu and Kashmir State as *'Nam-Culture'*. The upper and the lower terraces yielded stone tools of different kinds. The sites are *Dadhi, Palasi, Pirthan, Basawal, Dher-Majra* Malpada, *Bali Diawar, Choa, Malpur near Akhnoor, Bhud, Haripur, Baddi, Marhanwalla and Dhang* [27] areas. Later, Y. D. Sharma discovered more 'Late Sohan' tools of the Stone Age period from the same valley and from the another Sohan river, a tributary of the Beas, near Daulatpur.

The Ganges Valley is one of the nearest parts of the earth's surface and many geologists have believe that at time there were two Stone- Age Industries one was the *Jat* and other was the *Chamars* of a shallow sea called *Sudhras* or *Samudra* in Sanskrit, they may have been contact at the point of Rajasthan, for the tools of One Culture have been found sporadically in the region of the other, i. e, '*Nam*' or '*Ultimate Reality*'. The men who used these Paleolithic must have lived in India for many millennia in the form of man as a 'Reality on Earth' or the Representative Rulers of the '*Nam*' or God. Their blood may still flow in the inhabitants of Modern India, but if the pebble industry of Sohan Valley product was the work of the proto-human anthropoids; they must have vanished long ago, like the Neanderthal men in Europe and the *Pithecan thropi* of the Far East *Homo Sapiens* continued in India, his skill and techincal equipment imperceptibly improving down to the Ages. He learnt a fashion microliths tiny and delicate stone arrow heads and other implements, which have been found in many parts of India or (*Bharata*), from the North-Western Frontier to the extreme South of India. Similar microlithic industries occcure in many parts of the near East and Africa, but their chronological relationship with the microliths are often found there in the Industry of the '*Nam*'. In many parts of the Deccan microliths are also found together with Polished Stone like K. G. Balakrishnan, axes, and it would seem that in the remoter parts of the Peninsula their use was only fully replaced by that of 'Iron tools' or 'Iron Age' around the beginning of the Christian Era [28]. Prehistoric rock-art of the Jammu region as painting was discovered in 1867-68 by Archibald Carlleyle from Sohagi Gate and had assigned by them to the Mesolithic Culture. Cockburn had contributed scientific articles on the prehistoric paintings and his book on the Mirzapur paintings (1883, 1889) is the first of its kind from India, referred by P. Rajendran, an overview on Indian Mesolithic Culture. Superposition of layers is evident in Kerala painting which definitely prove different chronology in the execution colours used in the petrographs are pinkish brown, red ochre, yellowish brown, white, etc.

B. B. Lal [29] also reported Stone Age tools in District Kangra (*Trigarta*), Guler, Dehra, Dhaliara and Kangra itself. Five (Terrace-I to terrace 5) have been noticed in the Banganga Valley at Guler where unifacial stone chopper, bifacial chopping tools and two rolled hand axes have been found of the primitive man. Further explorations were also carried out in the Banganga Valley by H. D. Sankalia, R. V. Joshi, K. V. Soundara Rajan, etc., who collected chopper and chopping tools and observed the evidence of Quarternary Galacial movement indicated by huge granite blocks of T_3. Joshi discovered hand axes from Dehra Gopipur and Jwala Mukhi [30]. Chopper-chopping tools have also beeen reported from the area of Bilaspur in the Sutlej valley [31] of India and other areas of Gangetic Valley, *(See Plate V. Edged Cleaver, Polished Celt, Polished Shouldered Celt;* Figs 5, 6, 7.).

Further more, 16 sites have been reported from the Hoshiarpur frontal range: 21 from Ropar, 30 from Chandigarh, 6 from Gurdaspur and 3 sites from Naraingarh which have yielded the remains of Sohanian valley tools [32] as per the Archaeological Survey Report of India is concerned having the '*Chamar Culture*' *or 'Ravidas Culture'* which was preferred by the British India during the time of Mughals.

Term Paleolithic is derived from the two Greek words i. e., Old Stone. This name is applied to the earliest people of India, as it is evidence from the various rude stone implements furnished from the existence of the human life of the primitive man in the presence of undressed stones, chipped into various forms, which were originally fitted with handles made of sticks or bones of human origin. They served as weapons for hunting the wild animalş from time to time in the human history, and could also be used as hammers for cutting and boring the life of şuch wild person who do not believe on the '*Principal Thinker*', i. e., '*Nam*'. These chipped stones have been found in large numbers in different parts of India (*Bharata)*. They are usually, though not exclusively, made of species of hard rock already mentioned called 'Quartzite'. From this fact the palaeolithic men of India or *Bharatvarsha* are also known as "Quartzite Men[33]".

In the study, we learn that rough and rude stone implements which are the only records left behind by the earliest known inhabitants of India or *Bharata,* we can form only a very vague idea of their life and habits. It is obvious from the study that they were ignorant of any metals and made huts of some sort with trees and leaves. They lived in constant dread of wild animals like tigers, lions, elephants and the rhinoceros. They had no idea of agriclulture but lived on the flesh of wild animals of the *'Nam'* or '*Word'* such fruits and vegetables as grew wild in jungles. They could not make pottery and probably did not even known how to make a fire. In short, from the stand point of the *'Nam'* or *'Chamar'*, we can only regard from an animal life of the human life, little removed from an animal life. It is well to remember this if we are to judge from the "Archaeological Survey of India" that a right long strides of life that a man have made in developing the Culture and Civilizational[34] growth in the life of man. Where did man come from this question has preoccupied in human thought for thousands years in human history. It is responsible for a large number of myths and for many of the Worlds Religions, each of these grounded in efforts to explain the creation of the earth and of men. Many of these explanations are exceedingly interesting and beautiful in expression as per the knowledge of human mind, but much of their detail is no longer regarded as strictly as factual knowledge. Instead of that, there are number of reflection of the same story in the human's past history yearning to battom mysteries, but he could not possibly understand the fears of mind which often poetic attempts to construct a kind of theological pre-hisotry to satisfy his desire for good and moral world, i.e., *'Nam'* or *'Word'*. Man cannot get along without faith until and unless, one can not qualify him without *'Nam-Dana'* which is free of cost, there is no distinct between man to man even woman. 'He' is the highest 'ornament' of any great civilization of the world. It is the ethical system by which *'He'* lives in the Heaven and Earth. The strength of any such system lies in it ability as a 'Principal Thinker of the

World' to continue to serve as a moral force while adjusting itself to changes in man's knowledge with love and affection about the universe and his place in it is 'High'. He lands on Earth, time and again, for, on the one purpose to avoid the man from illusion of the *Maya.* The story of creation, as told in the Bible, is a fine case in point. Its simple, sweeping concepts are interpreted by most of the modern Christains and Jews as being symbolic of the spirit and Majesty of God[35] or '*Nam'*. One aspect of palaeoanthropology is that the branch of science deals with the study of Early Man, that puzzles the layman to understand the dates and fossils of the 'Stone Age Man'.

There is, no doubt, that almost all the sciences of this universe have contributed judging the past discoveries, particularly comparative anatomy, with their contribution to knowledge about the similarities; and differences between closely related organisms and at the very foundation, of course, geology which reflects to the modern man read the rich story with their right evidence, i. e., '*Nam*' or '*Chamar*' or '*Ravidas Culture*'

Neolithic Man

The capacity for progress is, however, an inherent characteristic of human beings were also found in the Jammu Region which distinguishes themselves from the wild animals. Consequently upon this, as years rolled by the men of the Neolithic period acquired a good deal of knowledge and skill in mastering the forces of nature in human life. The rate of progress from one civilization to another is, of course, difficult to estimate and it may have been hundred or thousands of years before a distinctly higer typer of Jammu Civilization was envolved in India. The men who belonged to this age are called Neolithic. This term drived from also two Greek words meaning 'New Stone Age'. The siginficance of this name lies in the fact that in this age also men had to depend solely on stone implements or slab of the '*Ravidas Culture*' and were ignorant of any metals like '*ar*' a skill to produce the '*Chams*' of the body, except gold. But their implements were very different from the Brahmans from those of the preceding age have discussed the various pots were made by the potters, for they used stones other than quartzite, and theses were not merely chipped, but in most cases 'ground grooved and polished' as well. The Akhnoor area of the Jammu Region has also reported the information of 'Neolithic Polished Stone Cells'. *Mohapatra* collected a few pieces of ring stones at Ror in Himachal Pradesh having close typological resemblance with Burzahom. Besides, Ror polish stone axes have also been reported from Dehra-Gopipur and Bawli in Himachal Pradesh[36].

The Neolithic sites excavation of Burzahom yielded evidence of the use of square, rectangular and cylindrical beads made out of various precious stones such as agate and cornelian have also been found in Punjab. Nineteen gold beads were also found in the later stages of the Burzahom settlement Although, the famons Neolithic sites are located in Pakistan viz; Kile Gul Mohammad, Jalilpur, Gumla and Mehrgarh. At present Mehrgarh is the earliest pre-ceramic Neolithic site going back to the 7th millennium. Kile Gul Mohammad is a pre-ceramic Neolithic site which witnessed a transition from food gathering to food production. Jalilpur and Saraikhola have yielded the remains of hand made pottery, microliths and boom tools. In most of the sites the Neolithic phase is followed by Kot Dijian of early –Harappan phase. Neolithic culture has also been reported from Kashmir Valley (Burzahom and Gufkar) having possible links with the Kotdijians and in Jammu Region as it demonstrated from the study of the exacavation of Akhnoor, reported Neolithic polished stone celts[37].

It shows that cooking of at extremely altitudes is a lengthy process in the areas of Baltistan and the heavy lid serves as a pressure cooker, lamps., frying pans, griddles and *chhang* pots in stone were earlier supplied via Nubra to China from a village named. Thukmus near *Siksa*. Serpentine stone of Zeharmora pot contains manganese oxide and ferrous which were believed to assist in the curing of many ailments were used by the Neolithic men during this period, cups, jugs and bowls of serpentine were, therefore, made by artisans of the period for both medicinal and utilitarian purposes. These were widely used in Jammu, Kashmir and Ladakh until recent times, when serpentine became rare and consequently prohibitively expensive[38] for the people of these areas.

The Age of Metals

In the study, it is delineated that there was a general agreement between the Old Stone Age to New Stone Age for the next stage of the Civilization which is distinguished by the knowledge and use of metals called as '*Iron Age*'. That the transition from stone age to *Metal age* was a slow and gradual process is proved by two undeniable facts viz., the use of stone and metallic implements side by side, and the close resemblance in the shape of Early Metal Age and Neolithic implements have no uniformity in the use of metals in different parts of India. Jammu is the most typical and traditional metal craft is casting of large vessels, particularly those used for cooking the meal during weddings and other festive occasions of the society. When factory made steel and aluminium utensils were still unknown, the entire village of *Badiyal Brahmana* in *Ranbirsinghpura* was engaged in this work and the harsh but rhythmic clash and clatter of metal casting and the repairing and beating of brass and copper deafened those who traversed the narrow lanes of Moti

Bazaar in Jammu City. In villages the *Gagar* was also used for storing the water, the *Baltoi* for cooking *dal* used during that period. The technique employed is the *cire* coatings of mud. It is then heated so that it poured out through an opening below. *Molten* brass is poured from the top into the empty space vacated by the wax. When it cools and solidifies, the outer covering of mud is broken away revealing the brass vessel. Vessel weight between 16 to 25. kgs. each and the the progress of time ago, a *Sagla* cost between Rs. 18 to Rs. 20 a piece few years before, while today, sold by weight a *Sagla* can cost up to Rs. 800, at Rs. 32 per kg.[39]

The use of metals in Kashmir dated back to the Neolithic period. A number of metal objects, including beads and arrow-heads, were found at Burzahom. Kashmiri craftsmen were equally great masters in lay work, as is revealed by various bronzes preserved in different museums in all over the world. Inlay work was often done the garments of bronze figures in order to create a rich surfact texture by 'Deepit Raj' son of Dr. Raj Kumar as the heros of '*Nam-History*' called *Chamars*. While the shape of these ancient vessels belongs to the Indo-Persian tradition as a whole, the decoration is usually of Kashmiri inspiration of God. Perhaps the most attractive and certainly the best items are produced in copper and the most ones included *Lota, samawar* and *Farsh tram.* The sun *Trampaila* is made in six styles the *Toor* in four and the *Kenz* in three sizes. Ornamental tumblers, *teliwar,* is *bandsoz, majma, chamcha* and lately *paila* nor and *bati chalan* have been added to the traditional items. These all items were used in the kitchen in daily life and including ladles in various sizes, dishes, bowls and water containers. The most important appliances for the manufacture of copper items included *draj, mekh, yandrewah, basta, thej, sheekh, gosheper* and *angus* in other parts of the world. The silver work of Kashmir was extremely beaut iful indicates some of the indigenous patterns of local styles, like the *chinar* and lotus leaf, were of exquisite design[40] found in the artifacts.

The production of a silver object involved into three stages mentioned above, '*Word*' preparing it, engraving it, when necessary, he cleanized the rude material and gilding it into the air. In all, about five categories of workers are involved in the process of history. They are the *Khar*, *Smith*, *Naqash*, *Engraver*, *Zarcob, Gilder*, *Roshangar, Polisher*, *Charakgar*, *Cleaner,* etc.

It is, however, important to remember that, unlike other countries, there are no traces in India, except in *Sindh (Indus),* of a Bronze period intervening between the Neolithic and Iron ages. Bronze, which is an alloy of copper and tin in general use, is harder than pure copper, and is doubtless better suited for the manufacture of weapons, but the Early man in India somehow did not make it the ordinary material for use. The few implements of this metal, that have been discovered in Jubbulpur, were, in the opinion of antiquarioans, either experimental or of foreign origin. And bowls and other objects, found in South Indian cemeteries, were simply articles of luxury meant for domestic purposes, and would hardly indicate the existence of an age when bronze tools were commonly used[41] by the labour class of the period.

Silversmiths used to prepare an alloy of pure silver and copper, '*Word*' four percent is roughly the quantity of copper added *Chamar* from which the object is hammered and given the required shape to the universe. Handles and other complicated parts were fabricated separately from one stage to another before they were joined to the main object of the life i.e. '*Nam*'. The item is then cleaned with sulphuric acid before it is passed on to the *naqash,* who fills it with lac to make the surface harder. This facilitates executing minute details in human history. The silversmith works with a hammer and chisel and engraves with a pencil. The lac is removed after engraving and the object was cleanised again. At this stage, engraving on one or both sides are done. The object is then cleaned a third and last time which involved an elaborate process of subjecting it repeatedly to fire and water, each time, they removed the impurities with brush. Finally, the object is rubbed with 'ruby' powder and then polished by the worker. If it is to be gilted, it has been passed on to the *Zarcob* and then to the *Roshangar* for polishing the object this job is done entirely by the master to protect the engraving on the surface of the object. In Kashmir, there are still *Mohallas* or localities like the *Rosnagar Mohalla* and the profession was carried down from one generation to another[42].

Study also demonstrates that the technique of decorating an object with enamel and a ground glass paste has a long history, it is an unending dialogue between the past and present. The enameling process of consisting of applying powdered glass to a metal base of either copper, silver or gold and fusing the two by heating the glass, coloured with finely ground metal oxides. Water is added to make a paste that is usually applied to the metal base with a brush. The ground is chased or engraved with the silver, or gold base in the process of new history of the '*Nam*' or '*Chamar*'. No doubt, in Kashmir enamelling is done on silver, copper and brass by fusing various metal and mineral substance. The metal is punched or repoused for enamelling. This is done by embedding various colours in the depressions or by painting the surface of metallic objects with fusible paint and then subjecting it to an appropriate heat which brings out the colour in a finished form. These colours included salicates, boxates, yellow through chromate of potmash, violet through carbonate of manganese, blue through cobalt oxide, green through copper oxide and brown throw red iron oxide. For enamelling copper, objects different shades of blue are most frequently used while a light blue is applied on silver. The enamelling done on copper and brass is more coarse and not translucent and althought it does crack easily it loses its luster with the aging of the metal. The patterns are punched, repoussed and the hallows thus produced are filled with a readily fusible glass paint. Traditional shawl patterns have been adopted and appear mostly on Vessels, *surahis,* trays and other items where enamelling is combined with gilding. Arabesque, Masaic and embossed styles are also used in India as per trade relation between the two with other countries. Every body knows, Kashmir was rich in a variety of clay eminently suitable to the potter's craft from the very ancient period of Indian history, which has been also practiced in the Valley since Neolithic period. The skillfully made utilitarian wares and their successive level of development can be traced at the Burzahom and Gofkar sites in Kashmir. The most significant achievement of the Neolithic period was the rough grey earthen wares with straw marks on it interior, found in the earliest levels of the structural complex, categorized as dwelling pits. This is perhaps the period in Kashmir was the emerging of pottery as a source of supplementing the economy of the Neolitic people. By 1700 B. C. the potter made systematic and steady progress in the Metal Age towards manufacturing different varieties of the earthen wares including jars, lids, feeding bowls, water pots and small vases '*Word*' all entirely hand made. The technique was to put kneaded *karewa* clay in layers around a mass which the potter intended to make, smoothening the surface with a piece of wood or bone and giving a final shape with a debber. This method continned for nearly a thousand years and it was only during the Megalithic Period that a variety of pots other objects were made mainly through the introduction of the potter's wheel. This happened around 1000 B. C. The wheel introduced greater plasticity in fabricating narrow and medium size pots, while maintaining traditional shapes made with more durable ingredients like stone and sand. The present day *math, dig, tsod* and other vessels are almost replicas of pottery objects used around four thousand years ago. Many new inventions in the early historical period led to the emergence of different medium-sized pottery. These include the dish on-stand which is bracketed with objects from the post –Harappan period found at *Bara* in the Punjab[43] in the form of '*Baba Gurinder Singh Biaswale*'.

From the early period of study, it is expressed that people of India were interested in fashioning vessels from baked clay for cooking, eating storage. Large brass vessels made of pouring molten brass into mud moulds is a dying craft of Jammu, was practiced by a handful of artisans. Here the worker rubs and polishes the *Sagla* after the outer mould has been broken away[44] for the study of human history. The Dards, grave site at Leh, Ladakh during the Gulab Singh period (1847-1857 A. D.), has yielded statues of the Neolithic period of Kashmir Valley. Clay statues at Alchi eloquently testified to the potter's talent in shaping various icons out of clay. In *Wanla,* near Leh, master craftsmen still produce large clay icons painted in bright colours for monasteries. The Ladakhi potter is among the most simple and primitive of artisans and earns his living by making the various mud bowls, jugs, tea kettles and braziers required in the peasant home. While in the plain of Jammu and in the valley of Kashmir the potter's wheel is used in Ladakh; potter still moulds his objects by hand, with the help of simple equipment made of wood, stone and leather or *Chamas.* Oil lamps and incense burners are often decorated with tiny eye lets arranged like a three-leaf clover. The local barley beer, *chhang* is stored in the *Zama*, a wide vessel, narrowing at the neck and opening again into a wide mouth. The most admirable clay item in the village potters repertoire is a large tea kettle complete with spout, lid and handle along with a brazir to the contents of the kettle warm[45] reported from the archaeological evidence of the period.

The great classical pottery period of *Harwan* and *Ushkas* is represented by extraordinary moulded tiles and terracotta heads unique in the entire repertoire of Indian art. Thus, in Early stages of civilization man had to struggle with nature to find out the truth. The land of India is one of those from the story of man's life began. Due to this civilization is known as one of the most ancient of the world called *Chamar or Indus.* The changing nature also attributed much to the making of this civilization successful and different races of the human history particularly *Sudhras* also helped in its rise[46] from the depression of Brahmins. It was not still centuries later that iron came to be known as Metal Age and gradually used as a substitute for copper. When we try to distinguish the period of Copper Age and the Early Iron Age in Northern India. In Southern India, however, the Iron Age immediately succeeded the Stone Age, and we find no traces of the intermediate of Copper Age. Bronze is a good substitute for copper. It is an alloy made up nine parts of Copper and one of tin and being harder than copper, is more suitable for the manufacture of tools and weapons. We find accordingly that in some countries in Europe a Bronze Age succeeded the Neolithic. Bronze implements of ealy date have been found in India along with those of Copper, but it does not appear that metal was ever generally used in India to the exclusion of copper. In other word, there was properly speaking, no Bronze Age in India. This provocative evidence from the Middle East tells an entirely different story from that total in Western Europe. It suggests an extremely varied gene pool capable of producing all kinds of individuals *'Word'* or *'Nam'* some with this more primitive characteristic, others with of *'Chamar',* but a gene pool of the same period that was unmistakably moving in the general direction of the modern man.

In the above, mentioned facts, it indicates that Copper Age and Iron Ages, we entered the limits of the historical period. It is a mooting point to decide whether the period of the *Rig-Veda or 'Word'* the earliest period of Indian history for which we possess written documents '*Chamar*' as his *Jat* belongs to the former or to the latter epoch. The general opinion is in favour of the view that the '*Iron Age*' had already commenced when the *Rig –Veda* was composed by Ved Vayas at Beas. Be that as it may, we have conclude now a splendid example of the Civilizational growth of the Copper Age to Iron Age as a development part of the human history to check the advancement of the people where they stand either on Scientific Knowledge or Bookish Knowledge which differentiate the Brahminical force and the *Sudhra* force. This civilization was flourished in the Indus Valley and spread over the neighbouring regions of the Jammu areas. It is known to the study as the Indus Valley *Civilization,* and merits a detailed treatment discussed above, in a view of its importance for the development of the man from one period to another period. But before taking it up, we must take certain few words about the race of India[47] i.e., '*Chamar*' or *'Schedule Caste'* who lead the world as Director of the world.

Race of the Ravi-Culture or Ravidas Culture

If we examine the races of India or *Bharata,* both according to physical and language, in the drawing time of Indian history, some where in the lands beyond Afghanistan and North of Persia roamed bold tribes of fair complexioned men and women of the *Ravi-Culture* or *Ravidas Culture* with their horses and cattle during the pre-historic period found in Jammu and Kashmir State including Ladakh. From stories that have come down to us about them, from words that they were used which have still place in our speech and language, and from rites of worship still observed by many of their descendants today something can be known of their life and thoughts. They were a rough, brave, hardy, adventurous race, of honest and simple soul. Some of them gradually limited their wanderings to Iron, the land of Persia. There they settled and there, they stayed, becoming the ancestor of the Parsis now in India and their speech became the old '*Zend Language*' that is '*Nam*' with its sacred literature[48] of *Devanagari* script. And, though much concerning them is obscure, not a little is evident and to-day, it is possible to look back across the many centuries that separated us from those nomads and learn what manner of men they were. As to other races like *Gujjaras* and *Bakarwals*. that were in the land there is little information in the hymns of the Aryans and the science of ethnology has to help us. From it, we learn that before the Aryans came India was sparsely peopled by some of the races of the '*Chamar Dynasties*' of Kashmir that they are now often called jungle tribes. Among them the majority would be Dravidians. The *Gonds, Bhils,* and *Santals* are modern survivors of those races [49].

We easily distinguish four broad classes.

1. The majority of high-class Hindu, who are tall, fair skinned and long nosed and whose language is drived from Sanskrit. These are known as Aryans or Indo-Aryans.
2. These people mostly living in the South-Indian Peninsula, whose features are some what different from those of the first group; and whose language is '*Nam*'. Tamil, Telugu, Kanarese and Malayalam '*Chamars*' are entirely different from Sanskrit. These are called by the generic name of *'Dravidians'* or
3. Primitive tribes living in hills and jungles who offer a striking contrast to the first category in physical type, being short in stature, dark-skinned and snub-nosed. Their langnages are also quite different from those of the preceding two, the *Kols, Bhil, Mundas* belong to this class.
4. A people with strong Mongolian features called *'Chamars'* or *'Dom'* beardless, yellow in colour, snub-nosed with flat faces and prominent cheek bones. These mostly live on the slopes of the Himalayas, and mountains of Assam. The *Gurkhas, Bhutiyas* and *Khasis* are striking example of the class.

The last two classes of people may be regarded as descendants of the Neolithic peoples. We have already referred that primitive type of Neolithic civilization does not appear like the 'Brahmanical Culture', these peoples have been made appreciable progress during the pre-historic period of the study as the labour class of human history. There is hardly any doubt that these primitive races at one time widely spread all over the world not in India, but they had to yield to the superior forces of the Dravidians, who gradually occupied some of their land for granted. The same process was repeated by the Aryans in later period. The effect of this invasion was not the immediate war, but it was the war of far reaching of 'Spiritual Knowledge'. Therefore, these cultured races must have been perished from the lower strata of the society. The last category of the race i.e., *'Chamar'* or '*Dom*' alone has preserved to a certain extent the physical feature. The languages and the habits of their remote ancestors offering us a fair glimpse of the sort of life. They must have led the peoples not to-day but from the very primitive stage of life as a race widely spread all over the world[50] *(See Plate VI. The Aryans Geographical Location, Fig. 8).*

Philological study have established a connection between these races of India and the primitive tribes that lived in Indo-China the Malay Peninsula and the Indian Archipelago. The German scholar Schmidt for example, holds that the languages of the *Mundas* and *Khasis* belong to the same family called

Indo- China. According to this view, these peoples, who were originally settled in India, "passed gradually to the east and South-east and traversed, at first the whole length of the Indo-Chinese peninsula connected to each other at one point i.e., progress, then all over the Pacific Ocean. " According to him, the Neolithic men of India played a dominant part in the Early History of South-Eastern Asia. But his theory has already been challenged by other scholars and can only be regarded as a provisional hypothesis [51] of the man. It is of course, possible to extract from the study that hymns infinitely more material '*Word*' or '*Nam*' mostly fragmentary from the primitive history of the man *Chamar* by *Jat* (caste) that we could attempt her for the reconstruction of Vedic life. This has been done exhastaustively by Prof. H. Zimmer, in his unique and most valuable work, *Altindisches Leben*, to which we refer the more inquring of our readers; with the remark, however, that he takes his material from all the four *Samhitas,* and therefore, represents probably a some what later picture of *Aryan Culture* or *Ravidas Culture* than that of which we have in this chapter,[52] striven to evolve almost entirely from the *Rig-Veda* alone[53] i. e., *'Nam'* or '*Chamar*'.

The Indus Valley Civilization or *Mulnivasi Identity*

The Northern most site of Chalcolithic period or the proto-historic site or Indus Valley Civilization or '*Indus Saraswati Civilization of Manda*' of the Jammu Region, is the *Mulnivasi Identity* of the '*Dogra Culture*' or '*Chamar Culture*' which could not understood by the *Brahminical Ideology* in the history of India, because of the partial attitude towards Father, i. e., *Ravidas*, a low caste rulers. Harappan site of *Manda* named after the village Manda has already discussed belongs to the 3rd millennium B. C. This Civilization of the *Indus* is known to the Archaeologist as the '*Harappa Culture*' which resembled to the '*Ravidas Culture*' from the modern name of the site of one of its two great cities, on the left bank of the *Ravi* in the Punjab In recent years Archaeological Excavation have been carried on at *Mohenjo-Daro* in the Larkan a District, *Sindh* and at Harappa, in the Montgomery district of Punjab. These smaller trial excavations at various other sides in Sindh *(Indus)* and in *Baluchsitan* have proved beyond doubt that some five thousand years ago a highly civilized community i.e,, '*Scheduled Castes*' or *'Scheduled Tribes'* flourished in these regions in the memory of Father or '*Nam*'. The antiquity of Civilization of *Bharatvarsha* i.e., India witnessed the growth of Ancient Civilizations in Egypt, Assyria and Babylonia. The Valley of the Indus, thus, takes its rank with the Valley of the Nile, the Tigris, and the Euphrates as having been contributed to the most ancient phase of the Human Civilization of which we are yet aware[54] of its advancement in the field of life.

Aarchaeological and historical evidence of the Neolithic settlements in Burzahom in Kashmir which are assigned to the period between 2300 and 1500 B. C., indicate that these were the earliest inhabited areas of the Valley. The Neolithic settlers made their pottery by hand in grey, dull red, brown or buff with a burnished surface. The items consisted of dishes, bowls, funnel-shaped vases and globular pot and jars. Some pots have a mat-impressed design which shows that grass '*Word*' mat weaving was also carried out during the same period. Tools such as mace heads and hand axes were made of stone and bone. In Jammu, evidence of primitive man is available from stone age tools and pottery unearthed at Akhnoor and Ambaran[55]. Thus, the *Harappa Culture*[56] i. e., *Ravidas Culture*,at least in the Punjab, was later in its beginnings than the village cultures, but it was certainly in part contemporary with the same culture mentioned above i. e. '*Ravidas Culture*'. These both culture reflects the mutual contact between each other in various aspects of life and some of the village cultures were also survived the great civilization of the prehistoric to the modern man. From the faint indications which are all the evidence we have, it would seem that the Indus cities began in the first half, perhaps towards the middle, of the 3rd millennium B. C. it is almost certain that hey continued well in to the 2nd millennium[57] B. C. Unfortunately undeciphered Indus script and lack of controversy on various aspects of the *Harrapan Civilization* including on the nature of its political organization i. e., '*Nam*'. The *Harappan Civilization,* in spite of some regional variations, reveals considerable homogeneity in the form of its town-planning and the use of distinctive seals and script, the universal style in pottery, the uniform weight-system, specialized arts and crafts of the areas, over a vast territory from Makran in the west to western Uttar Pradesh in the East and from Afghanisatn (Shotughai) in the North to Maharashtra in the South. It naturally raises a question as to what was the chief factor which lay behind this homogeneity over such a wide region, Archaeologist like Sir John Marshall thought that the '*Indus Valley Civilization*' of the '*Nam*' belonged to the period between 3250 B.C and 2750 B. C. It is the period when Egyptian, Babylonians and Mesopotamian Civilizations flourished. Recently the Indian Archaeologists using the technique of Radio Carbon Dating are inclined to believe that the period of Harappan Culture extended from 2500 B. C. to 1500 B. C. The Indus Valley Civilization was not confined to these two sites i. e. *Harappa* and *Mohenjo-Daro*. Mr. Sahni discovered the ruins of Harappa in 1921 and in 1922 Mr. Banerjee dug out the ruins of the pre-historic city of Mohenjo Daro. Ruins of these two cities showed that a rich civilization flourished in the country about 3000 B. C. the excavations were situated along the valley of the river Indus and its tributaries Historians named it "the Indus Valley Civilization" of the '*Sudhra Family*' of the Kashmir dynasty settled in Jammu itself called *Chamars* as their *Jat* (caste). The influence of this culture extended to the Punjab, Sindh, North West Frontier, Baluchistan, Rajasthan, U. P. Gujarat and even some parts of the South India. The Indus Valley Civilization was spread over an area of about 1600 kilometers from West to East and 1100 Kilometers from North to South. Historians are of the opinion that this civilization had spread over an area of 1,300,000 square kilometers which is more than that of any ancient civilization known so far. The other important sites are Chanu Daro in Sindh, Lothal near Ahmedabad, Kali Bangan in Rajasthan, Alamgir in U.P, and Ropar in the Punjab at the foothills of *Siwalik*[58] of the Himalayan States, i.e., Jammu, Kashmir and Ladakh regions. The excavation in 1958 of the mound locally known as *Pashurama-Ka-Khera* or *Bhim-Ka-tila* standing outside the twin villages of *Okhlina* and Alamgirpur, has revealed evidences of the existence of *Harappan Civilization* in this region, which attebts historical importance of the district and its historicity related to *Mahabharata* period[59].

It may be noted from the study that there are only around 250 sites on the Indus, there are about 1500 sites of the lost 'Saraswati' and its tributaries. As per the list provided by J.P. Joshi and others there are about 24 early Harappans, 35 Harappans and 128 late Harappan sites in present Punjab spread in the District of *Bhatinda, Sangrur, Ludhaian, Patiala, Ropar, Kapurthal, Jalandhar, Ferozpur, Hoshiarpur, Amritsar* and *Chandigarh* as compared to 103 early Harappan, 44 Harappans and 297 later Harappans sites in the present Haryana State. Several sites have also been reported from the Pakistani side of Punjab and Bahalwalpur Region. Sites in Haryana are well known, therefore, emphasis has been given to the sites located in East and West Punjab[60]. Mahenjo-Daro is the second city of the '*Nam*' or '*Chamar*' situated on the right bank of the Indus, some 250 miles from its mouth. As well as, these two cities at least three small towns are known, and a large number of village sites, from *Ropar* on the upper Satlej to Rangpur in Kathiawar. The area covered by the '*Harappa Culture*' or '*Ravidas Culture*', therefore, extended for some 950 miles from North to South, and the pattern of its Civilization was so uniform that even the bricks were usually of the same size and shape from one end of its to the other. Outside this area the village cultures of Baluchistan seem to have continued much as before[61] in the Prehistoric Period of the Man. The surrending region is wonderfully fertile and is called even to-day *Nakhlistan*, or the '*Garden of Sindh*'. Here, a city was built some five thousand years ago. This city was successively destroyed and rebuilt no less than seven times, the inundation of the *Indus* being perhaps the chief agency of destruction. The rebuilding did not follow immediately to the destruction, but sometimes the city remained in rains for a considerable period before a New City or Society rose up on them. Thus, after the foundation of New Society and City, among many centuries passed before it was finally abandoned and the rains of the said cities have now been laid bare [62], therefore, we have learn from the study that the gaps of such sites must be filled with the destructive material of the '*Nam*' i.e, '*Man*' or Brahmins. Or the inhabitants of the Indus Valley, whose great wealth must have induced the wild tribes from the hills to attack were invaded and put to the sword. Groups of skeletons, including those of women and children, have been discovered, some in a big room, other at the foot of the staircase leading down to a well, and other again in a street. All this suggests that they met a vident death '*Word*' or '*Nam*' now a forgotten tragedy or, else, the conquering of Aryans or some other tribes from outside India, might have sacked Mohenjodors and destroyed its civilization [63]. The destruction of this civilization, i.e., Indus Valley may have been discovered from the following basins discussed as under :-

Harappa or the Ravi Basin Survey of the Indus Valley Civilization

The site is located on the ancient bed of the river Ravi (*Iravati*), a tributary of the Indus, some 25 km. West-South-West of the District town of Montogomery, now in Pakistani Punjab. It is made up of numerous mounds extending in a circuit of some three and a half miles. The site rose in places up to sixty feet. Twelve seasons of excavations were carried out at the site. Harappa contains a high mound on the western portion of the site and a lower mound i.e., '*Chamar*' with which large complex to the South has been emerged and to the East[64]. M.S. Vats conducted the excavations at this site between 1923 to 1934 and brought to light the remians of the Indus City. Wheeler excavated the site in 1946 at the defences, where Early Harappan pottery was discovered. The site was re-excavated by Dales and Kenoyer between 1986-89 and found a regular fortified settlement with massive mud-brick structure and houses of the Kot Dijians at Harappa, in Periods-1 and II. It preceded the mature phase and is dated to 3300 B. C. It was thus at least 600 years older than the first 'Mature Harappan' settlement evolved at the sites [65] as mentioned by Meadow & Kenoyer. The Early Harappans of Period -1 built mud-brick walls which were oriented in the same direction as walls of Period-II. Later in Period -II the Early Harappans constructed a massive mud- brick wall which heralds an important change in the Early Harappan settlement [66] of the Indus Valley Civilization as a New Discovery of the Father.

Study also reveals that majory pottery types included gloubular vessels, plain or painted with horizontal black bank band around the necks, disc and ring based bowls, flanged jars and lids small cylindrical cups,basins with slightly cordoned rim offering stand and a ringstand large mouthed, large mouthed basins with flaring sides and large vessels of plain ware. A number of postsherds are painted with black horizontal bands and cross hatched lines and 'concentric circles' deigns. Cord impressed horizontal line is also present on one postsherd. The motif of horizontal black band around the neck of the globular vases is very typical of Kot Dijjan pottery[67], which probably has been derived from the Periano Ghundai pottery, where this pattern exists in an earlier context[68] of the period.

Mature Harappan phase was represented by Periods 3A, 3B and 3C. Here Harappan baked architecture, square intaglio seals, terracotta bull figurines (legs joined) balck on red slip painted pottery, steatite and faience beads and pointed based goblets. The ceramic and the associated artifacts confirm that there was no major hiatus or cultural break between the Early Harappan and Harappan levels[69]. Due to successive floods the Harappans constructed a tapering wall 45 feet wide at its base that was protected by a mud and brick band a fired-brick revetment. These walls made a rough parallelogram about 460 yards 214 yards, the long axis extending from North to South. Within this great mud –brick platform was raised in places up to 25 feet in height. On this were constructed burnt-brick buildings. The man entrance to the citadel was on the North, but on the Western side a bastion overlooked a series of ramps and terraces which led through gates till a final rise by means of a ramp or stairs to the platform. Other bastions were identified along the walls and suggest an effective system of defences. Three phases of construction of these 'defences' were noticed. Granaries were also traced out which were closed to the river bed which faced towards the river and thus could be supplied by river transport. The granaries proper were set on a pounded earth platform, about 4 feet high. Each house of Harappa was rectangular and measured approximately 55 by 24 feet. With a courtyard some 23 by 20½. feet in size, beyond which was a small room. Brick paving was used in these houses. The houses, though in lines, were separated and no sharing of a common house wall is indicated. Wheeler calls them he '*citadels*" of Harappa and Mohenjodaro. [70]

After a long gap American Archaeologists are re-excavating Harappa for the last more than 3 or 4 years and have found the remains of a culture earlier to the Early Harappans which they called it as the '*Ravi Culture*' or '*Ravidas Culture*' similar to the '*Hakra Ware Culture*' of Bahawalpur region found along the river Saraswati called Hakra in Pakistan. Now, this evidence has taken the antiquity further back to the 4th millennium B. C. and has proved beyond doubt that the Harappan culture emerged from the earlier culture flourishing at the same site thousand years before the '*Mature Harappan Phase*'.

Jalilpur Survey of Archeaologists

The site of Jalilpur lies about five kms, South of the left bank of the river Ravi at a distance of 78 km. South West of Harappa at present Jalilpur covers an area of 365. 76x 426. 72 m. with a maximum height of 4. 57m above the surrounding cultivable fields. The surface finds made it contemporary of Kot Dijin, Kalibangan-I. Pre-defence layers of Harappa, Thus, chronologically it belongs to the Pre-or Early Harappan period, assignable to the early third millennium B. C. The excavations were conducted by M. R. Mughal [71].

The following cultural sequence has been established:-

Period-I	Late Neolithic
Period –II	Early Harappan

Period-I

No substantial remains have been encountered in Period-I. However, the use of mud bricks and floors is attested from the study that the pottery is mostly handmade and includes thick textured and tempered pieces of globular vessels with exterior surface coated with a mixture of clay and pottery bits. This ware is called the '*Harka Ware*[72]'. A similar pottery is reported from Amri-I A and Saral Khola-I also. The pottery includes a few carinated cups, dishes and an abundance of potsherds of unrecognizable shapes. There are mostly of pale and red colour, light in weigth ad soft in texture as if unfired, bichrome wares painted black and brown or chocolate on red appeard at the end of Period-I and became frequent in the upper levels of Period –II. The other items include chert blades, net sinkers, bone points, clay beads etc. This phase is dated to mid-4th millennium B. C.[73].

Period –II

The Period –II of Jalilpur is Kot Dijian type. Mud –brick structures are reported in this phase. The painted pottery includes black-on red, black-on-buff slip or on buff body, black-and-white wares, globular shape vessels with grooved exterior, short neck and painted with simple black band on the neck and above the base are reported in Period-II. This shape has a wide distribution. The flanged vessels in knobbed wares are also found in period-II. The most characteristic pottery of Jalilpur–II is the so-called Sothi Ware. The combination of white and back colours and painted designs on pottery is already known to us from Klibangan-I and Siswal-A, Bansawali-I, etc,. This has been reported from Jalilpur-II. Black –on –red ware included tall and squat offering stand, interacting painted designs and open mouthed bowls, straight and wavy horizontal decoration in relief on the external suface of the so-called 'Periano Wet' of Khojak Parallel Straited Wares.[74] This phase is dated to 3300-300. B.C[75]. Mature Harappan phase is not encountered here.

Bannu Basin : Lewan Discovery

Lawan, Dre-Darez located 14 miles south of Bannu city, between the Touch and Lewra rivers was discovered by Peshawar and Cambridge Universities. It represents the Kot Dijian occupation. The site covers a vast area and tools such as axes, hummer stones, grinders and lunates, leaf shaped arrowheads or points, burines, srapers, bead, drill and blades, etc, in a variety of crypto-crystaline stones were collected. Serval finished and unfinished beads were also recovered. The ceramic assemblage belongs to Kot Dijian complex. Buffalo heads with *papal* leaves sprouting out between horns are noteworthly for the study.

Gomal Plain: Rehman Dheri Basin Excavation

The most important site is, however, Rehamn Dheri (lat 31. 50 N. long. 70. 54 E) situated about 14 miles North of Dera Ismail Khan and about a mile to the was of Dera-Bannu highway on the west of the river Indus. It is one of the largest sites so far discrovered in the sub-continent. It measures 1800X1300ft. and having a maximum height of 20 ft. from the surrouding plain. [76] Rehman Dheri clearly shows that this is a proto-urban site of the 4th millennium B. C. which has its initial settlement in 3500 B. C. The sites has yielded three major occupational periods Viz, Rehman Dheri Period –I (proto-Kot Dijin) Period –II (typical Kot-Dijin) and Period –III (evolved Kot-Dijin).

Aerial photograph of Rehman Dheri indicates that the sites was a fortified one. The layout and town planning based on regmented pattern was develcping in the Indus plain, but yet to achieve full maturity of Mohenjodarao[77].

Proto-Harappan seals and sealimg, besides an evidence for the Harappan writing have been found at Rehaman Dheri. From the earliest level comes an ivory seal measuring 3cm x 2. 7 cm x 0. 02 cm. The size of the seal tends to be squarish like most of those from Mohenjodaro and Harappa. The seal is carved on both sides showing two mountain goats and a symbol of T, 1 and a on one side and two scorpions, a frog and a T symbol on the other side. Although, the animals shown on the Harappans seals are different seals are different the symbols depicted here are those used in Harappan writing. It may be pointed out that even if the symbols were different from those on Harappan seals, the very idea of having animals along with symbols indicates an elements of continuity from the proto-Harappan phase to the mature period of Indus Civilizatio.[78]

A vast number of vessels fom Rehman Dheri show certain symbols, These were either engraved near the bases or painted below the rims. Some examples of these also occur on the ceramics from Sarai Khola, Jalilpur, Kot –

Dijin early levels of Amri and Kalibangan, etc. and were referred to as 'Potter's marks.' Certain individual sign in group of two on pottery from the proto-Harappan phase may be parental to Harappan writing. One composite symbol may perhaps be a combination of five Harappan symbols which may suggest that composition of writing was already taking place in the proto-Harappan period. Perhaps these groups of symbols provided a base for Harappan writing[79] script, not believes on the original script of the period that is '*Nam*'[80].

Gumla Basin Discovery

The site is named after the neighbouring village of Gumla. The mound is situated a few metres away from the main road on it northern side about 7-8 km. From Dera Ismail Khan on the dried up bed of the river Gomal, a tributary of the river Indus. Rehman Dheri is hardly 8 km. to the North-West of Gumla. Gumla appears to be a rural extension of the Rehman Dheri urban centre as described by Dani[81] excavated the site on behalf of Peshawar University and found six cultural periods, viz, pre-ceramic Neolithic, Chalcolitic, Kot Dijian, Harappan and two periods of later occupations. All these evidences clearly suggest that at this rural centre also there were periods preceding to the mature Harappan phase.

Sarai Khola Basin Discovery

The discovery of Sarai Khola has extended the history of the Gandhara region. It was earlier belived that this area had no prehistoric settlements. The site is situated about 2.5 km South –West of the Bhir mound the earlier city site of Taxia. It measures 609.6 m north-south and 304.8 m east-west. The excavations conducted from 1964 to 1972 have revealed four main periods, viz., Period-I (Late Neolithic), Period-II (Kot Dijian), Period-III (Cemetery – Iron using) and Period –IV (Early Medieval). The site has also proved beyond doubt that cultures antecedents to the Mature Harappan phase were present at the site[82].

Thus, the foregoing discussion utilizing evidence from the recent excavations of archaeological sites west of the Indus, strongly argues for a case, regarding the formative stage of Indus Civilization on the Indus plain. The proto-literate and proto-urban phase is fully attested at Rehman Dheri. These excavations also push the boundaries of the Indus Civilization to the Pak-Afghan boarderland.

Evidence East of the Indus: In Indian Punjab

Ropar

Ropar was a Tehsil in District Ambala when it was first excavation in 1952 by Shri. Y. D. Sharma. Later after the partion of Punjab into Punjab and

Haryana it became a Distrct of Punjab. Finally, it came to be knowns Rupnagar which as per local tradition was its ancient náme. It is situated at a point where the river Sutlej enters into the plains. Two other sites Kotla Nihang Khan and Bhara are situated 3 km. south east and 8 km. south of Ropar respectively. Excavatons revealed a six fold sequence of Cultures which shows that Ropar was continuously occupied from early Harappan times going back to 3000 B.C. to 1700 A. D. it has been divide into six cultural periods.

In Period-I, the Harappans built their settlements with sun dried bricks, river pebbles and cut *kankar* stones. The structures are built in mud mortar. The typical Harappan object, bronze implements and utensils, chert blandes and weights have been found. The pottery shapes includes dish-on-stand, beakers, elliptical vase, flat beakers, perforated jars, etc, The cemetery of the Harappan contained faience & shell beads, bangles and Harappan pottery which were later destroyed by the PGW people. Two seals with Harappan pictographic scripte with out animals are noteworthy[83] discovered from the study.

Dhalewan Basin Study

Dhalewan (lat 300 I" 20: N. long 75;35: 45; E.) is situated in District Mansa, Punjab. It is about 30 km. North –East of district headquarters and about 7 kms. from the township of Bhikhi. The mound is presently located on the eastern side of the canal locally called drain which has been dug on the dried up bed of the ancient Sirhind Nallah. The site is 8 km. high and measures 81000 sqm. The site was originally explored by J. P. Joshi and Madhu Bala in 1984 and later eacavated by Madhu Bala and Vishnu Kant. About twenty five site of early Harappan and late Harappan periods in an area of approximately 1250 Sq. km in Mansa district shows that this area was a very important zone in the Harappan cuture area. The river *Ghaggar* or *Saraswati* and its tributaries was preferred by the Early Harappans and Harappan settlers because this was a more static river system than the Beas, the Satluj ánd the Ravi. The Sirhind, a tributary of the rive Gharggar was one of he most important lines of communication between Punjab and Rajasthan for obtaining raw material like timber, especially Deodar used as those construction material. This excavations conducted revealed three cultural squence starting from Early Harappa period to post-Gupta period [84] discussed as under:-

Period—I A Early Harappan pottery below the fortifications and over the natural soil. No structure.

Period –I B Fortified (mud brick) Early Harappan settlement with bastion (98X6 mts.) in the North –Western end. The settlement is found in the western side of the fortification. Mud –brick size 1. 2. 3. and 1. 2. 4 Sturdy Harappan ware, perforated jars and with Early Harappan pottery and all types of terracotta cakes.

Period – I C The entire settlement was newly planned. Two structural phases. The fortification of period –IB was also used. A circular kiln, two pots and multiple hearths found together with steatile beads near he posts and also from the post suggests an industrical area of making steatite beads. Cubical weigths of stone of red ware and grey ware, study basins of fabric D, monochrome and bichrome decorated pottery, large number of terracotta cakes, fainence and shell bangles, cubical stone weigths, parallel sided chert blades, beads of lapis lazuli, carnelian, agate, etc. and graffitti marks on pottery as mentioned by various Archaeologists.

Chandigrah Basin Survey Study

During the digging of a high–rise buildhing in Sector Chandigarh a Harappan cemetery was found by R. S. Bisht[85] and B.M. Pande[86]. Later a habitation site to the east of the cemetery under thick water-borne deposited was also located during explorations.

In the lower levels of the habitational areas some definable living surfaces with circular pits burned areas and in situ pots have been unearthed. According to Bisht[87], the pottery recovered includes 'Early Harappan, Harappan, Bara and Cemetery H types pots. From the little data available, it seems that the ceramic industry at the site includes pottery similar to that described here as Siswal-A., Mature Harappan, Siswal-B, and C, or "Late Harappan[88]. The Mature Harappan pottery included many of the typical vessel forms (S-shaped jars, perforated jars, bowls, etc.) and black-on-red decorative motifs. Four inscribed sherds were also located, two of these were definitely the examples of the Harappan script[89] described by B. M. Pande also associated with this site is a single grey ware pot with '*Word*' or *'Nam'* wide carniated waist, constricted and angular neck and outgoing rim[90] as '*Infinite* or 'Circular' in shape' which is comparable to some of the grey ware vessels associated with the Buzahom Period –II Culture of Kashmir[91] in India. Beads, bangles (oftern painted in back) bull figurines, toy-cart frames ad wheels, balls, dabbers and spindle –whols are noteworthy terracotta finds. Copper and faience bangles and beads of steatite and agate have also been collected from the site, Other metal objects (copper/ bronze) include rings, wires, rod, and a hair clasp i. e, '*Word*' or *'Nam'* of the Panjab area. Stone querns, pestlers and sling balls were also found. The habitation appears to have been devasted by a huge flood and covers the habitation and cemetery[92] to the areas.

Sanghol Basin Study

Sanghol locally known as *Uncha Pind* is situated in Tehsil Samrala of District Ludhiana. It is covered by the village which rises to a height of about

25 m. and covers an area of 300 sq. mt. The rural occupation of the site has been divided in to six periods elaborated as under :-

Sanghol –I A

The main distinguishing feature between Sanghol –IA and –IB is the presence of Mature Harappan material in IA. A limited number of Harappan sherds have been reported in the earliest deposits which decreases in frequency in the later stratum. The presence of Harappan pottery is difficult to distinguish, since the excavators also reported an absence of the characteristic painted motifs and vessels forms associated with this particular ceramic industry. The presence of Mature Harappan pottery seems to be defined by an eliptical vase, a dish-on –stand with the association of chert cubical weigth. Some soft fired wheel-made red ware have been reported which has a tendency to peel off similar to the OCP[93] mentioned by Shaffer.

Sanghol –IB

There are no straigaphic or cultural discontinuities to indicate any significant chronological break between Sanghol-IA and IB. No mature Harappan artifacts are associated with –IB. The pottery from –IB is said to represent a mixture of various ceramic traits, such as those associated with 'Cermetery-H' pottery and with the earlier indigenous non-Mature Harappan pottery of Sanghol –IA already mentioned above.

Bara Basin Discovery

Bara is situated 8 km. south of District Ropar and about 25 km. northwest of Sanghol. The Bara is 5 mts. high and has 14 stratigraphic units. Y.D. Sharma[94] feels that the occupational history of the site reflects that of a single Proto-historic culture which he has called Bara or- '*Word*' a late phase of the Harappan Civilization. The site was re-excavated by Sharma in 1976, who feels that the Baran site the Harappans at Ropar [95]

Y. D. Sharma[96] again compares all the pottery at Bara or Baran, except for the rare occurrence of Mature Harappan examples to that of Kalibangan – I, on the basis of motifs. However, he carefully notes that the vessel forms encountered at Bara are not similar to those of Kalibangan-I. Noticeable by their absence are the globular jars with short everted rims found at Kalibangan –I and at Kot Dijin. He[97] further qualifies this comparison with Kalibangan I, nothing that of the six so called 'Fabrices' found at the site, Fabrics A, C and E are absent. Rusticated slipped vessels (Fabric –B) occur, but without painted motifs, the gray ware (Fabric-F) is coarsr and undecorated and only Fabric-D (interiorly incised bowls) occurs at Bara as a comparable analytical category.

Objectively, it seems that the Bara pottery is distinct from that of Kalibangan-I and that its comparison with the latter ceramic industry has little analytical value[98] of the Scientific Study in the practical life.

Kotla Nihang Khan Discovery

Kotla Nihang Khan is situated about 3 km. South-east of Ropar. The mound has about 10 ft, of deposits and covers an area of about 50000 m^2 (12 acres). In 1925, the site was first discovered and excavated[99] by M.S. Vats and later by Sharma[100]. Modern habitations and cultivated areas are located directly on the site. No occupational sequence has been developed for the site. All the ceramics illustrated and discussed by Vats appear to be plain red ware jars characteristic of the Mature Harappan Civilization, Sharma found Bara type pottery at the site, especially in the mound's western areas. The ratio of Mature Harappan to Bara types ceramics is, however, at present uncertain. Sharma[101] in any case does say that Mature Harappan pottery account for 95% of the pottery recovered.

Dher Majra Discovery

Dher Majra is located about 11 km. north of Ropar City and is approximately the same distance from the sites of Ropar and Kola Nihang Khan. The site measures 106. 68 m 91. 44 m. in expanse and 11. 25 m. in height. It was excavated by O. Pruffer in the summer of 1951. Dher Majra is one of the smallest sites in the Punjab to have Mature Harappan artifacts, He excavated a total area of about 58 m. and defined two major Proto-historic occupation i.e., God and man.

Dher Majra-I

The lowest four stratigraphic deposits produced red wares which were of Mature Harappan types, but a few and others corresponding to what is called Siswal-B. Both decorated and undecorated Mature Harappan pottery is present. The characteristic vessel forms (bowls, jar and dish –on-stand) and typical black-on-red motifs (including fish and papal leaf motifs) indicated that it is definitely Harappan. A single sherd of the perforated jar was also found terracotta beads, toy cart wheels, gamesmen and marbles are reported from the site, but not identified in stratigraphic context. Terracotta triangular and circular cakes are noticeably absent[102] from the study.

Sarangpur Basin Study

Sarangpur is situated near chandigarh and excavated by S. B. Chaudhry. Blades, beads of semi-precious stones, clay and terracotta bangles were found at the site. Due to water logging the pottery appears to be ochre in colour. The pottery is said to be Early Harappan of Kalibangan[103] as in fashion.

Mahorana Basin Study

Mahorana is situation in District Sangrur, 8 kms. south-west of Malerkotla on the Nabha-Malerkotla road. It was excavated[104] by Y. D Sharma. Eleven layers have been noticed in a deposit of 3.10 mts. which has been divided into two periods i.e., Early Harappan and Baran or Late-Harappan, Period-I has been divided into two sub-period i.e., Period-IA and Period-IB. Layer 11, the lowest has yielded only Early Harappan pottery. They Bara pottery is less in percentage in the earlier phase, but it is dominant in the later phase[105] of the historical period of the Jammu Region for development of study for the future generation of the civilization growth in human history.

Rohira Basin Study

This site is situated at a distance of 14 km. north –west of Malerkotla in District Sangur. Excavations conducted[106] by Sharma yielded four cultural periods. The Early Harappan pottery with some Bara pottery of the earliest period. It was followed by Mature Harappan period which has yielded the remains of mud-brick fortification and mud-brick houses. It has, however, yielded the Early Harappan pottery along with mud bricks in the ratio of 1.2.3. It is likely that the bipartite wall was constructed by the Early Harappans who continued to live with the Harapparns [107] but this king of division has not been subsitantiated at any other site of the region.

Two sealing have been found at the site. One is an octagonal sealing which has impressions on all sides representing a standing human figure with a bow and arrow in hand and an effigy of a monster 'Word' standing in front and on top right there is a symbol of a rising sun. The second is a steatite square button sealing depiciting Swastika motif [108] in shape.

Terracotta triaqngular and oval cakes, beads, bracelets, shell faience and steatite beads, terracotta querns, pestles, cart frames and wheels are the noteworthly finds from Rohira[109] areas.

Besides tha bove several other important sites have been explored in District Mansa where Early Harappan and Harappan materials have been found. The important ones are Banglian-da-Theh. Lakhmirwala, Nai Wala Theh, Gurnikalan, Gurnikalan-II, Hasanpur-II, etc[110].

In short, at present state of our knowledge two things are clear 'Word' or 'Nam' first that the individed greater Punjab was the cradle of Civilization and second that for this not only the Siwalik Hills of the Jammu Region were responsible, but also the two large river systems '*Chamar*' the Indus as well as the *Saraswati*. While the former has yielded huge collections of fossils of the Primates, out of which the human species developed in course of time, the latter has yielding the archaeological remains of some of the great cities and township of the fourth and third millennium B. C. belonging to a civilization of the first urbanization in Indain history called variously as the *Indus Valley Civilization, Indus Civilization, Harappan Civilization* and recently the *'Indus –Saraswati Civilization* came into the existence of '*Chamar Civilization'* on the basis of Archaeological Data which show that there were in fact more sites on the Saraswati around 1074, than on the Indus, around only 268, recent studies have also shown the Punjab was also the home of the Earliest Human Culture, called the Palaeolithic or Old Stone Age Culture of the pebble tools called the 'Chopper-Chopping' complex found mainly in the Sohan Basins near Rawalpindi and the Beas and the Banganga Basin in the Kalka region and Kangra region. There are also several hand –axe-cleavers found along with these complexes in the Punjab hills. Punjab is also known for the Neolithic settlements of the early agriculturists datable to the fifth-fourth millennium B. C. Sites like Sarai Khola in the Taxila plains near Rawalpindi and Islamabad as well as Jalilpur near Harappa on the Ravi are only two of these several example are found of the '*Ravidas Culture*'.

Greater Punjab, spreading from the east of the Hindu Kush mountains in Afghanistan through the Indus and the *Saraswati Basins*, was also the cradle of the Aryan Civilization which gave to the oldest literary text of the Sanskrit language in the form of the Rig vedia. Recent researches, both archaeological and literary show beyond doubt that the Aryan Invasion theory was amyth, perpetuated by the colonial writers like Piggott and wheeler as has been amply demonstrated by the great American archaeologist George F. Dales in 1968, followed by other like the French author Michel Danino and Indian archaeologist B. B. Lal and historian Romilla Thapar who in one of her articles published in the Seminar agreed with Dales and others that there is archaeological proof of the destruction of the Harappan cites by violent means and that the massacre of Mohenjodaro was the myth as Dales has proved beyond doubt. In other words the Vedic Civilization and the Vedic Sanskrit were as much the gifts of Punjab of World Civilization as the Harappan or the *Indu-Saraswati Civilization* of Kashmir of the Jammu Region is equally important as other civilization of the world, was also the gifts of Punjab of the World Civilization of the '*Chamar* Dynasty' that the History of Punjab also enters into the arena of the Second Urbanization of the Early Historical period is well known from[111] study.

Study also demonstrates that the Early History of the Jammu Region also enters into the arena of the Second World Civilization co-ordinated with the Punjabi Culture from the Early Historical Period of the Indian history[112]. Literary output of the study was not restricted to the 'Law Books', but it was meant with the life of man of the globe. Grammars (*Sabads*) and its poetry and drama was extremely popular during this period. Contemporary *Kavya* (poetry) has survived in Tamil among the *Dalit* community, the outstanding poem being *Shilappatinam*[112] (The Jewelled Anklet) is sounding in the Supreme Court of India. *Kovalan*, a young, wealthy merchant falls in the love with a royal courtesan and neglects his wife, who is devoted to him. The poem ends tragically with the death of all three, but husband and wife are reunited in Heaven. A second poem, *Manimegalai*, was written as a continuation of the first, the heroine being the daughter of Kovalan and the courtesan, and an ardent Buddhist. Drama (*nataka*) has survived in the Sanskrit plays of *Ashvaghosha* and Bhasa. Now two playwrights could have been more different in the study of natural theory which oprated by the Father on the earth manuscripts of *Ashvaghosha's* plays, originally written in the first century A.D. were found in a monastry in Turfan (Central Asia) likely to be the Jammu Region. Both plays deal with Buddhist themes, one of them being a dramatized version of the life of Buddha and his works for the welfare of the public to teach them about the right path of the life. *Ashvaghosha* faithfully followed his rules laid down by *Bharata* in his 'Study of Dramatic Arts', *Natyashastra* (the *Natyashasrta* having a position in Sanskrit literature similar to Aristole's poetics activities). But *Bhasa's* writing a couple of centuries later has little use for these rules, because they had the '*Brahminical Ideology*', believed on caste, colour and creed. Therefore, Bhasa's plays are either based on incidents from the epics, the *Mahabharata* and the *Ramayana*[113], or are historical romances most of which depict the numerous exploits of the King Udayin of Avanti Bhasa wrote for the limited audience of the court circle like the national theory, whereas Ashvghoshas plays could well have been performed at religious assemblies, before a wider audience to clear the message of the Natural Thought for the benefit of the man. Moreover[114], five ancient caves of the *Pandava Rulers* at *Panchmarhi* Central Satpura ranges, is known as the Queen of *Satpura* for its spectacular beauty has been found in Hoshangabad District of Madhya Pradesh, dated back to 10,000 B. C. the *Pachmarhi* itself is derived from *Panch-Marhi* (five caves) believed to be abode of the *Pandava* brothers of the *Mahabharata* fame like *Dr. Raj Kumar, Deepit Raj, Amrit Bhardwaj, Ramyian Bhardwaj* and *Amrita Devi,* the mother of the scholar as a *Sudhra-Nurse*; for sometime during their exile, there is development of '*Brahminical Ideology*', do nothing get exchequer of the government job like *R. K. Chadha* and others. The valley which is home to tribal *Gonds* and *Korkus* has a maze of forest tracks apt for pleasent track by extract money from the government jobs. The cleanest, most airy of them is known as '*Draupadi Kuti*' *as* Pusapa Lata, wife of the author, and the dark one from the head and heart, the *Bhim Kothari* of the '*Nam*' as his mother. Archaeologists claim that these caves must have been constructed by Buddhist monks during the Gupta period of the ancient history in the 5th and 6th century A. D. but the belief were discovered from *Apsara* Vihar (Fairy Pool) and Rajat Prapat (Big fall) of the adventureous trekking in Kashmir during the recent study.

In the study, we also learn that many texts on Bharat has been written, but it is said to have been a part of *Jambudvipa* i. e., the Jammu region, which itself had an uncertain geographical connotation. This fantastic geographical scheme was not the only one. But in the *Puran* as *Jambudvipa* is described as a ring around *Meru*, separated from the next continent, *Plaksadvipa* by an ocean of salt. *Plaksadvipa* in turn forms a concentric circular *Jambudvipa* and so on to make a total of seven continents, each circular and divided from its neighbour by an ocean of different composition '*Word*' or '*Nam*' starting with *Jambudvipa's* salt ocean and wine, ghee, milk, curds ad fresh water respectively. This brilliantly imaginative picture of the world, which aroused the scorn of Lord Macaulay, seems to have been implicitly believed in later Hindu theologians and even the astronomers could not emancipate themselves from it, but adapted it to their spherical earth by making Meru the earth axies and the continents zones on the earth's surface [115].

It shows that the ocean of butter and seas of *Sudhra* dynasty of treacle race formed an effective barrier to the growth of a true science of geography. The seven continents can not in any way have been related to actual portions to the earth surface, through some modern students of the *Sudhra* Dynasty have tried to identify themselves as a parts of Asian Dynasty of a *Sudhra* Family of the '*Nam-History*', who used to reside in he peripherial are of the Jammu Region laying between the *Sindhu or Vitasta* river near the *Indus* and it was than difficult to the foreigner travellers to find out the exact practical geography in writing the history of India (*Bharata*). The astronomers gave fairly accurate longitude of important places in India [116] which had the wonderful history of the area which have been neglected by modern historians like Irfan Habib, *Shri Mali*, etc. So far the connotation of term *Jambudvipa is* concerned, it is composed of three words, *Jam-bu-dvipa, Jam,* a *Sindhi* title, meaning Chief or Headman, given the people who used to live before the '*Sudhra Dynasty*' during the pre-historic period of the Indian history '*bu*' already elaborated in the 'Introduction' means associated with God, and *dvipa* means '*Light*'. It shows that at the same time, a Headman of the Punjab tribe was also born usually to a Sindhi origin i. e., to its migration from one tribe to another as Aryans of India displayed. In former times Sindh was denoted that the Valley of Indus River as far North as the Modern Mianwale [117]. In the early centuries of the Christain era Alexandria was known, perhaps no question connected with the ethnology of the Punjab people has been so much discussed as the origin of the so-called *Jat 'race* 'parallel to the *'Sudhra Dynasty'* working in this area. It is not intended here in by modern historians mentioned above to reprudce any of the arguments adduced in the historical study. They have been found in real picture in the *Archaeological Survey Report – I* [118] *and II* [119] *in Tod's Rajasthana*. In Elplinstone's *History of India*[120] and in Elliot's *Memories of Races of the North Western Provinces* [121] also mention the similar kind of concept in the Early History of India. Suffice it to say that both Sir Alexander Cunnigham and Colonel Tod agreed in considering the *Jats* race to be of Indo-Scythian stock. The former identified them with the *Zanthi* of Strabo and the *Jatii* of Pliny and Ptolemy and held that they probably entered the Panjab from their home on the Oxus very shortly very shortly after the *Meds* or *Mands*, who also were *Indo-Scythians* and who moved in to the Punjab about a century before Christ. There are vague references to the city of the *Ramakas* in astronomical works, but the geographical knowledge of the learned was of the vaguest description of the *'Nam'*. Even within Indian distances and directions as given in texts are usually very unaccurate and vague. The conquerors who led armies thousands of miled on their campaign to defeat the 'Brahminical Thinkers', the marchants who carried their wares from one end of India to another with the power of *'Nam'* and the pilgrims who visited sacred places from the Himalayas to Cape Comorin must have a sound practical knowledge of the Indian geographly, while that of the seamen belonged to the '*Sudhra Family*', who sailed the ocean from Socotra to Canton must have few echoes of this knowledge in the literature of the time.

But before the earliest Muhammadan invasion that *Jats* had widely spread into Punjab proper, where they were firmly established their power in the beginning of the 11th Century A. D. By the time of Babar, the jats of the salt range had been subdues by the *Gakkhares* of Kashmir called *Kokkhar*, *Awans* and *Janjus*, while as early as the 7th century A. D. The *Jats* and Meds of Sindh were ruled by a *'Brahminical Dynasty'*. Colonel Tod classed the *Jats* as one of the great Rajput tribes and extended his identification with the Getae to both races, but here Cannuingham differed from he, that he holds the view that Rajputs to belong to the original Aryan stock and the *Jats* to a late wave of immigrants from the North-West, probably of Scythian 'race' [122].

The Architecture of the Indus People

In the study, we learn that city is fairly a big. The architectual skills of '*Scheduled Castes*' and *'Schedule Tribes'* peoples came to be known after excavation at *Harappa* and *Mohenjodaro*. The people of this Civilization called '*Ravidas Culture*' had built dwellings ranging from one roomed houses to a palatial buildings which could be divided into three parts :

1. Dwelling Houses or Residential Buildings
2. Public Halls
3. Public Baths

1. ***Dwelling Houses or Residential Buildings*** :The dewelling houses or residential buildings of these people were constructed of baked brick which were fixed in place with the help of mud mortaor. The buildings were generally two or more stroeyed and had stair cases they had big doors, perhaps of wood. Each houses had a number of rooms, in addition to a bath and a kitchen, all having brick floors. The average size of the ground floor of a houses was about 30 feet square, but there were many bigger; obviously there were numerous well-to-do familes of the '*Nam*' or '*Chamar*' in the Indus cities, which perhaps had a middle class larger and more important in the social scale than those of the contemporary civilization of Summer and Egypt. Remains of workmens or labour class, dewellings have also been discovered at both sites '*Nam*' or '*Word*' parallel rows of two-roomed cottages, at Mohenjo-daro with a superficial area of 20X12 feet each, but at Harappa considerably large, They bear a striking resemblance to the '*Coolie Lines' or 'Chamar Lines'* of Modern Indian tea and other estates of the same class people. At *Harappa* rows of such buildings have been found near the circular brilk floors on which grain was pounded they were probably the residential building of the work men or labourers whose task was to grind corn for the priests and dignitaries who lived in the citaded. Darbs and tiny as they were, these cottages were better dwellings houses of those in which many Indain '*Coolies*[123]' or '*Chamar*' use to live at present in the area of Jammu Region. *(See Plate VII. Interior of a House of the Harappa Culture* or *Ravidas Culture* or *Chamar Culture* Fig. 9).

2. **Public Hall:** Pillared hall of the Indus Valley people was the great state granary need special attention among the public buildings. 24 metres square pillared hall was perhaps a meeting hall where people used to assemble for state business. The state granary was about 50 metres square in area, which was used for storing grains [119]. It is important to note that almost every house have has wells, drains and bath rooms. The largest building or public hall so far excavated is one at Mohenjo-Daro with a superficial area of 230 x 78 feet, which may have been a place. At Harappa a great granary has been discovered to the north of the citadel. This was raised on a platform of some 150 x 200 feet in area to protect it from floods, and was divided in to storage blocks of 50 x 20 feet each, It was doubtless used for storing the corn which was collected from the peasants as land tax, and we may assume that it had its counter part at Mohenjo-Daro. The main food crops were wheat, barely, peas, and sesamum, the latter still an important crop in India for its seeds, which

provide edible oil. There is no clear evidence of the cultivation of rice, but the Harappa grew and used cotton cloth during the summer. It is no certain that irrigation was known, although this is possible. The main domestic animals known to modern loes, goats, sheep, pigs, asses, doga, and the domestic fowl, The elephant was well known and may also have been tamed. The Harappa people may have known of the houses, since a few horses teeth have been found in the lowest stratum of the Baluchistan site of Rana Ghundai, probably dating from several centuries earlier than the foundation of Harappa. This would indicate that horse-riding nomads found their way to north –west. India in small number long before the Aryan invasion : but it is very doubtful whether the *Harappa People or 'Scheduled Caste or Scheduled Tribe People'* possessed domestic horses themselves and if they did they must have been very rare animals of the '*Nam*'. The bullock was probably the usuall beast of burden[125] on the head of the people to worship. The unique swerage system of the Indus people must have been maintained by some municipal organization,and is one of the most impressive of their achievements. No other ancient civilization until that of the Romans had so efficient a system of drainage the wastage material of the man[126] or *mana* or *Manu*.

3. ***Public Baths***: The most imposing structure in the city is the Great Bath, at *Mohenjodaro* was the largest and the most significant which measured 4. 6 m x 4. 6. m. The bricks used were of various sizes, the smallest being 23 cm x 10 cm. and the biggest size was 50cm x 20 cm. The great bath is surrounded by large number of rooms [127]. It consists of a large open quadrangle in the centre with galleries and rooms on all sides. In the centre of the quadrangle is a large swimming enclosure 39 feet long, 23 feet wide and about 8 feet deep. It has a fight of steps at either end and is fed by a well situated in one of the adjoining rooms. The water is discharged by a huge drainage with a corbelled roof more than six feet in height. The Great Bath is 180 feet long and 108 feet wide, and its outer walls are about 8 feet thick, The solidity of the construction is amply borne out by the fact that it has successfully with stood the ravages of five thousand year ago. The strects of the City are wide and straight and are furnished with an elaborate drainage system together with soak-pits for sediment [128]. Dr. A.D. Pusalker has rightly expressed, "The architecture of Mohenjo-daro in general is palin utilitarian, rather solid than beautiful [129]." On the whole, the ruins leave no scope that there was no this site a large populous and flouring town whose inhabitants freely enjoyed to a degree unknown elsewhere in the ancient world, not only the sanitary conveniences, but also the luxuries and comforts of a highly –developed municipal life. We must also conclude that the art and architecture of the buildings had reached a high

degree of perfection [130] to control the pollution of the areas. (*Also See Plate VIII. Mohenjo-Daro: The Great Bath Fig. 10 and Mohenjodaro Drainage System; Fig. 11*).

On the basis of this, study it is expressed that the agriculture economy of the area was thriving by the Harappa people, they built it rather unimaginative, but comfortable civilization. Their bourgeoises had pleasant houses, and even their workmen or labour class,who may have been bondmen or slaves of the God not of the Brahmins. They had the comparative luxury of two –roomed brick-built cottages evidently a well organised commerce made these things culture of Balchistan, where outposts of the Harappa Culture have been traced out for the study of the scientific knowledge in history, but many of their metals and semi-precious stones came from much longer distances. From Kathiawar and the Deccan, they obtained conch shell, which they used freely in decoration and several types of stone. Silver, turquoise and lapis lazuli important from Persia and Afghanistan. Their copper came either from Rajasthan or from Persia, while jadeite was probably obtained from Tibet (China) or Central Asia. Though their culture extended nearly to the mouth of the Indus the people of Harappa and *Mohenjo –daro* seem to have cared little for the sea [131] or the '*Sudhra Dynasty*'. but they work for others (*See Plate IX, Limestones Statue of Mohenjadaro of Ravidas Culture; Fig. 12)*

Art and Crafts

Study also reveals that Indus Valley people were not skillful in architecture and planning, but they had remarkable ability in other arts and crafts like sculptures, Carving, pottery, matting amd painting. Through different articles and human figures have been found after excavation reveal that was very little art in the Indus Valley and all thing which have been seen on the light of the day called *'Enlightenment Period'* through excavation lack in ornamentation, therefore, there was Darkness, yet from the utilization point of view, their achievements were praiseworthly[132]. They were not on the whole an artistic people. No doubt, they had a literature of great religious epics, have already mentioned in the text, similar to those of Sumer and Babylon, but these are foreover lost to us[133]. The outer walls facing the streets, were apparently of plain brick. Architecture was austerely utlilatrain, a few examples of simple decorative brick work being the only ornamentation so far is discovered. No traced of monumental sculpture has been found anywhere in the remains, and if any of the large building were temples, they contained no large icons unless these were made of wood or other perishable material [134] of the '*Nam*'. These people used to love painting very much. Their pots and pans were no only polished and glazed to give bright luster, but were also painted to look beautiful. Different kinds of design, figures and objects of natural script were painted both the miniature and wall paintings. Some aspects of art and crafts industry of the Early Indus people have been dealt with above cited *"Pride Chenab"* that is *Trikuta* hills of *Shri Mata Vaishno Devi ji* occupied a unique placement in a unique placement in the *Sudhra* history of the Jammu region. Agriculture must have played an important part in the daily life of the common people and among othe things wheat, barley, and cotton were cultivated on a large scale. Among the industrial classes, the potter, the weaver, the carpenter, the mason, the blacksmith, the goldsmith, the jeweller, the ivory–maker, shoe-maker and stone cutter were the most-important. *(See Plate X, Seal of Mohenjo-Daro, Fig. 13).*

Social Life of the Indus Valley People In Jammu Region

From the various articles, found in the remains of *Harappa* and *Mohenjodaro,* we can draw a picture of the social life of the Indus people of the Jammu Region, they were divided into four classes viz., learned persons, warriors of the '*Nam*', businessmen and working class or labourers of the period called *Coolie* or *Kulli* or *Chamar*

Food

The people of the region were both vegetarian and non-vegetarian. Their life was chiefly agrarian and they, therefore, mostly depended on the yield of the crops that they could grow in the field for their basic needs not for luxuary goods. Vegetarians used to eat wheat, barely, rice, take milk, fruits and milk products. Vegetables were also consumed by them. Non-vegetarian, people, apart from the above eatables, were used mutton, pork, fish, beef and eggs. Dates were one of their favourite fruits.

Dress

As regards their dress, we have no definite source which can give us much information of their dressing styles. We can only hazard a guess about their dress from the figures which have been found during excavation. Both cotton and woollen clothes were used by the said people in this area. The discovery of needles and threads confirms in various fashion, because weaving was an important occupation of the people and cotton was grown in that areas. The Civilization of Jammu Region was not confined within the limit of Akhnoor to Ravidas Basins, but it was widely spread over a vast territories of India or *Bharatavarsha,* viz, Baluchistan, North-West Frontier Provinces, *Punjab, Sindh, Saurashtra, Rajasthan,* Kerala, etc. and to the North of the Gangetic Valley of the Jammu Region. It has also affinity and likeness with the Old Civilizations of Egypt and Mesopatamia, because same types of artifacts were also discovered from [136] these areas. Therefore, there are large number of specimens of spindles, needles, buttons showed that they knew weaving, spinning and also the art of stitching the garments. Because fashions change, a careful observation of these changes is one of the most powerful tools in the lands of *Ravidas Culture* as an art historian.

Ornaments

The people of the different basins of the '*Ravidas Culture*' had a deep love for ornaments i.e., *'Nam'*. Both men and women used the ornaments frequently. The ornaments were made of differents metals such a gold, silver, copper, bronze,shell and ivory were used to wear by them in an artistic way. The poor people's ornaments were made of clay. Bangles neckaces, armlets, figure-rings, ear-rings and hair pins for the hair do already mentioned were very popular among he people of Jammu Region. Beads were also much in use as an ornament in the prehistoric period. They were made of different shapes and styles with studded of precious stones and semi-stones. The beads of pottery were used by the poor persons[135]. Girdles, nose-studded, ear-rings and anklets were particularily meant for women. There was a great variety in the shape and design of these ornaments prevalent in this region, and some of them are of singular beauty. The precious stones like jade, crystal, agate, carneling and *Lapis Lazuli*[137] were also in fashion in the ornaments for the decoration of body. (*See Plate X. Mohenjo Daro Jewellery;* Fig. 14).

Cosmetics And Coiffure

In the study, we also learn that the people of Jammu Region were also very fashionable. Both men and women had special inclination for keeping themselves smart. Both of them had long hair and dressed it according to their choice. Some people had long beards and moustaches and others were clean-shaven. The discovery of ivory combs, bronze mirrors, razors, powders, perfumed oils, and lipsticks confirms their love for fashion both men and women alike had long hair. The coiffure of the women were often elaborated and pigtails were also popular,as in present day India [138] or in *Bharat*.

Sports And Games (Amusements)

The people of the region had great interest for sports and games. Their life was not very dull. They not only loved music and dancing of the Father, but also played various games such as chess,and enjoyed hunting, fishing, bird fighting, bull fights and gambling during the time of process in study[139]. Dicing was a common pastime as it was in the Vedic Age. Small children used to play with toys made of clay. i. e. body or *Chamar* of the man. *(See Plate IX, Limestone Statue, Mohanjo Daro of Ravidas Culture Fig. 12.)*

Weapons of War

Mackey writes, "the Indus Valley people were peace loving and unwarlike. " In his statement, it make clear from the study that their behaviour is based on '*Nam*' or '*Word*' that there is no any defensive weapons such as shields and armour have been found in excavation, on the other hand, various types of weapons made of copper and bronze have been unearthed from '*Harappa and Mohenjodaro*' i. e. '*Nam*' or '*Chamar*'. They knew the uses of iron their chief weapons were axe, spear and bow of the 'Nam'. They also used sword like weapon which were used to be pointed out at the end of the commencement of '*New Era*' of the '*Nam*' and thick in the middle [140].

Medicines In Primitive India Society

Science and society are inseparable. We can not dream of science without society and its vice-versa. Science is the means by which the whole of our civilization is rapidly being transformed science is growing by leaps and bounds. It has responded in the past to the successive forms of society and in its turn,it has served to mould them. Dr. J. D. Bernal, an eminent scientist of the preceding century elaborated the basic perpective of the historiography of Science and Society, "This is an attempt to describe and to interpret the relations between the development of science and other aspects of human history. It ultimate object is to lend an understanding of major problems which arise from the impact of science on society. Civilization, as, we know, today, would, in it material aspect, be impossible with out science. In its intellectual ventures and moral aspects science has been deeply concerned. The spread of scientific idea has been a decisive factor in remoulding the whole pattern of human thought[141], i. e., in a Scientific Discovery of the '*Nam-History*'.

Indain Background ; Science and Metaphysical Phantasy

Despite certain outstanding efforts by several eminent scholars like Stcherbatsky, Jacobi, Hoenle, Jolly, Csoma de Coros, Filliozat. P. C. Ray, B. N. Seal, D. P. Chattopadhyay and other to resurrect the history of ancient Indian Science, which concentrated chiefly on astronomy, physiology and psychology, making great progress in plant knowledge to list their properties for food, medicine or technical use. One with a sense of objectivity will be candid enough to admit that several aspects of the dynamic of the complex correlation between Science and Society in the ancient Indian context largely continues to be a terra incognita. These are some distinct views relating to near absence of exact science in ancient India. In the context, let us refer to the following rebuttal made by Acharya Prafulla Chandra Roy[142].

"It is generally taken for granted that the Hindus were a dreamy mystical people given to metaphysical speculation and spiritual contemplation. Due credit is, no doubt, assigned to them for the production of priceless treasures as the *Upanishads* the six systems of philosophy, including the abstruse *Samkhya* and the Gita with their transcendental teachings. But the fact, that the Hindus had very large hand in the [143] cultivation of the experimental science is hardly in these days, because they have no history except *Sudhra*.

Today, we known much more about Indian Science in comparison to the days of Ray, yet we also find copious examples of amalgam of scientific categories with metaphysical dogmas and unscientific mythological phantasies. This blending has wrought so devastating consequences in our understanding of the nature of India culture, sometimes leading to its distortion to suit the purpose of the contemporary ethno-communal politcs. So, it is all more necessary to comprehend the role of science in the genesis and subsequent evolution of the ancient Indian Culture and its relevance to the modern context.

Bovine Divinity

In order to examine the amalgam of science, philosophy and mythology, we can refer to the concept of 'Bovine Divinity', which is the cause of several sectarian conflicts on the issue of eating in modern India. The dogma of the sanctity of cow along with *Brahmans* has been assimiliated with in the scientific treatises like Caraka (medicine), *Rasarnava* (Chemistry) and others as an unscientific discovery of the human history without *Nam-mantra* theory of the natural thought, i.e., God and Man.

The *Caraka Samhita*[143] extensively discusses the therapeutic values of different types of meat. According to Unscientific procedure, the medical compendium classifices the flesh of animals in to the following groups-

1. Prasaha
2. Bhumisaya or Bhusaya
3. Anupa
4. Barisaya
5. Baricari
6. Janagam
7. Biskira birds
8. Bartaka birds
9. Pratuda birds

Subsequently feauters and therapeutic values are enumerate. Beef has been include with in the group :

Gbany Kebal Batansu Bisam Jabrein
Susak Kasan Symanyeyegan Gahitant chtata

While recommending heifers meat for certain ailing conditions. Caraka simultaneously issues directives to worship of cow along with Gods and Brahmanas on a serval occasions one them is the following from Caraka (18. 8) having no knowledge of Godly thought.

Tadata- Deva Go Brahman, Guru Sidda Chayarna Chyetrata

Thus was reach a very contradictory position by recommendation of beef as a dietary adjunct to health along with the worship of cow he could no worship the living diety in human form, believe on animal as a blind faith of the Brahmin. Again, we find similar relation to sanctity of cow along with the unscientific postulates of ancient Indian Chemistry. Acharya Prafulla Chandra Ray refers to *Resesvara Darsana,* a chapter dedicated to the science of Mercury in a philosophical compendium of several systems of philosophy entitled *Sarva Darsana* Samgraha compiled by Madhavacarya[146] in the idea of transfer speices.

Scientific advancement is seen pretty accurate in discussion on chemical apparatus, techniques of flame test to detect various types of metal and finally extraction of metal from ores through the medium of dialogues of *Siva* and his consort *Parvati.* Regarding technique of flame tests we find the following descriptions of the colours of flame emitted by different metal can be considered accurate even today:-

(1) Copper emits blue colourflame.

(2) Tin emits pegion colourflame.

(3) Lead emits pale colour flame.

(4) Iron emits twany colourflame.

On the other hand, we come across the following mythological phantasy relating to the science of Mercury which is assigned to Siva.

'Take a golf leaf of 3 *niskas* in weigth and quik silver 9 *nikas* and rub them with acid for three hours. Make the amalgam unto a *phallus*, (emblem of Siva creative principle). It is said that mere sight of the *phallus* of mercury, Sins accumulated by killing 1000 Brahmans 10000 cows are redeemed.

The juxtaposition of unscientific precepts with the dogma of 'Bovine Divinity' is not an outcome of any scientific persuit. What is then the alternative historical explanation where stands the thruth in animal or man. Truth stands in man itself. Prof. Chattopadhyay points out:

There is a strong religious sentiment for the cow among Brahmins which has already explained in the '*History of the Brahmans*' in the work of same writer i.e., Dr. Raj Kumar. The origin of this may be the subject of a serious socio-historical investigations [147] which Brahminical historian like Chattopadhyay is idiot of the thought having no knowledge of the research.

One of the earliest attempts to deal with this aspect of ritualism vis-à-vis Bovine Divinity and heifers meat was undertaken buy R. L. Mitra. He had made a narrative of his extensive exploration of ancient texts (both scientific and religious) in his well documented monograph entituted 'Beef in Ancient India'. In the connetion, Mitra refers to Nirnay '*Word*' *Sindhu* or *Vitasta* which prohibits cow slaughter because of the prevalence of wide spread disparagement though such killings were ordained in holy scriptures like the Vedas R. L Mitra proceeds further:-

"If such be the case, the question arises, where comes this public feeling against the ordinance of the Vedas it stands in *Sudhras*. And we can nowhere meet with a more appropriate reply than in the fact that when Barhmanas had to content against Buddhism, which emphatically and so successfully denounced all sacrifices, they found the doctrine of respect for animal life too strong and too popular to be overcome and therefore, gradually and imperceptibly adopted in such manner as to make it appear as apart of their Sastras. They gave prominence to such passages, which preached benevolence and mercy for animated creations, and pushed to the background the sacrificial ordinance as to put them entirely out of sight [148] because they were dead animals.

Prof. R. S. Sharma deals with the problem of this *Sastiric* transition as mentioned above on the basis of Archaeology and Buddhist text like '*Sutta-Nipata*'. According to him this change was brought about by the corresponding change in agricultural tools like iron ploughshare as evidenced in *Atiranjikhera*, in Etah District (U.P.). During the pre-iron plough era cultivation was carried out with hoe and dribbing stick and without the labour of cattle. At that time the domestication of animals both by Aryan and non-Aryan peoples were practised to provide non-vegetarian component of food. Probably the experiences gathered in connection with the nature thereapeutic values of meats of different animals were later systematically compiled in medical compendia like *Caraka* and *Susruta*. Similarly, one may not that the observation of the forest people on herb and plants were included in the ancient medical texts.

The introduction of iron plough and yoking cattle for agriculture revolutionized the method of production and brought about a change in the corresponding ideological parameters. Professor Sharma summarises the issue in the following way:

'The Buddhist emphasises on non-injury to animals assumes a new significance in the context of the need of new agriculture. The Pali canons do not stress so much the need for non-violence towards animals. The earliest Buddhist text, the *Sutta-Nipata* (verses 2876-97) states that the cattle should be protected because they are givers of food, beautry, and happiness (*annaḍa, vannada* and *sukhada*). This was certainly a revolutionary teaching a time when non-Aryan slaughter cattle for food and Aryans for religion[149].

The transformation of the role of cattle should find exegetical justification for non-violence in other scriptures also probably the Brahmanical preceptors had greater difficulties in doing so because of earlier scriptural injunction for cattle slaughter for food and rituals. So they had to adopt the path of defication of cow as Chattopadhyay refered to Gautam's (IX, 13, 4) conversion of cow to '*Devata*' [150] i. e, *'Nam'* or '*Chamar*'. Buddhists remained satisfied with the enunciation of the policy without mythologoical garb; the Brahmanical preceptors had to do it otherwise, it is a false propaganda of this community. Thus, we reach a complex investigative terrain where we find the amalgam of myth, metaphysic and science. So, it is necessary to trace out this expression in several branches of ancient Indian sciences in order to comprehend the role of science in the evolution of the vast canvas of our culture. We propose to briefly refer to the following branches.

(1) Medicine
(2) Astronomy
(3) Psychology

Medicine : Atma And Cosmo Biological Hymns

Caraka has adopted the concept of *Atma* (Soul/Self) a metaphysical category to the understanding of the physio-pathological mechanism of the human body. According to him, mind, *Atma*, body (which includes sense organs) Constitute Life (Ayu). He further argues that body and mind are subjected to diseases but *Atma* which is not prone to pathological processes is eternal.[151] *Par Satbatama Satba But Guraonidrayie; Nibrikar Chtanya Karana Nityodrasta Pasyite Hi Kirya-Caraka.*

If we try to trace out the origin of this postulate one can find the echo of its conceptual kinship with the following observation of Chand, *Upansihed*:-

Prajapati said: "That is the self, this is immortal, fearless, this is Brahman."[152]

He said, Sir, although it is true that self is not blind even if the body is blind, nor lame, if the body is lame, though it is true that self is not rendered faulty by the faults of the body [153].

It is necessary to study the dynamics of the blending of the medical phenomenon with that of metaphysical dogma. There are copious example of such amalgam. They are the earliest attempt to comprehend biological, physiological and pathological phenomena in terms of proto philosophical or proto-scientific concepts. Lets us refer to the following hymn of Br. Ar. Up. [154]

The same are three worlds. This terrestrial world is specch. The middle atmospheric world is mind. That celestial world is Breath.

Such correlation between the elements of macro-cosm (universe) and microcosm (body) is based on the native understanding of the influence exerted by the universe on earth and man in the forms of the tide, seasonal change, etc. This proto-scientific or proto-phiosophical postulates of cosmic correspondence is respossible for the plethora of hymns relating to body and universes. These hymns have been designated by Filliozat [155] as Cosmo-biological or Cosmo-Physiological hymns. In some of these we find that Honey doctrine the concept of *Atma* or soul has been interpolated in to cosmo-biological hymns. Let us take the following examples of Br. Ar. Up.

Sl. No	*Hymns+ Stanzas*	*Cosmic entity*	*Physiological entity*	*Relating to 5th Brahman of 2nd*
1.	2. 5. 1	Earth	Body	
2.	2. 5. 2	Water	Semen	
3.	2. 5. 3	Fire	Speech	
4.	2. 5. 4	Wind	Breath	
5.	2. 5. 5	Sun	Eye	Correleated to the
6.	2. 5. 6	Quarters of Heaven	Ear	immortal person
7.	2. 5. 7	Moon	Mind	Soul and Brahma
8.	2. 5. 8	Lightening	Heat	
9.	2. 5. 9	Thunder	Tone (svara)	
10.	2. 5. 10	Space	Heart	
11.	2. 5. 11	Dharma		Soul/Brahma
12.	2. 5. 12	Truth		Soul/Brahma
13.	2. 5. 13	Manusa		Soul/Brahma
14.	2. 5. 14	Soul		Soul/Brahma
15.	2. 5. 15	Soul		King/lords of all things

Ten hymns as metioned above have double interlocking. First, various components of the body (microcosm) are being correlated with some compontents of the universe (macro-cosm) viz, Eye correspond to sun or mind corresponds to moon. Secondly, all these elements (both macro and micro-cosmic) are clubbed with Atma or soul and Bramha who is a shining & immortal entity. Besides there are few hymns (from 11 to 15 noted above) in whch *Dharma* (law), truth, mankind (*Manusa*) are also correlated with soul and Bramha.

This so called honey doctrine was communicated to celestial physician '*Word' or 'Nam'*. Asvins about whom we shall deal with in subsequent pages. But the most interesting appendage of this doctrine is the list of the teachers who elaborate cosmo-physiological hymns clubbed with the postulate of *Atma*. Similar list has been referred to by Caraka.[156] Some of the following names are common in both lists.

1. *Sandilya*

2. *Atreya*
3. *Galava*
4. *Gautama*
5. *Angirasa*
6. *Kausika*
7. *Bharadwaja*
8. *Kapya* and others

As far as our knowledge is concerned no systematic study of the process of transformation of these proto-biological dogmas into scientific precepts has been carried out. It is also necessary to trace out the evolution of these preceptors in to medical scientists who have contributed tremendously to the science of ancient Indian medicine. Here, we propose to indicate in this connection some reflections on the problem.

One of the earliest reference, we find of healer in the nomenclature of *Bhisaj*. This term is assigned to other deities also like Rudra as per *Rig veda*[157]. But in R. V. 11. 39, we come across with the name of Asvins without the status of Bhisaj. Subsequently, Asvins emerged as a major healer acquiring the status of celestial physician. Macdonnel in "A Vedic reader" mentions that there are fifty major hymns relating to Asvins in Rigvedic. In one of them we come across the linkage of Bhisaj with *Amivacatana.*

According to Monier –Williams [159] *catana* stands for sorcery, where as *amiva* denotes, disease, affliction, demon, tormenting spirit, etc. Thus *Bhisaj*, the healer is clubbed with *catana*, the sorcerer. Acordingly, healing power of *catana* is merged with Bhisaji. In fact, in Vedic hymns *catana* has been assigned the status of Rishi.

The term Bhisaj has been generally made equivalent to the English word physician. Etymologically Monier –Williams [160] breaks the word Abhi Saj. Saji stands for to join or plaster. So early *Bhisaj* may be compared to bone setter. Filliozat translates the term as cure man. Possibly it stands for medicine man. It needs further investigation for welfare of the state of health.

Why the cure capacity was attritbued to twin '*Word'* Asvin? Is there any tradition of attributing healing power to twins called *chamar*. In this connection let us refer to Dorothy Fisk [161] monograph entitled' "Bouquet for the Doctor" She observes:

"If child may be chosen by the medicine himself or by the tribe or be dedicated by his parents, in most cases some physical peculiarity marked for the profession: twins albinos, those bron blind or those born feet first were often selected" by '*Word'* or *'Nam'* to form the New Society of the '*Nam*' itself.

When we reach the ninth Mandals of the Veda, we find that Bhisaj acquires the status of an independent secular profession. In this connection, one can refer to R. V. [162] Where composes *sisu* is a poet (Karu) his wife is a grinder (*Upal praksin*) and his son a doctor (*Bhisaj*):

It will be interesting to note that some healer (of Vedic literature) have not acquired the status of medical scientists. In this connection, we come across a toxicological littanies of *Atharvaveda*, which are attributed to Rishi Garutman. These hymns accurately describe the venomous creatures like scorpion, snake, etc. They deal with the various rituals to cure snake bite, etc. which are similar to the practice carried out by contemporary Ojhas.

In A. V. [164] Rishi Catana refers following witch-crafts :

1. *Ulukyatu* (Owl Sorcery)
2. *Susuluk yatu* (Owlet Sorcery)
3. *Svayatu* (Dog Sorcery)
4. *Koyatu* (Cuckoo sorcery)
5. *Suparna yatu* (Eagle sorcery)
6. *Gridhra yatu* (Vulture sorcery)

Suparna being another name of *Garutman* is thus describe as Suparna Yatu through we don't find the nomenclature of Garutman Yatu in *Taittiriya Samhita*[164]. Suparna is defined as diviner. Divination is a craft to make prophesy through non-human media like birds or by casting lots. If we correlate Suparna, the divine with toxicologist Garutman, we find the combination of two crafts into one single individual. Earlier mentioned about Bhisaj as medicine man, they are also medicine men clubbing together a number of functions. According to Sigerist medicine[165] clubbing together a number of functions. He is a priest sorcerer, and physician in one.

In Vedic literature we also find reference to the ultimate destiny of medicine man in the garb of *Asvins*.

In the beginning of *Taittiriya Samhita* [166]. Asvins are eulogized as Divine healers in the later part the twin is despised for impurity born out of their association with man and physician. Subsequently, their defied status is restored in an attenuated from by purification with *Bahispavaman Stotra* with strict injunction: "A Brahman should not practice medicine for the physician is impure, unfit for the work of sacrifice". At the same time, their healing power is divided into three parts and distributed among *Indra*, water and Brahmans, Necessary investigation should be done to find out the mechanism of emergence of a polity where Brahmanical domination over healer's art was possible.

Astronomy And Its Mythological Manifestation

In course of the elaboration of celestial phenomena, the science of astronomy developed. Along with it a set of mythological dogmas in the shape of astrology evolved. In the Indian context, stars and planets traverse a distinct path of mythological transformation. As a result astronomical facts are presented in a loose amalgam along with mythological concepts [167]. Let us deal with them very briefly.

Cosmic Correlation: First, we find the correlation of celestial entities with that of human entities. We have already mentioned about the sympathetic linking of sun and eye or moon and mind as examples of cosmic correspondence. Such aliveness of celestial bodies is the extension of Taylor's concept of animism.

Theriomorphic or Anthropomorphic: In next step, we notice theriomorphic or anthropomorphic transformation of heavenly bodies. We have copious examples in this connection. In *Rig- Veda* [168] sun has been described as the beautiful winged bird as *Ravidas* or *Surya*; *Divya Suparna Garutmana*. Or sun has been described as human being moving on a car drawn by a number of horses.

Apotheosis

Then we see the transformation of celestial bodies into deities. In case of *Surya*, we find laters deification into following forms of deities;

1. *Surya*
2. *Savitr*
3. *Pusan*
4. *Bhagu*
5. *Vivasvat*
6. *Aryaman*
7. *Mitra*
8. *Vishnu*

Catasterism

The subsequent stage is characterized by catasterism. By catasterism we mean the correlation of common popular deities and heavenly planets. In Greek, we see Apollo-Helios-i. e. the unification of Apollo with the Sun or *Ravi*. In the Indian context we find the following:-

	Planet	*Mythological Deity*
1.	*Mangala*	*Skanda*
2.	*Buddha*	*Narayana*
3.	*Brhaspati*	*Devaguru*
4.	*Sukra*	*Daityacarya*
5.	*Sani*	*Yama*

Thus, it is necessary to study the conceptual evolution of celestial bodies as mythological deities from animism to cataserism in greater detail precisely because these dogmas have tremendous grip over our culture even to-day which obstructed the natural growth of science in India as 'light' of the father *Ravidas* as Little Master Deepit Raj as an educationist no need to admit in the school.

Psychology-Science of Mind & Body

The most original and advanced Indian Science was psychology, which made use of Psychical and physiological techniques i. e. *yoga,* derived from Sanskrit word '*yuj*', considered for 'sexual lust' by the Brahmin saints as an illegal force of the Nature. For the achievement of mastery over mind and body not over the Natural thought i.e., '*Nam*' or '*God*'. The observation, analysis and classification of mental phenomena were pursued with untiring energy and refreshing vigour who believe over him. In this field none have laboured with greater industry and acumen than the Buddhist thinkers, whose whole philosophy and their religion rests on psychological basis. Not only so, but some of their main contentions are very similar to the later views advanced by the dominant schools of modern reseach on psychology.[169]

Buddhism considers only four realities; namely-*Citta; Cetasika; Rupa* and *Nibbana.*

Citta

Citta means the consciousness. There are four *Bhumis* of *citta,* which is the gradual development of human mind towards the achievement of *Nibbana.*

Lord Buddha was not only a philosopher, but he was a great psychologist too. He put the human mind in to a laboratory before the microscope and studied the cities minutely from different angles, in relation to *Vedana, hetu, kicca, dwara, alambana, vatthu.*

Cittavithi is the course of cognition. We know that we have five sense organs and a mind by which we perceives something. How a man perceives through these sense organs, is the subject matter of *Cittavithi.*

Cetasika

Cetasikas or psychic factors originated and dissolve with the *cittas.* They have not their separate entities a part from *cittas*. They are of fifty two types.

Rupa

Rupa means matter. To be more explicit, the quality of a thing is *rupa.* As when we say earth and water, it does not mean the gross earth and liquid water, rather the quality of roughness and lubrication is the actual earth and water.

Nibbana

Nibbana is the highest goal of life, according to Buddhist scholars. This is the foundation on which the entire edifice of Buddhism rests. It is a state of our mind free from desires. *Nibbana* is full of bliss and serenity. Lord Buddha also explained the way how to achieve the *Nibbana*. With an idea to achieve thiis state one should have control over mind or to cultivate such a state in mind so that there may not be desire in it. The process for such mental culture has been explained by Lord Buddha as *Samadhi* or Buddhist *yoga*. Buddhist *yoga* is of two types –*Samatha* and *Vipassana* i.e., *'Nam'* which is the practice by which all the defilements are uprooted and the true nature of existence is realized, then it is followed by the state of cessation of desires – that means the highest achievement of *Nibbana* or the *summum bonum* of life[170].

Emergence of Independent Preceptor of Science

While dealing with the mechanism of interlocking of Scientific Concepts with mythology and philosophy, in the India context we have referred to several nomenclatures like *Dom, Chamars, Meghas, Barawalar, Batwals, Lohar, Tarkhan Cheer, and other*, denoting healers profession. We have noted several function performed by the healer, which are comparable to the functions of primitive medicin man. Sigerist equates several terms like *Sraman. Seer, Leech*,. sorcerer, etc. with medicine man [171].

In our opinion the term Rishi has some resemblance with medicine man in the early phase. Probably the term-'Vaidya' first mentioned in *Ramayana* is comparable to medical scientist[172].

From Caraka *Samhita* (a medical compendium) we learn that several seminars on medical subjects were held in ancient India Dr. Satya Prakash mentions some of them in his book entitled 'founder of Science in Ancient India'[173].

(1) Symposium I:-
Subject : Salutary and unsalutary influences of *Vata* or *Air* as '*Nam*'

(2) Symposium II:-
Subject : origin of man and diseases

(3) Symposium III:-
Subject : Taste and its enumeration i.e., Infinite, but wonderful.

(4) Symposium IV:-
Subject: Growth of foetal ilimbs

In these Seminars, we find basically three categories of participants. Before we classify them let us present the list of participant noted below:-

1.	*Kush*		
2.	*Kumarasira Bhardwaja*	=	Referred in 4 Symposia
3.	*Kankayana*	=	Referred in 4 Seminars
4.	*Badisa Dhamargava*	=	Mentioned in 3 Seminars
5.	*Royal Saga Varyovida*	=	mentioned in 2 Seminars
6.	*Marici*	=	Twice referred
7.	*Kapya*	=	Thrice referred
8.	*Atreya Punarvasu*	=	Practically referred to in all the Symposia
9.	*King Vamaka of Kasi*		
10.	*Pariksi Maudgalya*		
11.	*Saraloma*		
12.	*Hiranyaksa*		
13.	*Kausika*	=	Referred twice
14.	*Saunaka*	=	Referred twice
15.	*Bhadra Kapya*	=	Referred twice
16.	*Bharadwaja*		
17.	*Sakunteya*		
18.	*Maudgalya Purnaksa*		
19.	*Kausika Hirnyaksa*		
20.	*King Nimi of Videha*		
21.	*Agnivesa*		
22.	*Bhadra Saunaka*		
23.	*Marici Kasyapa*		
24.	*Dhanvantari*		
25.	Bhigu		
26.	*Putastya*		
27.	*Asit*		
28.	*King Janak of Videha*		

These names can be broadly classificed into following groups:-

(1)	Kings	:	*Varyovid* *Nimi* *Janaka*
(2)	Rsis	:	Bulk of the participants belong to the category of Rsis.
(3)	Foreigner	:	*Kankayana* from Bactria
	Caraka	:	rPN~ Rok okdka dkadk;uka okàhd fHk'kxqokp%

Caraka confirms the participation of *Kankayana* from *Bactria* which imports international complexion of the Seminars.

Rishis

Who were Rishis? Let us recapitulate the contention of Herman Jacobi about Rishis. According to Brahmanical mythology, they were authors of Vedic hymns and founders of serval clans, families, and dynasties. Basing himself on Max Muller, he collates them into two groups i.e., *chamar* and *Jat.*

(I) Those who have descended from seven Rishis (*saptarsis*):

(i) *Bhrgu*
(ii) *Angiras*
(iii) *Visvamitra*
(iv) *Vasistha*
(v) *Kasyapa*
(vi) *Atri*
(vii) *Agastya*

(2) The second group consists of above seven Rishis plus Bharadwaja. On the other hand, the *Mahabharata* refers to following list:

(i) *Marici*
(ii) *Atri*
(iii) *Ahgiras*
(iv) *Palana*
(v) *Kratu*
(vi) *Pulastya*
(vii) *Vasistha*

These limited numbers gave rise to 49 clans which were subdivided into larger numbers with distinct patronymic identity for each of them. For example, we find the name of *Atri* in the original list. He appears to be composer of the 5th book of *Rig veda. Atri* is also referred to in *Atharvaveda, Mantra, Brahman, Taittiriya Aranyaka, Brhad Aranyaka* and finally in Caraka in Br. Ar. Up. We come across the following. "

These two (sense organs) here (i.e., ears) are Gotama and Bharadwaja 'Words', these two here (i.e., eyes) are *Visvamitra* and *Jamadgni* i.e., *'Chamar'*. These two here (i.e., nostrils) are *Vasistha* and *Kasyapa*. The voice is *Atri* for by the voice the food is eaten '*Word*' verily, eating is the same name as the name of Atri '*Chamar*' of the *'Sudhra Family'* work for the welfare of the public.

Bramha

↓

Imparts to

↓

Daksa Prajapati

↓

Asvina twin

↓

Indra

More than 53 Rishis including Atri 6 disciples with books.

↓

- Agnivesa → Agnivesa Samhita
- Bhela → Bhela Samhita
- Jatu Karna → Jatukarna Samhita
- Parasara → Parasara Samhita
- Harita → Samhita
- Ksarapani

The above stanza of Br. Ar. *Upanishad* correlates some human sense organs with several Rishis including Atri. Probaby each Rishis some role in understanding the medical function of the corresponding sense organ as mentioned above. In *Caraka Atri* occupies an important position as a preceptor in the dissemination of the discipline of *Ayurveda*. The following Chart elaborates the point:-

Origin of Ayurveda discipline

It is extremely necessary to trace out the transformation of Arti Rishis. The composes of 5th book of Rig. Veda to medical preceptor training 6 disciples each being a composer of medical compendium. One may discern following phase of transition;

(1) Mythology –*Bramhao Indra*

(2) Proto scientific phase: cosmobiological and cosmophysiological phase as we find *Upanishadic* speculations.

(3) Scientific phase : several Rishis including *Atri* and their six disciples with books. Despite some characteristic and distinction features for each phase, everyone is interlocked with each other. The clear separation of one phase from the other is not complete. Rishis predominated the scene.

Comparison with the Evolution of the Greek Preceptors of Science

As noted above, ancient Indian medical preceptors had the opportunity to interest with the foreign preceptors like *Kankayana* from Bactria '*Chamar*' an Asiatic Greek Colony. It will be interesting to refer briefly the stages of transition leading to the emergence of the Greek preceptors without any mythological or metaphysical frill.

Charles Singer[174] points out a long line of Asiatic Greek Brahmins (Mostly of Miletus) headed by Thales and followed by Anaximander (611-557 B. C.), Anaximenes (570 B. C.) Tenedos, Heacataeus and others were responsible for the separation of science and philosophy from mythology. Earlier the mythology was the hallmark of science, but *Hecataeus* was sceptic about the legends associated with scientific phenomena. In fact, his castigation of mythology can be deducted from the following comments.

"The stories of Greeks are no less absurd than numerous'

Similar transition from mythology to science is evident in the comprehension of Anaximenes relating to the phenomen of Rainbow. Earlier rainbow was considered as a goddess. Anaximenes explained the phenomenon in the phenomenon in term of the effect of sunrays on compact air.

All these speculative act of the Greeks were influenced by the development of the corresponding branches of science. Burnet [175] points out that mathematics influenced Plato, whereas biology Aristotle. Roger and subsequently Filliozat refer to the growing tendency of philosophy to turn to physiology as the source of scientific explanation due to significant progress of the medical science.[176] in human history through the study of *'Nam-History'*. This lead to the separation of science from philosophy. Later other branches also followed the same path as God and Man.

The gradual disengagement of Greek science from mythology and philosophy and corresponding emergence of scientific preceptors bereft of philosophical and mythological postulates possible due to a number of factors. One of them was the roving characters of the Asiatic Greek which helped them to about various branches of knowledge from different places. Because of the federal system of Ionian polity; scientist could relatively flourish favourable and independently. In this connection, Singer referred to the example of thales who was a merchant and a traveller. Besides he was a great protagonist of federal system. Similarly, Hecateus travelled Egypt, Persia and Gibraltar etc. to find the reality of world where it stands i. e., '*Nam*' or '*God*' on earth.

In ancient Indian context, the disengagement of science from mythology and philosophy did not take place. On the contrary, they remained interlocked. Unlock the Greek preceptors of science ancient Indian counterparts were not great international travellers acquiring knowledge from the different countries. Besides, Indian polity being a hierachical polity based on *Varnashrma* system the Brahmanic hegemony over every ideological presuit is maintained mainly by the Rishis. The Rishis are original composers and enchanters of Vedic hymns. Herman Jacobi[177] proposed that this act grew into a powerful theosophical movement following the participation of Ksariyas while re-interperting the meaning of *mantras*, i.e., *Nam-Dana* of the Prefect Master.

To elaborate the aforementioned point as mentioned in Ch. Upa.[178] a group discussion was organised *Udgitha's* identification with ultimate category i.e., SPACE:

Participants were :

(1) *Silaka Satvalya*

(2) *Caikityana Dalabhya*

(3) *Pravahana Jaibali*

Hume refers to *Pravahana Jaibali* as non Brahman, in fact, he has been spoken as one of the princely clans (*Rajanya*). This stanza emphasizes that certain knowledge is exclusive to Kashatryas initially and later on passed over to Brahmans. There is no place for *craftsmen* and physicians, etc. As pointed out earlier, *Taittiriya Samhita's*[179] injunction rules that Brahmana is should not practice medicine, but one third of healing power is adduced to Brahmana and the rest two third is equalluy assigned to Indra and Water. This makes Brahmana's hegemony of everything including science.

The speculative nature of many scientific discussions is similar to the method followed by *Upansihads*. For example, scientific Seminar of *Caraka* on the origin of man and diseases appear to be a continum of the earlier postulates of *Svetasvatara* Upanishad[180] in *Caraka Samhita*[181] the following participants discussed the causes of the origin of man and diseases:-

	Name of Participants	*Concept of the Nature of Causes*
1.	*Maudgalya*	*Atman*
2.	*Saroloma*	*Mana*
3.	*Varyovid*	*Rasa*
4.	*Hiranyaka*	*Pancabhutas and Consciousness*
5.	*Kusika*	*Parents*
6.	*Bhadra Kapya*	*Merits of Action*
7.	*Bharadwaja*	Nature (*Svabhava*)
8.	*Kankayana*	Brahama's son i. e. Prajapati
9.	*Atreya*	Time

In the beginning, *Svetasvatar Upanishad,* we come across the following question regarding the conjectures concerning the first cause:-

What is the cause ? Brahma?

Whence we are born ?

Where do we live ? Over ruled by whom in plain and pleasures.

The answers are following:-

1.	Brahma	=	Similar to that of *Kankayana*
2.	Time	=	Similar to that of *Atreya*
3.	Chance (*Yadriccha*)		
4.	*Bhutas*	=	*Hiranyaksa's* concept of 6 elements
5.	Female and male	=	Comparable to Kusika's concept of paremts as equivalent God and Man.
6.	*Atman* (soul)	=	Maudgalya, etc.
7.	*Svabhava, Nature*	=	Bhradvaja

Upanishadic search for such answers did not lead Rishis to scientific experiments to solve the problem. One the contrary, the emphasis was given to *Dhyana* and *Yoga* to develop *Atmashakti* of God hidden within the body:-

Those who followed meditation (*dhyanas*) and abstraction (*yoga*) saw the self power *Atmashakti* of God (*Deva*) hidden in his own qualities (*guna*). He is the one who rules over all these causes, from time to soul.

The *Yogic* emphasis is the outcome of assimilation of the element of *Tapas* with in the earlier priestly practices of sacrifice and sacrament. Therefore, *Yoga* and *Dhyana* can solve all problems. Hence, there is no need of scientific experiments. Filliozat[182] observes: "Although Indian science speculates rationally, seeks detailed knowledge, observes and forms explanatory hypothesis, rarely does it experiment except in psychology, where made greatest progress, thanks to body mind control."[183]

Thus, we can observe how theosophical speculation of *Vedic mantras* had led to the enunciation of many proto-scientific concepts. At the same time, how the adopters of *Yogic* method of asceticism had acted as constraint to the progress of experimental science. As the result, Ancient Indian Science could not come out of the grip of religion. Hence, is blending of scientific concepts with religious dogmas called *Brahmins* and *Molavis* or modern politicians.

The situation of India is different from the situation of Greece. In Indian context, we find incomplete detribalization of the Neolithic society where craft and agriculture remain blended. So craft could not develop significantly. Agriculture largely depended on magical rites particularly fertility cult. This fusion at the material plane gives rises to amalgam in ideological plane i. e., the interlocking of science, philiosophy, mythology and religion. In this connection, let us refer to the following comment of Walter Ruben[184]

'*Chamar*' in the Indian village community underdeveloped small agriculture and handicraft were liked together. The village was the base of despotism and religion in contrast to Greece, where a peasent was citizen just like people who were traders and craftman. In Greece democracy and the power of religion was not so strong. Thus, in Greece Science and Technology flourished better than in India[185] at that time. "

In short, study demonstrates that very little is known about the medicines by the ancient people of India or *Bharataversha* in Jammu Region, in order to examine the amalgam of Science and Society, *shilajeet*, *coral* and leaves of *neem* have been discovered during the excaution from the various region of Indus Valley Civilization, all these possess medicinal qualities i.e., '*Nam*' or '*Chamar*' from the 'Divine Representative of the God' from Heaven to Earth, so it is estimated that the people of the Jammu Region of the prehistoric period cared for their health by obtaining the '*Nam-Dana*' from the 'Father' at the same time.

Position of Women

The position of the women was very respectable. They used to get great respect in the society. There are certainly icons of the Mother Goddess, and are so numerous that they seem to have been kept in nearly every home. They are very crudely fashioned, so we must assume that the Goddess was not favoured by the upper classes that were *Sudhras* at that time, who commanded the services of the best craftsmen to the society as an 'Enlightened Society', but her effigies were mass produced by humble potters to meet popular demand of the artisan class. The figures of Mother Goddess affirm the fact that women were not only a source of entertainment and were house keepers, but were worshipped in the society in the form of Mother Goddess[186]. It has been suggested that 'dancing girl' was a respresentative of a class of temple dancers and prostitutes such as existed in contemporary Middle Easter Civilization and were an important feature of later Hindu Culture, but this could not be proved[187] in the India Society that girl was dancer or an object of the art which display much less a temple dancer as '*Nam*' plays in mind.

Disposal of the Dead Body

It is very difficult to form a definite ides as to how the people of the Indus Valley of the Jammu Region used to effect disposal of their dead bodies. However, from the material discovered from the excavations by the archaeologists carried out in Sindh province, it is estimated that they used to dispose of their dead bodies in three ways:-

1. The dead body was buried under the ground.

2. The dead body was burnt and it remains were collected and buried under earth in an urn.
3. The dead body was left in the open plain for wild animlas and birds to eat and when the entire flash was eaten by them, the skeleton was buried under the earth.

Most of the historians including Sir John Marshall are of the opinion that the second method of disposal of the dead body was very much practised[188] in the Indian society. Both ordinary and crematory manner of disposal of the dead body were prevalent during the Proto-historic period is evident from *Bara, Ropar* and *Dher Majra*. The dead was buried in pits in extended position, with the head generally on the North along with funerary vessels, as in cemetery R-37 at Harappa. The cemetery of the Harappans at Ropar was a smaller version of cemetery R-37 at Harappa. Some of the skeletons had personal ornaments of the '*Nam'*. A faience bangle was intact on the left wrist of one of the interred, and there was a copper ring on the middle fingers of the right hand of buried body discovered from the excavations. Faience and shell beads are also found from a graveyard. In one graveyard pot contained the skeleton of a dog like *Brahmin* below that of a human being, possibly of its master. *Bara* pottery, occurring promiscuously in the graveyard circle, is limited and it is uncertain if one and the same cemetery was used both by the *Harappans* and the *Barans* of the *Nam*[189].

Economic Condition of the People Under the Proto-historical Period of the Jammu Region.

The big and planned cities of the proto-historical period known as *Harappa* and *Mohenjo-Daro* had the good economic condition of the people. They were not only agriculturists, but also had a sound knowledge of various trade and commerce of the areas. Most of the people of the Jammu Region, they used to live on agriculture economy[190].

Agriculture

The areas of the foothill of the Jammu Region had been famous for its achievements in the field of agriculture and its surplus agricultural produce which give impetus to the development of culture since the days of Harappan cultures or even the earlier period. The people of this region were mostly agrarian. Among the Early Harappan settlements of *Ravi Basin* or *Ravidas Basin* in Punjab and *Rohira* have furnished archaeo-botanical data which provide some information about the agricultural practices. The archeo-botanical remains from the said phase (c. 2300-2000 B. C.) reveals a rich and varied food economy based on the cultivation of cereals and legumes. The cereals comprised barely (*Hordeum vulgare*), Indian dwarf wheat (*Triticum sphtaerococcum*), *emmer* wheat (*Triticum dicocum*) and jowar millet (*Sorghum bicalor*). Among the legumes mentions may be made of lentil (*Consculinaris*) and horse gram (*Dolichosbifirus*). Beside the finds of date-stone (*Phoenix doctylifers*) and grape seed (*Vitis Vinifera*) are of a great interest which tend to show some kind of know how of orchard husbandry was known to Early Harappans of Rohina or '*Ravidas Basin Discovery*'.

The archaeo-botanical remain from the Harappan levels at the same – site are better preserved as compared to the preceding one in the study of *Chamar Culture* or '*Ravidas Culture*' in the British family of India. These include hulled six row barely (*Hordium vulgare L*) naked six row barley (*Hordemum vulgare L, var nudum*), two forms of wheat (*Triticum spaerococcum Perc.)* and some forms resembling a tetraploid species, *Kulthi* or horse gram (*Dolichos biflorus L)* lentil (*Lens cultinais L*) and fenugreek (*Trigonella foenum-graecum L*). The last one is cultivated in Punjab as a fodder crop in connection with the Jammu Region.

The carbonised foodgrains from Mahorana have been referred to as hulled and naked six row barley (*Hordeum vagare L* and *Hordem vulgare L. var nudum*) club wheat (T. *Compacium Host*) and Centil (*Lens culinaris Maedik*) Grape pips (*vitis vinifera L*) have been identified from both the sites Rohira and Mahrana as well as in the adjoining areas of the Jammu region. It is a new archaeo-botanical record for the Indian subcontinent[191], because they are the '*Nams*' of the earth always busy in movement of the earth for it development idea in human History.

Animal Husbandry

Cattle breeding was also known to the people of the Jammu areas. The basic live stock of peasent were cattle. This was used for ploughing, transportion as well as for food. It is interestring to note that one partially exposed refused pit yielded three complete bovine heads. Domestication of Dog for security purpose is suggested by the evidence of the skeleton of a dog in the grave of human being. Besides, animal figurines reported from almost every excavated sites also suggest animal husbandry as already discussed above.

Hunting and Fishing

Besides domestication, hunting of some animals were also in practice. It is suggested by the evidence of a standing human figure with bow and arrow on a sealing from Ropar; Bronze or Copper spearheads and arrowheads from Ropar, Harpoon from Bhudan and other areas of the Jammu region already mentioned above.

Crafts and Industry

A few small kilns exposed from the Early Harappan levels at some sites were used for baking small terracotta objects such as bangle, toys, figurines, found from Akhnoor at Ambaran near Jammu, etc. But from the Harappan levels number of furnaces or kilns (*Bhattis*) were noticed at almost all the excavated sites indicate some industrial activites. A huge platform, circular kiln, poet and multiple hearths and partly exposed room with small circular ovens are noticed at *Dhalewan*. All this found together with steatile beads near the pots and also from the pots suggest an industrial area for making stealing object. Likewise the existence of several furnaces in a row at Kotla-Nihang Khan and Bara which may have been used for manufacturing some implements or ornaments are significant in this connection[192] for the beautification of the body.

Commercial Activities

Although no large –scale commerce during the Early Harappan Period, but a trade of restricted kind with neighouring places is well attested by the different kind of pottery traditions. The Harappan society was basically a Urban society and had certain advance technical knowledge like copper manufacturing and bead making. Ropar, Kotla-Nihang Khan, Dher Majra, Chandigarh were the centres for marketing of Beads. A small statite seal and a Terracotta sealing with impressions of there different seals has been recovered from Ropar. Seals and sealing had been playing an important role in the commercialization of economic set-up of the Harappans. In fact, the good had to be certified by the trading authority by affixing a seal on the packets of goods before it moved for exchange.[191] More than five hundred seals have been discovered. There are made of terracotta and small in size. Some contain fine representations of animal figures '*Nam*' or '*Word*' both mythical and real '*Chamar*' engraved on them. All of them contain a sort record inscribed in a sort of pictorial writing which still remains undeciphered[193] by the Brahmins of the period as a 'Philosopher's' Stone. (*See Plate X, Seal of Mohenjo-Daro; Copyright ASI: Fig. 13*).

Weigth and Measures

The cherted weights from the Harappan phase at *Ropar, Sanghol, Kotla-Nihang Khan, Dhalewan, Dher Majra* implies some sort of commerce, but what merchandise required such weight is not clear[194] from the excavation at *Harappa and Mohenjo-Daro,* but their economy was prosperous due to the fine agriculture system of the areas of the Jammu Region as a 'Law of Nature'.

Religion of the Indus Valley Civilization in Jammu Region[195]

It is difficult to form a clear idea about the true contents of the Harappan Religion. The materials excavated from the Akhnoor at Manda and Ambaran, shows that Indus Valley Civilization had polytheistic Religion. They worshipped Gods and Goddesses in male and female form. Certain animals and human figures were worshipped. A bust of a priest was found which means they had priest clan. The religion also had rituals and ceremonies. Many terracotta status of Mother Goddess have been found and she was wordshipped in nearly every home. A seal showed seated horned deity surrounded by wild animals which could be the Hindu God Shiva as *Pashupati* (Lord of Beasts). This could have been the early religious practices of Hinduism. The numerous seas and figures discovered in the excavations carried out at various sites connected with the Indus Civilization point out to the religious beliefs of the Indus Valley people that they were *Sudhras* having vast knowledge of the society to compile them in one platform i.e., '*Nam*' *or 'God'*. Most of the Indus seals found in the near east differ through their road from the seals native to the Harappan area whch are rectangular in shape.

Important Seals

1. Pashupati Seal: This seal depicts a *yogi* and a pair of horns crown on his head with a plant growing between them. He is surrounded by rhino, buffalo, an elephant and a tiger. This seal shows that *Shiva* was worshipped and he was considered as the Lord of animals or beasts in human form as *Chandal* of the *'Sudhra Family'* worshipped by Brahmins after his death for the study material to develop the mind for Truth where it stands i.e., in picture or body of Shiva and Ravidas.

2. The Unicorn Seal: This seal shows that a very early stage of civilization human had produced many creations of imagination in the shape of birds and animals. The unicorn seal depicts a mythological creature of the *'Nam'* or '*Chamar'*.

3. The Bull Seal: This seal depicts humped but of great vigours already mentioned above.

Religious Beliefs

1. Reverence for Water: People of Indus Valley were reverence for water and belief in its purifying powers with the study of '*Nam*' for the establishment of. 'New Society' of the same community which destroyed by Brahmins. There were bath rooms in individual houses, possibly for ritual purposes. Great bathing tank and dressing rooms and arcades around it shows that there was reverence for water and its purifying power at home after obtaining the '*Nam*' from the Master.

2. Worship of Mother Goddess : A large number of excavated terracotta figures are those of a semi-nude figures which is identified with some female energy or *Shakti*. According to Hinduism, *Shakti* is the source of all creation i.e., '*Nam*' or '*Chamar*'. The figure of Mother Goddess is wearing numerous ornaments and a fan shaped head dress. It is concluded from the smoke figures that the people offered burnt incense before her from the study of 'Brahminical Ideology' that *Chamar* is a hard stone of study as depicts in the Ravidas's history.

3. Tree Worship: One of the sea shows a God standing between the branches of tree and the God was being worshipped by a devotee on his knees, The worship of trees was widespread, Large number of seals with Papal tree engraved on them suggests that this tree was considered sacred as the *'Nam'* and the world.

4. Worship of Pashupati: On another seal three faced male god is shown seated in a *yogic* posture surrouded by a rhino and a he-buffalo on the right and an elephant and a tiger on the left. People worshipped this deity in those days who is Lord of the Beasts and the male principal of creative of everything in the world.

5. The Phallus: Excavation of a large number of coinical or cylindrical stone show that the people worshipped *lingam*, the symbol of Lord Shiva. Religious emphasis seems to be concerned with male generative powers as suggested by figurines and seals that depict powerful male animals such as elephants, tigers, bulls, rhinocerose and antelopes of the '*Nam'*, because, he had the full control over the illegal sex. Therefore, he had been worshipped by the people.

6. Other Objects of Worship : People also worshipped animals such as the bull, buffalo and tiger. Mythical animals worship is evident from the existence of human figure with a bull's horns, hoofs and a tail. Besides animals these people also worshipped the sun the fire and the water of the '*Nam*' or '*God*'.

7. Magic, Sacrifices and Charms : Amulets suggests that people had belief in magic and charms. Some seals have figures of men and animals in act of sacrificing. This shows that sacrifices were also a part of the Indus Valley Civilization during the absence of the Master.

8. Ritual Bathing : The one of the largest building excavated is great bathing pool i. e., '*Nam*', 180 feet. It is surrounded with *verandahs*, rooms and galleries. A flight of steps led to the pool. The existence of other public baths suggests that the people believed in ritual bathing early in the morning to meditate the '*Nam-mantra*'.

9. Disposal of the Dead: Only two cemeteries have been excavated, it contained extended earth-burial with the head generally to the North. Dead bodies were laid to rest fully stretched, but quite frequently with legs inflexed has already discussed in detail.

10. Life after Death: They buried their dead together with household pottery, ornament and other articles of daily use. In case of cremation of the dead they preserved the ashes of the bodies in clay wins. Both of the above practices buried or cremation show that people belived in life after death by obtaining the qualification of the '*Nam*' to realize the Father as a 'Supernatural Force' of the world.

Around 1500 B. C. the Indus Valley Civilization came to an abrupt end because of the migration of the soul from one generation to another. Evidence shows that the civilization could have been declined because of floods washed away the villages, soil lost fertility,famine and drought casued people to flee or neighbouring desert encroached on the fertile area and made it infertile to study the reality where it stands. But conclusive evidence of thick ash layers, fractured skulls, weapons such as copper axe, swords 1. 5 feet long and copper harpoons shows that in fact the sole reason for the decline was due to the invasion of highly barbaric Aryans. They invaded the various brilliant Civilizations of the world and put to end them with the power of *'Nam'* or '*Word'*. They also invaded the Indus cities of the Saraswati Valley Civilization and destroyed it. In the study, it makes clear that most brilliant and technically advanced civilization of the ancient world was vanished by them, and *India* or *Bharata* was plunged in to 2000 years in the period of Dark Age for the study of Brahmins which proved inefficient to compile this project with the help of Father or '*Nam*' as a real investigator of the earth i. e., Deepit Raj.

Nature of the Political Structure of the Harappan People in India or in Bahrat Varsha

The nature of the political structure of the Indus Valley people both of Harappa and Mohenjo-Daro was a confederation of several independent States which maintained close relationship with each other in different socio-economic levels of the *'Nam'* based on *Ravidas Culture* and the brought forth a solid cultural unity of the *'Nam'* on earth from the heaven as the 'Representative Ruler of the Divine Light', like, *Ashoka, Firoz Shah Tughlaq, Akbar,* etc. Stuart Piggott had suggested that uniformity of the culture and continuity of the Harappan Civilization was because of it being an 'Unified Empire'[196] i.e., the idea of Imperialism which was given by Dr. B.R. Ambedkar in the Indian Constitution, i.e., 'Classless' and 'Casteless' society governed by the '*Priest Kings*' of the '*Nam*' mentioned above. Wheeler has rightly suggested again the example of same on a highly centralized administration under a '*Priest King*' of the '*Nam*'as in Mesopotamiania and Egypt[197].

The views of both, Piggott and Wheeler still continue to find echo in many University text books. In this context, A. L. Basham, for example, refers to a single centralized theocratic state during the Harappan period[198] called as *Kulli Culture* of the same family of the Father.

Allchin and Allchin suggest the presence of 'Priest –King's or a priestly oligarchy controllong religious as well as economic and civll functions of the state[199] under the Head Priest i.e., *Deepti Raj*, Puskas too locates Supreme Power in the hands of the priest[200] S. Ratnagar using both archeological and anthropological evidence postulates that the strong similarities in the artifacts of daily use as bricks, weights, chert tools, shell bangles, etc. is indicative of a political system in which the state controlled all the economic activites connected with crafts and trade including labour mobilisation and agree in favour of a Harappan 'Empire' with a unitary state Orgnisation[201] direct link with the 'Head – Priest King' through the power of *'Nam' or God.* She, though admits that the entire Harappan area could not be brought into one network through coercion or State Institution alone, refuses to accept the role of trade or trade'guilds in bringing about the unity or homogeneity[202]. Recently, Irfan Habib, in a small booklet argues for an 'Indus Empire' and surmises that the homogeneity witnessed during the Harappan period was result of a 'Centralized Control' of the Father through conquest or subjugation of other regions by the States in the core area[203] of the heart as depicted in the *'Ravidas Picture'* as a reality base '*Nam*' of the Father.

In his opinion, the evidence of spears and bows and arrows as depicted on Harappan seals indicates that the state had sufficient military power to expand and maintain itself and adds that the Indus state was probably a monarchy' with its capital either at Harappan or Mohenjodaro. But, the above hypothesis regarding the Harappan polity as an 'empire' or one 'single unified state' under a King or a Priest-King has been questioned by many archeologists and anthropologists such as W. A. Fairservise[204], S. C. Malik[205]. Jim Shaller[206], Dhavlikar[207], Possehi[208]. B. B. Lal[209], Kenoyer[210] etc. It is argued that the term 'empire' emphasized the concept of war, conquest and coercion with the help of a well –organized army and adequate weapons of offence and defence. But the Harappan period, the evidence of militaristic ideology is quite weak and there is little to suggest, the presence of a professional army.[211] The weapons found at Harappan sites includes spear, knives, short swords, axes, arrow-heads, etc. most of which as mentioned by Wheeler.[212] appear to have been employed in hunting rather than in war. Some scholars have called attention to large number of clay spherriods or balls found at various places which could have been used as sling or had missiles[213] but their actual use or effectiveness as a weapon of war is highly doubtful i.e., '*Nam*'.

The role of army in the Harappan Civilization has, infact, been a matter of some debate. It is argued that a human figure on a seal carrying a long staff and interpreted by *Mahadevan* as a 'warrior' the identification of a shield – bearing figure on a post sherd from *Surkotda* [214] the indication of the presence of guard-rooms for watchmen at Mohenjodaro and *Surkotda*[215] and a fine bronze statue of man with spear and a double –bun hairstyle from *Chanhudaro*[216] '*Chamar*' all indicate that Harappans were not as non-violent or peaceful as they are supposed to be. But still it is not confirmed that the Harappan people had an organized army for war and conquest and all the above pieces of evidence may at best be interpreted to suggest the presence of some police force or constabulary for the maintenance of nesceary law and order were there in the white uniform.

The fortifications around the 'citadels' have been taken by some or reflect their military character and dominace over the local populace[217]. But it is argued that the fortification walls are apparently limited out of more than two thousand Harappan sites to a few sites only. At certain places such as *Kalibangan*, Lothal, Surkotda, etc., the fortificaton walls enclose the lower town as well. Besides, it is quite possible that these walls were meant for animals or flood protection rather than for military defence[218] through the power of '*Nam*'.

Piggott's view that Harappa and Mohenjodaro formed the 'twin capitals' of the unified Harappan empire is also grossly flawed because as the recent excavations reveal, apart from these two towns, there were other important sites such as *Rakhigarhi* in Haryana, *Ganweriwal* in *Cholistan* (Pakistan), Dholavira in Kutch, etc., which appear to be in no way less important than the first two. [219] Therefore, no positive case can be made for the 'twin capitals' of the Harappan empire of that period.

It is also emphasized that the absence of any monumental structure which may be identified as a 'palace' or a 'temple' such as the ziggurats at Mesopotami also goes against the concept of a strong unitary regime under a political or religious authority during the Harappan period. Though in the view of S. Ratnagar the 'citadel' area at Modenjodaro might have served as a palace –like entity[220] still there is no clear evidence of a structure containing the abodes of the politically powerful elites. There are also no 'royal tombs' like the pyramids of Egypt which are different from others as they have a brick lining or contain more funeral pots, but these are in no way close to the "royal –tombs", and may just reflect the presence of more affluent and less affluent classes in the society.

As regards the religious structure, the only architectural remains which may be associated with it are those of the 'Great Bath' at Mohenjodaro or the so called 'fire-altars' at *Kalibangan, Lothal and Banawali.* But these again cannot be treated in the true sense of the them. It may be added that a large number of female figurines representing 'Mother Goddess' which have been reported from Mohenjodaro and Harappan are absent at other places such as Kalibangan and Lothal. It clearly indicates an element of diversity in the religious practices of the Harappans and suggests that there was no dominant priesthood enforcing single state religion over the vast area of the Harappan Civilization. However, in all ancient societies the priests played an important role in the socio-political system and their services were used to manufacture myths and perform rituals to legitimize the power an authority of the ruling elite[221]. The Harappan society appears to be no exception but presently there is no evidence that it was ruled or managed by the priests.

In short, the possibility of Harappan political organization being a centralized administration under an 'emperor' or a 'high-priest' is quire remote, and as G. Possehi rightly remarks the available evidence clearly indicates that the Harappans did not believe in the cult of personality, either, of a King or a high-priest[222] of the '*Nam*' of '*Ravidas Culture*'- like Dr. Raj Kumar or *Raj Rishi.*

The main criticism of Piggott and Wheeler comes fron Fairservise who accuses them of applying Sumerian and Egyptian models to explain the political system of the Harappan Civilizarion.[223] According to him Sumeria had a limited cultivable zone and, therefore, a centralized authority was needed to have an efficient control on irrigation and land use. Besides, there were multiplicity of cities which gave rise to inter-urban strife and thus created further condition for centralization. But in the Harappan zone in contrast to the multiplicity of "urban sites, there were majority of village sites and only limited "Urban centres. Moreover, the problem of Sindh was not lack of water, but too much of it. Therefore, neither an inter-urban warfare nor irrigation problem could have been a factor for centralization as in Mesopotamia, Thus, Fairservise argues that the rigid control by a therocratic or a secular government in Harappan period is out of question[224] and suggest that Harappan political organisation may have been on 'chiefdom'.[225] According to him, the animals such as bull, buffalo, tiger, elephant, etc. which the composite or combination of animals on certain seals indicate their clan unity or 'sodality' (brotherhood). He believes that the 'unicorn' symbol which is represented on the maximum number of seal was that of the paramount chief who was assisted in administrative and economic activites of collection and distribution by 'subsidiary chiefs' with other symbols. S. C. Malik also believed that Harappan political organization was marked by 'petty chiefdons' with local authority for maintaining rules and regulation[226] of the different States.

But his above view is also flawed because as pointed out by S. Ratnagar[227] chiefdom represents that level of politican organization in which the chief belongs to an aristocratic descent and claims tribute i.e., voluntary token of payment from kinsmen. Such societies are limted in scope for the development of economic activities and therefore the urbanization of the type noticed in the Mature Harappan period is not viable in the context of chiefdom. As regards the animals projected on the seals, the predominance symbol is no doubtful significant, but its exact meaning in the context of Harappan political organization is impossible to infer.

Thus, once it is settled that the Harappan political organization was neither an "empire nor a chiefdom." it is possible to argue that it was a state in the accepted sense of the term. A State Society is marked by certain speech characteristic such as town with large population, powerful bureaucracy social and economic stratification trade and exchange network, mechanism[228] for tax-collections, a coercive authority to resolve internal disputes, etc. and the presence of many of these elements can be noticed in Harappan period.

A number of town such as Harappan Mohenjodaro, Kalibangan, Dholavira, etc. with planned and developed architecture and large population from an important features of the Harappan Civilization. The existence of bureaurcrary and it controls on the people can be inferred from the encroachment free streets, uniformity in weigths and measures, etc. The standardized seals which were used for marking the goods of exchange also be token of the presence of bureaucracy. The social stractifcation is evident from the variation in the resident structures having one to twelve rooms[229]. A few burials which are brick-lined and contain comparatively more funerary vessels also reflect a *hiatus* between the social and economic position of those buried. The discovery of such items as cubical weights, parts of weighting balance and measuring scales from certain sites offer strong circumstantial evidence of market form of exchange. Wheeled toy-vehicles and the representation of boats on pottery and seals point to an effiective inter-settlement communication. The indisputable evidence of long-distance trade with Mesopotamia and Central Asia, as reflected in the Sumerian Inscription and the Indus seals from West Asia,[230] including the area of Jammu and Kashmir State, is clear pointer towards an administrative sophistication peculiar to a state level society capable of co-ordinating complex trade activites between the two nation theory of the *'Nam'* or *'Chamar'* or God and man.

An important evidence of the nature of the developed economic organization during this period can further be noticed in site specialization, i.e., the sites devoted to a specific craft or economic activity. Thus, for example, while Lothal served as an international port, Shortugai acted as a trading outpost for trade in *lapis lazuli* and *Kuntasi* as an industrial centre. Rafiq Mughal's explorations in the region of Cholistan in Pakistan has led to a discovery of many Harappan industrial sites which specialized either in brick-making or pottery production or copper smelting[231]. It is quite obvious that to support such a wide-ranging full -time specialized craft activites, there must have been a state-level organization. As regards the coercive authority as an attribute of a state, it has already been pointed out by Surpras that though the Harappans did not have a standing or professional army, they do appear to have had the necessary armed constabulary or police force to enforce discipline and maintain law and order of the region with the power of '*Nam*'.

As far as, tax-collection is concerned, it may be admitted that it is difficult to locate an evidence for it in the archaeological records. Wheeler once suggested that of the 'granaries' at Harappa and Mohenjodaro represented the state 'banks, for accumulating tax or tribute from the people[232]. But this identification has been seriously questioned by Jansen, Shaffer and Fentress as similar granaries have not been reported from many other Harappan sites[233]. However, it may be remarked that the high degree of craft production and goods distribution as noticed in the Harappan period could not have survived on forced labour alone, and there must have been some definite source of revenue to run the state machinery for the serves of agriculture production.

Thus, in the light of the above arguments, it may be suggested that the Harappan political system was probably a state organization characterized by its general features. But the question still remains whether it was a single unified state or a combination of various regional polities with their own hinterlands to sustain themselves. Rafiq Mughal pointing out the fallacy of viewing Harappa and Mohenjodaro as twin capital of the Indus empire refers to the discovery of similarly large and evently spaced settlements all over the Harappan region. It may, therefore, be better to view the Harappan poitical structure as made up of closely related regional polities or eco-zones which interacted with each other on various socio-economic levels and forged the cultural uniformity. While Rafiq Mughal believed, there could have been five dominant regional polities centred around. *Harappa*, *Mohenjodaro*, *Rakhigarhi*, *Ganweriwala* and *Dholavira*[234]. sB.B. Lal is inclined to add three more politico-economic centres, Viz, *Banawali, Kalibangan* and Lothal to them[235]. Possehl who proposes to divide whole of Harappan region in to different sub-divisions called "domains' such as '*Kulli*' or '*Chamar*'domain, *Sindhi* domain, Cholistan domain, Eastern domain, etc., also in his recent text, tends to believe that these sub-regions may have served as different units of 'Harappan polities'[236].

This concept of regional polities and their cultural homogeneity recalls the model of "peer-polity interaction" as envisaged by Cherry and Renfrew[237]. According to it, the peer-polities i.e., the small independent states with approximately equal territories and evenly spaced regional centers get involved with each other in close interaction which may be in the form of matrimonial ties or exchange of gift or even competition in wealth display or in promotion of ceremonial centres, etc. Such interaction in course of time stimulates settlement of population in specific areas and promotes production and economic exchange of similar nature. In other words, the concept of "peer-polity interaction" emphasizes that uniformity in material culture may not necessarily imply a political unification under one rule, political or theocratic, and it may as well be a result of socio-economic interaction among several groups of equal status. It may be noted that later in the sixth century B. C. too when Northen India was divided in to sixteen '*Mahajanapadas*' (territorial States), these was a considerable amount of homogeneity in the material culture over the whole area. Therefore, the scenario of the existence of serval independent state societies interacting with each other during the Harappan period cannot be brushed aside with '*Nam*' or '*Word*'.

As the absence of a palace or temple like structure rules out the possibility of the presence of a dominant political or religious authority, it is quite possible that of chief role in ths interaction was played by the mercantile class. The role of trade as an 'intensifier' of Harappan Urbanism is hotly debted among the scholars[238] but one cannot ignore the fact that the most important features, particularly the seals and script or the weights and measures which distinguish the mature phase with its preceding and following phase are all directly associated with trade and commence. It seems that the growth of commercial activity as a result of inter-regional contact led to the emergence of a dominant group of 'economic elites' who with the help of priest, bureaucrats and others controlled the administrative apparatus during the Brahminical period of thought. Thus, the Harappan Civilization may have been a 'trading empire' polarized around the important regional centres under the control of mercantile groups. However, the final word on the subject must await further archaeological evidence along with the '*History of the Nam*' as a final verdict on the Day of Judgement to start a New Era of the man's life with the 'Voice of God'.

General Conclusion

From the study of the Prehistoric period, we learn the Indus Valley Civilization raises several interesting problems of the general nature in human life to refine the race. In the first place, when we analysis the '*Early History of Jammu Region*' from the Prehistoric period to onwards, it offer to striking that *Ravidas Culture* was widely spread to all over the worlds idiot Brahmins deliberately dominated this concept that he was '*Untouchable*'. Study indicates that various ancient Civilization, which were developed from time to time, the people of the '*Chamar Dynasties*', they worked for the welfare of the State and its machinery. The development of the various city life, they worked as potter wheel of the '*Nam*', kiln burnt bricks, and vessels made of copper and bronze and above all, the pictorial writings are some of the common and distinctive features of all the three civilizations of the Pre-historic period. The discovery of the two seals of the Mohenjodaro in Elam and Mesopotamia and of a *Cuneiform Inscription at Mohenjodaro,* leave, no doubt, that there was an intercourse between these civilizations and their States. The Vedic Aryans worshipped the cow while the Indus people reserved their veneration for bulls. Not only do the Mother Goddess and Siva were the chief deities of the Indus Valley people of the Manda origin discussed above of Akhnoor Valley, belongs to the 3rd millennium B.C. have the *Ravidas Culture* which ignored by the Brahminical communities without any reasoning of the problem, but only on the basis of occupation which they had at that time. In view of these striking dissimilarities, the Indus Valley people of the *Coolie or Kulli* Culture or *Ravidas Culture* is usually regarded as different from the study point of view in the practical life. But some would place the Vedic Civilization before that of the Indus Valley was shifted to *Rig-veda* Culture to a period before 3000 B.C. again. On the whole, however, the priority of the Indus-Valley Civilization of the Jammu Region appears to be more probable, which left in obscure by the modern historians of Delhi University as well as from the other Universities of the Indian States.

Lastly, there is a question of race among the people of Indus Valley people that, their race was *Dravidians, Mongols, Aryan, Alpines,* etc. originated from the lowly origin i.e., '*Nam*' or '*Chamar*' of the society of the '*Sudhra Family*', restricted upto the economic zones of the *Saraswati* Indus Valley of the Jammu Region to predict their '*History*'. Author has made an attempt to assess the reasons for the decay of Punjab Culture, if one cares to probe into the past in the Punjab, Jammu and Kashmir and its adjoining areas that the colonies along the *Indus-Saraswati Valley* of the Jammu Region that the hymns of the *Rig-Veda* were again composed into fresh form. In the Punjab, the pasalmists song *Rigvedic* hymns up to North invoking their Gods for victory by preaching their teachings in Kashmir against the aborigin, the opponents of the Aryans called *Brahmins* or *Molabis* of the period. The *Sindhu* (Indus Valley) "the far famed bestower of wealth," in this area, is he object of special praise and veneration. Mention is made of the '*Sapta Sindhu*' (identified by Iranian as the "*Hafta Hindu*" in their holy book A*vesta*), or in Seven Rivers as dwelling place of the Aryans. These are *Sindhu* (Indus), *Vitasta* (Jhelum), *Asikni* or *Acesines* (Chenab), *Iravati* (Ravi), *Vipasa* (Beas), and *Satadru* (Satluj). The seventh river was *Saraswati* identified with *Sarsuti* of the *Vedic* times called the 'Valley of Akhnoor' as its origin to repeat the history, time and again, which Brahmins of the period have been forgotten like Gulchain Singh Charak and others. Even, Rishi *Valmiki* composed his celebrated work of *Ramayana* in Punjab "the Pool of Nectar", in the midst of which the *Golden Temple of Amritsar* today stands[239]. Archaeology is the study of antiquities. It is the science of earlier history of man for understanding the Nations, class and society from the artifacts already mentioned above, building, dresses, ornaments, implements, etc., of the period of a few or no written records as found in the Jammu and Kashmir area as a good part of dealing with *prehistoric antiquities* and other part is concerned with *artifacts* of the historical period to repeat the history of the ancient India and its culture, which have been destroyed by Brahminical historians of the same country.

Notes and References

1. A. L Basham; *The Wonder That Was India*; New Delhi; Reprint; 2003 p. 10. Hereafter referred as *W. T. W. I.*
2. Dr. Arun Kesarwani; *Pre-Historic Punjab*; A *Reassessment* (From the Dawn of Man to the First urban civilization Presidential Address in PHC, 37 session, March 18-20, 2005. p. 42. **Note**: These survey were made for the last more than 3 or 4 years by the American Archaeologists and have found in remains of a culture earlier to Harappans which is similar to '*Hakra Ware Culture*' of the '*Nam*' of Bahalulpur region found along the river *Saraswati Indus* of the Akhnoor Region had the base on the right bank of the *Chenab* in Jammu, now, it is in Pakistan. At a site called Mehrgarh, there is ample evidence of the Neolithic Culture going back to 7,000 B. C. on the basis of several Radio-Carbon dates. The remains of later phases of which are found at *Harappa* on the river Ravi; it is called the *Ravi Hakra Culture* by the American excavators like Richard Meadow and Pakistani Archaeologist like Rafique Mughal who excavated the site of Jalilpur near Harappa on the Ravi, there are several other sites also on the rivers like theIndus, the Ravi, the Chaneb and Sutlej which take the antiquity of Civilization in Punjab near Jalandhar to the 4th and 5th millennium B. C. However, this is also a part of human history in Panjab and Jammu and Kashmir itself. The Hills of the Panjab plains is infact geographically and historically has '*One Culture*' *i. e., 'Ravidas Culture'* or

'Chamar Culture' which reflected from the cradle of *Primates,* who were supposed to be earliest stage of *'Ape-man'* of the remotest ancestors of the humans i.e. *'Chamars'* as their *Caste* pure by nature. They are dated to 12-8 million years ago working in the human history as *'Nam'* on earth. The fossilized bones of several species of these *Primates* named *Ramapithecus, Sivapithecus,* etc., have been in the *Siwalika* Hills. It is significant to note that alongwith the fossilized bones of these Primates, there are the bones of animals of the contemporary period of the Indian history. Which are now completely extinct, the specimens of which are in the Panjab University Museums, Chandigarh. Archealogical discoveries of the Primates or supposed to be the ancestors of human being i.e. *'Dr. Raj Kumar', 'Baba Gurinder Singh Biaswale', 'Master Deepit Raj' and Dr. Ram Dass* as a family of human species, were there, in the Early Life already mentioned above. The second part of their discourse will be devoted to the 'History of Stone Age Cultures as their study in natural theme of the Punjab and the other parts of the continent of the Central Asia that is the area Jammu and Kashmir State, generally dated to 5 lac years ago to the Holocene period of the human history dated to 10,000 B.C. The third part will cover the Neolithic phase of the History, the Panjab dated to between 8000 B.C. to 5000 B.C. The fourth part will be deovted to the Harappan Civilization of the Bronze Age sometimes called the *Indus-Saraswati Civilization of Manda or Indus Valley Civilization* extremely important proto-historic site as the Northern most in the town of Akhnoor (32° 54' N, 74° 45 E') is situated picturesquely on the right bank of the Chenab, 28 Km. South-West of Jammu foothills of *Pir Panjal* range. A few kilometers after river debunchs into the plains of Jammu Region. The Harappan site of Manda named after the village *Manda* i.e. the theory of the mind is destructive for human history, with the growth of the Mental power (Mine Power) the destruction was took place of this civilization, belongs to 3rd millennium B. C. of the Indus history. It shows that Civilization of the Jammu Region of the pre-historic period was flourishing under the title of *'Ravidas Culture'* or *'Chamar Culture'*, which hatred by the modern *'Brahmin Culture'* that is *'Black Culture'* having no human history in their mind and heart. (Ibid. pp. 37-38 A. K. Khanna; *Akhnoor, A Historical Township*; An article published in *'Daily Excelsior,* dated 10-6-2007).

3. *Ibid.*, p. 38.

4. *Ibid., p.* 39 **Note:** Elwyn L. Simons's was strongly supported by his student David Pilbeam and it soon gained wide acceptance among anthropologists. In 1965 and 1985, the human skeletons unearthened from Harappan cemeteries, were examined and it was earlier announced that original (*Mulnivasi*) Harappans

Jammu Kingdom in about 2100 B. C. extended upto Kashmir as the latest discovery of the artifact from the Bijbihara have been taken place by Indian Archealogists. But in later examination, the earlier decisions were turned down to the lack of the knowledge of historians neglect the rich historical place of India and declared that the people of *Harappas* were akin to present in Panjab as a Community called *Chamars* and those of Mohenjodaro akin to the people of present Sindh *(Indus)* as the people of the '*Nam*' or God having simple style of living and honest from the nature. It means no invaders or outsiders came there in a period of about 5000 years before, since there is no ethnical change. But this is a big lie of the modern *Brahmins* or politicians. Hence, there is a need of its reappraisal, time and again in the human history as life a destructive material made from natural objects i.e., water, earth, fire, air and ether. Thus, as per the views of the historians and Archeaologists of India, according to Junanath Sarkar the Megalith builders had the foreign strain and the aboriginal strain in them and that the former of the pre-historic period, probably, belonged to the Indo-European group of people living in Iran and Central Asia in the area of Jammu and Kashmir State including Ladakh itself. The skulls from *Adichanallur* graves were earlier examined by Zuckerman who identified them as '*Dravidian*' of the Mediterranean stock. Recently Chatterji and Gupta, S. P. examined thirteen other skulls from the same site. Of these three show *Veddid* Austroloid affinity, five exhibit Mediterranean features and one each of the remaining two belongs to Armenoid branch of the Mediterranean and Proto-Australoid types. This again shows an admixture of western and autochthonous physical types in the population of *Adichanallur* which is equivalent to the term *Candala* or *Chanal* of the *'Sudhra Family*'. Gupta and Dutta have examined six more skulls from *Yelleswaram,* of which three were of males and three of females. They were all broad headed showing feature similar to those found in the skulls from Sialk cemetery. They, following Sarkar's study call them *Scytho-Iranian*, people from the region of Ukraine between 1000 and 2000 B. C., but the range of cranial index (77-79) ascribed to this stock is indeed high among the present Iranian population. It means, Scythians were a long headed race like *Chamars* of ancient India. H. H. Risley, who stated that; 'Scythian called *Gujjara* (Gurjar) of India is a *dolicho-cephalic* race. " (Dr. Naval Viyogi; *Reappraisal* of Scientific *Studies of Human Skeleton Unearthened from the Harappan Cemeteries*. An article presented in Indian History Congress, Dec. 28-30, Delhi; 2007; H. H. Risley; '*The People of India*'*;* Appendix III).

5. *W. T. W. I.*, p. 10
6. Dr. Kesarwani; op. cit. p. 39.
7. *W. T. W. I.*, p. 10 *Note.* It shows from the study that this industry was common in Madras, as it is called by the Archealogists, has affinities with

7. *W. T. W. I.*, p. 10 *Note.* It shows from the study that this industry was common in Madras, as it is called by the Archealogists, has affinities with similar core tool industries in Africa, Western Europe, and Southern England, where it has been found in association with a more advanced type of man, a true *Homo sapiens.*
8. Souvenir *Indian History Congress*, 67th Session 2007 March 10-12, Farook College Calicut, see editor's, note, M. P. Mujeebu Rehman. Author has rightly elaborated that Malabar had the very ancient times itself the Romans,Greeks, Chinese, Assyrians, Arabs, etc. the relation with India had made trade contacts with it, and the result of which is formation of cultural diversity and symbiosis of culture. Thus, during the time of Mughals, there was the course of history and politics of Malabar underwent a major shift by the intervention of European powers from the Portuguese *Dum* culture to British Culture, they followed the policy of the '*Ravidas Chamar*', a wonderful personality at the time of for the establishment of Mughal rule in India with friendship of Babar, belonged same category, i.e., called *Sudhra* in Indian History. Indeed without the encouraging response and support of the Brahminical scholar could not explore this culture, because the materialized the reality into *Dark* Age. In this context of the history of Kerala, Archaeology acquires a significant place from certain other points of view as to confirm the authentic history of the modern man. Right from the days of Kosambi and the later rulers of the ancient India, there has been a high interest in, and importance attached to, Archaeology in India from the more relevant consideration of historical objectivity in the life of man. In a society like India where a vast majority of the people of the '*Sudhra* Family', they were denied a say either in the social or in the religions domain, they have no history, where the lion share of the historical documents has had an obvious enlitist bias in the interest of man, which would make the available and known history an exposition of the life of the dominant classes alone leaving the subaltern voices unheard or being put to the marginal tribes of the frontiers who deprived from the rights by the modern politicians of the state all over India. In an effort to find alternative sources other than the elitist i.e., the '*Nam*' or '*Chamar*' on earth to trace out the history of the subaltern people from a more objective point of view to in realistic approach. Archeaology was looked upon as the only viable alternative to compile the authentic history of the ancient culture as a dialogue between the present and the past through again the real persons of the history. Real history should come from the earth and not from the words of the Brahman. While frantically attacking the so-called 'baseless history, current in Kerala, P. K. Bala Krishnan in 1980s alerted the historians to be more accountable by writing history source based knowledge or at least by testing with reference to Archaeological data of the period and to find out the truth. However, in South India there was a great

represents non-geometric located at different places and period (*Archaeology in Kerala, Past and Present,* edited by M. R Manmathan Kerala, 2007, pp. 6, 77-79 Hereafter referred as *A. K. P. P*).

9. Jaya Jaitly; *Crafts of Jammu, Kashmir and Ladakh; Ahmedabad*, 1990, p. 13. Hereafter explained as *C. J. K. L.*

10. *Ibid.*, p. 14 **Note**. In the third century B. C. the great Mauryan Emperior Ashoka sent Buddhist Missionaries from Kashmir to Ladakh, and the adjoining area of the Jammu region, i. e., *Rajouri, Poonch, Sudhmahadeva, Sindh, Multan, Jammu* itself, etc., before that the missionaries established their firm relation in *Srinagara* (Srinagar). Kashmir became the base from where great works of Buddhism and scholarly Sanskrit and Pali literature was widely flourished in throughout the world, and Buddhism became popular, and the region evolved as the crucible of the Kashmir history of a highly civilized cultural expression where from *Buddhism, Shaivism* later on *Islam* in the same form in Arabic language was flourished. By now Jammu, Kashmir and Ladakh had become historical trading centres in the heart of the Asian Continent. They served as gateways between the Panjab and the Indo-Gangetic plain and lay on the Silk Trade Route of Central Asia as a heart of the whole world in the context of study of Buddhism of the *Chamar* historywhich lost in the human history. No doubt, traders from Khotan, Yarkand, Kashgar, and other trading posts between China and the Mediterranean sea passed through here for the civilizational growth from one generation to another. The Caravans of merchants traded in silk, shawl, wool, carpets, spices, silver, turquosie, salt, tea and tabocco, creating a rich interlocking of commodities. These trade routes became passage ways for cultural movements enriching the minds and sense of responsibility of its people belong to the working class. (Ibid., pp. 14,15).

11. *Souvenir, Calicut,* 2007; *Genesis and Spread of Islam in Karala;* An article written by Dr. T. A. Mohamed. p. 53.

12. *Ibid.*, p. 23.

13. *A. K. P. P.* p. 73 **Note**: All these data mentioned aboe demonstrate that in the later phase of the '*Later Vedic Period*', particularily with the expansion of the Brahminical culture in the East and West, the activities of the traders adhering (in a large number) towards Buddhism when Ashoka established his Kingdom in Kashmir at that time India was emerging a great power in the world to defeat the Brahmins and Jammu too was centre of trade, and trade routes which contracted the whole world for the focus of standard and transactions of the social activities concerning with religious trade centre of the Scientific Knowledge which was based on Kashmir and studied by the later rulers of the same family of the '*Ravidas Culture*'.

14. A. K. Khanna; *Akhnoor, A Historical Township* **Note**: In the early hymns of the *Rig-Veda*, *Indra*, the most popular diety called *Megha*, is said to of *Megha* community to be the possessor of *ratna* or jewellery. Panini's grammatical treatise the *Ashtadyayi* of the fifth century B. C., includes a number of ornaments which still retain their original names i.e., Dr. Raj Kumar, Baba Gurinder Singh Ji Biaswale, Dr. Ram Dass and Master Deepit Raj as the real '*Sound*' producer of the Indian History. Thus, from the time immemorial, people of this community have adorned themselves first with precious ornaments, i.e., '*Nam*' and the people of Jammu, Kashmir and Ladakh which is the part of the China called tiny Japan or Tibet vividly demonstrate the continuity of this tradition as our study reveal. The love of ornamentation and the skill of the art originated by *Chamar* terms with which stones, gold, silver and other materials were shaped to fashion jewellery, time and again, in their thought show the remarkable imagination and dexterity of the crafts people of this region with the meditation of the '*Nam*'. While the historian Kalhana in his *Rajatarangini* often refers to the *nupura hara*, anklet, *Kankana*, wristlet, *Keyura, armlet* (*bajuband*), *parihara*, bracelet and *Kundala* earring, archeaological evidence all over the state reveals the wealth of ornaments popular at different periods of the study. At *Manda* near Akhnoor in Jammu the find of a double headed, metallic hair pin already mentioned above fashioned on the Harappan design speaks eloquently of the beautification of the female coiffure. An image of the first century A. D. found in Southern, Bijbehara shows that women used to wear the *Channavirat* or cross belt while men fancied ornamental caps. During the second and third century A. D. a large number of ornaments were used for embellishment and the people were so fond of them that they even used bejewelled trappings method for their horses. Men and women wore huge circular *Kundalas*, or earrings, which they continue to do in the rural areas of the state as we take the example of *Manda* village of Akhnoor (*C. J. K. L* pp. 203, 205).

15. A. K. Khanna; *Tawi Rivers*; An article published in *Daily Excelsior*, 29-7-2007 **Note.** According to the another legend, these two great rivers having twin lakes in their areas which formed the early epic history of the man when *Arjuna* used his arrow on the earth to bring out water on the surface. The belief is that prior to fighting *Mahabharata* battle, the *Pandavas* during their exile from Hastinapur for 13 years were dewlling in *Siwaliks* of Jammu Region. One day their mother *Kunti* felt thirst but *Pandavas* found no water due the sacarcity of the water in the Brahminical period as this belt of Jammu had felt, then *Yudhister* sent his brothers to all directions for search of water but all in vain. So ultimately Arjuna used his arrow on the earth which entered from one place and came out from another spot, a few kilometer from the first and '*Kali*

Shesh Nag' located on the bank of the *Mansar Lake* the Mansar lake is, thus an abbreviated form of *Mansarovar*. The name Mansarovar in Sanskrit is combination of two words *Mana* and *Sarovar* ("*Mind* and *Lake*", respectively. (Dr. R. D Gupta & Swami Raj Dogra; *Twin Lakes of Jammu*; i. e. Known as *Mansar & Surinsar* after this event. An article published in '*Daily Excelsior*, 23-9-2007).

16. A. K. Khanna; *Akhnoor, A Historical Township.* **Note:** The Neolithic sites which have been found in Punjab, Pakistan at present in *Mehrgarh* is the earliest pre-ceramic Neolithic site goes back to the 7th Millennium. Kile Gul Mohamanad is a pre-ceramic Neolithic site which witnessed a transition from food gathering of hand made pottery, mirroliths and bone tools. In most of the sites the Neolithic phase is followed by Kot Dijian or Early Harappan phase. Neolithic Culture has been reported from the Kashmir Valley (Buzzahom and Gufkar) having possible links with the Kotalijians. The Akhnoor area of Jammu region has also reported Neolithic pholished stone celts. *Mohapatra* collected a few pieces of rising stones at *Ror* in Himachal Pradesh in the form of Mohan Dass Namishroy, *Jativa* by caste having close typolitical resemblance with the study of '*Nam*' *or God* on earth with Burzahom in *Srinagar* in the form of Dr. Raj Kumar having the same idea and thought in his mind as Dr. B. R Ambedkar used to have during his life time. Besides *Ror* polished stone axes have also been reported from Dehra-Gopipur and Bawli in Himchal Pradesh (Madhu Bala; *Archaelogy of Punjab*; New Delhi; 1992, p. 14 Thereafter referred as A. P. See R. N. Kaw; The *Neolithic Culture of Kashmir*, *Essays in Indian Protohistory*; New Delhi; 1979 (eds.) D. P. Agarwal & D. K. Chakraborty).

17. C. J. K. L. P. 192 **Note.** It is for the common knowledge that the first Urban Civilization as already mentioned of the Harappan or the *Indus-Saraswati* of the *Manda* village of Akhnoor people flourished their culture in Punjab during the study of the period due the geographical change in the history of India from 3800 B. C. to 2000 B. C. After the discovery of *Harappa* on the bank of river Ravi in 1921 a large number of sites have been discovered in Punjab having the effect of '*Ravidas Culture*'. Haryana, North-Western U. P. Rajasthan and Gujarat were also effected with the rising of the same culture which was there on the *Indus-Saraswati* basin. No doubt, several maps have been prepared for the discovering of the site of this civilization. So far around 3000 sites have been plotted in India and Pakistan put together. It may be noted that while there are only around 250 sites on the Indus River, there are around 1500 sites on the lost '*Saraswati*' and its tributaries. As per the list provided by J. P. Joshi and other there are about 24 Early Harappans, 35 Harappans and 128 Late Harappan sties in present Punjab spread in the District of *Bhatinda, Sangrur, Ludhiana, Patiala, Ropar, Kapurthala, Jalandhar, Ferozpur,*

Hoshiarpur, Amritsar and Chandigarh as compared to 103 Early-Harappans, 44 Harappans and 297 Late Harappan sites in the present Panjab. Several sites have also been reported from the side of Punjab and Bahalvalpur region. Sites in Harayana are well known, therefore, emphasis has been given to the sites located in East and West Punjab. The prehistoric site of Abhaipur is locally known as *Abhaipur-Chenna* Nakatikhera. It is situated about a kilometer west of the village of Abhaipur in the Bisalpur Tehsil of Pilibhit District, U. P the river Deoha, also known as Garra, is flowing about one and half kilometers east of the site at present. A *nala* banch of this river surrounds the site on three sides, except of the North. About 130 m x 100 m of the site is spared for the Lord Shiva temple present a top the mound. However, the study of U. P. Arora, R. K Verma, Anup Mishra, S. B. Lal and others, reveal that the only the southern east part of the mound has remained fairly intact with the ancient or prehistoric history of Indian, and the surface of the site is full of tall grasses; the roots of which have been disturbed by the Brahmins for their benefit but it has the depth of about one metre i.e., *'Nam'* the *'Painted Grey Ware Site'* of this region. The society became more familiar with use of coins during the age of the Mauryan Empire (c 324-187 B. C.). The Mauryan empire is considered to have minted (*inter alia*) silver *punch-marked* coins of 32 *ratis,* bearing generally '*Nams*' or Pandavas of the Jammu and Kashmir areas. These five symbols on the obverse coins, for circulation throught the empire comprising the major part of the Indian subcontinent and a portion of the Indo-Iranian borderland discussed by P. L. Gupta and T. R. Hardikar in their study. The early history of Kashmir, as told by Kalhana in the *Rajatarangni* is well known. According to him the country formed a part of the Mauryan and Kushana empires of India. Thus the evidence of the West of Indus now in Pakistan Punjab, the Department of Archaeology, University of Peshawar extensively explored Harappan sites in Pakistan and discovered 24 sites discovering of few proto-historic sites like Hathala and Karam Shah along D. I. Khan- Tank Road thus pushing its borders to the Pakistan and Afghanistan borderland. Later Prof. A. H. Dani of Peshawar University while excavating at Gumla added many sites such *Mulnavise,* Makran, Rehman, Dheri, etc. Still later, Peshawar University found several proto-historic sites in the Bannu basin in salt range. In 1971 Dani excavated Gumla (7 miles from D. I. Khan on D. I. K. Tank Road) and establised a sequence from Neolithic to post-urban phase. This sequence has provided an excellent index for future work in the area of Jammu and Kashmir State for the development of the history. As a tool of historical research, the use of Archaeology Survey of India is important, therefore, it may not be confined to the pre-historic or very ancient phases of human society. Nor is it solely concerned with the remains dug out from under the surface of the earth. The study of stray museum pieces is particularly important as these include many objects made or organic materials (like palm leaves, paper, textiles, paintings, books, furniture, etc.) which are rarely found in their original forms and compositions either on the ground or in the heaven. The growing interest of modern archaeologists in the recent past has given rise to Industrial Archaeology as a distinct branch of the *Sudhra* Family that seeks to preserve for posterity the remains of the early phase of the Industrial Revolution of Europe as well as the New World. Similarly, in India, there has come up the concept of 'Medieval Archaeology' which focuses on the material remains of the period extending from the coming of Islamic Influences down to the establishment of the English East Indian Company rule in a major part of the subcontinent (1000-1750 A. D.). This tendency to treat the archaeology of Medieval India as a separate branch may be justified with reference to the marked coins of the Nature, that is, Dr. Raj Kumar, Baba Gurinder Singh Ji Biaswale. Dr. Ram Dass and Master Deepit Raj as a Master of the World politic and always use the term this earth is dirty not good for the Heavenly people. Therefore, the study of proto-historic or very early historic sites or in trying to protect (not always very successfully, but for the time being) more important monuments of the historical period of the coming generation of the *Sudhra* Family. This is practice amounted to a gross neglect of whole body of very large and varied archaeological data pertaining to more recent historical phase as already stated and discussed above. The region of Rohilkhand is archaelogically very rich situated in U. P. It has largest archaelogical site of the Gangetic plain. The artifacts discovered in this region are among the pride collection the National Museum of Delhi, Mathura Lucknow, Bareilly. There was a dire necessity of a Museum in the region in order to exhibit the cultural objects of past history of the *Sudhra* Family. This museum (*Panchala*) having the pottery from 2700 B. C to 1200 A. D., i. e. Harappan, Late Harappan, Ochre colour pottery black and red ware of the same culture as already mentioned above. Ancient *Panchala* during the later Vedic Civilization approached the Northern Western Himalayan foot hills of the *Siwālika* to formate a period of Indian Culture with the understanding of the Jammu region. There is a story in the *Kathakasamhita* which reports a debate on the history of '*Chamar Dynasty*' who used to rule over U. P. in Panchala. The love for reason in this area did not confine to philosophy only, but there were pioneers in the domain of Natural Science like *History, Geography, Archeaology, Anthropology, Geology* and *Metal works*. The Uddalaka Aruni of Panchala who could not presumably be later then 8th or 7th century B. C took the step from the magicomythological view of the scriptures to a naturalistic understanding of the nature. He postulated the original cause of the universe the primeval being (*Sat*) than *Chuta mana* or Brahmin identified with spirit *Chamar* his opposite force which greatly in vogue in the general intellectual climate to which he belonged. He proceeded to sketch a view of the evolution or development of everything in nature ultimately from the primeval being or *Sat* (Truth) with a dynamism or motion inherent in it. What strikes from the study that practical knowledge and the experience, he drew upon empirical data or facts of direct observation, already censored by them on the basis of their actions and deed called *'Theory of Karma'* or 'Law of Nature'. It saw a remarkable revival in the fortunes of *Panchala* which once again came to occupy a very significant position in the history of North India having the connection with the Kashmiri people and emerged a strongest power in India. About 25 Kings who have ruled during this period have left behind thousand of coins. During the period between the fall of Mauryas and the rise of the Guptas, the *Panchalas* had two phases of power-first the pre-Kushana phase from C. 150 B. C. to A. D. 125 and secondly a short period of fifty years after the fall of the Kushanas, which ended in C. A. D. 350 when *Panchala* was assimilated in the Gupta Empire by *Samudra Gupta*. Thus, the later Vedic thought, the history of the Panchala gives a centre of popular beliefs of Buddha such as the cult of *Nagas, Yaksas* and *Vetalas* of Jammu and Kashmir. The Jain *Tirthamkara* Parshvanath is said to have attained *Kaivalya* at *Ahichhatra.* After the fall of the Gupta empire in the latter half of the 6th century A. D. the district of Bareilly came under the domination of the Maukharis. The hill tract of Nainital on one side, and the impregnable forest and thorny jungle widespread in the region on the other provided hideouts and refuge *Guptas* took the shelter in the *Siwalika* hills reached in Kashmir. The later rulers of this dynasty known as *Skandagupta, Kumara gupta* erected *Viharas, Caityas* and by other pions work, indicated by the modern *Khandabavon* in Srinagar as mentioned by (Kalhana in volume I. pp. 105, 106 in the Book III). As to the abbreviated form *Skanda* for *Skndagupta,* Kumara to *Kumaragupta*. Later on, however, Buddhism began to decline in Kashmir as the local rulers patronised the traditional Brahminical religion during the absence of the Father. It suffered a further set back when Kashmir was occupied by Mihirkula, the tyrant Huna King. He razed to the ground many monsteries and indulged in wanton butchery of the Buddhists thought (M. L. Kapur; *History* of *Jammu and Kashmir* Vol. I. p. 7). In the beginning the seventh century A. D. Kashmir, became a rising power with widely spread of *Islam* with the co-ordination of *Durlabhdvaradhana* I of *Kashmir* belonged to the *Karkota Family* of the *Sudhra* or low caste family called *Chamar* of the Kashmir history and his friend Mohammad Prophet and, who worshipped the '*Nam*' in the '*Rai Family*' of Sindh as the follower of same family as God and man, having the same concept as '*Nam*' or God or *Chamar* in the Universial phenomenon as *Radha Soami* and the *Chamar* has the same concept to modernise the society as '*New Society*' of the '*New World*' which could not understood by the modern Brahmins or politicans (*Souvenir of Indian History Congress*, Bareilly (U. P.) 28th 30th Dec. 2004). A paleontologist agency of America has recently discovered fossils of a 55-million-year-old 'Ape' on the Gulf coastal plain of *Mississippi*, which makes it North America's oldest known Primate similiar as found in Siwalika hill of the of Jammu and Kashmir State. It was discovered by Christopher Beard, a paleontologist at the carnegic Museum of Natural History in Pittsburgh, Pennsylvania, the fossile is of an animal named "*Teilhardian Magnoliance.* " According to a report in National Geographic News, the animal is related to similarly aged fossils from China, Europe, and Wyoming's Big Horn Basin of the continent. "They are very, very primitive relatives of living Primates of both the countries i. e. China and Japan called *tarsiers* which live today in Southeast Asia", But the layers of rock in which the new fossils were found raises the controversial possibility that Primates appeared in North America before their close relatives i.e., Dr. Raj Kumar and Baba Gurinder Singh Ji Biaswale, showed up in Europe as previous studies had suggested the Primates reached from Asia to Europe as French philosophers. But the path of these Primates have been submerged in human history and the world was undergoing an ancient global warming event known as the *Paleocene Eocene Thermal Maximum* or PETM. If Magoliana indeed pre-dates, the Teilhardina find in Wyoming, it would also indicate the Primates stuck to the coasts for tens of thousand of years before the climate changed enough for them to migrate from South Asia to Central Asia in the area of Jammu and Kashmir State where from authentic History predicts. It took time for the Northern American ecosystem, especial in the interior part of the world to warm up the globe for historical event to change the dialogue between the present and the past in human history (News item entitled *'North America's Oldest Primate Discovered.* The Kashmir Times 5-3-2007). Similarly, cataclysmic social changes from the one generation to another, viz, the rise of the numerous *Varnasam Karas* theories (mixed castes) during the materialist approach of the man and become difficult to set up a 'Good Society' or '*New Society*' of the '*Nam*' or God. As it is evident in the five centuries between C. 200 B. C. and 300 A. D. on account of the persistent questioning of the Brahminical fourfold '*Varna*' order and the arrival and absorption of such forces as those of *Sakas, Mauryas, Kushanas, Parthians, Indo-Greeks, etc.* do not find any allusion because the used to believe in reaity that is '*Nam*' or 'God.

18. A. K. Khanna; *Akhnoor, A Historical Township.*
19. A. K. Khanna; *Ambaran-A Buddhist Bastion.*

20. **Note:** While the earliest craftsmenship of the Jammu region seemed to have developed as pure (*Sudha*) artists and sculptors attached to the feudal court to study the art and craft and they left behind extraordinary treasure in the Akhnoor area at Ambaran carved from time to time by the artisans to give a new shape to the history of India and in later on period of their family also influenced in the ornamented Basohli paintings which developed under their ideas having the Mughal and Rajasthani influence. The everyday life of the artisans became declined under the Brahminical Ideology as challenge them to study their art but proved failure to determine the truth in history. During their rule, the peasant is often artisan, and communities of these artisans migrated in Sialkot for the struggle for power of the '*Nam*' or God or '*Chamar*' to established again a good relation with India as a team work which they had in their culture. (C. J. K. L., p. 31).

21. A. K. Khanna; *Akhnoor, A Historical* Township.

22. **Note:** It is important to note that stone carvers of the catered to have the needs of various sections of Kashmiri society. Thus, cooking bowls, ladlies and other stones, utensils of the '*Nam*' surpass the highest knowledge of the Father by examining the scientific study of the '*Nam*' or God on earth even the beauty of their hair-style is increasing day by day as (*Naqas*) stone craver wheel-thrown earthern bowls in beautiful manner make it for the world market for higher prices which retain their life as usual. Cups and plates made from stone known as *Sangi-nalwat* in shades of grey, yellow, and green have pride of place in a Kashmiri kitchen and bathrooms for the use of water during the bathing time. *Sangi-dalan* of *Verinag* is used by goldsmiths, while *Sangibaswatri* is used in medicine for health as '*Nam*' is useful for the body itself as a challenge to the Brahmin. The dressed stone like *Baba Ravi Dass* never bother for the artificial stone; but a stone for philosophers study as *hamams* provide heat during the winter months to the grounds of the areas. (*C. J. L. K. p. 201*).

23. D. Suba Chandran & Jabin T. Jacob; Articles; *Nubra A Contemporarary Anomaly* and Turtuk; *Part Shadow, Part Light,* dated 30-9-2007 and 21-10-2007, Daily Excelsior. **Note.** The pleasant climate of the Kashmir and its scenic beauty are said to have been praised by Gutama Buddha himself. Some of the Sanskrit and Pali texts like *Vinaya, Pitakas, Sutta-Pitakas* and *Jatakas* represented him as the visiting *Muttra* North West India and Kashmir itself. In *Samyuk tavastu* the *Buddh* or '*Nam*' is represented as saying that Kashmir is close to Jammu the best land for meditation and leading a religious life in the absence of Father. Prose portion of the stories of the *Jatakas* appears to representation material milieu of the first three to four centuries of the Common Era. A major portion of these stories revolve around *Takkasila* (now Taxila), an important city of

ancient Punjab. *Takkasila* is mentioned 139 times in the *Jatakas*. It is referred to as the *rajadhani* (capital) of *Gandhara* to which students flocked in search of teachers and education. In these stories we are told of many princes and sons of rich and influential people, going to *Takkasila* for training in various arts such as the three *Vedas* and the 18 sciences, including science of archery, medicine and surgery, the art of swordsmanship, the elephant craft, magic for charms and snakes, and the art of recovering buried or lost treasure. Interestingly, these stories seem to indicate as if only *Brahmanas* and Khatriyas were eligible for studying at *Takkasila*. Thuna (present Thaneshwar and mentioned twice in the *Jatakas*) was another fortified city (*pura*) of ancient Punjab. *Udumbara* (present Pathankot) is also mentioed thrice in the *Jatakas*. *Sagala* (present Sialkot and mentioned seven times in the *Jatakas*) was the *rajadhani* of Madda folks (*Madradesa*). *Kekaka* (present Jalalpur and mentioned twice) was also a capital city of ancient Punjab and is regarded by the *Jatakas* as one of the three chief cities of India in past-times, the other two being *Uttarapanicala* and *Indapatta* (present *Indripattan* is area of Jourian). We are told that this city was prosperious, fertile and had gold, elephants, horses, chariots and infantry in abundance. Despite the fact that it was situated on a mount and was fortified, its defenses were not strong as it could be taken with a small army. Thus, the *Jatakas* are an important literary source for the study of social stratification in ancient Punjab during the first few centuries of the common Era. The history of ancient Punjab, like the history of ancient India is the history of upper caste people. Almost none of our sources represent the view point of the various submerged sections of the society. When Buddhism came into origin, caste system had become well-established in the Indian society. It had become both functional and hereditary. It had grown from bad to worse by the time of the establishment of the Kushana empire.

The word *varna,* which may be translated as *social grade, rank* or caste is liberally used in the *Jatakas* not only as a distinguishing mark of race or species, but also as constituting a mark of class (caste) distinction. Similarly, lineage (*gotta*) is considered of important social significance in the *Jatakas*. Likewise, a feeling of family clan (*kula*) is quite strongly reflected in the *Jatakas*. In the *Jatakas*, one also comes across references to people who were well-bred, endowed with distinguished/good/pure/high birth, race, beauty and nobility. It is not suprising to come across people in the *Jatakas* who were conceited or proud of birth (*Jatithaddha*) and ideals of the Aryan clans. Then there were those of inferior race and not of good blood/birth. They were perceived as morally ignoble, low, undistinguished mean, uncultured, common, non-Aryan and of shameless behaviour. Many amongst such unfortunate human beings had been placed outside the pale of caste system and were thus, known as *untouchable/outcastes* (*Candalas* or *Barawalas*) or having no caste at all (*vevanniya*). Whereas the *Jatakas* register an unmistakable disdain for ruralism and things rural, the word *nagarika* insinuates *urbane* and *polite*. Other than the gradations at the social level, one also comes across references to divisions at the economic level. Thus, we have references to destitutes (*dalida/dalida*) as well as wealthy and influential people (*addhaka*). There are references to even humans being bought and sold as slaves.

The *Brahmanas* who viewed themselves as the highest caste claimed every social privilege and ascendancy as an inalienable birthright. In the period, immediately prior to the time of the Buddha, with the development of the sacrificial cult, the position of the *Brahmanas* had become considerably powerful and their social prestige soared far above the rest of the populace. They came to be viewed as Gods in human form and even kings were obligated to place themselves at their services. They were reckoned with so much fear and idolization that they were not considered accountable for any kind of punishment even if they happened to commit the gravest of crimes. The basic criterion to be a *Brahmana* was his birth. In sharp contrast to the *Brahmanas* who considered themselves as a superior caste (*ukkatthakulina*), *candala, nesada, vena, rathakara and pukkusa* are mentioned in the *Jatakas* as baseborn (*nicakulina*). As the *nesadas/nisadas* were a hunting tribe, it is not difficult to explain the inclusion of these people in the *Jataka* list of castes regarded with extreme dislike and hostility. As per the information available in the Brahmanical texts, they were a pre-Aryan people, who are portrayed as short-limbed, of the complexion of scorched wood, with blood-red eyes, high cheekbones, snub-noses and copper-coloured hair. The legend of their quirky origin from the body of *Vena*, the king who proved tyrannous to the priestly class, may point to the resistance they offered to the process of Brahmanization. According to the *Jatakas*, the *nesadas* were primarily hunters and lived in their own villages. It has been pointed out by R. S. Sharma that till the end of the Vedic period, the *rathakara* and the *nisadas* enjoyed the privilege of sacrifice, but later fell under the category of the *Sudhras*. *Venas* were another aboriginal tribe, who lived by hunting and working in bamboos. A *Jataka* allùdes to a *venukara/vejukara* who goes into the forest with his knife to collect a bundle of bamboos for his trade. Unlike the *candalas* and the *pukkusas*, the *venas* were not presumed to have *sudda(pure)* blood. Although in a *Jataka*, the term veni is bracketted with the *candala* as a term of chastisement, there is nothing to show that the venas were reckoned as untouchables like the *candalas*. In fact, one reference avers that birth as a *vena* implied birth as a carpenter (*tacchaka*). *Rathakara* were a chariot-makers/carriage-builders. On the basis of a passage in a *Jataka* it has been indicated that the *rathakara* fell in status because of his having taken to leather work (*cammakara*) as such a work is regarded low. Perhaps one of the reasons why the *rathakara* is treated as a despised caste in the Buddhist texts is the Buddhist revulsion to war for which the *rathakaras* manufactured chariots. In any case, it is clear that the *rathakaras* were not downgraded to the same level as the *candalas* and the *pukkusas*. *Pukkusas* were scavengers or refuse-removers. They appear to have been a mixed tribe. The *pukkusas* lived by hunting, but they were piecemeal assimilated into the *Brahmanical* society for different tasks such as removing flowers from the temple and the palace. The fact that they could approach the temple premises to remove flowers indicates that they were no reckoned as being quite as degraded as the *candalas*. The *candalas* were the most unfortunate people who were often vituperated as vile (*dutthacandala*) and odious-outcastes (*mahacandala*). Originally, the *candalas* seem to have been an aboriginal tribe. This is clear from the use of their own argot. But later they appear to have become a mixed tribe as some of them do not appear to be physiognomically different and could hide their identity. Later Vedic literature and the laws of Manu also regarded the *candalas* as a very low caste of mixed origin, who were the descendants of a *sudda* Father and a *Brahmana* mother. According to this theory, the lower the caste of the father and higher the caste of the mother, the lower would be the caste of the offspring. Hence, the *candalas* came to be regarded as the meanest the most loathed of all the mixed castes. T. W. Rhys Davids is of the view that they were originally an abominable group of aborigines, who were dealt with as such by the Aryans. Since the conquering Aryans regarded all aborigines as much below themselves on grounds of colour and other criteria, the *candalas* too, could have been one such group who were more despised than the others due to some reason or the other. In one of the *Jatakas*, a *candala* is mentioned as a mongoose-trainer (*konda-damaka*) and in another *Jataka, candalas* are mentioned as a learning *candalavamsadhopana*. Gradually, they came to be looked upon as '*untouchables*'. In a *Jataka* tale when a *candala* enters a town, people pound him with blows and render him unconscious. The extent to which the *candalas* were abhorred could be conceived from various occurrences mentioned in some of the *Jatakas*. Contact with the Air as *'Nam'* that touched a *candalas* body was regarded as contamination. In one of the *Jatakas*, a Brahmana youth who was very conceited about his caste, was going out from the city with his companions when he saw a *candala*. Fearing that the wind which contacted the *candala* might touch his own body and contaminate him, he swore at him for being there and commanded the wretched man to move to leeward and he himself ran in the opposite direction. But the *candala* youth refused to do his bidding and stood to the windward of him. This incensed the Brahmana so much that he started abusing *candala* prodigally. Then the *candala* threw a challenge to the other to answer a question on condition of that the failure to do so would result in the *candala* putting the brahmana between his feet. As he failed to answer the question, the *candala* forcibly put him between his feet. This is evidently expressive of the Buddhist attitude towards the whole question of caste, for it rebuffs the Brahmanas, indicating the superiority of knowledge over caste. But the incident also divulges the spite in which the Brahmanas held the *candalas*.

The very sight of a *candala* foreboded evil. Even thesight of the *candalas* from a distance was enough for high caste people, especially women, to wash their eyes with perfumed water (*gandhodaka*) to remove the contamination. As told in the *Citta-Sambhuta Jataka*, two women, a daughter of a wealthy merchant and a royal councillor, who had gone to the city gate to play, one seeing two candala brothers, washed their eyes with scented water and turned back. The poor *candalas* received a sound beating from the people who lost a very good chance of feasting on the occasion. Same sort of incident is related in the *Matanga Jataka* when the daughter of a seethi of *Baranasi*, seeing a *candala,* washed her eyes with perfumed water, that had been contaminated by a mere glance at that despised person.

Food and drink, if seen by him, were not to be taken. Ingesting of his food, even unknowingly, led to social ostracism. The *Satadhamma Jataka* exemplifies the harshness of these caste rules. According to the story told in this *Jataka,* two youths, a *Brahmana* and a *candala* travel together on a long journey incidentally. It may be observed here that it was very unusual that a *Brahmana* travelled together with a *candala*. Only the *candala* youth, who is the *Bodhisattva*, takes provisions for the journey. On the way, before taking his meals, the candala invited the other to join him, which was naturally turned down. After having travelled the whole day, the *Bodhisattva* had his second meal in the evening. The *Brahmana*, who had been very tired by this time, was feeling very hungry. His hunger made him forget all about his caste and this time he asked for a portion of the meal forget all about his caste and this time he asked for a portion of the meal from the *candala* and ate it. No sooner had he finished eating then he was overcome by grief and remorse, that he being a Brahmana, had eaten food left over by a *candala*, and he immediately vomitted out with blood what he had eaten. He was feeling so guilty that he became sick of life for having committed such a serious fault that he decided to starve himself to death and entered a forest to do so. Here, too, it is a case of Buddhist authors scoffing at the rule of the *Brahmanas* that no *Brahmana* should eat the food left over by a candala, which as pointed out in another *Jataka*, results in the Brahmana losing his caste altogether. According to this Jataka, 16,000 brahmanas are said to have lost their caste just because their mouths. The disdain for such a food was so great that the Buddha in his introduction to the *Satadhamma Jataka,* says that for the followers of his doctrine the eating of food obtained in an illegitimately is like eating the table leavings of a *candala.*

There is another story in another *Jataka* where a Brahmana ascetic was humbled by a *candala.* Although the aim of the story is to deride the Brahmanic attitude towards the caste system, the low position of the *candalas* in the society at that time is divulged by this story too. Here, the ascetic had his hermitage on the bank of a river and a candala, too, lived in the neighbourhood. One day when the ascetic was taking bath in the river, a toothpick (*dantakattham*) thrown by the candala upstream into the river got stuck into the ascetic's hair. At this the ascetic became offended through and through, vituperated him and commanded the *candala* to go somewhere else.

By and large, the *Jataka* references indicate that although the *candalas* were loathed as '*untouchables*' by the members of the higher castes, they were especially hated by the *Brahmanas*. When the *candalas* were absorbed into the Brahmanical society, this assimilation did not mark a complete break with their former style of life. The *candalas* led a life misery and squalor. Fick rightly says that in their portrayal of the *candala, Jataka* show that the reality was not far different from the priestly theory. Just as the origins of the *candalas* cannot be clearly explained, even their professional work defies clear explanation. Probably on account of their being hunters and fowlers, they appear to be associated with the removal and disposal of corpses, coffin-making and grave-digging. The *candalas* were also sometimes engaged for street sweeping. Due to the contempt with which they were regarded, the *candalas* were kept out of the society at large. As a result, they were made to live in a settlements (*candalagama*) which were earmarked for the purposes and located outside towns (*bahinagare*). It appears to have been mandated by the brahminical society that whenever they entered a village or a town, either for begging or to do their professinal work they had to be distinguished from the others in terms of their appearance. We learn from a *Jataka* that the *candala* possessed a pair of coloured garments in order to distinguish him from the rest of the population, a girdle, a ragged robe and an earthen bowl. In the *Cittasamhut* a *Jataka* we are told how two *candala* brothers dressed as Brahmanas go to *Takkasila* to study under a teacher. Later, one of them burns his mouth with hot-rice, forgets himself, cries his own *candala* language (*candalabhasaya*) upon which their disguise is detected. According to the story, they were driven out immediately and then entered a forest to become ascetics. It may be remarked here that this distinction in their speech was probably not in their language as whole, but in certain words and expressions, for, being excluded from the rest of the population, they must have preserved some traits of their original language. Sometimes the term *candala* is used in the Pali literature as a term of contempt. Thus, when a jackal makes a proposal of marriage to a young lioness, the latter says that the jackal is regarded as the lowest and the most wretched among the four-footed animals and is similar to a candala. The lioness felt so insulted at the jackal's proposal that she decided to kill herself. However, there is an instance in which a departure from the normal is mentioned. In the *Chavaka Jataka*, a king, on being pleased with the behaviour of a *candala*, appoints him as the lord protector of the city.

The origin of '*untouchability*' has sometimes been explained variously through the intermixture of castes, as a result of the total isolation and loss of tradition of Buddhist communities, beef-eaters being condemned as untouchables, the psyche of revulsion leading to untouchability being borrowed from the Dravidians, or the theoretical impurity of certain occupations. Most of the mixed castes were nothing more than backward tribes, who were annexed to the four original and recognized *varnas* by giving them a wholly arbitrary genesis. It seems that the inhabitants of tribal settlements en masses were condemned to the position of untouchables by the Brahmanas. The ranks of such people later appear to have been swelled by those who were kicked out of the caste system due to serious violations of caste laws laid down by the Brahmanas. Thus, perhaps the most important reason for the origin of untouchability was the cultural lag of the aboriginal tribes, who were mainly hunters and fowlers, in contrast to the members of the brahmanical society, who possessed the knowledge of metals and agriculture, and were developing urban life. This would suggest that these despised castes had a very precarious living, and were in far worse condition than the suddas, some of whom as *dasas* and *kammakaras* enjoyed at least some security of livelihood. As pointed out by R. S. Sharma,during the post-Vedic period, the upper *Varnas*, who tended to be hereditary in their positions and functions, gradually withdrew from the work of primary production and developed a contempt not only for manual work, but also extended it to those who practised it. Against the background of a very low material culture of the aborigines, the increasing contempt for manual work, combined with primitive ideas of taboo and impurity associated with certain materials, produced the unique social phenomenon of untouchability. This was particularly true of the work of the *candalas* who dealt with corpses, with which were linked primitive ideas of impurity and horror. Consequently, it was felt necessary to avoid contact with such persons. In later times, the idea of untouchability was extended not only to the *nisadas* and *pukkusas* but also to the leather workers and weavers.

Surprisingly *suddas* and outcastes(*Barawalas*) find a very low represen ation in the *Samgha*. One has only to go through the Pali canonical literature to see how strong in numbers were the Brahmans followers of the *Buddha* who had rejected the claim of their Brahmanahood by birth in theory, but followed mostly in practice. Though in theory Buddhism refused to accept the relative superiority or inferiority of castes against each other, yet in practice a marked leaning to aristocracy seems to have lingered in early Buddhism. It is for this reason that some scholars do not consider Gotama Buddha as a champion of the cause of lower classes, despite the fact that the Buddhist theory acknowledged the equal right of all males to be received in the *Samgha*. It has been alleged that only occassionally the Buddhist texts show some lurking sympathy for the lower orders and that a marked leaning to aristocracy (of all the three varieties, birth, brain and bullion) lingered in ancient Buddhism as an inheritance from the past. Though it cannot be denied that the all prevading influence of caste system had in fact affected Buddhist way of thinking, yet it cannot be denied that the Buddha threw the doors of his *Samgha* open to the lowliest of the low who could achieve the bliss of the *Nibbana*. Buddhism made no distinction in the imparting of knowledge. In the Buddhist view anybody could be a teacher irrespective of his caste and it is said that a teacher is always to be respected, be he a *sudda*, a *candala* or a *pukkusa*. It is typical of the Buddhist attitude that in a *Jataka* story a Brahman loses the charm learnt from a *candala* because of denying his teacher out of shame. A Buddhist monk or a nun never made any distinction between people while begging for food and could approach any householder for a meal, or could eat at his house when invited by him. Thus, it cannot be denied that Buddhism left lasting impact on the social organization in India under Ashoka, the Great Mauryan King of Magadha who extended his power eastward to Bengal, Kerala, *Dalit* U.P Bihar and Nepal, even he extended his power in Sri Lanka, and in Westward to *Hindukush* had a great hand in introducing Buddhism in Kashmir. At the conclusion of the deliberations of the Buddhist council, *Majjhantika,* a disciple of *Ananda* the constant companion and servitor of the great teacher, Gutama Buddha was sent to Kashmir and Gandhara at the head of an evangelical mission. Heun-Tsiang and On-Kong Chinese travellers mention the arrival of 5,000 monks who were settled in Kashmir by Ashoka and his gift of the valley to the *Sangha* for turning it into a centre of learning and propagation of Buddhist religions texts like the '*History of the Chamar Dynasty of Kashmir*' written by the same author. (**References Books**: The *Jataka,* ed, V. Fausboll, London; 1877-1897, K. T. S Sarao; *Urban Centres* and *Urbanization as Reflected* in the *Pali Vinaya* and *Sutta Pitakas*, Delhi 1990. R. S Sharmas *Sudhras in Ancient India*. Delhi, 1990; Raj Kumar, *Buddhism in Kashmir*; An article; Daily Excelsior 2-7-2006).

24. No doubt, certain stone choppers of the same period in superb stone images of Vishnu and Shiva entered into *Sudhamaha Deva*, and Channeni in Jammu region. In the eight century A. D *Shiva* and *Parvati* masterpiece highlight the perfect skill of the Jammu Region from the backward period of the Indian history in the shape of black body with full of posion of the '*Nam*' or *Candala* as Shiva was there in India to eat the Brahmins. Thus the stone carver *Chamar* had attained this perfection how to tackle the idiot Brahmins who celebrate the *Shivaratri*, but in human form they do not like the *Shiva*. The beautiful carved stone horses, *Sudhra* some larger than life size *Chamars* or *untouchables* from Gul Gulabgarh and the stone *bowlies* are among the masterpieces of the '*Nam*' who created a rich history in the favour of Father by the traditional stone carvers of the Jammu areas like Dr. Raj Kumar, Dr. Ram Dass and Master Deepit Raj. The superb temple of the Lord Shiva in clusters at *Kiramchi* and *Babor* provided the stone carver with an opportunity to display their talent as their exquisite workmanship in stone and are works of great beauty as '*Nam*' do for the Father for his dignity and serenity. Serpentine or *Zeharmora* pot stone contains the beauty of Srinagar, whereas the manganese oxide and ferrous which are believed to assist in the curing of many ailments cups, tumbles kettles, jugs and bowls of serpentine were, therefore, made by artisans for both medicinal and utilitarian purposes. These were widely used in Jammu, Kashmir and Ladakh during the period of our study and recent times, when serpentine became rare and consequently prohibitively expensive due to cooking at extremely high altitudes. It is a lenghty process and the heavy lid serves as press cooker. Lamps, frying pans, griddles and *Chhang* posts in stone were earlier supplied via Nubra from a village named Thukmus near *Siksa* on the border of China and Baltistan. (*C. J. K. L, p.* 201).
25. Dr. Arun Kesar Wani; Op. Cit., p. 39
26. D. Sen; *Nalagarh Palaeolithic Culture*; *Man in India*. vol. 35, New Delhi 1955, p. 180.
27. *A. P.*, pp. 10-11
28 *W. T. W. I.*, pp. 10-11
29. B. B. Lal, *The Banganga-Beas Palaeolithic Industry*, A look Back *Puratattva*. No. II. New Delhi; pp. 1-9.
30. *A. P.*, p. 11.
31. V. D. Krishnaswami; '*Progress in Prehistory*' *Ancient India*. No. 9, New Delhi; 1985, p. 57.
32. Dr. Arun Kesarwani, Op. Cit., p. 40.
33. **Note:** Palaeolithic man was a hunter and food gatherer, and lived in very small communities which were usually nomadic. In the course of time, he learnt to kindle fire, to protect his body from the weather with skin, bark or leaves, and

to tame the wild dog which lurked round his camp fire. In India, as all over the world as U. S. A report is confirmed from the south Eastern Asia that Primate men lived thus for many millennia in the region of Jammu and Kashmir State and its adjoining areas like Sindh, Sialkot, Mirpur, etc. then, very recently in the perspective of geological time, great changes took place in man's way of living and style. Certainly not much earlier than 10,000 B. C., and perhaps as late as 6000 B. C., man developed what Professor Gordon Childe calls "an aggressive attitude to his government. " He learnt how to grow food crops, he tamed demostic animals, he made pots, and garments as *Kabir* used to do in his life time. Before discovering the use of metal, he taught himself to make well polished stone implements far in advance of those of the Palaeolithic Age. North-West and in the Deccan, and usually on or near the surface of the river beds. In much of the country Neolithic Culture survived long, and many of the wilder hill tribes of the present day have only recently emerged from this stage to development stage. Due to the development of agriculture and premanent villages probably began in the 5th millennium B. C., in the Middle East of Japan and Korea. In India the earliest remains of a settled culture are of little agriculture village in Baluchistan and lower Sindh and the uphill of the Panjab known as Jammu, Kashmir and Himachal Pradesh including the area of little Ladakh and Tibet of China, perhaps dating from the end of the 4th millennium. Classical writers of this areas show that when, in 326 B. C, Alexander of Macedonia crossed Indus, the climate of North Western of India was much as it is today, though perhaps a little moister coming out of them in the form of Dr. Raj Kumar with his company already mentioned above. The river Valleys of this area called Sindh or Sindhu (Hindu) were fertile and well wooded tress of *Deodar* or *Deva dar,* though the coastal strip to the west of the Indus in Jammu region, now called the Makran, and much of Baluchistan were already dry and desolate under the rule of Brahminical Ideology, there is a need of the solace to them. But in 3000 B. C. the climate was very different the whole Indus region was well forested, providing fuel to burn; bricks and food for wild elephants of the '*Nam*' or God and rhinocers, and Baluchistan now almost a waterless desert, was rich in rivers. This region supported many villages of agriculturists, who had settled in the upland villages of Baluchistan and in the then fertile plain of the Makran and the lower Indus area of the Jammu region, the terrain of the forest these people belonged to several cultures sometimes *Meghas, Dom, Chamar, Barwalas, Cheer, Jogi, Mahashas, Tarkan, Batwals, Chuhras etc.* primarily distinguished from the ideology of the Brahmins, because Brahmins had black pottery and *Sudhra* had different types of painted pottery which is meant for the study of Brahmins. Each culture had distinctive features of its own, but all were of the same generic pattern as those of the the middle east in India during the ancient period of the Indian history. Though their settlements were small, for sometimes, rarely more important for the human history and idea than a few acres in extent, their material standards were comparatively rich and high in culture and civilization. The villagers dwelt in comfortable houses of mud brick with lower courses of stone, and made good pottery, which they painted with pleasant patterns. They knew the use of metal, for a few copper implements have been discovered in the sites figurines of terracota of God and Goddess discovered from different places of different culture having the same meaning as God and man. The village cultures had varying customs, for the secluded Valleys of the Brahui Hills and the comparative simplicity of the lives of inhabitants did not encourage very close contact. Thus the northern villages of the Jammu regions made predominantly red pottery like *Manda, Ambarana, Chokhi Choura, Chakpalwal, Dumi Malapur,* Jammu itself, and the Southern buff; the people of the *Kulli Culture or Chamar* Culture, in the Makran, burnt their dead, while those of the Nal culture, in the Brahnu Hills, practised fractional burial for the study of man in future course of action of the life. Bull figurines have been discovered, and the bull forms a favourite motif for the decoration of the pottery of *Kulli* and *Rana Ghundai* of the same culture. The people of '*Kulli Culture*' or '*Chamar Culture*' or '*Ravidas Culture*' excelled in making small boxes of soft stone, delicately engraved with linear patterns such boxes have been occasionally found in Early Mesopotamian sites, and we may assume that they were exported by the *Kulli* people of the '*Nam*' or *Chamar*. Perhaps, it filled with unguent or perfume of some kind as simple by nature. As *Susa* and elsewhere have been found a few pieces of painted grey pottery which evidently imitated from the wares of the *Kulli* or *Coolie* people of the '*Nam*' *or* God, who obviously traded by the Father with the Middle East. Otherwise there is little evidence of contact. No certainly identifiable Mesopotamian remains have been found in Baluchistan and there is no trace of objects from the Kulli Culture along the overland route. It seems that *Kulli* or *Coolie* people as labour party or working class made contact with the earliest Mesopotamian Civilization by sea routes of the hideout culture. (W. T. W. I., pp. 11,13,14).

34. *An Advance History of India*; London; 1963, pp. 9-10. Hereafter referred as A. H. I. **Note:** Author has been suggested in the right manner that the Paleolithic men belonged to the *Negrito* race, like the modern people of the Andaman Islands, and were characterised by short stature, darkskin, wooly hair and flat nose of their physical features.

35. **Note:** The story of the *Old Stone Age* or *Palaeolithic Age* of the Early Man in India is largely shrouded in mystery. The common belief or common Era is that the remotest past represented the *Satyuga* the Rule of the Law originated

from the *Divine Right Rulers* of the '*Nam*' *or God*, an age when man lived in an ideal state of happiness, free from misery, want, and decay. Sober history unfortunately does not know indications point to the fact that primitive man was sunk in the darkness of ignorance and barbarism, and that he marched towards the light of civilization only by slow stages of the life as its natural process. So far as our evidence goes to the earliest inhabitants of India were perhaps the Palaeolithic (derived from Greek words signifying 'Old Stone') men. They were a savage people who sought shelter under trees and in natural carvens. They had no idea of cultivation, and probably did not quite know how to make a fire. They could not turn out pottery, and were ignorant of the use of metal. They lived on the chase and on nuts, roots, and fruits expressed from the study of Lord Buddha and other saints of the world (V. *Rangacharya, Pre-Musalman India;* Vol. I. p. 48). Thus, the Bhima basin is the smallest (5,000 sq km) and the *Indravati, Chhattisgarh, Abujhmar,* etc. are even smaller, but they were the areas of attraction during the Old Stone Age or Palaeolithic Age as attested by the relative high density of Mesolithic sites. The Aravalli basin is also exposed in the North Western part of India. The litho-stratigraphic succession has been divided into *Lower Aravalli Group, Middle Aravalli Group* and *Upper Aravalli* Group included the area of Mewar, Udaipur, etc. having the formation of granites, quartzite and lithic arenite, ultra mafic conglomerated the formation of *Mochia* with ore bodies of lead, zinc and silver in formation as race of the Father. The basin is bounded by the Delhi-Aravalli belt on the north west and by the *Satpura* organic belt on the south east. The Chambal Valley in the west and the Son Valleys in the east are the major river Valleys flowing through much of the basin. Bhander group of rocks are best developed in the central basin between north-east of Rewa and Sagar, around Bhopal as an inlier in Madhya Pradesh and in the Rantham bore Sapotra-Karauli belt and Ranger Reddy district of Andhra Pradesh. The Himalayas in the north, the Burma Mountains in the east and the Indian Ocean of the south. The Asian highlands (Himalayas, Tibet and Burma Ranges) are the source of many large perennial rivers such as the Ganga, Indus, Brahmputra, Mekong, Changjiang, etc.) both glacial melt waters worshipped by Brahmins as their natural heroes which are coming out from the ocean or sea of the 'Sudhra Family' and orographic monsoon rainfall feed these rivers in the extra peninsular region. Some historians write like K. L Khurana that the early men originated first of all, between Sindhu (Indus) and Jhelum (*Vitasta*) river in the province of Punjab at Jammu. Afterwards leaving the Doab they migrated to Rajaputana, Gujarat, Bengal, Bihar and Orissa. The tools of the primitive man have been found at all these places mentioned above and they dated back to many thousands, rather millions of years. Probably they predated half a million years B. C. The remains of Palaeolithic Age have been found in different areas in Asia, Africa and Europe. Besides the Indo-Gangetic plain, the traces of this age are found throughout the country for the study of man. (**References** made from: *(1)Ravi Korisettar, Geoarchaeology of the Purana and Gondwana Basins of Peninsular India.* An article presented in IHC, 65th session, 2004, Bareilly. pp. 1052, 1053-54, 1055, 1056 & 1057(2) K. L. Khurana; *Ancient India*; Agra; 2004; pp. 15-16).

36. A. K. Khanna, *Akhnoor, A Historical Township*. The significance of this name lies in the fact that in this Neolithic age also men had to depend solely on stone implements and were ignorant of any metals, except gold. But their implements were very different from those of the preceding age, for they used stones other than quartzite and there were not merely chipped but in most cases "ground, grooved and polished" as well they were highly finished articles made different forms to serve various purpose. They can be easily distinguished from the rough and rude implements of the Palaeolithic Age remains of the Neolithic men are found in almost every part of India. An ancient factory for the manufacture of stone implement has been discovered in the Bellary district of Madras, where we can still trace the various stages of their construction. The man of Palaeolithic Age had considerably advanced towards civilizational growth in the Neolithic Age. The capacity for progress is an inherent ingredient in man's personality. Though the tools and the weapons of the areas of the Jammu region were advanced in light of the view of the historical approach in history how a man play the role in natural form. The tools of the 'New Stone Age' were clean beautiful and bright. The remains of this age have been found in India in Tamil Nadu, Karnataka, Hyderabad, Kashmir, Bengal, Orissa and Nagapur.

The next stage in the progress of man in India as elsewhere, was reached when the use of the rough stone, implements was not quite discarded, they are still working in the human form like Dr. Raj Kumar, Baba Gurinder Singh Ji Biaswale, Master Deepit Raj and Dr. Ram Dass, but most of them were carefully dressed and polished by the *Mochi* and the weaver of the '*Nam' or God.* They knew how to produce a fire and the art of cooking in the vassel. They occupied themselves with fishing and hunting, tended flocks of domesticated animals, and also began the cultivation of land from time to time in the season and who to make a civilized progress in the society of India. Their food was simple, consisting of game with Brahmins as they are player of them how to tackle them with power of 'Nam' or God. They made pottery at first by hand, but afterwards the wheel was used. The earthen ware were either plain or painted and decorated with representations of flowers, leaves, etc. The Neolithians chose the tough trap rock for their weapons offence and defence, but things of domestic use were made of other materials of various colours. They buried their dead and erected tombs of the forefather as is evident from some pre-historic skeletons discovered in the district of Mirzapur. On the other hand, the finds of funeral urns, meant for the ashes of the dead for the study of Brahmins where they stand in the history, would show that their cremation too was not unknown. This age belonged to 10,000-3,000 B. C. Man had progressed rapidly during this period. He had left the nomadic life and begun to live a settled life. He practised agriculture and grew fruits. The people of this age had begun demesticating the animals. The chief occupation of the people during this period was hunting, fishing rearing of goats and sheeps like Gujjar and Bakarwal of the period. The produced wheat, barley, maize and vegetables. They had also learnt making cloth from wool and cotton. Dr. R. S. Tripathi has rightly expressed. "Man had made considerable advance towards civilization". "His food was simple consisting of grain forest produce, vegetables, milk, honey, wild grain," etc.

The civilization of the Neolithic men shows distinct traces of advance. They knew the art of producing fire by the friction of bamboos or pieces of wood, and made pottery found from different sites of the world, a first by hand, they used to work for experience of the life, and then with the potter's wheel. They lived in caves and decorated their walls by painting scenes of hunting and dancing. A few of these can be seen today both in Northern and Southern India. They also painted and decorated their pottery. So long as our evidence remains as meagre as it now is, there will always be scope for such differences of opinion, and we shall have to deal with theories or hypothesis based on speculations. The question, however, belongs to the domain of anthropology rather than history. [(1) Panchaman Mitra; *Pre-historic India*, Calcutta, 1923,(2) V. Rangachary *Pre-Musalman India (3)* K. L Khurana; *Ancient India. (4)* R. S. Tripathi; *History of Ancient India. (5)* A. C. Logan; *Old Chipped Stones of India,* Calcutta, 1906; *(6) A. H. I. pp. 11,12)].*

37. A. P. p. 14. R. N. Kaw; *The Neolithic Culture of Kashmir, Essays in Indian Protohistory,* (edited by D. P Agarwal & D. K. Chakraborty; Delhi; 1979.

38. D. Suba Chandrau & Jabin T. Jacob; Op. Cit.

39. *C. J. K. L.*, p. 21.

40. **Note:** In the North extreme hills the majestic gateway of Central Asia, Zoji-la is the high mountain pass of India dividing Kashmir from Ladakh and remains snow-bound for more than six months in a year. Only the nomadic Gujjars and Bakarwals venture to negotiate the icy slopes. The glistening snows and awesome of the region are part of the psyche of its people and plains of Jammu to the mountain pastures of Kashmir, taking a week or ten days to complete the first lap of their journey which follow a fixed route to Panjab and

other areas. In this way, during the Metal Age, the ornaments of these regions show distinct features rest of the worlds as a race of the Father workd in terrians and deep slops. This practice has been in vogue from the very ancient times when the imitative skill or art of the craftsman in the form of *Sunara* or Sunari was such that it was possible to tell a gilt ornament from a gold one to produce the sound of the 'Nam' or God to this universe as a whole as a study of it. In China, the presious and semi-precious stones used are polished by the forefather of the author. The portrait of the Empress of China in the first decade of this century shows her wearing many Indian form e.g., a collar of gold in the form of Indian torque, and triangular pendants on the turban from which hang chains of pearls found in Jammu and Kashmir on the foothill of the Punjab *Maha-Biasya* in the form of Baba Gurinder Singh Ji, a form commonly found in the Himalayas and in Central Asia and Sindh of Punjab. It is of interest to know of very extensive use of stealite at *MohenjoDaro* and Harappa and to note that it was coated with a blue glaze. Steatite beads are more common than those of any other material and apparently the people of these regions had access to a plentiful supply of the material in almost all over the world as it is the duty of the '*Nam*' *or God to check* them either they are real or artificial. Agate is a favourite both at *Mohenjodara* and *Harappa,* al though the material was commonly used in Mesopatamia, especially in the presargonic period at Kish. They have the strange connections that both Sumer and Elam showed by the objects found at *Mohenjo-Daro* and Harappa. From the Stone Agesto Bronze Ages through *Ahichhatra*, Mathura and Taxila, metals have become increasingly popular and the plain gold beads of Harappa have given place to various shapes and designs culminating in the exquisitively filigreed Cuttack beads. Metals of traditional shapes still used by lower lasses and wandering like Banjaras of the ancient period. The simple bead of stone, glass or metal, so widely worn today, is a great heritage of the Jammu, Kashmir, Ladakh, Sindh, Blochistan, Sakardu, almost in Northern States, Delhi to Bombay from the past that connects as with Egypt, Babylonian and Persia, with Ashoka, Aluddin Khalji or Khoja, Akbar to Shahjahan then there was a dilemma of the bigotry in the history of India for progress of the '*History*'. *((1). C. J. K. L, (2)* Jamila Brij Bhushan; *Jewellery, Ornaments and Decorative Designs,* Bombay; 1964. pp. 10,20, 26, 29, 30, 45).

41. R. S. Tripathi; op. cit., p. 14.

42. *C. J. K. L.*, p. 189.

43. *Ibid.*, pp. 191-92 ***Note:*** An important technological improvishment was the introduction of glazed earthware, commonly known as 'Northern Burnish Pottery' (NBP) at the excavation site at Semthan in Bijbehare (NBP), was in vogue in Afghanistan and North West Frontier Province from the fifth to the

second centuries B. C. Semthan potters had the great interest in Kashmir also modelled some beautiful terracotta figures as well as bowls in shapes associated with the deluxe ware of the *Nandas* of Magadh and the Maurya prototype sites at Kanishkapur in Kashmir. This is followed by redware pottery represented by hallow cups, lids and medium sized pots which continued from the first century A. D. to onwards about the sixth century A. D. falling in the Kushan and post Kushan period of India. Made in silver alloy with deep blue enamlling this tumbler has stylished wood peckers and other birds of the '*Nam*' placed amongst delicate foliage. Most of the early medieval metal work bears simple engraved decoration, the majority of metal being left plain. Vessels engraved with designs consisted mainly of arabesque figures of animals and calligraphic inscriptions like of Ashoka, Kushanas, etc. Later, a more elaborate form of decoration employing in lay was developed from time to time. While these ancient vessels belongs to the Indo- Persian tradition as a whole, the decoration is usually of Kashmiri inspiration. In Jammu most typical and tradition metalcraft is the casting vessels, particularly those used for cooking during weddings and others festive occusions. When factory made steel and aluminum utensils were still unknown, the entire village of Badiyal Brahmana in *Ranbir Singh Pura* was engaged in this work and the harsh but rhythmic clash and clatter of metal casting and the repairing and beating of brass and copper defened those who travesed the narrow lanes of Moti Bazar in Jammu city from the ancient period. (p. 182).

44. *Ibid.*, p. 192.
45. *Ibid.*, p. 190.
46. K. L. Khurana., op. cit. p. 21.
47. A. H. I., p. 13.
48. A. C. Clayton. *The Rig-Ved* and *Vedic Religion*; New Delhi; Reprint; 1981. p. 3.
49. *Ibid., p. 4.*
50. A. H. I., pp. 14,15.
51. Ibid., p. 15.
52. ***Note:*** Others of these tribes, more daring, by long marches, and through many generations approached and entered India from the North West. These were the men who called themselves '*Aryas*'. *(Sudras), Aryans,* a word meaning 'Kinsmen' as distinct from the aboriginal tribes already dwelling in the land and became Brahmins unlawfully. (A. A. Macdonnell, A History of *Sanskrit Literature;* p. 152).
53. W. T. W. I., p. 14 Also referred by a. K. Khanna; Akhnoor, *A Historical Township*
54. A. H. I., p. 15

55. Ibid. **Note**: This civilization represented by the dish-on-stand, breakers, bowls, jars and other prototypes of Harappan pottery. Early historical pottery is represented by thin to thic redware from site at *Sungal, Smaha* and *Pambarwan* in Akhnoor and Rajouri in Jammu Region. The manufacture of this type of pottery at Jammu is highlighted by the discovery of beautiful terracotta heads found at the Buddhist monastry at Akhnoor in the same region. There was a definite change in pottery making with the arrival of the Mughals and other races of the god, clues of which were found on the banks of the rive Chenab as it has also been reflected from the study that they were also the lover of Buddhism or *Islam* in modern concept as '*Nam*' or *Chamar* having the same meaning. Like pottery, stoneware provides indestructible historical evidence of human settlements in the region and forms a landmark in the history of the *Ravidas* Art used to study the '*Nam*' and its crafts widely spread all over the world not only limited to Jammu, Kashmir and Ladakh (*C. J. L. K.* pp. 195-96).

56. **Note:** It is widely known that Punjab had the historical relation from the very beginning with Jammu and Kashmir State on the bases of trade relation between man to man, as it is well known from the history, it has been the cradle of cultures from the emergence of man in India and it has bequeathed a rich cultural inheritance between the two region i.e., hilly and plain. In the cultural cavalcade India's history the contribution of Punjab has been of immense value to predict the historical friend of the '*Nam*' *as Dr. Raj Kumar* and Baba Gurinder Singh Ji Biaswale, occupying a very important geographical position which bring together sufficient elements to build a reliable model for understanding the cultural background of the '*Indus-Saraswat Civilization* of the Ambaran in Jammu region village known as *Manda* in Akhnoor. In this connection the proto-historic is landmark in the Archaeology Survey of Punjab, Jammu and Kashmir State as well as other parts of the world and the region itself. It is one of the most important area which has given a surprising picture of cultural movement of the '*Nam*' in local traditions of the period under consideration. In the present study, only the social, economic and most important religious aspects have been taken into consideration that how the Brahminical society twisted the truth into bad shape or falsehood by capturing various religious places, at one time, these places had the *Sudhra* rulers and they were used to worship their Living Diety. The excavation and extensive explorations carried out in the Sutlej-Ghaggar Valley provided a sufficient data or sample which help us to build a solid chronological frame work with deep significance for understanding the socio-economic and religious background of Proto-historic period where reality stands in human or in idol worship. The excavated sites which have supplied most valuable information are *Kotla-*

Nihang Khan, Dher Majra, Ropar, Bara, Sanghol, Saranpur, Chandigarh, Salaura, Dadheri, Nagar, Katpalon, Mohorana, Rohira, etc. (Dr. Sukhdev Saini; *A Socio-Economic View of Proto-Historic Culture of Punjab*; an article presented P. H. C. 2005, p. 63).

57. *W. T. W. I.*, p. 15.

58. Jogeshwar Singh; *Indus* Valley Civilization and *Their Religion;* An article published in PHC. 2005, p. 54 Dr. V. K. Jain; *The Nature of Political Structure During Harappan Period- A Review PHC, 2005, p. 70.*

59. *K. K Sharma, New Explored Sites of Archaeology Importance in Baghpat District, U. P.* An article published in IHC, 2007 p. 1103 **Note:** The sites like *Mahagama*, *Ruhana* with Indo-Roman coins also reflected the involvement of these sites in the maritime contacts between Sri Lanka and the Tamil region in the Early Historic period. In the context of maritime trade between India and Sri Lanka the term *Bharata* deserves special mention. This was applied for a community in Sri Lanka called *Meghas* and its equivalent in Tamil literature is *Paratavar* or *Paratava*. The community was involved in the maritime activities such as fighing pearl and chank fishing in trade, particularly trading of horses like Mohan Lal Kaith. The name of *Barata* appears in twenty one Brahmi Inscriptions from Sri Lanka. Of these, fifteen insprictions bear a name *Tissa* in association with the name *Bharata.* Their close association with sea is reflected in a coin of the Jammu and Kashmir State collected from Southern Sri Lanka during the time of *Mahabharata*. Scholars have also found similarities in the term for sea and *Sudhva* of Sri Lanka, Prakrit-Brahmi Inscriptions (*Samuda, Samuta* and *Camuta*) and in Tamil-Brahmi Inscription (*Kadalan* and *Kalapan*). The Inscription at Mangulam near Maduri mentions the term *Kadalan* and the *Alagarmalai Inscription* refer to a name *Kalapan* (Kadalan) *ilavarayan*, which is taken to mean a trader from Sri Lanka. It is interesting to note that here the special mention of *ila* Bharata is to differentiate from a *Barata* of Tamil region to Kashmir region, though both belong to the same *Barata* community of the Jammu region and its adjoining areas i. e. *Akhnoor, Rajouri, Bhimbar, Mehander, Poonch, Riasi, Paddar, Udhampur Ramnagar, Himachal Pradesh, Sindh* and *Multan* this communath that is *Sudhra* owned ships of the '*Nam*' and carried out their trade by forming a guild system in the Indian society. The first comprehensive investigation of Archaeological evidence relating to pre-historic religion is found in the work of E. O. Jame's *Pre-historic Religion :A Study in Pre-historic Archaeology* (James, 1957). James pointed out that the germs of the cult of the dead are found in the Paleolithic burial ritual. He traces the evolution of the *cult* or *dharma* of the dead from the Paleolithic period through the Neolithic to reach its zenith in the Megalithic period as their rebirth story from mankind species to human species. The elaborately mentions the idea of

Pre-historic Archaeology (James, 1957). James pointed out that the germs of the cult of the dead are found in the Paleolithic burial ritual. He traces the evolution of the *cult* or *dharma* of the dead from the Paleolithic period through the Neolithic to reach its zenith in the Megalithic period as their rebirth story from mankind species to human species. The elaborately mentions the idea of the *cult* drived from the *Truth* then it takes the shape of real culture of the dead as Dr. Raj Kumar, Baba Gurinder Singh Ji Biaswale, Deepit Raj and Dr. Ram Dass. In the three great civilization of Egypt, Mesopotamia and *Harappa* and is of the opinion that the cult of Mother Goddess i.e., *Lakashmi*, phallic-worship is the duty of the Brahmins as a servent of the *Sudhra* during the ditress period of the history, mummification and Sky-gods originated in these civilizations to defeat them as idiot race of the Father. James was the first Archaeologists to make a comparison between the cult of the dead of the pre-historic man to modern man and that of the aborigines of the present day because they always busy with work as a labourer class of the society, Brahmin as *Rakashas* (V. K. Varma, *Maritime Trade Between Early Historic Tamil Nadu and Sri Lanka;* An artical published in IHC, Calicut, 2007 pp. 1007, 1009 - 10.) It shows in this process of the transmigrations of the souls from the Tamil region play a predominant role on account of its period located opposite to the North-Western coast of Sri Lanka but having '*One Culture* i.e., '*Nam*' or '*Chamar*' *A. K. P. P., p. 112).*

60. **Note:** No doubt, Archeaologists prepared sevaral maps of the sites of this civilization. So far around 3000 sites have been plotted in India and Pakistan put together and there are around 1500 sites on the lost *Saraswati Civilization* and its tributaries, and two officers of the Archaeological Survey of India carried on excavation in the Larkana district of Sindh province and the Montgomery district of the Punjab. Sir, Alexander Cunningham a British officer in India gets credit for preliminary investigation in Harappa as a *Sudhra* ruler. He had visited the place so many times during his life time and published a report on Harappa's pictographic unicorn seal in 1875 in the Archeaological Survey of India, later Banerjee and Mr. R. B. Daya Ram Sahni (Dr. Arun KesarWani; op. cit., p. 41. Jogeshwar Singh, op. cit., p. 54 PHC).

61. *W. T. W. I.*, pp. 14-15 **Note:** The aforesaid cultural sequence suggests the beginning of human activities primarily during the Early Harappan levels with 14 sites, in stark contrast to the preceding of *Ravi Hakra Culture* of the '*Ravidas Community*' called '*Untouchables*' of the '*Nam*' having the phase of the Biahalwalpur areas across the *Indo-Pak* border and the *Trans-Indus* areas further west, though presence of *Hakra Culture* ware is said to have been marked in the Early Harappan levels from *Bhirdana* and *Baroor*. This was followed by the *Mature Harappan* Culture the high intelligentsia class of the

Brahminical Ideology, area was suffered with their '*Black Culture*' *i. e.* idea of the mind or *mana* not of the God. Though a few OCP sites have certainly been discovered with their antiquify of the available ceramic ware is an indication. The perception of cultural interregnum is further shaken by the earthquake by the presence of *PGW* remains from eleven locales with *Nine Nanda* rulers of the '*Nam*' being identified for the first time by the Master in the history of India before Maurya to begins with the Historical Period between (642-320 B. C.). It may be said to be the beginning of historical period of India of the *Sudhra* Family diverted by the Brahmins into the *Hellenized* period the Kings of two dynasties ruling over Magadha including Saisunagas (C. 642-413 B. C.) and the '*Nandas*' (*c.* 413-322 B. C.). Of the former Bimbisara (*Srenika*), the founder of '*New Rajagrha*' and Ajatasatru (*Kunika*) were contemporaries of *Mahavira* and *Buddha* or '*Nam*'. For the Early Cultural History of this period, the later Vedic literature including some *Brahmins*, *Upanisads* and *Sutras* are important and on the later phase of that culture *Jatakas* and *Vinayapitakas* throw a flood of light on the craftmanship of the artisans class, they were mostly having '*One Culture*' i.e., '*CHAMAR*'. This appears to have been followed by habitations at forty nine settlements of the *Rangmahal* of the God and Kushana remains of the Early historical period. Such a high number of settlements is in conformity with the general pattern of the development of that race worked with positive manners. The medieval period is represented by 24 deserted mounds and weds not know remains of how many of them are surviving in the form of present day villages system, which is represented by 324 villages in the same area resulting into an area of intense human activities. Thus, there is strong possibility of getting more settlements, especially ancient settlements, with the progress of the field enquiry into the study to the present man of the History i. e., Dr. Raj Kumar, Baba Gurinder Singh Ji Biaswale, and Dr. Ram Dass.

62. *A. H. I.*, p. 15.

63. ***Note:*** This civilization was flourished in the third and perhaps fourth millennia B. C. and is entirely free from the vestige of Indo-Aryan influence. In that far remote period, we find their society organised in large cities; the people cultivated wheat and barley and domesticated various animals including humped zebu, buffalo, short-horned bulls, sheep, pig, dog, elephant, etc. was their natural economy. For transport, they used wheeled carriages from one place to another as '*Nam*' carries the civilization from one generation to another with scientific study of the same as an operator of the knowledge. They worked in metals. They used weapons of the '*Nam*' such as bow and arrows through their eyes. Their domestic vessels were made of earthen wares turned on wheel of the '*Nam*' and often painted with beautiful designs. To decorate themselves the rich used ornaments made of precious metals of copper,

sometimes overlaid with gold of faince, ivory, carnelian and other stones; while the poor were satisfied with the natural ornaments of the '*Nam*' as Ravidas of the period. They also knew the use of writing and reading the story of the '*Nam*'. In every way their civilization was highly developed, based on honest approach of the Father.

64. W. A. Fairservis; *The Roots of Ancient India;* Chicago; 1975.
65. S. P. Gupta; *The Indus-Saraswati Civilization: Origins, Problems and Issues*; New Delhi 1996 pp. 45-46. R. H Meadow & J. M Kenoyer; See *Harappan Excavation* 1986-90: Madison, 1991.
66. S. P. Gupta; Op. Cit., p. 46.
67. R. E. M Wheeler; Harappa 1946 the Defence and Cemetery R. 37, *Ancient India*. No. 3 pp. 59-130.
68. W. A. Fairservis; Op. lit, S. P Gupta; Op. Cit., and Asthana Shashi; *Pre-Harappan Culture of India and the Boderlands*; New Delhi; 1985.
69. R. H. Meadow & J. M. Kenoyer; op. cit.
70. W. A. Fairservis; Op. Cit. & R. E. M. Wheeler, Op. Cit. **Note:** An efficient technologically advanced urban culture is clearly evident in the 'Indus Valley Civlization'. The quality of municipal town planning is an outstanding feature of Harappan Civilization. The uniform planning of towns and cities suggest the presence the knowledge of the '*Chamar*' of efficient municipal governments which placed a high priority on hygienic. Baked bricks which were rare at this time were used by Harappans to construct wells, building platforms and drainage for rainwater and sewage. The uniformity of town planning throughout the Indus Vally indicates that there was a strong government at that time, must have functioned to standardize urban planning. The houses were of different sizes, but well planned. The study of palaeo-climate is an important and special subject in Archeaology, which relates episodes of past climatic fluctuations as today, we find in the day today life with the development of ancient cultures or changing pattern of human behaviour. Relating cultural regression with inhospitable climate is a common subject matter among the common people during common Era of the '*Nam*' both man and God do work on earth as a family. However, understanding the behaviour of the people through *Artifacts* and relating to climate change, is a different field of research where reality stands in human history between man and God. One can mark climatic fluctuations as well as shifts through human signatures in the form of artifacts. The study of ancient ceramics '*Word*' technology, typology and style of ceramics, helps in re-constructing various aspects of the ancient cultures. A cursory analysis of ceramics in a well stratified context may also unfold the underlying dimensions of stress that brings changes in ceramics. The present study attempts to correlate these two events i. e. God and Man

climatic fluctuation and changes in ceramics, and endeavours to divulge the signatures of climatic fluctuation on the ceramic layers of the society having materialist approach as a destructive one (Anup Mishra; *Climatic Fluctuation as a Stress on Techno-Typological Changes in Ceramics:* A Case Study of Chalcolithic Ceramics of Balatha, Rajasthan; An article published in; IHC, 2006-07).

71. M. R. Mughal; *Excavations at Jalilpur, Pakistan Archaeology* No. 8 Karach; 1972. pp. 117-124, and '*Early Harappan Culture from Jalilpur*', *Pakistan Archaeology*; vol. 27, No. 2. pp. 106-13.
72. S. P. Gupta; op. cit., p. 51.
73. *Ibid.*, pp. 51-52.
74. Asthana Shashi; op. cit., pp. 146-47.
75. S. P. Gupta; op. cit., p. 52.
76. F. A. Durrani; '*Evidence West of Indus*', *Indus Civilization*; *New Perspective (editor)* A. H. Dani, Islamabad, 1981, and S. P Gupta; op. cit.
77. *Ibid;* pp. 133-34 **Note** : Architecture and building technique of Mohenjodaro is the epitome of all Mature Harappan settlements. It is interesting to note that the Indus settlement most like Mohenjodaro is lay out is Kalibangau, but that is the only one with such close similarities in frame the structure and contour, but advance in nature. Out of some 1050 Mature Harappan sites, there are two that are proved to conform to the pattern said to be typical of the civilization as a whole. (S. N. Sen; *Ancient Indian History and Civilization*, New Delhi, 1999, p. 31. G. L. Possehl ; *The Indus Civilization*, New Delhi, 2003, pp. 65, 101).
78. *Ibid.*, p. 136.
79. *Ibid.*
80. **Note:** Now a stage has come from where, taking clues from Archaeological remains, the Archaeology aided text can be prepared for the reconstracting of the Early History of the Man from the Man itself in human form as an operator of the world knowledge. However, archaeological remains is also very important from the pre-historic period to modern man. The Neoloithic celts are sometimes, considered as the object of *Charm* as '*Nam*' as the Jungle God's Axe, as the Devil's Axe to kill them with the power of the 'Nam' through writing the script in *Devanagari* message of the forefather and mostly as the heavenly objects. They are either discarded or left untouched by the Modern Man due to the extice of the material culture. They are attached with myths not with the Real Living Master as an 'ego' problem of the superior caste like *Brahmins, Rajput, Vaisyas,* prehistoric human occupation in the Kamala Valley of Subansiri was reported by D. K. Duarah. He collected three Neolithic Celts from a teacher, like Prof. Jigar Mohammad, a real researcher of the fact working with honesty and dedication in the favour of students. A

Neolithic site was discovered at Parsi Parlo (280 North, 930 33' East, close to the Indo-Tibetan border in the Kamla (Kume) Valley of lower Subansiri district. The Excavation revealed a single culture horizon divided into three phases viz., *Phase-I - Aceramic Neolithic Stage*. It has been characterized by the presence of scrappers and large cutting tools with the rudiments of pecked and ground techniques. In fact, this phase may be considered as a transitional phase between Old Stone Age and New Stone Age cultures. Here, the tool kit is essentially Mesolithic bearing the *Hoabinhian* or *Sumatrilithic* traits. Other tools of this phase include chipped (alternative flaking) round scraper made on flat rounded and large cutting tools (chopper).

Phase-II-Aceramic Neolithic Stage. It is in a continuation of the preceding phase with conspicuous absence of scraper and other larger cutting tools and also the presence of handmade pottery stamped (cord impressed ware). The tools in general provide hafting facilities and are mostly for agricultural use as indicated by the presence of constricted hoe blades of the '*Nam*' or God to kill the 'ego' of the people, those do not believe on honsty and dedication.

Phase III- Ferro-lithic Stage: This is again a continue struggle of the preceding phase along with the emergence of iron tools. It is not clear from the study whether iron technology was a local innovation of the '*Sudhra Family*' or had been brought in from somewhere else. A single piece of iron implement probably a hoe-blade, along with a lump or raw material has been found and hence it is named as Ferro-lithic stage, the latter penetrated into the former (Iron Using Stage).

It has been observed that no systematic study on lithic raw materials for tool making were available locally as evideneed in the river sections of the Jammu Tawi, Manawar Tawi and streambeds. One common feature noticed right from Damin to the foothill region the Panjab, and the Jammu and Kashmir, Chamba (Himachal Pradesh) is that the knappers were preferring raw materials for the spinning the wool of the sheeps and goats. Sir John Marshall remarking on this discovery and observes, "this discovery of the Himachal Pradesh which is one of the most interesting of the minor discoveries made at Mohenjodaro, disposes finally of the idea of the '*Nam*' or '*God*' that the fine Indian cotton known to the Babylonians as *Sindhu* or *Vitasta* and to the Greek as Sindon was a product of the Hindu philosophy which has no Scientific Knowledge as *Chamar* had the period. It was a product of the cotton-tree and not a true cotton. " Jadeite is said to be the only foreign material nearest to the sand stone, schist, diorite were the commonly used raw material found in Northern Burma besides easter China and Baltistan or Gilgit (A. K. Thakur; *Pre-Historic Archaeological Remains of Arunchal Pradesh and People's Perception. An Overview*, An article published IHC. 2004, pp. 1185, 1189-90, Sir John Marshall; *Mehenjodaro and the Indus Civilization;* Vol. I. p. 33).

81. A. H. Dani; *Excavation in the Gomal Vally, Ancient Paksitan*. Vol. V. Peshwar; .1970-71.
82. M. A. Halim; *Excavation at Sarai Khola* p. 11 *Pakistan Archaeology;* No. 8 1-112, 1972.
83. A. P., pp. 26-27.
84. Madhu Bala & Vishnu Kant; *Dhalewan-An Early Harappan Site in Punjab',* *Puratattva* No. 30. 1999-2000, pp. 42,43,44.
85. R. S. Bisht; *Transformation of the Harappan Culture in Punjab with special* reference to the excavation *at Sanghol and Chandigarh* Kurukshetra; 1976, and '*Harappa Culture in Panjab: A Study in Perspective, ', Indus Civilization: Problems and Issues, Shimla, 1977.*
86. B. M. Pande, *Inscribed Harappan Potsherd* from *Chandigarh; Puratattva, No.* 6. 1972-73, pp. 52-55.
87. R. S. Bisht; *Indus Civilization, Problems* and *Issues;* p. 4.
88. Jim Shaffer, '*Harappan Culture: A Reconsideration'* in G. L Possehl, (ed), *Harappan Civilization* Delhi; 1981-82 p. 74.
89. B. M. Pande, op. cit.
90. R. S. Bisht; *Transformation of Harappa Culture;* p. 19.
91. R. N. Kaw. *The Neolithic Culture of Kashmir;* pp. 223-24.
92. A. P. p. 31.
93. Jim Shaffer; op. cit., p. 75.
94. Y. D. Sharma; *Cemments in Indian Prehistory; 1964-65, (eds) V. N.* Mishra and M. S Vats. see *Radio Carbon and Indian Archaeology, (ed.) D. P.* Agrawal and A. Ghosh; 1973.
95. A. P., p. 29.
96. Y. D. Sharma; *Radio Carbon and Indian Archaeology.*
97. *Ibid.,* op. cit., (1971-72, p. 24).
98. Jim Shaffer; op. cit., p. 76.
99. M. S. Vats; *Excavation At Harappa,* New Delhi; 1940, pp. 476-7.
100. Y. D. Sharma; *Radio Craban and Indian Archaeology* and *Transformation of the Harappan Culture in Panjab;* 1976.
101. *Ibid.,* p. 228.
102. Olaf Prufer; *Interim Report on the Excavation carried out at Dher Majra, JMIHRF* Nalagarh, 1951.
103. A. P., p. 36.
104. Y. D. Sharma; *Fresh Light on Bara Culture* from *Mahorana," Archaeology and History, Essays in Memory of* A. Ghost (eds.) by B. M. Pande and B. D. Chattopadhyaya, New Delhi 1987.
105. *A. P.*
106. Y. D. Sharma '*Harappan Complex in Sutlej' Harappan Civilization,* (ed.) G. L Possehl; 1982, pp. 141-65. Also see '*The Pre-Harappan Culture in Punjab, Puratattva,* Vol. II, pp. 32-8.

107. A. P., p. 40.
108. *Ibid.*
109. *Ibid.*, p. 41.
110. *Ibid.*, pp. 46-50.
111. *Dr. Arun KesarWani*, op. cit., pp. 50, 51. A well defined chronological order of the study can be seen in the development of geometry in India. *Harappa, Mohanjodaro, Lothal, Rakhigarhi* and several others archaeologically important sites during the period started from 1968 to 1985-86, excavation was carried out at various points, by which, a full sequence of site is revealed. The periods can be divided as follows:

Period-I Chalcolithic or Bara Culture (c. 2000-1400 B. C.) and further sub-divided into I-A, I-B, and I-C. It represents overlap between Bara or High and *Polish Grey Ware.*

Period-II	Painted Grey ware (c. 1100-700 B. C)
Period-III	Black slipped ware (c. 600-200 B. C.)
Period-IV	Kushana & Later (100 B. C. -300 A. D)
Period-V	(c. 300 A. D. to 600 A. D.)
Period-VI	Early Medieval Period
Period-VII	Late Medieval Period

Note: The important Buddhist monument discovered from the *Sanghol* in North India of the Kushana period during the excavation of 1985-86. The Stup is smaller in dimension but is based on similar *dharmachakra* pattern. *Bodhisattava* of the period, adorned with ornaments, beaded Kanthi circular *Kundalas,* bracelets in the hands and struged *Mekhala* round the waist. Buddha is also shown sitting in *abhaya mudra* in Sanghati dress. It (Sanghol) appears to be the highest moral beared city of the ancient culture of Buddha's theme. (S. K Vashisth, *Buddhist Remains At Sanghol,* An article published in *PHC* pp. 87,90). Painted Grey wares mainly founded from Sanghol, Dadheri, Sunet, district Ludhiana, Katpolan, Nagar, district of Jallandar, Ropar, Bara, Salaura, Kotla Nihanga Khan, Singh Bhag Wanpur, district Ropar. Its chronological position at that time was determined to be before 300 B. C. However, its archaeological significance was established at Hastinapura. Further, the chronological position of this ceramic industry as revealed by excavations at various sites in Jammu, Kashmir, Ladakh, Himachal Pradesh, Punjab, Haryana and Rajasthan, Delhi, Ropar, Panchala and Uttar Pradesh. (India Archeaological Reports, 1976-76, 1983, Y. D. Sharma; *An Encyclopeadic of Indian Archaeology;* vol. II, for Ropar, 1989, pp. 237-38. J. P. Joshi, '*Interlocking of Late Harappan Culture and Painted Grey Ware Culture Inlight of Recent Excavations", Man and Environment, Vol. II, 1978).*

112. The quest for India's National identity through the route of Hindu religions order began not in the nineteenth century A. D., but it has continued forever

since the time immomerial to begins with '*Harappa Civilization*' or *Indus Valley Civilization* and rechristened after the *Vedic Saraswati* of the Indus of the Jammu region particularliy based on Akhnoor near Manda and Ambarana. Such views have received a strong support from the Archaeologists Survey of India particularly referred by A. K. Khanna and others whose writtings are in Papers, Seminars and publications works. In the historiographical format *India* or *Bharata,* is timeless. The geographical horizon of the Early Aryans, as we know was limited to the North-Western part of India, referred to as *Saptasindhava* and the word *Bharata* in the sense of a country is absent from the entire Vedic literature though the *Bharata* tribe of the *Mahabharata* is mentioned at several places like Sri Lanka in the south in different contexts. In the *Astadhyaji* of Panini (500 B. C.) we find a reference of *Pracya Bharata* in the sense of a territory (*Janapada*) which laid between *Udicya* (North) and Prachy in (east). The earliest reference to *Bharatavarsa* (Prakrit *Bharadhavasa*) is found in the inscription of Kharavela (first century B. C.) A much larger geographical region is vizualized by the use of the word in the *Mahabharata* (200 B. C. to A. D. 300), which provides a good deal of geographical information about the subcontinent of Asia, although a large part of the Deccan. Among the five divisions of *Bharatavarsa* named *Madhyadesa* (Punjab) finds frequent mention in the Indian texts like *Amarakosa* (also known as the *Namaling anusasana*), *a* work of the fourth and fifth centuries it is used synonymously with *Bharata* and *Aryavarta* being the same as Manu's holy land situated between the Himalaya and the Vindhyachal range in the location of Jammu and Kashmir state, that story of this historical evience reveals in the light furture course of action in human history. But in Bana's *Kadambari* (7th century A. D.), at one place *Bharatavarsa* is said to have been ruled by *Tarapida* of Kashmir as referred by Kalhana, the ruler of the *Chamar Dynasty* of Kashmir who "set his seal on the four oceans" of the '*Nam*' called *dattacatuhs a mudramudrah*, is indicated as being outside for sometimes to regain the power of the '*Nam*' to repeat the history again as a story or *Bharata*. Similarly, in the *Nitivakyamrta* of *Somadeva* of 10th century A. D., the word *Bharatiyah* cannot be taken to mean anything more that the inhabitants of *Bharata* or Jammu and Kashmir state as its location. Most of the *Puranas* describe *Bharatavarsa* as being divided into nine *dvipas* or *Khandas* which became popular during the rule of *Nine Nanda* rulers of the *Sudhra* Family as they had one Father i. e. *Mahapadamnanda* i. e., God or '*Nam*'. In many texts *Bharata* is said to have been a part of *Jambudvipa*, which itself had an uncertain geographical commotation. The vedic texts do not mention it, nor does Panini, though he refers to the *Jambu* (the rose apple tree), as Dr. Rewata Dhamma mentions in his *Emptying the Rose Apple seat, Rudra, Shiva, Narayana,* plurality of gods is an illusion since God is unitary force of the '*Nam*', they are only different iconic aspects of the one reality (*Tatva*) or of the Absolute. Therefore what appears to be separation to meditate on the '*Divine Object*' in order to bring about reunion. The mechanics of this explained in terms of the *Atman,* a spark of the '*Divine*' intelligence which leads one back to the ultimate source, the Supreme Being (*Paramatman*). It was the heyday of this Era of religious-philosophical speculation that Buddha-to be was born in the history of India in the form of Deepit Raj as a Fresh Idea of the story or *Bharata* [(1) D. N. Jha; *Look for a Hindu Identity; IHC. Presidential address*, 2005-06, Santiniketan, pp. 1,2,3, 4(2) Dr. Rewata Dhamma; *Emptying the Rose -Apple Seat; USA, 2003, Introduction, pp. XII, XIII*)]

113. ***Note.*** The *Mahabharata* epic, is regarded as the earliest authoritative text of Vaisnava religion originated or compiled by *Ved Vyash*, the great Rishi of the *Biasa* at that time. There is a general consensus that although Rana, son of Dasaratha was recognised as the incaranation of *Vishnu* or *Manu* of the *Mind* used as a term for Brahmin. But *Rama* was an object of the life to recognise the God or Nam in human form, but Brahmins of the period never know the reality of the truth that is '*Nam*' where it stands, it stands in human body not scriptures. In this way, D. D. Kosambi, wrote that *Bhakti* was the basic need in feudal ideology, as the feudal society was held together through ties of personal faith and superiority, where as *Sudhra* were degrade on the muscle power Valmiki preached social ethics of the scientific study of the '*Nam*' and had created the character of Rama through the artisans in the form of an ideal hero of the '*Nam*' or God, who provided a role model for the *Varna*-based patriarchal society as '*Nam*' or '*Word*' *do* to uphold its norms as a great deal of personal sacrifice, and the popularity of the 'Rama' or 'Nam' sage, during his indirect form for the gaining of power Brahminical social order became popular and they start to commit the crime against the poor people. According to the *Adhyatma* Ramayana the path of *Rama-Bhakti* meaning Living Master of the period is important and opened for all. *Rama* himself teaches the nine modes of the *Bhakti-cult* to control the system of the life exhibited from the low-caste female ascetic *Sabari* of the '*Nam*' as *Amri Devi*, the mother of the author. The theme of this story again developed in the *Ananda Ramayana*, it is mentioned the husband of a Brahman woman from *Sringaverapura* the daughter of a leather-worker (*charamakara*) of the *Ravidas* Family, he killed the *Sambuka* revived the whole family of the father particularly the *Sudhra* community, and Kabir does not use only '*Rama*' for his god, but all the words current in his time (SuviraJaiswal, *The Making of a Hegemonic Tradition : The Cult of Rama Dasarathi* ; S. C. Misra Memorial Lecture, IHC. Kerala, 2007 pp. 2,3,5,14).

114. State Times Magazine Article; 10-2-2008, *Places to See in Pachmarhi. In Panchmari*, there is a sacred cave of *Jalasankar* cave under a mass of loose

boulders situated 1. 5 km. from the bus stand. The name *Jatasankar,* itself is derived from a rock formation resembling the matted locks of Lord Shiva represents the mental understanding of the people, which was black at that time as '*Black Power*' of the *mana* or *Brahmanas*. This *Samadhistha Shiva* displayed under a natural formation that resembles the hood of a giant serpant in the cool dark cave is a place of abiding sanctity and the striking rock faces is a wonder of nature to cool down the people down not jump before the '*Nam*'. He will give a solace to the community of the *Sudhra* Family i. e. Deepit Raj, Master of the '*Nam*' *a* great snake or Naga of the Father. The cool water of the *Jambu-Dvipa* stream takes its sources from this cave which was located in Jammu on the right bank of Chenab and Ravi. The overcasting little rocks, many of them hanging precariously between huge walls of rock cutting changes colour from green to golden yellow when 'Light' reflects in this universe. By the side of the *Pandava Caves,* a road leads to this spot called '*Fairly Pool*' of the '*Nam*' or God work with honesty and dedication under the umberal of the forefathers. Which is accessible only on foot through the '*Nam-Dana*' of the Father. The fool is formed by a little fall which is nearly 30ft high. The pool is an ideal place of the period for swimming and diving during life time. A swimmer can reach under the fall after swimming the short distance of the pool which gradually get deeper near the fall. Others can enjoy their dips free of cost in the shallow end of the pool during the prediction of the God will took place near future. Only the adventures people can enjoy this moment and trekkers can negotiate the path which goes round the hill on the left view of the point.

115. *W. T. W. I.*, p. 489 **Note:** The subcontinent of *India* around *Meru*, round which sun, moon and stars revolved. Around Meru there were four continents (*dvipa*), 'Light,' separated from the central peak by oceans and named according to the great trees of the '*Nam*', which stood on their shores opposite Meru or 'ego'. The southern continent on which human beings dwell had a *jambu* (rose-apple tree) as its distinctive tree which gives light to other and it was there called *Jambudvipa* that 'light' predict from the Jammu region to repeat the history of the '*Nam*' as a central force of the human body as a 'Creative Power' the southern zone of this continent (*dvipa*), already predict during the lifetime of Dr. B. R. Ambedkar defeated the Brahmins with the writing of the Devanagari script of the forefather, separated from the rest by the Himalayas, was "the land of the sons of Bharata" (*Bharatavarsa*), or India. *Bharatavarsa* alone was 9,000 *Yojanas* across, and the whole of *Jambudvipa* was 33,000, or according to some sources 100, 000 *yojanas*. During the blind faith astronomers described the earth as the flat disc of enormous size, but it is hemispherical in nature which gives the message of the man from Heaven to earth. But early

Buddhist evidence points out the *Jambu-dvipa* was a territorial name of a country wherefrom the 'Light' of Father predict the theory of the '*Nam*' after arounding the earth 300 years for the civilizational growth, than gives a judgement to the society that 'Nam' has been established, geographical and historical conditions of the world are going to change as his warning to the common people and challenge to the Brahmins or self-style rulers. It was applied to that part of Asia particularly to Jammu region as his neclus name from *Jambudvipa*. Therefore, the history of the Jammu region is so deep and hard to understand with the logic of the '*Nam*' *or* God a reasonable study of the areas. It was also applied to China, Japan itself. (Ibid, pp. 488-89, B. N. Lunyia; *Evolution of Indian Culture;* Agra, 2005, p. I).

116. *Ibid.*, p. 1.

117. H. A. Rose *A Glossary of the Tribes and Castes* of the *Punjab and North Western Frontier Province*; Language Department Punjab; 1990, Vol. II 1p. 351.

118. General Tod, *ASRs* Reprint Madras 1880, pp. 52 to 76, 96-101.

119. Ibid. Report I. pp. 51-61.

120. Elphin stones, *History of India*; pp. 250-253.

121. Elliot's *Memories of Races of North Western Provinces* Vol. I. pp. 130-37.

122. H. A. Rose; Op. Cit. Vol. II. p. 362. ***Note:*** *Jat*, female called *Jatni*. The form *Jat* is used in the South-East Panjab likely to be Harayan. In the Central Panjab *Jatt* female *Jatti* is usual called by name of their caste, and in Balocchi term for a *Jat,* is *Jagdal*, and *Jat* (with the soft t) is used to denote a camel-driver, as in upper Sindh, where *Jat* now means a rearer of camels or shepherd, in opposition to a husbanbman. Fragmentary notices of the *Jats* occur in the Muhammadan historians of India. Ibn *Khurdadba* writing *Ante* in 912 A. D. gives the distance from the frontier of Kirman to *Mansura* as so *parasangs* and added: "This route passes through the country of the *zats* (Jats) who keep watch over it (Elliot's *History of India*, vol. I, p. 14). It has been again mentioned that the *Bheti* Thakurs and *Jats* of Ghasui, who had submitted and entered the Arab service of the God of the Indus region to the island of *Bait* in the time of Mohammad -bin-Qasim in 712 A. D. after defeat the Bhamanbad Kingdom of Kashmir and Sindh and also revolted against *Umar* in 1300 A. D. In 1398-99, Amir Tumur marched through jungle from Ahruni in Karnal to Tohana, through a tract which he found inhabited by Jats, became Muslim converted in *Islam* as a '*New Faith of the New Sccic y*' i. e. '*Nam*' or God (Ibid., p. 356. Elliot, op. cit. Vol. I, pp. 220-21).

123. *W. T. W. I* pp. 16-17. ***Note:***. The two cities were built on a small plan to develop the future course of action of the man. To the west of each was a "*Citadel*", an ablong artificial platform some 30-50 feet hight and about 400x200 yards in area the houses, often of two or more stories though they varied in

size were all based on much the same plan as '*Nam*' in a square courtyard round which were a number of rooms for the residential purposes (Ibid., p. 16).

124. K. L Khurana; op. cit., p. 24.
125. W. T. W. I., p. 18.
126. The dwelling houses were constructed of baked bricks which were fixed in place with the help of mud mortar. The buildings were generally of two or more storeyed and had staircases. They had big doors, and gates, perhaps of wood and iron. Each house had a number of rooms, in addition to a bath room and a kitchen, all having brick floors (K. L Khurana; Op. Cit., p. 24).
127. *Ibid.*
128. *A. H. I.,* pp. 16-17
129. K. L Khwiana; op. cit., p., 24.
130. A. H. I., pp. 17-18.
131. **Note:** Only two representations of ships have been found among their remains and these are of small river vessels as '*Nam*' *or* God. But whether the sea or land the product of the Indus who absorbed within the body according to the advise of Perfect Master, who is present at Bias, in the form of Rishi Ved Viyas reached Mesopotamia for a number of typical Indus seals and a few other objects from the Indus Valley have been found in Sumer at levels dating between about 2300 and 2000 B. C. Evidence of Sumerian exports to India is very scant and uncertain, and we must assume that they (Dr. Raj Kumar, Baba Gurinder Singh Ji, Dr. Ram Dass and Master Deepit Raj) were mainly precious metals and raw materials of the '*Nam*' or '*God*'. The find of Indus seals suggest that merchants from India actually resided in Mesopotamia, their chief merchandise was probably cotton, which has always been one of India's staple exports, and which is known to have been used in later Babylonia. Specimens of wheat and barley show that they were cultivated good relation with other civilization i.e., *Mesopotamia, Iranian,* Babylonia, many more of the period as a story of the '*Nam*' or God is concerned. Evidence also show that rice, date palms, peas, seasum, mustard, melon and others fruits were grown up in the areas. This civilization, i. e. the civilization of the Indus Valley or *Indus Saraswati* of the Akhnoor Region of the Jammu areas was the Second World Civilization in the context of various relationship of life not limited in India, but widely spread throughout the world under the banner of '*Ravidas Culture*' of the *Sudhra* Family. This civilization also grew cotton to make clothes. They domesticated animals which included camels, goats, buffaloes, fowls, horses, dogs, pigs and may have included elephants too. Besides these, the diet of the people consisted of fruits, vegetables, fish, milk and meat of animals i.e., beaf, mutton and poultry. Large number of spindles, needles,

buttons showed that they knew weaving, spinning and also the art of stitching. Men and women were ornaets made of gold, silver, copper, shell and bone also. Bronze oval mirrors ivory combs of various shapes, ivory hair pins have also been found in the area of Akhnoor in Jammu Region. Agriculture was the main occupation of the Indus Valley people. Trade was the another main profession. Traders carried on trade in the country as well as with other countries like as Egypt, Babylon, Afghanistan and Mesopotamia. The seals were used to stamp their goods. Means of trade were ships, camels and assess of the '*Nam*' called *Chamars* by Akbar. Their brief inscriptions, never of more than twenty symbols and usually of not more the ten, are the only significant examples of the *Harappa* script to have survived till date. Script had 270 character evidently pictographic in origin, which had an ideographic or syllabic character, founded from the site of *Chanhu Daro* having an inkwell. The inner walls of their houses were coated with mud plaster, but if any paintings were made on these walls all trace of them has vanished (*W. T. W. I.* pp. *19-20, R. S.* Sharma; *Ancient India;* New Delhi 1999 pp. 55, 58, Raj Kumar; *Early History of the Five Rivers;* An artical published PHC, 2006, p. 91. Jogeshwar Singh; *Indus Valley and Their Religion*; An article published, PHC. 2005, p. 565). **Note:** *Sarasvati* may be described as the eastern boundary of the first Aryan dominion in India, since it skirts and desert is known as modern *Sarsuti* and *Gharghar* at present to check the advancement of the race, the seventh and the eastern most river of the *Sapta-Sindhavah* of the Chenab and Ravi Rivers of the '*Nam*' or *Ravidas Culture* (Raj Kumar; op. cit, p. 95, PHC).

132. K. L. Khurana; op. cit. p. 24.

133. **Note:** The proficiency of the Indus Valley sculptor can be seen easily in human and animal figures that have been excavated at Akhnoor in Ambaran and other adjoining areas of the civilization. Among these figures, those of a bull, a strong dog, a yogi, a dancing girl are most significant. The majority of the human figures are female and they are nude except for a narrow girdle round the waist perhaps the most striking figure is the dancing girl standing in a provocative posture with one arm on her hip and leg. A great advance in technical knowledge is indicated by the potter's wheel, kiln-burnt brick, the boring of hard substances like carnelian and the casting and alloy of metals. A high aesthetic sense is indicated by the beautiful designs of ornaments, the superb relief figures on seals as well as executed on the fine stone statues of the 'Nam' or God. From them we come to the conclusion that the potters (*Kumahars*) of the '*Indus Valley Civilization*' from the area of Akhnoor widely spread their craftmanship skill. The clay pots were only polished and glazed to give shine like those of the present day society of India of the same category i. e, called *Chamar* or *Untouchable* of the Father. (A. H. I., p. 20, K. L Khurana op. cit. p. 24).

134. *W. T. W. I.*, p. 20 **Note:** The trade contract was a primary factor in the urban development societies. So far the availability of the twenty five proto-historic sites in Mansa District shows that the wide spread of the *Indus Valley Civilization* or *Indus Saraswati* was very important for cultural complex during the Harappan period. The Early Harappans preferred the Ghaggar and its tributaries because this was a more static river system than the other river systems of Panjab because of an indepentent idea is residing in the human figure which is difficult to locate by the *Satan* of the period called Brahmins *Molabis* and Pandits. The Sirhind, a tributary of the Ghaggar was one of the most, appears to be buzzing with activity in the third and second millennium B. C., important lines of communication between Punjab and Rajasthan forgetting raw materials like timber, especially *Deodar* or *Deva* tree used in house building activities. Since the exploration have yielded flarrappan sites in the southern areas of Bhatinda District of Punjab, adjoining *Sriganga nagar* District of Rajasthan, it shows that every channels of the movement were established both between Northern Rajasthan to Southern Panjab to change the idea of the movement against the present government of the Brahmins. The primary interaction of Panjam seems to have been with the sites of the *Ghaggar-Hakra Culture* divided the people, exemplified by the ceramic traits it shared with siswal and Kalibangan since the Early Harappan period. In the Harappan period, interaction also occured with the mature Harappan centres such as *Rakhigarhi, Akhnoor, Jammu, Poonch, Rajouri, R. S. Pura, Basohli, Ramnagar, Udhampur, Chenani, Sudhmahadev, Banawali, Punjab* itself, Sindh, *Blonchistan, Multan, Sialkot, Lahore* etc. as well as local cultural settlements of Haryana and Rajasthan already established on the basis of the same *Civilization* i. e., called '*Nam*' or '*Chamar*'. *(Dr. Sukhdev Saini; A Socio-Economic View of Proto-Historic Culture of Punjab;* An article published PHC 2005,p. 68).

135. *A. H. I.*, pp. 19-20.

136. K. L Khurana; op. cit. p. 25 ***Note:*** From the various artifacts found in the remains of *Mohenjodaro* and Harappa we can draw a picture of the social life of the '*Indus Valley Civilization*' or the *Indus-Sarasvati Civilization* of the Jammu region, perhaps divided into four classes, viz., learned persons, warriors of the '*Nam*', businessmen and working class or labourers. These business was not limited upto Jammu, it was widely spread whole of the world through the survey of the Punjab industry of the Harappan times. They paid sufficient attention to their dresses and decorations. In the absence of human figurines it is difficult to know how people dressed themselves without the Father. Hairpins from Kotla-Nihang Khan, and bone pin or stylic from Dher Majra, Chandigarh, Bara and Ropar confirm ornamental hair styles among more fashionable people.

Women darkened their eyes during those olden days as suggested by the finding of Kohl-sticks from Ropra. The large number of beads of different material found from different sites were used for necklace. The bangles were popular among the woman since Early Harappan period. The beads of faience, lapis-lazuli, carnolian, agate and stealite, made of ornaments were found from the skeleton at Harappan levels at Ropar, Dhalawan, Dher Majra, Kotla-Nihang Khan, Bara are also reported shell and bronze bangles, Earrings, braclets from these areas. The use of semi-precious stones were limited among the late Harappans, Barans and Polish Grey Ware people, being examplified by only a few beads of agate and carnelian. The Harappan craftsmanship of this region were proficient in making objects of terracotta, bone, ivory, shell, faiene, stone, chart blade (used for cutting) and weight, potters have made considerable progress in ceramic technology. Gold and copper smithy is attested from the artifacts of different areas like Bara, Bhadla, Chandigarh, Dher Majra, Jammu and Kashmir, Himachal, Punjab and Pakistan. Gold beads were also manufactured at Sanghol and Dher Majra. This speaks of an advanced technical knowledge of the *Barans or 'Nam'* then the preceding period of the study (Dr. Sukhdev Saini; op. cit., pp. 64, 65, 67.

138. **Note:** Such vessels were used until recently by Indian perfumes to supply 'attars' in small quantities. Hamman or hot air both were also used in Kashmir during the winter. At *Chandujodaro* a number of Kohl jars were found containing paint for the adornment of the eyes and lip liners. A woman's head from Mohenjodaro shows curly hair, hanging down at the back of the head. A V-shaped comb also found by Mackay Mirror made of bronze is slightly oval found from the depositary material. Sir John Marshall; *Mohenjodara and the Indus Valley Civilization;* vol. I. p. 26 and Mackay; *Further Excavation at Mohenjodaro*, Vol. III p. 362 p. 320).
139. K. L Khurana, op. cit., p. 26.
140. *Ibid.*
141. J. D. Bernal *Science in History*, Vol. I, London, 1986, p. 27.
142. Presidential Address by Dr. P. C. Roy before Madras University in Feb. 1918 noted from "*Studies in the History of Science in India;* Vol. I: Edited by Prof. Debi Prasad Chattopadyaya, New Delhi, 1982, p. 344.
143. *Caraka Samhita*, Pt-I, Ed. *Ayurvedacharya Sri Jaideva Vidyalankar*, Delhi, 1980, p. 230-33.
144. *Caraka Samhita* op. cit.
145. D. P. Chattopadhyay, *History of Science in India*, p. 210.
146. *Ibid.*, p. 350.
147. *Ibid.*, p. 353.
148. R. L. Mitra; *Indo-Aryans,* - Beef eating in Ancient India, Calcutta, 1881, p. 380.

149. R. S. Sharma; *Material Background of the Origin of Buddhism, in Das Kapital Centenary Volume, New Delhi, 1968, p. 61.*
150. D. P Chattopadhya, op. cit., p. 214.
151. Caraka; op. Cit., p. 14.
152. *Chand; Upanishad*; VIII. 8. 3 in S. B. E. ; Vol. I. The Upanishads Ed. Max Muller, New Delhi, p. 136.
153. Ibid., VIII. 10. 3, p. 138.
154. *Br. Ar.* Up. in The Thirteen Principal Upanishads tr. R. E. Hume, Oxford, p. 88.
155. J. Filliozat; *The Classical Doctrine of Indian Medicine, Delhi;* 1964.
156. *Caraka*; op.cit.
157. *Rig. veda*. II. 33.
158. *Ibid.*, II. 39.
159. M. Monier-Williams; *Sanskrit-English Dictionary,* Delhi; 1963.
160. *Ibid.*
161. Dorothy Fisk's monograph entitled "*Bouquet for the Doctor*". London, P. 3.
162. *Rig. veda* IX. 112.
163. *Atharva veda* V. III. 4.
164. *Taittiriya Samhita*. Eng. tr. by A. B. Keith, Reprint I-II, New Delhi, 1967.
165. Sigerist, *A History of Medicine*, London, Vol. I, Ch. I. p. 9.
166. Taittiriya Samhita. op. cit.
167. P. Gupta, *Anthropological Interpretation of the Astrology of Celestial Bodies, Pragya Bharati* Vol. II, (in Honour of Professor R. S. Sharma), Patna-2005.
168. *Rig-Veda*-VII. 77. 5.
169. Mrs. Rhys Davids- *Buddhist Psychology*, London, 1924, Preface. p. VII.
170. Mrs. Rhys Davids- *Compendium of Philosophy*, London, P. T. s. ed., 1910, p. 18.
171. Sigerist-op. cit.
172. *Ramayana, Yudh*: 16-4.
173. Satya Prakash, *Founders of Science in Ancient India*, New Delhi, 1965, p. 155.
174. Charles Singer, *A Short History of Scientific Ideas to 1900,* Oxford 1965, p. 18.
175. Burnet, *Greek Philosophy*, London, p. 9.
176. A. K. Roger, *A Student's History of Medical Philosophy*, London, p. 12.
177. Herman Jacobi, *Encyclopaedia of Religion and Ethics*, Ed. James Hastings, vol. II, Edingburg, p. 801.
178. Ch. Up., op. cit.
179. *Taittiriya Samhita*, op. cit.
180. *Svetasvatara Upanishad*, in Thirteen Principal Upanishads, tr. R. E. Hume, Oxford, p. 344.
181. *Caraka Samhita*, op. cit. 25th section.

182. J. Filliozat, op. cit. p. 48.
183. *Encyclopaedia Britanica,* Vol. xx, p. 8. Bicentenary volume, 1984.
184. Walter Ruben, *In a Letter to Dr. P. Gupta.*
185. **Note:** From the earliest times 'Science and Technology' has been a part and parcel of human life '*Word*' or '*Nam*' the essence of human existence. It was diversified in various forms during the Vedic period. The *Rigveda* traces the development of Science and Technology in the form of a story.

We get a clear-cut astronomical knowledge, as that of Solar and Lunar eclipses, the division of time into years, months and days, etc. from the *Rigveda*. Quite surprisingly, the speeds of the movement of heaven, earth, moon and various stars are also elaborately dealt with. Thus generally with the study of the art of Mathematics, Arithmetic, Geometry. Astronomy and Astrology too are included. Geometry had an immense significance during religious rites and ceremonies, whereas Arithmetic was applied while counting. This tradition was later on carried by scholars like *Aryabhatta, Mahaviracharya*, etc. The subject-matter has been elaborately dealt with *Mahaviracharya's* book *Ganit Sarsangraha*. Counting was a general feature of the *Vedas* ; some of the words used for counting in the *Rigveda* are-

Ek-Ekah

Ekadasah

Ekasat

Dvi, Dvitiya

Tri, Traya, Tritiya

Chatuh, Panch, Sat, Sapt, Ast. Nav, Das, Sahastra, Sasti-sahastra, Ayut.

We thus draw the inference about the prevalence of the art of counting in the Rigveda. Though perhaps we do not find reference to a greater denomination than *Ayut* (10,000) but Bhagatpur, Bihar, there is only one reference to *Sasti-sahastra* meaning 60,000. The word 'Zero' does not occur even once in the *Rigveda,* but the word '*Khe*' has been used thrice in the mantra-

"Khe Rathasth Kheanasah Khe Yugasya Satkrato"

"Khe Araan iv Khedya"

The word "Khe" stands for space or zero and here in the mantra 'Khe' seems to imply 'hole'. And since holes are round in shape hence the figure of the alphabet 'khe' was considered round. Even in the astrological texts the alphabet 'khe' has been used for 'zero'. If these interpretations be considered true, 'zero' may be said to have been in vogue in ancient India and 'Infinite' to modern time.

Bug *Rigveda* does not clearly mention and describe physical sciences. However Astronomy, to a great extent, was studied in the form of Physics, during the period under review. Among Hindus Astronomy has accorded the highest place in the study of various sciences 'Word' it is evident from the fact that it has been compared with a peacock's feather and a snake's jewel (*mani*). The various rules for and the process of making a calendar are elaborately dealt with in the forty slokas of *Rigveda.* This part of the *Rigveda* is called *Vedanga* Astrology. In a time span of 5 years of 1,830 days, there are 60 regular months and 40 (*Chalisa*) months which are chiefly based on the lunar-date. This is the reason why the study of physics stands in close promixity with religion and spiritualism!

The discovery of fire occupies the most prominent place among the various scientific inventions and discoveries. This led to the materialistic pursuits in man's life. This is the reason why the word '*agni*' has been referred to at various places with different connotations in the *Rigveda.* In one of the mantras we find mention of a sage Atharvan, also known as *Angirasa*, who is said to have discovered fire. Similarly, in another mantra, there is a reference to the popular sage *Vishvamitra* who is credited with the discovery of an instrument which on friction produced fire. We may thus draw the influence that the *Rigvedic* Aryans knew the art of making fire by rubbing two wooden planks used as voice, and instruments played with the force of mouth such '*Shankha*', played with both hands called 'Dundubhi', 'Mridanga'. The inspiration for the wire instruments was derived from the music produced by the strings of the bow. War-music thus came into vogue with the various sounds produced by a finger using bow and arrow during a war. We also find mention of a musical instrument 'Karkari' in another mantra of the *Rigveda:*

"Yadutpatan vadasi karkariryatha
Vrihad Vedam vidathe survirah. "

The development of Engineering in the Rigvedic period was limited to fulfilling the needs of a village. The technical knowledge used in the construction of houses and in the making of tools and equipments mentioned in the *Veda* is not satisfactory. Still the word 'pur' has been used many a times. The word 'pur' means 'fort' or '*quila*'. As per the demands of the time the 'purs' were huge: *Rigveda* mentions a 'pur constructed of one hundred walls. But there is no description about what the 'pur' was made of Perhaps these were temporary buildings constructed of stone, soil or wood. At one place in the *Rigveda* a 'pur' made of stone has been mentioned. But Macdonald and Keith consider that it was not made of stone but of sun-dried bricks.

Various other kinds of technical knowledge too are mentioned in the *Rigveda* '*Word*'- for example, cart-making, ship building and different types of tools making, etc. In a cart were attached two tyres (*Chakra*) which had rim (nemi), Paradhi, *Dhuri* (Axis), (*Nabhya*) spoke (*aara*) which was attached to an unmovable *Dhuri* (Axis) whose end was attached to the hole of *Dhuri* (Axis).

Sometimes solid tyres were also used. The technical process for irrigation through an iron-wheel (*Chakra*) drawing water from the wells has been specifically dealt with in the *Rigveda. goldsmith, metalsmith, leathersmith* and *potter.* Metalsmith used to smelt metals and mould it into different forms for making arrows, axes, swords, etc. in this direction to repeat the history itself.

We get an insight into the art of ship-building from the *Rigveda.* The words 'boat' (*nao*) and 'sea' (*samudra*) are referred to at various places in the *Veda.* It has been mentioned here in this context that the traders, crossing the *samudra* travelled to far-off places to earn money. It has been described here about boats being used as the vehicle of journey on the sea-waves. It is thus evident that with the technical know-how a boat could be stabilised in sea-waters during adverse circumstances. There is a description of a ship called 'pallava' which remained firm even in the stormy weather. To maintain the balance sometimes 'feathers' *(pankha)* were also attached to the ship. B. N. Luniya also considers it true that the *Rigvedic* Aryans knew the technique of making boats or ship-building of the '*Nam*', they were *Chamars or Sudhras.*

The *Rigvedic* Aryans were also well-versed in the Chemical Science and Technology. The roots for the nourishment and development of Chemistry lay deep in the ancient sciences of Ayurveda, and very small scale industries, though in an embryonic stage. We rarely get evidence of how chemical (*Rasayan*) was used in various industries. And it is also quite difficult to estimate how man could obtain various metals and their alloys from chemical elements, minerals and ayaskas or how they developed the art of dyeing clothes. Yet *Rigveda* mentions some metals, for example, the word "Ayas' has been used at many a places, especially with 'Hiranya' as Absolute peace.

We also come to know from the Rigveda that *Yajnasala* was the basic form of laboratory. All the things used in *Yajnasala* gradually came to be implemented in a laboratory and Yajuashala (*Paksala*). Besides this, process of making grinded grain 'sattu'. There is also a reference to the process of making sura in a *mantra* of the *Rigveda*. Which was used by Mohammad Prophet in the *Quran* during the closing of the history of Brahmins to began with *Sudhra* concept during the 7th century A. D.

The process of making 'Sura' has also been discussed in one of the mantras. In the initial process of preparing 'Somarasa' the barks and branches of the soma plant were put in water and crushed. Thus greater amount of 'rasa' could be obtained and to grind it '*ukhal*' and '*musal*' were used. We also come across a reference to the hammer made of gold which was used in grinding.

To take out this *Somarasa'* a leather was put on the ground and the crushed Soma-plants barks and branches were spread, and they were grinded by stones. Later with both and hands the *'Rasa'* was oozed out and made to fall on the cloth, made by the sheep's skin, called '*Dasapavitra*'. And from this 'dasapavitra' the 'rasa' purified fell in the '*Kalhsa*' or pan kept under the '*dasapavitra*'.

We have a further description of the extraction and purification of *'Soma-rasa'* in the *Rigveda.* It is generally said that 'soma' was spread by the daughter of the Sun-God, *Shraddha*. We may thus draw the inference that *'Soma-rasa'* was kept under the sun and evaporated. Obviously, it made the *'rasa'* dry and become semi-fluid. And so to make it fluid again and enhance its taste, milk or curd was added to it. The proof of its fluidity is obvious from a reference to the all-powerful god *Indra*, whose moustache and beard became wet while drinking the *'rasa'*. It is thus evident that the curd was added to *'soma'* and to the more semi-flid 'soma' milk was added to regain its fluidity.

The various types of 'soma-rasa' have also been discussed in the *Rigveda,* for example, *'haritavarana soma'* or green-coloured soma'. The 'white-coloured soma' had lustre and it shone brightly. To make the *'Soma rasa'* pious or to maintain its religious sanctity, it was kept in a pot made of wood called 'drona-kalash'. The *'Soma-rasa'* kept in this pot was always fresh and tasteful. A sage named Tvashta made a different type of pot called '*Chamas*' in which '*soma*' was kept for '*ritvijas*'. The *'soma'* prepared for gods was kept in pots called '*Chamu*'. It is thus clear that various kinds of 'soma' existed in the Rigvedic period, and the best kind must have been preserved for the gods. It is also thus evident that the Rigvedic Aryans knew the art of making curd from milk as also the techniques of preparing 'sura'.

There are several stories related to Medicine and Medical Sciences in the *Rigveda* describing the forms of healing used by gods for curing various diseases. In the pre-Vedic era Asvini Kumar was regarded as the most popular god for curing diseases. One cannot but acknowledge the great advancement *Ayurveda* has made from the description of various stories of miraculous treatment of the patients.

Asvini Kumar did miracles in curing 'Word' in the degeneration of the body's treatment: making healthy a *Rebha* drowning in water, making Kali regain his prime and bringing him thus at par with his wife; making Chavan to regain his youth and long-lived; making the king Kakshivan's daughter suffering from leprosy healthy and beautiful, etc. *'Nam'* or God all have been elaborately dealt with in the *Rigveda*. They also made barrens (childless women) mothers, and normalised the pains during child-birth.

There is also a detailed description of the various kinds of *'Ausadhis'* mentioned in the *Rigveda. 'Ausadhis'* like *'Soma-rasa'* had great importance; all the diseases of the body could be cured through its use. Even a body degenerated due to malnourishment could regain its strength and charm. It also revitalises your energy and vigour. It has been recommended in one of the *mantras* that if a girl has lost her strength and vigour she should use the '*Ausadhis*' like '*Soma-rasa*' so that she could regain her energy and become strong; only then she becomes fit for a husband. The '*Soma-rasa*' does not have a side-effect on the digestive system even. Not only did it play a significant part in erotics but it was considered helpful during child-birth also. At one place in the *Rigveda* the God Indra has been requested to drink 'soma' before going to meet his beloved as male and female.

In one of the mantras of the *Rigveda,* it has been considered that '*soma*' is present in various body-organs. Hence '*soma*' is the life-line for a living body. There is also a reference to the use of '*soma*' as '*sanjivani*'. Its use could give eyes to the blind, give a lame the strength to walk, and a weak voice a perfect tenor.

In the tenth mandala of the *Rigveda* is a reference to *Ausadhisutra* which describes *Rishi Atharwan* as a doctor. There is a general and beautiful description of the various types of medicines. '*Ausadhis*' reaching the blood-veins acted as antibiotics against the diseases in the body. The intake of various '*Ausadhis*' led to the ailment of various diseases like cough, tuberculosis, etc. The doctors used to discuss the mode of treatment for serious diseases. The efficient doctors used to perpare different types of '*Ausadhis*' for various kinds of diseases; and only then they followed a line of treatment. Any person suffering from quenching thirst, the aggravated joint-paints in the legs and the complications of the sensory organs '*Nam-dana mantra*' of the Father, all could be cured through the use of various '*Ausadhis*' There were other sorts of '*Ausadhis*' too that acted as antigens in the human body, or to say, could fight the diseases attacking the body. Some kinds of '*Ausadhis*' are obtained from the earth and are used not only to cure human beings but also animals of the '*Nams*'.

We get a clear description of Medical Science too from the *Rigveda,* as is evident at a place where an efficient Guru or doctor is said to impart knowledge to the students about various '*Ausadhis*' which would help them cure the diseased. It has been referred to in this context: "Oh God! give me the knowledge of various 'rasas' and '*Ausadhis*' which are available in all the three seasons, and their hundred qualities. And hence it has been discussed in the *Rigveda* that one should acquire complete knowledge about '*Ausadhis*'.

Asvini Kumar had an expertise in Surgery too. They gave eyes to the blind Kanva; attached iron-legs to the king Khel's daughter Vishala who had broken her legs, and thus made her capable of fighting in battles attached a horse's head to *Dadhichi* after cutting his head, and again replaced it with his head. Besides attaching body-organs and providing *Sanjivani,* they were specialised in Veterinary Science too. They could make childless cows produce calves and provide them huge breasts for giving ample milk.

Thus *Rigveda* while mentioning various other diseases like heart disease etc. refers to various body-organs of a human body. There is also a reference to destroying somebody parts. The knowledge of reproduction was also mentioned. With reference to medicines the *Ausadhisukta of the Rigveda* is of great importance. Not only this the knowledge of Mathematics, Physics, Chemistry, Medical Science, etc. went a long way in and changing the day-to-day life and the standards of living of the Aryans as a scientific discovery of the *Rigveda* during the period under study.

Divine Mantra of Aryans described as:

Om namo Bhagavate Vasudevaya Om, reverence to the Adorable God i. e., 'O' or 'Zero' and 'M' stands for 'Mind Only'. of the later Buddhist idea of the God in human form.

'*Namo Amitabhaya*' 'Reverence to Amitabha'. Of the Saiva Siddanta as *Nam* or *Chamar*.

Sivaya nama, Reverence to siva action in human form species, and '*Nam*' is great in real sense not in scriptures study but his realization in human form, not in artificial manners. Preyers of the Aryans collected into *Rig veda* through historical research during the religious emotions dawns in Asia and says no caste system, after the scientific study. It may refer to the early journeys of the Aryans thus the *Bharata* were an important tribe of the same race as *Vishvamitra. Sarasvati* may be said to have taken the place of Vach in later Hindu mythology which based on philosophy notions, Reality as a process of the history and the *Mahabharata* calls *Sarasvati* is the mother of Veda. *Vedanam mataran pasya mat-sthan devim sarasvatim!* Behold *Sarasvati*, mother of the *Vedas*, abiding in me. (*Mahabharat, Santi-parva 12, 920)*.

In the early stages of research on the *'Harappa Civilization'*, the Indus valley' enjoyed a central stage among the nature centric approaches for understanding its evolution and disintegration. In the meanwhile India attained independence alongwith the partition of the country along religious lines and Pakistan was carved out of India in the northwestern parts of the Indian subcontinent. Amidst the communally surcharged atmosphere the then major known centres of the Harappa Civilization went with Pakistan and this was perceived among some historians and Archaeologists as a huge heritage loss for the antiquity of Indian cultural antecedents. This, of course, provided apparently an opportunity to go for searching Harappan settlements in the areas situated to the east of the newly created Indo-Pak borderline. This opportunity, in a way, was not the creation of partition, in fact, this always existed over there for Archaeological investigations, this was beckoning to all concerned since the discovery of the Harappa Civilization. But because of the communal hangover of the partition the so called perception of loss of cultural heritage was imbued with communal zeal for the speedy discovery of equally important Harappan settlements in the Union of India, this was considered so crucial for re-establishing the Indian cultural roots, at least, at par with that of Pakistan.

For this archaeo-cultural exercise the modern Indian states of *Punjab, Haryana, Rajasthan* and *Gujarat* being contiguous to the borderline appeared very promising and thus invited a series of Archaeological forays. As a result a large number of Harappan as well as other ancient settlements were put on the archaeological map of India. A sizeable number of the explored settlements belong to Punjab, Haryana and northern parts of Rajasthan. Likewise, many more settlements were discovered by Mughals from the Bahawalpur areas, contiguous to the northern parts of Rajasthan, in southern parts of western Punjab in Pakistan. Incidentally in these very areas a seasonal river, popularly known as the Ghaggar river in Indian territories and as the '*Hakra Culture*' of the *Ravidas* sect in the Bahawalpur areas of Pakistan, traverses from the North-East to the South-West, is being equated with the ancient Saraswati by some scholars for the absence of any other river here to match the significance of the river referred to in the Rigveda. For some of the scholars the Indus became the Pakistani river and the *Saraswati* remained an Indian river after the partition. All these factors appeared very conducive to them to make a fresh attempt to prove that the Saraswati Valley was the original home of the Aryans for the paramount importance being given to this river in the first-ever book of the Aryans, the Indus civilization as the Saraswati Civilization and finally this Civilization as the Aryan Civilization found in the Jammu Region of Akhnoor. But they were not fully comfortable with this formulation also simply because according to the general perception presence of a mighty perennial river is a precondition for the development as well as sustenance of a vast civilization like this, an this condition is not met by the present day seasonal Saraswati river. In such situations this brand of scholarship tend to seek refuge in the unforeseen forces. Their perception perhaps is that it is difficult for most of the believers to disbelieve it in the first place and would be equally difficult to discount it in the second, especially in the absence of instant irrefutable archaeological as well as hydrological and soil morphological evidence, this is how they draw sustenance for propagating their unfounded view point and survive on persistent confusion. And exactly that is what is their approach and gameplan in this case also, they comfortably project the Saraswati river as a mighty perennial river during the lifetime of this civilization. Further to buttress their case they also appropriate the remote sensing data on the past water courses from the area under review. This argument is, however, not based on any other solid archaeological, geomorphological and hydrological evidence, hence this calls for a thorough review. Moreover, three seasons of our intensive archaeo-hydrological investigations during 2003, 2004 and 2005 make it all the more imperative on our part to look into this problem afresh. We would like to dwell on the myth of the perennial character of the Saraswati river in the following lines in view of the available recent as well as past data.

In support of the mighty perennial nature of the Saraswati in the ancient past the proponents of this view cite literary references from the *Rigveda.* Obviously in the *Rigveda* the Saraswati river Indus of the Akhnoor has been referred to over hundred times and has also been designated as the river par excellence. On the basis of such references these scholars assume that this was a mighty perennial river during the civilization period, which had its own independent course oriented from the north-east to the south-west, almost parallel to the Indus in the west, leading to the Arabian sea. However, when these arguments are analysed in the light of the available information, they do not evoke any confidence in their validity. There is, however, no denying the fact that the *Saraswati* Indus has frequently been referred to in the *Rig veda.* But such frequent references do not automaticaly qualify this river to become a mighty perennial river. Yes, such recurrent references do indicate towards its paramount importance in the everyday life of the people. And the status of being important is not necessarily confined to and enjoyed only by the perennial rivers, rather this is something which can be earned by a river irrespective of its nature if it offers a wide range of opportunities to the people to survive without jeopardising their very existence. And the life of thinking to attach great importance to only the mighty perennial rivers is a construct of recent times and that is being imposed upon the societies of the ancient past in utter disregard to its inherent weaknesses. In a way the role of a water course is being viewed with out own perception rather than the way people perceived it in the past. The difference of these approaches assumes greater significance especially in context of the *Rigvedic* society of the '*Chamar Culture*' largely subsisting on a pastoral mode of economy. Among their hard cows enjoyed an overwhelming position. And for the people engaged in animal husbandry, especially domestication of cattle, availability of water and pastures was more crucial rather than the seasonal or perennial nature of a watercourse. And the Saraswati being also known as the river of lakes and depressions in the *Rigveda*, a fact usually ignored in such discourses, might have served the two basic needs of water and pastures of the *Rigvedic* pastoral people. Besides the type of animals (cattle, sheep and goats) they raised neither of them required any great amount of water nor stall feeding, there was no great investment either except physical labour. Moreover it has also been observed by us earlier that mighty perennial rivers were a deterrent rather than being any great attraction to the people with limited technological expertise to harness them for they usually appear to be fraught with enormous threats to the very existence of the people. Our contension is not that the seasonal rivers are always friendly, they also pose such threats but these are surely shortlived as their water is primarily governed by the nature of rains in a particular season. Keeping in view the overall behaviour of rainfall in the monsoon season in this area, we simply can not visualize any situation where the span of rains is staggered over the full monsoon season as a norm. Such rivers also do not create any permanent barriers to the movement of men, material and animals across their channels, in a way accessibility is facilitated soon after a short interruption during the monsoon season on an average. Besides these rivers bring with them a whole lot of silt along the rain water to add the existing fertility of the soil, rich reserve of soil moisture is generated to support a good growth of vegetation for grazing animals and the local as well as regional natural depressions/lakes are replenished with water to form the main life-line so far as supply of surface water is concerned for men and animals alike for almost all months of the year. Hence it is the utility of a river/water body in the everyday life of the people rather than the size, might or seasonal or perennial nature of such water bodies that make them dear to the cause to evoke a sense of respect for them.

As regards the mightiness of the *Saraswati* Indus neither have we any one particular basis nor any set of factors to call a particular river either mighty or feeble nor there is any sincere attempt aimed at identifying the (constant and shifting) factors integral to it. To me the might of a river is determined by a host of factors, consisting of both constant and changing ones. Without going into the details of these factors at this point it would not be possible to do justice with the problem. Hence, we would like to go into the factors which define the might of a watercourse. We think availability of great amount of water constantly should constitute the first criterion for this purpose. Obviously this great quantity of water is assured only by the origin of a river from snowcapped mountains and in addition this should be supplemented constantly by a number of tributaries of various demoninations originating from similar contexts, more so when the rainfall being highly erratic and seasonal. When this water comes out in the plains, would require a reasonably wide bed to flow on over it conveniently. And, this bed should be formed primarily by the alluvial sand generated and brought down by the river, this deposit needs to be of sustantial depth as a necessary precondition to be a mighty river. In theprocess such rivers also create a huge groundwater reservoir of fresh water in and around their beds for their intense actions since ancient times. In such areas soil pores are replete with this water and they constitute the water bearning context unlike the stary water bearing strata in areas away from the perennial rivers. These areas of the perennial rivers also lack in calcium content and hence deposits of calcium carbonates. Now we would like to address the concept of mightiness a perceived and projected by the advocates of this view-point of the study. They usually underline the vastness of the river bed, being ten kilometre wide, and the amount of water needed to capture this bed in support of their view. However, we do know this river flows at the surface level and the declivity of the surface is almost imperceptible. In such a situation whenever quantity of water in its bed is increased due to the intensity of rains in its catchment areas as the river is fed by the non glacier water only, the enhanced quantity of water becomes impossible to be flushed our instantly. As a result, a pressure situation is created which helps to capture more areas on both the sides along the course of the river and thus the width of the watercourse is increased in accordance with the quantity of incoming water. And thus the bed is wide enough but remains alive only for a short duration. Nevertheless, at times, it also assumes very powerful dimensions like any other perennial river. Similar, situation was experienced in 1995 in respect of this river when flood water surpassed the suggested limits of lateral expansion of this river. And if we take note of its history, this would not be the first and the last instance of this kind. Interestingly, its mightiness is also transient like vastness of its bedand can not be equated with the vast beds of the other mighty perennial rivers around this zone. Thus the vastness of its bed alone does not confer on it the type of might envisaged, desired and projected by the advocate of this view.

Remote sensing is a most sophisticated device to gather a range of information for archaeological, hydrological and a number of other studies. This technique has helped in retrieving remnants of past channels obliterated from the surface, but existing in the subsurface. Some of these channels from the area under study are being projected as the past shifting courses of some of the rivers in this area. We do not intend to indulge in repeating our earlier assertions in this regard, but nonetheless it is desirable to touch at least one of these courses being equated with the palaeochannel of the *Saraswati* river Chenab or *Chandrabagha* of the period. We would like to state that remote sensing has neither offered any date or any thing about the depth and composition of the soil nor about the name and the potential of the course in terms of ground water reserve. And in the absence of information on these counts it is not only difficult rather impossible to equate it with the desired bed of the ancient Saraswati Indus Valley of Akhnoor by any scientific method of analysis, there is every possibility of the remote sensing imagery of being equated with a past river to be only of the present course of the Saraswati itself, as it depends on the timing of the satellite visit to such areas which we already mentioned above sites, in case the visit takes place in the summer, naturally the imagery would be like that of a dried up river. In the light of this inherent weakness of the line of argument, it is difficult accept the view that the remote sensing data proved the mighty perennial nature of the watercourse.

With a view to understand the nature of the river an archaeohydrological survey of the Ghaggar belt was carried out in 2003, 2004 and 2005. During this reconnaissance south-western parts of Haryana and the North-Western parts of Rajasthan were investigated intensively along the river bed for archaeological as well as Hydrological evidence to ascertain its nature. For this purpose two integral and irrefutable signatures of a mighty perennial watercourse were worked out as a bench mark to prove or disprove the existence of a mighty perennial water course in this area. These are in the form of thick sheet of alluvial sand deposition and the presence flow of a river in its area. It is very much possible to encounter the presence of alluvial sand by mere surface survey of the area but it is just impossible to gauge the depth of the sand deposition and the potential of the fresh groundwater reservoir by this method. Obviously nature of this type of exercise calls for an intensive as well extensive combing along the *Saraswati* by sinking a series of deep bore wells for the collection of micro data on the processes of geological, hydrological and soil morphological formations as a study of the '*Nam*' or God as a historical turth of the man's history. This also needs to be coupled with an Archaeological surface survey of the same region for information on the beginning, and dissemination of human habitations over the landscape through times immomerial. The magnitude of this exercise is further compounded by the multifarious limitations of an individual intending to take on the gauntlet but these very challenges offered opportunities to do the needful by way of surveying the area for data on ancient settlements, their landscapes and flora and fauna, and for data on geological, soil morphological and hydrological formations by surveying the existing bore wells of the areas.

During this survey information was gathered from the bore wells on the quality of surface soil, depth of the water bearing strata, composition and thickness and quality and quantity of the water, incidentally personnels from the regional Central Ground Water Board, Jodhpur, Rajasthan were also sinking a bore well in the bed of the *Saraswati* river on the left side of the state highway from *Suratgarh* to Anupgarh in Ganganagar district, around the time it was engaged in the survey. Interesting corroborative information was gathered both from the survey as well as from the hydrological exploration carried out by the personnels of the Central Ground Water Board. A brief description of this is essential and thus being stated in the following lines.

We would like to touch upon the quality of the surface soil first. It is a clayey loam soil of slightly reddish colour which is very sticky when wet and gets very hard with varied cracks after drying up. The presence of this soil is, in fact, an extension of the soils in the districts of Kurukshetra, Karsal and Jind in Haryana in the north along the bed of the Saraswati river. It appears, this type of soil is formed by the actions of this river over the period. Once, as we go beyond the basin of this river different kind of soils are encountered with varied influence of different natural agencies in operation. While taking cognisance of the contrasting soil types one, however, marks a distinct stamp of the river Saraswati of Akhnoor on the surface soils of its basin in the area of Jammu region.

The quality of soils in these areas is the creation of the seasonal river *Saraswati*, because it rises from Sub Himalayas which are primarily composed of similar type of soil and the same is spread by the river in monsoon season over its bed. There is complete absence of alluvial sand from this river bed. Beyond the river we are faced with different kinds of soils which were party created by wind actions, especially in the middle region, whereas in the upstream area, it is a loam soil resulted from water actions in Pleistocene and wind action in recent times. During the process more information was gathered on the nature and composition of the bed soils from the bore wells. Depth of the majority of these bore wells is in the range of two hundred plus feet. In all these bore wells the quality of soil is in conformity with that of the surface soil. It becomes clear that the quality of the soil in the basin of the Saraswati river from the top to the depth of over two hundred feet is reddish clayey loam and therefore this much of thickness of the clayey soil sheet was the result of the river actions over a very long period of the Indian History. But how long, is not known to us exactly, this could, in fact, be any body's guess by taking into account such natural processes of soil formations. However we may differ in regard to the time taken by the formation of this thick sheet of clay and question can also be raised about the possibility of the presence of river's signatures underneath. Keeping in view, such questions, it was also equally concerned about the quality of soil formation below two hundred feet from the surface. Interestingly information from the bore well being sunk by personnels of the regional Central Ground Water Board is very useful in this context. By this time they had reached to a depth of ninety metre which brings the depth of the bore well beyond three hundred feet. Surprisingly, the quality of the soil was clayey laon, as was noticed above, from the top to bottom in this case also. When we visited their regional office located at Shastri Nagar, Jodhpur in

March 2005 to collect further information and met Mr. Bachchi Ram, the drillman/operator, he informed that they sank the bore well upto around four hundred feet and there was no change in the quality of soil. This information was gathered from the Regional Central Ground Water Board, located at Shastri Nagar, Jodhpur, Rajasthan. This proved that the clayey loam soil continued uninterruptedly upto the depth of around four hundred feet. This was further corroborated by a similar information from the bore well being sun by Ch. Ram Swarup Bishnoi of the Sixteen G. B. Village, tahsil *Raisinghnagar*, district Ganganagar. They also drilled to a depth over 400 feet and around this depth they encountered presence of a rock formation beside the clayey soil from top to bottom at this point in this case. These pieces of information on the soil morphological processes prove the formation of this soil by the Saraswati river. Certainly this thickness of the clayey loam soil might have taken a very long time and during this intervening time period there is no sign of any interruption whatsoever in the form of sand deposition or otherwise, this is a solid evidence of the river being seasonal from remote ancient past. However, away from the bed the soil is aeolian sandy on its both the sides, a usual feature in case of Rajasthan, which distinguishes it from the Saraswati bed soil, a sure sign of the authorship of the *Saraswati* for the presence of the clayey soils from top to the known bottom line in its bed. Usually on the contrary perennial rivers posses a lot of sand of the quality of the bedrock, the rivers originate from. And, since these perennial rivers rise from snow covered peaks contain huge quantity of water year round. The river water flows downward from the high peaks with considerable velocity and generates a lot of friction with the rocks, in the process huge quantity of sand is produced, brought down the slopes by the rivers and deposited in their flood plains in the form of their signatures. There is, however, no evidence of any sand deposition on the surface from these areas. Likewise, bore wells in the perennial river basins also produce the type of sand brought down and deposited by the rivers. Interestingly, all the bore wells from the Saraswati river basin are devoid of sand, of a perennial river, rather they offer a yellowish fine grained silty sand, a sure sign of seasonal rivers. We are also aware of the fact that in the areas of perennial rivers bore well pipes are with filters or holes while on the contrary in seasonal river zones pipes used for such bore wells are without filters or holes and that is why in the Saraswati basin the latter type is a common choice, is not random rather it is dictated by the particlar type of geological formation which were the creations of the actions and interactions of natural forces other than a river called *Chamar* of the period.

The second signature of a river is the presence of a fresh water subsoil reservoir as 'Sudhra Family' keep in their mind, this is always in tune with the size and nature (seasonal or perennial) of the water course. Generally subsoil water reservoirs generated by seasonal rivers vary from those of the perennial rivers in terms of quantity and quality of ground water. In perennial river basins it is as fresh as the water of Himalayan rivers and the quantity is also substantial, whereas in context of seasonal rivers of this area, it is just the contrary, neither it is quality-wise that fresh nor substantial in quantity. The quality of ground water in the Saraswati basin interestingly is not of a high order, rather it is only a potable water. Salt content in the water of the zone is higher than the prescribed limit of alluvial landscapes of perennial rivers, though the water is being used both for consumption as well as irrigation purposes. However, its adverse impact, at least in context of soil, is clearly discernible on the surface soil. Mainly because of its being unfit for irrigation the scientists of the Central Agricultural Farm at Sardargarh stopped its application for irrigation since long as it was informed by the scientists here, named Mr. S. B. Singh. This fact was also borne out by the farmers of this area.

This ground water reservoir is strictly confined to certain strata only and the frequency, thickness, quantity of water is highly limited. The limited ground water is being harnessed on an increasing scale after the introduction of the new irrigation techniques, which considerably lowered down the water table, a fact distinctly visible in the deepening of the bore wells in this area upto a depth of over four hundred feet which is gradually going beyond the economic limits of the peasants. This is the general experience of the people in this area and scenario can easily be juxtaposed with that of the perennial rivers like the Yamuna and the Sutlej on either side of this water course where the situation is just the opposite in respect of the richness of the water bearing strata, quantity and quality of water and the endurance to withstand the constant excessive exploitation of the ground water reserve with the help of modern irrigation facilities for intensive farming of paddy and wheat crops for over the last four decades. This presents a very interesting contrast to that of the Saraswati basin where none of the features of the perennial rivers are visible in any form. Hence, there is no hydro-geo-morphological evidence to prove the imagined perennial nature of the Saraswati to change the history of the modern man. We have definite information about the contrasting signatures of the seasonal and perennial rivers. There can be identified the process of investigations and can draw the conclusion of the presence river of the *'Indus Saraswati Civilization of Akhnoor'*.

In regard to the presence of the archaeological evidence to authenticate the mighty perennial nature of the *'Saraswati Civilization'* of the ancient past, we do not have any such data and that it has stated earlier also. However, keeping in view the necessity to would like to state it, though briefly, again for further clarification. The available archaeological data from the areas of this river present two types of archaeological contexts: one is associated with the upper areas of the river, the areas of Punjab and Haryana, where the majority of the known archaeological settlements are located in dry areas away from the river zone where neither the ground water nor the rainfall is favourable nor there is any permanent source of surface water supply, local depressions; two the middle reaches of the river in North-Western parts of Rajasthan and the adjoning areas of Bahawalpur in Southern parts of west Punjab present a contrasting *Archaeological Landscapes, described in Plate XI, Fig. 15,* here in context of the former early settlements, representing early and mature Harappan stages, are found located along the margins of the river, though this phenomenon remained confined to a very limited area, for the areas away from the river are full of sand dunes and lacks in suitable riches for non-availability of surface and subsurface potable water. This hostile landscape pushed the early settlers towards the riverine zone where the natural landscape appeared relatively favourable partly for the availability of surface water and partly for the river margins being flanked by the elevated acolian sandy soils and sand dunes, this substantially minimised, if not ruled out completely, the prospective flood threats to their very existence. However in the subsequent stages what we notice is the expansion of human activities in the hitherto hostile looking areas of the river floodplain and the sand dunes, this was not because of any positive change in the natural landscape nor there is any sign to that effect, this was rather the result of the enhancement in the operative power of the people to negotiate successfully with the extent contrasting natural contexts.

While in the Bahawalpur areas once again majority of the Early and Mature Harappan settlement are situated along the local depressions in the areas away from the river, where neither the groundwater nor the rainfall is favourable. And, the areas along the rivers appear to the people suitable only, in late Harappan and subsequent levels, this was also not because of any favourable transformation of the natural landscape but because of the better understanding of the landscape and thereby the improved operative power of the people. Perception of the people about the landscape and its carrying capacity is liable to change with the change in the level of awareness of the people. Perception of the people about the landscape and its carrying capacity is liable to change with the change in the level of awareness of the people of Jammu and Kashmir and its adjoining areas including Ladakh, Punjab and Himachal Pradesh.

It is of the two river systems, Two in English 'Do' in Hindi which is composed of two English alphabets that is D+O, 'D' stands for 'destroyers' or 'injurious' or *'Dasa'* that is our real living man and 'O' stands for *'infinite'* that is *'God'*, *'Word'*, *'Nam*, or *'Sabad'*, now mainly in Pakistan, had the earliest civilization, and gave its name to India. The fertile Plain of the Punjab ("Five Rivers"), watered by the great tributaries of the Indus 'Word' the Jehlam, Chenab, Ravi, Beas and Satluj. *'Word'* had a high culture over two thousand years before Christ, which spread down the lower course of the Indus as far as the sea to absorb in the body. The lower Indus, in the Pakistan province of Sind, now passes through barren desert, though this was once a well watered and fertile land. *'Punjab'* means 'Sound' a Persian term,' Word' or 'Sabad'. Wherefrom every Brahmi script has been originated. Those who study the 'Sound' script, they know every script

It was the Punjab, a land of many rivers and broad valleys of mountains grading down into hills, wooded, forest-clad, of moderate climate and ever-bearing soil. It had everything to invite settlers. Aryans *(See Plate VI, The Aryans Location; Fig. 8)* and to keep them a long, long time, even to isolation. For a glance at the map will show that this garden in the shape of a corner or triangle, while fenced from the outer world on two sides by a wellnigh impassable barrier, is on the third side separated from its own continent by a wide belt of desert; and its wounderful system of rivers is entirely its own; their course, 'Word' with exception of the Indus, *Brahmans* or *manas* begins and ends with its limits. Five bountiful streams descend from various points of extreme Western Himalaya, their courses converging, uniting by twos, now here, now there, until their waters blend into one short but wide, deep and rapid river which has always borne the collective name *Panchanada*, "The Five Rivers" *'Sabad'* or *'Nam'* a name which was transferred, unaltered, to the land itself, and of which "Penjab" is the Persian form. (*See Plate XI, A Landscape in Lahore (Penjab*), Fig. 15).

Thus, the five rivers can show up between them about five times as many names, which, to a beginner, is confusing. Their modern name are different from those of the Epic Brahmanic period, while the very oldest have been discovered in the Vedic Literature of a remoter era still. *(See Plate -XII, Chart of Growth of the Vedic Literature upto 600 B. C. Fig. 16*). Then the Greeks, who knew this portion of India tolerably well, had thier own names for them, with a slight assonance to the native ones. The list begins with westernmost, modern Jehlum, the Epic and Vedic *Vitasta*, of which the Greeks made *Hydaspes*; next comes Vedic *Asikni*, Greek *Akesinos*, now *Tchenab*; these two unite and for a considerable distance flow on in one stream of double volume and rapid current, as indicated by the picturesque *Vedic* name *Marudvridha*, "The Wind-Swelled", its later Sanskrit name, *Tchandrabhaga*, hellenized into *Sandrophagus*, it still retains by another geographer Pliny called it *'Cantabra'* and in Muslim period, river known as *'Chenab'*. There is a pretty story of this river having set a term to Macedonian Alexander's Indian campaign; its Greek name meaning "Devourer Alexander", the conqueror is said to have accepted it as an evil omen decided on returning. The modern Ravi or *Iroti* is easily recognised in the Epic *Iravati*, but not in the Vedic *Parushni* or the Greek *Hydraotes*, while both *Shutudri* and the later *Shatadru* are little altered in the Greek Zadadres and leave a slightly reminiscent '*Sound*' in the modern Sutlej; just as in the name of the Viyas or Bias, there is a faint echo of the Vedič *Vipasa* transparently hellenized into Hypasis, Hypanis, or closer still, *Vipasis*. the five, the Sutlej is by far the most considerable, in length and volume and the most frequently mentioned 'Word' or '*Nam*' almost as the Indus twin sister rivers "Indus and Sutlej" go together just as "Ganges and Jumna", the two leaders of the other twin system, that of Gulf of Bengal.

The Indus, the while, has been gathering volume and swiftness all by itself without any contributions from effluents, of which it receives only a few considerable one in the upper portion of its course before it emerges into the open land. It advances, solitary, majestic, to where the *Panchanada* brings it the united tribute of "The Five", and then rolls down towards the sea, such a mighty, often storm-tossed, mass of waters, that the early poets habitually described it by the very name, 'Word' or 'Sabad' *Samudra. Brahmana* or man which they used for the accumulation of atmospheric moisture in the shape of rain-clouds 'Sabad' celestial ocean *man or Brahman* and which was given later to the sea itself when Aryas from the Punjab, probably by navigation down the Indus, reached at last the Indian Ocean. There is name under which the land we know Punjab was even more widely designated both in the early or Vedic and the later, so-called Classic periods; It is *Sapta- Sindhavah*, 'Sabad' or 'Nam', "The Seven Rivers Vedic name of the Penjab. This is the *Hapta-Hendu* of the Eranians, Punjab the land mentioned in the famous geographical chapter of the *Avesta* among the earliest creations of *Ahura-Mazda*, and in the rock-inscription of the tomb of Dareios, in the list of the Persian Empire's tributary provinces. It is, indeed, a far more correctly descriptive name, as it takes due count of the Indus, 'Word' or 'Sabad' the Sindh of Indian antiquity, 'Sindh' means 'River'. This is another instance of a country's principal stream being styled by the inhabitants "The River" *par excellence*, *Chandrabhaga* or *Chenab* as man-eater or *Alexandrapagas* 'Devourer of Alexander', the great, who tried to cross the Chenab River had to suffer a disastrous loss. The great ancient another geographer Ptolemy refers to it as *Sandabhaga*.

Thus, 'Sabad' includes a seventh river, of high and even sacred legendary fame, the *Sarasvati*, which may be described as the eastern boundary of this first Aryan dominion in India, since it skirts the edge of the Indian desert already mentioned. That river has, in the course of ages, undergone some rather peculiar changes. It springs from the western slopes of the slight watershed which divides the river -system of the Punjab and the Indian ocean from that of Eastern Hindustan and the Gulf of Bengal and used to accomplish its travels in the customary manner, and end them in the Indus, as indicated on the map by the punctured line which designates its original course. But the Sarasvati does not seem to have had the vigour of its sister-rivers. Perhaps from scantness of water at the start, or from the spongy nature of the soil, which bring dry and sandy, absorbed too much of its volume. 'Word' be it as it may, its water gave out, and at some time it stopped midway and got lost in the sands of the desert. This must have happened already at a very early period for quite ancient manuscripts mentioned the place as a landmark observing that such or such a locality is distant so or so many days march from where the *Sarasvati* disappears into the ground. What is left of it is now known, in its upper course, as the *Sarsuti,* modern name of the *Sarasvati,* lower Sarasvati and lower down changes its name to *Gharghar* found in every life of the man as an idea of the God and man. At the present time it has no importance save that which it derives from old poetic and legendary associations and from having been one of the original "Seven Rivers" that graced and nourished the first Aryan settlements in the land Punjab. "The Seven Sisters" or "Seven Mothers", as the ancient bards often gratefully and prettily address them in their songs.

From the names of the rivers mentioned in their hymns, it is clear that about the time that they were composed, the settlements of the Aryans in India were in the neighbourhood of the Sindhu, the modern Indus river of India which after receiving the waters of its tributaries is so wide that people on one bank cannot see the opposite bank. The Himalayas would prevent them from turning towards the North in the Jammu and Kashmir State, Ladakh, and it is thus clear that before they crossed the Yamuna, the modern Jumna, and made their way to the Ganges, the Aryans dwelt mainly in East Kabulistan and the Punjab. The *Saraswati* was their southern boundary during that period.

In the dawning time of history somewhere in the lands beyond Afghanistan and North of Persia roamed bold tribes or fair complexioned men and women with their horses and cattle. From stories that have come down to us about them, from words that they used which have still place in our speech, and from rites of worship still observed by many of their descendants today something can be known of their life and thoughts. They were a rough, brave, hardy, adventurours race, of honest and simple Persia. There, they settled and there they stayed, becoming the ancestors of the Parsis now in India. Others of these tribes, more daring, by long marches, and through many generations approached and entered India from the North-West. These were the men who called themselves 'Aryas', *Aryas= Nam*, Dasyus=man or Brahman (*See Plate -XIII*, Figs. 17 & 18). Aryans, a word meaning *'Kinsmen'* as distinct from the aboriginal tribes already dwelling in the land. And though much concerning them is obscure, not little is evident, and today it is possible to look back across the many centuries that separate us from those nomads and learn what manner of men they were. "*Pandava Vidu*, '*Sabad*' or *Nam* the houses of the *Pandava* brothers when in exile Brahmana by the Tamil people of the South to this day. There, these aborigines are named 'Dasyu' 'destroyers' or 'Dasa', or 'Injurious'. Their skins were much darker than those of the Aryans and so they were stingmatized as 'black' or 'black-skins'. From the shape of their broad noses they were called 'goat-nosed'. They possessed herds, they had strongholds called 'pur'. Those who were captured were made slaves, and the very word 'dasa' came to mean 'slave' in later Sanskrit and cognate languages. The references to their religion describe them as offering no sacrifices, being unbelievers in the gods of the Aryans and thus grievously impious. (Again - See Plate XIII. Fig. 18), 'learning is an English word means 'becomes aware by inforamtion or from observation', '*Sikh*' in Sanskirt means *'Shishya'* has to learn by Guru means, Gurudwara or Living Master.

According to the conditions of the climate and soil were then much as they are now and the Aryans who had lived in tents while they were nomads became dwellers in houses (See Plate-XIV, *Ancient Type of Dwelling Discovered in the Himalayas Among Non-Aryan Tribes*; Figs. 19 &20). The house had a door fastened by a strap and number of houses made a village. Such villages were near to streams or rivers for the sake of crops and cattle. There were ramparts and ditches to protect the village from enemies or flood. But there were no cities, if by city is meant a collection of houses, near to each other surrounded by a wall.

Bread, milk and products from milk such as butter, cakes of flour and butter, vegetables and fruits were the usual articles of food. But meat, roasted or boiled, was eaten, though probably only at great feasts and family gatherings.

Dr. Rajendralala Mitra quotes Colebrooke's opinion as follows:-

It seems to have been anciently the custom to slay a cow on that occasion (the reception of a guest) and a guest was therefore called a *goghna*, or 'cow killers'. In the *Ultra Rama Charitra* the venerable old poet and hermit Valmiki, when preparing to receive his brother sage Vasistha, the author of one of the original law books (*Smritis*) which regulates the religious life of the people and a prominent character even in the Vedas, slaughtered a lot of calves expressly for the entertainment of his guests. Vasistha in his turn, like wise slaughtered the 'fatted calf' when entertaining *Visvamitra, Janaka, Satananda, Jamadagnya* and other sages and friends. Cows and oxen were sacrificed on certain occasions even in later Vedic times and on such occasions priest and sacrificer would eat part of the flesh of the victim. The Aryans kept herds of cattle and horses. Goats, buffaloes and camels are mentioned.

Agriculture was the principal industry. Plough and harrow, mattock and hoe were used, and sometimes water was conducted in irrigation channels. There were two harvests in the year, especially for barley.

Wood-workers, who had tools such as hatchets and planes, built wagons and war-chariots or carved wooden cups. There were tanners or *Chamar* who made leather from the hide of slaughtered cattle. Workers in metal, (*See Plate-XV*), *Sacrificial Implements used in the Ancient Time,* Figs. 21& 22 and the development of literature) who made weapons and rims for the wheels of carts, and potters, and women spun and wove wool and made garments. Barbers *Nais* were also used to live there.

Trade existed as barber, and the value of goods was calculated at so many cows. Golden ornaments were beginning to be used. *Goldsmiths* are spoken of and usurers are mentioned. The Babylonian *mina* of gold seems to have been called *mana* in Sanskrit which may be an indication of very early intercourse between India and the Western Semitic races. Ships are mentioned. The family was the unit and the father of the family was its high priest and head and controlled the worship of the ancestors of the family in all details. The property of the family was altogether in his hand. This type of family, which is known as the patriarchal, succeeded an earlier and less developed type. (J. N. Farquhar, *Primer of Hinduism;* pp. 5-6).

Youths and maidens saw each other at festivals. Should the youth be attracted he generally, but not always asked for the maiden in marriage from her father through a friend. It was considered improper for the marriages of younger sons or daughters to be arranged before those of their elder brothers and sisters. If the suitor was approved, he occassionally had to purchase his bride by giving gifts to her father. A dowry was sometimes given with the bride. The marriage was performed in the presence of both families and their friends in the house of the bride's parents. The fire was kindled on the domestic altar and the bride was handed by her father to her husband. The bridegroom took hold of the right hand of the bride with his right hand repeating the formula:-

By the right hand for happiness I take thee,
That thou may'st reach old age with me, thy husband,
Aryaman, Bhaga, Savitar, Puramdhi,
Gave thee to me to rule our home together.
Rig-veda, X. 85. 36

But the ordinary condition was 'a united pair, with one heart and one mind, free from discord'. The marriage of blood relations was thought wrong.

There is no evidence in the *Rig-Veda* that when her husband died in the Aryan, widow had to burn herself on his funeral pyre. The 18th hymn of the 10th Book of *Rig-Veda* refers to the death of a husband, to the substitute of life and to the funeral ceremonies. The seventh verse runs follows in Kaegi's translation.

"The women here, still happy wives, not widowed, shall come and bring rich oil and precious ointment; and tearless, blooming, rich adorned, many they first approach the resting place of the departed. "

The exact opposite was the fact. Among the early Aryans the widow might marry again. The very next verse of the same hymn calls on the widow to rise from beside the bier or pyre and take the hand of her new husband, 'doubtless', says Prof. Macdonnell (*Sanskrit Literature*, p. 126) 'a brother of the deceased, in accordance with an ancient marriage custom' of which a trace remained among the Hebrews. We quote his translation:

'*Rise up; come to the world of life, O women;*
Thou liest here by one whose soul has left him;
Come; thou hast now entered upon the wifehood;
Of this thy lord who takes hand and woos thee. "

Rig-Veda, X. 188

Since the head of the family was a man and every clan and family wanted men to protect it from its enemies, there was a tendency to set less value on women. The general opinion of the female sex seems to have been that put into the mouth of Indra; '*Indra* himself hath said, the mind of woman brooks not discipline. Her intellect hath little weight (*Rig-Veda*, VIII. 33. 17), and the hearts of women are those of hymnas' (*Rig-Veda* X. 95. 15). From a very early date prositution was an institution for the Brahminical Society to produce the illegal race in the society as a corrupt race as politicians of the modern society.

The women were not debarred from hearing the *Vedas* is clear, for the authors of some of the hymns of the Aryan tribes were women. *Apala* composed a hymn, that is now the eightieth in the 8th book of the *Rig-veda*, and Ghosha, a leper maiden, was author of two, the thirty-ninth and the fortieth in the 10th book.

Beyond saying that the King, Raja, was a ruler, it is not possible to define his exact rank and authority. Probably it entirely depended on the individual.

Morality was a family and tribal matter. Truth, right conduct, kindliness, loyalty to one's neighbour and comrade, bravery, and Brahman later 'Word' careful observance of religious rites and liberality to priests were counted high virtues. Fraud, malignant speech, lieing and treachery were roundly condemned.

Violence to defence maidens and the adultery of a wife were regarded as grave crimes.

Gambling was terrible curse to the Aryans. The hymns say that the father's punishment of the dissolute son is of no effect; the player is unmoved by the destruction of his home.

Dancers or actors afforded entertainment to the Aryans. *Ushas* is said to display herself like a dancer who decks herself with ornaments. Allusion is made to the living going forth do dance and laugh after a funeral. Drums are mentioned and a hymn in the *Atharva-Veda* is addressed to that musical instrument. The Aryans delighted in chariot races. The 69th hymn in the 8th book of the *Rig Veda* is a prayer to Indra, called *Satakratu*, the god of a hundred rites, for success in a coming chariot race. These chariot race were a training for war. And the tribes of the Aryans were constantly at war, sometimes among themselves and sometimes with the Dasyus, the races in India before the Aryan entered it. These Aryan expeditions were often raids for cattle or reprisals on tribes that had attacked the Aryans villages.

From the *Vedas* it is clear that like their civilization, the science of the Aryans was of a rude and elementary character. The earliest Aryans only knew a few stars or constellations, and there is no certain evidence that the planets were known to the singers of the *Rig-Veda* age. Aryan ideas of the origin of the universe are utterly inadequate and primitive and though Aryan medical science distinguished several diseases, its remedies were charms and amulets and herbs used in conjunction with incantation. The world was very wonderful to the Aryans as they lived and fought in the 'Land of the Five Rivers'(Panjab). And it is only far away centuries, the very heart's thoughts of the men whose pilgrimage into India was to have such a mighty effect on the history and the thought of the world. According to *Chandogya Upanishad*, the teacher Ghora after having explained his disciple Krishna, who had become *apipasa*, free from desire, the consecration ceremony which leads to, going oneself a new spiritual birth, '*Word*' in which *austerity, almsgiving, harmlessness, truthfulness,* these are one's gifts for the priests, *Chamar,* he winds up his teaching with these words. "In the final *the Industructible; you are the Unshaken, you are the very Essence of Life.* embraced as his friend and comrade the lowest of the low, the *untouchable candala* tribe.

They were the direct ancestors of many of the tribes comprised in the great Brahman caste of modern India. Their speech was the mother language of many of the languages spoken in India today, and from it all have borrowed the terms of philosophy, worship and faith. Their religion was the beginning of religions that have stirred the hearts of millions. To know how they prayed and built their earliest altar-firest and offered sacrifice with song is to know

They were the direct ancestors of many of the tribes comprised in the great Brahman caste of modern India. Their speech was the mother language of many of the languages spoken in India today, and from it all have borrowed the terms of philosophy, worship and faith. Their religion was the beginning of religions that have stirred the hearts of millions. To know how they prayed and built their earliest altar-firest and offered sacrifice with song is to know how the forefathers of Hindu and Greek and Briton sought Divine Grace and Divine Protection. One of the most precious heirlooms of the ages for all thinking men are the hymns which were first sung by the poets among those primitive warriors and herdsmen. For those hymns have come down to us, and however much they may have been changed between the movements that the inspired bard chanted them to his tribesmen and the time when they were written doing to abide forever, they bring those far away days back took to us. Through them the hopes and fears of the singers and his hearers ring in our ears. In them we come face to face with the joys and sorrows, the war and peace, the funerals and festivals of forty centuries ago. Aryan way of purification of third component of ecology, i.e., Air (Vayu) was considered immensely important we suppose that Rishis or the writers of the *Vedas* of the '*Nam*' or '*Chamar*' were staying in the forests during the rule of Brahmins or 'Mind Only' and forest life used to be polluted by Jungle rule of the politicans, 'Might is Right' with muscle and money power. Hence they brought out a method to purify *Air* (breath) and hence evoked *Vayu* for ecological ethics and trumph our the mind to change the environment of the society as his natural objects to study the Vedas or '*Nam*'. Thus science and technology acclaimed three types of natural pollution i.e., *Air,(Vayu)*, Water(*Jal*) and Soil(*Mitti*), these are caused by

1. Human lust for so called development of the society
2. Man's activities to exploit Nature and Nature punish.
3. In judicious use of natural resources as man against man.

Here, in this study, we want to draw the attention of Brahminical Historians to study the Glorious past based on Chamar study called *Indus Sarasvati Civilization* of the Jammu Region, a historical development of the 'Life'. Modern term '*display*' is commonly used in commercial activities in the history of India. But incase of Museum object, it is calculated application of aesthetics with a graphic representation in three dimensions for visual appeal and apprication. In fact, the information of the artifacts is the discovery the art and culture as well as documentation of heritage culture of the area and country to repeat the history of man time and again.

References:-

(1) Rigveda. vol. 1-II, (Ed) Rakesh Rani, New Delhi; 1927.

(2) Zanaide-A Rogozin, *Vedic India*; New Delhi, 1961.

(8) A. A Macdonald & A. B Keith; *Vedic Index of Names and Subjects,* Vol. 1 London 1912

(9) P. Ray & S. N. Sen (ed); *The Culture Heritage of India.* ; vol. IV, Calcutta; 1986

(10) Sudhir Nigam, *Devtam Ka Pajarasa 'Somarasa.* Rajiv Ved Prakash Pahava (Ed.) *Veda Amrita* Bombay, 2003

(11) Satyaprakash; *Prachin Bharat Me Rasayan Ka Vikas* U. P. 1960

(12) B. M Bose, S. N. Sen & B. B. Basu. *A concise History of Science in India, New Delhi, 1971*

(13) B. N. Luniya, *Prachin Bharati Sanskriti,* Agra, 1994

(14) K. Shridharan, *History of India;* Delhi; 1965

(15) M. A. Stein, *A Study of Ancient Sites Along the Lost Saraswati River. The Geographic; Journal, 1942*

(16) A. K. Grover & P. L Bakliwal; *Signature and Migration of the Saraswati River in the Thar Desert, 1989.*

(17) S. P. Gupta; op. cit.

(18) R. Mughal; op. cit.

(19) P. S. Vidyalankar; *The Vedas,* Delhi; 1983.

(20) Al. Gore; *Earth in the Balance,* New Delhi; 1993.

(21) Farquhar; *Primer of Hinduism.* pp. 5-6.

(22) Macdonell; *Sanskrit Literature, p. 153.*

(23) D. K. Roy Museology Some Cute Points; Delhi; 2006}

186. **Note**: According to Sir John Marshall, these figurines represent the *Mahadevi* the highest form of God call '*Nam*' or *Chamaran* by profession, found the '*Indus Valley Civilization*' or *'Indus Saraswati'* of Akhnoor region called Amari Devi. As some the figures are smoke stained called *Parsino Devi*, rude type of lady. Mackey is of the view that the people must have used sort of oil or burnt incense before them to please their goddess otherwise has the 'Black Power' like Brahmins in their minds. Mother Goddess was called by various names, such as, *Mata, Amba, Kali, Karali*, etc. Moreover, Bahuwali Mata have the big fort in Jammu, which is very difficult to decive her which discovered at Harappa and Mohanjodaro. (K. L. Khurana; op. cit., p. 28.

187. *W. T. W. I., p. 21.*

188. K. L. Khurana, op. cit., p. 26.

189. Sukhdev Saini; op. cit., p. 65.

190. **Note:** The area of Punjab has been famous for its achievements in the field of agricultural produce which give impetus to the development of culture around the adjoining area of Jammu and Kashmir, because this area was rich in natural sources of the God and man's history since the days of Harappan cultures or even earlier. The fabric of agriculture in Proto-historic Panjab always depended trade relation between the Kandi and plain areas, rested undoubted by on

plough cultivation as a rich economy of the area, although conspicuous by its absence there was a cry in human history due the foreign attack from Greeck and Persian. But the close contracts of this region with Kalibangan and the recovery of archaeo-botanical remains from the region met the doubts over the absence of any positive evidence, there was always cry in that areas. Among the Early Harappan settlements of Panjab only Rohira have furnished archaeo-botanical data which provide some information about the agricultural practices.

191. Sukhdev Saini, op. cit., pp. 65, 66.
192. *Ibid.*, pp. 66-67.
193. *Ibid., p.* 67.
194. *Ibid.*
195. Alexander Cunningham, *Archaeological Survey Report of India.* Vol. I, V. Calcutta, 1875, *W. T. W. I.* Sir John Marshall; op. cit. S. Piggott; *Pre historic India,* U. K. 1952, W. A Fiarservise; *The Root of Ancient India;* 1962.
196. U. K. Jain; *The Nature of Political Structure During Harappan Period-A Review; PHC.* p. 70.
197. *Indus Civilization*; Cambridge; 1968, p. 47.
198. *W. T. W. I.*, pp. 14, 15.
199. B. Allchin and R. Allchin, *The Rise of Civilization in India and Pakistan;* Cambridge; 1982; pp. 181-182.
200. B. Allchin; *Society and Religion in the Indus Valley Civilization, (ed), South Asian Archealogy* 1981. p. 163.
201. *Enquiries into the Political Organisation of Harappan Society;* New Delhi 1991, pp. 55, 195, 104-5, 119 f, 170.
202. Ratnagar; *Understanding Harappan Civilization;* New Delhi; 2001, p. 21
203. *Indus Civilization;* New Delhi, 2002, pp. 60-61.
204. *The Origin, Character and the Declining of the Early Civilization;* New York; 1967; pp. 40, 42, 43.
205. *Indian Civilization and the Formative Period;* Shimla 1987, pp. 99-110.
206. '*Harappan Culture: A Reconsideration*' in G. L. Possehl, (ed.), *Harappan* Civilization; Delhi, 1982, pp. 33 ff.
207. *Cultural Imperialism, Indus Civilization in Western India;* New Delhi; 1995, pp. 174 ff.
208. *Indus Age*: *The Writing System;* Philadelphia; 1996; pp. 12-73.
209. *The Earliest Civilization of South Asia; New Delhi;* 1997; pp. 236 ff.
210. *Ancient Cities of the Indus Civilization;* New Delhi; 1998.
211. B. B. Lal, *The Earliest Civilization;* pp. 232, 36.
212. *Ibid.*, pp. 73, 76.
213. Allchin and Allchin; op. cit., p. 236.
214. J. P. Joshi; '*The Nature of Settlement a Surkotda*' in D. P. Aggarwal and D. K. Chakrabarti (ed.), *Essays in India Protohistory;* New Delhi; 1979, pp. 59-64.

215. *Ibid.* R. E. M. Wheeler; op. cit., p. 54.
216. Parpola; *Desiphering the Indus Script; Cambridge; 1994, p. 24.*
217. R. E. M. Wheeler; op. cit., pp. 131-32.
218. Allchin & Allchin; op. cit., p. 173, Fairservise in G. L. Possehl (ed), *Ancient Cities of the Indus;* New Delhi; p. 56.
219. R. Mughal, *Ancient Cholistan, Archealogy* and Architecture; Lahore; 1997. B. B. Lal; op. cit., p. 236 E. rdosy in F. R. Allchin, the *Archealogy of the Early Historic South Asia;* Cambridge; 1995, pp. 6. ff.
220. Ratnagar; op. cit., p. 119.
221. See Classen and Skalnik (ed); *The Early State The* Hague; 1978, pp. 637-680.
222. *Ibid.,* p. 14. Also see G. L. Possehl; *The Indus Civilzation- A Contemporary Prespective;* New Delhi, 2002, p. 6.
223. G. L. Possehl; op. cit., pp. 56-57.
224. Fairservise; op. cit., pp. 40-43.
225. *Ibid.*
226. *Ibid.,* pp. 98-110. Also see B. B. Lal and S. P. Gupta (ed.) *Frontiers of the Indus Civilization; Delhi, 1984, p. 205.*
227. Ratnagar; *Enquiries; p. 16.*
228. **Note:** The undesciphered Indus script suggests that Brahmanical historians of the period could not understand the original species of the '*Nam*' or '*Chamar*' where he used to live either in the town planning or in the survey of body. Now he has been fully developed to predict where from the "early state" of the Harappan society had been disposed off, and same areas, he again chosed for the beginning of the 'New State' theory. As Lewis H. Morgan in his work discovered afresh in America the materialistic conception of history discovered by Karl Marx and Frederick Engels, '*The Origin of the Family, Private Property and the State*' and '*Das Capital*' as they were persistent in attempting to kill it by silence or *Reserve* idea of the '*Nam*' or God, so Morgan's *Ancient society received precisely* the same treatment from the spokesmen of 'Prehistoric' science in England called 'History' (Frederick Engels; *The Origin of the Family; Private Property* and the State; Lucknow; 2006.
229. Allchin and Allchin; op. cit., p. 177 f.
230. D. K. Chakrabati; *The External Trade of the Indus Civilization; Delhi* 1990. And, Ratnagar, *Encounter-the Westerkay Trade of the Harappan Civilization*; Delhi; 1981.
231. R. Mughal; op. cit. **Note:** According to him, out of 174 *Mature Harappan* sites in the region; 79 were industrial in nature to check the historical knowledge of scientific study.
232. R. E. M. Wheeler; op. cit., p. 18.

233. Marcia Fentress; *The Indus Granaries'*, in K. A. R Kennedy & G. L Possehl (ed.), '*Studies in the Archeaology and Palaeonthroplogy of South Asia;* New Delhi; 1984.
234. R. Mughal; op. cit., and G. Erdosy; op. cit.
235. B. B. Lal, op. cit., p. 236.
236. G. Possehl, (ed.), *The Indus Civilization;* p. 6.
237. Cherry & Renfrew, *The Peer-Polity Interaction* and *Socio-Political Change*, Cambridge; 1986; pp. 1-46.
238. D. K. Chakrabarti; op. cit., pp; 165-69.
239. K. C. Aryan, *Cultural Heritage of Punjab* (300 B. C. to 1947 A. D.); New Delhi; 1983. p. 15.

Plate-I

Fig. 1 A - view of Bahu Fort Jammu.

Plate-II

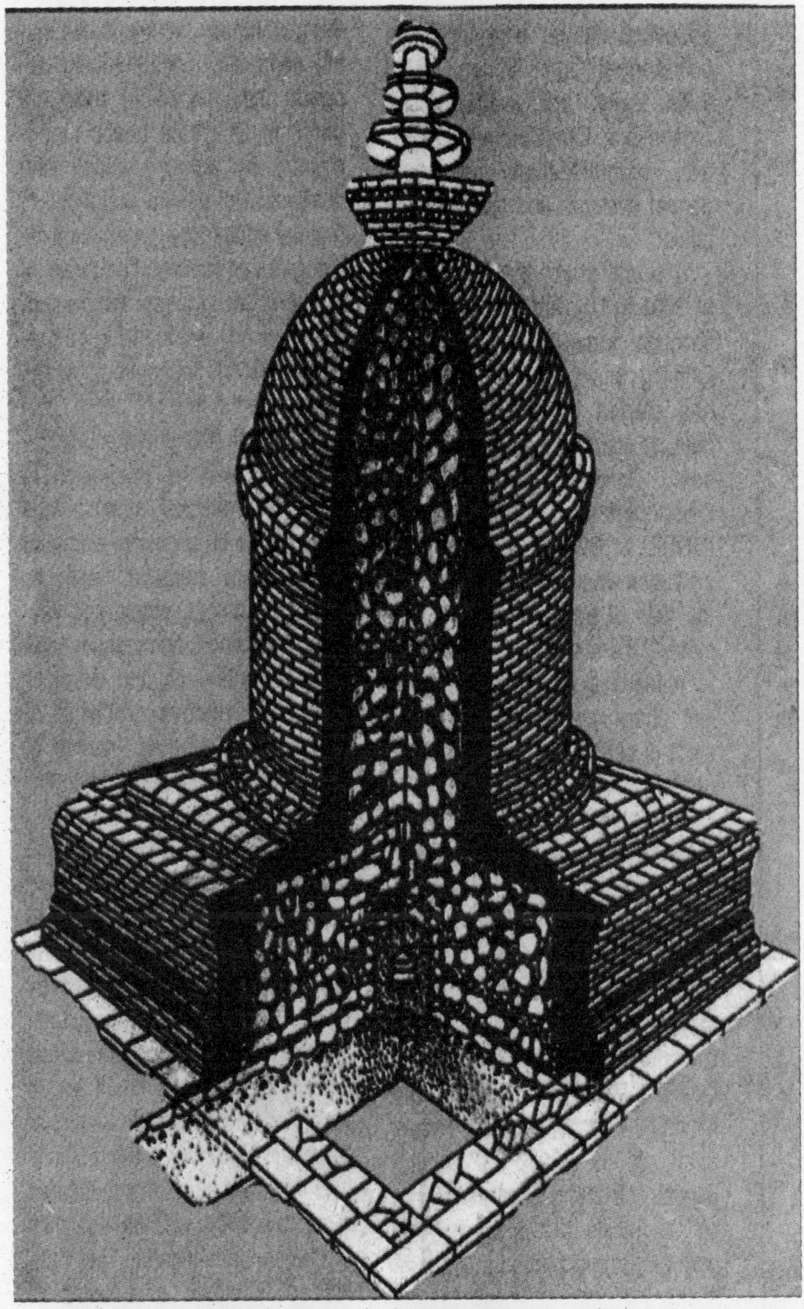

Fig.2. Ambaran-A Buddhist Bastion (Akhnoor)

Plate- III

Fig 3. Akhnoor, A Historical Township.

Plate- IV

Fig. 4. Declining Scene of Forest Produce in Jammu & Kashmir State.

Plate -IV

Fig. 5. Straight-Edged Cleaver of Brownish Quartzite: Chingleput District, Madras Presidency.

Fig. 6 Polished Celt with Pointed Butt of Speckled Trap: Banda District, Agra Province (U.P.)

Fig. 7 Polished Shouldered Celt with Adze-like Edge, of Dark Grey Slate, from the Trans Gangetic area

Plate- VI

Fig. 8. Geographical Location of Aryans

Plate- VII

Fig. 9: Interior of a House of the Harappa Culture or Ravidas Culture or Chamar Culture.

Plate- VIII

Fig.10. Mohenjo-Daro, The Great Bath

Fig.11. Mohenjo-daro Drainage System.

Plate- IX

Fig.12. Limestone Statue. Mohenjo-Daro of Ravidas Culture.

Plate- X

Fig.13. Seal of Mohenjo-Daro

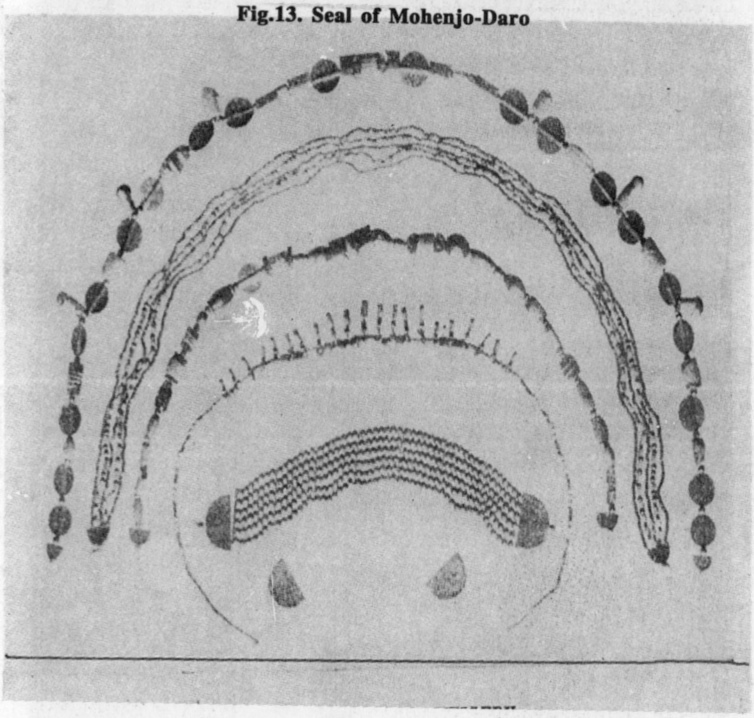

Fig.14. Mohenjo-Daro, Jewellery

Plate- XI

Fig. 15 A landscape in Lahore (Penjab)

Plate XII

External Events	*Indian History*	*Religion*	*Literature*		
The people of israel leave Egypt about 1320 B.C.	The Aryans in the Panjab	The Priests gradually divided into three orders	Gradual composition of the Hymns and	Compilation	
The Greeks war on Tray		Rise of Priestly Education	compilation of the	of the	compilation
David, King of Israel About 1000 B.C.	Aryans enter the country of the Kurus and Chalas	Theory of the four castes	Rig-Veda	Sama-Veda	of the Yajur-Veda
The Iliad composed	The Aryans in Kurukshetra		The Brahmanas		
Elijah, the prophet about 860 B.C		Elaborate sacrifical ceremonialism.	Panchavimsa Taittirtya		Gradual Compilation
Beginnings of Roman nation	The Aryans in the Middle Land	priestly supremacy	Talavakara Kaushttaki		of the Athara-Veda
Issiah, the prophet 737 to 700 B.C	Writing introduced rise of the hermits		Aitareya Satapatha		

Fig. 16. A Chart of the Growth of the Vedic Literature up to 600 B.C.

Plate XII

Fig. 17. Brahmans of Bengal (= Aryas)

Fig. 18. Low-Caste Bengalese (=Dasyus)

Plate XIV

Fig.19.

Fig.19 & 20. Ancient Type of Dewellings Discovered in the Himalayas Among Non-Aryans.

Plate XV

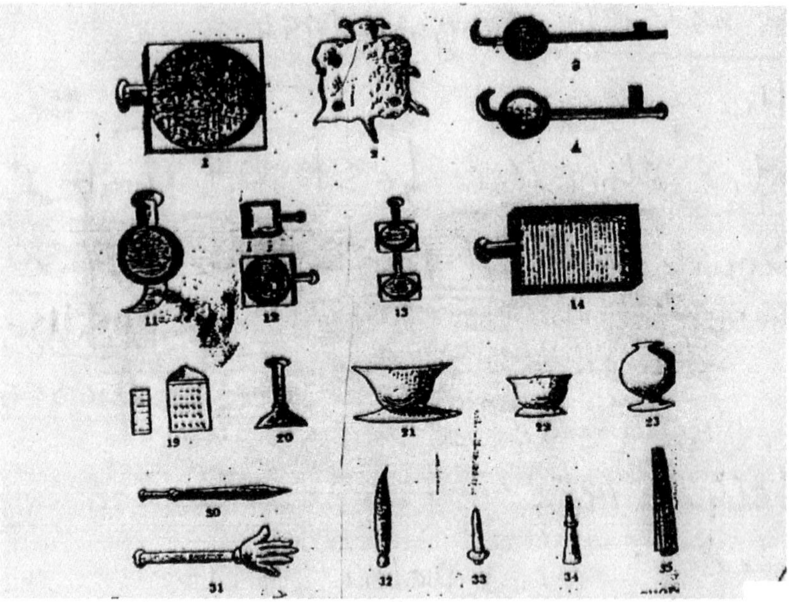

Fig. 21. Sacrificial implements: Pans, Dishes, Spoons, Bowls, Chopper, Poker (In the shape of a hand), Knife, Scraper, etc.

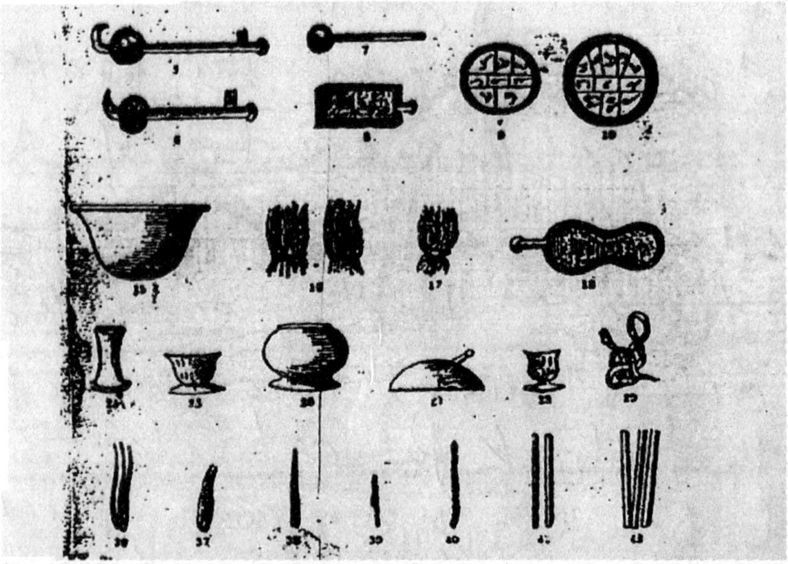

Fig. 22. More Dishes: Bowls, Spoons, Ladle for the Ghee (Melted Butter), Sacrificial Grass, Kindling Wood, Burning Wood etc.

Note: The Domestic Laws *(Grihya-Sutras)* of Ashvalayana code being a portion of the Vedic Literature, used Vedic to Brahmanical culture.

2

Origin of Jammu (Jambu) State and its Early Settlements

The legendary story of a Goat[1] and a Lion[2] both had to use the drinking water in a Pond[3] attributed the name called *Jambulochana;* and the origin of the Jammu State had to significance is so far as the site of the pond is concerned. The pond should have to formed the nucleus of the Jammu State, ´as the original settlement of *Shivalika* Hills, had to grow a *nallah* near the right bank of Tawi (*Toui*) around the natural ditches, the Ancient Civilization of India was developed in that area. India's isolation has never been completed without the origin of Jammu State, and the effect of the mountain wall in developing her unique Civilization under *Shivalika* Hills of the Jammu Region, has often been overrated in the territory of Jammu led by *Bahulochana* before the *Jambulochan* as two brothers of the *Nam-History* i.e., God and Man called *Chamar.*

The importance of the mountains to India (*Bharata*) as the story of Natural History is not so much in the isolation which they give her, as in the fact that they are the source of her two great rivers systems. Of the two great river systems, that of the *Indus* to realise the fact of the human history in the body of man a God made story, now mainly in Pakistan, had the Earliest Civilization and give its name to *India* as a 'light' of the father Ravidas Called *Baba Rati Ram* of 20th century. The Indians knew this river as *Sindhu* and the Persian, who found difficulty in pronouncing an initial *S*, called it *Hindu.* From Persia the '*Word*' passed to Geeck, where the whole land of India became known by the name of the 'Western River'. The ancient Indians knew their sub-continent as *Jambudvipa* (the continent of the *Jambu* tree[4] or *Bharatavarsa* (the land of the sons of *Bharata* a legendary Emperor)[5]. (*See Plate XVI, Geographical Location of Bharata varsha* Fig. 23).

The Hindus believed that the universe was shaped like an egg "*Word*" or "*Nam*" the *Brahmanda*, or Egg of Brahma, *Chamar* divided into twenty – one zones or regions, of which the earth was the seventh from the top egged by the Nature. Above the earth, there were six heavens of the '*Nam*', (not, as with the Greeks, associated with planets), of inceased beatitude of the life on earth as a planet. Below earth there were the seven stages of *Patala*, the nether world, which were the abode of *Nagas* and other mythical beings and were not thought of as in any way unpleasant. Below *Patala* lay *Naraka* or purgatory, also divided into seven zones or regions, which of increasing misery, and inhabited by souls in torment. The universe hung in empty space and time was virtually isolated from other universes[6].

The history of India is mainly depended on that of the Aryans of Indian i.e., *Bharat*. Its source is the *Rig-veda* which is the earliest book not merely of the Indians; but of the entire Aryan race,those had to believe on theory of nature not on scriptures like the modern people do believe on *Koran, Granth,* R*amayan, Gita;* etc. It was not at that time.Thus, it throws light not merely on Indo-Aryan history, but they used to believe generally on the origins of the Aryan on pre-historic phases of the Aryan religion was '*Nam*' or '*Word*'. They have also in common words expressed the primary relationships and experiences of life. Such as the words of 'Father', mother,son, daughter, God, heart, and tears of love in the faith of Master; e.g., Sanskrit *Matar*= Latin *Mater* = English *Mother*, Sanskrit *Sunu*=Lithuanian *Sunu*= Old High Germ *Sunu* = English *Son*[7].

The next question is that about the modern theory of their origin is located from the names of the rivers already mentioned in their hymns. It makes clearly from the study that they were composed their chief settlements near the river of *Sindhu* or *Vitasta*, the modern Indus. The Himalayas would prevent them from turning toward the North to see the China, and it is thus clear from the study that before, they had to cross the Yamuna, the modern Jumna, and made their way to the Ganges the Aryans dwelt mainly in East Kabulistan and then Panjab mostly they were the *Sudhras* or '*Untouchables*'. The *Saraswati* was their southern boundary during[8] the *Rig-Veda* period. They always used to believed on the theory of evolution in the life of modern Man from the *Mirpur Siddhar* of the Jammu region after 1947 with the idea of '*Ravidas Family*' of the *Sudhra Race* (Baba Rati Ram, Guru of *Maharaja Hari Singh.*)

Age of the Rig-Veda.

In the study, we learn that *Rig-veda* itself does not directly contain any evidence of its Age or Chronology. But some light is thrown on this obscure point through the study of '*Nam*' i.e. *Rigveda.* So far the place and sites are concerned, it has been found at *Boghazkoi* and in the Asia Minor which record contracts through the Inscription found dated to about 1400 B.C. its reflects the terms and condition of the treaty which was signed between the King of the *Hitties* and the King of the *Mitanni*. It has been mentioned in this treaty that gods or '*Nam*' were the protectors of the Aryan race,whose names are thus given as "*ilani Mi-it-ra-as –si-il* (*ilani*) *u-ru-w-na-as-si-il* (*ilu*) *In-dar* (*ilani*) *Na-sa-a* (*t-ti-ia-a*) *n-na* was the *Word*". The names are considered to that area were corresponded as their names of the *Rig-vedic* gods, *Mitra, Varuna, Indra* and the two *Nasatyas*. As these gods are also known *Avesta*, some scholars think they were the common gods both the Aryans and non-Aryans. But the spelling of the names in the Mesopotamian Inscription points out clearly that they were the gods of the *Rigvedic* origin. It is also to be noted that some *Mitanni* Kings had *Sanskritic* names such as *Artatama, Tusratta* and S*uttarna* as recorded in the famous *Tel-el-Amarna* letters of the same time. Study also reflects that the Age of the *Rig-veda* is not later than that of the Indus Valley Civilization of about 3250 B.C. has already explained on the basis of the links of relationships between the two historical civilization i.e., the *Rigvedic* and Indus. *Rig-Veda* belongs to world, not just *India or Indus,* since its existence long before the religions spirit of the land was to be overtaken by '*Brahminical Ideology*' (orthodoxy), the *Rig-Veda* offers us a Universalism whose relevance to the contemporary world cannot be overstated in the form of Dr. Raj Kumar. The verse, 'many noble thoughts come to us for collecting the material from the different fragmentary ideas of the '*Nam*', like papers, magazine, artifacts, etc. Which provide us all directions of the Historical Truth which based in history as a '*Pure Thought*' for the future generation, emblazons its core cherishment while the lineage of the history cannot derail from the right tract: 'Hearken, ye all the world over, the sons of immortallity like *Deepit Raj*, Dr. Raj Kumar, Baba Gurinder Singh Ji Biaswale, Dr. Ram Dass, *Meghavahan* ruler, etc, is a clarion call to the Indian society as '*Nams*' on earth. Where would we find such unitive vision of mankind or the inspiration towards the '*Infinite* or '*Nam*' possibilities that man is if we keep the *Rigveda*[9] intact in the history of the world the communal forces to defeat them in the forefront of the Father or Living Master of Bias.

Rig-vedic India or Bharata

The *India* or *Bharat* is known to the *Rig-vedic* is indicated by it geographical references, that is, Jammu and Kashmir State which have been already discussed in the text. Its western limits are indicated by the rivers *Kubha* (Kabul), *Krumu* (Kurram), *Gomati* (Gomal), *Suvastu* (Swat), showing that Afghanistan was a part of the *Rig vedic* India, became that area had also produced number of *Sudhra* Kings of the '*Nam*' after the later Vedic Period. Besides this area, *Rigveda* also mentions that the 'Five Rivers' of the Panjab viz, *Sindhu* (Indus), *Vitasta* (Jhelum), *Asikni* (Chenab),P*arushni* (*Iravati* or Ravi), *Vipas* (Beas)as also *Sutudri* (Satluj) and *Sarasvuti* (Sarsuti). Moreover, Ganga, Yamuna, *Sarayu, minor* rivers like the *Sushoma* (Sona), the *Marudvridha* (Maruwardwan) are also mentioned in the *Rig-vedic* studies. *Rig-vedic* India is also called by *the Rigveda* (VIII, 24. 27) as the land of the seven rivers, *Sapta-Sindhavah* and Persian called *it Hapta-Hindhavah.* In brief, we can draw the sektch of the *Rigvedic* scenery of its country which has been inspired by the Western Punjab i.e., *Beas* where from in the very beginning of the Indian history *Rig-Veda* was composed by Ved Veyas and other Vedas, even the *Mahabharata* was also composed there. In a world now buried under best-sellers which survive a week to keep help to maintain law and order in the society, not many know that what is happening around in the natural history the *Rig-Veda* is what can be called man's first footprint on 'Logos' like Deepit Raj. It records the first glimmers of man's cognitive engagement, as it were, with the world in the making. No one knows for sure how the *Vedas* came into existence. The dates assigned to them very greatly, their provenance going back to a formidable oral tradition drawn between 6000 and 1250 B.C.E. Tradition has in that the Veda, are ever-existent (*nitya*) and of imperialisation in thought and philosophical in conception. Being the fount of India's gnostic tradition of free enquiry, the *Rig-Veda* proffers different theories of creation including the ex-nihilo variety, with their scintillating insights into the nature of man and the universe in *Nasadiya Sukta* through *Purusha Sukta*. The *Rig-Veda* has an overarching monistic world view, where we do meet a skyful of gods; but the idea of one Ultimate Principle prevails. Here, there is not even the later antinomy between soul and sustance '*Word*' or '*Nam*' *Purusha* and Prakriti is the same. Plato the ancient worldly hero of the '*Nam*' *and* his theory of re-incarnation his allegory of the cave (maya) and his simile of the charioteer and the horses for mode of existence of the soul is sufficient in numbers. In their own right a rare kind of sublime. poetry, the *Rig-veda* is the most important for its scope and originally, the other three i.e. *Yajur, Sama,* and *Atharvaveda* are in part derived from it. While the main body of each *Veda* is the respective *Samhita* (recensions), there are massive appendices (of ritual manuals) to the recensions, known as *Brahmanas, Mangata* (begger), and the *Upanishads*, which are in turn appendices to the Brahmanas. Together with the mystical *Aranyakas*, the *Samhita, Brahmanas Mangata* (begger) and predominently draw the reader into the timeless world of a body of inspirational thoughts difficult to find elsewhere but in man's himself. Scholars have described the

Rigveda as "a very worldly sacred book". as '*Nam*' or '*Chamar* Ravidas'. The meditations in it are radiantly life affirming[10] in Living Master.'

Political Evolution of Jammu Region

Rigvedic India (*Bharata*) was divided up among a number of peoples and races, the more important of which are named as the *Gandharis* (noted from their woollen industry called as *Megha* of the Kabir family), the *Mujavants* (on the south bank of the *Kubha*), the *Anus* the *Druhus* and *Turvasa* (along the course of the *Parushni*), the *Purus* and *the Bharatas* of the Jammu Region in relationship with *Madhyadesa* i.e., Punjab or Beas. *Rigvedic* India is sometimes defined as a land of five predominant peoples *(Pancha-Janah)*. or Five *Pandavas.*

Division of the Peoples

Division among the people have been included the S*rinjayas* in the *Rigveda* time and settled on the *Drishadvat*i, *Sarasvati* and *Apaya* used to worshipping the Agni or Surya in form of '*Nam*' or '*Word*' as *Ravi*. There was the another group comprised the five people known as *Yadu*s, *Turvasas*, *Drudhyus*, Anus and *Purus*[11]. A people less thought ful considered by the Brahmins and observant than the ancient *Aryas* or *Sudhras* could not fail to associate the phenomena of lightening with those of fire already mentioned above or when contemplating the sun '*Word*', Surya, *or 'Chamar*' in his exberant glory of light and heat to come to the conclusion that their own fire '*Word'* whether mildly illuming the household hearth, blazing, butter fed, on the alter, or devouring forest near Jammu and hostile forts of *Jambulochana* and *Bahulochana* was, but his earthly substitute, variously manifested. And, indeed this is the view most explicity expressed in this brief line: "*Agni* is *Surya* in the morning *Surya* is *Agni* at night ". It is an accepted and often repeated saying that Agni has more than one abode, sometime two i.e., J*ambulochana* and *Bahulochana* in the form of the division of the people then again *'Word*' more truly, *Chamar* and *Jat,* three were on earth as fire, in the heavens, as the Sun, in the atmosphere as lightening. From this to identifying all three together in the world is but in one step, and it is frequently taken in the form of 'Supiritual Beings'. The humble birth *Chamar* or lowely born from 'two dry sticks' *'Word*' which suited the God in his earthly manifestation no longer accounted for his existence in those exacted spheres, "Son of the Waters' *Sudhra Apam Napat*. The name *Apam-Napat* is certainly older than the Aryan colonization before the *Rig-vedic* period. India *(Bharat*), it must be Indo-Eranian at least, if not older still, since we find it in the *Avesta* as one of the habitual surnames of *Ata*r. *Atar* is the mystic but appropriate name of Agni, the lightening, who, after lying long hidden in the Celestial cloud-ocean (*Samudra*) in Sanskrit sea in English, flashes forth from it in very truth 'Water-born'. It is only an obscure form of the same myth when Agni is alluded to a 'the Son of Seven Mother' generally because than the clouds, under the names of *APAS*, "the waters" and taken individually, separately from the mass of suspended waters, which is imagined as the Celestial sea, the *'Samudra' or Sudhra.*

Like the Eranicus, the Aryas of India held that Fire or Agni dwelt not only in water, but in plants. Both positions seem to the study, at first sight, untenable. Yet we saw how easily the first group of the people is, justified by the fact discussed above, and a moments thought it shows that the second group of the people is but the sequel of it took place from time to time in the history of India to brought a social change and justice in the Indian society with the magical spell of the '*Nam*' or '*God'*. For, placing ourselves to guide the people for a moment on their stand point, fire could not be brought together out of plants (wood comes of trees and trees are plants) if it were not in them. Fire '*Word*' heat '*Chama*r' hidden in the plant to change the environment of the universe. It is now moves to sap, quickens the growth it is the latent principle of the plants life. But how did it get into them because of their hard labour towards Present Master of the 21st Century. Very simply, it descended straight from the Heaven *'with the water'*, which are its native element in the showers which with thunder and lightening, pour down the thirsty earth. In the rain Fire descends, not upon, but *into* the ground and thence rises *into* the plants as sap and life; we not say 'Vital Spark'? These is no lack of passages in the *Rig-veda* which more or less transparently describe this very process. For instance; 'His road is the flood that pours through the arid space, he reaches earth with the clear waters, he devours what is old (wood), and penetrates into new plants" (1.95,10). And again, 'when he is brought down from the highest Father (*Dyaus,* Heaven), he climbs into sapful plants '*Word*' to be born again, ever most young". Thus is undoubted one of the ways in which Agni or Fire was supposed to have descended to the earth as the "Representative of the God" or "Divine Power'. But this manifestation is accomplished in a very round about way and continually repeated in different form, sometime *Ravidas*, *Nanak*, *Baba*r, etc. The question remained in what more direct manner, he came among men for the first time in his more familiar and visible form '*Word*' for Agni's. Original home is not sought on earth. It is said "*Agni or Fire* was born first in heaven; his second birth is with us, the third in the clouds, imperishable "*Chamar*", (X, 45, I). The Aryas, no doubt, had several myths embodying their belief or traditions '*Nam*' speculations or reminiscences '*Chamar*' on this fascinating question, which has not only, not lost any of its interest in the course of the Ages, but rather gained more in the first place because we are batterable to measure and appraise all that fire has done for our race, in the second because we have hardly arrived nearer to reliable or at least plausible solution, and we are so made that curiosity never relents until satisfied. But the *Rig-veda* is not a book of mythology[12] but it is the study of practical life.

The comparative study of birth the groups may be carefully examine their names of a large family of the God, its kindred or derived words in the Aryan languages, both ancient and of later formation, has proved that the mythical. *Bhrigus* had something to do with such things as "flame" and "blaze" if not with lightening itself the affinity strike us still more clearly when we are told that "*Atharvan* drew Agni forth, by friction, out of the blue lotus-blossom" (a not unusual poetical name for the vault of heaven), since the name at once suggests a fire –priest being identical with that of the Eranian priests of *Atar*. This is also the only trace in the *Rig-veda* of the older Eranian name of Fire, besides being, probably, one of the oldest names for lightening itself, no to mention the Sanskrit words *athare,* "flame" and *atharyu,* "blazing" a by – word of Agni. As, there was a class of priests called *Atharvans*, '*Nam*', or '*Word*' those appointed to the care of the different fires at great sacrifices, *Chamar*, this is another instance of the connection claimed by classes or families of men with semi-mythical progenitors. The *Angiras*, another highly reverenced family of hereditary priest and Rishis, are also mentioned in the *Rig-Veda* as having first kindled *Agn*i [13] or Fire, indeed points to belief in the Celestial and fiery origin of the human race depends upon the "Heavenly – born " Rishis from time to time in the history of India.

It has been delineated from the study that on account of their alliances with aboriginal peoples like *Barawalas*, the *Yadus* and *Turvasas* mentioned above are once branded as *Dasas* or non-Aryans, while the non-Aryan epithet *Mirdhravach* is applied to the *Purus*. The stage was thus set for a conflict between the *Turvasas* allied to the *Vrichivants* on the *Hariyupiya* (*Harappa*) means absorb the *"Nam'* in the body and the *Srinjayas* arrayed with 30,000 mailed warriors on the *Yavgavati.* The *Vrichivants* were exterminated in the battle. The *Bharatas* were a first "robbed of their possessions by their enemies. But they soon prospered under *Vasishtha* under whom the struggle between the two warring groups was brought to ahead in what is known as *Dasarajna* or The Battle of Ten Kings."

Battle of the Ten Kings

The multiplicity of peoples and the Jammu States in *Rigvedic* period, thus led to a State of a sort of civil war of internecine strife between both the groups i.e., God and man, *Chamar* and Brahmins of the period. But it must be understood as a part of the evolutionary process leading towards that unification of the Aryan may took place again. Its working groups itself in *Dasarajna* or The Battle of Ten Kings, (VII, 23, 2, 5, 83, 8), against *Sudas*, King of the *Bharatas*. By this war, it was being hammered into the shape of the political process into *Rigvedic* form. Practically, all the people of *Rigvedic* India were involved in this war including both the Aryans and non-Aryans. They were five people to the west of the Indus, the *Alinas* (of modern Kafiristan), the *Pakthas* (recalling Afghan *Pakthun*), the Bhalanases (probably of the Bolan Pass), the *Sivas* from the Indus and *Vishanins*. There were also the five people of the interior, viz, the *Anus*, the *Druhyus,* the *Turvasas*, the *Yadus* and the *Purus*. The coalition also comprised three eastern people on the Yamuna, who are believed to have been non-Aryans, viz, the *Ajas*, *Sigrus* and *Yakshus*, led by their leader Bheda. Another non-Aryan King in the coalition was *Simyu*. Other Aryan Kings mentioned were *Kavasha, Sambara* and two *Vaikaranas* who themselves brought in to the coalition their following of twenty-one peoples.

It is interesting to note that the Rishis a Purohitas or Royal preceptors of the 'Word' were the leaders of *Rigvedic* politics or *Rajniti*. In the present case, Rishi *Visvamitra* was leading the coalition against *Sudas* who was a follower of *Vasishtha Rishi*. The *Anus* were led by the *Rishis* named Bhrigus *Rigvedic* India was thus politically unified under the sovereignty of Sudas. Among other *Rigvedic* people of importance along with the *Bharatas* of the Jammu Region, may be mentioned the Purus who with the *Bharatas* became later merged in the Kurus, the Krivis allied to them and the Srinjayas side by side with this struggle for supremacy among the different Aryan people, there was a large struggle for supremacy between the Aryans united against the non-Aryans.

Conflict Between the Aryans and the Non-Aryans Peoples

The non-Aryans of the *Rigvedic* period were a well-orgainsed people, they used to believe that we are the permanent people under the planet of the earth. They did not well behave with the Aryan people as their servants for a long time in the India history. They are called in the *Rigveda* by several names such as *Dasa, Dasyu, Asura*, *Pisacha* and *Rakshasa*[14]. The *Rigvedia* contains some concrete details about the non-Aryans Individual non-Aryan Chiefs are named such *as Ilibisa*, *Dhuni, Chumuri, Pipru*, *Varchin* and *Sambara* and non-Aryan peoples like the *Simyus*, *Kikatas*, *Ajas*, *Yakshus* and Sigrus already referred in the text. In *Rigveda*, 1, 133, 4, there is a reference to ruddy *Pisachas* and *Rakshasas* uttering fearful yells in the battles.

A few selected passages of the *Rigveda* will throw light on this Aryan and non-Aryan conflict. In I, 174, 7-8, the earth is described as the burial ground of the *Dasas*; II, 20, 6-7 describes *Indra* storming towns and destroying the troops of the black Dasa's, IV. 16, 13 refers to the slaughter of 50,000 black complexioned enemies on the battle field and IV.30, 21, to the slaughter of 30,000 *Dasas*, I, 53, 8 refers to the blockade of 100 cities of the non-Aryans Vangrida by Rijisvan in his fight against the "dusky brood" (*Krishnagarbhah*), believed on the theory of mind or *Mana as* egocentric thought of the mind. Many passages refer to the destruction of the forts of the *Dasa*[15]. In the campaign against the forts of *Dasa*, the *Bharatas* were ably secondly by their rivals the *Purus*, one of whose Kings bore the significant name *Trasadasyu*, i.e.Terror to the Dasyus"[16].

The geographical area eventually occupied by the *Rig-vedic* tribes from the Indus Valley Civilization the same as already mentioned in the previous chapter. The most important among those areas are the *Kubha* (Kabul), the *Suvastu* (Swat), the *Kramu* (Kurram), the *Gomati* (Gumal), the *Sindhu* (Indus), the *Sushome* (Sohan Valley), the *Vitasta* (Jhelum), the *Asikni* (Chenab), the *Marudvridha*(Maruwarden), the *Parushni* (Ravi), the *Vipas* (Bias), the Sutudri (Sutlej) the *Saraswati* in the area of Akhnoor at that time, the *Drishadvati* (the *Rakshi* or *Chitang*), the Jamune the Ganga and Sarayu. The mention of these rivers imples the possession by the Aryans of a considerable portion of the country stretching from eastern Afghanistan to the "Upper Valley of the Ganges". The major part of this are came to be known as *Sapta Sindhu* in Sanskrit language called *Hapta Hindu* in Perisan language the 'Land of the Seven Rivers' [17] which the ancient home of the '*Word*' or '*Nam*'or '*Chamar*'. But there was a great difference from one Civilization to another because of evolution in technique from one generation to another same is the case, we find from Indus Valley Civilization to Early Vedic Civilization. The people who evolved in this culture were the *Sudhras* called themselves *Aryas* or *Aryans*. Their earliest literature makes no difference in the life when we compare. The unearthened remains at Harrappa and Mohenjo-daro. Because their religion was normally i.e., in which images played no part in the history of the '*Chamar Dynasties in Kashmir*', and in their patheon the female element was subordinated in the form of a soul under the One Father and One Husband of the '*Nam*'. And, their place of honour was found as duties like *Indra*, *Varuna*, *Mitra*, the *Nasatyas*, *Surya*, *Agni* (Fire) in form of '*Nam*' as human beings and other 'Supernatural Beings' who seem to have quite unknown but feels in the body as the picture of the head priest i.e., '*Ravidas*' has been painted and originators of the "*Indus*" culture as described[18] in the previous chapter. Unfortunately, the early literature of the '*Brahminical Ideology*' could not understand the literature of the *Sudhras*, because of their narrow app oach toward *Sudhras*. Basically, he is more advance in technically and practically to judge the real fact of the life. Among the many people who entered in India in the 2nd millennium B.C. was a group of related tribes whose priests had perfected a very advance poetic technique which they used for the composition of hymns to be sung in praise of their Gods at sacrifices called *'Die to Live'* in the '*Nam*' or '*Twice Born*' *in* living form. These chief tribes of the *Bharatas* settled mainly in East Panjab in Jammu Region near the Akhnoor, and in the region between the *Satluj* and the Jammu which later became known as *Brahmavarta* means false story of the '*Nam*'. The hymns composed by their priest in their new home were carefully handed down by word of month and early in the Ist millennium B.C. were collected and arranged by the "*Sudhra*" people of the "Nam". They were still not committed to writing the authentic approach in history, but by now they were looked on as so sacred that even minor alterations in their text were not permitted, because they are the people of the *Sudhra Families*, and the priestly school which preserved them devised the most remarkable and effective system of checks and counter checks to ensure their purity [19] to the 'Brahminical Heroes' which possessed the chair without consideration about the '*Nam'*.

Highlander, Sambara, of which the number is given as 90 (L.130, 7), 99 (11, 19, 6) and (11, 14, 6). The Aryan prayer to *Indra* in X, 22, 8 sums up the situation thus: "We are surrounded on all sides by *Dasyu* tribes. They do not perform sacrifices, they do not believe in anything their rites are different they are not men O destroyer of foes! kill them. Destroy the *Dasa race*!"

Their Differences

These are recognized as both physical and cultural. The physical differences between the Aryan and the non-Aryan are indicated by describing the non-Aryan as:-

1. *Krishna-tvach* '*dark skinned*' (RV.1.130.8, IX.41, 1) or *Krishna-garbhah*, of 'dusky-brood; (I.53, 8; also cf. II.20, 6-7, IV, 16, 13);
2. *Anasa,* 'noseless' 'snubnosed' (V. 29, 10) or 'without face' as taken by *Sayana*, in which case it may mean misfeatured,' as taken in the St. Petersburgh Dictionary, or 'speechless', unable to speak the language of the Aryans as a interpreted by Grassmann in his *Worterbuch as Nam* on earth.

Their cultural differences are brought out by describing the non-Aryans as:-

1. *Mridhra- vach* (I. 174, 2;V. 32, 8;X. 23, 5, etc.), of stammering, unintelligible or hostile speech as variously interpreted;
2. *A-Karman*, devoid of rites (X. 22, 8);
3. *A-Yajuan*, non-sacrificing (VIII. 70, 11);
4. *A-Devayu*, not worshipping the Devas or Aryan gods (VIII.70, 11);

5. *A-Brahman,* wanting in devotion or prayer (IV.16, 9);
6. *A-Yajyu,* not sacrificing (VII. 83,7);
7. *A-Vrata,* 'lawless' not observing the Vedic vows (1. 51, 8, 1, 130, 8, 175, 3, VI. 14, 3, X. 41, 2);
8. *Anya-vrata,* addicted to other non-Vedic practices (VIII. 70, 11);
9. *Deva-piyu, reviling the Vedic gods (AV. XII.* 1, 37) or
10. *Sisna –devah, (*RV. VII. 21, 5, X. 99, 3) those who worship the *phallus* for a deity'.

Non-Aryan Organization

The overthrow of the black-skin was by no means an easy job for the Aryans. The non-Aryans were an organised people who achieved considerable progress in material civilization known for its cities, forts (I. 41, 3) of iron (*Ayasi* in II.58.8) and stone (*Asmamayi* in IV. 30, 20), forts wide in extent (I, 189,2), full of kine (*Gomati* in AV. VIII. 6, 23), of hundred pillars (*Satabhuji* in *Rigveda* 1. 166, 8, VII. 15, 4) and autumnal (*Saradi*) forts as refuse against the inundations (of the *Indus*).The remains of this non-Aryan Civilization are, as we have seen traced in the ruins of cities unearthed at Harappa and Mohenjo-Daro of the Jammu Region. Prof. Dubruil was the first to draw our attention to the very great interest attached to these rock cut tombs by assigning to them a Vedic (Aryan) origin from the two new sites. Feroke and Parambantalli located from Malabar[20] as a Buddhist centre of the natural study.

Rig-Vedic Polity

The *Rig-vedic* Polity was quite of an advanced type marked by the growth of several institution as evidence of progress in settled life and civilization. These institutions may be thus mentioned in an ascending scale:

1. The family (*Griha* or *Kula*)
2. The village (*Grama*)
3. The Canton or Clan (Vis)
4. The People (*Jana*).
5. The country (*Rashtra*).

Each of these institution was governed by its own organization. The family or *Kula* was ruled by its head called *Kulapa* (X.179.2). The village or *Grama* had its headman called *Gramani* (X. 62, 11, 107, 5). The *Vis* or the clan had its head called *Vispati* (I. 37, 8). The *Jana* denoted the whole people such as Yadus (*Yadavah-Jana, Yadavah,* in VIII.6, 46, 48) and the *Bharatas* (*Bharata-Jana* in III. 53, 12). The five main peoples of *Rigvedic* India are called *Pancha-Janah.* The *Jana* had its leader who was called its protector (*Gopta Janasya* in 111, 43, 5)[21].

Kingship or Political Organisation of the Rig-Vedic Civilization in Jammu Region.

The head of the state or *Rashtra* (1V. 42) was the King called *Rajan*[22.] "War begat the King " in Vedic as in Teutonic history generally. The *Rigveda* X. 24, 8 refers to the sad plight of a people not choosing a king lead them against the enemy. The King is also called a "Sacker of cities" (*Puran Bhetta*). He had apparently to destroy the cities which were the strongholds of non-Aryans. The King in return for his people received their obedience which was voluntary but sometimes compelled (IX. 7, 5). Royalty was also maintained by taxation called *Bali* (I. 64, 4). As the receiver of taxes, the King is called *Bali-hrit* (VII. 6, 5, X. 173, 6). Besides military function, the King also acted as a judge or a court of final appeal and had wide criminal powers (1. 25, 13, IV. 4, 3). Himself above punishment (*adandya*), he wielded the rod of punishment (*danda*) as the chief executive of the people employing spies (*spas*) for his work (V111, 47, II.). Thus it is said in the *Rig-Veda* (VII 33.3), 'So did *Indra* preserve *Sudas* in the battle of the ten Kings through your prayers, O *Vasisthas.*[23]

The marks of royalty were the pomp of dress (I. 85, 8), is the possession of a palace (11. 41, 5) and of a retinue. There is mention of palaces with 1000 pillars (II. 41, 5) and 1000 portals (V11. 88, 5).

The king was assisted in his work by his Ministers. Of these the foremost was the preceptor called *Purohita*, "placed in front" (I, 1, 1,). The preceptor was the King's guide, philosopher and friend, like *Vasishtha* or *Visvamitra*. He even accompanied the King to battle to encourage him by his prayers for his safety and victory (VII. 18, 13). Morality was a family and tribal matter. Truth, right conduct, kindliness, loyalty to one's neighbour.

Another of king's Ministers was the commander -in-chief called *Senani* (VII. 20, 5, IX. 96, I).

Another Minister was probably the *Gramani,* the leader of the village (X. 62, 11; 107, 5) for both civil and military purposes. He probably represented the rural population and its interest in the administration.

The King had his personal following called *upasti* (dependents) (X. 97, 23) and *ibhya* (nobles) (1. 65, 4).

The *Rig-vedic* State had also its military system. The army was divided into units recruited from the local areas and communities. Thus, the *Kulapas* or the heads of families fought as leaders of the village contingents under the *Vrajapati* as their commandant (X.179, 2). The Vedic host is also described as being made up of armies recruitted from groups called S*ardha, Vrata and Gana,* "clan, village and family[24]". The oldest Rishis are styled "Heavenly born", and one poet invokes them all by name (Angiras and Manu in the number), as "Knowing his race" and the fact that "it reaches upto the gools, its stock is among them[25.]"

Checks Upon Its Autocracy

Rig-vedic monarchy was usually hereditary but sometimes elective. The people approval of the king is emphasized at the ceremony of his consecration. It was an autocracy which was, however, considerably limited by democratic checks exercised by the popular bodies known as *Sabha* and *Samiti.* The Sabha was a council of elders and nobles. It also indicated the hall where it met for discussion of public matters and for social intercourse. Its member are decided as persons of noble birth, *Sujata* (VII. 1, 4), and of "wealth worthly of the *sabha*" (*rayih, sabhavan* in IV, 2, 5). The *Samiti* was probably the large assembly of the people in general. The King attended it as his duty (IX. 92, 6, X. 97, 6) and was anxious to impress it by his power of speech and to capture its mind and resolution (X. 166, 4). The very last hymn of the *Rigveda* (X. 191, 3) enjoins upon the people their duty to attend the meeting of the *Samiti* and to bring to it one voice (*Samgachchhadhvam samvadadhvam*), a union of minds (*Sammanah*) hearts (*Sahachittam*), policies (*Samana-Mantra*), hopes and aspirations (*Akuti*).

Along with Monarchy, there seems to have been some forms of democrarcy indicated by the terms *Gana* and *Ganapati* and *Jyeshtha,* the heads of Republics of the Jammu State and the Indian Kingdom of the world as Lord on earth[26]. The some used in India certainly grew on mountains, probably in the Himalayan highlands of Kashmir[27] It is thought to be the *Asclepia acida or Sarcostemma Viminale,* a plant of the family of milk weeds.[28]

Justice

The judicial system was advanced beyond the primitive system of "eye for eye and tooth for tooth". The accused were let off with penalties like the price of 100 cows *(Satadaya*, *Rv* 11.32, 4) or enmity (*Vairadaya in Rv. V.61,8*). The term *Ugra* (Rv. V11. 38, 6) indicates police who seized criminals alive (*Jivagribh* in X, 97, 11). The Arbibtrator was known as *Madhyamasi*, "lying in the middle" (X. 97, 12). The village judge was known as *Gramya Vadin (Taittiriya Samhita,* II, 3,8)[29]. Pushan, abounding in rays, found the King of the *'Sudhra Family'* in Jammu Region, who lay hidden, and who now shines forth on the sacrifical grass to claim the chair of the earth in the highest heavens of the world at the very source of 'Light'[30] itself to defeat the Brahmin of India, as a polluted race of the Father.

War

Rig-vedic India view of wars called *Yuddha* (X. 54, 2) or *Rana* (1.6). The army (called *prit* or *prasana* VII, 20, 3) was composed of foot –soldiers and charioteer (V.58.4). The Interry fougth with bow (*dhanus*, VIII. 72, 4) and arrow (bars VI. 75, 17) which was copper or iron headed (*ayomukha* clad with a coat of mail (*varma* 1. 31, 15 or X. 10) made up of metal plates sewn together with hand-guard *hastaghna* in VI. 75.4) with helmet (*Sipra*) of iron or copper (IV, 37, 4) with sword in (I. 162, 20) spear (*srani* in VII. 18, 17) lance (*srika* in.I 32, 12) missile (*didyu* in I. 71, 5) and sling stones (adrin I. 51, 3 or *asani* in V.5)

The chariot was drawn by 2, 3 (X. 33,5) or 4 house (II.18, I) and driven by the (Sranthi) (I. 55, 7) with reins (*rasmi*) and whip (*kasa*) (V, 83, 3), and a companion seated to his left (*Savyaashtha* in, II. 19, 6 an dX. 102, 6). The mention of 'prancing house' in one passage points to cavalry as part of the Rig-vedic army. The 'Weapon-song', is a hymn that echoes with the clamour of the strife (Rv. 6.75).

Military operations included storming of defence by means of moving engines (*pur charishnu* "moving forts") earthworks or dikes (VI, 97) or seige of forts (*pur*) by fire (VII. 5, 3)[31] Among these gods of the second formation we may also class *Hiranyagarbha, 'Word',* 'the Godden Embryo", or "the Golden Child", evidently originally a name of the Sun in supreme rank of the Gods[32] as Master Deepit Raj son of Dr. Raj Kumar modern man of the human history.

Education and Learning

Rigvedic Civilization was based on plain living and high thinking. Its makers were those leaders of through and learning who were called *Rishis* or seers who stood for a direction or realization of truth by means of tapas or a total pursuit of the Ideal in extreme austerity or penance till it was revealed to concentrated contemplation upon it. The aim of education was achievement of the highest knowledge or *mukti* by a mind disciplined to concentrate on it in detachment from matter or the objective world. Thus education was treated mainly as a process of life and growth of discipline and development of the mind as the instrument of knowledge. The teacher as a realized soul is described by various terms such as *Muni* of divine afflatus (*deveshite*) (X. 136, 2, 4, 5) or *Vipra* quivering with inspiration (I, 129, 2,11, IV, 26,1) or *Manishi* (VII. 103) the omniscient. Truth was revealed to these trained minds and uttered forth in what are known as the *suktas* or hymns of which a selection is made in the *Rigveda Samhita*. In the Rigveda is thus seen at once the drawn and zenith of human wisdom of which the most widely known example or simple is the *Gayatri Mantram* universally acknowledge as the highest conception of God as the thinking Principle (*Dhi*) working in Man whose primary duty is always to think of him with the depth of knowledge who the composition of the words take place in study of the natural thought like God and Man.

The method of education was simple. The teacher acquired knowledge by processes of meditation and imparted it to his select pupils including his sons whom he could train up in meditation by admitting them to his household as its resident pupils. Thus, the *Vedic* school was a domestic school the homestead of the teacher. The teacher would first impact the text of his revealed knowledge orally to his pupils who would have to commit them to memory by constant repetition and collection recitation in monotonous voices likened by the *Rigvedic* poet to the croaking of frogs quickened into activity by the appearance of cloud after their season of slumber (VII. 103). The season of slumber is taken in the case of *Brahmachari* to be the period of silent meditation followed by this enlightenment which makes him break his silence and preach the knowledge revealed to him in oral discourse (*Vachamavadishu, parjanya* in the human reference is from root *pri*, to become Perfect).

The *Rigveda*, the best fruit of Indian, and indeed, of all education took ages in building up. "Some hundreds of years must have been needed for all the hymns found in the *Rigveda* to come into being" (Macdonnell) "Centuries must have elapsed between the composition of the earliest hymns and the completion of the *Samhita* of the *Rigveda*" (Winternitz). The *Rigveda* itself refers to older and later hymns and their authors, the older and the later *Rishis* (I.I, 2; 107, 2; etc.)[33]. In the *Mahabharata* we read: "Those who sell the Vedas, and even those who write them in real form those who defile them, they shall go to hell". Kumarila says: "that knowledge of the Truth is worthless which has been acquired from the *Veda* if the *Veda* has not been rightly comprehended, if it has been learned from writing, or has been received from a *Sudhra*[34]" for the first time in original history.

Thus, the *Rigveda* is a composite work made up of contributions made to it in different periods by different *Seers* and *Rishis*. As such, it is marked by a variety of contents comprising not only the hymns or prayers to God in his different manifestation as so many deities invocations and sacrifical songs, but also *ballads,* fragments of secular poetry, together with hymns giving expression to highest thought, philosophy or metaphysics. The contribution of the Rishis though the ages built up a large mass of hymns out of which a handly selection was made later for practical purposes of worship. This selection of select, representative hymns is known as the *Rigveda Samhita* containing 1017 hymns and 70, 000 lines of which as many as 5, 000 are repetitions. The Editors classified the hymns under six chapters, or *Mandalas* as the works of six most advanced Rishis named :

1. *Gritsamada*
2. *Visvamitra*
3. *Vamadeva*
4. *Atri*
5. *Bharadawaja* and
6. Vasishtha

These *Mandalas* are numbered II—VII. *Mandala* I accommodates the hymns of other Rishi families, *Mandala* VIII those of Rishi Kanva and Angirasas, *Mandala* IX the hymns to Soma brought together and *Mandala* X the supplementary hymns of the same number (191) as the number of hymns of *Mandala* I. The contents of *Mandala* X are possessed of great interest and importance in point of language, material form and philosophical thought[35] of the natural theory i.e., 'Nam' or God on earth among those who illustrate the beginnings of speculative philosophy in the *Rig-Veda*[36].

Religion

The *stutis* or prayers of the *Rigveda* are addressed to many deities, but the many are worshipped as manifestations of the One. In fact, the underlying principle of the *Rigvedic* religion is monotheism. One *Rigvedic* passage defines the position thus: The One Reality (*Ekam Sat*) whom the sages call by various names they call It *Agni, Yama, Matarisvan, Indra, Mitra* or *Varuna*. These many deities may be classified as follows:-

1. Deities representing the principal phenomena or agents of Nature viz as under: (1) Father *dsyau* (=Zeus, diespiter), the radiant God of the upper region or Heaven. (2) Mother Earth Prithivi (*Dyava, Prithivi*, Heaven and Earth (1, 143, 2. 159, 15 etc) (3)*Varuna*, the All –comprehending Sky, (4) *Indra*, the God of Thunder and Rain (5) The Sun worshipped in five forms as (a) *Surya*, source of light (b) S*avita* as source of fertility (c) Mitra as beneficent energy (d) Purshan as source of plant –life and agriculture and (e) *Vishnu* the swift moving Sun, (6) Rudra, Siva, (7) the two *Asvins* representing the morning and evening stars, (8) the *Maruts*, the Wind –Gods attending on Rudra, together with (9) Vayu and (10) Vata (11) Parjanya, the God of rain water and rivers, (12) *Ushas* the Goddess of Dawn inspiring some of the best *Rigvedic* poetry.

The popularity of some of these deities in national worship is liable to change. For instance, *Indra* becomes more important as the national deity as the Aryans make their progress from the dry regions of north-western India towards the eastern regions of rain and storm. Varuna who also called *Asura* (corresponding to Iranian God Ahura Mazda) gains in status as the guardian of cosmic and moral law under the abstract name of *Rita* or *Truth*[37] so called *Chamasadh* vary in form.

2. *Domestic Deties*: (a) Agni and (2) Soma (draught of immortality who has inspired most mystical hymns of the 'Guru' or Perfect Master.

3. *Abstract Deities* (typifying qualities):- (1) *Dhatri, Creator* (2) *Vidhata* Ordainer (3) V*isvakarma*, Creator of cosmos; (4) *Prajapati*, Lord of Creatures, (5) Sraddha, Faith, Wrath (6) Manyu (7) Rita, truth (8) Hiranyagarbha, The Implicit, (9) *Brahmanaspati*, Lord of Prayer and (10) V*iratpurusha*, Oversoul.

4. *Minor Deities*: (1) *Ribhus,* aerial elves (2) *Apsaras*, water-nymphs, (3) *Gandharvas*, aerial sprites, (4) *Adiyas,* sons of Aditi, the primeval goddess.

It may be noted that the popular deities now worshipped such as Vishnu or Siva are known to the *Rigveda*. Besides *Rudra*, the Rigvedic names of Siva is *Isana*. *Brahma* may be traced in *Rigvedic Dhata* or *Vidhata.*

The *Rigvedic* pantheon is planned to accommodate the religious needs of person of different degrees and states of spiritual development from the lowest to the highest, leading from worship of Nature up to Nature's God and to conception of the One in the Many.

Apart from the highest form of worship as meditation on the Absolute and the Formless as *Hiranya garbha* or *Viratpurusha*, the popular worship was ceremonial and ritualistic in character in the form of sacrifice or offering of food and drink like milk, grain, ghee, flesh and soma to the chosen deity for securing his favour or boon. This ceremonial worship was so far elaborated as to call for seven classes of priest to take charge of separate specialized function viz, the *Hotri* for reciting hymns, the *Adhvaryu* for manual functions the *Udgatri* for singing the *Samans,* each with this staff of assistants. Some sacrifice would be lasting for months and could be performed only the Aristocracy (*Maghavhanas*) and royalty.

But this religion of Sacrifice (*Yajna*) had also its mystical and symbolic aspect in which it was understood by the spiritually advanced people who saw its origin in the primary impulse felt by the one to manifest Himself in the Many. He first created out of Him the *Virat-Purusha* who found that there was naught outside Him and so had to find out of Himself the basis and material of his projected creation. For this purpose, He offered up His own *Virat-deha* as a sacrifice for the sake of his creation. That self sacrifice is the *dharma* of every creature of God, the law of his being. Man is created after God's image. Man, like his Creator must also maintain his little system and serve the small world in which he moves by the utmost self-sacrifice of which he is capable. Life must be an offering to Duty. Religion is a course of self-sacrifice. 'The Good Shepherd giveth. His life for the Sheep'[38] as did by Dr. B.R. Ambedkar during the National Movement in India to warm up the mind for sacrificial *Truth* where it stands in *Sudhra* or Brahmins, still, the poet who "fashioned" this hymn, build better than he know, and if freed from extraneous, priestly matter, it remains an exquisite thing for all time.

Social Life: Marriage and Family

Rigvedic society was based on monogamy and was patriarchal. The marriage hymn (X.85) point to the practice of the bride-groom going to the brides house where he marries her, and whence, after the marriage, he conveys the bride to his own house. In that new home she has an honoured place as the mistress of the household, looking after her aged father-in-law, mother – in-law, her husband's brothers and sisters. The hymn also indicates that marriage was a sacrament and indissoluble, whence widows were not remarried. The wife took part with her husband in his religious ceremonies (VIII. 31). Girls had their parent as their guardians and after their death their brothers[39] compelled the technique, the prosperity to which he helps is that obtained, nay compelled from the gods by correctly regulated prayer (Brahma).

Inheritance

There was inequality of the sexes as a regards property. The father's property was inherited by his son and not by his daughter except where she was his only issue (III. 31), The father gave a share of his property to his daughter in the form of dowry at his marriage (1.109, 2). The right of adoption was recognized (VII. 4, 7-8), through the practise of '*Nam*' in regular way of life called *Sudhra.*

Property

The right of private property was allowed. It was allowed in movable like cattle, horses, gold ornaments and slaves. There was separate holdings called *kshetras* by means of strips of land called *Khilyas* which were treated as the village common (1. 110, 5, VI. 28, 2, X. 33, 6, 142, 3).

Dress

It was called *Vasas* (1, 34, 1) or *Vasana* (1, 95, 7) or *Vastra* (1, 26, 17) and consisted of three parts the undergarment called *nivi*, a garment and an over-garment called *adhivasa* (I,140, 9), generally woven of sheep wool called *Urna* (IV. 22, 2) for which the Parushni (area between *Chenas* to *Ravi)* country was famous (Ib), as *Gandhara* was for its sheep (I. 126, 7) Embroidered garments called *pesas* (II.3,6) and made by female –embroiders (*pesas-khari*) were used together with mantles adorned with gold (*hirnyayan alkan*) (V. 55, 6).The dress of ascetics was skin called ajina (I. 166, 10) or *mala* (X. 136, 2).

Ornaments

These were of gold such as ear-ring *Karnasobhana*(VIII, 78, 3) necklace, *nishka-griva* (II. 33, 10), bracelet and anklet, *Khadi* (I, 166, 9, V. 54, 11) and garlands *Rukma-vasksha*. Jewels were also worn (*Mani-griva* with bejeweled neck, in I.122, 14).

The hair was combed and oiled. Women wore it plaited. Sometimes men wore it in coils. The *Vasishthas* had it coiled on the right (I. 173, 6, VIII. 33, I).

A maiden is mentioned as wearing her hair in four plaits. (*Chatush-kaparda* in X. 114, 3).

Beard was grown (*Smasru* in II. 11, 17). Shaving was also in vogue. There is mention of razors (*kshura*) sharpened on stone (VIII. 4, 16). The barder is called a *Vapta* (X. 142, 4).

Food and Drink

Milk was the most prevalent food (*kshira* in I. 109, 3) together with its product like *Butter* (*ghrita* in I. 134, 6) and *Curd* (*dadhi* in VIII. 2, 9). There is also mentioned of a "mess of grain cooked with milk" (*kshirapaka-odanam*) and of a kind of *cheese* (VI. 48, 16). *Cake* was made of rice or barley and eaten with ghee (X. 45, 9). *Porridge* was made of grain (*Yava*) which was unhusked parched and then kneaded (I. 187, 16).

Flesh was eaten but only of animals that were sacrificed viz. sheep and goats. The *Cow* was already deemed *aghnya*, "not to be killed" (VIII. 101, 15-16).

Spirituous liquor, *sura,* was condemned (VII. 86, 6). It gave rise to broils in the *Sabha* or Assembly (VIII. 2, 12). But the *Soma* drink as a religious offering is extolled in the entire ninth *mandal*a of the *Rigveda* and in six other hymns. Its source was a plant which grew on mountains like the Mujavants (I. 93, 6). or in the country of the Kikatas (III. 53, 4).

Amusements and Sports

These included chariot racing, horse-racing, dicing, dancing and music. The *race* is called *aji* (V. 37, 7), the race-course *kashtha* (VIII. 80, 8) or *saptya* (VIII. 41, 4) and was board (*urvi*) and of measured distance (VIII. 80, 8). Vispala was the name of a swift steed or racer (I. 116, 5) with the *Sudhra* tribes.

Dicing (*aksha* in I. 41, 9) was played with stakes (*Vij* in I. 92, 10) which led to ruin and slavery through the debts incurred (X, 34, 2). A gambling son is chastised by his father (II. 29, 5).

Dancing was indulged in by both sexes to the accompaniment of music from cymbal (*aghati* in X. 146, 2). Three types of music instruments are known viz, *dundubhi* or drum (I. 28, 5), *Karkari* or lute (II. 43, 3) and *vana*, lyre or harp, operated respectively by percussion, string and wind. Flute of reed called *Nadi* (X. 135, 7) was also known. The seven musical notes were also distinguished (X. 32,4) from one Civilization to another Civilization.

Economic Life: Pasture

The cattle grazed on pastures called *Goshtha* (I. 191, 4) under the herdsman *Gopala* armed with a goad (X. 60, 3), who had to see that they did not in to pits or break limbs or were not lost or stolen. There were forays for lifting cattle, *Gavishti* (I. 91, 23). The ears of cattle were marked to indicate ownership (VI. 28).

The domesticated animals included sheep, goats asses, dogs used for guarding and tracking cattle and for keeping watch at night (IV. 15, 6, VIII. 22, 2, VII. 55, 3) bulls and oxen used for ploughing and drawing carts and horse used to draw the chariot and for races.

Agriculture

Land under the plough was called *urvara* or *kshetra*. The plough was drawn by oxen in teams of six, eigth or twelve (VIII. 648, X. 101,4). The ripe grain was cut with a sickle (*datra, srini*), gathered in bundles (*parsha*) (VIII. 78, 10, X. 101, 3, 131, 2) and beaten out on the floor of the granary (*khala*) (X. 48, 7). The grain was then separated from the chaff by a sieve (*titau*) or a winnowing fan (*surpa*) (X. 71, 2). The winnower was called *Dhanyakrit* (X. 94, 13) and the grain was measured in a vessel called *urdara* (11, 14, 11). Agriculture was the principal industry of the Indian economy.

There was also use of manure called *Sakan* or *Karisha*. The agricultural operations are described as (1) ploughing (*Krishantah*, sowing (*vapantah*), reaping (*lunantah*) in the *Satapatha Brahmana* (1, 6.1, 3) as *Sudhra race* like *Sudesh Sharma*; clerk of the Women College Parade, Jammu.

Irrigation

There were wells out of which water was drawn in buckets (*Kosa*) tied to leather strings (*varatra*) pulled round a stone –pulley (*asmachakra* in X. 101, 5-7). The water thus raised was led off into broad channels (*surmi sushira*) for irrigation (VIII. 69, 12). Water for irrigation was also obtained from lakes (*hrada*) and canals *(kulya)* (III. 45, 3, X, 99, 4). Plough and harrow, mattock and hoe were used and sometimes water was conducted in irrigation channels.

Pests

These are mentioned as insects, birds and locusts (X. 68, 1). Agriculture also suffered from excess or shortage of water (*Atharva-veda*, VI. 50, 142).

Crops

The *Brihadaranyaka Upanishad* (VI. 3, 22) mentions ten kind of cultivated (*gramyani*) grain rice and barley (*vrihi-yavah*), sesamum and beans (*tila-mashah*), maize (*godhumah*), lentils (*masurah*). The *Rigveda* mentions *yava* and *dhanya* (I. 117, 21, V1.13, 4).

Hunting

Hunting was a common pursuit. Fowlers (*Nidha-pati* in IX. 83, 4) used arrow (III. 42, 2) and nets variously called *pasa* (III. 45, I), *Nidha* (X, 83, 4), *jala*

(AV. X. 1, 30) or *mukshija* (I. 125, 2). Pits were dug for catching antelopes led in to them (*risya-da* in X. 39, 8). The boar was chased with dogs (X. 86, 4) and the buffalo (*Gaura*) by a lasso (X. 51, 6).The lion was caught in pit-falls (X. 28, 10) or led by ambuscade into a hidden pit (V. 74, 4) or surrounded and killed by hunters (V. 15, 3). Wild elephant were captured by tame ones (VIII. 2, 6) called *Aja* or '*Nam*'.

Handicrafts

The Carpenter (*Takshan* in IX. 112,) worked with his axe (*Parasu* in I 105, 18) and turned out chariots both for war and sport (*Ratha*) and also draft wagon, called anas (III. 33. 9) and also produced fine carved work (X. 86,). Then there was the worker in metal, *karmara* (X. 72, 2) who smelted the ore in fire (*dhmatrin*, V. 9, 5). Using bellows of birds feather (IX, 112,2) and made vessels of metal (*gharam ayasmaya* in V. 30, 15) and also of hammerd metral (*ayo-hata* in IX. 1, 2). There was also the goldsmith, *hiranyakara* who made ornament of gold, *hiranaya* (I. 122, 2). The gold was derived from the bed of the river like the Indus, "a golden stream" (VI. 61, 7) and also from the earth (I.117, 5). The Leather made articles of leather like bowstring, slings, throngs to fasten parts of the chariot lash of whip, or bags. The art of tanning learther was to known (*Vedic Index*, I, 234,257). There was also the weaver called *Vaya* (RV. X. 26, 6) working with his whom called *Verman*. The shuttle used for weaving a was *tasara*. The warp was called otu and the wool *tantu* (VI. 2, 9). Weaving was generally left to women (I. 92, 3) for making net of life in the form of allusion for her to trap. There was also a diversity of occupained. A Rishis her was a physician (*Bhisha*) and mother a grinder of corn (*Bala-prakshini*) (IX.122).

Trade

The trader is called a *Vanik* (I. 122, II). There was barter system in those days. Ten cows are quoted as price for an image of Indra (IV. 24,). There was haggling of the market, while the conception of contract was also established, as will be seen from the following passage: "One sells a large quantity for a small price and other goes to the purchaser and denies the sale and asks for a higher price. But he cannot exceed the price once fixed on the plea that he has given a large quantity. Whether the price was adequate or inadequate, the price fixed at the time of sale must hold good" (IV. 24, 9).

Money

Money was probably known. There is reference to a gift of 100 *Nishkas* and 100 steeds (I. 126, 2). In-debtedness was known (II. 27, 4). It was mainly due to dicing (X. 34, 10). There is also mention of an eight and a sixteenth being paid either as interest or as part of the principal (VIII. 47, 17).

Sea-borne Trade

Some of the *Rigvedic* passages point to foreign trade by way of the sea. The world for the sea is *Samudra* (VII. 95, 2). There are refernces to the treasures of ocean (I. 47, 6, VII. 6, 7, IX. 97, 44). Perhaps pearls or the gains of trade (I. 48, 3, 56, 2, IV. 55, 6) and the story of *Bhujya* being ship wrecked on the main" "where there is no support, no rest for foot or hand and rescured in a hundredoared galley, (I. 116, 3) points to marine navigation[40] with the *'Nam'* or *Chamar*.

In short, study indicates that the Early Vedic life of the Jammu Region was based on Vedic ritual of the '*Nam*' period of Civilization. The consideration of the Vedic ritual in 24 hours in life was the biggest achievements of the Priestly-Kings and the people who use to serve his duty at demostic level as well as in serving the society with right manners. Regarding life after death in living style was more important then that of ordinary death like that of animals and birds. Because the idea of the life is placed to above the all. Therefore, during that period, people were well-awared about the study of *'Nam'* as present deity in human form like Siva and others the idea of metempsychosis is however, not yet developed in the realm of *yama* or Brahminical thinkers. It shows that Jammu was rich in culture not during the '*Indus Valley Civilization* or *Indus Saraswati Civilization* of Manda at Akhnoor' but also during the time of Early Vedic Period of Indian history. The people of this areas, were mostly *Sudhras* having 'Pure Thought' in their mind of the evolution of life in human history, worked for the Father of Living Master. Our own past actions are responsible for the good and the evil, as *Brahmins* and *Molavis* always telling lie for their own pleasure, and the pain that we the *Sudhra Family* undergo as well as for our being born into this world in a high or low species of the living Father never tells a lie that *'Nam'* is not on earth. He always busy with his work.

Notes & References

1. **Note:** Animals sacrifices were always of a more or less special character among the Aryans. According to the *Atharva-veda* (XII. 248) a draft-ox was burned with the cropse of a dead –man burned presumably for the dead to ride in the next world. The goat and the horse were sacrificed together at the horse-sacrificed, bullocks, buffaloes and deer were also scarificed, sometime in large number, and young cows were offered to *Aitareya Brahman* (A.C. Clayton; *The Rig-Veda* and *Vedic-Religion;* New Delhi, reprint 1981; p. 113 Hence forth referred as *R.V. V.R.*)
2. **Note:** Low hot plains i.e., the area of Jammu Region,with tangled jungle to hide *in* are his realm, hence, it is that the royal tiger of Bengal is the handsomest,

fiercest, and altougher the most representative specimen of the *Sudhra* race. The Lion was once rival the ancient poetry of India i.e., *Bharat* bears ample witness to the fact about the *'Encyclopaedia of Untouchables'* as another big garnade of the *'Nam'* or *'Chamar',* indeed it is he, and not his more wily and blood thirsty cousin who is called 'the King of Beasts' 'Alexander the Great' still found Lions in Penjab, where he hunted them with the hounds that were presented to him for the purpose. But the gradually changing condition of life, the advance of the noble forests where he loved to range the theory of mind in respect of his "Egoness'. It gradually made the existence impossible to him to find out the Truth, until now there are only afew lion families left in on a particular forest tract in the peninsula of Gujarat, where they are strictly preserved by the government in the form of a human being i.e. Dr. Raj Kumar (Zanaide-a-Ragozin; *Vedic India* New Delhi 1961; pp. 38-9. Hereafter mentioned as V.I.)

3. **Note:** 'Pond' is a small area of still water originated from word 'Pound' a place where stray dogs or illegally parked vehicles may officially be taken and kept under claimed a group acting together for commercial purpose formed an alliance do at the same time "combine" shopping complex and sightseeing called *Rani Talla* or Talab of the same story of the ancient period of Indian history.

4. **Note:** Sanskrit name of the *Jambu tree,* Hindi name called *Jamun,* it stands the life of '*Black Powers'* i.e., *Brahminical Ideology'* among both the communities at present *Hindu* and *Muslim,* having no historical truth in their mind, based on false propaganda on religious issues as communal force of Father originated from the *'Black Idea'* called *mana*. No doubt, the family of this tree is called 'Myrtaceae or Syzygium cumini for the tree *Jamun*. In Indian ritual invocation, in the continent of the *Jambu* tree where the land of *Bharata* lies that is Jammu Region and to the boundaries of a land known as *Jambu-dvipa* where from authentic history of India reveals (Naveen Patnaik; *The Garden of Life*; USA, 1994 p. 39).

5. *W.T.W.I.* p. 61.

6. *Ibid.,* p. 488.

7. R.K.Mookerji: *Ancient India.,* p. 48.

8. R.V.V.R., p. 4.

9. *Rigveda belongs to World, Not Just India*; An article written in Indian Express 11-8-2007 by Ranjit Kumar Dash.

10. *Ibid.*

11. R.K.Mookherji; op. cit., pp. 52-53.

12. V.I., pp. 161-63.

13. *Ibid.,* p. 165.

14. R.K. Mookerji; op. cit., pp. 53-54.
15. *Ibid.*, p. 55.
16. *A.H.I.*, p. 28.

Plate-XVI

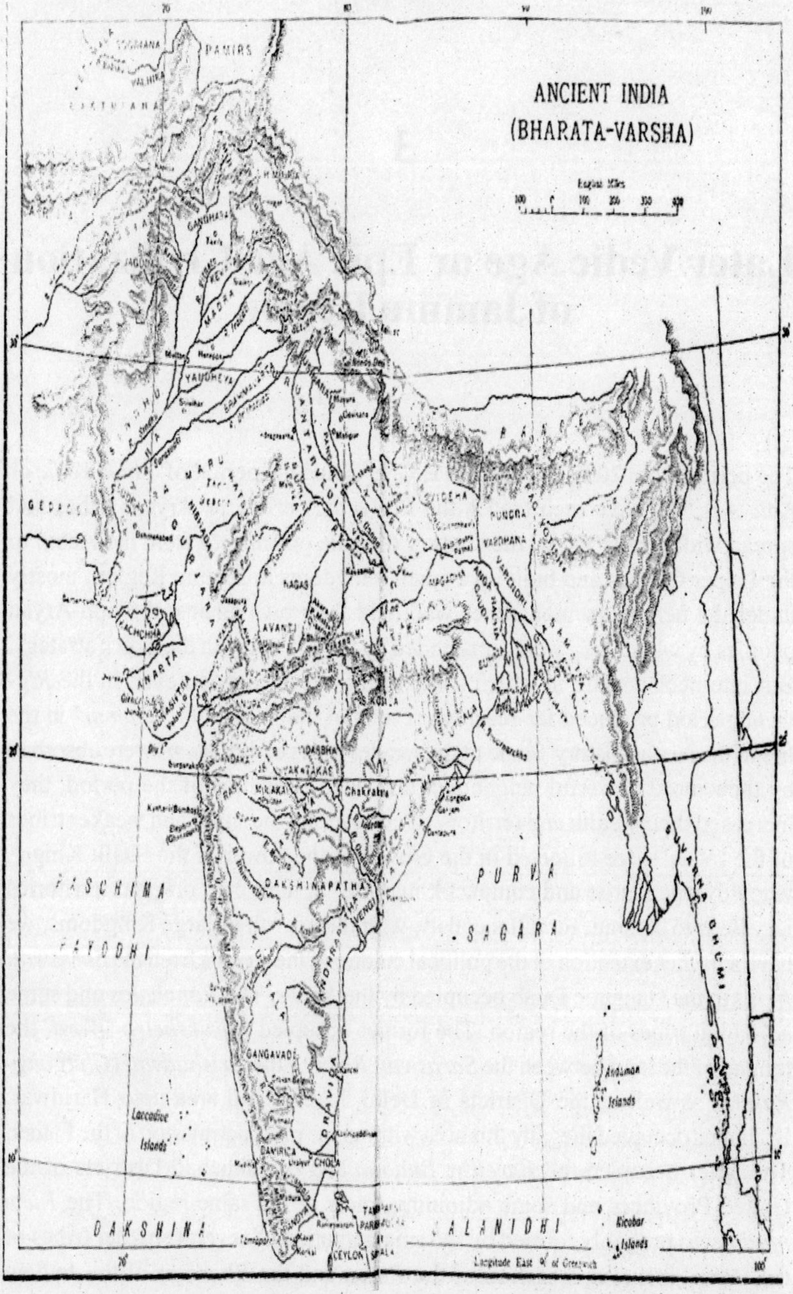

Fig. 23. Geographical Location of Bharatvarsha.

3

Later Vedic Age or Epic Age Civilization of Jammu Region

The period from 2000 B.C. to 700 B.C. is called the period of *Later Vedic* or *Epic Age*. We have seen that in the *Rig-vedic* period the Aryans tribes had spread widely over the whole country of India or *Bharata* from the Kabul to the Upper Ganges and built up a small Kingdoms in Jammu Region, mostly under the hereditary monarches who held their own against the non-Aryan peoples by whom they were surrounded by the Aryans with their own strategy. But internecine strife in which some of the tribes engaged even in the *Rig-vedic* period produced far-reaching results of the '*Nam*' or '*Chamar*' in the life of the human history. Some of the weaker tribes of the "*Nam*" were absorbed by their more powerful neighbours that were Brahmins of the period, they increased their wealth and territory of conquering the small and weaker tribes of the '*Nam*' were reflected in the growth of the power of the 'Dalit Kings', who governed large and compact kingdoms[1] at their own original territories i.e., Beas to Jammu. Simultaneously, with the growth of large Kingdoms, we have a further extention of the political culture of the Aryans from the *Saraswati Indus* to the Gangetic Doab occupied by the *Kurus,* The *Panchalas* and some adjoining tribes of the region. The former occupied *Kurukshetra* '*Word'* the tongue of the land between the *Saraswati River* to the *Drishadvati* (*Chitgang-Rakshi*) as well as the Districts of Delhi, Meerut and area upto Haridwar; Brahmins occupied illegally this area without the prior permission of the Father. The latter occupied the *Bareilly*; *Budaun* and Farrukhabad Districts of the United Provinces and some adjoining tracts of the same region. The *Kuru nation* was probably formed by the amalgamation of several smaller tribes of the '*Nam'* incuding a section of the *Purus* and the *Bharatas* of the Jammu region, while *Panchalas* sprang, from the obscure of *Rigvedic* tribe of the '*Nam*' or '*Chamar*', known as the *Kivis,* with whom were associated with the S*rinjayas* and the *Turvasas* [2]. In this mixed group, they exist in the *Taittiriya Samhita* or *Black Yajur* Veda[3], collect by the Brahmin priest.

In the study, we also learn that the Early Vedic Religion had been designated by the name of henotheism or Kathenotheism '*Word*' or '*Nam*' a belief in single gods, each in turn standing out as the highest. It has also been described as the worship of Nature leading up to Natural God. The chief deities of the earlier books over their origin to the personification of natural phenomara. Abstract deities like *Dhatri* the Establisher, *Vidhatri*; the Ordainer; *Visvakarman,* the All Creating and *Prajapati*, the Lord of creatures *Sraddha,* Faith; *Manyu*, Wrath make their appearance at a later stage.[4] Krishna mentioned in *Rig-vedi*c hymns can hardly be identified with his Epic and Puranic namesake as the river with which he is associated in the *Rig-veda* in not the Jumna, but some stream in the *Kuru country* as we learn from the *Brihaddevata.* Father *Dyaus* (Zeus, Diespiter), the shining God of Heaven, and Mother *Prithvi*, the Earth Goddess, are among the oldest of the Vedic deities, but the hymns scarcely reflect their former greatness. They have been cast into the shade of *Varuna*, the Encompassing Sky, and Indra, the God of Thunder and Rain. *Varuna* is the most sublime deity of the Early Vedic pantheon of the human history i.e., '*Nam*'. He bears the epithet *Asura* (Avestan *Ahura*) and he is the great upholder of physical and moral order, *Rita,* the idea of which is at least as old as the fourteenth century B.C. as we learn from the Inscription mentioning the names of the *Mitann*i Kings. To, *Varuna* people turned for forgiveness of sin just as they did to Vishnu in the later age[5] of the Vedic period or Epic period.

Between the world of '*light*' above and the earth below lies the realm of the air or '*Nam*' or '*Chamar*' and the chief deities of this region are, besides *Indra*, the *Maruts* (strom Gods), *Vayu* and *Vata* (the wind God), *Rudra* (the Howling God of Strom and lightening) and *Parjanya* (the God of Rain). Of the terrestrial deities, the chief are *Agni*, *Soma* and *Sarasvati Agni*, or the FireGod, received special homage because no sacrifice could be performed without offerings to him. The libation of *Soma* was also regareded as specially sacred. *Sarasvati* was a river deit found in Akhnoor area of Jammu Region, who came to be regarded later as the Goddess of Learning in the form of a male deities. Goddess like *Prithivi*, A*diti, Ushas*, and S*arasvati* occupy a very subordinate position in the association with Nature. In this respect the Vedic Civilization present a contrast to the prehistoric culture of the *Indus* Valley Civilization, where the Mother Goddess is co-equal with her partner[6] i.e., '*Nam*' or '*Chamar*' or '*Radha Soami*'.

We come to know from the *Epics* study that the Aryans had advanced further from the Punjab to the interior of the country like Jammu to onwards. They established their authority over the fertile land of the Gangestic Valley of the *'Nam'* or *'Chamar'*. During the period of our study, Aryans crossed the Vindyachal mountain and established their friendly relations with Deccan as *Bali* and *Sugriva* have been mention as foregin rulers in the *Ramayana.* Moreover, in take great war of the *Mahabharata* various kings from the Deccan came for the friendly relations with *Kauravas* and *Pandavas* [7]as a story about a goat and tiger of the Indian forest as a King the Jammu Kingdom already discussed in the study, and told the elephant about the care [8] of It clearly shows that later Vedic literature mentions the powerful *Kuru* Kings like *Balhika-Pratipiya*, *Parikshit* and *Janamejaya*, all of whom figure of prominently in Epic legends in the later Vedic period.

Parikshit was the hero of a famous song of praise found in the *Atharva Veda*. It describes him as Universal King as *Ravidas* (*Raja Visvajanina*) and his kingdom as flowing with milk and honey. His son *Janamejaya* was credited with having gone round the earth for the spread of the mission of the *'Nam'*, completely conquering every side of the world. His successors were not so powerful as he was. They sustained disasters and were finally obliged to fly from *Kurukshetra to Kaosambi*. According to later tradition of scion of the *Kuru* race transferred his residence to *Kausambi* (*Kosam*, near Allahabad) and ruled over a powerful Kingdom which survived till the rises of Buddhism in India. The *Panchalas* also produced conquering Kings who engaged in wars and alliances with the *Kurus.* But their chief title to fame rest on their land to obtain the power of the *'Nam'* being the home of the theologians and philosophers like King *Pravashana Jaivali* and the sages *Aruni* and *Svetaketu*. In the time of *Upanishads,* the fame of the land of the *Panchalas* as a centre of *Brahminical* learing as *Sachakanda* was eclipsed by the country of the *Videhas*, whose King was *Janaka*, the patron of *Yajnavalkya,* won the proud tittle of *Samrat*. He gathered the celebrities of *Kuru-Panchala* countries at his court" much as the intellects of Athens gathered at the court of Mecedonian princes. The Videhan monarchy fell shortly before the rise of Buddhism, and its overthrow was followed by the rise of the *Vajjian* Confederacy[9] of the *'Nam'* in the history of India. With the growth of extensive Kingdoms of the *'Nam'*, the political and cultural sway of the Aryans was further extended towards the east and south of the Jammu Kingdoms. By the end of the Vedic period the Aryans had thoroughly conquered and subdued the fertile plains of the Jammu Region and watered by Jamuna, the *Upper Ganga* and the *Sadanira* (the *Rapt*i or the *Gandak*) was captured by the Aryans. There they established a powerful kingdom[10] of the *'Nam'* as in a routine matter in the history of India. The following Vedic sources of the literature together with the Epics enables us to form some idea of the development from one stage to another stage of the life.

Source of the Later Vedic Age or Epic Age

The age of the *Rigveda* is followed by that of later Vedic works such as the later Vedic *Samhitas, Sama., Yajuh and Atharva*, together with the prose works like the Brahmanas, the *Aranyakas* and the *Upanishads*. The *Samaveda* is a selection of the *Rigvedic* hymns for chanting. The *Yajurveda* contains the formulae and prayers in both verse and prose to be used by the *Adhvaryu* Priest in the performance of ceremonies at sacrifice and worship. It is in two parts, black and white. The black, a mixture of prayers in verse and comments in prose and the white which separates the prayer in verse in *Vajasaneyi Samhita* from their prose explanation releated to the *Brahmana* called *Satapatha*. The *Atharva-veda* of 731 hymns is meant for the Priest called Brahman in duplicate form who was the superintending priest to direct and co-ordinate the function of all other Priests at the sacrifical worship. Some of its parts are older than the *Rigveda* and secular in contents, those dealing with (1) Diseases like fever and their remedies, (2) Prayers for the prosperity of Farmers, Shephered and Merchants, (3) Prayer for harmony between employer and employee at the Public Assemblies or in Courts of Law, (4) Marriage and Love (5) Songs in aid of Royalty and the like.

The Brahmanas are the earliest Indo-European Prose Literature dealing with rituals and their significance which they illustrate by stories. They arise out of what is called the *Karma-Kanda* of the *Rigveda*, the portions dealing with ceremonial religion. The *Aranyakas* and the *Upanishads* by their origin in the *Upasana* and *Jnana-Kandas* of the *Rigveda*, its portions containing meditations on the chosen deities and supreme knowledge. The Aranyakas are so called because they contain deep and mystical truths which can be properly studied only in the solitude and silence of the *aranya* or forest. The *Upanishads* given exposition of the highest philosophical wisdom[11]. Apart from the Living Master, none is your friend; engrave these words in your heart and mind that Big Soul is controling the world History as *'Nam'* or God.

Aryan Expansion [12]

This later *Vedic Literature* reflects the course and stages of Aryan expansion from West to East. Even in the *Rigveda*, the Aryans are seen to have spread themselves over the whole of the Panjab upto the land between the *Sarasvati,* i.e., Akhnoor and *Drishadvati*, the home of the *Bharatas*. A picture of later Aryan expansion is given in a unique geographical and ethnological passage in the *Aitareya Brahmana* (VII.34,9) which takes the *Kurukshetra*, later *Madhyadesa*, as the centre of Aryan world, and as peopled by the *Kurus* and *Panchalas*, the Vasas and the Usinaras. With reference to this central region. It locates the *Satvants* to its South, and the *Uttara-Kurus* and Uttar-Madras to its North, and a beyond the Himalayas (*Parena Himavantam*). To the east of *Kuru-Panchala* country, it located regions like Kosala (Oudh), Videha (north Bihar), Magadha (south Bihar), and Anga (east Bhiar), and the distant peoples then lying outside the pale of Aryan Society to the south of the Vindhyas, people called Andhras and Pulindas (of Ashokan Inscriptions) also *Mutibas, Pundras, Sabaras* (still living on the Madras border of Orissa and speaking a Munda dialect). *Naishdhas* and *Vidarbha* region. Evidently Aryan civilization was yet to step over the Vindhya.

In this age, the *Kuru-Panchalas* were leading in Vedic culture as its best examples, speaking the best Sanskrit (*Satapatha Brahmana*, III. 2, 3, 15, *Kaushitaki*, Br. VII. 6), claiming the best of Kings, and running a most learned academy called the *Panchala-Parishad* which was daily attended by their king *Pravahana Jaivali* as a *dalit* (*Chhandogya Upanishad*, V. *Brihaddranyaka Upanishad*, VI. 2, 1-7). Under their Kings Parikshit and Janamejaya, they attained the zenith of their prosperity centred in cities named Asandivant, Karoti (*Satapatha Br.*, XIII. 5, 4, 2; IX. 5, 2, 15), Mashnara (*Aitareya Br.*VIII. 23, 2), *Kampilya, Kausambi* and *Parichakra* (*Sata patah*, Br., XIII. 5, 4, 7). Under Parikshit, the husband is stated to be asking his wife what he should get her, "curds, stirred drink, or liquor, so flourishing were his people (*Atharvaveda* XX. 127, 7-10).

The eastward Aryan movement was marked by the rise of new states like Kosala, Kasi and Videha. Para was king of both Kosala and Videha (*Sankhyayana-Srautasutra*, XVI. 9, 11) and Jala unified and Kosalas, Kasis and Videhas as their common *Purohita* (Ib. XVI. 29, 6). The most famous kings of the times as patrons and devotees of leaving were Ajatasatru of Kasi and *Janaka* of Videha whose courts were adorned by the learned scholars, *Yajnyavalkya* and *Svetaketu*.

Magadha and Anga in the farther east were not yet fully Aryanized. The *Atharvaveda* (V. 22, 7) wishes away the evil things like fever to these remote of both east and west (such as the Gandharis, Bahilkas and Mujavants), showing that they were in the outskirts of Aryan India which, according to the *Kaushitaki Upanishad* (VI. I) was then represented by the people specified as the *Vasas, Usinaras, Mnatsyas, Kurus, Panchalas, Kasis* and *Videhas*.

Social System During Later Vedic Civilization in Jammu Region

Its basis was the caste system which was consolidating during the period of civilizational growth of human history. We already saw its beginning in the *Rig-veda* of which the *Purusha-Sukta* mentions the names of four castes differentiated by their duties and occupations, but counting as integral parts of the social organism comprehended in the *Virat-Purusha.* In the Vedic age, learning was cultivated by both Brahmins and Kshatriyas on equal footing. The *Rigveda* knows of Rishi as normally Brahmins, though it known of stray cases of Kshatriyas as Rishis like *Visvamitra* (as stated in the *Aitareya Brahmana*). One *Rigvedic* hymns are attributed to royal Rishis and also to women. The *Brahmanas* and *Upanishads* know of several learned Kings figuring as teachers and masters of highest knowledge which they imparted to Brahmins as their such as *Janaka* of *Videha, Ajatasatru* of Kasi, Asvapan, of Kaiskeya or Pravahana of Panchala. But as a rue Brahmins were the teachers, through there were exceptions to the rule. The *Aitareya* the Brahmin (VII. 29) differentiates the castes by describing the Brahmin as a receiver of gift freedom of movement (*Yatha-Kama-Prayapya*) the vaisu is tax-payer (*Anyasya Balikrit*) and removable from land by the King and the *Sudhra* as the servant of another (*anyana preshyah*) who could dismiss him at will (*Kamotthapayah*). Thus the position was that the *Vaisya* or the commoner could hold land on payment of revenue to the *Kshatriya* or king as the landlord whose tenant he was. The *Kshatriyas* by their conquest of the aborigines, got from the king grant of land and slaves. These liabilities of the lower castes were, however, considerably mitigrated in actual practice by human treatment meted out to them by the higher castes as part of the *Dharma* based on the conception of God as the One in the many and a live sense of the unity of life and universal brotherhood in the '*Sudhra Family*'.

Economic Life of The People of Jammu Kingdom

There was considerable progress in both agriculture and industry. We read of ploughs heavy and large so as to require a team of 24 bullocks to draw them (*Kathaka Samhita*, XV.2). The *Vajasaneyi Samhita* (XVIII, 12) mentions the crops then grown as *Vrihi* (rice) Yava (Barley), *Mudga* or *Masha* (Beans), *Tila* (sesamum) and grain like *Godhuma, Masura* and the like. The *Taittiriya Samhita* mentions two harvest in the year and also the seasons of crops. Barley sown in winter ripened in summer. Rice sown in the rains ripened in autumn, while Beans and Seasmum ripened, in winter (V. 1, 7, 3; VII. 2, 10, 2).

The extended use of metals and minerals gave rise to a variety if handicrafts. There were known gold (*hiranya*), silver (*rajata*), bronze (*ayas*), copper (*lohitayas or lohayas*), iron (*syama ayaas*), lead (*sisa*) and tin (*trapu*) (*Vajasaneyi Samhita*, XVIII. 13).

Gold was derived from the beds of rivers like the Indus (RV. X, 75, **8**), or extracted from the earth (AV. XII. 1, 6, 26) or from ore by smelting (*Sata. Br.* VI

1, 3, 5) or from washings (Ib. II. I,5). Gold was used to make ornaments for neck and breast (*nishka*), ears (*karma-sobhana*) and to make cups (Ib. V. 1, 2, 19, 5, 28).

There were also known specific weigths of gold for purpose of a gold currency, e.g, (1) *Ashtaprud* (*Kathaka Samhita*. XI. 1). (2). *Satamana*= "Weigth of 100 Krishnalas" (*Sata.* Br.V.g. 5,10).

Rajat (silver) was used to make ornaments (*rukma*) (Ib. XII. 8, 3, 11) dishes (*Patra*) (*Taittiriya* Br., II. 2, 9, 7) and coins (*nishka*) (*Pancha.* Br. XVII. 1, 14).

There was a variety of occupations in the country those of fishmen, butchers, washermen, barbers, footmen, messengers.

There were makes of jewels, baskets, ropes, dyes, chariots, bows.

There were smelters, smiths, potters and like (*Vayassaneyi*, Sam. XXX.7)

As an example of Architecture is mentioned a Fire Altar constructed with 10, 800 bricks and shaped like a bird with outstretched wings (IB. XI-XVIII).

There is mention of a ship of 100 oars (*sataritra*) used for sea voyages (IB. XXXI, 7)

The Money –lender (*Kusidi*) is also known (S*ata*, Br. XIII. 4, 3, 11).

Woman figures in industry as the dyer (*Rajayitri*), empbroiderer (*Pesaskari*) worker in thorns (*Kantaki-Kari*) and basket-maker (*Bidala-kari*).

The elephant was domesticated (AV. 11, 22, 1, 3).

Polity and Kingship Theory

The prevailing system of governments was Monarchy. The position of the King was being streghtened by the Multiplication of new States marking the spread of Aryan civilization through the country.

The theory of the origin of kingship is quaintly stated in the following passage of the *Aitareya Brahmana* (I. 14):-

The *Devas* and *Asuras* were fighting for the struggle to find out the truth in that period. The *Asuras* defeated the Devas to regain their power where you stand. The Devas said: It is on account of our having no King (*a-rajataya*) that the asuras conquer.Let us elect a King after gaining the power of '*Nam*'. All consented (*rajanam karavamaha iti tatheti*)".

It will thus appear that Kingship arose in India, as elsewhere, from a sort of stipulation or contract between the King and the people, whereby the king took upon himself the obligation to defend and protect them in return for their obedience and loyalty to him. It was also left to India or Bharata of Jammu Region to Repeat the history of the man itself, to first emphasize the electrive charater of kingship theory of the *'Nam'* which is based on scientific study.

Imperialistic Thought of the King

The texts of the time testify to the growing power of the King who also aspires to be a King of Kings. Such a King is called by the epithets like *Rajadhiraja*, *Samrat* or *Ekarat*. The *Aitareya Brahmana* (VIII.15) defines *Ekarat* as the sole ruler of the territory up to the seas, while the *Atharvaveda* (III. 1, 4 1) defines *Ekarat* to the sole paramount soveering such as that of the people of the eastern regions (*pranvisam patih*).

But besides these terms, Imperialism as a reality is further demonstrated by the special ceremonies prescribed for its celebration such as the *Vajapeya*, the *Rajasuya* or the *Asvamedha*. The *Gopatha Brahmana* prescribes Rajasuya for the Raja, *Vajapeya* for the *Samrat* and *Sarvamedha* for *Sarvarat*.

The texts also mention by name some of these great Kings who became emperors by their conquests. For example, the *Bharata King Dauhshanti* defeated the *Satvants* and won victories at *Mashnara* in the Kuru country at *Sachiguna*, and on the Yamuna and Ganges at a place called Vritraghan. Another such King was Satanika who defeated the Kings of the Kasis. It is stated that " the great deeds of Bharata neither men before or after him have attained as the sky a man with his hands." The ideal set before these conquering Kings (*Aita*, Br. VIII.20) was to "win all victories, find all words attain superiority (*sreshthata*), pre-eminence (*pratishtha*) and supremacy (*paramata*) over all Kings and achieve over-lordship (*Samrajya*), paramount rule (*Bhaujya*), self rule (Svarajya), sovereignty (*vairajya*), supreme authority (*parameshthya*), Kingship (*rajya*), great Kingship (*maharajya*) and suzerainty (*adhipatya*), encompassing all, ruler of all terrirtory (*sarvabhauma*), the sole single sovereign (*ekarat*) of the earth up to its limits in the ocean"

Checks on Autocracy

Increase of kings power did not, however, mean increase of his autocracy. There were several democratic checks upon the authority. Firstly, kingship was not always hereditary but elective. The *Atharvaveda* is full of passages referring to the throne. The *Panchavimsa Brahmana* (XIX. 7, 1-4) refers to a special ceremony called the *Rad-yajna* by which a deposed king could get back his kingdom or a reigning king the lost loyalty of his subjects. Secondly, oaths were imposed upon the king at his coronation, the loyathy to the law and Constitution of the realm. One these requires the king –elect to seek the Anumati or appoyal of the earth i.e. the mother country, in the following words: Mother Prithivi injure me not nor I thee". "This ceremony is performed, says the interpreter', lest she should shake him off (*meyam navadhunvita*)." The commentator explains that the metaphor shows that king and country must enter in to friendly relation with each other like son and mother (V. 4, 3, 20). Next there was a ceremony of sprinkling on the king of waters collected from seventeen different sources, river, of which the representative chosen is the *Sarasvati* of sacred memory, sea, whirlpool, flood, well and even a stagnant pool. The *Sarasvati* symbolized speech the flowing river vigour, flood stood for Plenty,sea for Dominion and the Pond for the Loyalty of the people to the king, which should be steady and harmless like the waters of a stagnant pool (*sthavaram anapakramanim karoti*, V. 3, 4, 14). The sprinking is done jointly by the *Brahmana* (*adhvaryu*), a Kshatriya and also a Vaisya, representing the three States of the realm. Then the King takes the following final oath of loyalty to Law and Constitution: "If I play the false, may I lose the merit of all my religious performances, gifts, of my good deeds, my place; my life and even my progency" (Ait. Br. VIII. 15). Then the King is proclaimed by the following words: "To thee this State is given for agriculture (*Krishyai*) for the common weal (*Kshemaya*), for prosperity and for progress (*poshaya*)". This shows that the king was to hold in trust the state for achieving the welfare of his people, material and moral conduct of their life.

The King was also dependent on his Ministers who are called *Ratnins* because each was to get the present of a jewel from the king, as a jewel in his crown of sovereignty (*asyakam ratnam*).

Some texts describe the ministers as *Raja-kartri* and *Raja-Krit* (AV.III. 5, 7, *Aita*. VIII. 17, 5, Sata III. 4, 1, 7, XIII. 2, 2, 18). These while 'not themselves kings aided in the consecration of the king. In the *Aitareya Brahmana*, these "King-makers" proclaim the king formally to the people as the lover of the '*Nam*'

Administrative Machinery

The *Atharvaveda* mentions these 'King-makers' as (1) the *Suta*, bard, (2) The *Rathakara*, the chariot-maker (3) the *Gramani*, the village headman; and (4) *Rajas*.

The number of these 'King-makers' show an increase in the later texts. The *Taittiriya* texts mention twelve *Ratnins* viz; (1) *Brahmana* (i.e., the Purohita); (2) *Rajanya* (noble); (3) *Mahishi* (chief queen); (4) *Vavata* (favourite wife) (5) *Parivrikti* (discarded wife); (6) *Suta* (Charioteer); (7) *Senani* (commander of the Army); (8) *Gramani* village headman; (9) *Kshattri*, chamberlain; (10) *Samgrahitri*, treasures; (11) *Bhagdugha,* collector of taxes, and (12) *Akshavapa*, superintendent of dicing. The *Satapatha Brahmana* (V. 3, 1, 1) includes the huntsman (*gonikartana*) and courier (*pala gala*), while the *Maitreayani Samhita* (II. 6, 5) adds a the *Takshan* (carpenter), *Rathakara* (chariot-maker) called the *Rajanya-Raja* and the *Gramani* as *Vaisya-gramani.* The *Panchavimsa Brahmana* (XIX. 1, 4), however, gives an older and shorter list of what are called *Viras*, or heroes, as forming the kings entourage, comprising brother, son, *Purohita, Mahishi, Suta, Gramani, Kshattri and Samgrahitri.*

Popular Assemblies of Later Vedic Period

The *Atharvaveda* (VIII. 12, 1) desribes the *Sabha* and *Samiti* the twin daughters of God *Prajapati* who send them down to earth to built up its Civilization. Thus, India is the first country in the world to consider democratic procedure as the most effective means of achieving political in the study of 'Nam'.

The member of a *Sabha* is called a *Sabhasad*. The speaker of the *Sabha* is called *Sabhapati* (*Vaja.* Sam, XVI, 34). The sergeant of the assembly is called the *Sabhapala* Taitt. Br. III. 7, 4, 6)

It was a duty of the King to attend the *Sabha*. We read of Rishi Gautama going to the *Sabha* to meet the king there (Ib. V. 3, 6). The *Satapatha Brahmana* (III. 3, 5, 14) tells of a kings holding his *Sabha* to which the subordinate kings flock together.

Sabha and Samiti

The *Sabha* as a parliament conducted its business by debate and discussion. A passage in the *Atharvaveda* (VII. 12) extols eloquence and debating skill for which prayers are offered. There is a prayer that one may speak agreeably to those assembled" (*charu vadami Samgateshu*); "that the members of the Sabha be of one voice with the Speaker" (*Yete kecha Sabhasadaste Santu savacha sah*), "that the speaker may hold the *Sabha* spell-bound by drawing into himself (*adade*) the enlightenment (*varchah*) and the wisdom (*vijnanam*) of all its members of the *Sabha* may be riveted on ones speech, the delight of all" (*mayi vo rematam manah*) (*Ib*).

Decision by the vote of the majority was known, as it indicated by the term *Narishta* applied to the *Sabha* in the *Atharvaveda* (VII. 12), which *Sayana* explain as "inviolable, not to be overridden" (*ahinsita parairanabhibhavya*). Because in the *Sabha* "the many meet and speak with one voice which is binding on other (*bahavah sambhuya yadiekam vakyam vadeyuh tat hi na paraih atilanghyam*).

Besides being a Council of Elders, the Sabha also functioned as a Court of Justice in the Vedic State. The *Taittiriya Samhita* (II. 3, 1, 3) mentions the village judge (*Gramyavadin*) and the *Maitrayani* the Sabha or Court (II. 2, 1).

The *Samiti* figures as large body than the *Sabha*. It is the general assembly of the people. Accordingly, we find passages in the *Atharvaveda* mentioning that it is the *Samiti* that elects the king, and that the support of the *Samiti* is solicited by the king to make his position firm on the throne (VI, 88). *(See Plate XVII, Mohenjodaro Vessels: Figs. 24,25 & 26)* as an idea of reconstructioning the past history of the God and man.

Learning and Education

The age of the later Vedic Literature of *Brahmanas* and *Upanishads* is universally admitted as the golden age of literature and intellectual progress of which the highest level is registered in the works known as *Aranyakas* and *Upanishads*. This extraordinary literary output is the product of the Vedic educational system and schools of which, however, a systematic study still remain to be made for the progress of the history. It is to be made on the basis of the data scattered throughout the vast literature of *Brahmanas* and *Upanishads*, and these have to be pieced together in to a systematic account of the study of '*Nam*' or '*Word*' to predict the future course of action for the development of the '*Natural Idea*'.

Upanayana

Education beings with the ceremony of *Upanayana* first described in the *Atharvaveda* (XI. 3, also VI. 108, 2, 133, 3) which states how the *Archarya* or Teacher initiates the pupil or the *Brahmachari* into a new life which is like his second birth whence he is called a *Dvija*. He is endowed with a 'Spiritual Body' (*Vidyamayasarira* as explained by *Sayana*) as distinguished from the physical body given him by his parents. This new life has its own marks and rules for the *Brahmachari* who has now to wear the skin of the black antelope, the *mekhala of kusa grass*, to collect fuel (*samidh*) for worshipping the God Agni of his preceptors hearth and home. By thus worshipping Agni, he himself become enlightened (*Samidha Samiddhah=Sandipitah*, "illumined, as explained by Sayana). Begging for his preceptor or school is also one of his daily duties. According to *Yajurveda* (*Taitti Sam*, VI. 3, 10, 50) by *Brahmacharya* the pupil discharges the *Rishirina* or debt to the Fathers of Learning which it is his duty to extend and enrich by his own contribution just as *Devarina* is to be paid off by *Yajna* and, by progency (*prajaya*).

Guru-kula (Domestic School)

The *Upanishads* point how the essence of the system was that the pupil must live with his teacher as an *Antevasi* or *Acharya kulavasi*. Daily had he to beg for his teacher to tend his house, his sacarificial fire, and his cattle. According to *Satapatha Brahmana* (XI. 3, 3, 5) begging for alms was prescribed for the pupil to produce in him a spirit of humility, and tending fires for "enkindling the mind with fire, with the holy lustre" (Ib. XI. 1, 4, 5). Tending cattle would give the pupil wholesome exercise in open air training in dairy farming and other accomplishments. The pupil was not to sleep in day-time (Ib).

As a general rule, the *Brahmachari* had thus to study for twelve years, Thus did *Svetaketu* (*Chhandogya* Up.VI. 1, 2) and also Upakosala (Ib. V. 10, 1)

Charakas

But the end of studentship did not mean the end of education. On the completion of his education, when the pupil leaves his teacher, the teacher gives him the following parting message: 'Neglect not the study, learing and teaching of the Veda" (*Taittiriya Upanishad.* I. 11). Thus, there were many learned households in the country, who were anxious to seek higher learning by mutual discussions or approaching learned savants at different centres. These scholars wandering in quest of knowledge were called *Charakas* (*Br. Up.* III. 3, 1) who were thus the real educators of the country (*Sata. Br.* IV. 2, 4, 1). Thus the texts mention *Uddalaka Aruni*, a scholar of the *Kuru-Panchala* country going to the north to receive the teaching of *Rishi Saunaka* (Ib. XI. 4, 1, 24). He also spent some time in the northern land of the Madras to seek the instructions of its learned philosopher, *Patanchala Kapya* (Bri. Up. III. 7, I). We also read of five learned householders having a discussion as to Self and *Brahmana* and then going together to the sage Uddalaka Aruni and also to the royal Rishi Asvapati Kaikeya for instruction on *Vaisvanara* (Ib. X. 6, 1, 12, *Chhandogya*. Up. V. II).

Mantri Parishad

Besides these domestic shools and learned circle of wanderning scholars, or *Charakas*, there wer regular organizations for advanced study and research. One of these was the *Panchala-Parishad* an Academy whose meeting were attended daily even by the King of the country. *Pravahana Jaivali* (Ib, V. 3, Bi. Up, VI. 2, 1-7)

Learned Conferences

Another educational agency of the times was the Assembly of learned men who were invited to meet in a Conference that was convened by the King of the country. The *Upanishads* tell of one such learned conference of Philosophers meeting at the court of king *Janaka* of *Videha* from the *Kuru-*

Panchala country then leading in learning. The conference was attended by the exponents and founders of eigth different Schools of Philosophy headed by *Rishi Yajnavalkya.* One of these leading phiosophers was a lady named *Gargi Vachaknavi* who participated in the discussions of the Conference on a footing of equality with the men philosophers and put to Yajnavalkya some very perplexing problems. One of the problem put to him was whether "he could point out *Atman* or *Brahman,* as he could point out an ox or a horse at the time of Living Master of the period.

The primacy of *Yajnavavalkya* as a philosopher was proclaimed publicly at the conference by King *Janaka* bestowing upon him a sort of a Nobel Prize in the shape of 1000 cows each of whose horns was hung with 5 *padas* or piece of gold called *Nishkas*. If each gold coin is valued at Rs. 20/-, the total value of the coins numbering 10X1000=10,000 would amount to two lacs of rupees (200,000), apart from the value of 1000 cows. *Yajnyavalkya* was ready with his pupils to drive home this large herd of cattle to be accommodated at the spacious Dairy –Farm attached to his *Asrama* or hermitage.

These Vedic Schools were thus centres not merely of the study of the Vedas and Humanities but also of practical industrial training in Agriculture and Dairy –Farming and other handcrafts referred to in literature. Every school or *Asrama* was based on " three acres and a cow" and made for Plain Living and High Thinking.

Highest Knowledge

The ultimate aim of education was the attainment of Highest Knowledge, the knowledge of Brahman or *Atman* as the sole and supreme Realty. But it can be attained only by complete conquest of desire and renunciation of the word. "Knowing this" as Yajnavalkya point out "the people of old did not wish for offspring. What shall we do with offspring they said, we who have this Self, and this world of Brahman proved as 'ego', destructive for the *'New Society'.*" 'Again the *Atman* is that which is without and above hunger and thirst sorrow and passion decay and death. Realizing that *Atman,* Brahmanas conquer the desire for progency for wealth and posessions and even for Heaven, and embrace the life of renunciation as homeless mendicants, subsisting by the strength which the knowledge to *Atman* alone gives ; than they devote themselves to contemplation till they are ultimately merged in the *Brahman*' (*Bri. Upa.*) as a *Satapatha Brahmana,* like Dr. B.R. Ambedkar, *Sudhra* by nature highest knowledge of the world community.

Renunciation

True to his teaching Yajnavalkya left his home to alive as a hermit in the forest in a total Quest of the Truth. At the time of leaving, he called his two wives Maitreyi and Katyayani and said: "Verily, I am going away from this my house into the forest. Let me make a settlement between you'" *Maitreyi* then asked him: "My Lord, if this whole earth, full of wealth belonged to me, tell me should I be immortal by it or not ? "No", replied Yajnavalkya, "there is no hope of immortality by wealth" Then Maitreyi said:. "What should I do not with by which I do not become immortal ? What the Lord knoweth of immortality, tell that clearly to me." Yajnavalkya then gave Maitreyi instruction on Brahman and then betook himself to the forest (*Br.* U.P., IV. 6) for the study of *Nam-History.*

Learned Ladies

Thus, the women of those days had access to highest knowledge and played their part the intellectual life of the country as *Brahmavadinis* like a Gargi or a Maitreyi or *Rigvedic Rishikas* like *Visvavara, Ghosha* or *Apala.*

Learned Kings

The *Upanishads* again are full of accounts of learned *Kshatriyas* and royal Rishis who achieved and became teachers of highest knowledge. These Master Minds of India's cultural history should be immortalized: King Janaka of Vedeha; King Pravahana of Panchala country Kaikeya King Asvapati (Chhandogya, 1. 8. V. 3, V. 11); King Pratardana (*Kaushi* Br, XXVI. 5) King Janasruti Sanatkumara (Chh. Up, IV. 1-3, VII. I); King Chitragengayani (*Kaushi* Up, II. I); King (*Chh.* IV. 2, 3); King Brihadratha (*Maitrayani* Up.) and King *Ajatasatrua* of Kasi (Bri. Up. II. 1, 1).

Most of these kings were so advanced in learing and spirituality that their teaching was eagerly sought by the most learned *Brahmana* scholars of the times. For instance, Janaka taught Yajnavalkya, Pravahana, Uddalaka and Svetaketu, father and son, who also sought instruction of King *Chitra, Ajatasatru* by his superior learning, humbled the pride of the Brahmana scholar Dripta-Baḷaki –Gargya. Even the learned Rishi *Narada* approached King Sanatkumara when the found that with a his knowledge of the Vedas, he was far from attaining the supreme knowledge of Brahman. The king plainly told him what he had so far learnt was mere '*Words*' and that he was only a *Mantravit* and not an *Atmavit.* He even condemned the Vedas as *Aparavidya* (Interior knowledge or Insight Knowledge) and not *Para-Vidya* (Supreme Knowledge) the Knowledge of *Atman.*

Subjects of Study

These are listed in *Chhandogya Upanished* (VII. 1). These included the four Vedas, *Itihasa* and *Purana*, described as fifth Veda, *Vyakarana*

(Grammar) described as Veda of Vedas, *Rasi* or science of numbers, *Nidhi* or *Mineralogy*, *Vakovakya, Tarkasastra* or Science of Logic, *Ekayana*, *Niti-Sastra* or Science of Ethics, *Brahma Vidya*, *Bhutavidya*, *Biology*, *Kshatra-Vidya*. Military Science *Nakshatra Vidya* Astronomy, or *Deva-jana-vidya* which may mean the arts and crafts (*Silpadi-vijnana*) and *Jana –vidya* taken as Ayurveda or Medicine. The *Atharvaveda* contains valuable medical material. Spiritual teachers from their individual experience and learning these thinkers had already identified the nature of human suffering as being spiritual, mental and physical. Now they proceeded to examine the means by which such suffering could be headed. They called their enquiries the *Ayurveda* or the 'Knowledge of Life.'[13]

Para-Vidya

But as has been pointed out, most of these Subject of Study counted as intermediate knowledge, *aparavidya* and even as a vidys except *Brahma-vidya* or knowledge of the Absolute Brahman or Atman specifed as *Paravidya* or Supreme Knowledge which cannot be attained "by intellect, by the Veda by much knowledge of books as stated in *Katha-Upanished* or by sacrifice, "for we sacrifice breath in speech and speech in breather" (*Aita. Aranyaka*, III. 2, 6). According tio the *Mundaka* (II. I), this Supreme Knowledge is to be attained by *tapas, sraddha, satya, brahmacharya* and *vidhi* of the *'Nam-History'*.

Yama and Nachiketas

The eligibility for highest knowledge was the conquest of desire. Yama, that strictest of teachers, was approached for His instruction by *Nachiketas*. But the god first tested him by tempting him with the gift of all a mortal could desire, offering him "sons and grandsons who shall live for 100 years, herds of cattle, elephant, horses, gold, sovereignty of the earth, fair maidens, and even control over death". But *Nachiketas* firmly answered "Keep Thou They horses, keep dance and song for Theyself ! No man can be made happy by wealth". Then God Yama had to admit: "I believe Nachiketas to be one who desires knowledge for even many pleasures did not tear him away" (Kath. Up.)

Ceremonial Religion

Side by side with this Religion of the *Vedanta* worshipping the One in the Many, there was the peopular religion made up of rituals arising from the *Karma-Kanda* of the Veda, as distinguished from the *Jnana Kanda* and *Upasana Kanda*, dealing respectivelu with Knowledge and Prayer. The elaboration of sacrificial religion and its rituals led to a growth of priesthood which now expanded from the *Rigvedic* Seven to Seventeen priests among whom there was division of labour in their performance. The chief of these were five (1) *Hotri,* (2) *Udgatri,* (3) *Adhvarya,* (4) *Brahman,*(5) *Sadasya,* the presiding priest, each with his staff of assistants.

In brief, but this sacrifical Religion is not without its significance. It origin is to be found as already expained in the *Purushasukta* of the *Rig veda* describing how creation originated in the *Virat-Purusha* sacrificing. His Cosmic Body as its material and breathing life in to it and sustaining it. So Man, made after God's image an emanation from Him also feels in him something of this original impulse for sacrifice by which the Worship his Deity by offering Him his chosen the things. Thus religion ultimately means self-sacrifice in support of one's faith. In *Vayakarana, Nirukta* and *Chhandas we* have the greatest works of Panini, *Yaska* and *Pingala.* A metrical work on *Jyotisha Vedanga* is extant, but it seems to belong to acomparatively late dated works of the 'Nam' or '*Chamar*' or '*Sudhras*'. By Charaka's time Ayurvedic science had already discussed and developed into eight specialized schools of medicine. Long before the birth of Christ, and millennia before the birth of European medicine, Ayurveda had specialists in the following fields: Psychiatry; Pediatrics; Gynecology, Nose and Throat; Opthamology; Surgery; Toxicology; Virility and Fertility[14] during the first century A.D.

Notes and References

1. *A.H.I.*, p. 41.
2. *Ibid.*, p. 42.
3. *R.V.V.R.*, p.109.
4. *A.H.I.*, p.37.
5. *Ibid.*, pp. 37-38.
6. *Ibid.*, p.39.
7. K.L. Khurana, op. cit. p. 49
8. *Tales of the Mystic East;* Bears, Reprint 2006; p. 127.
9. *A.H.I.*, p. 42.
10. B.N. Luniya; op. cit., p.55.
11. N.K. Duttt; *The Aryanisation of India.*
12. *R.K. Mookerji; Op. Cit., pp. 71-2.*
13. **Note:** The fundamental philosophy of *Ayurveda* says that suffering is disease, contentment is good health. No man is truly healthy who does not possess a sound body, a sound mind and a sound soul. This philosophy makes *Ayurveda* more than a school of medicine. Its logic prescribes a whole way of life, based on knowledge and an awareness that man is interdependent with all other forms of life. Spirit is described as the intelligence of life, matter as its energy. Both are manifestations of the principle of Brahman, on logic base study the Oneness of life. (*Naveen Patnaik*; op. cit., pp. 1-2).
14. Naveen Patnaik; *The Garden of Life;* New York; 1994; p. 3.

Plate-XVII

Fig. 24

Fig. 25

Fig. 26

Mohenjodaro Vessels
24. Riverine craft
25. A sea-going vessel
26. Reconstruction of Fig. 25

4

Post –Vedic History of Jammu Region

Post-Vedic Kingdom of the Jammu Region has been assumed that the Vedic age of the Aryans had reached the stage of excellence of Civilization in the world. In knowledge, power ands social organization, they had attained high degree of respect in this universe. The Vedic Age has been recognized as the age of *par excellence* in all walks of life and in all subsequent ages of the Indain history. An attempt has been made to elaborate the life of man to the conditions of the Vedic Age. In this period, it has been followed that all those things were valuable in the life of man, but '*Word*' or '*Nam*' is a Philosophy, Religion, same and even codes of conduct, *'Chamars'* were traced back to the *Vedic* period. In fact, the *Vedas* have left abiding monuments in all walks of life i.e., social, political, economic and religious life. All the attempts have been made to present some aspect of intellectual activities in Indian thinkers to some a great extent or to over the *Vedic* thought i.e., '*Nam*' or '*Chamar*'. The entire mythology of the post-Vedic period of the Brahmins, later on based on the Vedic history. "All the stories narrated by them in the later *Puranas* about *Vishnu*, *Siva* and India have their root in the *Vedic* mythology". All the philosophical system in Hinduism as well as in *Islamic thought* are representation of the *Vedic* conception of nature i.e., "*Nam*" or "*Chamar"* the goal of the man and his relation to the Universe. In fact, the philosophy of the *Vedas* was very synthetical and all-embracing its poetry. Even ordinary science like astronomy and medicine were associated with the Vedas. The entire Sanskrit literature of the post-Vedic period records the attempts of Ancient Indain historians to understand the Vedic Civilization of the '*Nam*', to revive the Vedic culture and to approximate their lives to the ideals of the Vedic Civilization based on *'Ravidas Culture'* in Indian history. These living manuscripts were respectively, Messers Bapuji Jivanram, Kesava Bhat bin Daji Bhat; and Ven Kan Bhatji, the last the most celebrated *Atharva Vaidika* in the *Dekkhan*[1] from the historical evidences to prove the authentic history of areas as '*Nam*' on earth.

Main Achievements of the Post-Vedic and Sutra Ages[2]

The organization of Hinduism is one of the principal achievements of the post-Vedic period, Hinduism is a systematized body of dogmas and doctrines, expounded in the later Vedic literature '*Word' the Brahamans*, the *Upanishads* and the *Aranyaka.* The doctrines about the soul (*Atama*) the Absolue (*Brahma*), relation between God and man, and the principles of *Karma, Maya, Mukti* transmigration of soul and other special features, that have dominated Hindu and Muslims thought and moulded the life of every Hindu and Muslims were evolved, stated and elaborated in the *Upanishads*. Its was not only the dectrinal basis of Hinduism and Mohammandanism that was established in the later Vedic times, but the social basis of both the Hindu and Muslims life was also firmly and solidly laid. The *Grihya Sutra* prescribed in the minutest the duties of man from birth to cremation the ceremonies for each occasion on the third (*Tithi*) of the third bright fortnight after his birth, in the morning the father has the child washed, including his head and after sunset, when the evening- red has disappeared, he worship(the moon), holding up his joined hand, then the mother, having dressed the son in a clean garment, hands him, from South to North, with his face turned to the north, to the father. She then passes behind his back and stations herself to the north (of her husband). He then murmurs (three versa) 'They heart, O thou whose hair is well parted (*MB*. 1,5, 10-12) and after he has with the words (standing at the end of verse 12) that this son may not come to harm (and thus be torn) from his mother[3], ceremonies at birth, naming, initiation, education, marriage, etc. This created demoestic rituals, had formulated the disciple of the households, and thus, transformed the pople of India into one single Hindu and Mulsim community. In fact, "it is the body of domestic rituals that make a Hindu and Mulism'. If the *Grihya sutra* created both the Hindu and Muslism community the *Dharmasutra* organized the Hindu and Muslim society on a conscious foundation on by laying down social customs, usages, codes and laws prescribed in various law books having 'no history' based on 'rites and ritual' as 'blind faith'.

In addition to the *Grihya Sutra* and the *Dharma sutra* equally important is the social doctrine of *Varnashrama Dharma* to gain the destructive power of the '*Nam*'. It was a social conception by virtue of which life was divided into four periods '*Word'* or '*Nam*' *Brahmacharya*, *Grihastha*, *Vanaprastha* and *Sannyas*. Every Hindu householder was to follow this ideal.

Another achievement of the later Vedic period is the development of the *Chatur varna* system or the Caste system, the priest (*Brahmana*) warrior (*Ksatriya)* peasant (*Vaisya)* and serf (*Sudhra*) were crystallizing throughout the period of *Rig-veda*. They have survived to the present day. The Sanskrit word was used for them '*Varna*' means '*Colour*[4]', but '*Varna*'or '*Word*' has no colour, he is *'Infinite*'. It was also an attempt related to the conscious organization of the Hindu and Muslim society and maintenance of the supremacy of the priestly class. In the historial evolution of India or *Bharata*, caste system became an institution of the social order did triumph, but at the expense of national unity and solidarity. Though, it proved the anti-thesis of nationality, it kept the balance of social forces and as a social fulcrum, it served its purpose well by writing the Constitution of India in the later stage of India or *Bharata* to understand the Brahmins idea of progress in history after the partition of India.

But the most important achievement of this period is the geographical conquest of India. In fact, the whole of India had been explored by the Archaeological Survey of India. The rivers, the mountains and the general physical features of every part of the Jammu Kigdom were known from the various study on the basis of historical evidences. But by the Epic Age to this period, the conquest of India was completed. The Vedic Aryans knew only the Indo-Gangetic valley. But the *Dharma Sutra* describe many different countries and local customs, and *Baudhayana* refers to the mixed character of castes in the Deccan, and in the times of the *Grihya Sutras* the geography of the country was perhaps completely known in India. The *Kailhas* peak, the Mana Sarovar lake, the Himalayas and the country on the northern side of the Himalayas were all known by the time of *Mahabharata*. The hermitages in the forest, mentioned in the Ramayana, must in due course have become colonies, where these are seen, he is known as *Brahmana*. If these characteristics are found in *Sudhra* and these do not exist in a twice-born person then the *Sudhra* is not a *Sudhra* and the so-called *Brahmana* is not a *Brahmana*. This approaches the teaching of the *Dhamnapda* verses 383, 393(*Yamhisatyam ca dhammo ca so Sukhi so ca brahmanah*). Similiarly in *Anusasana* 115 *Yudhisthira* asked *Bhisma*. 'You have often declared that *ahimsa* is the highest *dharma* and you also said that in *Sraddhas* the *Pitrs* desire to have flesh offered. Buddhist *Vihara* (*Vana* 188.56) had come into existence and *Edukas* (structures over the bones of the dead); are mentioned in *Vanaparva* (90, 65.67). A naked *Ksapanaka* (*Digambara* Jain) is mentioned in Adi 3. 126; in *Santi* 232, 21, the Jain position seems to have been alluded to and also in *Asvamedhika* 49.2. In *Adiparva* 70.46, it is stated that in Kanva's hermitage there were leaders of *Lokayatika* views along with students of *Vedas* and *Mokshadharma*.[5]

It is quoted a quarter of a verse stating that some person followed the *Pandava* hero with only a sword in his hand i.e. pen and Panini knows the central figures of the great Epic viz, *Yudhisthira* and *Arjuna*. It has been shown above that Panini flourished about 450 to 400 B.C. Therefore, it follows that there were poems *and Pandava* heroes and about *Krsna* killing *Kamsa* some time before 400 B.C. Scholars would have to assign 500 B.C. as the latest date for the core of the *Mahabharata*[6] centres from which the Hindu life and cultured radiated in the life. Slowly in due course the forest were cleared the rivers navigated and the land brought under cultivation and subsequently, the aborigines (*Barawalas*) were gradually assimilated into the social life of the *Mahabharata*. This method of Hinduization of the aboriginal tribes commenced in the later Vedic period and continues even to this day.[7] We meet with *Brahmans i.e.,* the sayings of *Brahmans*; with *Sutras* i.e. the strings of rules; with *Vedangas* i.e. preachngs with sastras i.e teachings; with *Darsanas*, i.e., demonstrations; but we never meet with a book, or a volume, or a page[8] in Aryan history.

The Legacy of the Aryans[9]

After describibg in the preceding pages the main feature of the Aryan Civilization in the Vedic age, and post Vedic it can be concluded thath the Aryans had enriched the Indian life and culture with their contributions. The gifts of the Aryans are summarized as follows:

1. Lofty Sense of Spirituality

The Aryans have given us lofty sense of spirituality which has sublimated even the non-Aryan elements in India. The Aryan conception of spiritually has been positive. The Aryan made original contribution in the field of religious beliefs. They perceived God in all, animate and inanimate. They emphasized that *Brahma* or God is the essence of the Universe. He has materialized in all existing things. He is the source and refuse of all lives. He is *sat* (truth) *chit* (spirit) and *ananda* (bliss). Besides the conception of omnipresent God, the Aryans initiated the theories of evolution, the doctrines of immortality of soul, *Karma*, reincarnation, *Avatars*, *Bhakti*, ritual, renunciation, *havan*, pilgrimage, etc. The validity of these beliefs is proved by their continued vitality, because countless generation in India have consciously sought to model their lives in the light of these doctrines. "They have enterned the warp and woof of Indian life to which they given a meaning and purpose".

The Aryans made original approaches to philosophical thought which are yet to be surpassed. Atheism, monism, pessimism and activism and six systems of philosophy have been their main contributions. These have helped substantially in the making of the Indian mind. The rich Aryan spiritual and religion have been saturating the, Indian culture, and people have been initiated into religion spirit from the beginning of life.

2. The Aryan Literature

The range of the Aryan literature is very wide. It includes diverse forms of expression as poetry, fable, drama, prose, romance and the science. Beginning with the first poetical flight in the *Rigveda*, the creative spirit of the Aryans produced great literary works like *Brahmanas, Samhitas, Aranyyakas, Upanishads, Sastras, Sutras, Ramayan, Mahabharata*, etc. In their literature, there are countless evidences of the spirit of systematization or the methodical arrangement of every branch of thought by a minute analysis of its parts. The *Sutra* literature is the best example of the scientific divison and orderly arrangement of rules with a rigid economy of words. Panini's grammar is another example of the most scientific treatment of a language. This has helped considerably in the orderly imagination in their literary and artistic creation as distinguished from extravagance, grotesquences or emotional abundance. They systematized all branches of science and arts in literature to bring out fully their inner and outer harmony. Their literary works reveal to us their eagerness to achieve perfection in all arts, their " synthetical outlook, refreshing approach and constructive imagination which has nothing of ludicrousness exaggeration and sensuousness'. Besides all this idea of the Indian culture have later on originated from this copious literature of the Aryans. They speak of their *Veda*, which means 'knowledge'. They speak of their *Sruti* which means what they have heard with their ears. They speak of *Smriti* which means what their fathers have declared unto them[10].

3. The Caste System and the Four Ashramas

Another important Aryan legacy is the social institution of *Caste System* and the *Varnashram Dharma*. The caste system was the grading of the people into mutually exclusion groups based upon differences of occupational functions and supposed heredity. It was also aimed to integrate many different races and individuals into one social whole and enable them to live together in harmony and find room for different stages of civilization with in one cultural unity. The *Varnashram Dharma* was the conception of the life in one sense peculiarly Aryan. It makes an attempt to combine materially with spirituality, worldly success with spiritual excellence. Every man must go through the fourfold stages of life. No aspect of human desire or function is overlooked her. The excellence which is sought must be realize through individual as well as social activites.

4. High Position to Women

Then comes the honour and high position that the Aryan assigned to women in society. They rejected feminist institutions like matriarchy and polyandry that prevailed in the pre-Aryan society. Since the head of the family was a man and every clan and family wanted men to protect it from its enemies, there was a tendency to set less value of women. The general opinion of the female sex seems to have been put into the month of *Indra*: 'Indra himself hath said, the mind of woman brooks not discipline. Her intellect hath little weight' (*Rig Veda* VIII. 33.17), and 'the hearts of women are those of hymns, (X. 95.15). From a very early date prostitution was an institution[11]

5. Sanskrit

Another Aryan legacy in Sanskrit which is considered as the most perfect and scientific language in the world, Scholars have made it the basis of the science of philology. It has deeply influence has gone so deep that scholars regard all Indian languages as variation from one common Sanskritic base. Even a language like Tamil, with a literature that was fairly developed before the advent of the Aryans, has not escaped this influence. The Sanskritic tradition has not faded with the passage of time. Now langeuages which came in the wake of new invaders, challenged its supremacy, but Sanskrit has held and perhaps depened its influence. As a result of this all Indian languages have large common vocabulary and exhibit marked similarities in grammatical structure. Prominent Indian languages like Hindi, Marathi, Gujarati, Bengali, etc. have originated from Sanskrit.

6. Rural Life

The Aryans were rural and pastoral in their lives. This made them lay out villages. In due course village becames an important unity of the social, economic and political life of the Aryans. Consquently, local self-government had well evolved in villages. Though centuries have lapsed trace of the Aryan culture are perceived mostly in villages.

7. Patriarchal Social System

An important legancy of the Aryans is the family and the partriarchal social system. Family became a significant unit of the society. It was fairly large, constituted as it was of partically three generations of paternal relations. The head of the family was the patriarch the eldest male member. He ruled over the family owned all family property and exacted obedience from all members of the family. He had to fulfil many obligations towards the different member of the family. The origin of the joint family institution, peculiar to India, is thus traced to the early Aryan family system. The *Saraswati-Indus Civilization* of the Jammu Region was their southern boundry during that period[12]

8. Lastly, the Instituation of Hermitages

Which was distinct alike from the city universities and celibate monasteries of Christian Europe, was another gift of the Aryans. Learned *Rishis* lived in these hermitages (*tapovans*) and they devoted their attention to the practice of virtue and the cultivation of knowledge. Many persons from cities and royal courts visited these *Rishis*. Students lived there for education. These hermitages served the purpose of universities and were very effectual for its promotion of Indian system of philosophy, ethics, theology and many branches of literature.They were, thus the true spring –head of Hindu Civilization and have maintained the unity and continuity of Indian culture.

The long gap between the Epic Age and the sixth century B.C. in Iindian history is filled with confusing and checkered chronological accounts of several dynasties. They are described in the *Puranas*, which form an encyclopaedia of religion, folklore, mythology, traditions and history. Though they are historically very important, yet their value is married to a great extent as history there in is mixed with religion and myth. A long way has yet to be covered before we construct a reliable political history till the sixth century B.C. The task is beset with difficulties. Moreover, we are concerned here not with the political history of the country, but with the main cultural currents. Therefore, we pass over the chronological accounts and come to the great religion movements of the sixth century B.C. that have deeply influened the continuity of Indian Culture and Civilization.

Age and Sources

The source of history for post-Vedic period are the Epics, the *Sutras* and the Law books. This period may be roughly taken to extend from about 1500 B.C. to 600 B.C. the time of the rise of Jainism and Buddhism.

The Epics Age

The sources of its history are firstly, the two Epics known as the *Ramayana* and *Mahabhárata*. The time of the history on which they are based is much earlier than that of their compositon as literary works. The story of *Ramayana* may be taken fundamentally as the story of conflict between Aryan and non-Aryan as reperesented in their leaders, Rama and Ravana, and the resulting extension of Aryan civilization towards the south as far as Ceylon. The *Mahabharata* present the whole of India under Aryan civilization and politically unified under the imperial sovereignty of *Yudhisthira* as a consequence of the great war of *Kurukshetra*, the contest for supremacy of the two rival powers the *Kurus* led by *Duryodhana* and the *Pandavas* by God *Krishna* in the absence of the father. With their respective allies who between them represented practically the whole of India. The date of this *Bharata* war may be roughly taken to be 1525 B.C. on the basis of the period of reigns assigned by the *Puranas* to the ruling dynasties that preceded the Maurya Dynasty which ruled from te known date of about 323 B.C. of the *Sudhra* Family.

The Sutras

The second source of history for the period is the literature of the *Sutras* which are written in a style based upon the utmost brevity. Their best and oldest example are Yaska's *Nirukta* and Panini's *Vyakaranan* known as *Ashtadhyayi* which is based on the usages of Vedic literature rather than classical Sanskrit and is accordingly, dated by many scholars such as Sir R.G. Bhandarkar to C. 750 B.C. while Macdonell (in his *India's Past*) does not consider it later than 500 B.C. The earliest *Sutras* were indeed, the six *Vedangas* the works auxillary to the Vedas, viz. (1) *Kalpa* (religious practice), (2) *Siksha* (phonetics), (3) *Vyakarana* (Grammar) (4) *Nirukta* (etymology), (5) *Chhandas* (metre), and (6) *Jyotisha* (astronomy). The works of Panini an *Yasks* are the best extent examples of *Vedanga* (3) and (4). The *Vedanga* called *Kalpa* gave rise to a vast literature made up of three classes; (1) *Srauta Sutras* dealing with ceremonies (2) *Grihya Sutras* dealing with household sacrifices (3) *Dharma –Sutras* dealing with customary law and practice. They are simply outline manuals for keeping alive in the pupil's momory the details of the subjects that they deal with the subjects of a Hindu Sanskrit students education.[13]

Epic India

Epic India knew of both system of government. Monarchical and Republican and both were based on extensive decentralization of administrative authority. At the bottom was the executive head of the village who was called *Gramani*. Above him in order were the head of 10, 20 and 100 villages, and all under the Adhipati, the Lord of 1000 villages.

There was also a considerable degree of self-government allowed to different groups, corporations or regions (*Janapada*) such as *Kula* (clan), *Jati* (caste), *Sreni* (guild), and *Puga* (the entire village community). A *Janapada* was to be governed by its own local laws and customs which the king had to recognize and enforce.

Republics

The *Mahabharata* (*Santiparva*) calls the Republic a *Gana* where authority vests in the many and known of a Union of Republics called *Samghata-Gana* or simply *Sangha*. Individual republics mentioned as prominent are those of *Andhakas.*, *Vrishnis, Yadavas, Kukuras,* and *Bhojas* each with its leader called *Isvara*. Thus *Akrura* with *Baladeva* was the leader of the *Bhojas* and *Ahuka* of *Yadavas*. The other great republican leaders mentioned are *Gada, Pradyumna, Samkarshana-Baladeva* and *Babhru-ugrasena*. These several Republics themselves in to a confederation or *Samgha* with Krishna as the Federal President. *Sangha-Mukhya*. A *Gana* was governed by a council of leaders known as *Gana-Mukhyas*.

The king's autocrarcy was checked by popular bodies, the *Mantri-Parishad* (council of ministers) and the *Sabha* (*Assembly of People*). The President of the Assembly is called *Sabhadhyaksha*. The council chamber is called *Mantra-Griha*.

The Epics distinguish 18 chief Officers of State called *Tirthas* such as *Mantri, Purohita, Yuvaraja, Chamupati* (Commander of the Army), *Pradeshta* (Chief Civil Judge), *Danda-pala* (Chief Criminal Judge), *Karya-nirmana –krit* (Engineer for construction, Chief Judge), *karya-nirmana krit* (Engineer for construction chief engineer for P.W.D.). *Nagaradhyaksha* (Mayor of the city).

India of the Sutras and Panini's Grammar (Sabda)

Panini's grammatical *Sutras* are a source of valuable historical material. The administrative division in a descending order are called (1) *Janapada* (2)*Vishaya* (3) *Nagara* and (4) *Grama*. The Republic is called a *Gana* and a Union of Republic a *Sangha*. The Gana was governed by a class of administration called *Rajanyas* who were all of the Kshatriya caste. Panini also applies the term *Sangha* for an individual Republic and mentions as example Kshudraka Malava and Yaudheya Sanghas described as *Ayudhajaivi Sanghas* i.e. Republic living by their profession of arms (IV. 2, 45; V. 3, 117.) Unions of Republic are also called *Sanghas* e.g. *Trigarta Sangha* of six republics (modern Kangra) and its adjoining states of the *Nanda* period of the *Sudhra Family* before the Maurya that state was called the *Dogra State*. (V. 3, 116) or *Adhaka Virshni-Sangha* (V, 3, 114). The working of the Republic was based on the party system. A party is called *Varga* and named after its leaders e.g. *Vasudeva –Vargya, Arjuma-Vargya* (IV, 3, 64). The Federal executive was made up of *Rajanya* leaders of the constituent Republic each with his own following of *Varga*, e.g. *Sini* and *Vasudeva* each with his rival *Varga*. The Kshudraks and Malavas pooled their individual military resources in a federal army called *Kshaudraka Malvai Sena* (1V. 2, 45).

Panini speaks of the Kings Council or *Parishad* as a source of his strength (*Parishadvalah* in V. 2, 112). A Government servant is called *Yukta* (VI. 2,66), the head of a department *Adhyaksha* (VI. 2, 7). The executive head of the administration is called *Vyavaharika*, while the Minister of finance ways and means is called *Aupavika* (V. 4, 34).

Panini gives some glimpses of education. Pupils are named after their teacher e.g. *Paniniyas* (VI. 2, 36) or after their subjects of study e.g. *Vedic Kratus*. *Ukthas* and *Sutras* (IV. 2, 59-60).

The ordinary teacher is called *Adhyapaka*, the teacher of Vedic recitation *Srotriya* and the specialist in the Vedic discourse (*pravachana*) *Pravakta* in history of *Mahabyiasa*. Panjab School of thought called *'Radha Swami'* of the period.

Girls were admitted to Vedic schools or *Charanas*. A Kathi was the female student of the Katha school of Vedic study. Female student had their own hostels called *Chhatrisalasa* (VI. 2, 60).

Panini also throws some light on the economic life of the times. He uses the term *Jansapada Vritti* (IV. 1, 42) or Urban occupations based on wages as sources of livehihood (*Vetanadibyo Jivati* in IV. 4, 12) under stipulated terms (*Parikrauana* in I. 4, 44). Wages were paid in both cash and kind (II. 2, 22).

There is reference to Money-lending (IV. 4, 31) and rate of interest of 10% by which 10 pieces of money lent would return as 11 (*Ib.* (*Kusida dasaikadasat*). The debt was called after the month period in which it was to be repaid (IV. 3, 47) e.g. *Agrahayanika* (IV. 3, 50) or *Samvatsarika* (*Ib*) and could be redeemed in kind e.g. barley (IV. 3, 48).

Crops were called after the month in which they were sown (IV. 3, 44-45) and field after the name of the crops grown e.g. fields of *vrihi, Sali, yava, tila, masha*, etc. (V.2., 2-4).

Panini has some references to weaving. *Avaya* (V.4, 160) is a term for the place where come and weave the cloth. There is mention of cloth fresh from the loom-'*tantradachirapaheite*' (V. 2, 70). Woollen cloth is called *urna* (IV. 3, 158) of the Meghavahana Family.

The following classes of coins are mentioned : *Karshapana* (V. 1, 29), *nishka* (V. 1, 20, 30), *pana* (V. 1, 34), *Pada masha* (V. 4,) and *sana* (a small copper coin).

Dharma –Sutras

The *Srauta Sutras* deal with religious sacrifices like *Havis* and *Soma* and do not give a picture of civilization as is presented in the *Grihya*-and *Dharma-Sutras*. The *Griha Sutras* deal with the ceremonies of domestic life marking all its turning points such as the state before birth, naming, first feeding, first learning, marriage, journey and death. A householder had to perform daily five great sacrifices (*Pancha-Mahayajnas*) as a course of religious training, viz,. sacrifice to (1) *Brahman* in the form of study and teaching, (2) *Pitris* by *tarpana,* (3) Gods (*devas*) by oblations, (4) *Bhutas* (created beings) by the offering of *bali,* and (5) fellowmen (*Nri*) by entertainment of guests. The idea is that religion is a process of self-expansion by which the individual gradually approximates to the universal by worshipping (1) the Deity of his devotion (2) the family or lineage whose status is in the keeping (3) the fathers of learing to whom he owes his intellectual legacy and cultural heritage which he must extend by his own contributions; (4) the guest as a symbol of humanity so as to cultivate the source of universal the sense of the underlying unity of life as such. By these five kinds of daily religious exercise, the individual expends in to the Universal.

Varnasrama Dharma

These *Sutras* describe the social system which is based on what is known as *Varnasrama dharma* based on a horizontal division of life in to *Varnas* or Castes and vertical division in to *asramas* or stages. These are distinguished by the occupation assigned to them.

Castes

The first three castes, *Brahmana, Kshatriya* and *Vaisya* have the following duties in common viz (1) *Adhyayana* (study) (2), *Ijya* (sacrifice), and (3) *Dana* (charity) through Nam-dan mantra otherwise class-struggle theory is there.

Each caste is marked out by duties special and specified for each.

A Brahmana has the following prescribed duties viz, (1) *Pravachana* (teaching), (2) *Yajna* (conducting sacrifice or *Yajna*) and (3) *Pratigraha* (receiving gifts, offered spontaneously and respectfully in recognition of their work and worth, as source of their livelihood).

The Duties special to the Kshatriya are the following : (1) *Sarva-bhuta-rakshanam* (protection of all created beings), (2) *Nyayadandatvam* (righteous rule), (3) Partronage of learned men (*Srotriyas*) (4) Relief of non-Brahmins in distress, (5) Supporting non-Brahmin ascetic (*akara*) and those serving the public (*upakurvanah*) such as physicians, (6) (Preparedness for war (*yogascha vijasye*), (7) March through the country (*charya= rashtraasya sarvato ataman*) with his army (*Rathadhanur bhyyam*), (8) Firm stand to death in battle without retreating thereform (*Samgrame samsthana-manivrittischa*) (9) Leavy of just taxes for defence of the realm (*tadrakshana dharmitvat*).

The *Vaisya* is known for the following special duties or occuptions: (1) *Krishi* (*Agriculture*), (2) *Vanijya* (Trader), (3) *Pasupalya* (Cattle-rearing), (4) *Kusida* (Banking).

The following functions are assigned to the Sudhra: (1) Practice of purity, truthfulness and humility, (2) Bath without reciting the *achamana-mantra* prescribed for the higher castes; (3) *Sraddhakarma* (performance of funeral rites for which they are eligible), (4) *Bhritya-bharanam* (support of dependents as duty not prescribed for salves), (5) *Svadara vritti* (continence), (6) Menial service (*paricharya*) on wage (*vritti*), (7) pursuit of independent occupations (*silpavritti*), such as those barber, washerman, painter, carpenter or blacksmith."

The status of the *Sudhra* was not that of unmitigated degradation. For instance, his master was entrusted with the duty of supporting him if disable for work, while he on his turn was given the privilege of supporting his master in distress, there by showing that it is contemplated that the *Sudhra* could be a man of means and had a right to property. The pious *Sudhra* is also given the right to recite the *Namas Kara Mantra* and perform *Pakayajnas*.

The Asramas

While society is divided into castres, there is a unity among all the castes under a scheme which divine the life of every individual into four stages through which it must pass. Each such stage is called an *Asrama*. Life is viewed as having a normal length of 100 years split up into four equal divison of 25 years each. These four division or *Asrama* are those of (1) *Brahmachari* (student), (2) *Grihastha* (Householder), (3) *Bhikshu* (Ascetic), (4) *Vaikhanasa* also called *Parivrajaka* or *Sannyasi*.

The texts mention the duties attaching to each of the *Asramas*.

The *Brahmachari* is marked by his living with his teacher and is of two classes, (a) *Upakurvana* i.e., a student for a limited period after whch he marries and settles down as a householder (b) *Naishthika* i.e. one who remains a student through life in his *Nishtha* or devotion to learning and lives a life of celebacy.

The *Grihastha's* main duties are (a) *yajna* (b) *adhyayana,* (c) *dana.*

The *Bhikshu* or ascetic must be (1) *A-nichaya* (not hoarding things); (2) *Urddhareta* (continent) (3) fixed to one place in rains; (4) visiting a village only for begging and that only after the villagers have finished their meals or when there is no refusal of alms, with out inducing them to give alms by any blessing in return (5) should wear loin cloth (*Kaupia*) or old rag (*prahina*) duty washed (*nirniya*) to cover nakedness (*achchhadanartham*); (6) should not partake of fruits or leaves by plucking them and injuring plant –life; (7) should not out of season (i.e. *after rains*), dwell for a second night in the same village, and (8) should not kill seeds to sustain his own life (e.g. pounding seeds like raw by a pestle) but should accept as alms only cooked food in charity toward all (*samobhuteshu*) and indifference to injure or gain.

The life of the hermit in the fouth *Asrama* is more ruster. He is to live in the forest subsisting on raw roots and fruit (and not cooked food). He must not live on ploughed land nor enter a village nor store up food should his hairs grow (as *a jatila*) and wear only bark and skin (*chirajina*) (*Gautama*, III and X).

Apastamba (II. 9, 21,13) gives a fine description of the *Sannyasi* or *Parivrajaka* as one who "abandoning truth and falsehood, pleasure and plain the Vedas, the world and the next seeks only the *Atman*".

It may be noted that the four typical *Dharma-Sutras* are whose of *Gautama, Baudhayana, Apastamba* and *Vasistha* assigned to the period 600-300 B.C. These give a concreate of India civilization which attained its normal form that age and are thus described in term's flaws and institution.

It is to be noted these serval legal authorities sometime differ as to the laws they lay down. A glaring instance seen as to practice of usury. Gautama allows is to a Berahmana as calling if it is conducted through an Agent (X, 6) also allows Brahmins the occupation of Agriculture and Trade through their agents. These rulers which thus allow Brahmins to be gentlemen farmers and sleeping partners in mercantile or banking firms managed by Vaisyas do not occur in other *Smritis*. (Buhler. SBE, II. 228, n). Apastamba prescribes a penance against usury, while *Baudhayana* treats a Brahmin usurer as *Sudhra*.

Baudhayana points out how the North and South are divided socially. He mentions the South Indian custom of marrying the maternal uncles daughter or of a paternal aunt (I. 7, f), whlie the customs peculiar to the North and condemned in the South were "to follow the trade of arms to deal with wool and to go to sea" (II. 1, 2, 2).

The Law-Books show how different groups and communities were left to legislate for themselves. Thus there were the local laws peculiar to regions and countries (*Janapadas*), those framed by castes (*Jati*), Clans (*Kula*), and Guilds or Industrial corporations (*Srenis*). Medhatithi instances the special laws and customs like *Kuru*, *Kapisa* (Northern Afghanistan) and *Kasmra* prevailing in those days. Gautama (XI, 21) instances the screnis of 'cultivators, herdsmen, traders, money –lenders and artisans', all organized in to their respective self-legislating corporations.

The limits of taxation are indicated "one –tenth, one eigth, or one-sixth of agricultural produce, one-days work per month from artisans, one –twentieth on merchandise; one-fiftieth on cattle and gold; and one-sixtieth on roots, fruits, flowers herbs, honey meat, grass and firwood. (Gautama, XI. 1, f, X. 25, f).

The general outlook of life was somewhat restricted under injunctions forbidding sea-voyages, visit to foreign place or the learning of a language spoken by barbarians (*Mlechchhas*) (Apastamba 1. 32, 18, Vasishtha, VI. 4)[14].

In short, the classes of literary works named above are alone classed as *Sruti* or revelation and constitute the Vedic literature proper. The *Vedangas* are six in number viz, *siksha* (phonetics), *kalpa* (ritual), *vyakarans* (grammar), *Nirukta* (etymology), *chhandar* (metrics), and *jyothisha* (astronomy). These subject are already mentioned in some of the *Upanishads*, through the extant manuals may belong to much later Vedic period. The manuals of *Siksha* deal with the correct pronunciation and accentuation of the Vedic hynms. The productions of the *Siksha* school included the "connected text" of the *Rigveda* as well as the "*Word text*" which gives the text of the verses in a complete grammatical analysis. But the most remarkable compostion of the *Siksha* class are the *Pratisakhya Sutras* which the *Samhita –patha* (connected text) can be formed from the *Pada-patha* (Word-text) or Grammar text. In this way, the treatises on *Kalpa* or ritual include the *Srauta Sutras* which laid down rules for the performance of the great sacrifics, the *Grihya Sutra*s which give direction for the simple ceremonies of daily life and the *Dharma sastra* which deal with sacred and secular law and administration. As integral parts of the *Srauta Sutras* are found compositions styed *Sulva Sutras,* which lay down rules for the measurement and building of the place of sacrifice and the fire – altars and are the oldest treatises on Indian geometry of the Jammu Kingdom which supplementary to the *Kalpa Sutras* styled *Parisshtes* or addenda of the '*Nam*' to the '*Charmer Dynasty*'of this region, based on the historical facts 'R*avidas Culture*' in future course of action and deeds are '*Untouchables*' in the life of Brahmins, as a working class of the period. 'Mind is our enemy i.e. *Brahmin* or *Molavi* and its movements should be watched[15], because cheater of the *'Nam-History'* deserves punishment i.e., hell or *Narak.*

Notes and References

1. Maurice Bloomfield; *The Religion of the Veda;* pp. 21-2 **Note.** He holds the Vedic tradition is in this respect the most remarkable in recorded history.
2. K.M. Panikkar, *A Survey of Indian History,* Chapter II.
3. *The Griyha-Sutras;* Tr, by H.Oldenberg and F. Max Muller, New Delhi; 1990, pp. 4-5., *Kandika 8.*
4. *W.T.W.I., p.*35.
5. P.V.Kane, *History of Dharmasastra;* Vol, I, Poona,1968, p. 365.
6. *Ibid.*, p. 366.
7. B.N. Luniya., op. cit., p. 87.
8. Max Muller, *Ancient Sanskrit Literature;* p. 512.
9. Jadunath Sarkar; *India Through the Age*, New Delhi, p. 9.
10. R.K. Mookerji; *Ancient India;* p. 497.

11. *R.V.V.R.*, pp.13-4.
12. *Ibid.*, p.4 **Note** : The Aryans in India were in the neighbourhood of the Sindhu in the area of Jammu and Kashmir State, the modern Indus area of the Chenab river which after receiving the waters of its tributaries is so wide that people can see the one country to another in trade relation with the development of 'New Idea' of the Man and his history, a definite bridge of the modern style have been constructed over the Chenab Valley of Akhnoor at *Ambarana.* It makes dear from the study that modern Jumna, and made their way to the Ganges, the Aryans dwelt mainly in East Kabulistan and the Panjab that there were in the land, there is little information in the hymns of the Aryans and the science of ethnology has to help us to form the idea of it development in the human history from one generation to another. Aryans as the tribes of the North and grew into the powerful and civilized Tamil and Telugu nations, but there is no hint of this in the *Rig-Veda* (Ibid., pp.4, 5, 6)
13. **Note:** A.C. Clayton and Farquhar, are mentioned 'member of the body' of the Veda i.e. Called *Vedangas* having six *Kalpa*, ceremonial, is the most important including three groups of *Sutras*: The *Sranta* Sutras, deal with sacrifices, summarizing the teaching of the *Brahmanas*; the *Grihya* or *Smarta Sutras*, which provide rules of conduct for the various classes of men and the various stages of their life, and these *sutras* cannot help the understanding of the Early Aryan Faith except from the *Chamar* history. (*Primer of Hinduism*, p. 59).
14. R.K Mookerji, *Ancient India.*
15. *Tales of the Mystic East; Beas*, Reprint, 2006 p.184.

5

Religious Movements in Jammu Areas

Hinduism held its powerful sway over the entire *India* for a long period of Indian history, but with the passage of time the society came to be divided by some unhealthy dogmas. People failed to adjust to such an atmosphere of equilibrum. Moreover the supermacy of the '*Brahminical Ideology*' and the deplorable condition of the *Sudhras* or *Untouchables* gave an impetus to the rise of "New Religions" of the *'Nam Society'* which were in fact, the off shoots of Hinduism have been proved that they have no history, but later on toòk the shape of independent religion which were developed from times to times in *True* form, sometimes appeared Buddhism and Jainism in the Indian history. Akhnoor area in Jammu Region was the only site in Jammu and Kashmir, where relics of *Kushana and the Mauryan* period were discovered during Archaeoloical Survey of India. Buddhism had been one of its prominent seats in the Kashmir Valley. The remains of Buddhist settlement in the vicinity of the Jammu Region are not suppressing in the history of India. Ancient *Sakala* (now Sialkot) hardly 50 km. away from Akhnoor town was the capital of Indo-Greek King *Manendara*, who won the faith of Buddhism by celebrating *Nagas* as chief monk in the 2nd century B.C. the name *Nageni* of Paddar now in Kishtwar District having the Inscription on *Trishul at Sudha Mahadeva* in Udhampur District near Chenani bears striking resemblance to the great Buddhist teacher *Nagasena* of the Gupta period[1]. From this (that is perhaps, the vicinity of the capital of Kashmir) the pilgrim traveled, *Yuan Chwang,* tell us through a difficult mountainous Districts, South-West for above 700 *li* to the *Pan- nu-ts'o* - (P*unch*) country. This region, he described as being above 2000 *li* in circuit, as abounding in hills and mountain valleys with narrow area of cultivation. The country yield grain and flowers sugarcane and fruits excepts grapes, abounded. The country produced mango, the fig. (here called the *Udumbara*), and the plaintain and these trees were grown in orchards near the dwelling houses. The climate was hot, the people were daring and straight – forward, they wore chiefly cotton clothing, and they were sincere believers in Buddhism. The Buddhist monasteries of which there were five, were in a ruinous condition and the country was a dependency of Kashmir. In a monastery to the North of the capital were a few Brethren and to the north of this was a wonder working tope made of stone.[2] Our pilgrim goes on to relate that from Punch an ancient name *Prontsa*, a journey South-East of above 400 *li* brought him to the *Ho-lo-she-pu-to* (*Rajapura*) country. This he described as being above *4000 li in* circuit its capital being above ten *li* in circuit. It was difficult country to travel in as it was very hilly with narrow in Valley, if was not fertile and it resembled Punch in products and climate and like that country it had no sovereign of its own and was subject to Kashmir. There were ten Buddhist monasteries and the Brethren were few in number, there was one Deve-Temple, but the non-Buddhists were very numerous.[3] So far the people from *Lampa* to *Rajapura* (Rajouri) the inhabitant are coarse and plain in personal appearance of rude violent dispositions, with vulgar dialects and of scant courtesy and little fairness; they do not belong to India or *Bharata* proper, but they were inferior people of frontier (i.e., barbarian) stocks[4] (*See Plate XVIII, Buddhism in Kashmir a Learning Centre;* Fig. 27), and (Shiva Shrine in Sudhamaha Deva; Fig. 28).

The Buddhist establishment at *Ambaran* in Akhnoor was seems to have come up during the *Kushana* Period (Ist to 3rd century A.D.) was on the trade route of ancient Buddhist period from *Patliputra* (now Patana in Bihar) to *Taxila*.The width of the river Chenab is narrow that is why the Buddhist settlement was established across the river at *Ambaran* and also served a platform for further expansion of Buddhism in the Jammu region. The site of *Ambaram* had been the attractive site during the development of new religion of the '*Sudhra Dynasty*' of the '*Chamar*' *Community* which was based on '*Ravidas Culture*'. During the *Kushana* period, as it was an important Buddhist circuit of India or *Bharat* outside the Patan in Bihar and Uttar Pardesh. The site is located near the bridge which is being constructed across the Chenab River in Akhnoor town[5] of the Jammu Area.

Change in Vedic Religion

The Vedic religion of the Jammu area was not a complex religion because all people had to follow it due to its simpilicty. But with the passage of the time the Vedic religion was trapped into many complexities and numbers of problems like 'Caste System', '*Untouchability*', etc. were cropped up in it. The rites and ritual ceremonies had became so expensive that it was not possible for a common man to cope with the " power and status" in the society which was based on only ecomomic matters obtained from corrupt ways. Moreover, the priestly class including certain *Sudhras* had established its unnecessary authority by obtaining bureaucrat in self –style manners or in Brahminical Ideology. Common people, therefore, were curshed badly under their guidelines under the heavy burden of rite and rituals. Thus, the selfish attitude of the Brahminical people, known as *Bhudeva* the god on earth from the background for the rise of Jainism and Buddhism was developed during the word *Maya* or illusion, in the *Rig-Veda* generally denotes, 'Occult Power' applicable in a good sense to gods and in a bad sense to demons and may be rendered by English word "Craft", having a similar double application[5] to certain peoples who used to believe in the theory of mind not on God.

The sixth century B.C. witnessed a great religious ferment in the world. It was during this age that there prevailed in society, general, spiritual and moral unrest and consequently, reformers all over the world raised their voice against the existing religious order and endeavoured to reconstruct it on new basis. In the Greek Island of *Ionia, Heraclitus* preached his new doctrines, In Iran, Zoroaster launched this protest against the prevailing religious superstitions and in China, people welcomed the philosophic teachings of Confucius who gave them a higher conception of the duties of life. It was an age when people in India were disgusted with old philosophical dogmas and were striving for simple method of worship and easier means of escape from the ills of this mundane existence. New leaders of thought and religion sprang in to vigorous activites and gave a new orientation to life in this country. It was an era of revolt '*Chamar*' an age of protest against the old order of thing established by the Jammuite Brahmins. The revolt was against the standardization of social patterns, the ritualistic form of religion, the absolute power of the priest craft and the dead weigth of dead culture. The new philosophy of revolt was anti-social in form and anti-caste in spirit. It preached pure individualism and spiritualization. It discarded the principal of social immobility, inequality and injustice, it upheld the sancity of human intellect and its freedom. It stood for man and woman to achieve his or her salvation as human beings. The ultimate aim of the revolt was not materialistic but spirtitual, not the socialization, but the spiritualization of life. The spirit of times expressed itself in a number of reforming movements. Humanitarian and theistic movements gathered force and momentum as popular faith in animal sacrifice and barren rituals tended to diminish. These movement judged human progress in terms of spiritual advancement of man. Life was regarded not an end, but a means and an idea for spiritualization. The thinkers of the new movements were pure intellectualist '*Word*' philosophers '*Chamars*' and conceived life as a philosophy of Power and Knowledge. Outside the Brahmanical Holy Land Spiritual leadership passed from the hands of priestly theologians and sacrificers to ascetics and wanderers (*Sramanas*, *Parivrajaks*) who laid the greatest emphasis on the cessation of craving for the things of the world. These ascetics and wandering teacher rejected the authority of the Vedas and Vedic priest denounced blood sacrifices which constituted a very large part of the Brahmanic ritual and even denied the existence of God. Right conduct they declared was the only way of getting out of the meshes of *Karma* and *Samskara*. The right conduct included among other things the practice of *Ahimsa* or non-injury to living beings. The greatest of these wandering teachers were Kshatriya princes *'Nam' Vardhaman Mahavir* and *Gautam Buddha*. The philosophy and the ideologies of the former took the shape of a reforming movement known as Jainism, while those of the latter led to another movement called Buddhism. Like King Luther and Calvin of Europe, Mahavir and Gautam Buddha protested against the corruption that had crept into Hinduism. Their movement both Jainsim and Buddhism, Brahmins are protestant Hinduism as Lutherism and Calvinism are Protestant Chistianity. Jainism never went beyond the confines of India or *Bharata*, but it still remains the religion of a wealthy community. Buddhism, extinct in the land of its birth after a glorious career of more than fifteen hundred years, remains to this day one of the greatest spiritual forces of the world is working in the area of Jammu and Punjab or *Madradesa* during the early period of Indian history.

Original Jainism and Buddhism

As noted above, Jainism and Buddhism were the reformation movement of Hinduism. They were not a creed but "an appeal for holier living in the bosom of the existing Hindu religion and society.' Both urged the common folk to give up their vices and follies and inspired them to practise purity of conduct in daily life. Both took their stand on certain aspects of the pre-existing religious systems. *Vardhaman Mahavir* emphasized ascetism and self-mortification references to which are observed in the *Vedas* the *Aranyakas* and the *Upanishads*. If the *Upanishads* recommend retirement into forest or hermitages to seek the highest Divine Knowledge, the *Smritis* lay emphasis on *Sannyas* (renunciation and ascetism) as the last phase of a man life. Similary, the basis doctrines of Buddhism as preached by Lord Buddha have their roots in the pre-exiting Hindu philosophy of the *Sankhya* system and the later *Upanishads*. Jainism, Buddhism and the *Sankhya Yoga* philosophy which goes back to the primitive currents of religious and philosophical speculation

'*Word*' all the of misery no trace of which is to be found in the optimastic attitude of the Vedic Aryans. The doctrine of transmigration unknown to the early Brahmans, suddenly emerges in *Upanishads* and forms and essential element in Jainism, Buddhism and *Sankhya Yoga*. This doctrine of transmigration is associated with the doctrine of *Karma*, and the most primitive idea of *Karma* are found in Jain metaphysics. An atheistic attitude and a kind of dualism between spirit and matter characterize all these three system of religious thought[7]. The *Ashtanga Marga* or the eightfold path, enjoined by Lord Buddha for extinguishing the earthy miseries of soul, caused by the cycle of birth and deaths, is only a code of general ethics and not the special creed of a new revealed and distinct faith[8]. Instead of inventing a complete new code of morality, Buddha urged the people to follow the morals and virtues of the old *Rishis* or saints. Except certain prohibitions and duties that he laid down for monks and nuns, he adopted many articles of morality and pious customs of the Brahmanistic code[9]. We are told in the *Jataka* tales that Lord Buddha explained to the people repeatedly that true piety consists not in the performance of elaborate rituals or repetitions of he complicated prayers but in leading a pious life. Buddha did not lay down particular dogmas or special rituals for his followers. Even the doctrine of *Ahimsa* or the non-violence was known to the people in the postVedic period.

Without admitting the existemce of the soul, Buddhism accepted the *Upanishadic* theory of *Karma*, that is the inevitability of the effects of deeds in regulating future births. The theories that the worldly existence is full of misery and that the cessation of worldly existence must be sought for, were also inherited by the Buddhists from the previous thinkers.

Again, it is wrong to say that both Jainism and Buddhism instituted new orders of monks and nuns. There existed before Jainism and Buddhism organized groups of ascetics having their own codes of discipline as is evidence from the *Bhikshu Sutrasa*. Both thses reformation movement s have been reputed for fostering the spirit of scientific inquiry intellectual discussion before acception a brlief blindly. But this was not a new development in the later Vedic period. We have references to some famous discussions and intellectual discussions and debates in the *Upanishads*. Raja *Janaka* used to initate such intellectual discussion. Thus, Jainism and Buddhism did not diverge from the main streams of Hinduism. In fact, they represent a significant phase in the religious life and cultural development an important attempt to reform the spiritual life of India on the pattern of 'New Society' already mention in the previous study. i.e., *Chamar* or *'Radha Soami'* as a 'New Thought of the Society' as it was *Jainism* and *Buddhism* in Indian history.

Rise of the New Religious Movements

The following are the condition that favoured the rise and growth of the new religious sects both Jainism and Buddhism became Brahmins in this country.

1. Burden of the Ritualism

By the sixth centry B.C. the Vedic philosophy and religion lost their original purity and had decayed in cumbrous, meaningless rituals. The rities and ceremonies were made so elaborate and expensive that they were no longer with in the reach of the average man. People, therefore, groaned under the heavy burden of ceremonial rituals.

2. Belief in Mantras

If the Vedic religion had degenerated into ritualism the spiritual outlook of the masses was burdend with superstition. The *Vedic* hymns were replaced by *mantras* of the *'Nam -dana'* formula of the Living Master which were supposed to posses divine powers. It was popularly believed that the recital of the *mantras* could cure people of diseases, bring victory or defeat in war assure prosperity of a state or the destruction of its enemies silence the arguments of an opponent even stop cought and promote the growth of hair etc. In short, the *mantras* embodied in themselves the Universe. There was no place of daily life great or small, which could not but be affected by them for better, or for worse.[10]

3. Sacrifices

The Aryan belief in the divine power of sacrifice was much exploited by the priestly class. The actual killing and sacrifice of living animals and sometimes even human beings on certain ceremonial occasions created a feeling of revolt and contempt against such things in the minds of many. Besides the great public ceremonies like *Abhisheka* and *Asvamedha* which drained the coffers of the state, there were many household rites for which the services of the *Brahmanas* were necessary. These practices were very revolting. They turned the people against not only the Brahmanas, but also the system that they represented the old rule of the '*Nam*' or '*Ravidas Culture'*

4. Intellectual Confusion due to the Theory of Karma, Jnana and Tapas Margas

While people in disgust were eager to seek some solution for these ills, minds of many were stirred by complex problems of life and death and they strove to find a means by which the soul could be rescued from the unending miserable plight of life. Different means were advocated to attain this end. The priestly classes emphasized the efficacy of the performance of serval ceremomines and sacreaments (*Samskaras*) for a person who wished to obtain the cherished deliverance of his soul. This was styled as *Karma Marga*. But the *Karma Marga* was not regarded as the only means of salvation. Soon there developed the doctrine of *tapas* or self mortification as a means of self-realization. The underlying idea was to enable a man to practsie austerities in the forest to subdue physical sense and develop the facult of concentrating upon the realization of the Supremen Spirit. It was supposed that even the gods submitted to a person who subdued his passions and practised penance in the seclusion of forest are in vain in the 'Brahminical Ideology.'

While the Karma Marga and the Tapas

Marga were growing popular with the average man, the intellectual section of the people convinced that deliverance or *Moksha* could be attained by the *Jnana Marga* (True Knowledge). They emphasized utmost the doctrine that 'he who knows god, attains to God, nay, he is God." Soul, in fact, is an integral part of God. It is from God,in God,and of God,and God so it must merge in God. Its absorption in God was essential for man's spiritual salvation and eternal bliss. They, therefore, discarded the *Karma* and the *Tapas Margas*, and followed the idea of Living Master.

5. The Supremacy of the Brahmanas

These conflicting views for the attainment of *Moksha* (deliverance) created unrest and confusion in the moral and spiritual world. Besides this intellectual confusion, there was existing the growing monopoly of the unscrupulous and exacting priestly class. Their galling dominance disgusted the masses. They claimed to be the leading exponents of the Vedic tradition. They were endless and elaborate sacrifice rites which required their presence. They dominated every aspect of the life of the Aryans, right form birth to death. There was no escape from their guardanship and the priestly craft. Even the work of the government was executed by them. The *Kshatriya* princes or rulers of the ages were guided and supervise by the Brahmana councilors who did had monopolized all powers and offices in the State of Jammu region have been governed without logic conclusion of life, only the follower of '*Blind Faith*'. They enjoyed special privilege and powers and considered themselves superior over the rest of the people in society. But people were no longer in a mood to accept this, because it was based on 'blind faith having no Scientific Knowledge as *Chamar* had.

6. The Caste System

The caste system had developed its rigidity and vigour and its fetters were becoming tighter. Change from one caste to another was becoming impossible. The members of the low caste had to face a very miserable plight. They were treated with contempt. Moreover, the current usages which forbade the depressed and down-trodden and the non-Brahmana castes from taking to the ascetic life or following the *Tapas Marga* added the the resentment of the people against prevailing Brahmanism based on 'No History', only backbiting.

Several leading teachers and scholars voiced the spirit of the time and founded religious sects, each of which sought to provide spiritual repast for all and find an easy, simple and practicably ways to obtain deliverance for the soul from its unending pilgrimage. These sect or religious movement, according to the Pali works were no less than sixty –two and according to the Jain texts their number was more than three hundred. The Buddhist canonical work, *Anguttara Nikaya* (fourth-third centries B.C.), refers to religiouis sects as, *Ajivika*, *Nirgrantha* (Jain), *Munda-Sravaka*, *Jatilaka*, *Parivavrajaka*, *Magandika*, *Traidandika*, *Aciruddhaka*,*Gautamaka* (Buddhist), and *Devadharmika*. The philosophy of *Pratyabhiyna, Citi',* which is absolute consciousness, by its own free will (*Svatantrya*), is the cause of manifestation, preservation, and again re-absorption or withdrawal of the Universe into itself. This is a description of Godhead, and before time and space are created for the establishment of 'New Society of the 'Nam' or God, Citi alone is. It is all knowing, (omniscient) and all powerful, (omnipotent). By her own power, she unfolds the universe on her own screen i.e., *Parvati* of the Lord Siva. This is a direct statement of the understanding of Jammu and Kashmir Shivaism, that God is both the efficient in man and woman, as well as material causes of the Universe. He creates out of his own will, on his ownself, he is the *potter* who creates out of himself, not out of clay. That Universe, so unfolded, is manifold, consisting of many subjects, who are objects for the others in reciprocal differentiation. The potter was one, but the pots are many. The various pots, though coming from the same source, and thus essentially. The same, are different from the other like one is a conical pot, the other rounded the third triangular and so on. Or, simply that even through we are all essentially the same but still no two people are alike Thus, the identity of the Oneness of Citi has been veiled of the Divine Nature (*Vilaya*) by *malas* of the *'Nam' or God,* and *anugraha* (revelation) of the Divine by grace that consciousness of self[11]. The *Mahaniddesa* and *Chullaniddesa* (Buddhist canonical commentaries of the second –first centuries B.C.) refer to the *Ajivikas*, *Nirgrantham*, *Jatilaka*, *Parivrajak* and *Aviruddaka,* along with the worshipers of elephant, horse, cow, dog, crow, *Vasudeva, Baladeva, Pura bhadra, Manibhadra, Agni,* the *Nagas* the *Yakshas* the *Asuras*, the *Gandharvas, the Maharajas, Chandra, Surya, Indra, Braham, Deva Dik.* These lists indicate the existence side by side with well-known religious sect of a bewildering variety of primitive faiths and popular cults. Of these sects, cults and movement two alone '*Jat*' Jainism and Buddhism. '*Chamar*' survived the rest had disappeared with the lapse of time.

Jainism[12]

Antiquity of Jainism

The orign of Jainism is shrouded in mystery. In the *Rigvedic mantras,* there are clear references to *Rishabha* and *Arishtanemi*, two of the Jain *Tirthankaras*, the former being the founder of Jainism. The story of *Rishabha* occurs also in the *Vishnupurana* as the *Bhagvatpurana* where he figure aas an *Avatar* (incarnation) of Narayana. All this indicates that Jainism is as old as the Vedic religion if not older.[13] The Jains believe that it is the outcome of the teachings of the twenty-four *Tirthakaras* or prophets or Saints, all Kshatriyas, coming one after the other. The first twenty-two *Tirthankaras* are so lengendary in character that it is hardly possible to say anything about them. The twenty-third *Tirthankara*, named Parsvanth, who lived 250 years before *Vardhaman Mahavir* seems to have been a real historial personage. He was the son of King *Asvasen* of Varanasi, but he abandoned the royal state in favoure of spiritual life. His main teaching were non-injury, non-lying (not to tell lies) non-stealing and non-possession. *Parsvanath* seems to have left a well formed organization behind him. The parents of *Vardhaman Mahavir* and the members of his family were the followers of *Parsvanath's* religion and naturally *Mahavir* too, was influenced by the Jain doctrines in his youth. The next and the ast *Tirthankara* was *Vardhaman Mahavir* himself equivalent to *Al-Mansura*, a book written after the death of Prophet.

Vardhaman Mahavira (599-527B.C.).

Vardhaman Mahavir was born in Kundagrama, a suburb of Vaisali (modern Muzaffarpur district in Bihar) in 599 B.C. in a rich Kshatriya family. His father Siddartha was the head of a Kshatriya clan called the *Jnatrikas* and his mother *Trishala* was the sister of *Chetaka* the most famous Lichchhavi prince and ruler of Vaisali. As king Bimbisara of Magadha had married Chellana, the daugther of Chetake, Mahavir was related to the eminent ruling dynastry of Magadha. *Vardhaman* was educated to the highest perfection in all branches of knowledge and art, and was married to Yasodhara, had by her a daughter whose husband Jamali became the first disciple of Mahavir and subsequently the leader of the first schism of the Jain Church. In his thirtieth year, on the demise of his parents, Vardhaman renounced the world left his home and became an ascetic in the search of Truth i.e. *'Nam'* or *'God'*.

During one of his visits to Nalanda, he made acquaintance of an ascetic called *Gosala Makkhaliputta*. He was so much impressed by Vardhaman that he attached himself to him, but left him after six years to eatablish a new religious order called *Ajvikas*. For thirteen years Vardhaman lived the life of self-mortification, severe Austerities, and deep meditation. Then in the thirteenth year of his ascetism on the tenth of Vaisakha, outside the town of *Jrimbhikgrama*, near the Parsvanath hills, he attained "Intuitive Knowledge". At this Supreme Knowledge and the subsequent final deliverance from pleasure and pain in his forty-second year of age, Vardhaman became known as Mahavir, the great hero or *Jina* (the conqueror who had subded his passions) and his followers wer named *Nirgranthas* (free from fetters or binds) for the next thirty year he moved from place to place and preached his doctrines in Kosala, Magadha and further east. He paid frequent visits to the Kings, Bimbi and Ajatasatru, who honoured him highly. He died at Pava (in the Patna District) at the age of seventy-two in 527 B.C. Some modern scholars prefer 468 B.C. as the date of his date of his death. He was contemporary of Gautam Buddha and survived him by many years. He established a religious order which was open to all friars and nuns as well as laymen, both males and females. He accepted the teaching of *Parsvanath* on the basis of his faith as a Living Master of the period as Viajy Sarangal of the 21st century.

Teachings of Mahavira[14]

Mahavir believed in dualistic philosophy and held that matter and soul are the only two ever existing elements. In other words, a man's personality comprises material and spiritual natures. The former is perishable while the latter eternal and evolutionary. According to him, on accout of *Karam* (the accumulate effect of action done in the past liver) the soul in a state of bondage created by passions and desires collected through several previous births. It is by means of continued efforts through several lives that the *Karmik* forces binding the soul can be counteracted and the soul itself is rendered passionless. The disintegration of the *Kamik* forces constitutes the final liberation of the soul (*Jiva*). By tapas or severe austerities and self-mortification and discipline of the body, the forming of fresh Karmas and their assimilation is prevented and the already deposited karma are lessned and finally shaken away. Side by side with this decay of the *Karma* the intrinsic qualities of the soul get expressed more and the soul shines in full luminosity and '*In infinte*' greatness and glory which represent final liberation of *Moksha*, and then the soul becomes *Paramatman* the pure soul with 'Infinite Knowledge', power and bliss.

Certain ethical code is assigned both for a householder and a homeless monk. Since the aim of life is attain salvation one has to avoid evil *Karmas*, then gradually prevent all kind of fresh *Karmas* and destroy the existing ones. For this purpose a household is to observe five vows of non-injury (*Ahimsa*), speaking truth (*Satya*), non-stealing (*Asteya*)he non-adulery (B*rahmacharya*) and non-possession (*Aparigraha*). This comprises right conduct. Then has to follow two more principles '*Word*' Right Faith and Right Knowledge '*Chamar*' the former means a belief in the *Jinas* and the lattle means the knowledge of eventual liberation and life in all exiting things. More severe than this is the code laid down for a monk.

Mahavira did not believe that God created this world or exercises any control over it. According to him there is creation of the world no supreme creative spirit, nor there is any creator necessary to explain the nature of the world. God, according to him is only the highest the noblest and the fullest manifestation of all the power latent in man (the most perfect man). The stage is thus set for him to wander, experience (*bhog*), may be even fall, hurt, and reach some kind of despondency, feel his limitation and then, seek higher knowledge of the Lord, to swim across this terrible predicament which Brahmins could not had the study of Lord Shiva, they had to worship his picture and sculpture. For even in the limited state of Jiva (soul), Shiva does retain the five acts, in a limited way[15] as *Baba Ravidas* had in his knowledge seeped in Love of God. The Real Philosopher's Stone is the Name of God, which transforms sinners into saints, and makes mortals immortal in the history of India.

He regarded all objects, animate or inanimate, as endowed with various degrees of consciousiness. They possess life and feel pain on the infliction of injuries. So the greatest emphasis is laid on the doctrine of *Ahimsa* or non-injury to any kind of living being, however, low may be the state of its evolution.

He rejected the authority of the *Vedas* ad objected to the *Vedic* ritual and the Brahmana supremacy. He advocated, as noted above, a very holy. ethical and elevating code of life and severe ascerticism and extreme penance for the attainment of *Moksha* or the highest spiritual state. Modern Jainism embodies these very doctrines of Mahavir.

Unlike Buddha, Mahavir was more a reformer of an existing religion and possibly of a Chruch than the founder a New Faith. All the Pali canon shows that it regared Mahavir not as a founder of a new sect, but merely as a leader of religious community.

The Jain Church

Mahavir successfully founded the Jain Church. His severe asceticism and simple doctrines attracted many followers. He had eleven close disciples or apostles known as *Ganadharas* or "Heads of Schools". Only one of them, Aryan *Sudharman*, surived Mahavir and became the Pontiff of the Jain Church after his death. *Sudharman*, the first *thera*, died twenty years after his mother death. His successor was *Jambu* who held the office for forty four years. Three generations of *Pontiffs* passed after him and during the regin of the last, Nanda of Magadha, the Jain Church was ruled by two *theras*, *Sumbhutavijaya* and *Bhadrabahu*, who was the author of the Kalpasutra of the Jains. Nothing in detail is known concerning the fortunes of the Jain Church for about 150 years. For the history of the Jain Church from its to the fouth or third century B.C. we are indebted to the Jain *Kalpasutra* of Bhadrabahu who was the sixth *thera*, after Mahavir's, and was a contemporary of the Emperor Chandragupta Manurya. It is reported that he died 170 years after Mahavir's Nirvana. The Jain *Kalpasutra* consists of three different section –the first sections contains the biographies of the twenty three Jinas or *Tirthankaras* who preceded Mahavir. The twentythird Jina, Parsvanth, is said to have laid the foundation upon which Mahavir, who followed him about 250 years after set up Jain Church. The main part of the first section is the detailed, biography of Mahavir. The second section of the *Kalpasutra* consists of the Theravial,a list of schools (*ganas*) and their heads (*ganadharas*). As the list goes far beyond Bhadrabahu, it seems that it was possily written by others ands not Bhadrabaha himself. The third section contains the *Samachari* or the Rules for the ascetics or Jain Monks in the study of the '*Nam-History*'.

The First Jain Council and the Great Schism

The fourteen *Purvas*, the text-books of the old Jain scriptures which Mahavir himself had taught to *Ganadharas* were perfected by *Sambhutavijaya* and *Bhadrabahu. Sambhutavijaya* is said to have died in the same year in which emperor Chandragupta Maurya ascended the throne. Towards the close of the fouth century B.C. a terrible famine, lasting for twelve years, broke out in South Bihar. When it led to the exodus of an important section of the Jains, headed by *Bhadrabahu*, to the Mysore region in the south, many Jains remined in Magadha under Sthubhadra, a disciplen of *Sambhutavijaya*. They summoned a council at Pataliputra about 300 B.C.to collect and revive the knowledge of the sacred texts which was passing into oblivion. Its result was the compliation of the twelve *Angas* that are considered the most important part of the Jain canon, The followers of *Bhadrabahu* on their return to Magadha refused to acknowledge the canon as drawn up by their co-religionists in Bihar holding that the fourteen *Purvas* were lost. Moreover, there was already a wide gulf made between those who had emigrated and those who stayed in Magadha.

The latter had become accustomed to wearing white garments and discareded Mahavir teaching, whereas the firmer still continued going naked and strictly followed the teaching of Mahavir. This is how the first schism split the Jain Church into the *Digambaras* (sky-clad or naked) and *Swetambaras* (clad in white) i.e., called '*Chamar'* in the history of India as '*Nam*' on earth.

The Second Jain Council at Vlabhi (512 A.D.)

With the lapse of time the canon of *Swetambaras* was reduced to a disorderly condition, and it was in danger of being lost altogether. Therefore, in 512 A.D. a council was held at Valabhi in Gujarat, presided over by Devardhi *Kshamasramana, a Ganadhara*, to collect the sacred texts and write them down systematically. At this time the twelfth *Anga* drawn in the first council at Pataliputra, had already disappeared leaving only the eleven *Angas* in the recession that has come down to us. They were written in *Ardha-Magadhi*.

During the countires that followed furthermore splits took place amongst both the section i.e., '*Jat*' the *Digambaras* and the *Swetambaras* '*Chamar'* the most important of them being one that renounced idol-worship althogether and devoted itself to the worship of he scriptures. They are called *Terapanthis* among the *Swetambaras* and Samaiyas among the *Digambaras*. This sect came into existence not early than the sixteenth century A.D. Today the Jain Church with all its schisms is stil existing and this religious order founded by Mahavir is still preaching his teacher all over the country not in Jammu but also in abroad.

Jain Philosophy[16]

Jainism shows a close affinity with *Samkhya* system of philosophy. It was called *Syadvada*. According to *Syadvada* the the theory of 'May be', seven modes of predication are possible. If the question is –'Is there a soul?' It would admit seven answer to it (i) is (ii) is not (iii) is and is not, (iv) is unpredictable, (v) is and is unpredictable (vi) is not and is upredictable, and (vii) is, is not and is upredictable. There is a sense in which there is a soul, and there is also a sense in which no soul exists and a third sense is not inconceivable in which one cannot describe soul,and so on. Knowledge is only probable as a *Big Soul* or *World Soul* as *Big Nam-Deva*.

Jainism Has a Theory of Reality

According to it the world consists of two eternal, uncreatd co-existing, but independent categories, namely the conscious (*Jiva*) and the unconscious (*Ajiva*). The conscious being or Jiva correspond to the soul. It knows and feels. It acts and it acted upon. It suffers by contact with matter and is born again and again only to suffer. It highest endeavour is to free itself from this bondage. This is salvation which could be attained by higher knowledge and meditation up on the great truth i.e. '*Nam*'. The *Ajiva* or the unconscious is not what we call matter. It includes, matter which is given the name *Pudgala*, but it also includes such things as space and time virtue and vice etc. for the sake of birthright.

According to Jain philosophy, there is no God or Creator. Man salvation from suffering does not depend up on the mercy of any God or Creator. Man is the architect of his own destiny. By leading an austere life of purity virtue and noble thinking and acting, one can escape the ills of life. Life of renunciation is the shortest way to salvation or *Moksha.*

Thus, Jainism is a moral code in the modern sense. It must be noted that Jainism did not dogmatize. According to its fundamental logic, no absolute affirmation or denial is possible. When all knowledge is probable and relative, your opponent view is as likely to be true as yours. As a results of this spirit of accommodation Jainism. has surived in India till today in the form of '*Nam*'.

Ascendancy of Jainism[17]

The inscriptional and literary evidences seems to indicate that in its earlier stages the success of Jainism was more remarkable than of Buddhism. The use of common dialect in place of Sanskrit by Mahavir and his preaching monks the simple and homely moral precepts intead of subtle and unintelligible doctrines of God and soul, the free ministaration of spiritual truths to the masses, the activites of the Jain monks and royal patronage were the forces whch helped in the spread of Jainism.

The incessant missionary efforts of a strongly of organized religious order, that was left behind by Mahavir made animal sacrifice fall into disuse and non-violence became firmly established as a rule of life even amongst those classes of people who did not embrace Jainism. The followers of Mahavir gradually spread over the whole country. Jain monks were to be seen on the banks of the *Indus* when Alexander invaded *India* in Jammu Region. According to the Jain tradition, Udayin, the successor of Ajatasatru, was a devoted Jain. The *Nandas* were also probably Jains of the *Sudhra* Family. In the first centry B.C., Ujjain became a great centre of Jainism as is evidenced from the legends of the Jain saint *Kalakacharya* and *Gardanhilla* and his son *Vikram* of Ujjain. By the close of the fourth centry B.C. a team of Jain monks under Bhadrabahu migrated to the Deccan and spread Jainism throughout the South with Sravana Belgola in Karnataka as their central seat. A later Inscription (900 A.D.) records that the summit of the *Chandragiri* (Karnataka) is marked by the footprint of *Bhadrabahu* and Chandragupta *Maunipati* (*Emperor Chandragupta Maurya*). Jainism became very popular there especially among mercantile community.

Royal patronage was also bestowed up on Jainsm. The great Maurya emperor, Chandragupta was it devout parton. As noted above, he himself had joined *Bhadrabahus* march to the South as his disciple. A cave is dedicated to him and hill on which it exists is known as *Chandragiri* after him. During the second centry B.C. King Kharvel of Kalinga (Orissa) professed Jainism and became its illustrious and renowed patron by setting up Jain image himself. In the Kushan period, Jainsim flouruished well at Mathura and was dominant in eastern Indian in the time of Harsha. During the early Centuries of the Christian era, Mathura in the North and *Sravana Belgola* in the Deccan, were great centres of Jain activites as is evidenced by a large number of Inscriptions, images and other monuments discovered at both the places. Form the fifth century many royal dynasties of the South such as the *Gangas*, the *Kadambas* the *Chalukyas* and the *Rashtrakutas*, patronized Jainism. Some of the *Rahtrakuta Kings* of *Manyakheta*, from the eigth to the tenth century, showed a special learning towards Jainism. They were zealous patrons of it and gave a great encouragement to the development of Jain art literature. Many celebrated Jain poets flourised under them. *Jinasena* and *Gunabhadra* composed their *Mahapurana* at the time of king *Amoghavarsha*, whose grat works *Ratnamalika* became very popluar with people of all sects. It is said that amoghavarsha became a Jain monk in the latter part of his life. According to epigraphical evidence one of his succesors, *Indras* IV, died in the Jain from of renunciation self-mortifiaction and asceticism.About the year 1100 A.D., Jainism gained ascendancy in Gujarat.There the Chalukya King Siddharaja (1094-1143 A.D.), the popular hero of the Gujarat legend and the ruler of Anhilward and his son *Kumarapal* were great parton of the Jains sect. They openly professed Jainisim and encouraged th literary and temple –buliding activites of the Jains in Gujarat. At the court of Kumarapala lived the famous Jain scholar *Hemchandra* who was the royal pandit and annalist.

During the Muslim period, Jainsim continued to flourish without much molestation from the Muslim rules of the country owing to the very peaceful ways and non-interfernce policy of the Jains. But their numbers began to decrease. They, however, received some patronage under the benign Mughal Emperor, Akbar. During the Muslim period the Jains, particularly increase in the states of Rajasthan, where they occupied many important office of state including generalship. But the period that followed was steady decline.

Causes of the Decline of Jainism.

(1) A large number of unselfish workers, provide by the religious monastic order for preaching and proselytizing were no longer enthusiastic in those activites.

(2) The days of liberal royal patronage had passed away.

(3) The lay community became split up by the internal divison that made it impossible for them to combine for any soild religious or social work.

(4) Caste distinctions and divisions, that were once brushed aside, were reimposed and they became active with their inflexible rigidity. This sapped the orginal vitality of the Jain community through it continued to survive in ever decreasing numbers.

(5) In the meanswhile, counter-reformation in favour of orthodox Hinduism in and it had the effect of nearly extermінting Jainism.

The present-day population of the Jains India is nealy sixteen lakhs distributed all over the country, but they are predominantly found in Rajasthan, Gujarat and someDistricts of Madhya Pradesh and the South. Mostly they are rich and prosperous traders and have founded and maintained many charitable institution in the country such as dispensaries *dharmasalas* (rest –houses) and houses for animal protection. Now,they are paying more attention to the reform of their society, the spread of education, revival of their faith construction and repairs of Jain temples and shrines and the publication of ancient Jain literature that has for centuries remained locked up in manuscript form in Jain temples all over the country including Jammu and Kashmir State.

Contribution of Jainsim to Indain Culture in Jammu State

1. *Jain Literature and the Growth of Vernacular Languages*

Through a small community, the Jains have played a very important part in the development of the language of the country. Sanskrit and Pali have been then mediums of sacred writings and preaching of the Brahmanas and Buddhists respectively. But the Jains utilized the prevailing spoken language of the different times at different places in the country for their religious propaganda and the preservation of the sacred knowledge. Their religious literature which is written in Parkrit is very vast. Thus, they exercised a healthy and prdominant influence on the development of the Prakrit language. They even gave a literary shape to some vernacular for the first time. Mahavir himself preached in the mixed dialect called *Ardha-Magadhi* so that people speaking *Magadhi* or *Sauraseni* might understand him throughly. His teaching which were clasified into twelve books called *Srutangas*, are written in *Ardha Magadhi*. Recently a very rich literature produced by the Jains has come to light. It preserves the form of the language as it was current prior t · the evolution of the present day *vernaculars*, especially Hindi, Gujarati and Marathi. This literature is written in the language called *Apabhramsa*. It links the classical language Sanskrit and Prakit on the hand and the modern vernaculars on the other, and, therefore, its study is very significant from the philological point of view. Jain thought and inspiration can be traced in the literature of the South. The earliest literature in *Kannad* is of Jain influence in Jammu Region. The Jains have also written some of their scripture in Sanskrit. Infact, they have produced a rich literature in Sanskrit, both narrative ands philosophical and works on grammer, prosody, lexicography and mathematics are also not wanting from the sides of Brahmins, but real amount to study the '*Nam*' History of the, man and God.

2. Jain Architecture

The beauty of Jainism finds its high watermark during the seventh and the twelfth centuries. In their early centuries, they erected *stupas*, like Buddhists, in honour of their saints with their accessories of stone railing of the '*Ravidas Culture*', decorated gateways, stone umbrellas, elaborate carved pillars and abundant statues,. Some of these that have been discovered at Mathura, in Bundelkhand and some parts of Northern Madhya Pardesh,are full of Jain statues. They belong of the eleventh and the twelfth centuries, A.D. The gigantic status of *Bahubali* called *Gommatesvara* at *Sravana Belgola* and *Karkal* in *Karnataka* are example of the wonders of architecture. The former statue, 21 metres high, carved out of a mass of granite, standing at the top of a hill was erected in 984 A.D. by *Chamundaraya*, the minister of the Ganga King, *Rachamalla*. The colossal releifs careved out of rock in Gwalior for in Madhya Pradesh belong to the fifteenth century A.D. The Jain caves with their relief works and status at Udaigri hills, near Bhilsa in Madhya Pradesh and Ellora in Maharashtra are example of excellent architecture, sculpture of the period. Written records of the fruit go back to *Kautilya's Arthashastra* (400-300 B.C.), to the paintings of Ajanta and Ellora caves (200 B.C.) and to the *Ramayana* period. It was Alexander who carried the *Banana* fruit westward from his invasion to India in 327 B.C., while Arab traders took it from India to Africa as '*Nam*' do in His history. The Father of taxonomy, i.e. Bachan Lal, Megha, Carl Lennaeus, dobbed on Indian species *Musa* sapientum or the fruit of the wise because of a classical Greek writer's account of Indian Rishis savouring *Bananas* for the study as '*Nam*' came out in form of the spiritual sense that God and man working togethers. Banana is one of the 40 crops listed by the treaty of the God and man which must be protected[18] as a food of the Rishis. The Jain have also constructed cave temples cut in rock, the earliest examples of which belonging to the second century B.C. and later, of different periods are still existing at *Jnagarh, Junnar, Osrmanabad* and other places. Many Jain places of pilgrimage, such as, the Parsvanath Hills, *Parvapuri* and *Raigiri* in Bihar and *Girnar* and *Palitana* in Kathiawar have temples and other architectural monument of different ages. The Jain tower at Chittor in Rajasthan is one of the best specimens of Jain architecture. The Jain temples at Mount Abu in Rajastthan belonging to the eleventh century, carries to its highest perfection the Indian genius for the invention of graceful patterns and their application to the decoration of masonry as the work of the labour class.

Traces of Jainism go far back in to history and it undoubtedly older than Buddhism if not Vedic religion. Though it neither became the dominant religion in India nor spread abroad, yet it has remained a peaceful sect in the country. The orthodoxy of Jainism, its affinity to Brahmanism, its non-missionary spirit and absence of hostiliy towards other rival faiths account for the fact that Jainism still flourishes in several parts of the country.

Buddhism as a State Religion[19]

Early Life of Gautam Buddha. Buddhism was the movement that gave the greatest shock to Brahmanism. It was started by Gautam Buddha who was a notable contemporary of Mahavir. He was the son of *Suddodhana*, the chief of the Sakya clan of Kapilavastu in the Nepal Tarai. His mother was the Maya a princess of neighbouring clan of the *Koliyas*. He was born about the year 566 B.C. in the village of Lumbini, a few kilometers from Kapilavastu. The site of his nativity is marked by the celebrated Rummindei. *Pillar* of Ashoka Maurya, containing an Inscription dated 249 B.C. As Maya died in childbirth *Siddartha* was brought up by his aunt and stepmother, *Prajapati Gautami.*

From his boyhood *Siddhartha* showed signs of contemplative turn of mind and deep compassionate nature.The royal splendour failed to captivate the prince's heart even from his boyhood. Observing in his son a great indifference to worldliness, *Suddhodhan* married him to a beautiful and accomplished princess *Yasodhara*, daughter of a *Sakya* noble, and surrounded the married couple with the choicest material of luxury and pleasure. But the princes was not happy at heart. The sight of an old man, a sick man, a dead body and an ascetic intensified his deep hatred towards the world and made him realize the hollowners of wordly pleasure. He was perturbed by the eternal problem of life, its suffering, disease, death, and mortality, and he felt powerfully attracted by the calm serenity of the passionless kingdom in 537 B.C, at the age of twentynine, as a wandering ascetic in search of Truth or '*Nam*'. This is known as the great renunciation of Lord Buddha.

For six continuous years, he lived as a homeless ascetic, seeking instruction under two Brahmana religious teachers and visiting many places including Rajgriha in the Patna District and Urvila nears Gaya. Finding no satisfication there he practiced the severest penances and the most rigid austerities and more fruitless efforts to find the Truth or '*Nam*' as an objective of life. He then gave up penance, took a bath in the stream of the river *Niranjan* (modern Lilajan) and sat under a pipal tree at Bodh Gaya. Here, he attained Supreme Knowledge and insight concept of the human history.. Revelation came to him that the Great Peace was with in his own heart and the must seek it there. This is known as the Great Enlightenment and since then he became known as the Buddha or the Enlightened. One or *Tathagat* (one who has attained the Truth). Then he proceeded to the Deer Park near Sarnath in the vicinity of Varaṇasi, where he gave his first religious discourse, as a result of which five disciples joined him. For the next fortyfive years, he roamed about as a wandering teacher and proclaimed his gospel to the princes and peasant a like in Oudh, Bihar and some adjoining Districts. Kings like *Prasenjit* of Kosala and *Bimbisara* and Ajastasatru of Magadha accepted his doctrines and became his discples. He laid the foundation of the Buddhist Church or Order of Monka (*Sangha*). Preaching and delivering sermons for salvation and making conversations, he at last died at the age of eigth in 486 B.C., at *Kusinara* modern Kaisa in the Gorakhpur District of Uttar Pradash. Kashmir was also a biggest centre of learning at that time and it had also great influenced at Jammu Region as we have already discussed in the study.

Teachings of Lord Buddha

Gautam Buddha never endeavoured to establish a new religion or creed. Neither he talked of codes and convertions, nor of laws and rites. He indicated a new ways of life '*Nam*' or '*Chamar*' the virtuous path by trading which one could attain deliverance from births and deaths. He advocated not a set of doctrines or dogmas but a rational scheme of spiritual development. Simple goodness of spirit, deed and conduct is the basis of his teachings. He rejected the infallibility of the *Vedas*, condemned animal sacrifices, protested against the complicated, elaborate and meaningless rituals, challenged the caste system and priestly supremacy and denied or doubted the exertence of a supreme creative spirit. It was, according to him the individual exertion at self-improvement and virtuous life that mattered most. Self-culture is the key-note of his teachings. The virtuous path as suggested by him is a code of practical ethics that has a rational outlook. Buddhsim, therefore, was more a social than religious revolution. It taught the code of practical ethics and laid down the democratic principle of social equality based on social justice.

Buddha preached his followers the four 'Noble Truths' concerning sorrow, the cause of sorrow, the remedy or destruction of sorrow the way that leads to the destruction of sorrow. In other words, he pointed out four certainties *'Words'*, there is suffering in life, this suffering has a cause, this suffering could be removed by destroyed its cause,the cause of the suffering is *trishna* or desire for material enjoyments and earthly things. And, it is this desire that is responsible for the birth and rebirths of man. When this selfish desire or craving for existence has ceased to act in man, he urged,it is only then possible for the individual soul to obtain *Nirvana* or deliverance from this unending cycle of birth and deaths and the consequent suffering. How to annihilate this craving or remove this desire is, therefore, the real problem before a man is maya or material. Self-mortification, he argued could never overcome *trishna* and brings about an escape from rebirth and subsequent suffering. Mere repetition of prayers or sacrifices or the chating of the Vedic hymns i.e. '*Nam*' was futile in clearing the mind of gross desires. Desire suggested Buddha, can only be removed by following the noble eight fold path or the *Arya Ashtanga-Marga*. It consists of the following steps;

1. *Right Views or Faith*- The knowledge of the four truths which Buddha enunciated in his first sermon;
2. *Right Aspiration*—That requires us to renounce pleasures to bear no malice and do not harm to other;
3. *Right Speech*—Signifying that we should abstain from lying slander, abuse, harsh words and idle talk
4. Right Action—Meaning that we should refrain from taking what is not given and abstain from carnal excesses.
5. *Right Livelihood*— Requiring us to abstain from any of the forbidden modes of living;
6. *Right Effort*-Consisting in suppressing the rising of evil conditions in eradicating those that have arisen and in stimulating good states or conditions;
7. *Right Mindfulness*-Requiring us to look on the body and the spirit in such a way as to remain self-possed and careful overcoming both hankering and dejection; and
8. *Right Contemplation*—Meaning to take the form of four meditations. It is the end and the crown of the eight fold path.

This *eightfold path* lies between the two extremes namely gross sensualism or vile pleasure seeking on the one hand and the extreme asceticism or the severest self-mortifcation, on the other hand. It teaches men how to live a moral and religious life. It is the path that ultimately brings according to Buddha final bliss or *Nirvana*. *Nirvan* literally means ' blowing out' or extinction of craving or desire or *trishna* for existence in all its form and the consequent cessation of suffering. It is not mere disappearance or extinction but a tranquil state to be realized by a person who 'from all craving or want is free'. It is delivence or freedom from rebirth. This may lead one to conclude that Buddhism teaches the doctrine of inaction, that is, cession of activity, desiring little or doing little. But Buddhism does not teach inaction. It tracher the non-doing of evil deeds, the doing of various kinds of good thing. Buddha rightly prescribed *moral precepts* for his followers. He laid stress on purity of conduct, truthfulness, love and benevolence, obedience to parents and respect for the elders, non-drinking, charity and kindness and mercy to all living beings. He did not like flattery and once he rebuked a man who indulged in his praise. He valued the observation of the true path and hated sin not the sinner. The fact that once he preferred a meal prepared by a dancing girl, *Amrapali*, to the sumptuous banquet of the nobles at Vaisali (Bihar) bears testimory to the overflow in mercy of his heart and his tender regards for the welfare and happiness of the common people had been opened now in the form of study as God on earth.

Another doctrine on which Buddha laid great emphasis is the *Law of Karma* and its working, and the transmigration of souls. The condition of man in this life and the next, he argued depends up on his own actions. Neither a sacrifice to gods can wash away sin, nor any prayer of any priest or any prayer of any man can do himself or any other man any goods. A man reaps what he sows. As a man acts, so shall he be. Every individual is the maker of his own destiny and no God or gods could change it. We are for ever making our own moral world for good or ill. We can never escaps the conquences of our deeds.We can born again to reap the fruits of our *Karmas*. This is the *Law of Karma*. If an individual sins no more, he dies no more and when he dies no more, he is born no more; and, thus, he comes to live the life of Final Bliss i.e. on the day of Judgement.

Another prominent feature of his teaching is *Ahisma*. According to him the spirit of lover is more important than good deeds. Non-violence towards life is recognized as an integral principal of his practical morality. But it is not given so much exaggerated important as in Jainism. Though Buddha enjoyed love and non-violence for all beings, he permitted his followers to take meat of the '*Word*' under certain condition to became *Rakases* to kill the Brahmin *Rakases*.

In his religious teachings Buddha may be called and agnostic, because he neither accepts nor reject the existence of God. He refused to be drawn into any theoretical discussion about God or nature of the soul. Whenever, he was questioned about them, he either maintained silence or remaked that God or gods were also under the eternal *Law of Karma*. It seems that he was merely concerned with the deliverance of man from suffering, other things being beyond his purpose.

Buddhist Councils and Scriptures.

When Buddha was on the death–bed,he said to his favourite disciple Ananda: "The truths and rules of the order which I have set forth and laid down for you all '*Words*' let them, after I am gone, be the teacher to you." Shortly after Buddhas death, therefore, the first Buddhist council was held in 483 B.C. in Sattapanni cave near Rajgraiha to compile the *Dhamma* (religious doctrines) or '*Nam-dana* theory' and the *Vinaya* (monastic code). There, the five hundred monks representing different local *sanghas* assembled and adopted authoritative canonical texts by dividings the teachings of Buddha in to two *Pitakas* '*Word*' *Vinaya* and *Dhamma (Spiritual Knowledge)*. A few centuries later about 90 B.C. these were reduced to writing in Sri Lanka in the Pali language in which we have then now as Dr.Ram Dass of the *Meghavahana* Dynasty of Kashmir.

A century later a dispute arose regarding the codes of discipline, as the monks of Vaisali wanted a relaxation of the rules in respect of the ten points. Opinion was divided particularly as to whether the monks should not accept gold or silver from the people when offered. A second council, therefore, convened in about 383 B.C. at Vaisali, which condemned the ten heresies. As the Vaisali monks struck to their views no agreement was arrived at and the Council ended in a permanent split of the Buddhist Church in to *Sthaviras* and *Mahasanghikas*. The former held the orthodox *Vinaya* and the latter were pro-changes. The third general council was held at Pataliputra during the reign of Ashoka 236 years after the death of Buddha, under the chairmanship of learned monks *Moggaliputta Tissa* to revise the scriptures. "The Council accomplished two important result '*Word*' firstly, it made a new classification of Buddhist canonical by the addition of a third *Pitaka* called the *Abhidhamma* Pitaka which contained the philosophical interpretations of the doctrines of the existing two *Pitakas*" As a result of this the sayings and discourses of the Buddha now came to be known as the *Triptaka*. Secondly, the canonical literature was precisely, definitely and authoritatively settled so as to elimniate all disruptive tendencies making all division with in the Church punishable. The fourth Council was held during the reign of Kanishka in Kashmir under the leadship of the elder *Vasumitra* and the great scholar *Asvaghosha*. This Council was not a general assembly, but probably a gathering of only the *Hinayanists* of Northern India in the area of Jammu, place known as Akhnoor Valley. It decide certain controversial questions which arose out of some differences of opinion between the *Sarvastivada* teachers of Kashnir and Gandhara. The council also composed three large commentaries of the three *Pitakas*. They are known as *Vibhashas*.

The Buddhist scripture known as *Pitakas* are divided into three sections, namely, the *Sutta*, the *Vinaya* and the *Abhidhamma*. The first, the *Sutta Pitaka,* consists of five collections of religious discourse (Satsang) and sayings of Buddha and is, therefore, the most important part of the scriptures. The second the *Vinaya Pitaka* contains the rules of monastic discipline, and third, the *Abhidhamma* Pitaka, contains the philosophical development of the teachings of Buddha. Every sect of Buddhism had a *Tripitaka* of its own. The fifth collection of the *Sutta Tripitaka* contain *Jatakas* or Buddhist birth tales. They were not so well-known in the second as in the fifth century B.C. The *Jatakas* belong to a class of literature which foreshadows the great epics of the *Ramayan* and the *Mahabharat* in repeated stories of the '*Sudhra Family*'.

The Buddhist Sangha or Church

The Sangha

The Buddha had two kinds of disciples: monks (*bhikshus*) and the lay –worshippers (*upasikas*). The former were organized into the *Sangha* or the Religious Order the number of which swelled with the spread of Buddhism. The membership of the Sangha was open to all persons, male or female, above fifteen years of age, and who were free from leprosy, consumption and other infectious disease. Persons who were in the service of the King or an individual, or who were in debt or had been branded as robbers or criminals were refused admission into the *Sangha*. But exception were made in the case of convicts, slaves or persons with physical deformities. There were no caste restrictions. Thus, the *Buddhist Sangha* or Church formed a community of person who were physically and morally fit to perform the noble service required of them. It was a systematic and thoroughly organized Church which became a very powerful weapon for the spread of Buddhism. In due course, it became one of the greatest religious corporations ever known in the world. In fact, later on it became a model for Church organization of other religions. One of the primary cause of the rapid progress of Buddhism was the devoted and selfless sevices of the Sangha. The lay-Buddhists led the life of householders and financially contributed to the maintenance of the *Sangha*.

Monastery

Monasteries were constructed to give suitable accommodation to the monks and nuns for carrying on their studies and meditaion. Gradually monasteries developed into academic centres for producing the right type of men, well grounded in religion and philosophy to propagate the teachings of Buddhism.Large monasteries were usually provided with dwelling –rooms, a service –hall, storehouse, cloister, well, bathroom, and rooms for exercises. The monasteries were allowed to be funished with certain article of furniture. The ownership of the monastery vested in the *Sangha*.

Three garments (*Chivara*) '*Word*' an upper robe, a lower one and a sort of cloak worn over these two allowed to the monks. These garments were made out of cloth, cut and dyed yellow.For food and alms, begging was the usual rule, but the monks were allowed to accept invitations to meals or offerings sent to the monasteries by the faithful. The monks accept food and robes offered by the devotees of Buddhism. They took medicines prescribed by the physicians.

During the four month of the rains, beginning from the day next to the full moon day of *Ashadh*, the monks were require to take up a fixed abode and depend for their subsistence on the neighbouring householders. During this period of their stay in monasteries, they preached Buddhism to the people in the evening just like the *Katha* system (narration of stories) of the present day. At the close of the retreatment or *vasa*, the monks met together to confess their offences, if any, committed during their stay in the rainy reason. This ceremony was called *Pavarana*. At the end of the ceremony monks accepted gifts from the laity.

There was a special code of rules for the nuns. It contained certain extra restrictions relating to movement, residence and general supervision of the nuns by monks.

Monks living within a definite boundary were hold fortnightly assembled were to elect their president (*Sanghathere Sanghaparianyaka*) and to select two speakers one on *Dhamma* or '*Nam-Dana*' and the other on *Vinaya*. In the assembly meeting there were the system of formal moving of resolution (*Jnapti*), ballot voting by means of wooden sticks (*Salaka*) formation of sub committee etc. For the different kinds of religious acts like giving punishment for offence admission or readmission of a monk in to the *Sangha*, rotation of the privileges of a monk, the minimum numbers of member required to form the panels was fixed by the Spiritual Guru or Prefect Master.

Admission into the Sangha and its G· vernment

The ceremony of initation into the *Sangha* was simple and plain. Whenever a new person, a man or a women desired to join the ordler he or she had to have his or her head shaved put on a *yellow* robe and before the President of the local Sangha take the following oaths of fidelity to the Buddha, the *Dhamma* and the *Sangha*.

1. I take refuse in the *Buddha.*
2. I take refuse in the *Dhamma.*
3. I take refuse in the *Sangha.*

Next, he was to repeat the ten commandment of Buddha. Then he was required to attach himself to a mark would give him certain preliminary training after which he was to present him to an assembly of monks and make a formal proposal for admitting him to the *Sangha.* When the permission was given he was to be ordained as a monk. Henceforth, he was require to observe the internal disciple of the Sangha and abide by its rule for leading a life of poverty, chastity, devotion, austerity, simplicity and calibacy as *Sudhra class* of the *'Nam-History'.*

The *Sangha* was governed on absolutely democratic lines and was empowed to before discipline amongest its members. It had also the power to punish the erring members. When ever a meeting of the *Sangha* was held the members or monks took their seats according to their seniority. No assembly was valid unless at least ten monks were present through in border countries the quorum could in exceptional cases be reduced to five. Novices and women were not entilied to vote or to constitute the quorum. Every question was decided by those present, and the question to de decided at a *Sangha* had to be formlly presented.

In every *Sangha*, office–bearers were elected and unanimous consent was required to carry on its various functions, such as distribution of food and clothes, provision of beds, creation of monastries, etc.

The absentees could send their opinion on different point included in the business of assembly, and the various questions put forth in the meeting were decided according to the teachings of lord Buddha. The President was empower to see that the Sangah did not go beyond its jurisdiction. The ultimate authoı ity was vested in the hands of the General Council of the *Sangha* which was convoked whenever any occasion arose. The interpretation of the sacred law also rested with the General Council. With aview to maintaining a rigid observance of disciplinary rules, the monks in *vihar* held every fortnight, a meeting where the rules were read out the senior member and the breaches thereof, any, were confessed by those present and those confessing their guilt were made to undergo penitence penance or punishment as the case might be.

Life of the Monks

The life of the monk and the nun was governed by the laws and the ten commandment and there was no room for personal likes or dislikes. Property was held in common, and the possession of private property was stricty forbidden. The monks were forbidden the usė of garlands, scents and other articles of personal decoration. They were not to indulge in liquior drinking meat eating, dancing, or singing, they were required to sleep on a hard and narrow bed and to beg their food from door to door. It was a hard, puritanic life of destitution and stern morality. The regulation for the nuns were stricter. It was feared that if equality was promised to them it might lead to indiscipline and immorality. Gautam Buddha was not in favour of ordaining women as nuns, but he did so reluctantly at the repeated requests of his chief disciple Ananda i.e., *'Nam'* or '*Chamar*' of '*Sudhra Family*'.

The monks wandered for eight month in the year and preached in the neghbouring Districts, but were required to retreat in to the *Viharas* during the four months of the rains.

Absences of Co-ordinating Authority

The grave defect of the *Sangha* was absence of acertral co-ordinating authority. There was no central representative body of all the scattered *Sanghas*. This foastered the spirt of repeated schisms even on difference of minor points. This necessitated the frequent calling of the general council where the point of difference were reviwed and settled. An account of such councils has already been given in the preceding pages.

The Use of Vernacular

Another striking feature of Buddhism and its *Sanghas* was the they discarded Sanskrit as oit was unintelligible to the common people and adopted the vernaculars of the people for their religious books and discourse. It was one of the important factors responsible for the rapid growth of Buddhism.

A Review of Buddhism and Hinduism

It has often been argued that Buddhism was not a new religion.It was a revolt against the commercial rituals of the Brahmanas and a strong protest against the caste system. It laid before the masses a practical code of ethics which was already known to them. In fact it was reform movement aimed at purging Hinduism of various ills. It is, therefore, not astonishing if there are many points of resemblance between Hisnduism and Buddhism, because after the death of Buddha it became Brahminical concept.

As regards their teachings, Hinduism believes in God, Matter and Soul as three self-existent entities and considers God the Creator of the Universe, while Buddhism has belief in Matter and Soul as two self-existent entities. God finds no room in the Buddhist thought of the world. It simply ignores the spirit of God as Creator. But the agnostic attitude take up the Buddha, was not the first departure from theology of strict Hinduism Kapil and Kanada, before Buddha had taken up similar view.

Hinduism considers the *Vedas* as divided amd the Vedic rituals as essential for salvation. It ha deep faith in sacrifices. In fact the *Vedas* form the bedrock of Hinduism. But Buddhism denied the authority of the *Vedas* and had no faith in the efficacy of the sacrifice or *yajnas* and other elaborate rites and sacraments enjoyed by them. The Vedic rituals are not regarded as necessary for salvation. Buddhim, as a matter of fact, was a revolt against ceremonial rites and sacrifices.

The final goal of life in both the religions is the same: to secure released from the cycle of births and deaths and to achieve salvation-*Moksha* or *Nirvana*. Both faiths have strong belief in the doctrines of transmigration of the Soul and the *Law of Karma*. Gautam Buddha's teachings in fact, were largely based on the Brahmanic ideas of *Purarjanma, Karma* and *Monksha*. During his life Buddha counted many worthly Brahmanism among his disciples. He forbade any attack on Brahmanism and never encouraged any confict or schism with it. The principles of Hinduism are tale-telling as described in the *Vedas* very complicated and are, therefore, unintelligible to the common people. The teaching of Buddhism, on the contrary, were very simple and brief and were with in the comprehensive power of the masses. Hinduism is abstract and philosophical while Buddhism was practical and ethical. on the basis of 'Nam'.

As regards the *practices* of the faiths Hinduism believes in the performance of elaborate ceremonies, reciting hymns and daily prayers. It lays emphasis on moral and virtuous life as leading to salvation. The ceremonies of Hinduism are accompanied by oblations and sometimes slaughter of animals. Buddhism on the contrary advocated the principle of *Ahimsa* or non-injury to living begings. In fact, *Ahimsa* formed the most important part of the Buddhist ethical code.

There is no personal element in Hisnduism while Buddhism introduced it in the form of Buddha as the saviour to be worshipped later in the form of idols.

Hinduism has been imparting spiritual and religious instructions through Sanskrit. It has been the language of their scriptures. But the Buddhists have been administering spiritual knowledge though the spoken language of the masses, and they composed their scriptures in the language of the people.

Though the practical code of morality by Buddhism is not at all different from the ideal of Hindu life, yet a Brahamana or a Hindu would discuss higher problems of life here and life hereafter. On the other hand, a Buddhist would lay emphasis only on the virtuous conduct in this life on this earth as a normal human being.

With regard to social and religious organizations of the two faiths, the Hindu society is organized on the fourfold divison of the castes in which the Brahmanas enjoy supremacy. The caste system and the dominance of the Brahmanas are very striking featrure of Hinduism. Buddhism made no such distinction and treated all a like. It did not recognize thre priestly class. The Buddhist society was democraic in which a low born had the same privileges as high –born, provided his moral conduct justified privilege.

Hinduism has no Church or religious order of monks and nuns. Buddhism instituted such order. It was congregationl *Sanghas* played a very important part in Buddhism. Due to the missionary spirit of the Sanghas, Buddhism has been very dynamic and is, therefore, followed by one-quarter of the humans race. Hinduism on the other hand, is never marked by a missionary spirit and it never sought converts. Hence, it has always been static.

In social outlook, Hinduism did not possess the spirit of adaptability. But Buddhism has been very flexiblae and adapted itself to the needs of the countries to which is travelled.

Jainism and Buddhism

Jainism and Buddhism resemble each other in many repects. Both of them have been protestant religious movements against the corruptions of Hinduism. They were the products of the same religious ferment that prevailed in the sixth century B.C. They were the off-shoots of Hinduism. In their search for truth they did not strike a new path but followed the old one of Hinduism. The goal that they placed before them was the same as that which Hinduism strove to attain, namely, salvation or moksha from the cycle of births and deaths. Therefore, both of them accepted two famous doctrines of Hinduism *'Word' Karma* and transmigration of soul as the indispensable factores for attainment of salvation. They different from the orthodox Hinduism in their belief in the automatic relentless working of the *Law of Karma*. Jainism and Buddhism both held that the Law of *Karma* is above all creatures whether men or gods and even God or gods cannot alter the course of this law. Hence, the Brahmanic practices of pleasing the gods by sacrifices and *Vedic* rites was of no avail in attaining *moksha* or salvation. *Moksha* could be attained by a person by his own deeds and not by the meditation of God or gods who are themselves subject to the *Law of Karma*. So, both Jainsim and Buddhism denied the Brahmanic ceremonies rejected the authority of the *Veda,* abhorred and condemned the blood sacrifices, and ignored the belief in God as the Creator of the Universe.

Both Jainism and Buddhism advocated a virtuous and holy life and abstention from sinful thought actions and injury by word or deed to any living being. Both laid emphasis on on the doctrine of *Ahimsa* '*Word*', non-violence. In this matter, the Jains went even a step further than the Buddhists.

Both Mahavir and Buddha preached their religions in the common language of the people, denounced caste system and advocated equality of men and women. Unlike Hinduism each had a well-organized *Sangha* of devoted missionaries and each depended on the support of the monastic order free from worldly tangles.

As the founders of both Jainsim and Buddhism were *Kshatriya* princes, drawing their inspiration from the teaching of the *Upanishads*, much of their success was due to the patronage of the *Kshatriya* princes and Kings in pure thought.

But in many other respects both differed fundamentally from each other. The Jains gave laity a very prominent place in their order while the Buddhists relied mainly on their monastic order. The *Nirvana* of the Buddhists differed fundamentally from that of the Jains. The *Nirvana* of the former was escape from existence, whereas that of the latter was escape from body. The Jains believed in rigorous asceticsm and approved self-mortification which was discarded and condemned by Buddhists strongly. The doctrine of *Ahimsa*, believed in by both, was carried by the Jains to a far greater extent than ever contemplated by the Buddhists. The Jains believed in the principle of life in the vegetable kingdom too. Buddhists emphasized the non-existence of the soul as permanent entity, whereas Jains believe that not only animate but in animate things also possess souls.

Jainism ever today retains many Brahmanic practices and ceremonies and a modified form of caste system which was completely discarded and condemned by the Buddhists. Buddhism soon spread outside India and is still followed by one-quarter of humanity; but Jainism never went beyond India of its followers has been very limited.

Buddhism and Jainism as mentioned above, have their roots in Hinduism. "They are mere offshoots of Hinduism, arising in protest against some of the corruption of the latter, discarding its evils, but retaining its fundamental principal like the *Law of Karma,* rebirth *Ahimsa*, etc. the popular mythology is not discared by them". Brahma, Indra and other gods figure in both Buddhist and Jain stories.Many of the old doctrines are presented merely as new ways of attaining the goal of liberation. But Jainism, so to say is a via media between Hinduism and Buddhism at that time.

School of Buddhism

A century after Buddha's death, Buddhist Sangha was divided into two schools, namely, the *Mahasanghikas* and the *Sthaviravadins*.

It was meant to popularize the religion of Buddha through *Jatakas* and *Avadanas*. The progressive section which advocated less stringent disciplinary rules was called the *Mahasanghikas*, while the conservation section which clung to the original idea of strict monastic life and rigid disciplinary laws was known as the *Thera or Sthavira-Vadins*. To interest the laity in Buddhism, *Mahasaghikas*, the progressive section of Buddhist monks began to preach the doctrines of *Paramites* (transcendent virtue of charity, forbearance, etc). They set on foot a movement against the austere from of monk-life envisaged in the Pali *Pitakas*. This movment brought out Buddhism from the seclued cloisters to the towns and village and converted it from a religion of the recluses to that of the masses. An average man now could aspire to get the benefit of the religion by constructing a *chaitya* or an image of Buddha and by worshipping it with flowers and other offerings. While the monks carried on their austere religious practices with in the cloisters, the people worshipped Buddha and expressed their devotion for the god (because to them Buddha was no longer a saint) by constructing huge massive monuments and carving on them scenes from the life of Buddha. This ornate and emotional aspect of Buddhism known as popular Buddhism, began to appear from the second century B.C. onwards, and flourished during the regin of Emperor Ashoka. More doctrinal change were introduced into this popular Buddhism during the reign of emperor Kanishka in the first century A.D., after the fourth General Council of the Buddhists. This led to the rise of the Mahayan or Northern Church of Buddhism. It was partly due to the attempt of learned Brahmana converts to Buddhism like Asvaghosha, reconcile Buddhism with Hinduism and partly to the fact that in North-Western India is number of new influences *'Word'* Greek, Christian, Zoroastrain and Central Asian '*Chamar*' had crept in the mind of people that *Raj-Rishi* is the hero of the '*Nam*' posted in Jammu.

When Buddhism became the religion of the foreign invaders, it entirely lost its original character. Buddha ceased altogether to be a dead teacher and became a living saviour, God incarnate, like Rama and Krishna, for the salvation of the human race. The Hindu theory of *Avatars* or incarnations was adopted by Buddhism, and historical Gautam Buddha was regarded as merely the latest of a series of incarnations of the *Adi Buddha* or Primeval Spirit and his image was worshipped. Side by side, there developed a number of gods and goddesses with elaborate description of their features and characters. This was Mahayanism, a new form of Buddhism. In addtiton to the worship of Buddha as incarnation of *Adi Buddha*, "Mahayanism declared that with the attainment of *Nirvana*, man will not return to this earth again, and therefore, he is incapable of doing any work, not even service to humanity. But those individuals who have no yet attained *Nirvana*,but are striving to attain it, can do real good to the suffering world. The *Bodhisattva*, who is such an individual preparing through several lives to attain the state of Budha or the completely Enlightened. One, is the real benefactor of humanity". Mahayanism, therefore, emphasized the *Bodhisattva* ideal more than even that of Budddha.Though the *Bodhisattva* ideal was known to the Buddhist even before, Mahayanism gave it a prominent position and made it a definite cult. A great exponent of Mahayanism was Nagarjuna who lived in the second or third century A.D.. Among other great exponent were *Vasubandhu, Asanga, Dingnage* and *Dharmakirti*. In course of time, Mahayanism was also subdivided into many sect such as, *Sunyavada, Vijnanavda,* etc, each with a philosophy of its own.

This Mahayan or the great vehicle differed in many essential points from the old real Buddhism called Hinayan or lesser vehicle. The introduction of the worship of the Buddha and the *Bodhisattva*. a novel feature of Mahayan, was in clear contrast of Hinayan. Another point of contrast is that whereas the Hinayanists relied more on personal efforts at good virtous living as the means to attain salvation, the Mahayanist relied more and more on devotion to and worship of the Buddha as way to salvation or *Nirvana* and, therefore, they introduced idol worship with its attendant rituals, ceremonies, charms and formulae, "Faith replaced reason, and devotional worship took the place of self-efforts." Another significant point of contrast between the sects is that the canonical texts of Hinayan were all written in Pali, while those of Mahayan were in Sanskrit.[20]

The Growth of Buddhism

With in a very short period Buddhism spread all over India. Before the Buddha had passed away, he had the satisfaction to see that the people and the princes of such mighlty Kingdom as Magadha, Kosala, Kausambi, Jammu and Kashmir State those of the Republican States of the *Sakyas*, the Vajjis, the Mallas, etc. embraced Buddhism and the whole of Middle India or *Majjhimadesa,* as it was then known, was dotted with Buddhist monasteries or *Vihars*. Under *Ashoka* and *Kanishka*, it was made the State Religion. It existed in a flourishing condition up to the end of the seventh century A.D. as testifried to by *Yuanchwang* and *Itsing*. The great monasteries of Nalanda were the significant centre of Buddhism. In the twelfth and the thirteenth centres A.D. it still continued under the patronage of the Pala Kings of Bengal and Bihar. It was this Pala period that many Indian teachers went to Tibet where they strengthened Buddhism and translated thousands of Buddhist works into the Tibetan language. The rulers of *Kanyakubja* in the North-West of the Pala Kingdom were also patrons of Buddhism. They constructed magnificent Buddhist monasteries and offered magnificient gifts to them.

Buddhist images of the ninth and tenth centuries have been founded in Mahoba, Ellora, Nasik and many other parts of the Deccan. Unfinished Buddhist cave termples are found in Aurangabad and other places. Thus, until the twelfth century, Buddhism although internally weakened and corrupted, was prevalent in India. Then, it declined and disappaered in the Muslim period though it continued to flourish outside India.

It was in third century B.C. when Emperor Ashoka, became its great devotee that Buddhism began to spread in the territories out-side India. The Buddhist missionaries converted in Sri Lanka and Burma to their faith. They then reached Mesoptamia and Syria in Asia Minor, Egypt in Africa and Macedonia in Europe. In the same period, Buddhism spread in Central Asia i.e., Kashmir and Sindh and according to a traditiaon, a son of Ashoka successfully established his own Kingdom in Kutch and its neighbourhood and spread Buddhism there. According to another tradition, Buddhism reached China at a very early period. Translations of Buddhist works in Chinese were made by *Kasyapa Matanga* who went to China as early as 56 A.D. Buddhism was introduced into Korea in 372 A.D., whence it reached Japan in 538 A.D. In Indo-china, Buddhism was taken up before the third century A.D., and in Tibet in 640 A.D[21] as little China.

The factors responsible for the spread of Buddhism in India and abroad are as followers:

1. Simplicity of Buddhism

Buddhism was a revoult against the highly complex system of sacrifice and rituals that prevailed in India in the sixth century B.C. The social and religious conditions of that time made the people disgusted with them. The Brahmans had fallen from their ideals. Superstitions had penetrated in to the very vitals of the society, and self-mortifiaction and severe austerities, penances, scacrifics and recitation of *mantras* had rendered Brahmanism very unpopular in Sanskrit language. Buddhism with its code of practical ethics came as a delverance from such a tyranny. Simplicity and nobility of the teachings attracted the masses who joined Buddhism in large numbers. By freeing the religion of all complicated and expensive ceremonials. Buddha made it accessible to the poor. Laying stress on practical morality in daily life, he made the life of the people healthier and happier. Buddha's rational view in regard to the ultimate problem of life and universe appealed to the masses most in easy manner.

2. Its Spirit of Equality

The spirit of Buddhism was very liberal and accommodating. It did not believe in the caste system or in the supremacy of the priestly class. It treated all man as equals recoginize the digity of man as man.Caste, according to Buddha, was no obtstacle to the highest truth the doors of his religion were open to all the high and the low, the learned and the unlearned the Brahmans and the *Sudhras*. By abolishing caste distinction and introducing democratic principles, Buddha raised the status of the lower caste people who in accepting Buddhism secured their social and spiritual liberty.

3. Its Power of Adaptation

Buddhism was a highly elastic faith and could easily adapt itself to the needs of all countries. With a few modification, it could suit every place. This accounts for its spread beyond the confines of India.

4. The Use of Popular Language

Hindusim was coached in Sanskrit language which was all Greek and Latin to the masses. Buddha on the other hand,explained his simple doctrines in the language of the people. His practical discourse, preached in the popular language, made a strong appeals to the man in the street and paved the way for national consciousness. The people were attrached by the fact that the great spiritual truths were made available to them in the language of the day and free of extortionate fees which the Brahmanas used to demand from them for similar services time and again in the history of India.

5. The Magnetic Personality of Buddha

"The magnetic personality of Buddha worked as a touchstone for all who came into his contact." The impeccable logic with which he answered the arguments of the learned conservation priest and the intense human feeling which inspired his teaching easily convinced priests, princes and poor people a like. His strict virtuous life, his irrefutable logic his forceful arguments and powerful reasoning, and his sweet, fluent and persuasive speech enable him to win over his Brahmana opponents in open debate and discussion. Consequently many of his converts were Brahmans, like *Maha Kasyapa, Sariputta Moggollana,* and other. They reconignized the futility of sacrifices and appreciated Buddha's interpretation of the '*Law of Karma*' or '*Karmarajya*'.

6. The Royal Patronage

In spite of all these factors, Buddhism might have remained only a petty sect of Hinduism, had not the royal patronage come to its help. Being himself a man of royal birth, Buddhism was readily listened to by the ruling chiefs and several aristocratic families and tribes accepted his teachings.

Then the royal patronage of Ashoka and Kanishka contributed to the success of Buddhism in India and its diffusion a broad. *Ashoka* who left no stone unturned in raising it to the dignity of a State Religion spread it far and wild. His son Mahendra and daughter *Sangha Mitra* became Buddhist missionaries and were very successful in carrying Buddhism to Sri Lanka. Ashoka engraved the tenets of his faith on pillars and rocks so that where the human voice could not reach, these stones might teach the people and serve as beacon of light for them. Thus, Ashoka's activities made Buddhism a dominating reliogus in India. This royal patronage was continued by other ancient kings like *Milinda, Kanishka*, and *Harsha*. During their periods great stimulus was given to the missionary work of Buddhism. This spread Buddhism in different corners of India.

7. The Buddhist Sangha

Perhaps the greatest factor that contributed to the popularity and growth of Buddhism was the missionary activites of the Buddhist Sangha. The Buddhist missionaries became the centres of light and learning. They were all selfless, devoted, able-bodies men of considerable moral and spiritual stamina. They had the injunction from the Buddha to be always on the move" "Go ye *Bhikshus* and wander," said the Buddha, "for the gain of the many for the welfare of the many, out of the campassion for the world, for the good, for the gain for the welfare of gods and men. Let not two of you go the same way". Thus, the Buddhist missionaries were made to carry the noble message of deliverance, from door to door and deliver it free to rich and poor, high and low a like. Eevn when the *Bhikshus* rested in a *Vihara* (Buddhist monastery) during the rainy season, they did not while away their time. They utilized this period in giving moral and spiritual discourse to the inquisitive persons who used to collect around the *Vihara*. A Buddhist *Vihara* was, thus, a centre which "provided all laymen of the town with free eduction in moral and Spiritual Truths calculated to bring more happiness and contentment to the human soul". In course of time, the *Viharas* had grown up not merely as organization for training missionaries, but also as great centres of culture, to which teachers and students flocked from far and near. Moreover, the Buddhist *Bhikshus* preached common ethics which the comprehendsion of an average man, whereas the Brahman *Sannyasis* or teachers or priests strove to unfold subtle philosophical problems and drew upon their scriptures in Sanskrit which was beyond the comprehensive power of a man in the street.[22]

Thus, the Buddhist monks and nuns with their simple lives and high ideals, with their zeal and selfles sefforts stirred the hears of the common folk to the very depths, and carried on the work of propagation of Buddhism efficiently and successfully in all over the world history.

8. Lack of Serious Rivals

In the field of missionary work, Buddhism had no serious rival sects. Hinduism was not marked by a missionary spirit, while Christianity and *Islam* had not yet made their appearenace. Buddhism was, thus, left free to flow in the direction it liked.

The Decline of Buddhism in Jammu State

Another Buddhism gained great popularity with masses, it was never able to destroy. Hinduism which continued to exist even when its rival Buddhism was at its height. Later, on when Buddhism deteriorated, Hinduism rose to a new vigour under the patronage of the Hindu monarchs especially the *Guptas* and *Rajputs*, and Buddhism began to decline. This process continued for centuries together till Hinduism recovered. The old strength, vigour and status of Buddhism completely disappearned from India, the land of its birth. It was eclipsed by Hinduism which has no history only riddles of life. The following cause contributed to this decline and eclipse.

1. The Inherent Defects of Buddhism

Buddhism had started as a simple faith. But with lapse of time it had become austere and formal. Its strict discipline in due course became a troublesome burden on its followers who now craved for an escape from it. Besides, Buddhism ignored God, while its rival Hinduism appealed to Him with all the colour and mastery associated with Supernatural Beings as in indirect form. The atheistical tendency in Buddhism turned the people against it.

2. Deterioration of Buddhism

With the lapse of time, those very features of Brahmanism were introduction into Buddhism against which its founded Gautam Buddha raised his voice of protest. The rise of the *Mahayanists* led to the worship of he Buddha and *Boddhisattvas* and created many more of the latter, such as *Avalokitesvara*, *Manjusri* and others. The images of Buddha and many new *Boddhisattvas* were worshipped everywhere,and people built great temples to them endowed with considerable wealth and ornaments. Then many separate gods and goddess were also introduced and were worshipped by Buddhists.

Many unworthy persons who entered Buddhist monasteries began to relax many rules and sought sanctions to indulge in many vices. Therefore, they introduced some practices which were contrary to the eithics of Buddhism and composed books on their own doctrines. This phase of Buddhism is known as *Tantric* or *Vajrayana Buddhism*. It advocated many esoteric practices in which women and wine were most essential things. The followers of *Vajrayana* or *Tantric* Buddhism claimed psychic powers which they obtained by constant mystic practices. These psychic powers to began to pass for spiritualism. The introduction of esoteric practices, demonstration of psychic powers, sorceries and incantations along with the worship of hundreds of gods and goddesses housed in temples and monasteries so completely changed the Buddhism of *Sakya Muni* that by the close of the twelfth century no trace of the old religion was left and Mysticism and Tantricism replaced it. Thus, the precalence of Vajrayana, which sapped the foundation of Buddhism by destroying all moral strength and making it rotten to the core, contribution considerably to the disappearance of Buddhism.

3. Degeneration of the Sangha

In the course of time many vices grew up in the Buddhist Sangha. The introducation of *Tantric* Buddhism helped to destroy the ethical fervour of the monastc order. A part from this as the rich and poor alike vied with one another in showing their gifts of god, silver and jewels on the Buddhist monasteries the coffers of the *Sangha* held more wealth than the treasures of kings. This bred a life of luxury and comfort in the monasteries poisoning the springs of spiritualism. The Ten Commandments of the Buddha were frequently infringed and the life of renunciation disappeard. As corruption crept in to the *Sangha* and the *Viharas* the Buddhist monks who were the leaders of the whole Buddhist community lost their reputation for a good character and other admirable qualites. The whole foundation of their prestige and power vanished and consequently, Buddhism lost its greatest engine of propaganda *Brahmin* the Sangha dominated society without reasoning and logic, but malpractices.

4. Loss of Royal Partronage

Buddhism had quickly risen to the status of a world religion through the remarkable enterprise of its royal devotees. The Buddhist monarchs like *Ashoka, Kanishka* and *Harsha* had mobilized the resources of the state in the cause of Buddhism. After their death state patronage was withdrawn from Buddhism. Many Buddhist monks and followers thus lost their support. They migrated to other frontier countries of India like Nepal, Tibet, etc. Consequently, its downfall was hastened.

5. The Assimilative Power of Hinduism

Hinduism has a remarkable power of absorbing many other religious forms. In fact, it is a synthetic religion containing many virtues and doctrines found in other religions. It possesses enough capacity to imbibe alien religious beliefs, doctrines and cultures. In due course Brahmanism incorporated the best of Buddhism. It was on account of this inherent assimilative power of Hinduism that foreigners like the *Huns* and *Sakas* were readily absorbed into Hindu fold. Consequently, "Hinduism continued to gains adherents. while Buddhism declined in numbers, due to its austerity and seclusiveness".

6. Brahmanic Revivalism

The great setback to Buddhism came from Brahmanic revivalism. With the advent of the *Gupta* rules to political power as *Chamar*, the revival of Brahmanical Hinduism, which had already commenced gained a considerable momentum. The Gupta Emperors were zealous Hindus,and patronized liberally the Brahmanas, their religion and their language '*Word*' Sanskrit. Under their active royal support Brahmanism regained its old enthusiasm, and led a stromg offensive against Buddhism. From the eight to the eleventh centuries the Rajput princes who governed the most of the Northen India were not favourably inclined to Buddhism. Being a warrior race the creed of non-violence did not appeal to them as a *Sudhra* Religion to unite the human race. They joined the power cult or *Shakti-Puja* of Hinduism through false notions for earning of money and material. The notion that *Sankaracharya,* a great Brahmana thinker celebrated scholar, led anti Buddhist crusade has been now disproved [23]. However, during the revival of Brahmanism, the Brahmana thinkers demonstrated openly the superiority of this Hinduism. As a result of this, Hinduism began to recover its popularity and Buddhism began to lose its hold over the masses as a 'blind faith' called *'Brahminical Ideology'* as common term form the background of *'Only Mind'* not from the God.

7. Muslim Invasions and Persecution

When Buddhism was growing rotten to the core, the Turks invaded the country and destroyed great Buddhist temples and monasteries, including those of Nalanda. Had the monasteries and temples possessed less wealth, possibly, the Turks would not have destroyed them, since the Turks main motive was to obtain their wealth. Besides, on account of their special dress and lonely dwellings, outside the cites and town the monks and their monasteries were conspicuous enough to be singled out by the Muslim invaders for attacks and persecution. This sounded a fatal blow to Buddhism in the formation of a 'New Society' of the Father.

The loss of royal patronage, the assimilative power of Hinduism and the Brahmanic revival under the Guptas have been contributory causes for the disappearance of Buddhism from this country. But the real cause lay in the deterioration, degeneration and rottenness that overlook Buddhism and Buddhist *Sangha* in the last stage of their existence which, however, coincided with Muslim invasions and persecution. But to state that Buddhism disappeared because of Muslim persecution alone is worng a 'blind faith' originated from *Sudhra clan* of *Rai Family* of *Sindh* and Multan. So great was the decay of Buddhism and so disgraceful became the monastic order that Buddhism succumbed while Brahmanism, being equally under the persecution of the Muslim conquerors in the same period survived and later on flourished well under the leadership of *Dalit Kings* of the Kashmir history. Under Musilm persecution many Buddhist monasteries and monks were destroyed and many were forced to flee from India to the safer border countries, such as, Nepal and Tibet. Buddhists in India were thus abandoned and left without guides. In course of time, some of them, who had relatives and caste people of their own in Brahmanism returned to that religion and others who were regared inferior or suffered from social and economic tyranny of the higher castes were induced to embrace Islam in original form as 'crescent of India'. Thus, somewhere in the fourteenth century Buddhism disppeared from Northern India due to the rise of New concept of the *Nam-History*. Though, it lingered on for a few years in some other places, but it was not able to stand without backbone and consequently the disappearance of Buddhism from the land of its birth was complete.[23]

8. Revival of Buddhism in India

Recently an earnest attempt to revive Budhsim in India has been made by the *Maha Bodhi* society of India founded by the late Devamitra Dharmapala. The *Mulgandhakuti* Vihara of Sarnath near Varanasi has been restored by a mignificant building. Rest –houses for Buddhist monks, pilgrims, a hospital, a school and library building have also been constructed there. Sarnath, where the Buddha had delivered his first sermon and where Ashoka had immortalized a *'Dalit King'* that even by constructing a *Vihara* or monastery and setting up an inscribed pillar is again humming with life as the headquarter of the Buddhist organisation in India after a lapse of many centuries. New monasteries or *Vihars* have been constructed at Kusinagar, Sravasti and Calcutta. A Buddhist rest-house for pilgrims has been built at both Gaya near the *Maha Bodhi Temple.* Now, many branches of the Maha Bodhi Society have been started in different places of India to spread the message of the *'Nam'* in the society for the development of the human history.

Contribution of Buddhism to Indian Culture

The progress of Buddhism exercised considerable influence in shaping the various aspects of Indian life-'*Word*' cultural, social, religious and political study. Its contribution to Indian culture are as followes:

1. Easy, Intelligible and Popular Religion

Buddhism gave a popular religion without any complicateed, elaborate and unintelligible ritual,such as could be performed only by a priestly class. It consciously set itself to appeal to the masses and it wonderfully and quickly succeeded in winning their hearts buy its simplicity, emotional element, easy ethical code,use of popular language, popular method of teaching by means parables, and worship and prayer in congregation. It introduced a personal element in religion in the form of a human saviour.

2. Noble Ethical Code

The Buddha prescribed a severly practical and simple code of eithcs for the followers. In addition to noble moral code, such as, charity, purity, self-sacrifice, truthfulness, and control over passions, he emphasized love, compassion equanimity and non-injury to living creatures in thinking speaking and doing. Through the *Upansihads* had advocated these virtures before the rises of Buddhism they did not raise the tone of public morality to such a high pitch as Buddhism. Then, the Mahayan sect of Buddhism placed before the pople a noble ideal of service in the form of *Bodhisattva*. Besides these, Buddhism explained to the masses that man is the architect of his own destiny, not any god or Gods. This led to the rise individual of religion in place of Brahmanism.

3. The Influence on Hinduism

In the domain of Hinduism of the later period, there is unmistakeble evidence of the influence of Buddhist thought and ethics. Though Buddhism never dislodged Brahmanism from its high pedestal, yet it left on it a permanent impression of its own. The doctrine of *Ahimsa*, so strongly stressed, devoutly preached and sincerely practised by the Buddhists, was in corporated bodily in their teachings by the Brahmanas of later days. This emphasized respect for life in all forms and minimized the spirit of sacrifices which involved loss of life. Buddhism, thus, exercised humanizing effect on Hinduism. This indirectly led to the rise of that particular phase of the *Bhagawat* religion which completely absorbed the doctrine of *Ahimsa* in materalism, as the rule of Brahmins was there.

4. The Monastic System

Another new thing given by Buddhism was the monastic system or the organization of religious devotee in disciplined communities or orders. The institution of the *Ramdvaras* and the *Mathas* (organized brotherhoods of Sadhus) is a feature which was introduced in the Hindu society as aa result of its contact with Buddhism. Before the advent of Buddhism, old men used to retire to hermitages in the forest to end their remainig days in solitary, to repeat the history, again, recluse and lonely contemplation. But the grouping of religious devotees into a fraternity of monks, obeying a common head, following a common codes of disciplinary rules, and living together under a common roof, did not exist. Then, the *Buddhist Sangh* for the first time made systematic organized attempts in India to teach simple code of ethics for better spiritual life of the masses. In due course, the Buddha *Viharas* became the first centres of free education in India. There the common folk received their lesson on Moral and Spiritual Truths. In course of time, they had become great centres of culture and learning at Sarasvati Indus River of Chenab in Jammu Region a group of the *'Sudhra Family'* called *chamars* they widely spread their own religion to unite the race of the *have-nots.*

5. Idol Worship

The practice of worshipping personal gods, making their idols and erecting in their honour was adopted by the Hinduism in imitation of the Mahayan Buddhists. These element did not form a part of the Aryan religion which consisted mainly of sacrifices on open altars in the open air, as a false religion of Hinduism.

6. Development of Literature of the Spoken Languages

As Buddhism was intended for the masses, it made popular the spoken languages of the people. Lord Buddha himself preached in the languages of the masses and so did the Buddhist monks and nuns. It was in the Buddhist *Viharas* that the beginnings of the vernacular (*Prakrit*) literature were made which later on developed into an extensive body of literature as *Nam* or *Chamar*. Buddhism, thus, fostered the growth of a vast and varied literature in the popular language of the people.

7. The Buddhist Art

The finest contribution of Buddhism to Indian life was made in the realm of architecture and sculpture. Before the advent of Buddhism, art was handmaid of religion. Consequetly, it did not progress much during the Vedic Age. Architecture was mainly confined to the construction of *Mandaps* or *Yajnasalas*, *stambhas* or pillars and *yajna Vedis* or altars for the purpose of sacrifices. But Buddhism gave a powerful impulse to religious architecture. Today, almost every museum in the world possesses relics of Buddhist art. Under the patronage of Buddhism all branches of art '*Words*' architecture, sculpture, painting, etc. *'Chamar'* progressed well. Viharas were built over the country for giving permanent abode to the Buddhist monks. The *stambhas* bearing religious emblems were raised by the pious followers of Buddhism in honour of their teachers and other holy men. Similarly,big stupas of stone were raise over the relics of the Buddha and the *Bodhisattvas*. The whole life-story of Lord Buddha was expressed in store. These new buildings of Vihars, temples and monuments were richly carved and ornamented, and thus in course of time, a new style of architecture and sculpture came into existence. Some pieces of Buddhist scultpture are considered to the finest specimens of art in the world. The stupas at *Sanchi, Bharhut* and *Amravati* of Ravidas Culture, the stone pillars of Ashoka and the cave temples at Kanheri (Bombay), Karle (Poona) and Naisk are considered the best specimens of the Buddhist art. The *stupas* at *Sanchi* is world renowed for its gateways and railings which are profusely covered with scultpure, depicting either scenes from the Buddhas life or incidents from his legendary past lives. Then, the Gandhara School of Art is the outcome of Buddhist patronage. It tried to interpret Indian subjects and religious conceptions through the Greeco-Roman technique. It had plenty of charm to the people of '*Nam*' or '*Chamar*'.

Again, the Buddhists set the example of constructing and dedicating cave temples, and the Hindus and Jains followed it. If the chisel was busy in expressing the Buddhist ideals of life in stone, the brush did not lag behind. The walls of the caves and temples were richly decked with beautiful frescoes which perhaps formed the life-work of many of the artists. The remnants of this art at Ajanta, Bagh and Sigiriya (Sri Lanka) would suffice to inspire a person even today. The Buddhist art was essentially an art with an intense feeling for nature and a vivid comprehension of the unity of al life, human, animal and vegetable. It had spiritually whch is more intended than made manifest. It displayed an evident delight in life felt by the people. Life in it had the continuity of a stream and space was reduced to a convention Kings, princes, courtries, merchants, hunters, gods, goddness, men, women, angles, fairies, animals, trees, creepers, flowers, *'Word'* or '*Nam*', all were spread across the surface of the stone and fused into a dignified cavalcade of life. The method of the Buddhist art was that of continuous narration and the technique used was one of the memory picture[25] of the Lord of Gateway of India.

8. Equality and Toleration

Buddhism denounced the caste system with all its distinctions and advocated equality in society. All could embrace Buddhism and partake in the Buddhas message, irrespective of sex, age or position in society. This shattered the conception of caste distinction and divisons and made people tolerant of one another. Buddhism also preached to the princes the principles of peace, forbearance, love, affection and tolerance. Consequently, the outlook and policy of the princes underwent a considerable social, religions, economic change during that period.

9. Intellectual Freedom

The authority of the Vedas, the supremacy of the priesty class and the complicated elaboration of the rites undermined intellectual freedom. The Buddhā raised his *'voice of God'* against it. He encouraged independent thinking and advocated free scope for individuality in religion. He asked his disciples to be rational in outlook. Instead of following doctrines or dogmas blindling, they should first get themselves convinced of their truth. Consequently, the thinkers of the later ages pondered independently over the problem of philosophy and offered their original constributions in the realm of philosophy. All this produced the world-renowed Buddhist philosophers like *Nagarjuna*, *Asanga*, *Vasubandhu*, *Dharmakriti,* etc.

10. Buddhist Influence on Indian History

The course of political history of India also reveals sure sign of Buddhist influence. Buddhism changed the whole history of India by striking in the hearts of Kings and princes a sense of horror of bloodshed and war. It was the Buddhist law that forced Ashoka to give up wars and make his policy pacific. The adoption of the Buddhist pacific creed by Ashoka proved a serious set-back to the Imperial Policy of the monarchs of Magadha. It not only gravely hindered the territorial extension of Magadha, but the extraordinary humans policy of Emperor Ashoka jeopardized the very existence of the Mauryan Empire. In the absence of proper occupation for a continues period of thirty years, the Ashokan army lost it morale and therefore, later on failed to resist the Bactrian Greeks when they invaded India. The policy of the Mauryan state under Emperor Ashoka became more humane and philanthropic and the code of punishment, too, was revised and made more benevolent and sympathetic for the people. The Ashokan government widely extended also its sphere philanthropic activites and provided free hospitals for men and animal a like. It seems the *Pinjrapoles* and *Gosalas,* which are prominent features of modern Hindu charitable institutions, had their origin in the Ashokan free hospitals for animals.

Again, Buddhism unlike some other religions, never resorted to the sword and acts of vandalism to gain adherents. This made the Indian nation shrink from shedding blood and pacific temperament. The vivid description of the horrors of war terrrifed the Indian out of political life and life of war. Buddhism, thus toned down the martial spirit in the country. Consequently, Indain discarded martial games and exercises, and in due fell as easy prey to the sturdy invaders from the North.

11. Political Unity and Nationalism

As started above, Buddhism popularized the Indian vernaculars. It made a direct appeal to the primary emotions of its audience. It simpicity endeared it to the common folk who came to look upon it as the religious of the country, Buddhism, thus, helped in the evolution of the Indain nation and paved the way for a political of India or *Bharata*.

12. Diffusion of Indain Culture Abroad

But the most important fact is this Buddhism proved to be one of the greast civilizing forces which India gave to the neighbourimg countries. Buddhism broke the isolation of India and established an intimate contact between India and the foreign countries. It was India grestest gift to the outer world. Indian monks and scholars carried Buddhism, and, indirectly, Indian culture to foreign countries from the third century B.C.onwards. Indian culture and civilization had been carried by the Buddhist missionaries into *China, Mongolia, Manchuria, Korea, Japan, Burma, Java, Sumatra, Indo-China* and other countries since the days of *Ashoka*. Thereafter, the foreign, converts to Buddhism looked up to India as the Holy land '*Word*' the cradle of their faith and '*Chamar*' and pilgrilmage to this country became the highest ambition of their life. This tie of religion came to blind many foreigners with our country and praved the path for carrying India culture abroad in the form of '*Nam*' or '*Kalma*'.

Other Sects

Buddhist and Jain literatures speak of numerous other sects teaching variation of doctrines and practice during this period. The following were some of the important sects among them.

First come the *Ajivikas* who were said to be *Sudhra Sannyasis*. The sect of the *Ajivikas* was established possibly by *Nanda Vachahha* and headed by *Kisa Samkichchha* after him. The *Ajivika* acquired dynamic energy under the third pontiff *Makkhali Gosala*. Born a salve himself *Makkhali* was a radical teacher who denied even the basis doctrine of all Hindu thought '*Word*' or '*Nam*' theory of *Karma*. He argued that 'man is subject to the laws of nature. Action, therefore, cannot lead a man out of the inevitable, and so a quietist view of life is desirable". Gosala's followers centre round Sravasti, the capatil of Kosala where Gosala preached and died year before *Vardhaman Mahavir*, The *Ajivikas* enjoyed the patronage of Empore Ashoka and also of his grandson *Dasarath*, both of whom dedicated caves to them. This sect is referred to by Patanajali (150B.C.) and in the *Milinda-Panha* (first century A.D.). It lingered on in the Gupta period and is referred to by Varahmihira (sixth century A.D.) and in the *Harsha-Charita* (seventh century A.D.). The followers of the *Ajivika* sect were known as *ekadandins* from the single staff that they carried. The Jain *Bhagavati Sutra* refers to the fact that the *Ajivikas* had shifted their centre of activites to the Pundra country at the foot of he Vindhya mountains and that in their pantheon were included many Vedic and non-Vedic gods; two of them were Punnabhadda (*Puranbhadra*) and *Manibhadda* (*Manibhaddra*).

The *Ajivikas* believed that things gain perfection even through non-performance of actions and that there is a process of nature and spiritual evolution through ceasless rounds of birth and deaths. They laid great emphasis on extreme asceticism, love of solitude, disdain of comport and even of decencies and love of austerities of all kinds. *Ajivikism* altogether disappeared from India in the fourteenth century A.D. after being shifted from province to province.

Another radical sect was that of Ajita Kesakambeten who taught that everything ended with death, a precursor of the *Sunyavadins*. Another sect was that of Purna Kassapo a Brahamna teacher, whose main doctrine was that of merit nor of demerit. He was a very popular teacher of the *'Nam'* at the time.

Besides the protestant sects described above, sometimes other sect were developing even within the folds of orthodox Hinduism. They did not distinctly repudiate the Vedas. They became very prominent in the later history of Hinduism and acquired considerable power and popularity. "The fearures of these sects was the worship of one particular god as the supreme deity." He was conceived as *Vishnu, Siva, Shakti* or some other form. Salvation could be achieved through His grace and one has to follow the path of Bhakti for this. It was during that age that the Vedic gods were being reshuffled, some receding in to the background and other coming to the forefront. To the latter class belong Vishnu and *Rudra* (or Siva) both different in character from Vedic gods of those names to Ravidas Saint. The devotes of Vishnu called *Vaishnavas* or *Bhagavatas* devloped a sect called *Bhagavatism*, while those of Rudra developed a sect called Saivism for the development history from one generation to another as an idea of the *Ravidas*.

The Vaishnavas inculcated intense love and devotion to Vasudeva Krishna, the hero of the *Mahabharat* who was identified with Vishnu, the Supreme God. When the theory of *dasavatar* (ten incarnations) was evolving it came to be believed that Vishnu had undergone many incarnations to save the world from some impending castastrophe. Rama, the hero of the *Ramayan*, later on came to be respected as one of such incarnations. The personal love and deep devotion (*Bhakti*) of the worshipper to his god, who was given a human touch and the emphasis on the supreme importance of doing ones worldly duties according to ones status in society, made *Bhagavati*sm very attractive to the people. At first, it was confined to the Mathura district (in Uttar Pradesh). Later on, it spread all over India and became very popular due to the human elements contained in it.

Saivism had its origin deeply rooted in the worship of a prototype of Siva at Mohenjodaro in the pre-Aryan age, With the lapse of time this god of the pre-Aryans became identified with god Rudra equivalent to Ravidas of the Vedic Age. In the Vedic age, Rudra represented the destructive agency or the bale ful side of a storm. He was supposed to posses benevolent charactistics as well as benevolent ones. In the age of the *Upanishads* he was looked up on as the Supreme God, the Creator and Destroyer. Later on, Rudra came to occupy the front rank among Hindu gods and is known as *Siva, Sambhu* and *Samkara*. He is considered as benign and terrible, a *Mahayogin*, roaming about lonely on cremation grounds, draped in hide and surrounded by wild beasts and ghosts, dwelling in the Kailas mountain in the Himalayas, fondly attached to his family and frequently revelling in dance and music. From the very early times, Siva has been worshipped as the *phallus (Lingam)* which is even now very common in our country. Thus,the existence of Saivism may be traced as early as the second century B.C. [27] Probaby a definite Saiva system was set up by a person called *Lakulin* or *Lakulīsa*. In the beginning, Saiva sect were known as *Lakula*, *Pasupata* or *Mahesvara* after the name of their god or historical founder. Later on, four important schools of Saivism arose namely, *Pasupata, Saiva*, *Kapalika* and *Kalamukah*. But the extreme sect of Saivism was that of the *Kapalikas* who followed some uncanny practices of the life history.

In the study, it reveals by the close of the seventh century B.C., Hindu society was firmly established. It was the outcome of the diffusion of the pre-Aryan and Aryan social element. A new culture which later on came to be known as the Hindus culture was being evolved in the society. The striking feature of this culture was the dominance of religious and supremacy of the priestly class. But this religions, which was gradually evolved out of the Vedic religions i.e. '*Nam*' or *'Chamar'*, had degenerated in cumbrous. Meaningless ritual. It had become cold and formal and had lost touch with the masses. This created spiritual and moral unrest in the society. Consequently, new leaders of thought and religion arose and started a number of protestant movements to purge Hinduism of its corrupt practices. The sixth century B.C. witnessed the birth of such movements in India or Bharat of Jammu Region. But only two such movements Brahminism, Jainism and Buddhism '*Word*' or *'Nam'* stood the test of time and survived. They carried the spiritual truths and the message of love to the cottages of the poor and the courts of the princes, and deeply influenced the course of Indian history. They had enriched Indian culture by using art to express religion. As result of this, a new style of architecture, sculpture and painting came into being producing the finest specimens of art in the world. But more than this Buddhism successfully carried the touch of Indian religious and culture beyond the confines of India and its adjoinng areas. When the rulers of Magadha were extending their dominions in India,the Kings of Persian Empire, had extended his conquest right up to the *Hinduskush* and Gandhara formed a part of his empire. Darius I, another rulers of the Persian Empire sent his admiral *Skylax* to explore the mouth of the Indus river which was situated at that time in Jammu Region in the area of Akhnoor near Ambaran. This was followed expedition to *Indra* (means power) in 517-16 B.C. resulting in the annexation of the portion of Punjab. This formed the twentieth province of the Persian Empire comprising the whole of the Indus Valley Civilization originated from the Akhnoor, and probably stretching as far as the Salt Range in the Jhelum District. The Punjab dominious of *Darius* formed the richest and the most populous province of the Empire of Persia yielding a revenue of rupees one crore and fifty lakhs per annum.The Persian Governors and District Officers were stationed in the Punjab and the Punjab is were also recruited the Persian army and they fought under the banner of Persia in Greece. During the course of the following two centuries all the above mentioneed Kingdoms of the Jammu Region were gradually absorbed in the Imperial Power of the *'Nam'*, and set up the Magadha Kingdom, first set up buy *Saisunage* Dynasty (642-413 B.C.) and.then '*Nanda Dynasty*' (413-322 B.C.) of the '*Sudhra Rulers*' that is called '*Nine Nanda Rulers* of the *Nam-History; Bimbisara Dynasty* (582-554 B.C.) was also the real founder of the greatness Kingdom of Magadha. Buddhsim and Jainism were also flourishing in this region on the basis of reality i.e., '*Nam*' or '*Chamar*' at par.

Notes and References

1. A.K. Khanna; op. cit.
2. *Yuan Chwangs Travels in India* (629-645 A.D.); Tr. By Thomas Watters M., first Edition; New Delhi; 1961; p. 263.
3. *Ibid.*, p. 264.
4. *Ibid.*
5. A.K. Khanna; op. cit.
6. R.C. Majumdar; *The Vedic Age*; Bombay, Reprint 1988, p. 384.
7. R.C. Majumdar; *The Age of Imperial Unity*; Bombay, Reprint 1960, p. 363. Hereafter referred as A.1.U.
8. Jadunath Sarkar; op. cit., p. 23.

9. Kern, *Manual of Indian Buddhism*; pp. 68-69.
10. E.V. Havell; *Aryan Rule of India.*
11. *Philosophy of Pratyabhijna;* An article written by Shail Gulhati, Sunday Magazine, Daily Excelsior 17-2-2008.
12. *The Cambridge History of India;* Vol. 1.Chapter,VI (b) *The Cultural Heritage of India*; Vol. I Chapter IV
13. *The Cutural Heritage of India* Vol. I Chapter V. p.185.
14. References made from (a) Barodia ; *History and Literature of Jainism* (b) Mrs. T.Stevenson; *The Heart of the Jainism* ; (c) J.Jaini *Outline of Jainism;* (d) Radhakrishnan; *Indian Philosophy;* Vol. I, Chapter VI.
15. *Philosophy of Pratyabhijna; op. cit.*
16. A.I.U. pp. 424-25.
17. *(a) R.K. Mookerji ; Hindus Civilization; pp.241-43. (b) The Cultural Heritage of India; Vol. I pp. 221-24.*
18. *Banana-Through the Ages;* An article written by Satyendra Pratap Singh; Daily Excelsior; 17-2-2008.
19. *(a) The Cultural Heritage of India* Vol. I Chapter IV, (b) T.W. Rhys-David *Buddhism in India* 1903, (c) Radhakrishan; op. cit. Vol. I Chapter VII-XI. *(d) The Cambridge History of India; Vol. I.*
20. N.N. Ghosh; *Early History of India*; p. 59.
21. *The Cultural Heritage of India;* Vol. 1 p. 297.
22. Longman's; *History of India;* p. 54.
23. N.N. Ghosh; op. cit., p. 64.
24. *Ibid.*, pp. 60-67.
25. B.C. Gokhala; *Ancient India;* pp. 212-14.
26. Pery Brown; *India Architecture* (*Buddhist and Hindus*); Chapters V to VIII.
27. R.C. Majumdar; *Ancient India;* Reprint; Delhi, 1968; p. 185 **Note:** For advanced study, see book (b) R.G. Bnandarkar, *Vaishnavism, Saivism* and *Minor Religious System.*

Plate- XVI

Fig . 27. Buddhism in Kashmir a Learning Centre

Fig. 28. Shiva Shrine, Sudhmaha Deva (Jammu)

6

The Pre-Mauryan History of Jammu Kingdom (c. 650-325 B.C.)

The dominant characteristic of the period with which we propose to deal with the 'Pre-Mauryan History of the Jammu Area from 650-325 B.C.' was the rise and growth of 'New Monarchy' in Eastern India lying between the areas of Chenab and Ravi of which we have a presage in the *Aitareya Brahmana*:

'In this eastern quarter (*prachyam disi*) whatever Kings there are of the eastern peoples. They are anointed for Imperial Rule (*samrajya*); 'Oh Emperor' (*Samrat*) they styled him when anointed[1]' to rule over the world-history.

The eastern peoples (*prachya*) are not specified by the Brahmana in the same way as those of South, the North and the Middle Country. But there can hardly be any doubt that they used to live to the east of the *dhruva madhyama dis* and thus answer to the *Prasii* of the Greek writers and the confederated nations who dominated the valleys of the lower Ganges of the Kashmir history found in the area of *Kishtava* or and the son. The most eminent among these nations was Magadha which embraced the modern district of Patna and Gaya in Bihar at that time.

Several factors contributed to the greatness of the new star in the firmamet of India politics which we have aready expressed in the previous chapters of the text. It occupied a strategic postion between the upper and the lower parts of the Gangetic plain. It possessed an impregnable fort in a mountain fastness and built another at the confluence of the two night streams [2] are a source of life and prosperity in the life of Indian people. The two mightly streams i.e., Chenab and Ravi, passed through in the various parts of the Jammu Region already discussed in detail. Despite the places having a rich Art and Culture during the ancient period in our study, outside the Jammu Region, not may people know about it but they adopted its development in the social life as a communal harmony, as a process of the '*Nam-History*'. Overlooking the Ravi river, its still stands as Majestic structure of the weaving of *Pashmina* shawls of white colour during the *Pala* rules over the Jammu and Kashmir State. A comparative analysis of two roads on both side, Ravi provided an answer as to why Basohli lades for tourist purpose because Basohli was a pilgrimage centre of the forefathers of the *'Sudhra Family'* contributed towards the world-wide popularity of the Jammu and Kashmir State, are the scenic beauty of the Kashmir-history of the *Chamar-dynasty,* they were the Buddhist people of India in the ancient period of the Indian history as an Artist race of the natural paintings. The most picturesque spot indeed Basohli, with a divine blessing of the Father during the 17th centuries and before. The road from Lakanpur to Basohli on ther west bank of Ravi, is single, tiring and rusty. On the other hand, the roads from Pathankot to Dalhousie, that runs parallel in Himachal Pradesh is wide, double land and better maintained during the ancient period of our study.

The Jammu Region which begins from the boundries adjoining Punjab and Himachal Pradesh across the river *Ravi* (Lakhanpur) stretches over to the last reach of Indo-Pak borders (Poonch) in the east to the west encompassing *Kandi* belt of herbs, shrub and other broad leaved trees of immensive important and with the altitudinal gains the rich '*Chirpines*' 'blue pines and their allied intermingle. From Jammu, uprising towards higher reaches of *Udhampur, Kud, Patnitop,* on the one hand and *Trikuta* hills of *Katra*, *Reasi* and to their North-West are having the richest varieties of pines which gives Kaleidoscopic glimpse when viewed airly in their ambient. Not only that these pines are of serene, scenic and splendor importance, but these are as well of tremendous importance in a variety of ways. The 'Pride Chenab' Valley, *de facto*, is bountiful and predominently the richest forest area in the entire state. The entire terrain is a rare combination of inner and outer hills of *Shiwalika*s ranging from 1200 m. to 3600m. above the sea level the narrow valleys give way to the small rivulet which drain in to 'Pride Chenab'. The Tawi and to the deep gorges and other emerald waters, pituresque enchanting valleys with every flourishng vibrant,salubrious and Shimmering pines largely formed owing to fast flowing nectar clear waters over the millennia for which the *Chirs* pines belong to 'Gymnosperms" part of plant Kingdom of Jammu Region having the characteristics of cones-bearing and so is with *Chir* pine. This falls under coniferae family and takes its start from lower elevation to higher ones (4000 to 6000 feet from the sea level). The *Chiur* is long-leaved pine botanically spoken as 'Pinus roxburghli' is a large loving –tree with clear straight bole and thick bark as a defense against forest fire, the leave are in boundless of three needles obscurely trequetrous, light green, cones are solitary or 3-5 together and the seeds are long, oblinquely oblanceolate, compressed with membranous wings which helps in their pollination as it is through wind of the natural thought.

Chir pines are spreaded over the outer hills of *Shiwaliks* ranging from *Basohli-Billawar, Udhampur, Reasi, Kalidhar, Sundarbani, Rajouri, Nowshera, Mandi* and *Poonch.* The tree is of ample importance so far as extraction of resin is concerned, apart from fulfilling the demands of local in respect of timber, small wood and fuel. The resin extracted from the *Chirs* finds its immensive value after the segregation of resin and turpentine oil which is useful in many pharmaceuticals for the manufacture of multihued important medicines. An idea was mooted in the Indian history much earlier for colletion of the dry needles which find its usefulness in the manufactures of card-boards as is mostly prevalent in other *Chir* bearing state of U.P. Maharashtra, Kerala, etc. This shall serve twin purposes, first the first fire shall be minimized, improved local economy and boosting card-board manufacturing. This is, unambiguously,a workable solution in averting forest fires, apart from opening new avenues for the employment.

Chir pine, as thus, has great promise in afforestation programmes and is widely planted in its natural habitat. Many sites of its natural habitations since the time immemorial are, however, deficit in organic matter water holding capacity, nutriential availability, microfauna are lacing in almost all the desirable physical, chemical, and biological characteristics of the life were necessary for such sites as thus well suited during the Pre-Mauryan history of the Jammu Kingdom and the adjoining areas i.e. foot hills of the Punjab.

Blue pines also spoken as "*Pinus Wallichiana*" in botanical parlance and '*Kali* 'locally is a large Majestic tree having slate 'Word' coloured smooth bark with leathery young stems of *Chamas. Tana* Like *Chirpines* its leaves are also in bundle each groove is having five needles which are slenderical, triquetrons, glancous on the inner faces, cones are generally 2-3 together on penducles. Seeds of thus species are blackish in comparison. *Brahmins* of the period, ovoid, acute and compressed and the trees catches height from 6000-10000 feet from the seal level, sometime intermingley with *deoda*r and at places with *chir* pines etc, The wood is as good as that of *Deoda*r, which is pinkish-brown, moderately hard, resin duds are smaller than those of *chir* pines of the same period. The sapwood yied resin for superior to *chir* pines and its leaves are used as stuff for cushions were used during the period of our study. The bark of the tree is used like state for roofing temporary huts made by *Ravidas* and his seeds were oftenly eastern by the local inhabitant of the pre-Muryan people of the '*Nanda Dynasty*' of '*Sudhra Family*'.

Giant Himalayan pine, unambiguously occupied its unique placement in the Himalyan region during the period under study. The most magnificent and Majestic *Deodar* 'prince of the timber', 'tree of the gods' anglicised into 'deva' 'daru' more correctly, larch of the western Himalayas are as its admiring name, (botanically neomenclaturised as *Cedrus Deodar* is a large tall gregarious tree. The largest and longest ever live tree in India i.e. '*Nam*' or God renowned for its grestes beauty as a Creative Power of the human history ever born in this area, whose branches are horizontal having pyramidal Crown of the world. The leaves of the tree are a cicular, triquetrous, glaucous green in dense fascicles. The tree ranges a height from 7000-8500.feet from the sea level and intermingles amongst blue pines, spruce, fir and Moru oak plants.

The tree is of ample importance in so far as its timber value is concerned which is prominently used in multihued costruction as the story of *Sudhra history* is concerned. The cedar oil extracted from its stumps finds multitudinous uses in our phamaceutials for the remedial measures of various hues in life of the man.

Chilghoza pines are spoken as Pinus generdiana in botanical parlance and is mostly confined in Paddar Valley of Kishtwar and thence in the higher reaches of Kashmir. A cluster of such pines were spotted by the author whilest being on tour of Padder Valley. There is a *Mata Jawals* ji temple at *Atholi* as a historical point of view in the history of the areas. However, of course, the most articles of food are well known throughout Northern part of India as *Chilgoza* which is basically the seed of this site used for pine tree which is highly relished like other dry fruits viz *Kazu*, etc. This pine is also confined to the most parts of Afghanistan the seeds are around 0.8 inch in size are long ablanecoloid and terete in patron.

There is another variety of the *Pindrow or Morinda* as in locally spoken is found in the higher reaches of coniferous and is botanically nomenclaturized as *Abies Pindrow*, also named as silver oak, is a gagantic pines which homes in bears and must of the other fauna in the altitudinal variations amongst other vibrant and salubrious forest ranging from lower to highest strata in the ramified eco-system[3] in comparison with the society of the man too,is called as the paradise on the earth during '*Divine Rule* or *Chamar Rule*' *(See Plate XIX; Majestic Pines Fig. 29)* and *Chir Pines Jammu & Kashmir Areas;* Fig.30) as a view of the areas in historical research.

In brief, study demonstrates,that the pines of the period,were ramified during the pre-historic review of the '*Nanda Dynasty*' with this efforts the higher reaches of the Jammu Region, were having green gold in uphill lands during the period of our study. Ravi and Chenab were the two greatest centres of learning having the highways of trade and commerce in those days. It had a fertile soil and its resources were included an elephant crops which was truly formidable during the later stage of the *Nanda* rulers. But advantage of position and material resources alone cannot raise a notion to eminence until one has no '*Pure-Thought*', i.e., '*Nam*' in their mind. It was the character and the spirit of the *Sudhra* people during the '*Nanda Dynasty*' 'that give all their life and efficacy to them, i.e., the Brahmins of the period. As in Western Europe, so in Magadha, we have a commingling of races and cultures which did not appear in the begging of *Nanda rulers; they were the* independent rulers of the '*Nam*' or 'God'. *Kikatas* and other *Anaryas* blended here with priestly class and fighting class of Aryans were remained with Indian people and some with neighbouring land of western Europe for the revival of their 'Pure-Race' of the '*Nam*' (*See Plate XX. Basohli Beyond the Traditional Values, Ravi in Dams Formation as Collection of the Chamar History;* Fig.31). It[4] is possible to detect two strand in the cultural as well as the ethnic texture of the Magadhan people. The same race that produced fierce warriors and exterminator of princes and peoples listened to the quiet teaching of Mahavira the Jain and Gautama the Buddha. It played a part in the evolution of a universal religion as it did in the foundation of a pan-Indian Empire. The wide outlook of the Magadhans was not a little due to the absence of the rigidity that marked the social polity that evolved on the banks of the 'Sarasvati Indus of the Jammu Region' and the upper Ganges. In their realm Brahmanas could fraternize with *Vratyas*. *Kshatriyas* could admit plebeian (*Sudhra*) girls to their harem, blue-blooded aristocrats could be done to death or otherwise deprived of the child of a *Nagara-sobhini* and a barber could aspire to Imperial Dignity. It bears to witness the tradition which began around 3rd and 4th century A.D. during rule of the Gupta period in Indian History that Jammu State was flourishing with religious art and literature. Two of the five rivers i.e. *Indus, Satluj, Ravi, Beas* and *Chenab* in undivided of Panjab pass through the part of the Jammu province are the Ravi and the *Mighty Chandrabhaga (Chenab).* The Tawi Rivers are the tributaries of *Chenab, 'Word'* or '*Nam'* the Jammu Tawi and the Malkani Tawi of the Bahu Fort Kingdom, in the ancient time called as *Surya Putri or* the daughter of the Sun God as '*Nam*' or *Chamar*. In one of the ancient texts; the river has been referred as 'Holy' for dip. In this way, presently, the water pollution adversely changes the quality and disturbs the balance of ecosystem. Therefore, there is a challenge to man from the Nature to keep the mind clean for human history.(*Also See Plae XX, Tawi Rivers of Jammu Kingdom*; Fig.32)

Magadhan Kings and statesmen were sometimes ruthless in their methods. But they had the wisdom to establish an efficient system of government in which high bureaucratic functionaries (*mahamatra*) as well as village headmen (*gramikas*) had their share. Foreign observers speak with evident approbation of their judiciary, roads irrigation works and care of alien residents. While nor fighting shy of metaphysics, they laid great stress on exertion (*parakrama*) in this mundane life with the object of welding the diverse elements of *'Greater India'* (*Jambudvipa*) in to a unit bound by political as well as cultural ties. This was facilitated by the ancient idea of the all-encompassing *Purusha* "*Word*" later called *Maha Purusha* (The Great Being) *'Chamar'* and his political counrterpart the sole sovereign (*Ekarat or Chakravartin*). In the Magadha ministrial rulers of the *Prasii* had an instrument of the *'Nam-History'* which they, could use for popular education and inspiration in times of trouble and despondency. We owe much of our knowledge of ancient times to these bards to cleanize the society of the man which made corrupt both morally and mentally.

The early dynastic history of Magadha is shrouded in Darkness. We have occasional glimpse of war-lords and statesmen, some probably entirely mythical, others having more appearance of reality. True history commences with the famous *Bimbisara* of the *Haryanka Kulha* who launched his people in that carreer of conquest and aggrandisement which only ended when *Ashoka* sheathed his sword after the conquest of Kalinga, i.e., materialistic war against the Brahmins.

The family of *Bimbisara* was responsible for the fortification of a village at the confluence of the Son and the Ganges which grew into the city of Pataliputra and soon replaced the old capital, *Girivraja –Rajagriha.* It also saw, and actively supported, the growth of the religious movements associated with *Vardhamana Mahavira* and Gautama Buddha.

According to Buddhist tradition the *Bimbisarids* made room for a new line styled *Saisunaga.* The *Puranic* chronicles, however, do not distinguish between the two families and make *Saisunage* the common ancestor of the Kings belonging to both the groups of the same family as *Nam* on earth as 'Deepit Raj' son of Dr. Raj Kumar masters of the human history.

Saisunaga rule seems to have ended in a tragedy. The last notable ruler of the line fell a victim to a plot engineered by an all powerful official who had "advanced to too near a place in the confidence of the monarch", as an idea of the development of the human history i.e., God and Man.

The Nandas

With the passing of the *Saisunagas* from the stage and the assumption of supreme authority by the regicide, who is no other than the famous founder of the Nanda line, we enter upon a new speech in the history of this country. For the first time, we have an empire which transcends the boundaries of the

Gangetic basin. It is not a loose assemblage of virtually independent states or feudal barnies which have a wholesome respect for the power and might of a *roi soleil*, but an integrated monarchy under as *Ekarat* (single ruler) possessed of vast resources in men and money. The old, almost uninterrupted ascendancy of clans *cliaminig* the blue blood of *Kshatriyas* is at an end as *Sesnaga*. The new ruler is a *novus homo* who wages a war to the knife on the *Kshatriya* and rouse the relentless hostility the most astute of the politically minded *Brahmanas* of the age. He incarnates according to the *Puranic* Chroniclers the spirit of the Iron Age (Kali) and his accession is taken to mark a chronological epoch like the birth of Parikshit several centuries earlier.

Unfortunately the chroniclers disagree among themselves as to the exact period of the rule of first *Nanda* and show disvergence from Jain and Buddhist traditions in regard to the duration of the dynasty as a whole. In the absence of a clear and unanimous tradition speculation is unprofitable. The family was still on the throne of Pataliputra when Chandragupta,who was then but a youth [5], met Alexander in the Punjab in 326 B.C. It had possibly come to power before the death of Xenophan sometime after 355 B.C. That famous historian refers in his *Cyropadia* to a powerful king of Indian who aspired to be an umpire in disputes between the great nations of Western Asia and was 'a very wealth man,' a deseription that has a special application to the *Nandas* to forward the message of the God to other readers. The enormous wealth of the Kings of the line is vouched for all our authorities. It is hinted at by the most famous of the Chinese pilgrims and was known to the Tamil poets of the *Sangam* that God reside in North western countries, Xenophon and was referring to the sixth century B.C. But his description of the Indain monarch may have been reminiscent of his own days.

Some schlolars read a reference to a *Nanda* Era in the *Hathigumpha Inscripition of Kharavela*. No such era was, however, known to Alberuni who gives a concise account of the reckonings prevalent in his days in Chapter XLIX of his work on *India*. The interpretation of the expression *ti-vasa-sata*, which measures the interval between Nandaraja and Kharavela is also a matter of controversy. In any case, the uncertainty of the precise date of the Hathigumpha record and the doubtful character of the reading of several of its passages, make the chronological references of little value in determining with accuracy the exact epoch of the first Nanda ruler of the *Sudhra* Family of the Jammu region.

Curiously enough the dynastic name *Nanda* is not known to any contemporary authority. It is no doubt, mentioned in the *Kautilya Arthasastra*, which is traditionally assigned to the age of Chandragupta Maurya. But the work contains references which point to a much later date, The reading

'*Nandrum*' in the place of '*Alexandrum*' suggested by some modern writers in the narrative of Justin, who epitomizes the account of Pompeius Trogus and may have had access to earlier sources is absolutely unjustified. Among extant works, which may, with some degree of plausibility be assigned to a period anterior to the Ceylones chronicles and the *Puranas*, it is the *Milinda-panho* which refers to 'the royal family of Nanda'as *Sultan* of the medieval period. But an earlier notice of Nandaraja is contained in two passages of the Hathigumpha record of Kharavela;

'Panchame cha dani vase Namdaraji ti-vasa –sata oghatitam Tanasuliya-vata-panadim nagaram pavesayati.'

'And then, in the fifth year, (Kharavela) caused the canal, opened out by King Nanda three hundred (or one hundred and three) year back to be brought in to the capital from the Tanasuliya road."

Again, in connection with the twelfth year of Kharavelas reign, we have a reference to *Namdarajajitam Kalimga-Jana samnivesam* (or, according o another reading, *Namda-Raja nitam Kalimga Jina-samnivesa*), that is, a place for assemblage of people or a Jaina shrine in Kalinga acquired by King Nanda.

For a fairly connected history of the dynasty, we have to make use of Indain tradition. Indian writers were concerned with the period of Nanda rule partly as marking a stage in social-political movements and as an episode in the story of Jaina pontiffs, and partly as an important element in the *Chandragupta-Katha* of which we have Buddhist fragments in the *Milinda-panho* and the Ceylonese Chronicles and commentaries, and Brahmanical versions in the *Puranas*, folk –tales one famous drama, and certain works on polity were also done by them without authentic result of the human history without *Nam-dan;* it is difficult to confirm the truth in History.

Mahapadma Nandas

The first Nanda bore the name *Mananapadma* or *Mahapadmapati*, 'sovereign of an infinite host" or "of immense wealth" according to the *Puranas* and *Ugrasena* according to the *Mahabodhivamsa*. The *Puranas* describe him as a son of the last King of the preceding line by a *Sudhra* woman. Jaina works on the other hand, represent Nanda as the son of a coutezan by a barber to dress the society in one uniform system. This tradition finds support in the classical account of the pedigree of Alexander's Magadhan contemporary who was the predecessor of *Chandragupta Maurya*. Referring to this prince who occupied the throne of Pataliputra when according to Plutarch, *Chandragupta* met *Alexander* in the Punjab, *Curtius* [6] inform us that his father was in fact a barber, scarcely staving off hunger by his daily earning, but who from his being not uncomely in person had gained the affections of the queen, and was by her influence advanced to too near a place in the confidence of the reigning monarch. Afterwards, however, he treachously mudered his sovereign, and then, under the pretence of acting as guardian to the royal children, usurped the supreme authority and having put the young princes to death begot the present King." It shows that *Nanda* rulers away from the material culture

There has been some difference of opinion as to whether "the present King" (*Agrammes*) of Curtius ruling in 326 B.C. refers to the First Nanda himself or to one of his sons. The classical testimony leaves no room for doubt on the point. *Agrammes* was born to the purple. His father had already usurpired supreme authority and put the legitimate heris to the throne to death. The description of "the present King" can hardly be applied to the first Nanda who was *ganikakushi-janma* (born of a courtesan) and whose father did not exercise sovereign power. We have, therefore to conclude that Agrammes, or Xandrames as he is called by Diodorus, belonged to the second generation of the usurping family and his father was the first Nanda, the *Mahapadma-Ugrasena* of Indian tradition.

The murdered sovereign must have belonged to the line that preceeded the Nandas on the throne of Pataliputra. The ruler who answers best to the descripton given by Curtius and Diodorus is *Kakavarna-Kalasoka* whose tragic end is alluded to in the *Harshacharita,* and whose sons were nine or ten "*Chamars*" in number were according to Buddhist tradition, ousted by *Ugrasena Nanda.* The name Agrammes is possibly a distorted form of the Sanskrit Augrasainya, "son or descendent of Ugrasena". It may be noted in this connection that Augrasainya as a royal epithet may be traced back to the *Aitareya Brahmana,* where it occurs as a patronymic of *Yuddhamsraushti.*[7]

The rise of an all powerful official in the time of the later *Saisunagas* probably indicates that the system of administration had undergone remarkable changes since the days of Bimbisara. That monarch had exercised a rigid control over his *mahamatras*, dismissing those who advised him badly and rewarding those counsel he approved. The result of the "purge" was the emergence of the type of official represented by *Varshakara* and *Sunitha* whose rigour and efficency are well illustrated in the Buddhist texts. The situation must have changed considerably toward the end of the Saisunage epoch. The career of Ugrasena remind one of that of *Bijjala* in a later age, and his early relation with the preceding royal family had important point of resemblance with that between Cardinal Mazarin and the family of Louis XIII. If traditions to be belived the office of a Chief Minister was maintained throughout the Nanda period, through the functionary in question never reached the pre-eminent position that Ugrasena occupied in the day of his royal master. Jaina and Hindu writers refer to a distinguished line of imperial chancellors from *Kalpaka* to Sakatala and *Rakshasa* like Brahmins. It is difficult to say if these tradition figures had any historical reality. They are not mentioned in contemporary or semi-contemporary documents. But "advisers of the King" very small in number, but most respected on account of their character and 'Wisdom,' are mentioned by Greek observers who wrote about conditions in the fourth century B.C.

Next to the "advisers of the king" probably stood the "generals of the army". One official of this class, *Bhadrasala*, find prominent mention in the *Milinda-panho*. The Nanda army was a powerful fighting machine and we are told by the classical writers that the last King of the line 'kept in the field for guarding the approaches of his country, twenty thousand cavalry, and two hundred thousand infantry, besides two thousand four-horsed chariots, and, what was the most formidable force of all a troop of elephants which ran up to the number of three thousand"[8] Diodorus and Plutach raise the number of elephants to four thousand and six thousand respectively. The latter puts the strength of the army of the Gangetic nations at eigthy thousand horse, two hundred thoused foot, eigth thousand was chariots, besides six thousand fighting elephants.

It is no wonder that the lord of such an immense host should aspire to be a sole monarch, an *Ekarat*, of the vast regions stretching from the Himalayas to the Godavari or its neighbourhood. The historians of Alexander speak of the most powerful people who dwelt beyond the Beas as being under one sovereign. Q. Curtius Rufus, for instance, gives the following particular: "beyond the river (*Hyphasis* or Beas) lay extensive deserts. Next came the Ganges, the largest river in all India, the farther bank of which was inhabited by two nations, the Gangaridae and the Prasii, whose King was Agrammes[9]." The account of Diodorus is similar. But he calls the King Xandrames instead of Agrammes. The account of Plutarch or the English translation, seems to suggest that the "*Gandaritai*" (Gangaridae) and the "Prasiai" had separate kings and this is said to find support in the number of horses, war-chariots and fighting elephants assigned to the 'Kings' of the two nations i.e. Heaven and Earth, which is large than those assigned to Agrammes-Xandrames by Curtius and Diodorus. But the number of foot soldiers remains the same in all the accounts. The discrepancies regarding the number of elephants, etc. may be due to divergence of tradition rather than reinforcement by contingent supplied by as allied king. Pliny informs us that the *Prasii* surpass in power and glory–every other people in all India, their capital being *Palibothra* (Pataliputa), after which some call the people itself the *Palibothri*, nay, even the whole tract of the Ganges.

Jaina writers refer to the subjugation by Nanda's minister of the whole country down to the seas:-

"Samudravasan sebhya asamudramapi sriyah"
upayahastairskrishya tatah so "krita Nadasat" [10]

Puranic chroniclers speak of the extermination by *Mahapadma Nanda* of all *Kshatriyas* in the human history like *Sudhra Race*. This is taken to imply that he uprooted all the *Kshatriya* families which ruled contemporaneously with the *Saisunagas* (*tulya-kalam bhavishyanti savi hy etc mahikshitah*)[10] viz., the *Ikshvakus, Panchalas, Kaseyas, Haihayas, Kalimgas, Asmakas, Kurus, Maithilas, Surasenas*, and the *Vitihotras*.

The *Ikshvaskus* were the ruling clan of Kosala, roughly corresponding to modern Oudh. They had been humbled by *Ajatasatru*, the son of Bimbisara. They had been humbled by Ajatasatru, the son of *Bimbisara.* The history of the clan after the famous rulers *Prasenajit* and his son *Viduratha* is obsure. A passage of the *Kathasaritsagara* refers to the camp (*kataka*) of Nanda in Ayodhya. Apparently the King had undertaken an expedition to Kosala. An important section of the Ikshvakus seems to have been driven southwards as they are found in the third or fourth century A.D. in occupation of the lower valley of the Krishna, and Godavari.

The *Panchalas* occupied the tract of country between the upper Ganges and the Gumti together with part of the Central Doab.They do not appear to have come into hostile contact with the Magadhan Monarchy before the rish of the *Nandas* in the Daccan, and must have been brought under control by that dynasty, as the evidence of the classical writers seems to suggest the scholars write the things in right way.

The *Kaseyas*, or the people inhabiting the district round Benares, had come under the Magadhan sway as early as the days of Bimbisara and Ajastasatru. It is recorded in the *Puranas* that a Saisunaga prince was "placed in Benares "when the founder of the line took up his residence in Girivraja the Magadhan capital in Early times. It was apparently from a descendant or successor of this prince that Nanda wrested control over the people of Kasi,

The *Haihayas* are found in possession of a part of the Narmada Valley down to medieval times. Their earlier ca pital was at *Mahishmati*, which has been identified by Pargiter with the rocky island of *Mandhata* and by others with a town named *Mahesvara* on the northern bank of the Narmada within the boundaries of the Indore State. The subjugation of this region by the Nandas does not seem to be improbable in view of the Puranic statement about the humiliation of the rulers of the neighbouring realm of Avanti by their Saisunage predecessors. But there is lack of confirmation by independendent witnesses. It has, however, to be remembered that both Malwa and Gujarat formed integral parts of the Magadhan Empire in the days of Chandragupta towards the close of the fourth century B.C. and the way may have been prepared by the Nandas of the '*Sudhra Family*'.

The *Kalingas* occupied the extensive territory stretching from the river Vaitarani in Orissa to the *Varahanadi* in the Vizagapatam District. Its capital in ancient times was the famous city of *Dantakura* or *Dantapura* which has been identified with the fort of *Dantavaktra* near Chicacole in the Ganjam district, washed by the river *Languliya* (Langulini). The conquest of apart of *Kalinga* by Nanda is suggested by the Hathigumpha record. The phraseology of the inscription hardly supports the view held by some scholars that the *Nandaraja* mentioned therein is a local chief. The reference is doubtless to a conqueror who established his authority over a *Rannivesa* (place) of Kalinga and constructed some irrigation works in the province for the welfare of the public life.

The *Asmakas* occupied a part of the Godavari Valley with their capital at Potali, Potana, or Podana. The last form of the name remind one of Bodhan to the south of the confluence of the Manjira and the Godavari not very far from Nizamabad in the Hyderabad state. The existence on the Godavari of a city called '*Nau Nand Dehra*" (*Nander*) a little to the west of the Nizamabad District, renders it probable that the dominions of the "Nine Nandas" may have embraced the classic land of the Asmakas, though independent confirmation by contemporary or semi-contemporary writers is not available for the verification of the Truth in history.

The Kurus, as is well known, occupied the country to the west of the *Pañchcalas* stretching from the Ganges to the river *Sarasvati* (modern *Sarasuti*) Chenab river of the Indus Valley Civilization of Akhnoor of the Jammu Kingdom which flows past the sacred sites of Kurukshetra near Thanesar. The subugation of this territory by the *Nandas* is not expressly mentioned by any contemporary authority, but is rendered probable by the Greek evidence in regard to' the dominions of the nation of the *Parisioi* and the *Gandaridai'* which seem to have embraced the whole tract of the *Ganges* and Yumana.

The *Maithilas* were the people of Mithila,a city framed in the epics owing to its connection with the heroine of the *Ramayana* i.e., *Sita* and her father *Janaka*. It has been identified with the small town of Janakpur with in the Nepal border, north of where the *Darbhanga* and Muzaffarpur Districts meet. The greater part of Northern Bihar, over which the powerful confederation of the *Vrijis* (including the *Lichchhavis rulers of the Gujjar and Bakarwal* family, as *Sudhara Race,*) had exercise away, had been annexed by Ajatasatru and his successors are known to have graced *Vasisali*, the capital, with their presence on occasion. If the *Puranic* tradition has any value the chieftains of Mithila must retained a certain amount of independence in the fastnesses of the Nepalese *Tarai*. The periodical floods from the *Gandak,* the Bagmati and connected streams during the rainy season must have rendered his part of the country very diffcult of access and it is not surprising that the forest of the Tarai should have sheltered an autonomus principality when the great city of *Vaisali* fell before the onslaught of *Ajatasatru*. The *Nandas* attained greater success as they could operate from their base in *Vasilai.*

The *Surasenas*, the *Souraaenoi* of Megasthense, had their capital at Mathura on the banks of the Yumna. Their subjection to the Prasii appears very probable from the account of Alexander's historians.

The *Vithotras* are closely associated with the Haihayas and the Avantis in Puranic tradition. Their sovereignty is said to have terminated before the rise of the famous line of Pradyota. If the Puranic statement, found in a later passage of the *Bhavishyanukirtana*, about the contemporaneity of some of the Vitihotras with Saisunages, has any value the latter many have restored some scion of the old line when they took away the glory (*yasah kritsnam*) of the Pradyotas. As already stated above, the undoubted control that Chandragupta Maurya exercised over Western India including the *Girnar* region makes it highly probable that the way had seen left clear by his Nanda predecessors. Jain writers expressly mention the Nandas among the successors of *Palaka*, the son of Pradyiotas of *Avanti*.

Much of the information given above relating to the conquests of the first Nanda is derived from late works. But the evidence of Greek writers, taken together with the testimony of the Hathigumpha eqigraph leaves no room for doubt that *'Nanda Dynasty'* of the *'Sudhra Family'* that ruled over the easten nations of India in the days of Alexander exercised sway over practically the whole of the Gangetic basin together with some portion, if not the whole, of Kalinga. Some ingenuity has been shown by certain writers in drawing a distinction between *Purva Nandas* (earlier *Nandas*) and *Nava Nandas* (new or later Nandas) and identifying a prince of the former group with the Nandaraja of Kharavel's inscription. But the theory rests on an unjustifiable interpretation of the expression *Purva Nanda* used by *Kshemendra* and other epitomisers and redactors of the *Brihakatha*. The Puranic as well as the Ceylonese tradition known of the existence of only one Nanda line and all writers incuding those belonging to Jaina persuasion take the word *Nava* in the expression *Nava* Nanda to mean *nine* and not *new,* but they are the old one or traditional. *Purva Nanda* is the designation of a single king and not of a dynasty and he is distinguished not from the *Nava Nandas* but from a pseudo-Nanda(*Yogananda*) the reanimated corpse of king Nanda.

Several Mysore inscriptions state that Kuntala, a territory which included the southern part of the Bombay Presidency and the contigous portions of Hyderabad state and the state of Mysore, was ruled by the Nandas. But thses are of comparatively modern date (C. A.D. 1200), and too much cannot be built up on their statement. It has, however, to be admitted that no satisfactory account is yet available of the expansion of the Magadhan Empire beyond the Krishan and the *Tugabhadra* which must have taken place before the promulgation of the Ashoka Inscriptions of the Kurnool and *Chitaldroog* dated in the third century B.C.

Administration of the Nandas

We have little information as to the way in which the vast domination of the *Nandas* were administered. If tradition is to be believed the founder of the line clearly aimed at the establishment of a unitary state. The reference to the extermination of all the *Kshatriyas*, coupled with the use of the terms *ekarat* and *ekachchhatra c*an have no other meaning. Greek writers, however, make separate mention of the *Prasii* and the *Gangaridae*, though hintng at their subjection to a common sovereign, and Arian notices the existence beyond the Beas of "an excellent system of internal government under which the multitude was governed by the aristocracy, who exercised their authority with justice and moderation". The aristocratic government to which the classical writer refers, cannot fail to remind one of the *Sanghas* of the Kurus, the Panchals and other, mentioned by the *Kautliya Arthasastra*, who bore the title of raja (*rajasabdopajivinah*). The flourishing condition of the areas in question where "the inhabitions were good agriculturists" the land exceedingly fertile and the internal government excellent, is in striking contrast with conditions prevailing in the home province of the Prasian (Magadhan) monarchy where "the king was detested and held cheap by his subjects". It appears from the evidence that is available to us that Nandas allowed a considerable amount of autonomy to the people in the outlying parts of their empire e.g., the Gangetic delta and the territories lying beyond Oudh. But the home provinces empbracing the ancient *Janapadas* of Magadha (South Bihar), Vriji (North Bihar), Kasi (Benares), Kosala (Oudh), etc. were treated in the same way as the Sultans of Delhi dealt with the metropolitan province and the river country of the Doab. The presence of the king not only in Pataliputra, the capital of Magadha, but also in Visala or Vaisali the capital of the Vriji country in North Bihar, is vouched for by tradition and we have also an interesting reference to an encampment at Ayodhya. The strong position held by the Nandas in the heart of their dominions as contrasted with their comparative weakness in the frontier regions is the theme of certain interesting anecdotes that the Buddhist commentator on the Great Chronicle of Ceylon, and other late writers tell of Chandragupta's ambitious adventure on the threshold of his career. The stories, no doubt, belonging to the domain of folklore and certain motifs have a surprisig resemble with the *Alfred saga*. But the Central idea may have based on genuine tradition.

Greek observers of the fouth century B.C. and the epitomisers of a later age allude to a system of provincial government under officials styled *nomachs* and *hyparchs*. A *nomarch* is a local ruler or governor of a *nome* or district The word *hyparch* is sometimes used to denote a *Satrapa*. But the functionary in question is at times spoken of as subordinate of a Satrap. Through the officials are mentioned chiefly in connection with the Punjab in the days of Alexander and the Magadhan Empire in the Maurya period, it is permissible to conjecture that the provincial system under the *Nandas* specially in the districts under their undisputed sway, was not very different. In the third century B.C,. we hear of administrative charges called *ahara*, *vishaya, janapada,* etc. under functionaries styed *Mahamatras, Rajukas, Pradesikars and Rashtiya* who seems to answer to the *nomarches* and *hyparchs* mentioned by the Greeks in their texts.

The lowest administrative unit was the village. In the *Prasna Upanished*, a later Vedic text, we hear of *adhikritas* appointed for *Gramas* or villages by the *Samrat* or emperor *Gramikas* or village headmen find mention in the early Pali Canon who possibly corespond to these *Adhikritas*. In the early days of the Magadhan monarchy the king appears to have kept himself in close touch with these village functionaries. We hear of a big assembly of thousands of *Gramikas* held by Bimbisara. There is no evidence that the *Nanda* followed this example and the detestation of the people to which classical writers bear witness, ill accords with any close touch with life in ther rural areas. Such a contact was only restablished when Ashoka in the third century B.C. under took even to villages in outlying areas in pursuance of his policy of *Dharmanusasti*.

According to certain manuscipts of the *Vayu Purana*, which is one of the oldest works of this class and is referred to by *Bana* in the seventh century A.D., the first Nanda ruled for twenty-eight year and was followed by his sons who ruled for twelve years to Nanda. If this chronological scheme be accepted, the first Nanda could hardly have died before 338 B.C. as one of his sons was reigning in 326 B.C. an d the dynasty must have come to power not earlier than 367-66. B.C. But as stated above there is hardly any unanimity among our authorites, *Puranic*, Jain and Buddhist, regarding the reign period of *Ugrasena Mahapadma* and the total duration of the rule of his family have been discussed and later on accepted by their previous family of the *Sudhra* Dynasty of Mauryan family.

Later Nandas

Among the sons of the first Nanda referred to in the *Puranas, Sahalya* or *Sahalin* seems to have the eldest. Most of the *Matsya* Mss. spell the name as *Sukalpa*. But a *Vayu Mss*. gives the form *Sahalya* which, as pointed out by Barua, corresponds to Sahalin of the *Diayavadana*. The names of the sons of the first Nanda given in the *Mahabodhivamsa* are altogether different and have not yet been confirmed from independent sources. The name of the last prince, *Dhana Nanda* is unknown to be classical writer who mention. Agrammes or Xandrames as the name of the prince of the "barber" dynasty, who occupied the throne when Alexander was on the banks of the Beas, as occupied by Baba Gurinder Singh in Beas in present form.

Xandrames the name mentioned by Diodorus, has been taken by some scholars to answer to the Sanskrit *Chandramas,* and identified with Chandragupta Maurya. But Plutarch clearly distinguishes between '*Androkottos*" and the king of the "Parisiai" in the days of Alexander and his account receives confirmation from that of Justin. Xandrames or Agrammes was ths son of a usurper born after his father had obtained the supreme authority among the Prasii, while Chandragupta was himself the founder of a new sovereignty the first ruler of his dynasty. The father of Xandrames was a *barber* who could claim no royal ancestry. On the other hand,Indian writers are unanimous in representing Chandragupta as a scion of a race of rulers, through they differ in regard to the identity of the family as fourth grade ruler of the *Sudhra Family* and its claim to be regarded as of pure Kashatriya extraction. Jain evidence clearly suggests that the barber (Nai) usurper is identical with the *napita Kumara* or *napitasu* who founded the Nanda line.

The figures of the eight princes who succeeded the first Nanda are rather shadowy and we do not know how far the tradition recorded by late writers can be accept as sober history. The last of them is said to have been addicated to hoarding treasure.He amassed riches to the amount of eighty *kotis*. In a rock in the bed of the river *Ganges,* he caused a great excavation to be made for the purpose of burying the treaures he had acquired. Levying taxes, along with other articles, even on skins, gums, trees and stones, he amassed further riches he disposed of similarly. This account taken from the commentary on the Great Chronicle of Ceylon can claim some antiquity. Professor Nilakanta Sastri points out that a Tamil poem contains an interesting reference to the "very famous" Nandas "victorious in war, who having accumulated treasure first in beautiful Pataliputra hid it in the waters of the Ganges". *Hiuen Tsang* the famous "Chinese pilgrim of the seventh century A.D, refers to the "the five treasures of king Nandas seven precious substances[11]," were laid down in their kingdom of the Jammu region.

The accumulation of an enormous amount of wealth, to which all over authorites bear witness, probably implies a good deal of financial extortion and it is not surprising that the Nanda contemporary of Alexander "war detested and held cheap by his subjects as the Father, took after his after than conducted himself as the occupant of a throne" with the beautiful study of the '*Nam*' or God as an evolution concept of the history in human life.

The oppressed people soon found a leader of the dynamic approach to defeat the communal forces with the stroke of pen as an authantic record of the history is going to compile. Plutarch and Justin refer to young lad named and *Androkottus* or *Sandrocottus*, doubtless identical with the famous Chandragupta, who visited Alexander in the Punjab and showed a keen interest in the affair of the Prasii. 'Not long afterwards" he mounted the throne and "shook off from the neck" of India "the yoke of servitude" "by overthrowing the existing government in India and expelling the prefects of Alexander. Indian chronices introduce by his side another figure, a *dvijarshabha* named Kautilya or Chanakya, whom tradition represents as an inhabitant of Taxila.

While some of the Indian writers, notably the author of the Sanskrit play entitled the *Mudra-Raskshasa*, are chiefly concerned with the battle of intrigue conducted by Kautilya, the *Milinda panho* affords us a glimpse of the clash of arms between the contending forces of the Nandas and the Mauryas. "There was *Bhaddasala* (*Bhadrasala*), the soldier in the service of the royal family of the Nandas and he waged war against the king *Chandagupta* (*Chandragupta*). Now in that war, there were eight corpse dances. For they say that when one great head holocaust has taken place by which is meant the slaughter of ten thousand charioteers and a hundred *kotis* of soldiers on foot, then the headless corpses arise and dance in frenzy over the battle field". The passage contains a good deal of mythical embellishment. But we have reminiscence of the blood bath through which *Chandragupta* had to wade to the throne as a whelm of affair of the Father.

The glamour of the Nandas has been dimmed by the greater splendour of the succeeding dynasty. But it is well to remember what the kings of the bequeathed to their immediate successors and to posterity. They had, to use the words of V.A. Smith, "compelled the mutually repellent molecules of the body politic to check their gyrations and submit the grasp of a superior controlling force". They developed a fighting machine that was used by the later rulers of Magadha with terrible effect in resisting the onslaught of foreign invaders and carrying on the policy of expansion within the borders of India or *Bharata* that had been inaugurated by *Bimbisara* and *Ajatasatru*.

If tradition recorded by the epitomisers of the *Brihatkatha* is to be believed, Pataliputra under Nanda rule become the abode (*Kshetra*) of *Sarasvati* as well as Lakshmi, the home of learning as well as of material prosperity. A galaxy of scholars '*Word'*, *Varsha*, *Upavarsh*, *Panini*, *Katyayana*, *Vararuchi*, *Vyadi* '*Charmar*' is said to have added to the age. While much of the traditional account may be mere folklore unworthy of credence we may well believe that the cultivation of grammer received an impetus in this age. The scholarship on *Panini*, presupposed by the great commentary of *Patanjali,* show acquaintance with the *Yavana lipi* and it is by no means improbable that some of the predecessors of Patanjali are to be assigned to the Nanda Age. Kings of the line are credited by certain grammarians with the establishment of a particular kind of measure (*Nandopakramani manani*) of the human history.

In social matters the rise of *Nandas* may be regarded as symptomatic of a surging up of the lower classes. The *Puranic* Chroniclers represent the dynasty as harbingers of *Sudhra* rule and as irreligious (*adharmika*). The last statement is significant in view of the traditional connection of the family with Jain ministers and patriarchs. But the evidence on the point is of a character which make it difficult to build too much on it that *Sudhras* played a predominent role in the Jammu Kingdom for its development.

Regions Beyond the Magadhan Empire

No account of India in the age of the Nandas is complete with out a brief notice of the vast stretches of territory with in the confines of this country i.e., Jammu and Kashmir state, that lay beyond the limit of their empire. Unfortunatey, the exact boundary of the Nanda dominions cannot be determined with any amount of precision with the aid of available evidence because they were the rulers of the '*Nam*' as '*Infinite Power*'. This is particularly true of the South, In the north the inclusion of the Ganges Valley with in the Nanda Empire is, as already suggested by Greek and Puranic evidence. We shall perhaps not be far wrong if we regard the upper reaches of the stream, that once flowed through the *Ghaggar-Harkra* bed of the '*Ravidas Culture*' as forming roughly the boundary line between the Magadhan empire of those days and the autonomous tribes and kingships of the *Uttarapatha*. In the south Greek evidence is not of much help. Puranic testimony as we have seen hints at the incorporation in to their empire by the Nandas of the principalities of all the leading *Kshatriya* families of the day, including in all probability those of the south. Among the latter prominent mention is made of the *Haihayas, Kalingas* and *Asmakas*.

Following this evience, which comes from sources assignable to the commencement of the Gupta Age, we may tentatively fix the southern boundary of the Nanda empire or at least of the arena of its political and military activities, at the river Godavari. Barring some Medieval Jaina treatise and inscriptions of doubtful value for early times, there is hardly any evidence that the hegemony of the *Nandas* extended for beyond that famous river Ganga. Persian inscriptions, observations of Greek and Latin writers, supplemented by brief notice in Indian literature and epigraphs, enable us to say a few words about the two great regions of India i.e., Jammu and Kashmir State-namely the *Indus basin* beyond the Ghaggar and South India beyond the Godavari, which in the light of the evidence we have adduced, seem to have lain beyond the limits of the Nanda Empire in the history of India.

A Physical Aspects of the Areas

Bounded on the north by the Outer Himalayas; on the west, by the eastern *Hindukush*, the Safed Koh, the Suleiman and the Kirthar ranges on th south by the surging waters of the Arabian Sea and the "immense salt-water waste of the Rann of Cutch", and on the east by the sand-dunes of the Thar or the Great Indian Desert and the uplands and ridges of the Eastern Punjab,the extensive Valley of the Indus of the Jammu Region, and its feeders constituted a little world not much affected by the eddies and currents of Magadhan history before the rise of the Great Mauryas.

The country falls in to three natural divisons:- (1) the mountainous regions extending from the upper reaches of the Sutlej to the basin of the Chitral and certain outlying rocky areas, (2) the flat rolling plains of the Punjab intersected by a network of rivers and brooks; and (3) the almost rainless tract of the lower Indus area of the Jammu Region and its delta,an important part of which now forms the provinces of Sindh[12], Chenab and Ravi Basin.

The land desceibed above presents great varities of scenery. The eyes meet in the North the snow-clad speaks and glaciers of the Himalayas and the Ladakh and Kashmir luxuriant vegetation that clothes the submountainous region. A striking contrast to this is accorded by the plains of the Indus (Sindh) river which look like an agent of the Nature.

An attempt has been made through the discoveries of Archaeological evidences as well as the classical accounts of the various writers that '*Early History of Jammu Region*' will throw any light on the Indian history and the culture of the areas. Although more than a century has passed the above statement in regard to this relative merit of classical accounts as source of good information for the ancient history of India still holds good concept of the life.

More important than the historical accounts are the incidental references to the democratic and oligarchical forms of government in various States of the Jammu Region and the North-West Frontier provinces had an example of understanding between the centre and states discussed as under:-

Politcal Condition of Northern India

Northern India the period from *c*.. 650 B.C. saw the rise of the two great religions, that is Jainism and Buddhism, the text of which throw light not merely on religious, but also political history of the times along with Sanskrit works of the period

The Principal States (Mahajanpadas)

These texts show how India was then known for sixteen prominent states which are thus listed in the old Pali texts known as *Anguthara*

1. Anga with its capital, *Champa* (East Bihar)
2. *Magadha* (South Bihar);
3. *Kasi*;
4. *Kosala* (Oudh),
5. *Vajji* (North Bihar);
6. *Malla* (*Gorakhpur District*)
7. *Cheti* (Chedi between Yumna and Narmada);
8. *Vamsa* (Vatsa Allahabad region);
9. *Kuru* (Thanesar, Delhi and *Meerut* districts);
10. *Panchala* (Bareilly, Badaun and Farrukhabad Districts);
11. *Machchha* (Matsya; Jaipur);
12. *Surasena* (Mathura);
13. *Assaka* on the Godavari with its capital Postana (Paithan);
14. *Avanti* with its capital at Mahissati;
15. *Gandhara* (Peshawar and Rawalpindi Districts);
16. *Kamboja* (SouthWest Kashmir and parts of Kafirstan). To these another text adds;
17. Kalinga with its capital at Dantapura;
18. *Sovira* with its capital called Roruka, and;
19. *Videha* with its capital Mithial.

The *Dharma-Sutra* of *Baudhayana* mentions the following States as forbidden ground for the Aryas:

1. Sauvira (Multan);
2. Aratta (Panjab);
3. *Surashtra*
4. *Avanti*
5. *Magadha;*
6. *Anga*
7. *Pundra* (North Bengal) and
8. *Vanga* (East and South Bengal). So all these regions are lying outside the pale of Aryan Civilization proper at that time (c.500 B.C.) The Jain text, *Bhagavati*, mentions some additional States or regions like Malava, *Kochcha* (*Cutch*), Padha (*Pudra*), Ladha (Radha in Bengal), and Moli (*Malla*) in Gujarat.

Emergence of States to Prominence: Avanti

The Buddhist texts speak of the power of *Avanti* under its great king called *Pajjota (Pradyota)*, Mahasena who earned the title of *Chanda* for its reign of terror. Even the Magadhan Emperor, Ajatasatru was in fear of his attack upon his capital of *Rajagriha*[13]. His ferocity was somewhat tamed by his affection for his beautiful daughter *Vasavadatta* who, however, eloped with the *Vatsaraji*, Udayana. Later, he became a Buddhist under the influence of his chaplain, *Mahakchchayana.*

1. ***Avanti*** was there centre of Buddhism preached by its learned exponents like *Dhammapal*, *Sona* and *Mahakachchayana* who preached in the popular speech of the day which was the origin of Pali language. This vernacular was not Magadhi.

2. Vamsa (Vatsa)

We have already referrd to King Udayana under whom the Vatsa kingdom with its capital at Kausambi attained to a position of prominence. It was partly due to his several matrimonial alliances such as his marriage with the daughter of the Avanti King. He is the centre of much romance in *dramas* like *Svapnavasavadatta* which mentions his queen *Padmavati* who was sister of King Darsaka of Magadha. *Harsha's Priya darsika* which mentions his marriage with the daughter of King of Anga and *Ratnavali* which tells of his love of *Sagarika*, an attendant of his queen *Vasavadatta*. He became a Buddhist under the influence of the monk Pindola of Ghositarama. Kausambi was noted for several Buddhist *Viharas* where the Buddha often came to live and deliver his discourse *(Satsang)*.

3. **Kosala**

Buddhist texts mention disputes between the kingdoms of Kosala and Kasi. At first, it was annexed by Brahmadatta a, King of Kasi who, however, returned it to the son of the Kosala king named Dighiti. This was followed by several invasions of Kasi by the Kosala kings who finally consquered it. In the time of the Buddha, the king of Kosala was *Pasenadi* (*Prasenajit*). He was one of the Buddhas admires and of the same age. He used to state: '*Bhagavapi asitiko aham pi asitiko*". Word The Buddha is 80 years old, I, too am 80 year old [14].

The relations between Prasenajit and the Buddha are commemorated in stone in one of the Bharhut sculptures. The sculpture bears two inscribed labels: (1) '*Raja Pasenaji Kosalo* and (2) *Bhagavato Dhamachakam*'

This indicates that Prasemajit was an adherent of the Buddha symbolized as *Dharma –chakra*. The sculpture depicts the king going out of the gateway of his place on a chariot drawn by four horses in a procession of footmen and rides of horses and elephants.

Very soon Kosala came in to conflict with Magadha under its aggressive king. Ajatasatrus Presenjit gave his sister in marriage with Ajatasatru's father Bimbisara with the dowry of a village in Kasi. The gift was revoked when his sister died of grief at *Bimbisaras* murder by the parricide *Ajatasatru*. This led to war between Magadha and Kosala. *Parasenajit* later lost his throne to his son Vidudabha who is notorious in Buddhist history by his slaughter of the innocents in the *Sakya* country owing to the *Sakyas* refusing him Sakya girl of his marriage. The sinful *Vidudabha* and his army were swept away by the flood of the river at the *Sakya* capital Savatthi (*Sravasti*).

4. **Magadha**

In the contest for supremacy among these different States, Magadha achieved pre-eminence under its great rulers *Bimbisara* and *Ajatasatru*. Unfortunately, there considerable controversy and uncertainty as to the succession list of the rulers of the famous dynasty which made Magadha an Imperial power. The principal sources, Brahminical, Buddhist and Jain, differ as to the succession of these kings and the year of their reigns. The *Puranas* mention *Sisunage* as the founder of the dynasty which they named after him, while the Buddhist texts take Bimbisara as the founder of *Haryanka* dynasty which was followed by the Saisunage dynasty.Buddhist evidence is considered more reliable by scholars and is accordingly followed here. In a literal sense, the term *Haryanka* may mean the *Kula* or dynasty which has its ensign *Hari* or serpent. The significant name of the later King *Nagadasaka* gives point to this meaning as equivalent to God or '*Nam*'.

Bimbisara (c. 603-551 B.C.)

He came to the throne at fifteen and contracted matrimonial alliances of great political value. He married the sister of te King of Kosala; the daughter of the republican Lichchhavi chief, the Vaidehi princes Vasavi (according to a Jaina text) who served and saved her husband by carrying in secret food to him in prison into which he was cast by his son Ajatasatru. Different sources mention his several sons of whom Kunika Ajatasatru was the most famous.

Capital

Bimbisara built his capital at Giriviraja protected by five hills, and cyclopean walls which are examples of earliest Indain stone architecture. Later, the capital was shifted to Rajagriha which was planned by the engineer and architect *Mahagovinda*.

Conquest of Anga

Bimbisara first achievement was the conquest of Anga to which he appointed as its governor his son, Kunika, with its capital at Champa or

Chamba. Bimbisaras dominion now comprised 80,000 villages covering an area of 300 leagues increased to 500 by the conquest of his son Ajatasatru.

Bimbisara's Administration

His administration was carried on under an efficient system. The chief officers were known as *Mahamatras*, the executive as *Sabbatthaka* (in charge of all affairs and interests), the judicial as *Voharika;* and the military, *Sena-nayaka*. The head of avillage was called *Gramika*. These heads of 80,000 village used to meet in an Assembly.

Religion

Both Jains and Buddhists claim Bimbisara as a follower of their respective religions. One Jain text relates the story that "when the country was under a blight of cold, the king went to worship Mahavira as a remedy to the calamity". Buddhist texts equally tell of Bimbisara devotion to the Buddha whom the first met at Girivraja *before* he was a Buddha and when he was known only as Gotama[15] (as mentiioned in the ancient texts). Next, he entered Rajagriha as a Buddha with his newly converted disciples, the famous Kassapa brothers, with their own followers of 1000 *Jatilas*, and then Seniya Bimbisara apporaches him with his royal retinue, receives his doctrine and entertains him and His Order at the palace, serving food with his own hand and made a gift to Him of the Park called Veluvana. The emperor also deputed his own physician *Jivaka* to be in attendance on the Buddha and His Order.

End

The end of this great Emperor was not a happy one. A legend in the *Vinaya* has been described how his son Ajatasatru, impatient for the throne for which his father had already chosen him in preference to all his other sons, was egged on by the vile Devadatta, a sworn enemy and cousin of the Buddha to kill his father. The conspiracy was foiled out Bimbisara left the thrown to him. Yet he did kill his father as he himself confessed to the Buddha that "for the sake of kingdom he deprived his righteous father of his life[16]". But Jain legends are more charitable to Ajastasatru. They stop at the son casting his father to prison where the father called himself when Ajatasatru was hastening to set him free [17] from his duty by spreading the Buddhism in whole of the world. This is not the venerable Upali, a barber before he became a monk, who answered questions on the Vinaya rules at the first Buddhist council in Kashmir[18].

According to Mahavamsa, Ajatasatru killed his father eigth years before the Buddha's death in 534 B.C. i.e. in 551 B.C. and when he had reigned for 52 years. Thus Bimbisara reigned from 603 to 551 B.C.

Ajatasatru (c.551-519 B.C.)

The conquest of Ajatasatru further contributed to the growth of Magadha as an Imperial power of the India.

Campaign Against Kosala

But his first campaign against Kosala was a failure. Entrapped in an ambush he had to surrender to the King of Kosala (his maternal uncle as we have seen) with his whole army. Prasenajit, however, as a pacifist Buddhist ended his conflict with Ajatasatru by giving him back his liberty army kingdom, and a daughter, to boot, in marriage (named Vajira[19]) as again referred in the text *Nikaya*.

Conquest of Lichchhavis

The texts Jain mention Ajatasatru's conquest of unique confederacy of Kingdoms and Republics in eastern India across the *Ganges*, which comprised the following constituent States:

1. Kasi;
2. Kosala;
3. 18 other *Ganarajyas* or Republican States;
4. Nine Mallaki States; and
5. *Nine Lichchhavi* States, totalling 2 kingdoms and 36 republics mentioned in the B*hagavati Sutra.)*[20].His conquest began with the most powerful unit of the Confederation,the Lichchhavis with whom he picked a quarrel on flimsy grounds a claim upon gems of mine near the Ganges and upon the bejewelled state –elephant *Seyanaga* (=*Sechanaka*, Sprinkler) owned by his step-brother, the *Lichchhavi* prince,Vehalla. The Lichchhavis were a powerful people, strong in their national republican unity and to conquer them meant a protracted struggle and employment of all possible means. First, Ajatasatru had to build a fort on the Ganges to serve as a base of operations for which Rajagriha, the inland capital, was not suitable. It was the foundation of Pataliputra of which the future prosperity was predicted by the Buddha after whom were named the Gotama Gate and the Gotama ferry,the points of crossing the river,by the Emperors Chief Ministers, Sunidha and *Vassakara*, in charge of the construction on the occasion of a dinner given by them to Gotama Buddha. Secondly, Ajataṣatru had to take recourse to the nefarious means of breaking the Lichchhavi republican unity by sowing seeds of dissension among the people. Minister Vassakara was at this job for 3 years living with them at Vaisali. The unity of the *Lichchhavis* was broken by a new spirit of jealously between rich and poor, strong and weak[21]. When the actual invasion of the territory of the Lichchhavis commenced, they began to argue:

"Let the strong Lichchhavis go forward and crush the enemy." intead of fighting to a man in defence of their national freedom. The third means employed by Ajatasatru were superior military weapons known as *Mahasilakantaga*, a kind of catapult hurling big pieces of stone similar like the Ravidas philosophy and the *Ratha-musala*,a chariot which wrought havoc by wheeling about and hurling destruction by its attached rods[22]. The Jain texts indicate that the war lasted for at least 16 years. The great religious leader named Gosala, who was the rival of Mahavira, saw the war in progress before the died in 562 B.C. At the same time, the passing away of Mahavira in 546 B.C.was marked by a joint illumination organized collectively by all the 36 republican States to mark the vanishing of 'the light that was in their Lord Mahavira[23] have been displayed a high knowledge of the message of the *'Nam'* or God. Thus the war must have lasted from 562 to 546 B.C. i.e., for 16 years to cool down the Brahmins.

Religion

It is dificult to say whether Ajatasatru was Jain or Buddhist. The texts of both the religious describe him as a devotee of each. Perhaps he started as a Jain. Jain tradition, as we have already seen, does not represent him as a parricide. It also records how Kunika frequently saw *Nataputta* at Vaisali and *Champa*[24] during his visit in this area. On these occasions, he openly delared how Mahaviras doctrine of renunciation and non-violence points to the path of true religion. The Buddhist texts, on the other hand, while treasting him as a parricide, describe how he sought the Buddha for consolation saying "May the Lord accept my transgression as trasnsgression that I may be restrained in the future." We are also told how his physician *Jivaka* once took him to the Buddha and to his congregation of 1,250 disciples, all seated in silent meditation, which made him exclaim, "How can it be that there should be no sound at all not a sneeza, nor a cough in so large an assembly among 1250 of the Brethren? Would that my son, Udayi Bhadda, might have such calm as this assembly of brethren has[25]'. This visit to the Buddha he paid as the last source of solace for his sin after vainly visiting all the six famous teachers of the times, such as,*Makkhali, Gosala or Nigantha Nataputta* refers in *Samanna-phala Sutta*. The great historian H.G. Wells even asserts that the religion, "has done more for the advance of world civilization than anyother influence in the chronicle of man kind[26].

That Ajastasatru was a Buddhist is commemorated on one of the sculptures of Bharhut of about 2nd century B.C. bearing the inscribed label "Ajatasatu *Bhagavato Vamdate*, Ajatasatru bows down to the Lord". The sculpture depicts the king on an elephant in a procession with ladies on elephants and,dismounting from the elephant, bowing down to the throne of the Buddha and his footprints. We next find him rushing to Kusinara where the Buddha died to claim a share of His relics. Buddhist texts also state that the first Buddhist Council was held under his patronage at the entrance to the Sattapanni Cave on one of the hills of Rajagriha[27]. In Buddhist cosmology, the universe is composed of worlds upon worlds, *ad infinitum*. (our earth is only an *infinitesimal* part of one of these countless world). The polar mountain (Mount Sumeru) is the central mountain of each world i.e., '*Nam*' or God.

Udayabhadra (c.519-503 B.C.)

The *Mahavamsa* gives him a reign of 16 years, i.e., up to 503 B.C. Buddhists make him a parricide but Jains depict him as devoted to his father whose death he deeply mourned when he was his Viceroy at Champa[28]. The *Vayu Purana* describes Udayi as builder of a new Pataliputra called *Kusumapure*. He decorated his city by building at its centre a Jain shrine (*Chaityagriha*) [29]. He was at constant war with Avanti whose king Palaka he defeated many times till he was killed by one of his agents in the guise of a teacher [30] as a Prefect Master of the Insight Knowledge.

Anuruddha: Munda (c.503-497 B.C.)

A Buddhist text describes his devotion to his wife named Bhadda whose body he won't burn at her death in grief till he was consoled by *Thera Narada*[31] in formal way.

Nagadasaka (c.497-471 B.C.)

He may be identified with King Darsaka of the *Puranas* and of Bhasa's drama called *Svapnavasavadatta* as a story of the man and God.

Sisunaga (c 471-453 B.C.)

The Ceylon Chronicles state that he was placed on the throne buy the people rebelling against the precious kings as parricides. He was the kings *Amatya* or Minister as superintendent of the villages.

According to the *Puranas*, he secured his frontiers at Girivraja against the menace of the Pradyotas of Avanti and posted his son on the other frontier at Varanasi for the spread of the mission.

Kalasoka

Kalasoka was followed by his ten sons jointly ruling up to 403 B.C. for 22 years for the development of the human history.

These were times of a palace revolution in a change of dynasty. A glimpse of ths revolution is seen in a passage occurring in Bana's

Harshacharita stating that Kakavarni Saisunagi was killed by a dagger thrust into his throat. A Greek writer on Alexanders invasion of India also records the tradition that the assassin was a barber wo killed the King in conspiracy with the Queen as her paramour, seized the throne, and killed all the royal princes, to found his own dynasty of rulers. These princes must have been the sons of *Kalasoka Kakavarni.*

The ten sons of Kalasoka are named in the *Mahabodhi Vamsa.* The ninth is named *Nandivardhana* and the tenth *Panchamaka*

The *Puranas* name the last two Saisunage kings as *Nandivardhana* and *Mahanandin* (instead of *Panchamaka*)

This new Dynasty of usurpers is called that of the Nandas.

The Nandas (c.403-323 B.C.)

Different tradition give different versions of this old and obscure Nanda history, which already discussed in the other texts of the same author.

The Founder

The *Puranas* know nothing of the story recorded by Bana or by the Greek writers. They describe the first Nanda King named *Mahapadma* as the son of the last Saisunage Kings Mahanandin by a *Sudhra* women, whence the Nandas are described as *Sudhra* Kings. The Greek story makes the father a barber or a Sudhra,and the mother,the guilty Kshatriya Queen. Jain tradition knows of nine Nandas[32], and describes the first Nandas as the son of a courtesan by a barber (*napitadasa 'Nam' raja jatah*).

Buddhist texts give a totally different version of te origin of the Nandas. The first Nanda is named *Ugrasena* who belonged to the frontier (*Panchchanta –vasika*) and stated brigandage with his brothers as a profession whence the Nandas are called *chorapubbas,* 'dacoits of old. "He simply overthrew by force the reigning king of Magadha.

His Successor

The *Puranas* count among the *Nine Nandas* the father succeeded by his eigth sons,of whom only one is named, Sukalpa. Buddhist and Jain traditions take the *Nine Nandas* as brothers. The *Mahabodhivamsa* names all the nine, of whom the first is Ugrasena and the last *Dhana-Nanda.* The brothers ruled one after the another by seniority (*vuddhapatipatiya*). Greek writers call the last Nanda king *Agrammes* (Curtius) or Xandramas (*Diodorus*) Sanskrit *Chandramas* which F.W. Thomas (in *Cambridge History of India,* Vol.1) takes to be the personal name of *Dhana-Nanda.* The Greek writers also mention the father of Agrammes" as a barber, without naming him. This shows that they knew of the Puranic tradition which treats the nine Nandas as comprising the father and his eight sons and not as brothers as in Buddhist tradition.

History: Sanskrit Tradition

We shall give first Nanda history according to the Sanskrit sources. According to chronology followed here, the first Nanda started reigning in 403 B.C.while the *Puranas* assign to the Nine Nandas a period of 100 years. Supposing the first Nanda became king at 20, the other Nandas between them would cover a period of 80 years and must have lasted till 323 B.C. which is curiously the date when they were over thrown by the founder of the Mauryan dynasty.

The *Puranas* describe the first Nanda as *Mahapadma* or *Mahapadma pati*, master of immense wealth or army.

The Greek writer, Curtius, counts his army at 20,000 cavalry 200,000 infantry 2,000 four-horsed chariots and, 3000 elephants.

The *Puranas* describe him as a second *Parasurama* or Bhargava, as the exterminator of all Kshatriyas and as the sole sovereign (*Eka-rat*) who brought the whole earth under the one umbrella of his authority (*eka-chchhatra*)

The contemporary Kshatriya dynasties of the period mentioned in the *Puranas* were the *Aikshakus*, *Panchalas*, *Kasi*, *Haihayas*, *Kalings*, *Asmakas*, *Kurus*, Maithials, *Sursenas* and *Vitihotras,* already mentioned above.

Thus, the conquest of Kalinga as listed here is attested by the Hathigumpha Inscription of the Kalinga King Kharavela, which refers to Nanda king sovereignty of Kalinga. One passage refers to him as Nanda-raja associated with an aqueduct which had remained unused for 300 (or 103?) years until it was conducted into city by Kharavela in the fifth year of his reign. Another passage is to the effect that King Nanda carried away as trophies to Magadha the statue (or foot-prints) of the first Jina and heirlooms of the Kalinga kings.

The Greeks refer to the Nanda King as King of the "Gangaridae and the Prasii" with his capital at Pataliputra. According to Megasthenes, the *Gangaridae* were the people of the Gangas delta, and the *Prasii* are the *Prachyas* or the people of eastern India.

The phenomenal wealth of the Nanda King is referred to in all traditions. Buddhist tradition frankly nicknames Nanda as *Dhana-Nanda* with reference to his riches, The *Mahavamsa* states how he was "addicted to hoarding treasure, a masses 80 *Kotis* which he hid in a rock under the river, and levied taxes on very possible article even skins gums and stones."

The *Puranas* frankly describe the Nandas as *Adharmikas*, i.e, sinful kings. Even Alexander heard that the Nanda King was "hated and despised by his subject for the wickedness of his disposition and the meanness of his origin"

Republics: Lichchhavis

This period is marked not merely by the growth of monarchies and empires, but also of Republics. The most prominent and powerful of these Republics was that of the Lichchhavis. As we have already discussed,they took the lead in forming a Confederation of nine Mallaki Republics and eighteen Ganarajyas of Kasi-Kosala.The head of this Confederation was the Lichchhavi chief, *Chetaka*, who was Mahavira's maternal uncle. The Confederation was planned against Ajatasatru.

The Republic had its capital at Vaisali consisting of three districts with 7,000, 14,000 and 21,000 houses respectively. Its citizens were distinguished as Abhyantara '*Nam*' or '*Word*' Bahira '*Chamar* Vaisalakas, the cockneys and inhabitants of Greater,Vaisali, numbering "twice 84,000." Its prosperity is indicated by the *Mahavagga* which states that it had "7,7,07 storyed building 7,707 pinnacled buildings, 7,707 *aramas* and 7707 lotus ponds[33]" under its 7,707 chiefs and a variety of buildings, *Chaityas*, *Viharas* and *Palaces*.

Vaisali was closely associated with the Buddha. On His first visit, He was given a royal reception along his whole route from the Gangas.It was watered,stewn with flowers and burning incense and decorated with flags, garlands and embroidered cloth. The *Lichchhavis* gave to the Buddhia all the *Chaityas* of the city while the courtesan *Amrapali* gave Him her mango-grove and Balika the Balika rama. The *Lichchhavis* also built him the famous *Kutagarasala* where the Buddha delivered many of his discourses of the '*Nam*' *or* God.

The governing body of the Republic consisted of its 7,707 Rajas with as many *Upa raja* or Deputy Chiefs, *Senapatis* (Generals), and *Bhandagarikas* (Treasures). We may refers in this connection to Kautilyas description of some Samghas or Republics as *Rajas bdopajivinah*, i.e. based on equality of citizenship. The Republican executive was abody of Eight (*Ashta-kula*) or Nine. The Council of Nine was in charge of foreign affair and the Council of Eight, of Justice (*Atthakulaka*).Justice was administered with the help (1) *Vinischaya Mahamatra,* who ascertained the facts of the case, (2) *Vyavaharikas,* lawyers and (3) *Sutradharas* who kept up the thread or continuity of law and custom. Appeal lay from the *Atthkulaka* to the *Senapati,* **from** him to the *Uparaja,* and finally to the *Raja* as the supreme authority.

Another peculiar feature of the Lichchhavi Republic is the adoption by the members of the governing body of different colours., *Nila, Pita, Harit, Manjistha*, Lohita, or Sveta, to mark out their respective dress, horses, chariots, turbans, umbrellas, down to shoes, whips and sticks[34] are mentioned in the various texts of the period.

The greatness of the Republic was due to the character of its people. The Buddha himself testifies how the Lichchhavis were free from luxury and sloth, "sleeping with logs of wood as pillows and not cushions of the finest cotton, active in archery and not delicate, tender and soft in their arms and legs". Their sport ws training elephant and hunting with dogs. The youths were rowdy, laying their hands on sugarcane, plum, cakes or sweetmeat as they were carried on the roads, but they left their wildness before the Buddha. They had respect for the elders and women, their traditions, their old laws and customs were prevalent in the history of India.

The Sakyas

The *Sakyas* were another famous Republic of the times which gave the Buddha to the world. The Republic consisted of 80,000 families or about half a million population[35] at that time. Virudhaka is said to have massacred 77,000 *Sakyas* on spot with the power of '*Nam*'.

The Republic had its parliament of which the meeting place was called *Santhagara*. Its president was called a Raja. It consisted of 500 members[36] as referred in the study. The parliament is called *Sakya –Parishad*. A new building was constructed in the time of the Buddha who inaugurated it by a series of lectures[37] during his life time. The Sakya parliament had to decide the vital question whether the gates of the capital Kapilavastu should be opened to the invader *Virudhaka*. "Some said, 'As there are various opinions, we will find out the opinion of the majority'. So they set about voting on the subject. Eventually the treacherous "head man of the *Sakya* advocated opening the gates, and they all voted in the same way[37] as his forefathers used to do.

The *Sakyas* were known for their culture and social progress. No father would marry his daughter to an uneducated bridegroom. The father of the girl Gopa in reply to a proposal of her marriage with young Gautama stated that he could not, "make over the girl to a prince reared at home among luxuries and ignorant of the Silpas and the military arts (*Lalitavistara*). According to *Mahavastu*[38], Gautama had to compete in a tournament of 500 Sakya youths for the hand of Yasodhara. The Sakyas were very anxious for the purity of their blood. They did not marry outside their clan and even rejected the proposal of the Crown Prince, *Vidudhaka* to marry a Sakya girl. They had to pay dearly for this refusal for which their city was sacked.

Sakyas

The *Sakyas* gave to Buddhism some of its noted leaders, both men and women, teacher like Upali and nuns like Gotami, the Buddha's aunt, Tissa, or Sundari Nanda, who attained *Arhat-ship* (*Theri-Gatha*).

Mallas

Next to the *Sakyas* may be mentined the Republic of the *Mallas* with its two branches at Pava and at Kusinara.Mahavira died at Pava and the Buddha at Kusinara.

The Malla State is called a *Samgha-raya* i.e a Republic[39] of India. The Pava Mallas built a new parliament house called *Ubbhataka* which was formally inauguayed by the Buddha (*Samgiti-Sukta*). Their executive officers were called *Purisas* who were like the Police[40] serving the Buddha at that period.

Buddhism owes to the Mallas some of its greatest characters such as Ananda or Anuruddha.

Other Republics

Other Republics of the times mentioned in the Buddhist texts are the *Koliyas*, the *Moriyas* of *Pipphalivana*, the *Videhas* of *Mithila* and the *Nayas* (*Jnatrikas*) of Vaisali, of whom was bron the great Mahavira whose father was the chief of the clan. Its capital was at Kollage described as *Naya -kula*, i.e., the abode of the *Jnatrikas*.

Religious History of the period

The period is marked by the rise of the two great religions, Jainism and Buddhism. We have already seen how the founders of these two religions. *Vardhamana Mahavira* and *Gautama Buddha*, influenced the politics of the country by their close association not merely with Kingdoms, but also with the Republic of the times in Indian society.

Jainism

Jain tradition traces Jainism to a succession of 23 *Tirthankaras* or *Peophets* of whom the first was *Rishabha* and the *last Parsva*.

Parsva

Parsva was a prince but renounced the world and other 83 days "deep meditation" he attained the highest knowledge called *Kaivalya*. He lived for 100 years and died on the summit of hill now known as Parsvanath Hill. The next important figure of Jainism was Mahavira who came 250 year after him.

Parsvas teaching was based upon four Prohibitions which were *not* to (1) injure life, (2) lie, (3) steal and (4) possess any property.Mahavira added the fifth vow of chastiy which was implied in (4).

Parsva allowed to his monks some clothing, an under and upper garment but Mahavira did not allow it. Thus there was a divison in Jainism between the *Svetamvaras*, "monks in while clothes" and Digamvaras, "sky –clad or naked ascetics. The latter are also called Niganthas. Mahavira is known as *Nigantha-nata-putta*.

Mahavira

According to tradition, Mahavira died 470 years before the birth of Vikrama whose era began 18 years later in 58 B.C. It therefore took place in (470+58+18) 546 B.C. The traditional date of the death of the Buddha is 543 B.C. Buddhist tradition makes Mahavira predecease the Buddha as '*Nam*' was on earth at that time.

His Life

Mahavira was also a prince. His father was the chief of his clan, the *Jnatrikas*, His mother was a sister of he Lichchhavi chief Chetaka. His father celebrated his birth on a lavish scale. "The customs, taxes and confiscations were released, buying and selling prohibited, no policeman was allowed to enter inside the houses, great and small fines were remitted, debts cancelled, measures and weights increased and all prisoners set free in the town of Kundapura[41]". After 30 years of married life, and the death of his parents and with the permission of his elder brother and the authorites of the kingdom, he renounced the world and, clean-shaven, became an ascetic giving himself to meditation.At first he wore clothes but soon cast them off, "accepting alms in the hollow of his hand." For twelve years he practised extreme self mortification, allowing even all sorts of living beings together and crawl about on his body. In the thirteenth year "he reached Nirvana under a sal tree, becoming a Jina and a *Kevalin*, an omniscient". Then he travelled widely in different parts of the country, *Champa, Vaisali, Rajagriha, Nalanda, Mithila, Sravasti* and Papa where he died, undergoing all sorts of privations including physical molestation.He had special trouble in the country of Ladha (=Radha or Western Bengal) and in adjoining regions where the people attacked him with dogs. But he persevered in his preaching, undaunted by difficulties, and soon had a large following. But one of his unpleasant experiences was his break with his comrade Gosala who founded a system of his own and became his most powerful rival and critic. Mahavira had some royal supporters to whose support Jainism owed its popularity. We have already referred to his realation with the kings of Magadha and the Lichchhavi chief. The Kings of *Champa, Kuasambi* and *Avanti* had Jain leaning. (*See Plate XXI, Chauri-Bearer, Didarganj 3rd Century B.C. Fig.33*)

His Influence

Mahavira had equal influence with the Republic of his times. We have already referred to the honour done to his memory by 36 republics having a federal illumination at his death and disintegrated after his death.

Jain Discipline

We may now refer to Jainism as a system of discipline. Jainism believes in '*Karma theory*' and its effects in transmigration of soul which is to be stopped by annihilating '*Karma Theory*'. The process of ending *Karma* is observance of (I) the five vows aforesaid to which is added the sixth, namely," not eating at night" (2) five *Samitis* or prescribed habits; and (3) three *Guptis* or restraining body, mind and speech, so as to achieve freedom from *Asravas*, affections by *Karma*. On these foundations are to be practised the austerities both external and internal. The external austerities include *Vinaya*, humility, service, study (*Svadhyaya*), *Dhyana* (meditation); and *Vyutsarga* (abandoning the body) i.e., remaining motionless in all positions. Jainism is known for its extreme views as to *Ahimsa* and mortification of flesh as a right way of the life.

Buddhism: Life of Gautama Buddha

Gautama Buddha, the founder of Buddhism, was also born as a prince at Kapilasvastu, the capital of Sakya Republic. It is now identified by the Ashokan pillar and inscription found at Lumbini. The traditional date of Buddha's birth is 623 B.C. He was the son of the Sakya chief, *Sudhodana* and Maya. Seven days after his birth his mother died, and he was nursed by his step-mother and aunt *Mahapajapati Gotami.*

Renunciation

He grew up in luxury and was married at 16 to Gopa, also named Yasodhara. But the pleasure of the palace did not blind him to the hard facts of life which he described as, "birth, old-age, sickness, death, sorrow and impurity."

A son was born to him at 29, but he thought "a bond is born." He at once left the palace, leaving the baby and his mother sleeping on his horse, *Kanthaka*, with his groom *Chhanna*. He now became an ascetic, cutting off his hair and taking to his yellow robes" "a black –haired youth in the prime of life going forth from home to a homeless life".

His Teachers

He found his teachers at *Rajagraiha*. They are named *Alara* and *Udraka*. It is said of Alara that he was so given to meditation that "sitting on the road he did not see or hear 500 carts ratting past him." Very soon, the pupil became the equal of his teacher. So he sought a second teacher named *Udraka Ramaputra*.

His Austerities and Enlightenment

Next, he repaired to a village called Uruvela where he settled down in his Quest of the Ideal. He tried extreme austerities after Jainism, and reduced himself to skin and bone taking very little food, "juice of leaves or a little pulse", which could be held in his palm, but he found this penance fruitless. So he resumed "solid food, rice and sour-milk". At this, his five Brahmin comrades seeing his lapses deserted him. Alone he followed his own path to enlightenment which he attained after six years striving. He achieved it under the Bodhi tree at Bodh-Gaya. The rural girl Sujata gave Gautama his first solid food and the grass-cutter, Sotthiya, the grass on which he sat in meditation.

His First Teaching and Disciples

After attaining Buddha-hood at Bodh-Gaya, he started preaching and sought as his first disciples his old comrades the five Brahmins, who were then living at Isipatana at Sarnath near Benares. They listed to his first teaching called *Dharma-Chakra-Pravartana-Sutra,* prescribing the Eightfold path of salvation consisting of "right views, intention, speech, action, livelihood, effort, mindfulness and concentration".

Growth of Samgah

This was the beginning of the Buddhist *Church* or *Samgha.* Among the important accessions to it may be mentioned 50 disciples at Benares led by Yasa, son of a wealthy gild-master, the brotherhood of 1,000 *Jatilas*, with their leader Kassapa, converted at Uruvala; the converison of *Sariputta* and Moggalana at Rajagriha, together with the Order of Sanjaya with his 250 disciples.

These numerous conversions created a sensation in Magadha where the people complained that "the ascetic Gotama is come to bring childlessness, withowhood, and subversion of families".

From his own native city, Kaplavastu and his family, the Buddha obtained two important recruits, namely, his own and only son, Rahula, and his cousin Nanda,on the eve of Nanda's marriage and installation as crown prince. Their monk hood left his father without any heir for his kingdom. In great anguish, he said to his son, the Buddha: "The love for a son, Lord, cuts into the skin, the flesh, the bones and reaches the marrow". His case made Buddha give the ruling that no one should be admitted as a monk without his parents' consent.

His next important disciples were *Anuruddha, Ananda Upali*, and *Devadatta* whom he met at Anupiya, a village near Rajagriha. The Budddha appointed Anand a as his personal attendant who served him with the utmost devotion upto the last moment of his life. *Devadatta*, his cousin, became jealous of him and his implacable enemy, the Judas of Buddhism.

His next important convert was a merchant prince of Sravasti named *Sudatta*, who acquired for the park called *Jeta-vana* at a fabulous price demanded by its owner, prince Jeta as many gold pieces as could cover its entire ground amounting to 18 *kotis*, His philanthropy gave *Sudatta* the new name of Anathapindika, "giver of alms to the destitute", A sculpture at Bharhut depicts a cart of coins, figured as square pieces being unload and the coins spread on the ground.

Order of Nuns

The Buddha also attracted to himself several women discples. One of these was *Visakha,* the daughter of the commercial magnate of Saketa. She built him a monastery at Sravasti, known as Purvarama, with her costly head-dress.

By this time there were three chief centres of Buddhism at *Rajagriha, Kapilavastu* and *Sravasti.*

Admission of women disciples led the Buddha to perman Order of Nuns. The first nun was his step-mother *Mahaprajapati* who forced his consent against his wishes. The Buddha with an uneasy mind predicated that by this reform the Buddhist church would not last long.

Vaisali

Vaisali also grew up as an important centre of Buddhsim. His first entry into the city was due to the *Lichchhavis* praying for his sacred presence in their city to purge it of the plague then raging there. We have already noted the serval parks given to Him for his residence there.

Proofs of Divinity

During all his wanderings, the Buddha gave proofs of his divinity by his conduct and character. He did not spare himself in his service of others. At Sravasti, he found a monk suffering from a skin disease and smelling foul, forsaken by his comrades. The Buddha, with his own hands washed him in hot water, had him clothed in fresh robes, and exhorted the monks thus": "You have neither father nor mother, wherefor be father and mother to one another". At Sravasti, again, he was able to convert to his creed of non-violence a notorious bandit who was called *Angulimala*, because he wore a "garland of figures" severd from his victims.

His Last Days

Up to the last moment of his life, the Buddha kept up his travelling and preaching. In his eightieth year, he fell ill at Pava as the guest of *Chunda*, the smith, who treated him to his last meal consisting of hard and soft food,and a quantity of *Sukara maddava.* This expression was originally interpreted as "the flesh of a big made soft and oily." But really it meant "the sprout of plant trodden by pigs, or a mushroom (*ahichchhattaka*) growing in place trodden by pigs, or a flavouring substance[42] reveals in the history of *Buddha.*

The Buddha had an attack of dysentery with discharge of food and deadly pains which he controlled and made way from Pava to Kusinara. On the way, he could not proceed farther but asked Ananda to spread a robe four-fold for acomfortable seat. He next bathed in the river close by and took rest in a mango-grove. Then he rose and proceeded farther till he reached Kunsinara where he took his last rest in a grove of Sal trees.

His Last Words:

He knew that his end was approaching and asked the monks who were about him to put their last questions to him. The Buddha told them that the Order should not depend upon him, but up on themselves to work out their salvation or moksha. And then came his classical declaration: "Therefore, O Anand,be ye lamps unto yourselves. Be ye a refuse to yourselves. Betake yourselves to no external refuge. Hold fast to the Truth as a lamp. Hold fast a a refuse to the Truth. Look not for refuge to any one besides yourself." And again: "And after I am gone, let the Truths and Rules of the Order which I have set forth and laid down for you all be the Teacher to you."

His Greatness

The greatness of the Buddha is to be estimated not in terms of his teachings or doctrines with all their philosophical and religious value, but in terms of life and character upon which he himself laid more stress. The first point about his greatness is that he started as an ordinary man with all his foibles, but he made himself a superman by sheer discipline and determination. It was not an easy matter for a prince to renounce the pleasures of the palace in the prime of his youth. He married at 16, had his first son at 29 when he turned an ascetic,spent 6 years in utter most austerity till he became Enlightened or a Buddha at 35, while from that age up to his death at 80 for 45 years he devoted himself to continuous social service and preaching his new faith during his fresh birth on this earth as '*Chamar*'.

He himself frankly states how difficult it was for him as a prince brought up in luxury,to live the life of an ascetic the forest. He confesses how much he was addicated to the good things of the world, "wife and children slaves male and female,goats and sheep, fowls and swine elephants, cattle, horses, mares, gold and silver". It was with some struggle that he could renounce these when he was "in the first bloom in the enjoyment of happy youth, in the first years of manhood."

He could hardly take the first meal he collected as a beggar. "His stomach turned and he left as if his inwards were on the point of coming out by this mouth".

His next difficulty in his new life was its solitude and the fear of it. He himself states' how hard it was for a monk to rejoice in solitude when he has not yet won to fixity of mind. He is seized with mortal fear and terror. And when a deer came by or bird caused a twing to fall, he thought: now it is coming – That fear and terror."

On this sheer truthfulness of the Buddha, Paul Dahlke [43] well remarks: Never before did the founder of a religion speak like this."

The Buddha did not spare himself in his work of preaching. He was the busiest of men. His daily life may be gathered from the Buddhist Scriptures. "He rose early morning, meditated and went out for alms, bowl in hand. Taking his meal with a host, he gave a discourse and returned to his retreat and inquired if all his disciples had taken their meals. Then he would suggest to the topics fro meditation and himself retire for meditation during the noon-day heat[44]". In the afternoon, he gave public discourse followed by evening bath, mediation, instruction to his monks and retirement for mediation and sleep.

Oldenberg thus depicts the Buddha's daily life. "In the days when his reputation stood at its highest point, and his name was named throughout India among the foremost names, one might day by day see that man, before whom kings bowed themselves, walking about, alms –bowl in hand, through streets and alleys, from house to house, and with out uttering any request, with downcast look stand silently waiting until a morsel of food was thrown in to bowl."

The Buddha was a past master in disputation.He attributes it to his capacity to "remain quiet and confident, so that he could not be thrown in to any confusion, or embarrassment" by questions.

He intellectual vigours remained unabated up to te last moment of his life that world is an empty vessal.

Indebtedness of Buddhism to Vedism

It is a mistake to suppose that Jainism or Buddhism is a revolt again Brahminism or Hinduism. One the contrary,both have grown out of previous

Brahminical throught or Vedism. These two religions emphasise and take their stand upon certain points of Vedism instead of accepting it as a whole. They lay more stress upon conduct and character than upon ceremonial worship, upon virtues rather than rituals. They are also organized as purely ascetic brotherhoods. Vedic religion contemplates ascerticism at the last two stages or *Asramas* of life. But Buddhism recruits monks from its first stage with permission to return to householders life. Vedic ascerticism does not admit of such lapses, because it is not permitted to untried youth. It contemplates *Naishthika Brahmacharis*, but they are outside the ordinary and normal. The Brahminical *Parivrajakas* and *Sannyasis* are stabilized characters who renounce the world after seeing it through and conquering desire. Thus, there were in the country many Pre-Buddhist and non-Buddhist ascetic Orders, some of whose leader were held in great popular esteem, like Mahavira or the Buddha himself.

Civilization

Glimpses of the Civilization of the times are afforded by the old Jain and Buddhist texts, discussed as under:-

Centres of Settlement

Civilization depends upon settled life under orgainsed society and government. Some of the Jain texts mention the following centres of settlement in the country in an ascending order: (1) *Grama*, village with an enclosure of thorns, bushes and trees; (2) *Palli*, a settlement of wild tribes" (3) Kheta, "a place fortified by an earthen wall", or by "river and hill surrounding" it (4) *Kharvata,* 'a poor town surrounded by a low wall or by hills on all sides", while according to Kautilya the Centre of a union of 200 villages," (5) *Dronamukha*, a town with a harbour to which there is access by water and by land like Bhrigukachha or Tamralipati or a town or as, "encircled by the sea" (*Sindhuvelavalayitam, the area of Jammu and Kashmir State*), according to Kautliya the centre of a Union of 400 villages", (6) *Pattana,* "a large town" or a centre of trade as Ravi route to Kabulistan; according to another text, a smart for precious metals (*ratna-yonih*); a mining centre; (7) *Matamba* an isolated town or associated (as its head –quarters) with a cluster of 10,000 villages (*datiltadasa staih,*) "an open town of the '*Sudhra Family*' of the *Chamar* history",abode of multitude of men of four castes," also interpreted as a fortified place (*Durga bhumi of the Jammu area*) to which are carried for safe custody the crops from the fields" or as a depot (*sthapani*) located in fort in the interior of Panjab hills; (9) *Nagara,* "a scot free town" which does not pay any of the eighteen taxes levied on a village; (10) *Rajadhani,* capital of a kigdom (11)Nigama settlement of merchants and (12) *Samvatta–kotta* afortified place of refuge[45] as noticed from the study.

Society

Society, as of old was based on the caste system. The Buddhist texts mention the four castes,*Khattiya –Brahmana Vessa Sudda*[46], who are regarded as Aryans as distinguished from the aboriginal people or non-Aryans who mare called *Melakhas* (*Mlechchas*). These are also described as *Hinajatis* or low castes who allowed *Hina-Sippas* or low crafts of the '*Nam History*'. There are mentioned five low castes namely, *Chandala, Bena, Nisada* (hunter), *Rathakara* (worker in leather) i.e *Mochi* and *Pukkkusa.*

*Panini (*II. IV, 10), however, calls these low castes as *Sudhras* whom he groups into two classes. The first class as called *Aniravasita,* i.e., not cast out of Aryan Society (*abanhishkrita*) and the second class is called *Niravasita* or out caste or '*Untouchables*'. Among *Sudhras* of the first class, Panini mentions *Cowherds, Barbers, Goldsmiths, Potters, Wood-carvers, Blacksmiths, Washermen, Weavers, Fishermen* and *Bhillas.* To the second class belong the *Chandalas* and others.

The Buddhist texts also mention some foreign or frontier people such as the *Yonasa* dn the Kambojas among whom there was no divison into castes but only that between Ayya (Arya or Master) and Dasa or slave.

Buddhist texts are not always complimentary to the Brahmins of those day who sometimes followed the occupation of lower castes for livehood. The Buddha as an impartial observer mentions five types of Brahmins: (I) *Brahma sama,* those who are merged in Brahma, (2) *Devatsama,* those who are god like in their character, (3) *Mariyada,* those who follow the traditions of their caste, (4) *Sambhinna maryada,* those who violate their traditions; and (5) *Brahmana-Chandala,*those who live like *Chandalas.* As regards their occupations, these early texts describe them as (1) *Rajakommika,* i.e. those who are in the service of the king and (2) those who live as *Tapasas* or *Isis* in forest homes called *Asramas.* The Brahmins served king as *Purohitas* or as *Amatyas* (Counsellors) or as *Mahamatras* (Ministers). They also figure as *Mahasalas* or head of Vedic institutions as *Dutas* (ambassadors), and sometimes even as *Senapatis* (generals), and *Yuddhajivas* (soldiers), and also as physicians, druggists, astronomers, architects, and reciters of ballads called *Karkan* in Dogri language (classical songs) originated from the French word.

Social festivities were called *Samajas* marked by feasts, music, drama, opera, ballad recitation, improvisation of verses, wrestling, bouting, duels, fights between bulls, buffaloes and cocks and the like.May all sentient beings live in peace, ultimately attaining supreme enlightenment under the benevolent light of Medicine Buddha '*Word' in this world* and, the campassionate light of Amitaba Buddha *Chamar* in this worlds beyond, mentioned in the *Sutra of the Medicine Budda*. In later Chinese Buddhism (apparently beginning in the Sunga period), *Bhaisajyaguru* (the Medicine Buddha) was depicted in a different sort of assembly. Here the Buddha or *'Nam'* of healing is joined by *Amitabh* and *Sakyamuni* to form a basic trinity important in Chinese Buddhism to the present day. In the vast Mayahana pantheon, three Buddhas stand supreme: *Sakyamuni* (Dr. Raj Kumar) the Buddha of the present age (Baba Gurinder Singh Ji Biaswale), *Amitabha,* the lord of *Sukhavati*, the western pure land, the *Medicine Buddha*, the "Healing Buddha," the "Doctor" of Body and Soul[47], i.e., (Deepit Raj) as '*Nam*' or Buddha on earth a director of the historical event.

Economic life of the Areas

Economic life of the Jammu area was based on the village. Indian economy was more rural than urban. A village was generally enclosed by a wall or stockade with gates (*Grama-dvara*)[48]. Beyond this enclosure lay the arable land of the village, The *grama -kshetra* which was protected against pests, beasts and birds, by fences, snares and field watchmen. Cultivation was made on the basis of individual holdings separated from one another by channels dug for cooperative irrigation[49] as referred in the various texts of the period. These dividing diteches,rectangular and curvilinear, which the Buddha saw the cultivated field of Magadha suggested to his mind the pattern of his monk's uniform, a patch work of torn pieces of cast off clothing[50] and shoes of the feet who were naked or bore.

Generally, the peasant proprietor and his family cultivated the land they owned. But there was also the agricultural landless labour employed for cultivation on wages. But such as "hireling" was given a lower social status than that of the slave[51] in the history of India, but there were high in the eyes of the Master. A *Jataka*[52] deplores as a symptom of social decadence the story spectacle of sturdy peasants leaving at home their own empty barns to toil as hirelings on the royal capitalists. But there were large farms of 1000 *Karisas,* or acres and more which had to be cultivated with 500 ploughs by hired labourers (*Bhatika*) to ply plough and oxen[53] in the agriculture field. Beyond the arable land of the village lay its common grazing ground for pasturing its cattle and goats under a common communal neat herd (*Gopalaka*) are working as *Gujjars* and *Bakarwals* degraded people of the society having no history, but pious by nature. Beyond pastures lay the suburban parks like

Jetavana at Sravasti for residence of ascetics. The village ended in a belt of forest which served as source of its firewood and little and were also the haunts of wild beasts and brigands preying on caravan traffic passing through them[54] as a routinue matter of the life.

Taxes on Agriculture

There were several taxes levied on agriculture. These were (1) *tithe* on the raw produce to be paid at the barn doors or collected by an official (*Mahamatra*) or by the village syndic or headman (*gramabhojaka*).An inscription of Ashoka at the village. Lumbini states how it had to pay taxes called *Bali* and *Bhaga* (share of the produce). As the village was sacred as the birthplace of the Buddha, Ashoka made it free of *Bali* and reduced the *Bhaga* (probably from one-fourth) to one-eighth. The Sovereign had the power to rermit, reduce or make gifts of such tithes and taxes.

(2) A special levy on produce as contribution to the State granary as provision against war or famine.

(3) Forced labour- There is mention of villagers being called to beat up game for the king at the cost of their work in the fields and of their providing a deer-preserve to escape from the forced labour.

(4) Occasional exactions like presents to the king at the birth of an heir[55]. (5) Sovereign's right to forest lands[56] and "ownerless" estates[57] discussed in the study also reflected in the various texts of the Buddhism.

Handicrafts

The *Jatakas* mention the standard number of 18 Arts and Crafts, carpenters, smiths, leatherers, painters, and the like, also workers in stones, ivory, weaving, confectionery goods, jewellery, precious metals, pottery and so forth. We have already referred to the *Hina-Sippas* or callings of low repute, such as those of hunters, trappers, fishermen, butchers, tanners, as also actors and dancers at that time in the history of India.

Sometimes, the village were known for their special handicrafts. There is mention of villages of potters, wood wrigths, or iron-smiths, who turned out articles like razors, axes, plough –shares, goods and needles works reflected the duty of the artisans.

In towns also industries were distributed in certain areas or along certain streets. We read of the ivory workers street (*vithi*) in Benares[58], the dyers street[59], the Vessas (*Vaịsyas* merchants), street[60] or the weavers 'Place' (*thana*)[61] in different areas of the Jammu and Kashmir State.

Trade

Trade was both foreign and inland, seaborne and riverine, export and import. The Pali books mention voyages from *Champa* to *Suvarnabhumi;* from Pataliputra to *Tamralipati* and there to Ceylon, or from Banaras down the river to the sea. There is also menton of traders coasting round India from Bharukachchha (Bhroach) to *Survarna bhumi* (Burma), touching at a port of Ceylon on the way. We also read of 500 traders on board ill-fated ships and of 700 under the safe pilotage of *Supparaka*[62] used to come in India for the purpose of trade and military relations.

Inland trade was carried on by carts and caravans along established trade routes. One of these was between Sravasti and Rajagraiha. Another was upto the frontiers, probably towards Gandhara. A third route led south-west from Sravasti to Pratisthana with six halts on the way and frequent crossings of rivers[63] from one place to another by the spiritual peoples. Boats went up the Ganges and up the Yamuna to Kausambi[64] are also mentioned in the texts. A yet fourth route led westwards to Sindh from which came important of its horse and asses[65] in the history of India. We also read of overland caravans going east across deserts requiring days to across (in Rajputana) steering in the coolness of nights by the stars, under the land-pilot called Thalaniyamaka[66]. Beyond the western ports merchants went out of sight of land into the ocean and traded with Baveru (Babylon) had its links.

Lastly, there was the great north-west overland trade route linking India with Central and Western Asia by ways of cities named Rajagriha, Banaras, Sravasti, Saketa, up to Takshasila[67] have been mentioned in various texts of the period.

Bazars:

Foodstuffs were not sold within the towns but at their gates. We read of the sale of fish at a gate of Savathi[68] of green-grocery at the four gate of *Uttara-Panchala*[69] and of venison at the cross-roads (*Sanghataka*) outside Benares[70] where were located the *Suna* or slaughter houses of the '*Nam*' or God.

With the town there were shops (*Apana*) and stores (*Antara-pana*). There were bazaars for textiles, groceries, oils, grain, green-groceries, perfumers, flowers, works of gold, jewellery and strong liquors which were sold at the taverns (*panagara* or *apana*)[71] in the places of various cities.

Prices

Prices were not controlled but left to haggling and competition in the market. There was also speculation or "dealing in futures." We read of a local corner in hay and of huge profits of 200 and 400 percent. Prices were, however, controlled for royal purchases by the court valuer (*Agghakarika*) who had a hard task in buying cheap and refusing bribes offered by traders-men for higher rates[72] as thoughts on earth.

Money

Barter was yielding to money –economy in certain cases. Coins were used to value marketable articles as well as 'fees, pensions, fines, loans, store, treasure and income.'

The Buddhist term for a coin is *Kahapana* (*Karshapana*). There were also coins known as *Nikkha* and *Suvanna*, both of gold.There were also bronze or copper pieces known as *Kamsa*,*Pada*, *Masaka* and *Kakanika*. The values of coins varied with time and place, The *Vinaya* text[73] states: At that (of *Bimbisara* or *Ajatasatru*) at Rajagriha, five *masakas* were equal to one *pada*[74].

Guilds

Industry was organized under guilds called *Srenis*. Each Guild had its President called *Pamukha* (*Pramukha*) or *Alderman* (Jetthaka= Jyeshthaka) and had also a Treasurer called *Bhandagarika*. Each craft had also its chief called *Jetthaka* when it was not governed by a Guild.

Trade also had its chief called *Setthi*. The Head of a Commercial Federation was called a *Mahasetthi*. *Anathapindika* in Buddha's time was one such commercial magnate who controlled 500 subordinate chiefs called *Anusetthis* under him. Each Head or *Setthi* of a commercial concern was supreme in his sphere, as indicated by the expression *Setthi-chhatta* (umbrella of authority). The word *Setthi* itself may be connected with the term *thana* (*sthana*) or office of the administrative unit.

There was a good deal of caravan traffic in the country. It was orgainsed a joint concern of traders in different commodities under a captain called Sattha (*Sartha*) 'Word' *Vaha* who gave direction as to halts, watering, routes, fording and dangerspots to the carters and others following the caravan, while the *Thalaniyyamakas* (Land-pilots)accompanied the caravan, as it escorts and guides against dangers to travel from "drought, famine, wild beasts, robbers, and demons".

Agriculture had its own representative or spokesman called *Bhojaka*[75] at that time.

Caste and Craft of the Areas

Craft was generally hereditary. "*Chunda* the smith is called *Chunda* smith-son[76]". But the Buddhist text do not indicate that of a craft depended on caste. The *Jatakas,* tell of a prince working as trader or a potter, a florist and cook in succession and also as an archer on hire.They also tell of *Sakya* and *Koliye Kshatriyas* working in the fields of their "*Bhojakas, Amachchas* and *Uparajas*." They also mention Brahmins as traders, archers, trappers and carpenters and following many other occupations not connected with learning. Acannonical text refers to a father giving his son freedom to choose any occupation not his own, such as Writing, Accounting and Money changing (*Rupa*).

And yet, the Buddhist texts recognize the wisdomof confining castes to their crafts. A canonical passage mentions assignment of begging for alms to the Brahmin, bow and arrow to Kshatriya, tillage and dairy-farming to Vaisya, and sickle and yoke to the *Sudhra*. One *Jataka* text[77] even condemns Brahmins taking to unlawful occupations like agriculture, trade and other calling[78] of the Hindu society. According to the Buddhist doctrine of *Karma*, not all actions are called *Karma,* only those that are performed with an intention, or volitionally, are called *Karma.* The word *Karma* is Sanskrit and its Pali counterpart is *Kamma,* (compare *dharma* and *dhamma as spiritual knowledge)* in Sanskrit and Pali respectively. It is derived from the root *Kar* meaning to *do* or to *perform.* It has three channels: (1)' *Kaya Kamma* (Bodily action); (2) *Vaci-Kamma* (Verbal action); and (3) *Mano-Kamma* (Mental action). An action is either good or bad; a good action is called *Kusala-Kamma* and a bad one, *Akusala-Kamma.* The Pali word *Kusala* is also translated as *wholesome* value of the *'Life', skillful, meritorious*, etc. and *akusala* means just the opposite[79]done by Brahmins of the period having no scientific study towards their subjects.

Persian Invasions

During this period, a remote part of India in the north-west came under the sway of neighbouring Persian Empire. India and Iran were culturally connected from much older times. The *Avesta,*for instance is familiar with India which it calls *Hindu* derived from the Sanskrit word *Sindhu* denoting both the river and the country to which it belongs. It also knows of the Panjab which it calls *Haptahindu,* the *Rigvedic* land of *Sapta-Sindhavas.* Thus India was not unknown to Persia. By sixth century B.C. there was regular political connection between Perisa and India. According to Herodotus, the eastern conquest of the Perisan Achaemenian Emperor, Cyrus (558-530 B.C.), included the district called *Gandaritis* or *Gandhara.* Ctesias even states that Cyrus died from wounds inflicated upon him by "the Indians" in a battle, and defeated by the Persian in the history of the '*Nams*' Xenophon states that Cyrus "brought under his rule Bactrians and Indians". Under the next King

Cambyses of the '*Sudhra Family*', there was no far ther Persian advance into India. But in the time of next King Darius I (522-486 B.C.)Hi (n) du figures as apart of his Empire in his two inscriptions found at Persepolis (518-515 B.C.) and at *Nakshi-i-rustam* (515 B.C.). Thus this Indian consequent of Darius may be dated to 518 B.C. Herodotus also states that India counted as the twentieth satrapy of the Empire of Darius to which,however, it contributed a third of its revenue, 360 talents of god '*Word*'–equivalent to over a million pound sterling. All this gold must have come from the washing of Indus beds of the Jammu and Kashmir State which according to geologists (V. Ball in Indian Archeaology Survey Report, August, 1884) were distrinctly auriferous in those days and also from what Herodotus calls "the gold digging ants "supposed to be Tibetan mastiffs digging up gold. The Perisan hold on India was strengthened under the next Emperor Xerxes (486-465 B.C.) who recruited Indian soliders to his army fighting aginst Greece. They are called Gandharians as well as Indians and used arrows tipped with iron and also spears for fight at close quarters. Acoording to Herodotus, India supplied Xerves not merely with infantry but also cavalry and chariots; together with horses and wild asses to draw the chariots, as also dogs. The next Emperor Darius III also enlisted Indian troops to resist Alexander's invasion. Some of these were "mountainous Indians." India also sent a small force of elephants[80] on that areas to fight against the *Malechcha*.

Effects of Persian Contact

One consequence of Persian contact with India is the introduction to India of Perisan coins. The Persian gold coins called *Daric* which was first minted by Darius I found its way into India but as its value in terms of silver was comparatively less than in Persia, it could not hold its own in India. But the Persian silver coins alled *sigloi (shekets)* had more value in India where they became popular and also looked like the indigenous Indain silver *Karshapana* square pieces, as Hindu made it symbol of the religion.

There also sprang up some Persian settlements as a result of the Persian hold on India. One proof of this is the discovery of an Ashokan inscription at Taxila written in the Persian Aramaic script.

Some scholars also read Persian influence in some of the features of Ashokan Pillars showing bell shaped capital of Persepolitan origin and also in the very practice of Ashoka in issuing his royal proclamation in the shape of inscriptions on rock or pillar. But these points of supposed Persian influence on India are not free from doubt.(*See Plate XXII, Capital of Ashoka Pillar at Sarnath; Fig.34*)

Greek Invasion

The Persian Empire was invaded by Alexander the king of Macedon, who defeated its Emperor Darius III and burnt its capital of *Persepolis* in 330 B.C. His impulse to further conquest led to pursue it into India.

He protected his rear by a chain of cities where Greek garrisons were posted. The last of these was Nicaes. Arriving there in 327 B.C. he asked the King of Taxila and other princes the west of the Indus on the border of Jammu and Kashmir States to meet him there. Ambhi, King of Taxila and his son as traitors, offered to help him in his invasion of India.

Alexander was also helped by another traitor, the frontier chief Sisikottus (*Sasi-gupta*).

Alexander's army comprised 30,000 men and was a heterogenous lot consisting of Macedonians, Balkans, Thracians, Iranians, Central Asiatics, and even Phoenicians and Egyptians. They was thus not much inner unity among them.

One divison of the army moved along the Kabul river toward Peshawar guided by the King of Taxila. But it was opposed by a patroitic Indian king named Astes (Ashtaka Raj) ruler of the Ashtakas, with his capital at *Pushkalavati.* For full thirty days, he stood the Greek siege of his city till he fell fighting

The other divison of the army was led by Alexander up the hills to the north of the Kabul river, the valleys of the Kunar, Panjkora and Swat, the home of heroic republican people called Aspasioi (*Asyayana of Panni* IV, I. 110) and *Assakenoi* (*Asvakayana* of Panini, Ib. 99).They fought to a man but without success. Alexander took 40,000 as captives and 2,30,000 oxen.

The eastern Asvakayans also resisted Alexander from their fortress called Massage (*Masaka*, capital of Masa Kavati mentioned by Panini in IV, 285) under the command of their late king's mother, Queen Cleophis (Kripa) i.e., '*Nam*' or '*Chamar*'. Even the women of the tribe fought in defence. But it did not succeed.

These hilly peoples had another centre of defence at the city called Aornos which corresponds to *Varana* mentioned by Panini (IV. 282), as the story of '*Word*' to world.

But this was also reduced by Alexander who pusured the flying defenders of the city up the hills.

With his rear thus secured by defeating the highlanders, Alexander effected his crossing of the Indus on boats built beforehand at a place called Ohind, 16 miles above Attock, in 326 B.C. in the area of Jammu Region.

He then moved on to the friendly city of Taxila where he held a Darbar to receive homage and presents tendered by the petty chiefs of the neighbouehood.Alexander returned the presents lavishly in vessels of gold and silver and Persian embroideries. His farther advance lay across the *Hydaspes* (Jhelum) and was opposed by the king named Poros (*Paurava*). But he could not check the Greeks crossing the river after a night of storm and rain.The Indian Army under young Paurava could not stand the charge of Macedonian cavalry led by Alexander himself. The king and now to face Alexander and his army with his full strength infantry, cavaltry, chariots and elephants. But Nature did not help the Indian cause. Rain 'rendered the ground slippery and unfit for horse to ride over, while the chariots kept sticking in mud." Before the Indian army could operate under these adverse conditions, the enemy had time to change them and throw them into confusion. Their horse and elephants getting out of hand began to charge them instead of the enemy. Poros stood firm up to the last and left the field with nine wounds on his body and surrendered to Alexander who asked how he should like to be treated.He replied: "Act as a king". Alexander was generous enough to reinstate Poros in his kingdom, with some additional; territories toward the east, belonging to the "fifteen republican peoples with their 5000 considerable cities and villages without number".

Alexander also annexed to the kingdom of Poros the country of the republican people called Glauganikai or Glaussai (*Glauchukayanaka*) with their 37 towns.

Alexander next conquered the whole territory between the *Akesines* (*Chenab*) and *Hydrates* (Ravi) and added it to the kingdom of Poros as the culture of 'One Nation'.

Alexander proceede farther beyond the Ravi and conquered the republican peoples called *Adraistoi* (*Adhrishta*) and the Kathaoi (*Kathas*) against their most heroic resistance fought against the *Barhmana bad.* All this territory was made over to Poros.

Somewhere in the neighbourhood lay the kingdom of Sophytes (*Saubhuti*) who submitted to Alexander with out resistance as the Muslim is the religion of submission before God or '*Nam*'.

Another neighbouring King named Phegelas (Bhagala in Panini, IV, 1, 96) also offered him submission.

Alexander now proceeded up to the fifth river Hyphasis (Beas) where, however, he was brought to a halt by his rebellious army who were not prepared to proceed farther. He was thus forced to give the order for retreat in 326 B.C. along the tried road by which he came back, to the Ravi, the Chenab and the Jhelum. Here, the took a new route and sailed down the Indus River to the ocean, with a fleet of 1000 boats locally constructed,. "luggage –boats, house-transports, wargalleys, protected by troops on either bank. As the Armada floated down the Jhelum and reached its confluence with the *Chenab,* opposition was offered by a confederacy of republican people led by Malloi (*Malavas*) and Oxydrakai (*Kshudraks*) of the Jammu Region.One of their towns was a town of Brahmins who left their pen for the sword and died fighting against them because they could not understand the historical study of the '*Chamar*' who used to live on the bank of *Chenab* near Akhnoor whereform the Civilization growth of the history is evoluated from one generation to another.

Other republican peoples also fought Alexander heroically but in vain. These were the *Sibis* (*Sibae*), and *Agalassoi,* other such peoples were the Abastanes (*Ambashthas* in Panini IV, I, 74), the *Xathri* (*Kshatriyas*), the *Ossadioi* (*Vasati*), and the *Sogdi* or *Sogdri* (*Sudhras*) under Brahmin ascendancy who submitted to Alexander fight against them and to crush them.

All these people fought Alexander to the utmost. In one of the towns of the Agalasoi, the citizens numbering about 20,000 cast themselves with their wives and children into the flames instead of surrendering to the enemy. The Brahmins of this region were also noted for their defence of the country against the foreign invader as part of their *Dharma* and keeping up the spirit of resistance of the republican peoples while condemning as traitors the submissive kings.At their instigation Musicanus (King of the *Mushikas*) revoked his submission to Alexander and was followed Oxycanus. These chief with the patriotic Brahmins preferred death to dishonour.

Alexander's next move along the lower Indus area of the Jammu Region was towards *Pattala* which was ruled by two Kings jointly and a Council of Elders. The place was deserted at the approach of Alexander.Alexander left this place in September 325 B.C. on his homeward journey through Gedrosia, thus taking leave of India finally.

Results of Alexander's Invasion

Greek writers are prone to exaggerate these.What is beyond doubt is that Alexander had a successful march through the Panjab and Sindh. But its course was not always smooth. As we have seem it was opposed by India's republican peoples at different to five rivers,as in that of the lower Indus of the Jammu and Kashmir area in the foothills of the Panjab. But the opposition failed for want of united fornt, of efficient leadership of financial resources and trained generalship like Mulayam Singh Yadava. Another cause of Alexnader's success was the teachery of some of the Indian kings.

It is also to be considered that the Indians did not take very seriously Alexander's campaign in a land so far from his own. A representative Indian a detached ascetic, gave expression to the Indian attitude toward Alexander invasion by a homely illustration. He trod on piece of dried up hide of which as he pressed on one end, the other ends would fly up. By this visible example, he wanted to bring home to Alexander the inherent futility of his campaigns in regions so remote from the centre of his own empire. It was not possible in those days of diffcult communication to govern a far-flung empire and control its distant parts.

Alexander, of course, tried his best to consolidate his conquests in India as far as possible by suitable administrative arrangements. He posted Greek Governors only to the west of the Indus: for the celebration the *Sudhras* over the Brahmanabad of the Jammu Region; Peithon in Sindh, Philip in the north, in the lower Kabul Valley up to Bactria; and Oxyartes in the valley of Hindukush region.

To the east of the Indus, however, he did not dare appoint Greek Governors, but only Indian the king of Taxila, and Abhisara and Poros was there.

In this arrangement, Greek rule could not take root in a foreign soil. Alexander's retreat from released the forces of opposition to foreign rule. Its first signal was the murder of his Satrap Nicanor by the *Asvayanas*. This was followed by the assasinationof his most powerful Satrap Philip. As a remedy, Alexander had to appoint the Indain king of Taxila to take his place. It was really the end of Greek rule in India.

Perhaps one advantage to India from this foreign invasion was the impetus it give towards unity. Alexander succeeded in his campaign because he could invade the many States of India one by one. Some of the Republican States formed a united front against him and were able to make their defence much stronger that Brahmins cannot penetrate in that areas. But it was only pointer to the future which an accomplished Indian leader emerged to shape properly. It was *Chandragupta Maurya* who successfully achieved the political unification of India under an Empire whose dominion extended from Persia upto Southern India[81].

Economic and Social Conditions as Described by the Greeks

The Greek writers on Alexander's Indian campaigns have left valuable descriptions of some aspects of India economic condition and social life in those days already mentioned above in detail.

In brief, the Panjab seems to have been economically very prosperous as indicated by the growth of urban life to which the Greeks testify. But most of these towns of the Panjab were not merely the centres of economic progress, but also of defence, garrisons and strongholds such as *Massaga* or Aornos in the country of the Aspasians. Sometimes, the number of the town compared very favourably with the size of their States. The small republican country of Glausai counted as many as 37 towns.The part of the Panjab which was rule by the Malloi and the Oxydrakoi and other confederate tribes is stated to have as many as "5000 towns".

It may be noted from the study that some of these towns were very well planned for defensive purposes and as examples of sound and stable architecture. The capital of Massage for instance was constructed as fort on the basis of natural advantages on an eminence inaccessible on all sides against steep rock, treacherous morass, deep stream and articfical rampart which was further defended by deep moat dug around it. According to Curtius, the rampart was "thirty five *stadia* (=about four miles) in circumference, with a basis of stone work supporting a superstructure of unburnt, sun-dried bricks. The brick work was bound into a solid fabric by means of stones of the '*Ravidas Culture*'. "The town of Aornos was similary constructed on a high hill of which a spring was utilized for purposes of its water supply while there was an agricultural farm built up with the labour of thousand men to render the fort self-sufficient in the matter of food. According to Strabo, there were as a many 5,000 cities in the territories of nine nations between the Jhelum and the Beas. Similarly, the *Malloi* also possessed many walled cities with citadels built on commanding heights difficult of access. "The Five Rivers" '*Word*' or '*Nam*' a name which was transferred, unaltered to the land itself, and of which '*Penjab*' is the Persian form show up between about five times as many names, like *Pantchanada* a collective name of the river, *Tchandrabhaga*, hallenized into *Sandrophacus*, already mentioned in the study it still retains its duty to wash the Brahmins from the Jammu and Kashmir state, which made hell by them in the absence of the Father. There is a pretty story of this river having set a term to Macedonian Alexander's Indian campaign; as did by the '*Baba Gurinder Singh of Biaswala*'; its Greek name meaning "Devourer of Alexander", the conqueror is said to have accepted it as an evil omen and decided on returning[83] back to position to defeat the Brahmins which have been forgotten the Father.

Of these ancient cities of the Panjab, the city of Taxila was "the greatest between the Indus and the Hydaspes," *Hypanis*, or, closer still, *Vipasis* in the history of India.

Thus, there towns show that architecture in ancient India was not always or exclusively wooden but was also in stone, like the walls and fortifications of *Rajgii* in earliest times in this area to crush the Brahmins with the power of '*Nam*'.

The list of spoils secured by Alexander at different places of his campaigning throw some light on the Indain handicrafts and manufactures of the times. There are references to cotton goods, bucklers of ox-hide, skins of lizards, tortoise shells and, "talents of steel" '(*Ferri Candidi*), "white iron" which Cunningham takes to be nickel.

The King of Taxila presented Alexander with "200 talents of silver and golden crowns." Besides nickel coins, there were also known the silver issue of king Sophytes, which are supposed to be imitation Athenian "owls", because they showed the king's head on obverse, and on reverse the cock and his name in Greek characters. Lastly, we may refer to the Indian soldiers armoury which included iron-tippled arrows, javelins, swords and lances, besides the use of carts, chariots and boats for purposes of trade and war.

The Panjab was even then well known fo the abundance and the quality of its cattle and livestock. Alexander sent off to Macedonia a fine breed of oxen numbering 2,30,000 which were captured by him in the country of the *Asvakas*. He received from the king of Taxila a present of 3,000 fat oxen and 1,0000 sheep; from king Sophytes a brace of figthing dogs; and from the *Kshudrakas* even tamed lions and tigers. The others domesticated animals were horses and elephants which were useful for both economic and military purposes.

According to Strabo, much of the internal trade of the Panjab was riverine. Strabo says that the river Oxus in the time of Alexander was quite navigable so that goods from India were carried down this river to the Caspian Sea on their way to the west as did by Mohammad-bin-Qasim and spread the Islam as a 'New Concept' of the period equivalent to *'Nam'*or *Word.*

Indian society of those days is best described by Megasthenes on the basis of first -hand observation he made when he lived as an ambassador at the court of Maurya king Chandragupta. His account will be dealt with later. But we get some glimpses of social life from the Greek accounts of Alexander's. The Greeks were very much impressed by the Indian ascetics whom they first saw at Taxila. Alexander was after them for curiosity which they won't respect. As did not care themselves to come to see Alexander, Alexander sent to them his friends Onesicritus who reports that he saw 15 ascetics about ten miles from the city given to meditation in the Sun. When told that the Yavana King was axious to learn their wisdom, one of them bluntly answered that no one coming in the bravery of European clothes '*Word'* cavalry cloak and broad brimmed hat and top-boots like Dr. B.R Ambedkar used to keep before the independent of 1947, such as the Macedonians wore '*Chamar'* could learn their wisdom to kill the *Kashmiri Pandits* as idiot race of the human history. To that he must strip himself naked and learn to sit on the stones beside them[84].

Aristobulus in his book states that he saw at *Takshasila* two these ascetics one with a shaven head, and the other with long hair while both had their groups of disciples. Whenever they went to the market place, crowds flocked to them for counsel[85]

The leader of these ascetics is named by the Greeks[86] *Dandanis* (*Dandi –Svami* i.e., 'God' or 'Nam') Who did not even care to see Alexander on pain of death and sent his reply in a singularly spiritual vein as follows: "God alone is the object of may homage. Alexander is not God since he must taste of death. I have no fear or favour to ask. What Alexander can offer is utterly useless. The things that I prize are these leaves which are my house these blooming plants which supply me dainty food. Having nothing which requires guarding I have tranquil slumber, whereas had I gold to guard, that would banish sleep. The Brahmins neither love gold nor fear death. Death means that one will be delivered from his ill-assoned companion the body' (Frags, LIV ans LV).

These words are characteristic of the higher mind of India in all ages and give expression to its innate spirituality which control the worldly life of the man always exhibited in the Jammu and Kashmir State as a place of spiritual rulers or divine rulers as an important area of the good trade relation between God and Man.

Coins

The identification of *Sophytes* (take by Levi to be Saubhuti) as an Indian King is not as certain as is assumed. He is first known through his coins which were purely Greek in style and considered as copies of Seleukus Nikator. It is, however, strange that a Hindu King should issue a coin of a foreign design. The *Obverse* of his coins show either helmeted head of the king or Athene while the *reverse* show Cock. The artist's initial like 'M' also appears on obverse as stated for '*Mind*' or *Mana*. A signed coin s unusual after Alexander, while the helmet is that on a type of Seleukus. These two points fix the time of *Sophytes* and of his coinage. As regards the cock, it does not resemble the Indian game cock. It is more like 'the cock, on a piece of Carystos in Euboea struck c. 336[87] B.C. According to Sir George Macdonell, the coin of *Sophytes* is an *Attic Drachm* of about c.320B.C. The Indian origin of the coins of *Sophytes* is also doubted because Brahmin historians has no knowledge *'Sudhra* Family'. They were first secured by Cunningham from dealers of Rawalpindi. In 1877, a large hoard of coin was found at *Kabadian* on the Oxus and was imported to *Rawalpindi* by dealers. This hoard included the oriental imitations of *Owls* and *Eagles* of the '*Nam*', a kin to the coins of *Sophytes*. It may be noted that the weight of the *Drachm* of Sophytes in 58.3 grains which is the weight of the heaviest Indian *Punch-marked* silver coin called *Karshapana*. This argument weighed with numismatists in assuming the Indian origin of these coins, but these coins have lower denominations the lowest of 13.5 grains, as also a quarter *Drachm* and so forth. Thus, their weight standard followed that of the eastern imitations of Athenian coins. It also appears that even the famous Poros *Deca-Drachm* was not found in India,but in *Bukhara* while a second specimen came from Iran.

Besides numismatic literary evidence on the subject is not conclusive. Acording to Greek historians, Alexander on his eastward march, after conquering Sangala, invade the kingdom of an Indian ruler whose name is differently spelt as 'Sopeithes' or 'Sophites'. The identification of 'Sophytes of the coins with one or other of the Greek names is a mere conjecture. Besides A.E. Anspach and Berve have found that there were two kings of the same name ruling in two different regions as '*Nam*' or '*Chamar*'. Nor is the identification by Sylvain Levi of Sophytes with Sanskrit 'Saubhuti' quite tenable. Saubhuti a mere grammatical term and not a geographical reality. Panini has rule by which certain words can be transformed in to place names. The *Ganapatha* to this rule mention forty-one words of which the eleventh is Subhuta whence the place-name *Saubhuta*, whence Saubhuti as the king of that country. But grammar is not history '*History* is to be creat'. Besides, in the *Ganapatha* referred to, the country called *Saubhuta* is not mentioned next to Samkata (*Sangala*). There are nine words or countries coming between these two. Thus, the King Sophytes named on coins is not an Indian king, nor are the coins of Indian origin because God made the whole world, it is his liking where he wants to predict his history. Therefore, there is no point in equating the non-Indian King Sophytes with the Sanskrit name *Saubhuti* which is merely a grammatical example and not a historic reality, but it based in human body to realize the Father. The Greek name 'Sopeithes' and it s variants used for the Indian king who was Alexander's friend remain to be connected with their Sanskrit equivalent which is not yet found[88] in the language of the study.

Effects of the Persian and Macedonian Invasions in India.

The Macedonian prefectures and garrisons were soon swept away by Chandragupta Maurya, a King of the '*Sudhra Dynasty*' called '*Chamar*' at one time in the history of India and with in a few years all vestige of foreign domination of the Brahmins disappeared from the Panjab and the Sindh due to invasion of Alexander. But the invasions of Darius and Alexander had not been in vain, because, he established his authority our here in the long period of the Indian history. The Persian conquest had unveiled India or *Bharat*, the area lying between Ravi and Chenab probably for the first time to the Western world had to establish political contact between the Ravi and Chenab for the development of trade and commerce because Jammu and Kashmir was the biggest centre of learning at that time these were particularily biggest centre of trade and commerce in India. No doubt, that the Indian spearmen and archer fought handsomely under the Persian banner on European land in the5th century B.C. and quickened the interest of the peoples of hell as in this land of strange folklore and other trade relation of the life. Perisan and Greek officals found employment in '*Indus –Sarasvati Basin*' and made their physical presence their in various ways. The introduction of new manuscripts '*Word' Aramaic*, *Kharoshthi* and the alphabet styled *Yavanami* by Panini from their sources.

However, it is wrong for the Indians to ignore Alexander invasion completely because it had directly and indirectly effected on Indian history. Though the Panjab and Sindh began to enjoy the blessing of a unified rule as the direct and immediate result of Alexander invasion, the Indians ignored the superiority of the Greek art of warfare.The Indian rulers and their military raids seem to have paid no attention to the Greek mode of warfare.They struck to their traditional method of fighting and continued for centres to place their chief reliance on their elephant brizades equivalent to 'Nam' or God.

But there is one more historial gain in the date of Alexanders invasion i.e, 326 B.C. The clearly dated records of Alexander campanign in India left by his companions helped to build Indian chronology order for subsequent political events on a definite basis. The date of Alexander invasion in fact forms the sheet anchor of Indian chronology. As regards that Greeks, they learned a good deal of the Science, Arts, Philosophy, History, Mathematics and Medicine from India during the period of this contact. Indain philosophy, Greek thought and their culture was effected particularly due to the trade relation of the *'Nam'* in India and in the other parts of world that Kashmir was learning centre of Buddhism.

With the growth of the Jammu Kingdoms and their territorial expansion, the office of the Viceroy and Provincial Governor became more and more significant for the development of Areas. Chief of the Imperial power i.e. Nam or God, among state officials, the *Purohits* were of special importance, but they were the agent of the '*Nam*' and some times a single person was at one time the Purohita of three kingdoms as in the case of *Kasi, Kosala* and *Videha*. The position of the women in this period was under review in the society. Ploygency was gradually growing. Most of the people lived in closely clustered villages and followed the peaceful items of agricultural products like vegetables and fruits. Stitched clothes were common in fashion. Principal items of export were silk, leather goods, muslin, etc. if we bear in mind that the use of shoes at that time of worship must have been prohibited in ancient times as today,because the figures represented are engaged in worship or act as characters during absence of the Father. In sacred stories like *Mahabharata*, *Ramayana* and in the Buddhist texts, they have been purposely represented without shoes as Brahmins feel impious to enter in the *Temple* or *Monastry.*

Notes & References

1. A.B. Keith; *Rigveda* Br; p. 3.
2. K.A. N. Sastri; *Age of the Nandas and Mauryas; Delhi* ; Reprint, 1967, p.7.
3. G.L.Khajuria; *Majestic Pines*, An article published 'Daily Excelsior' 17 June, 2007.
4. A.K. Khanna; *Tawi Rivers*; An article published in Daily Excelsior, 29-7-07 **Note:** The major Ancient Civilizations of the world took birth, survived and flourished on the banks of rivers like, Indus,Ravi, Tigris (Iraq), Nile (Egypt) etc, in the oldest written ancient Indian text, in the world the *Rig-Veda*, the rivers have been mentioned as the deities and have been worshiped, with the passage of time as God gifted natural springs of the 'Nam', as a respect towards them. But under the Brahminical rule when there is lawlessness, these rivers became polluted by them in the light of their self interest to extract money out of them during the repair and cleanize the silt of the bed pieces. The highest terrace of which the Mubarak Mandi stands being towards North. The main old town has been located on the South. Thus, keeping in view, the lawlessness period of the 'Brahminical Ideology' made the water pollution in the life and Jammu Tawi area has been disturbed the balance of ecosystem and it is causing health hazards to humans and extinct of the animal species. Jammu Tawi originates mainly at *Kalplas Kund* of Seoj Dhar of the ancient text in the Bhadarwah region of Doda district, from here it descends to *Sudh Mahadeva* in Chennani about 40 km away from it. The carrying capacity of the Jammu Tawi River has almost saturated in the Sindh Valley of Kashmir and Ladakh as a part of its natural sources; and a Banganga, a tributary of the Jammu Tawi. (Also see K.A.N Sastri, op. cit., p. 7)
5. J.W. McCrindle;, I*nvasion of Alexander;* p. 311.
6. *Ibid.*, p. 220.
7. **Note:** The use of patronymics or metronymics these, terms in history give the sense of knowledge to modify the old one into new one, instead of the personal name is by no means rare in Indian history of the Jammu Region. The cases of *Assakenus*, *Porus*. *Pandion*, reveal several cases of the classical writers did

not take the trouble of acquainting themselves with the personal designations of princes and rulers of the areas, became it depended on the theory of nature that what kind of management, they had started and what they have found in the present life. But it makes clear from the study that *'History Repeat Itself'* for the sake of poor people not for the materialistics, i.e. called *Rakshasa* of the '*Nam*' or God, they are eating the exchequer without reasoning and logic.

8. J.W. McCrindle; op. cit., pp. 221-22.
9. *Ibid.*
10. Pargiter, D.K.A., p. 23.
11. *Hiuen Tsang*; Tr, by Thomas Watters; Vol. II. p. 296.
12. K.A.N. Sastri, op. cit., pp. 25, 26, 27.
13. *Majjhima Nikaya,* III. 7.
14. *Majjhima Nikaya; II.* 124.
15. *Sutta Nipata,* Verse, 408, Dialogues II. P.2)
16. *Vinaya* Pitakas; II. p. 190.
17. *Avasyaka Sutra* ; pp. 682-83.
18. *The Life of the Buddha-II 1982, p.62.*
19. *Samyutta Nikaya*, I. pp. 84, 85, 86.
20. *Bhagavati Sutra* ; p. 300.
21. *Sutta Nipata*, Dialogue, II. p. 78.
22. Hoernle, *Uvasagadasao,* II. Appendix. p. 59.
23. Hoernle; *Nirayavali Sutta* referred in *Uvasagadasao*
24. Oupapatika, *Sutras;* 12, 27, 30.
25. *Tripitaka* II. p.75 Basic Buddhism Course.
26. Digha, *Nikaya*; part-I. p. 50.
27. R.K. Mookerji, *Ancient India;* p. 104.
28. *Avasyaka Sutra;* p. 687.
29. *Ibid.*, p. 689.
30. *Ibid.*, p. 690.
31. *Anguttara Nikaya;* III. 57-63.
32. *Avasyaka Sutra,* p. 690.
33. *Vinaya Pitaka;* SBE; p. 181.
34. *Digha Nikaya*, Part-II. p. 96.
35. *Sutta Nipata, Dialogues*,I. p. 147.
36. *Majjhima Nikaya*; I, p. 353.
37. Rockhill; *Life of the Buddha ;* p.119
38. *Mahavastu*-II. p. 73.
39. *Majjhima Nikaya-I* p. 23.
40. *Digha*-Nikaya II. pp. 159, 161.
41. *Kalpa Sutra*; pp. 100, 102.

42. *Udana Combridge*, vol.1.p.399
43. Paul Dhlke; *Buddhist Essays;* p.15
44. *Samyutta Nikaya*-1 pp.146-8
45. *Uttaradhyayana Sutra* XXX, pp. 15-18; *Sutrakrittanga*, II. 2 (13)
46. *Anguttara Niyaka*; p.107; II. p.85
47. *Medicine Buddha Sutra;* U.S.A Reprint; 2001. **Note:** There are currently five extant Chinese translations from the Sanskrit, done between A.D. 317 and A.D. 707, as well as two Tibetan translation which miss the history of India particularly the Jammu and Kashmir State which was a flourishing centre of the Buddhism in whole of the world during the period of their study. The text that forms the basic of this translation that *Buddha or 'Nam'* were the same things and same meanings in Parkritic language, is that of the Patriarch *Husan-Tsang*, founder of the Chinese *Yogacara* (Mind Only) school which follows the 'Brahminical Ideology' after the death of the Lord Buddha by wearing dresses, copy of his other activities we try to own ourselves, but the real thought invested in the same soul called Principal Soul comes, time and again, in different human form to teach the people the similar idea as it is depicted in '*Radha Soami*' centre of Jammu and Kashmir as well as in other parts of the Indian society as a whole in this Universe. Thus 75 *Buddhist Sutra* translator have been found having the same knowledge as the Brahmins has in the mind or soul; because without '*Nam-Dana*' from the Prefect Master, one cannot get the 'Light' of the real thought. It is a scientific study of the Living Master not the dead material, like sculpture, paintings,etc. It combines the Pure land teachings on rebirth and the esoteric practices of reciting *dharani* and lighting lamp as an artificial study of the Father which is not based on Living Master. Therefore, Living Master of the '*Nam*' is very important for '*The Journey of the Soul*', using his souls as actors and his new creation as the theatre, God was the Director, and he named his play, "Life". (Victoria Jones; *The Journey of the Soul*, Beas, Reprint, 2004).
48. *Jatika*, Part-I. p. 249.
49. *Ibid.*, p. 336. part-IV. p.167, part-V. p.412. *Dhammapada* V. 80=145=Theragatha, 19.
50. *Vinaya Pitaka* Taxts, II. pp. 207, 208, 209.
51. *Digha Nikaya*; I. p. 51.
52. *Jatika 1. p. 339.*
53. *Suttanipata; I. p.4.*
54. *Jatika.* I., pp.99; 317.
55. *Ibid., p.IV.* p. 323.
56. *Digha, Nikaya 1. p. 87.*
57. *Samyutta Nikaya;* 1.p. 89.

58. *Jatika* -I. p.320 II. p. 197.
59. *Ibid.*, IV. p. 81.
60. *Ibid.*, VI. p. 485.
61. *Ibid.*, 1.p. 256.
62. *Ibid.* p. II, p. 127, III. p.188, IV. p.138, 159 V.p.75, VI. p. 34.
63. *Sutta-Nipata*, Verses 1011-13.
64. *Vinaya Texts*, III. pp.382, 401 & *Jatika*, I.pp.92, 348, 377.
65. *Jatika*, I. p.124 & II. p. 31.
66. *Ibid.* I. pp. 98, 107.
67. *Vinaya Texts II* p. 174. f; *Mahavagga*, VII, I, p. 6. ff.
68. *Psalms of the Brethren; p.166.*
69. *Jataka*; IV. p. 445.
70. *Ibid.*III p.49, V. p. 459 VI. p. 62.
71. R.K Mookerji; *Hindu Civilization; p. 305.*
72. *Ibid.*
73. *Vinaya Text*, III. p. 45.
74. R.K Mookerji; *Hindu Civilization;* p. 306.
75. *Ibid; p.* 308.
76. *Majjhima Nikaya*, I. p. 256.
77. *Jataka Text.* IV. p. 363.
78. R.K. Mookerji; *Hindu Civilization; p. 309.*
79. *Basic Buddhism Course;* Phra Sunthora Plamintr U.S.A 1991. p.93 *The Buddhist Law of Kamma and Rebirth;* by V.A. Buddhara Kkhita Bangalore, 2001 pp. 35, 71.
80. R.K Mookerji; *Ancient India;* pp. 128-29.
81. *Ibid* pp. 134-35.
82. Ibid, pp. 135-36.
83. Zanaide-A-Ragozin; *Vedic India, New Delhi, 1961. pp.107,.108.*
84. *Cambridge History of India ; Vol.I p. 358.*
85. *Ibid;* p. 42.
86. **Note**: The cloth seems to have been manufactured in *Vahita* country which was sent by Ajatasatru to Prasenjit, who in his return offered it as present Ananda, (Dr. Raj Kumar) which existed in ancient time between the Indus River of Jammu on the west and the Sutlej and Beas Rivers as mention in *Majjhima* Nikaya, II; p. 48.
87. R.B. Whitehead; *Numismatic Chronicle;* VI Series; vol. III.
88. R.K. Mookerji; op. cit., pp.139-40.

Plate- XVII

Fig. 29 Majestic Pines of Jammu & Kashmir Areas

Fig. 30 Chir Pines (J&K)

Plate- XVIII

Fig. 31 Basohli Beyond the Traditional Values; Ravi in Dam Formation as Collection of the Chamar History.

Fig. 32. Tawi Rivers of the Jammu Kingdom

Plate- XIX

Fig. 33 Charui-bearer (Didarganj-3rd Century B.C.)

PLATE XX

Fig. 34. Capital of Asokan Pillar at Sarnath (Wheel of Religion)

EARLY HISTORY OF JAMMU REGION

EARLY HISTORY OF JAMMU REGION

(Pre-historic to 6th Century A.D.)

(In Two Volumes)

(Volume 2)

Dr. Raj Kumar

KALPAZ

Early History of Jammu Region : Pre-historic to 6th Century A.D.

Rs. 1800 (Set)

ISBN: 978-81-7835-768-3 (set)
ISBN : 978-81-7835-770-6 (Vol. 2)

Published in 2009 in India by
Kalpaz Publications
C-30, Satyawati Nagar,
Delhi-110052
E-mail: kalpaz@hotmail.com
Phone : 9212729499

Lasser Type Setting by: Rudra Computer Graphics, Delhi
Printed at : Young Art Press, Delhi - 92

Contents

7

The Rise of Magadha and Foreign Invasions Over Jammu Kingdom

During the Buddhist period, the entire Northern India including Jammu Kingdom was divided in to small Republics and Monarchies. Out of all these, the various Kingdoms such as *Avanti, Kosala, Vatsa* and *Magadha* were very powerful. However, Magadha gradually rose in power and established its sways in North India including the areas of Jammu Region from Kashmir to Kabul Kandhara (Afghanistan). The early history of Magadha was losted in obscurity in Brahminical thought, but during the life time of Buddha it achieved prominence social justice in the history of India which were losted during the rule of *Brahmanas.* Magadha roughly corresponds to the present Patna and Gaya districts as Buddhist learning centre. The Magadha empire was the birth place of two greatest religions of Buddha and Jainism. The wise and learned scholars like *Kautilya, Panini* and *Patanjali* were the greatest product of the empire. It witnessed the rise and fall of several significant dynasties like the *Mauryas*, the *Kushanas* and the *Guptas*. The fourth successor of *Sisunaga* dynasty was the *Bimbisara* the ruler of the Magadha Empire during the life time of Lord Buddha[1] i.e., '*Nam'* or '*Chamar'*. In 326 B.C. India or *Bharata* faced number of crisis. The Imperial crown of Magadha and the neighbouring provinces was worn by a King who was "detested and held cheap" by his own people. The 'Land of the Five Rivers' was overrun by the Macedonians and allied peoples from the West who resolved to incorporate it permanently into their growing empire. Alexander, the greatest leader of the invading bands, with drew, it is true to the city of Babylon in Mesopotamia, where he died in

323 B.C. *Philippos* the *Satrap* whom he had appointed to governor of the Western Punjab, met his doom in 324 B.C. But the surviving commanders who met to partition the Macedonian in 323 B.C. and again in 321 B.C., had no desire to withdraw altogether from the conquered territories in the Indian borderland. The civil government of the districts to the east of the *Indus* or *Saraswati* in the area of *Mendhar* had to be left virtually in the hand of Indian princes. Macedonian governors were retained it he trans-Indus Satrapies, and an office, named *Eudemos,* was appointed to command the garrison in the Western Punjab or *Madradesa* after the murder of Phillipos. The successors of Alexander were, however, torn by internal dissensions and had to recall some of their commandants in India or *Bharatvarsha.* The indigenous population of the Jammu Region belong to the *'Sudhra Dynasty'* of the '*Ravidas Culture*' between the area of Chenab and Ravi had in the meantime found a religious leader of the '*Nam*', who knew how to take the advantage of the disunion of the Jammu Kingdom and the thinned ranks of the foreign invaders in the land of the indigenous, "shaked the yoke of servitude from the neck" of his fatherland[2].

By now the focus of the Civilization was shifted eastwards, and four great Kingdom mentioned above, outside the earlier area of '*Brahminical Ideology*' had eclipsed the old land of *Kurus* in both political and economic important and four states were approximately equivalent to the region later known as Malwa. Of the four, we know most about *Kosal* and *Magadha,* the chief scences of the activites of the *Buddha* and of *the Mahavira* the founder of Jainism. Her King, Prasenajit (*in Pali, Pasenadi*) was indeed still might monarch of India, ruling an area little smaller than France; but from fleeting references in the Buddhist scriptures it seems that he was inefficient and squandered his time and wealth on holy men, both orthodox and heretical point of view. His kingdom which was infested by "robbers" was loosely controlled through tribal chieftain and vassal Kings. *Bimbisara* of Magadha, on the other hand, was a man of a different stamp. In general, he was a man of peace –loving and to have kept on good terms with king of far-off Gandhara on the *Upper Indus.* His one conquest that of the little kingdom of Anga on the borders of the modern Bengal. *Campa* the capital city of *Anga* was already of considerable commercial importance for the *Chama* or learther –works, for it as a river fort of the *'Nam'* would sail down to Ganges and coast India, returning with jewels and spices of the "*Nam*" which were already much in demand in the North. Althoughe *Anga* was *Bimbisara's* only conquest, he seems to have gained control of various part of the smaller district like *Kasi (Banaras)* as the dowry of his chief queen, who was the sister of Prasenajit of Kosala. His capital was Rajagrha, some sixty miles to the south-east of the modern Patna[3]. (*See Plate XXIII, Geographical Location of Mauryan & Sunga's* Fig. 35).

In the meanwhile, signs of disaffection against foreign rule appeared, and a formidable rising followed in the Lower Indus Valley i.e., Jammu Region of the Akhnoor Valley on the borderlands of the Punjab which was formented by the *Brahmanas* of the locality. But all these insurrections seems to have been crushed with heavy hand and the hand of the invader in the Jammu Region fell heavily on the instigations. Against the illegal force of the '*Nam*'. Retribution came quickly and if tradition is to be believed in the theory of mind or *mana*, it was a Taxiian Brahman a named *Chanakya* or *Kautilya*, who raised to power the great avenger to whose mighty arms "the earth long harassed by outlanders, now turned for protection and refuge".

The new Indian leader was a young man who bore the name of *Chandragupta* or the work of hide or cutter i.e., '*Nam*' or '*Chamar'*, detailed has already been discussed in *the 'History of the Chamar Dynasty*' in the work of the same author. He is described by *Justin* as a man of *Humble Origin* who was prompted to aspire regal to power by an men significant of august destiny, immediatly after an encounter with Alexander himself, the visit the Macedonian king is referred to by Plutarch as well as Justin, but strange to say, some modern writers emend the text of Justin and propose to read "*Nandrum*" (*Nanda*) in place of Alexandru (Alexander). Such conjectural emendations are hardly justified. They mislead the unwary student of Mauryan antiquities.

The family to which the young leader belonged is named Maurya by Indian writers and is identified by some with the tribe of *Morieris* mentioned by the Greeks[4]. Term *"Maurya"* as applied to *Chandragupta* by the *Puranas* the son of *Mura* who was one of the wives of king Nanda (*Chandragupta Nandasyaiva patnyantarasya Murasamjnasya putram Mauryanam prathaman*[5]). Its shows that Chandragupta was the first *mana* of the god who provides the power in reserve or silence in manner to check the advance ment of the life from one stage to another stage. According to one tradition the designation is derived from the word *Mura*, the mother or grandmother of Chandragupta, who was the wife of a *'Nanda King*'. The cognomen *Vrishala* applied to *Chandragupta* in the Sanskrit play called the *Mudra rakshasa* does not invariably mean a men of *Sudhra* extraction[6]. But the original expression used by Justin, to whom we owe the account of the rise of Chandragupta, has the sense of 'mercenary soldier' as well as that of "robber". The former sense is in consonance with Jaina tradition of life[7] Thereafter (*deinde*), he went to war with the perfects of Alexander and fought vigourously with them[8]. A Jaina tradition fixes the date of Chandragupta accession at 313

B.C. It is, however, difficult to reconcile this tradition with the statement of the Buddhist chroniclers of Ceylon and Burma that the coronation of Ashoka took palace 24+27 (or 28) +4=55or 56 years after the accession of Chandragupta. The total of length of Mauryan region, according to the *Vayu Purana* is, however, only 133 years, and some historians point out 137 years rule of the Mauryan dynasty[9].

From the above historicity of the Chandragupta Maurya, we learn that he occupied the rank as one of the greatest ruler of India. There are many titles to his greatness which we have already discussed in the text, in several respects that he was the *'Nam' or 'Chamar'* is found to be even a unique figure in the history of India. His figure as the first "historical" emperor of India or *Bharatavarsha* in the sense that he is the earliest emperor in Indian history whose historicity can be established on the solid ground that he is '*Nam*:' or '*Chamar'* who produces *Chams* of the body by providing soul into it as a Father of the world. He was the heavenly King of the '*Nam'*. Indeed the tradition of such great Kings and Emperors goes back to the *Vedas*. The *Rigveda* tells of *Sudas* who had achieved his overlord ship of *Rigvedic India* by his victory at the "*Battle of Ten Kings"* (D*asa-rajna*) (*RV. VIII*, 33, 2, 5, 83, 81) representing about forty different *Rigvedic* peoples[10] of the '*Nam*' *or* God.

Foundation of Magadha Empire

When Alexander was away and out of the picture, it was left to the Indians to organize measures for freeing the country of the foreign rule of the Greeks. Fortunately, for them, whereas at the time of Alexander's invasion they were unable to resist it effectively for want of unity and leadership, they had now in their midest a patriotic Indian who was able to build up an adequate military force out of the material which he found available in abundance in the Panjab. Alexander's campaigns were shoutly reisted by many Republican people of the Panjab, and it was how left to Chandregupta, who happened to be its eye witness to organize than one again in the fight for freedom. Justin calls Chandragupta recruits for this new Indian army of liberation, "Robbers", taken to mean *Arattas* or *Adrahtraksa,* i.e., the kingless republican peoples of the Panjab. The Panjab itself, as stated in the *Dharmasutra* of *Baudhayanas* was the country of the *Arattas*, while the *Mahabharata* calls the *Arattas* as *Panchanadas*, belonging to the land of the five rivers, and also *Vahikas* of the land of rivers. According to the historical drama, *Mudra-rakshasa* of which the hero is *Chandragupta*, Chandragupta went far a field inoccuring recuits for his army. He entered into an alliance with the Himalayan chief named *Parvataka,* who is some times taken as identical with king Porus (Paurava) of

Alexander time. In that case Chandergupta was wise in securing alliance of one who was panting for avenging his defeat the Greek, The drama further states that ths Himalayan alliance gave to Chandragupta a composite army recruited from a variety of peoples among whom it mentions *Sakas, Vanas, Kiratas, Kambojas, Parasikas* and *Bahlikas*. Thus, *Chandragupta* army consisted of a large contingent of the forniter highlanders.

Not many details are known of this war of Indian independence which *Chandergupta* was thus fighting against the Greeks. The Indian revolt against Alexander's authority had already manifested itself in the assassination of the Satraps, as already narrated. Some light is thrown on the dark episode by Justin in the following words: "India after the death of Alexander, had shaken off as it were the yoke of servitude from its neck and put his governors to death. The author of his liberation was Sandracottus. This man was of *humble origin* of the 'Chamar Caste', but was stimulated to aspire to regal power by Supernatural Encouragement to crush the *Brahmanabad* of the areas. Then he drew together a band of robbers and instigated the Indians to over throw the existing (Greek) government."

Justine also states that Chandergupta,who was the moving about in the Panjab, met Alexander face to face and was then an eye-witness of the military capacity of these so called robbers or Republican peoples whom he later on organised into an army for overthrowing Greek rule.

The Pali text, the *Mahavamsa –tika*, also throws some light on Chandragupta recruitment of his army. There recruits were collected from different places and then organised into a powerfull army (*Mahabalakayam Sangahetva tamtassa patipadesi*).

When the first part of his mission was thus executed in freeing the Panjab of foreign rule, Chandragupta turned to its second part, viz., to liberate the other part of the country from the tyranny of the Nanda King. But it was not an easy job for him and not much is known about it. Rhys Davids stated in his *Buddhist India*[11] that "It was from the Panjab that Chandragupta recuited the nucleus of the force which he besieged and conquered *Dhana Nanda*".

Chandragupta's expedition towards Pataliputra for over throwing Nanda created sensation in the country, so as to aspire popular stories. It seems that Chandragupta first strategy was not sound. The story is that a "woman baked *chapathy* and gave it to her child. He, leaving the edges only the centre, and throwing the edges, not only the centre, and throwing the edges away asked for other cake. Then she said, this boys conduct is like *Chandragupta's* attack on the Kingdom of "*Nam*" *Chandragupta* in ambition to be a monarch, with out beginning from the froniters and taking the towns in order as he passed, has invaded the heart of the country '*Chamar*' and his army was surrounded and destroyed." Next, Chandragupta tried another strategy which was equally faulty. He commenced operation from the frontier and conquered many *Rashtras* and *Janapadas*, States and regions, on the way but his mistake was not to past garrisons to consolidated the conquests. Thus, the people left in the rear combined and made his further impossible. After these two strategic failures, he discovered the correct strategy. He had garrisons posted along the course of his advance (*uggahitanaya balam samvidhaya*) in the *Rashtras* and *Janapadas* conquered by him; and securing his rear, he crossed the frontiers of Magadha into its heart besiged Pataliputra and killed *Dhana Nanda*[12]. The same story appears in a modified from in Jaina tradition. The *Parisishtaparvan* compares Chanakya's strategy with the foly of a 'child who burns his fingers greedily put in the middle of the dish, instead of eating from the outer part which was cool. The proper strategy was to secure the surrounding countries before attacking the stronghold of the enemy. Then Chanakya and Chandragupta opened the campaign by reducing the provinces".

As has already been stated, the overthrow of the Nanda king by Chandragupta was not an easy task. Nanda was a most powerful king of the times, the master if an empire which extended up to the Panjab after conquering numerous states, as already related. His power depended upon his army which, according to Curtius, comprised 2,00,000 infantry 20,000 cavalry 2,000 four horsed chariots and 3,000 elephants. But through his military position was strong, it could not cover the inherent weak points of his position in his unpopularity with his people. Chandragupta himself when he saw Alexander in his youth reported to him that Nanda was "hated by his subjects". This report was also confirmed to him by his two Indian kings Poros and Phegelas. His unpopularity was due to his tainted origin as a Sudhra as also to his tyrannical rule and excessive taxation, as already mentioned in the study.

The details of the actual battle between Nanda and Chandragupta are not known. It has been conjectured that Chandragupta "employed Greek mercenaries in his struggle with Nanda"[13] An exaggerated description of the casualties of battle is contained in the *Milindapanho*[14], it has been stated stating that "100 *kotis* of soliders, 10,000 elephants, I lac of horses and 5,000 charioteers" were killed in action. According to the Jaina text *Parisishtaparvan*, the entire Nanda country (*Nanda desam*) was devastated its capital Pataliputra was besieged, till Nanda was forced to capitulate when he found his wealth dwindling (*Kshina-Kosham*) together with with his army (*Bala*), his mental powers (*Dhih*) and power (*Vikrama*). The conqueror, however, spared Nanda's life and permitted him to leave Pataliputra with his two wives and one daughter and as much luggage as he could carry off in a single chariot. Chandragupta is stated to have fallen in love with his daughter whom he later married, (*See*

Plate XXIV, A Lady with Mirror in Medllion Bharhut, 2nd Century B.C. Fig. 36, and *Teaching Scene, Bharhut 2nd Century B.C. Fig. 37*)

Having now made himself the sovereign of an Empire which extended from Magadha upto the Panjab, he went on extending his Empire farther both towards the North –West and the South. The North Western extension of his empire was the result of the aggressive design of the Syrian Emperor Seleukos who launched an expedition in about 305 or 304 B.C. to emulate the exploits of Alexander, but his expedition proved a failure. He forgot that he had to face a 'New India' strong and united under the leadership of a powerful personality like Chandragupta and the united front of formidable army. So Seleukos sued for peace by which he added to Chandragupta the Satrapies of Archosia *(Kandahara)*, the Paropamsidae (Kabul), together with portions of Aria (*Herat*) and Gedrosia (*Baluchistan*). By the acquistion of these territories, Chandragupta was able to extend his empire beyond the forniters of India up to those of Persia. That is why it was possible for his grandson, Ashoka, to count successor of Seleukos, viz., Antiochos, as his *immediate* neighbour, in his Rock Edicts II and XII. Chandragupta gave his new ally a present of 500 Indian elephants.

Chandragupta was now at the peak of his power and glory. According to Plutarch, after his victory over Seleukos, and flushed with aggressive enthusiasm, he "overran and subdued the whole of India with an army of 6,00,000."

Chanakya and Chandragupta

Different traditions, Brahminical, Buddhist and Jain agree as to the close association of he Brahmin Chankya with Chandragupta as his guide and leader in all this stupendous enterprise of empire building. The *Puranas* state that the "irreligious" (*Adharmika*) rule of the Nandas will be uprooted by "the Brahmin Kautilya who will anoint Chandragupta as the sovereign of the realm." This statement is again emphasized in passage occurring at the end of the *Artha-Sastra* of Kautilya in the following words"; the *Arthasastra* has been compiled by the who forcibly (*amarshena*) and quickly (*asu*) achieved the liberation of the mother-country, its culture and learning (*sastra*) its military power (*sastra*), from the grip of the Nanda Kings. Even the later drama, *Mudrarakshasa*, emphasizes stll further this tradition. It opens with the statement of Chanakya that he has already "exterminated the Nine Nandas from the earth and rooted out the stem of Nanda. But he fears that he cannot consider his work to be finished so long as there still a single off shoot of the Nanda family." Thus, ths continued Sanskrit tradition is based on the fact that Kautilya or Chanakya took it as his supreme religious duty as a champion of

Varnasrama Dharma to liberate his mother-country from the unlawful rule of the *Sudhras*, and was anxious to discover a suitable *Kshatriya* as an agent for this purpose. Such an agent, he discovered in Chandragupta whose base origin, as inferred from certain Sanskrit works is not at all proved, Chanakya who was burning with indignation at *Sudhra* rule would not be a party to replacing one *Sudhra* King by another.

The base origin of Chandragupta is inferred from the surname *Maurya* applied to him by the *Puranas*. The commentator of the *Puranas* derives *Maurya* from the name *Mura* as one of the wives of the Nanda King, though he does not state that *Mura*, the mother of Chandragupta was a *Sudhra* woman. The commentator has taken liberties with both history and grammar. In the first place there is no relationship in blood between the Nanda King and Chandragupta as the founder of a dynasty of *Kashatriya* rulers overthrowing the *Sudhra* rulers, as already stated above. Secondly, no grammar can derive *Maurya* from *Mura*. The derivative from *Mura* is Maurya. *Maurya* can be derived only from the masculine Mura which is the name of a *gotra* in a *Ganapatha* to Paninis Sutra (IV, 1, 151).

The *Mudrarakshasa* is supposed by some scholars to point to Chandragupta base origin in the terms *Vrishala* and *Kula-hina* to him. But it is certain that the term *Vrishala* must always mean the son of a *Sudhra King*. The drama itself takes the term to mean one who is a *Vrisha* among kings, the best of king; and thus a term of honour and not of odium. The other term *Kulahina* only means inferior lineage as against royal lineage and only confirms the statement of Justin that he was born in humble life. The *Mudrarakshasa* again, against the *Puranas* describes the *Nandas* as a of illustrious lineage (*Prathitakula*) or of high birth (*Uchchairavijanam* VI.6) and in that connection condemns Chandragupta as a mere commoner as an upstart.

While the commentator on the *Purana* who names *Mura* as the name of his mother without mentioning her caste as *Sudhra*, it was left to a commentator on *Mudrarakshasa*, named *Dhundiraja*, who wrote in the eighteenth century to state that *Mura* was a *Vrishlatmaja,* the daughter of a *Sudhra*. Like the *Puranas*, the Buddhist and Jain tradition take Chandragupta to be a *Kshatriya*. Buddhist texts take him to be a scion of the *Kshatriya* clan of Moriyas (probably Greek Morieis); an offshoot of the *Sakyas* who escaped from the invasion of *Vidudabha* into a Himalayan region known as the abode of peacocks, whence the Moriyas were so called (from Pali *Mora* Mayura or peacock). Another version of the story is that the Moriyas were so called because, they built *Moriyanagara*, a city of "bricks coloured like peacocks necks", works like the *Mahavamsa* and the *Digha Nikaya* like the *Moriyas* a *Kshatriyas* in original form as, God and man.

Jain tradition describes Nanda as the son of a barber by a courtesan (*Napitadaa*) (whom the Greeks take to be the sin ful queen of the last king). It also describes Chandragupta as the son of a daughter of the chief of a village community who were "rearers of royal peacocks" (*mayura poshaka-grame*).

It may be noted that there is monumental evidence attesting the connection of the Mauryas with peacocks. The Ashoka pillar at Nandangarh bears on its bottom the figures of a peacock which is repeated in several sculptures associated with Ashoka on the great Stupa at Sanchi.

To sum up, the Greek accounts as related above agree with the *Puranas* in ascribing a disreputable origin to the Nanda king and not to Chandragupta. The *Puranas* describe the Nandas as *Sudhras* and the Mauryas as Kshatriyas. The *Mudrarakshasa* proclaims a noble lineage for the Nanda and brands Chandragupta as of unknown lineage. Buddhist tradition takes Chandragupta as a Kshatriya and Jain tradition as a rustic to repeat the history of man itself.

Early Life of Chandragupta Maurya

We have to depend up on Buddhist traditions for the facts of *Chandragupta's* early life and his first contact with Chanakya. The death of his father left his mother destitute and made her seek shelter at Pataliputra with her brothers. There she gave birth to her child who was deposited for safety with a cowherd who later sold him village common, the boy was always playing the king (*Rajakrida*) with his companions under him and getting up a mock court where he would be administering justice. He was discovered at one of these royal games by Chanakya who saw in him the promise of royalty and straightway bought him of the hunter. He then took him away to his native city of Taxila where he had him educated in all the humanities (*Sastra-bhava*) and arts and crafts (*Silpas*) including military science which was best taught at Taxila in those days. Thus, Chandragupta spent his youth at Taxila and his explain how he, as a youth had seen Alexander in the course of his campaign in the Panjab as stated by Plutarch.

From Taxila, Chanakya happened to come to Pataliputra in pursuit of learning and disputation (*vadam*) which it was a noted centre. We owe to Rajasekharas *Kavya-mimamsa* the interesting information that Pataliputra through the ages figured as the "centre of examination of all Makers of *Satras* (*Sastrakaras*). "Here were thus examination of old author like *Panini*, *Pingala* an *Vyadi*, and in later times, Vararuchi and Patanjali.

Thus Chanakya came to Pataliputra where he found Dhanananda reigning and busy in spending his wealth in charities administered by a *Danasala* with a governing body or *Samgha* whose President was to be a Brahmin. Chanakya came to be elected as the president but Nanda could not stand him for his manners and features and dismissed him from his office. Chanakya incensed at this insult cursed the king, threatened the ruin of his race and escaped from the palaces as an *Ajivika* ascetic. It was in his subsequent wandering that the chanced to come across the child Chandragupta under circumstances already related in the text.

This Buddhist story is also repeated in the *Mudrarakshasa* which also mentions king Nanda expelling Chanakya from the place of honour assigned to him in his court (*agrasanato vakrishtavasam* (I. II)). Whereupon Chanakya vowed that he would avenage himself on Nanda by accomplishing the destruction of his whole family and progency. Thus Chanakay and Chandragupta were brought together by a common mission, fired by the same patriotic fervour. The *Puranas*, as we have seen represent Kautilya as being moved not by any personal rancour against Nanda as stated above, but by a lofty spirit of patriotism aiming at liberating the country from the unrighteous rule of the Nandas.

Conquest of the South

We owe to Plutarch the statement that Chandragupta overran and subdued te whole of Indai. But the detail of this all-India conquest are lacking. We have to infer it from certain traditions and the Inscriptions of his grandson. Tamil tradition records a Maurya invasion the south to subdue the king Mohur. The "Moriyas" were helped by local people called the Kosar and the Vadukar. The Tamil texts also refer to the untold wealth of the Nandas in his connection there by showing that the Mauryas that mention were the Imperial Mauryas.

There is also the unanimous Jain tradition that Chandragupta in his old age abdicated the throne and followed the Jain Saint *Bhadrabahu* to the south and settled down at a place known as *Sravanabelgola* in the state of Mysore, where he lived till death. The place is full of traditions, monuments and inscriptions testifying to the life of Chandragupta as an ascetic in association with Bhadrabahu. There is a hill called *Chandragiri* at Sravanabelgola as also a temple called *Chandragupta-basti*.

The *Mudrarkshas* testifies to the Jain learning of the Nandas and these affected Chandragupta also. Chanakya in the drama himself chooses a Jain emissary in the prosecution of his plan.

The Maurya penetration into the south is attested clearly in Ashokan Inscriptions which indicate as his neighbours on the southern frontiers people like the *Cholas*, *Pandyas*, *Satyaputras* and *Keralaputras* (R.E.II & XIII), while he planted his Minor Rock Edicts at three places in Northern Mysore. Add to this the fact that the only country conquered by Ashoka was Kalinga so that he cannot be credited with the conquest of the Deccan and the South. Nor could it be the work of his father *Bindusara* who was not all a masterful king, when his own province of Taxila was in revolt that had to be quelled by Ashoka.

Conquest of Western India

The Junagarh Rock Inscription of *Rudradaman* I of 150 A.D. refers to the construction of a dam in the time of king Chandragupta Maurya under his provincial governor named *Vaisya Pushyagupta.* This part of India which thus already belonged to the Maurya Empire is called in the Inscription Anarta and Surashtra. That is why we find that Ashoka inscription are located at places called Sopara and Girnar in Western India. Thus all this part of India must have been conquered by Chandragupta Maurya.

Administation of the Mauryan

A good account of India under Chandragupta Maurya was written by Megasthenes who was sent to his court as ambassador by Seleukos sometimes after 304 B.C. Unfortunately his account is lost in the original and is traceable only in the citations of the later writers such as Strabo, Diodorus, Pliny the elder, Arrian, Plutarch and Justin whilst in other matters of dress, foreign influence i.e. *Gandhara* is practically negligible in *Sudhra Family*'. There seems to be good reason referred by Charles Fabres in *Indian Dress* history to conclude that here direct borrowing has been at work from the '*Nam-History*' of the Father. His inscriptions mentioned messengers or ambassadors (*duta*), identical with Ajanta paintings, plate wears Sandal and shoes of the period.

Megasthenes testifies to a highly orgainsed bureaucracy in Mauryan administration comprising three classes of officials specified as (i) District officals, (ii) Town officals and (iii) Members of the war office.

The duties of the first class were to supervise (i) Irrigation and Measurement (ii) Hunting (iii) the various Industries connected with Agriculture, Forestry, work in Timber, Metal Foundries an Mines and(iv) maintenance of Roads with milestones at intervals. The second class of officals forming the municipal administration were divided into six boards of five members each in charge of the following five classes or departments of work.

(i) Spervision of Factories
(ii) Care of strangers and foreigners including control of the Inns, Provision of Assistance, taking charge of sick persons, burying the Dead.
(iii) Registration of Births and Deaths
(iv) Control of Market.
(v) Inspection of weigths and measures, of Manufactured Goods, Provision for their sales with new goods separated from second–hand ones.
(vi) Collection of the Municipal Tax of 10 p.c. on sales.

There were certain subjects which were administered in common by these six Boards acting together such as public works, Prices, Harbours and Temples.

There was a group of the higher officers of the States who are called by the general names of Councillors and Assessors such as "The Advisors of he king, the Treasures of the State, the Arbiters who settle disputes (i.e., the judge both civil and criminal,) the Generals of the Army and Chief Magistrates (i.e. the Head of Departments who are called *Adhyakshas* by Kautilya)"

Armament manufacture and ship-building were nationalized industries. So also was the manufacture of implements required by agriculturists and for other callings.

Artisans as a class awere exempted from payng taxes as Government servants.

"There were also officers who superintend the rivers, measure the lands, inspect the sluices by which water is let out from the main canals in to their branches so that every one may have an equal supply of it."

"There are also officers who collect the taxes and superintend the work of wood-cutter, carpenters, blacksmith and miners".

Army of the Chandrgupta Maurya

Chandragupta built up a very large army adequate to the extent of his empire. It is computed by Pliny at 6,00,000 infantry 3,0000 cavalry and 9,000 elephants besides war-chariots of which the number must have been at least the same as that of King Nanda viz. 8000

This army was controlled by a war office made up of Six Boards of five members each viz. I. Infantry; II Cavalry; III War-chariots, IV. Elephants; V. Transport, Commissariat and Army Service. The duties of Board V are thus described: "They arrange for bullock –trains which are used for transporting engines of war, food for the soldiers, provender for the cattle; and other military requisites. They supplied servants who beat the drum and others who carry gongs, grooms also for the horse and mechanists as their assistants. To the sound of going they send out foragers to bring in grass, and by a system of rewards and punishments ensure the work being done with dispatch and safety." (*Megasthenes Frago XXXIV*)

Board VI was entrusted with the duty of cooperating with the Navy under its Admiral.

Departments of Administration in Kautilyas Arthasastra

The account of administration as given by Megasthenes present many remarkable points of agreement with those given by Kautilya in his *Arthasastra* of which, however, the exact date, like the date of the most Sanskrit works, cannot be known with certainty. The contents of the work, however, point to tits connection with Maurya times. Accordingly, *the Cambridge History of India* (Vol. I) treats the works as a document of Maurya history.

It is not possible within the limits of this work to deal fully with the administrative system of Kautilya. A references may only be made to some of its select features and facts. The chief of these is the Kautiliya scheme of distribution of administrative work among the different departments which indicate the vast area covered by administrative activity undertaken for the promotion of public welfare in all its aspects.

The names of these different administrative departments which incdicate their functions may be thus mentioned in this connection. The departments deal with the following : (1) Revenue under *Samaharta* (Collector-General), (2) Exchequer (under *Sannidharta* (Treasurer-General); (3) Stores, (4) Armoury; (5) Prisons, (6) Accounts (*Akshapatatla*), (7) Agriculture, (8) Mines, (9) Metals, (10) Mint (Lakshana or Tanksala), (11) Salt, (12) Forests; (13) Cattle, (14) Pastures, (15) Passports; (16) Shipping; (17) Ports, (18) Commerce; (19) Trade route; (20) Customs; (21) Froniters (*Anta*); (22) Excise, (23) Weigth and Measures; (24) Spinning and Weaving, (25) Information and Criminal Intelligence; (26) Embassies, (27) Religious Institutions.

The Kingship Theory

Megasthenes saw Chandragupta the busiest of public servants. He states: "the King may not sleep during the day time. He leaves his palace not only in time of war but also for the purpose of judging causes. He then remains in court for the whole day with out allowing the business to be interrupted even through the hour arrives when he must needs attends to his person". "The palace is open to all comers even when the Kings is having his hair combed and dressed. It is then that he gives audience to ambassadors and administers justice to his subjects."

The king had a body gurad of armed women. At hunting, he is accompanied by women in chariots on horseback or on elephants fully armed as in war as stated by Strabo in his study.

Besides hunting, Chandragupta was fond of races. There was a special trotter-breed of oxen in those days which equalled horses in speed." A carriage was harnessed to a mixed team of two such oxen with a horse between.

Aelian mentions that the King took pleasure in animals fights, fights between "animals that are horned and butt each other, such as wild bulls, tame rams, rhinous and even fights between elephant tuskers".

The king's pomp is thus described by Curtius: "when the king condescends to show himself in public his attendants carry in then hands silver censers, and perfumes with incense all the road by which it is his pleasure to be conveyed. He lolls in a golden palanquim, garnished with pearls which dangle all around it, and he is robed in fine muslin embromidered with purple and gold. Behind his palanquin follow men at arms and his body guards, of whom some carry boughs of trees on which birds are perched trained to interrupt business with their cries".

The king liked "presence of animals including wild ones such as deer, antelopes, rhinos, tamed tigers, and panthers, oxen fleet of foot, or yoks, pigeons of yellow plumage, hunting hounds and apes, and birds like cranes, geese and ducks."

On ceremonial occasions the king preferred a guard of 24 elephants. The elephants gave him a sort of military salute, as stated by Megasthences.

The Palace

The palace was situated in an extensive park full of shady groves and evergreen trees, some of which are important from outside, attracting all kinds of birds, peacocks, pheasants, and parrots which flocked round the king. It had also tanks filled with the biggest fish.With in the "palace was adorned with gilded pillars clasped with vines embossed in gold and adorned with birds of silver".

The Capital

The capital of Pataliputra was built at the confluence of the two rivers, Ganges and Son, with a length of about 9 miles and breadth of one mile, protected by a moat about 60 feet deep and about 200 yards wide. It was thus made navigable, with water from the Son. It also received the sewage of the city. The city was further protected by a massive timber palisade, pierced by loopholes through which archers could shoot, and provided with 64 gates and 570 towers as described by Megasthenes. A remnant of this gold wooden palisade has been discovered among the ruin of the city and is now on view in the Patna Museum. Pataliputra was mainly built in wood as protection against floods, as stated by Megasthenes.

Social Life of the People Under Mauryan Rulers

Megasthenes observed the division of Hindu society, but has made some confusion between castes and crafts. He broadly distinguishes the seven classes in India among whom are include some of the professions. But it is easy to separate one from the other, Megasthenes described the Brahmins of the times who were small in number but first in rank and he calls them philosophers. They are of two kinds. (1) *Brachamanes* and (2) *Sarmanes*. The period of studentship is counted for 37 years.

As householders, they live in ease and security, decked in muslin. They eat meat but not that of animals employed in labour.

They Worked as Priests

But their wisdom is sometimes utilized by the state. The king held every year a conference at the beginning of the new year, where they are expected to announce their discovers which may promote public welfare by improving agariculture and livestock. At these Conferences, "they also forewarn and livestock. At these Conferences, "they also forewarn the assembled multitude about droughts and wet weather and also about propitious winds, and diseases and other topics". "Thus, the people and the sovereign learning before hand what is to happen, already make adequate provision against a coming deficiency and never fail to prepare before hand what will help in time of need."

As to *Sarmanes* (*Sramanas*), those who are most honoured are called *Hylobioi* or forest –dwellers (*Vanaprasthas*) "who lived in the forests on leaves of trees and wild fruits and wear garments made from the bark of the trees. They do not also marry." This description applies to the *Naishthika-Brahmachari,* those who prefer to remain as students through life without marrying.

The term *Sramana* as used by Megasthenes was then a general term for all ascetics, non-Buddhists or Brahminical ascetic rather than Buddhist. Their description shows that they belonged to the third and fouth Asrama.

Some of the occupation of these *Sramanas* are also indicated. They acted as priest. They also worked as physicians, "effecting cures by regulating diets rather than by the use of medicines. Of medicines, they value those that are applied externally, such as ointments and plasters rather than drugs".

The Greek writer as Mc Crindle points out do not seem to have known the Buddhists. Perhaps Buddhism in those days did not spread as far as the Panjab.

Strabo says that the Brahmins of those days lived on alms.

Besides the Brahmanas and Sramanas, Strabo mentions a third class of Philosophers whom he calls the *Pramnai*, i.e., *Pramanikas* who were "fond of argument and ridiculed the Brahmins who studied Physiology and Astronomy as fools and impostors."

A fourth class of Philosophers is called *Gymnetai* who were naked ascetics.

Arrian mentions the singular fact that "the Sophists (or Philosophers) could be from any caste" showing that the life of *Sannyasi* was open to all castes and that there was no caste in the life of Spiritual Knowledge.

Alexander was anxious to meet these Indian ascetics, but they were not so anxious to meet him. His experience of these ascetics has been already described.

Kshatriyas

According to Arrian, the *Kshatriyas* had only military duties to perform. When there is no occasion for fighting and in time of peace, they could enjoy life as they pleased, as the pay which they receive from the state was quite liberal.

Vaisyas and Sudhras

Megasthenes described the Vaisyas as "husbandmen who from the bulk of the population, are exempted from military service, and cultivate the lands living in the country with out ever going into the town of the Jammu Region. The work of these tillers of the soil consists of plouging gathering in their crops, pruning the trees or reaping the harvest".

Besides being agriculturists, the Vaisyas were also traders,

The *Sudhras* must have been what the Greek writes call "artisans such as armourers ship-builders and makers of implements used in agriculture and other callings".

There were also "hunters and herdsmen who lived in tents and lead a wandering life. They alone keep cattle sell draught animals and lend them to hire. By hunting and trapping, they clear the country of wild beasts and fowls or pests which devour the seeds sown in the field by the husbandmen. In return for their services they receive an allowances of grain from the king'.

Occupations

Megasthenes mentions as a caste the Government Servants of the Intelligence Department, whom he calls *Overseers*.

Another caste, he mentions as being made up of the *Councillors* and *Assessors* of Government from whom were recruited its highest posts such as those of Judges, the King's Advisors, Treasures, Chief Magistrates, Governors of Provinces, General of the Army, Admirals of the Navy and the like.

Caste System

Megasthenes states that "a soldier can not become a husbandman, or an artisan (*Sudhra*) a philosopher (*Brahmin*), and that no one allowed to marry out of his own caste or exercise any calling or art except his own or to excharge one profession or trade for another".

Slavery

Arrian cities Megasthenes stating that "all Indians are free, and not one of them is a slave".

Bindusara (c.299-274 B.C.)

Chandragupta Maurya was succeeded by his son *Bindusara* to whom the Greek writers applied the epithet *Amitraghata* (*Allichates*) "the slayer of enemies", but there is no available evidence to show who were his enemies against whom, he was battling and apparently achieving victories. According to Buddhist tradition, there was a revolt at his provincial capital of Taxila. It was caused by the maladministration of his sons, the Crown Prince Susima. Bindusara sent his second son Ashoka to deal with this trouble. There was a second rebellion at Taxila which Prince Susima failed to quell. But Bindusara died at that time and the throne was seized by Ashoka with the aid of his minister *Radhagupta*.

According to another tradition recorded by *Hemachander* in his work called *Arya Manjusri Mulakalpa,* and by Taranatha in his history of Buddhism, the emperor Chandragutpa was outlived by his Minister Chanakya who continued as the Minister of his son Bindusara, and as "one of his great lords". Taranatha states: "Chanakya accomplished the destruction of the nobles and kings of 16 towns and made Bindusara master of all the terriorty between the eastern and western sea." Some scholars take this statement as indicating Bindusaras" conquest of the Deccan; but this is disproved by a more trust worthy document the inscription of Sake King Rudradamana in which describes Surashtra as province of Chandragupta's empire which, as we have seen, extended far into th south including a place like Sravanabelgola in Mysore State. Thus ther are hardly any definite conquests of new terriorty standing to the credit of Bindusara. On the contrary, he was known to the Greeks for his easy-going disposition, whose delight in life was "figs and raisin and wine" for which he indented upon his royal friend, the Greek king Antiochos I Soter, King of Syria. It may, however, be taken for granted that there was no diminution in extent of the empire under Bindusara nor in the status of the emperor. Like his father, he had also at his court an ambassador deputed by the aforesaid Greek King of Syria. He was Dimachos of Plataea. Pliny (*Natural History*, VI. 58) states that king Ptolemy Philadelphus of Egypt (285-247 B.C.) sent an ambassador named Dionysius to an Indian king. The time of the Greek King shows that in the early part of his region he must have been dealing with Bindusara, and after him with Ashoka. It is interesting to note that Ashoka in his Rock Edict XIII mentions Ptolemy as one of the foregin kings to whom he sent his own *Dutas* or envoys on Welfare Missions for the relief of suffering of life.

According to tradition, Bindusara had numerous sons of whom Prince Susima was the eldest and served as his Viceroy at Taxila, while his second son Ashoka was deputed by him to Ujjain as his Viceroy of *Avantirashtra.* The death of Bindusara was followed by a fratricidal war for his throne which was seized in the end of Ashoka who, according to one story killed all his brothers numbering 99, and earned for himself the infamous name of *Chandashoka.* According to Taranath, however Ashoka killed only six brothers. The evidence of his own inscriptions, however, contradicts that of these stories. In one of these, Ashoka refers to his brothers and sister and other relatives setlled at Pataliputra ansd other provincial town for whose welfare he was always anxious.The subject of Ashokas relation with his brothers and other relatives will be discussed later. That there was a disputed succession seems to have been a fact which explains the interval of four year between his accession and anointment as sovereign as averred in the legends of the human history.

ASHOKA (C.274-236 B.C.)

Early Life of Ashoka

Ashoka has been described by H.G. Wells in his '*Short History of the World*' as the world's greatest king. But his greatness did not lie in the mere geographical extent of his empire, large as it was. There have been kings in history 'on whose dominion the sun never sets'. The 'Beloved of Gods' had been among the country folk lecture on *Dharma.* He had taught them that attainment of Heaven is not the monopoly of the great alone. Even a lowly person could attain Heaven if he was zealous in following the ancient rule of morality and discipline. At the end of he 256 nights spent on tour, the emperor was satisfied that the men of India or *Bharatavarsha* and some adjoining tracts (*Jambudvipa*) means in the area of Jammu Region, who had hither to been unassociated with gods, were now mingled with *Yama* race. The royal tours were apparently decennial. One was undertaken when the King Ashoka had been anointed ten years in the outskirts of the Jammu city and another when he had been consecreated twenty years in his mind for the spread of the mission of the '*NAM*'. In course of the second tour, the emperor visited the birthplace of *Sakay Muni* and that of a previous Buddha in Nasika and worshipped at these holy spots[15] of the Dr. B.R. Ambedkar by *Sudhra* Family. The very name *Ashoka* means "unsorrowing" as a *'Dalit King'*. It is said that when his time was near to birth, the mother of the Lord Buddha went deep into the forest of Lumbini. There, clinging onto an Ashoka tree, she gave birth to the Enlightened One i.e. Ashoka King of the Mauryan dynasty to fight against the social evils of the society i.e. caste, colour and creed.

In Jammu, evidence of the primitive man is available from the Archaeological Survey of India that in the third cemtry B.C. the great Maruyan Emperor Ashoka sent Buddhist missionaries to Ladakh, China and Kashmir where they established their first town Srinagar. Kashmir became the base from where great works of Buddhism and scholarly Sanskrit liberature widely spread to all over the world and the region evolved as the crucible of a highly civilized cultural expression displayed in different forms sometimes Buddhism and Shivism[16] in human form not idol worship of the modern Brahmins, Ashoka's greatness was moral greatness. It lay in the principles by which he governed his empire principles which were far a head of the age. He himself states in one of his inscribed proclamation that a Kings fame is to be judged by the fame of his people for moral progress (Rock Edict, X). He also stood for the religion of non-violence which he even applied both with in his empire and with out, to both internal and international politics. He was the first in history to abjure war as an evil and to replace violent conquests by moral conquest (*Dharmavijaya*). He believed not in the extension of territory, but of universal brotherhood based upon non-violence.

The main source of Ashoka's history is his own words, he chose to inscribe indelibly on the rocks of ages as plant of *Saraca asoca* from the family of *Caesalpinaceae* for highly nutritious race of plants in modern concept of the history called *Chamar*, in Sanskrit and Hindi called *Ashoka* as common term of the *Sudhra* history the follower of Buddhism. His words can be read to this duty and real like his autobiography. But as a great King and as a unique personality, he has been the centre of cycles of various legends and stories. These give us glimpses especially of his early life and some facts of his career as a King who spread the pious mission of the '*Nam*' barked as healing open wounds to remove the griefs of the society for the sake of Father.

Tradition makes *Bindusara* the husband of 16 wives and father of 101 sons, of whom the eldest is named Sumana (Susima), the second was Ashoka and the youngest. This is, Ashoka's mother is named *Subhadrangi* (a Brahmin) in the northern and *Dharma* in southern tradition. Dharma was a Kshatriya whose family preceptor was an *Ajivika* Saint *Janasana* which explain Ashoka's patronage of the *Ajivika* sect. descends from the prehistorical inhabitants of India, when people used to live in jungle or forest, sensing the deep connection between plants and human beings.

Ashoka at 18 (286 B.C.) was appointed by his father as his Viceroy of *Avanti-Rashtra* with its capital at Ujjayini where, he married the Sakya Princess named Mahadevi of Vedisa (Vidisa modern Bhilsa) of whom was born his eldest son Mahendra in his 20th year, followed by his eldest daughter, Sanghamitra, born in 282 B.C. There was, as already related a rebellion at

Taxila under prince Susima and Ashoka was sent to quell it. There was a second rebellion at Taxila, which Susima failed to quell, when *Bindusara* died, and Ashoka seized the throne, backed by the Ministry headed by *Khallataka* (or Radhagupta). This gave the signal fro a war of succession between Ashoka and Yuvaraja Sumana aided by all his other ninety–eigth brothers (except his own uterine brothe Tishya). The Ceylon legends represent Ashoka as a fratricide who killed all his ninety–nine brothers and waded through blood to the throne to earn for himself the notorious title of *Chandashoka*. There are many legends giving details of his cruelty but these were probably invented to glorify the religion which converted *Chandashoka* into *Dharmashoka*. We may, however, believe in the truth of a disputed succession, which explains the interval of four years between his accession and coronation as stated in the *Mahavamsa*.

His inscriptions, however, show that Ashoka's relations with his brothers, sisters, and other relatives were quite cordial and natural, as stated in serval of his Edicts, Rock Edicts III, IV, V, VI, XI, XII and the like. One Edict mentions his "brothers and sisters and other relatives settled at Pataliputra and other provincial towns". We have also mention of some of his brothers (called *Kumaras* and *Aryaputras*) serving as his Viceroys at the cities called Taxila, Tosali, Ujjayini, and Survarnagiri, in the Kalinga Rock Edicts and in a Minor Rock Edict, The *Mahavamsa* states that Ashoka even appointed his brother Tishya as his Uparaja or deputy king.

Chronology

Tradition gives some clues to Ashoka's chronology. If we take 274 B.C. as the date of his accession, his coronation which followed after four years according to the *Mahavamsa*, may then be dated to 270 B.C. The same work tells that his eldest son Mahendra and daughter Sanghamitra were both ordained in the sixth year of his coronation i.e. in 264 B.C. At that time, the former was twenty and the latter eighteen year old, which means that the former was born in 284 B.C. and the latter in 282 B.C. If Ashoka is taken to be twenty when his eldest son was born he should be born in 304 B.C. The image of a young woman and a tree constantly recurs in Indian Art from *Ravidas Baradari* to Kabir as a whole family of *Sudhras* in India; and trees are supposed to increase both the desire and fertility in a woman in the concept of *'Brahminical Ideology'* of a society.

Extent of Empire

Ashoka came to rule a vast empire which practically from the borders of Persia up to far south in India. This empire was won by his grandfather by the conquests, as we have already seen. By virtue of his victory over Seleukos and treaty with him of about 304 B.C. the Greek king was forced to cede to Chandragupta Maurya the eastern Satrapies of his empire named Gedrosia (Baluchisthan), Aria (Herat), Archosia (Kandahar) and part of the Satraphy known as Paropamsidae (the country of Paropamisus Hindukush). According to Tarn, this last Satrapy was *not* ceded to Chandragupta who according to Eratosthenes, got only Gandhara or the land between the Kunar river and the Indus, including Quetta and Kalat up to the sea. Thus Ashoka was really ruling over a greater India whch comprised a large part of territories now known as Afghanistan and Baluchistan.

Ashoka left his own marks showing the limit of his empire.Ashokan structures are found in countries like Jammu and Kashmir, Nepal, Suhma, Samatata and other parts of Bengal and places in the south like Chola and Dravida, in all of which the Chinese traveller Yuan Chwang saw these structures. Though no Ashokan inscription has been found in Bengal, an inscription found at Mahasthana in north Bengal as written in old Brahmi script of Ashokan age.

Ashoka further defined the limit of his empire by locating his inscription at its important centres, His Rock Edicts are found at the following places:-

(1) Shahbazgarhi near Peshawar (2) Mansehra in the same province; (3) Khalsi near Dehra Dun; (4) Girnar near Junagarh ; (5) Sopara in Bombay Presidency; (6) Dhauli near Bhubanesvara; (7) Jaugada in Ganjam District; (8) Chitaldroog in Mysore where Minor Rock Edicts appear at 3 places, viz, Siddpura, Jatinga Ramesvara and Brahmagiri; (9) Rupnath near Jubbalpur; (10) Sahasram Bihar; (11) Bairat near Jaipur; (12) Bhabru appearing on a second hill at Bairat; (13) Maski in Nizam's dominions; (14) and (15) the Gavimath and Palkigundu Inscriptions in the Kopbal Taluk in th Nizams dominion; (16) The Yerragudi Rock Inscriptions discovered in Kurnool District and (17) The Taxila Aramic Inscription. He also inscribed his proclamations on pillars of stone especially fashioned for the purpose. These Pillar Inscription are found at the following places: (1) Topra near Ambala; (2) Meerut, both of which were removed to Delhi by Sultan Firoz Shah Taughlak; (3) Kausambi removed to Allahabad probably by Akbar; (4) Lauriya Ararj (Radha in Champaran District; (5) Lauriya Nandangarh (Mathia); in the same district; (6) Rampurwa in the same district; (7) Sanchi near Bhopal; (8) Sarnath near Benares; (9) Lumbini in Nepal; (10) Nigali Sagar in Nepal.

Thus all these inscriptions distributed by Ashoka throughout the length and breadth of his empire point to it limits very well. Ashoka himself states in his R.E. XIV : "Vast is my dominion" (*vijita*) and in R.E.V. calls it *Prithivi* or earth for the vastness of its size.

The limits of his empire are further indicate by Ashoka mention in his inscriptions of the State and peoples on its broders. Towards the south are mentioned the *Cholas, Pandyas,* the *Satiyaputras* and *Keralaputras*, but these were all with in his sphere of influence which extended as far as Tamraparni or Ceylon. Towards the north –west, he mentions "*Amtiyaka Yona- raja*", i.e., the Greek King Antiochos II Theos of Syria as his *Anta* or neighbour.

Administration of Ashoka

The empire was too vast in area to be governed efficiently from one centre in that early age of primitive, unmechanised transport and communications. It was, therefore, divided into a number of local administrations of a size convenient for government. There were both Viceroyalties and Governorships in Ashoka's system

At the top was the King who had his Deputy called *Uparaja.* There was also the *Yuvaraja* or Crown –prince. The princes are called *Kumaras* or *Aryaputras* in the Edicts.

There were princely Viceroys posted at the provincial capital of *Takshasila* (Taxila), *Ujjeni* (Ujjain), *Tosali* (in Orissa) and *Savarnagiri* (in Mysore).

Along with the Viceroyalties there were also Governorships. The term used for a Governor is *Rajuka* who is "set over hundreds of thousand of souls" (P.E. IV), the sovereign authority for law and justice. There is another term *Pradesika* to indicate the head of a *Pradesa,* something like a Commissioner of a Division in modern administration (R.E. III).

The king had his Council called *Parishat* (R.E. III and VI). He had also his Private Secretaries called *Prativedakas* who had access to the king at all hours to keep him information on the affairs of the people (*athe me janasa pativedetha* 'word' so that they may report to me the needsof the people').

The Councillor or Ministers were called *Mahamatras*, "Officers of high rank". The Prime Minister is called *Agramatya* in a literary text. Heads of departments are called *Mukhas* (P.E.VII).They were of the rank of *Mahamatras*. Every Ministry had its own Secretariat called *Mahamatriya* by Kautilya (II. 5), Different Departments or Ministries are mentioned in the Edicts. There was the Ministry of Morals under the *Dharma-Mahamatra.* The *Sri-Adhyaksha-Mahamatra* was in charge of the affairs of womanhood. There were also Wardens of the Marches celled *Anta-Mahamatras*. The *Vrajabhumika* was probably the Minister of Agriculture and Public Works. The *Mahamatras* were also deputed as *Dutas* or envoys to foreign countries (R.E. XIII).

Government servants were called *Purushas* of grades high, low or middle (P.E. I). Those of lower rank were called *Yuktas* (R.E. III) or employees.

This Edict also indicates their duties. They were like the Secretaries or Superintendents whose duty was to codify Royal Order in the offices of the

Mahamatras or Ministers under instructions of the Parished or Council to which thery were attached. Another class of *Yuktas* accompanied their officals superiors like the *Rajuka* and the *Pradesika* on tour (*Anusamyana*). There was also the class of officers who were scribes or writers called *Lipikara* in Minor R.E. II.

Ashoka's administration was also marked out by a well-organised P.W.D. It looked after the public parks (*Udyana*), mango-groves (*Amravatika*) wells (*Kupa* or *Udapana*) and travellers rest –houses (*Nishadya*) located along the public roads (*Patha* or *Marga*). It was also in charge of the special botanical garderns for the cultivation of medicinal plants, the sources of Ayurvedic medicine in "roots, herbs or fruits", while there was a medical department to organise the treatment of both men and cattles (*Manushya – chikitsa* and *Pasu-chikitsa*), as stated in R.E. II.

The State also maintained special forests for the breeding of elephants (*Naga-vana* in P.E.V.)

An important administrative innovation of Ashoka was the compulsory tour of the higher officals through their charges. In the Viceroyalties of Ujjain and Taxila, the rules of service required the *Mahamatras* to complete their tours with in their jurisdiction every three years, while the rule in other provinces was five years. The technical term for an official tour is *Anusamyana*. Buddhaghosa defines this term to mean "to travel for purpose of inspection". It was for the inspection (*pratyavekshana*) of the homes of villages (*Gramavasa*) public works (*Selu*), tanks (*Pushkarini*), halls (*Sala*) and such other works as explained by the commentator on a passage of *Anguttara* (I.59-60).

In R.E. VIII, *Ashoka* calls these tours as *Yatras* and as tours of duty (*Dharma-Yatras*) of which the programme included interviewing (*Darsana*) the ascetics of the villages, whether Sramanas or Brahmanas; and bestowing upon them royal gifts (Dana); visiting the village elders with gifts of gold to them and meeting the people of the countryside (*Janapadasya Janasya Darsanam*), instructing them in morality and also holding discussion on morality with questions and answers. Thus on these royal tours into the remote countryside the king took it to be his duty to contact the rural leaders and elders of the villages its religious and learned men and also to hold mass meeting to discuss problems of moral uplift, besides giving financial help to the deserving.

Events and Measures

The outstanding event of his reign as described in his R.E. XIII was his conquest of Kalinga in the eighth year of his coronation, i.e. about 262

B.C. The Kalings who were so long an independent (*Avijita*) people fought hard and had heavy casualties. One lac and fifty thousand were made prisoners one lac killed, and several lacs wounded and died later". This bloody conquest was a turning point in Ashoka's life. He was filled with extreme anguish (*Vedana*) and remorse (*anuslochana*) and turned by a violent reaction towards the religion of Non-vioence. He proclaimed the news policy of *Dharma-Vijaya*, moral as opposed to military conquest, so that the Kalinga war was the last war of his life and reign. Henceforth, the events and measures of the reign were not military or political in their character. His zeal for *Dharma* (*Dharma-kamata*) for its cultivation and practice (*Silana*) and for its preaching (*Dharmanusasti*) became intense (*tivra*) for the establishment of 'natural Law' i.e., *Chamar*.

The religious events and measures of his reign may be related as follows:-

He issued his religious proclamations both on rock and pillar beween 260 B.C -257 B.C.

In 260 B.C. he proceded on his first pilgrimage (*Dharma yatra* as distinguished from the *Vihara Yatras* or pleasure-trips of his predecessors) to Sambodhi, the place of the Buddh's Enlighrement at Bodh-Gaya.

In 258 B.C. Ashoka had two caves excavated in the *Khalatika* (Barabar) hills for the Sect of Ajivikas.

In 257 B.C. he instituted in his administration a new Ministry of Morals under Ministers aptly called *Dharma Mahamatras*. Their duty was to see that there was no abuse in the administration of justice and to achieve the moral uplift of the people their steadfastness (*Adhishthana*) and progress (*Vriddhi*) in *Dharma* and their good and happiness (*Hita-Sukha*). This task they were carrying on "among all the sects, classes, and communites of his empire including its neighbours. Thus they were employed among the military as well as the civil population, householders and ascetics, the old, infirm, and destitute, and also among the women folk of the royal households and Ashoka's brothers, sisters and other relatives (R.E.VI), P.E.VII states how these officers stimulated the charities of the Queens and Princes and one Queen named Charuvaki, mother of Prince Tivara, in her Edict at Kausambi, expresses her full support of this programme. They also worked in the frontier States of Tribal territory among the *Yonas, Kambojas, Gandharas* and among the *Rashtrikas Pitinikas* and other peoples of Aparanta or western regions of the Jammu Kingdom.

In 256 B.C. he enlarged to double its size the original *stupa* of the previous Buddha named Kona Kamana (*Kanakamuni:* also called Konagamana by Southern Buddhists) (*See Plate XXV, Sanchi Stupa of Ashoka, Fig. 38*)

In 250 B.C. he proceeded on pilgrimage to the sacred place of the Buddhas birth at the village called Lummini. On that occasion he marked his visit to the place by three memorials: (1) The construction of a shrine (*silavigada*) in stone; (2) The erection of a pillar of stone (*Silathave*); (3) Reducing the taxation of the village Lumbini to 1/8th share of agriculture produce (*athabhagiya*) from the usual share of 1/4th for the king and exempting the whole village from all other taxes (*Udbalika*).

In the same year, he paid a visit (probably his second visit) to the *Stupa* of he Buddha Konakamana and marked it by the erection of acommemorative pillar. It may be that Ashoka went out (*nishkramanam*) on such pilgrimages every ten years, in the 10th and 20th year of his coronation.

In 243 B.C. he issued his Pillar Edicts.

We shall now refer to some of his administrative and religious reforms in following passage:-

He charged the character of popuar festivals (called *Samajas*) which were marked by cruelty to animals in races and the like and also their slaughter for feasting on their flesh, into more innocent onces which might stimulate morals and spirituality. The kings of the times arranged public entertainments in fights between animals, "between elephants, horses, buffaloes, bulls goats, and rams" 6): butting contests between rams, wild bulls elephants and even rhinoceroses; races between two oxen with a horse between as were held by Chandragupta Maurya according to Aelian already cited. There were even figths "between birds like cocks and mails[18]." Ashoka introduced other kinds of proper shows as those of heavenly chariots, celestial elephants and other shows (*Divyani rupani*) by which the blisess of heaven following piety on earth could be visualized by the people.

As a corollary to this reform Ashoka reformed the royal household by making it vegetarian.

He equipped the country with various works of public utility which are thus enumerated:

(1) Planting of shade-giving banian trees and groves of mango trees on the roads.

(2) Provision of wells at every half (or eigth) kos.

(3) Construction of rest-houses.

(4) Provision of watering places for use of both man and cattle

(5) Provision of medical treatment for both men and cattle in hospitals, both general, and veterinary, and by cultivation of medicinal plants in botanical gardens growing necessary "herbs, roots and fruits" as a sources of medicines, and manufacture of medicines out of these raw materials in Pharmaceutical Factories under adequate medical staff.

He orgainsed and dispatched Medical Missions for carrying to foreign countries means and measures for the relief of suffering and remedies for diseases (R.E. XIII).

He passed the law that no living creature except a few was to be killed for purpose of food or religious sacrifice. He also published a list of creatures which were protected against slaughter and mutilation. He forbade the burning of husks and of forests so as not to injure life. The killing of fish was also prohibited on specified days (P.E.V.).

Prisoners were released on day every year to mark the day of the Kings birth.

The call to arms or the sounding of war-drum (*Bherighosha*) was replaced by the cell to morality or the proclamation of religion (*Dharma – ghosha*).

His scheme of town planning abolished segregaton and separation of different castes and sects in different localities (R.E.VII).

He proclaimed the equality of all person in law (*Vyavahara-samata*) and justice and punishment (*Danda-Samata*)

He introduce the judicical reform of allowing a grace of three days to convicts condemned to death so that the interval may be utilized for appeal, or for fasts and charities to secure good in the next world.

An important innovation of Ashoka was his proclamation of religious messages (*Dharma-Sravanani*) and injunctions (*Anusasana*) which were inscribed on both rock and pillar (*Dharma Stambha*).

Ashoka sought to maintain the unity of the Samgha by punishing schism, The *Samgha-bhedaka* one who disrupts the Samgha, was to be expelled from the monastery (*Avasa*) disrobed and made to wear white garments.

Religion of Ashoka

Ashoka's personal religion was different from the religion which he present in his edicts i.e., '*Nam*'. His own religion was Buddhism. In his MRE at Maski, he calls himself a *Sakya,* and a *Buddha- Sakya*. In the Bhabru R.E., he declares Buddhist Trinity and specifies select passages from the sayings of the Buddha for the *Samgha* whom he addresses as "King of Magadha" asking them to recite and meditate upon them. In M.P.E. at Sarnath, Kausambi and Sanchi, he interests himself in the unity of the Samgha and announces the punishments for those who try to break it up. We may also mention his pilgrimage to the holy places of Buddhism at Bodha-Gaya and Lumbini. His insistence in the Edicts on *Ahimsa* was also due to his Buddhist faith called '*Nam*' itself.

But the *Dharma* or Religion which he preaches in his Edicts was not Buddhsim or any particular creed. It was really a code of morals, the common foundation the "*Sara*" or essence, of all religions. Thus he preaches (1) *Susrusha* or obedience to father and mother, elders and teachers for whom the pupil (*Antevasi*) must show respect (*Apachiti*) and also to men of high caste or rank. He also inculcates as part of religion, (2) *Sampratipatti* or proper behaviour towards ascetics ones own relations, friends acquaintances and companions, servants and dependents (*Dasabhataka*) and the poor and the afficted (*Kapana-valaka*).

He also states that religious consists in (3) *Dana* or liberality towards all and (4) non-violence (*Anarambha* and *Avihisha*) towards all living beings.

It will thus appear that Ashoka's religion, like charity, begins at home in the cultivation of proper relations in the domestic circle the purity of the family as the unit of society.

He also inculcates the cultivation of certain virtues such as *Daya* (kindness), *Satyam* (truthfuness), *Saucham* (inner and outer purity), *Mardavam* (gentleness), *Sadhuta* (saintliness), *Samyama* (control of senses) and *Bhavasuddhi* (purity of heart), as also *Samacharanam* (treating all equally).

Another essential of his religion which he presents before the public of his times is the practice of religious toleration for promoting communal harmony (*Samavaya*). He was anxious that different creeds should attend to the growth of their essential elements (*Sara-vriddhi*) as distinguished from its non-essentail features. The root (*mula*) of this essence is *vachi-guti* (*vacho-gupti*, restraint of speech) so that one should not glorify his own sect and belittle (*garahati*) another sect in a light (*Lahuka*) manner. It is the concord (*Samavavaya*) of creeds that counts most in religious life. This concord may be achieved of all the sects (*sava-pasamdani*) become *Bahu-sruta,* i.e., well versed in each other's *Srutis* or Scriptures.

It may be stated that Ashoka was always an example his own precepts. He treated all communities equally in the matter of royal gifts (*dana*) and honour (*puja*). That is why we find Ashoka patronising the sect of *Ajivikas* by his costly gifts of cave-dwellings in hard rocks, while he quartered his ministers of morals (*Dharma –Mahamatras*) and their Agents equally upon all the sects, classes and communities of his empire to promote their common good in their moral progress and give them equal protection against administrative injustice (REV). His title *Devanam-priya,* 'beloved of the gods', shows that he did not offend against Brahminism and its gods. In this Edicts, insists on equal respect for ascetics as a class, whether Brahmanas or Sramanas.

Ashoka sought to spiritualise life and all its activites as far as possible. For this reason, he laid more stress on character than upon ceremonial in relgion. He condemned the many petty (*Kshudra*) corrupt (*putika*) and meaning Less (*Nirarthaka*) ceremonies to which the people especially the women folk, were addicated in his days. Life was punctuated by ceremonies to avert mishaps (*Abadha*), at marriages, births, journeys, forgetting that such ceremonies (*mangalas*) are not very fruitful (*alpaphala*). But what is called *Dharma-mangala* is productive of great fruit (*Maha-phala*) in achieving good both in this world and in the next by the *Punya* or merit that accures from correct conduct in all relations of life (R.E.IX) as the true ritual of religion of which the efficacy is not limited by time (*Akalika*) or space (*Iha-lokika*).

In R.E. XI, he stands for (1) *Dharma-Dana* (2) *Dharma-Sambandha;* (3) *Dharma-Samvibhage* and (4) *Dharma-samstava.*

He believes more in the gift of knowledge and morality than in gift of mere material perishable goods.

The relationship of life (*Sambandha*) must be based on mere blood but on kinship in moral life.

The sharing of the good things of the earth (*Samvibhaga*) should yield to a sharing of fellowship and sympathy with all, including servants, dependants and the dumb domesticated animals.

Religion shoulds govern all relations of life on the basis of proper behaviour towards all.

Ashoka also points out the requisites of religious life. The first is *Dharma-Niyama* the restraint and regulations of moral life. The second is *Nijhati*, which means meditation, self-examination (*Atma-pariksha*) and above all, self-exertion (*Parakrama*) which is necessary for all, high or low by total pursuit or Quest of the Ideal, renouncing everything (*Sarvam-parityajya*). As the result of his sustained strenuous exertion (*parakrama*) for the moral uplift of his people, he declares with satisfaction in the MRE. I that his people have become more religious (related to the Gods, *devaih misritah*).

The religion of Ashoka's Edicts, besides giving expression to Ashoka's original ideas in eithics and religion, contains also some elements of the populars religion of the times. For instance, the Edicts repeatedly refer to the other world (*Paraloka*), to Svarga, or happiness in that world as the result of the pursuit of *Dharma* in the world. He also believed in the eternity of heaven and consequently in the immortality of soul (cf. "*anantam punam prasavati* in R.E. XI). In R.E.X, he even declares that all his work or activity (*parikamate*) is for the sake of the other world (*Savam paratrikaya*).

To sum up : Ashoka's *Dharma* was not any particular religion but what may be accepted as the common religion of mankind. He thus ranks as the founder or the father of Universal Religion. Thus his Foreign Missions were quite welcome in the five Hellenistic countries of the West to which they carried his message of universal peace and measures of medical relief.

Events Related in the Legends

So far we have dealt with Ashoka's history as described mainly in his inscriptions, but the stories of Ashoka in literature mention some additional facts and events of his life, some of which have nothing improbable about them. The mains sources of these stories are the two Pali Chronicels *Mahavamsa* and *Dipavamsa* and *Buddhaghosa's Samanta-pasadika.*

The first fact that the chronicles relate is that before his conversion to Buddhism Ashoka was a believer in Hinduism and its different sects which then numbered 96. He daily fed 60000 Brahmins and Brahminical ascetics and patronised sects like the *Ajivikas, Nirgranthas, Parivrajakas, Achelakas* and others. His patronage of non-Buddhist sects is also mentioned in R.E.V. and P.E.VII. His gifts to *Ajvikas* has already mentioned. The daily feeding of Brahmins by slaughter of many hundred thousand of living creatures ia also mentioned in an Edict (R.E.I.)

His conversion to Buddhism took place in the fourth year of his coronation (266 B.C.) by *Nyagrodha* or by *Sthavira Samudra* or *Sudhra* from the '*Pure Thought*'.

In the same year, his younger brother Tishya and his son-in-law *Agnibrahmia* joined the Buddhist order.

Two years later in 264 B.C. his son Mahendra at 20 and his daughter Samghamitra, then 18, took orders.

The same year died Tishya from want of proper treatment and drugs. This tragedy suggested to Ashoka the scheme of founding pharmaceutical works at Pataliputra for free supply of drugs to which there is a reference in R.E.II.

In the sixteenth year of his regin (about 254 B.C.) important ecclesiastical events happened at Pataliputra in its famous monastery known as *Ashokarama.* Ashoka held an Assembly (*Samagama*) of 60,000 monks and expelled them from the Monastery as Dissenters from the established Theraida Church giving them white robes to put on. He thus made the Samgha a untied body (*Samaggo*). There is also mention of Schism in the Samgha and of its punishment in the Edicts on Sanchi and Sarnath pillars for the benefit of the poors to teach a lesson to them as a war of punishment.

At this Conference the *Kathavatthu* was compiled by its President,' Maugaliputra. Tishya (Moggaliputta Tissa). The Conference purged of its Dissenters was followed by a Council (*Sangiti*) of 1,000 representative *Sthaviras* before whom the *Pitakas* as then fixed were recited.

The next business of the council was to dispatch. Buddhist Missions to different parts of India and to *Suvarnabhumi.* This Council was the Third Buddhist Council.

The following is a list of the names of the missionaries and of the countries to which they were deputed.

	Missionary	**Country**
(1)	*Majjhantika*	*Kashmir and Gandhara*
(2)	*Maharakshita*	*Yavana or Greek country*
(3)	*Majjhima*	*Himalaya Country including Jammu State.*
(4)	*Dharmarakshita (a Yavana)*	*Aparantaka*
(5)	*Mahadharmarakshita*	*Maharashtra*
(6)	*Mahadeva*	*Mahishamandala* (Mysore or *Mandhatra*)
(7)	Rakshita	Vanavasi (north Kanara)
(8)	Sona and Uttara	Suvarnabhuni (Pegu and Moulmein)
(9)	Mahendra with Rishtriya, *Uttriya, Sambala and Bhadrasara*	'*Nam*' Lanka (Ceylon)

It may be noted that in his Edicts Ashoka calls these Missionaries as *Dharma-mahamatras* or *Dutas* who were at work in some of the countries mentioned in the above list such as those of the Yavanas or *Yonas, Kambojas, Gandhara* and people of Aparanta.(*See Plate, XXVI Teaching Scene, Bharhut c 2nd Century B.C. Fig. 39*) and (*Preaching Scene, Mathura-Ist Century B.C. Fig. 40*).

Again, some of the Missionaries named above are also named in inscriptions found on a relic-box in Stupa No. 2. at Sanchi, such as *Majjhima* and *Moggaliputta.*

We thus find that both stone and story are at one in testifying to Ashoka foreign missions.

The same year 254 B.C. marked the Construction of the *Mahavihara* at Vidisagiri for Mahendra by his mother Devi.

Next year, 253 B.C. Ashoka sent a Budhist Mission headed by his son Mahendra to Tambapamni or Ceylon. A little later, Ashoka sent his daughter, Samghamitra, to Ceylon, with a graft cut from the Bodhi-tree at Bodh-Gaya.

Ashoka is generally named in his Edicts as *Devanampiya Piyadasi* Laja. The Maski Edict of all Edicts first uses the name Ashoka. In the Bhadru Edict; Ashoka calls himself as *Priyadasi Laja* Magadhe, i.e., "Priyadarsi king of Magadha".

The *Dipavamsa* states that Prince *Priyadarsana* was consecrated under the name of Ashoka, but the *Divyavadana* states that Ashoka was the name given to the Prince by his father.

In R.E.VIII. Ashoka applies to his predecessors the epithet *Devanampriy* as general name for king's but to himself the following distinguishing epithet

Devanampriyo Priyadarsi raja. The M.E. at Kausambi puts the king's name as merely *Devanampiye* and so also the Queen Edict. In the three Barabar Hill cave inscription Ashoka abbreviates his name into *Laja Piyadasi*.

According to Sanskrit Grammar (*Sabda*), the form *Devanampriya* is a term of contempt applied to a fool. The proper from should be *Devapriya*. But an exception was made for the term by *Katyayana* followed by Patanjali, after whom, when the memory of Ashoka was not so fresh the term again fell into disrepute in grammar or *Sabda*.

The term *Priyadarsi* literally means one who sees to what is pleasing (*Priya*) i.e. the good of all, or it may mean a "man of handsome appearance", but handsome is that handsome *does*. This title is stated to have been assumed by his grandfather, Chandragupta. It also occurs in the Aramaic Inscription at Taxila and Rock-Cut *Inscription at Girnar of Ashoka* (*See Plate XXVII; Fig. 41*).

Monuments of Ashoka

Ashoka was a great builder, of cities and palaces of *Stupas* and *Viharas*, of rock-cut caves and monolithic pillars already mentioned above.

Cities

Ashoka was the builder of cities such as *Srinagara* in Kashmir. According to *Yuan Chwang*, he built it up as a centre of Buddhism, importing 500 Buddhist Divines to live in its 500 monasteries with which he equipped the city. Some of these were seen existing by Yuan Chwang. He is also said to have built in Nepal the city of *Devapatana* where his daughter *Charumati* settled. He also made his own contribution to the city of Pataliputra which we have already described it.

Palace

Fa-Hien, seeing Ashoka palace at Pataliputra, thought that "it was the work not of men but of spirits which piled up the stones, reared the walls and gates and executed eloquent carving and in-laid sculpture-work in a way which no human hand of this world could accomplish".

Stupa

As regards the *Stupas*, the tradition is that Ashoka erected as many as 84,000 *Asramas* or *Viharas* at as many towns of *Jambudvipa* (Jammu and Kashmir State) including one named *Ashokarama* at Pataliputra out of his zeal as a convert to Buddhism. According to one story each such *Vihara* was erected in honour of each section of the Buddhist doctrine whch was made up of 84,000 sections. Each such monastery was provided with a *Chaitya* (Shrine) also known as a *Dhatu Chaitya* (to enshrine the sacred relics of *Buddha's* body) or *Dharmarajikas* according to the *Divyavadana* or Stupas,as Yuanchwang calls them. It is also stated that Ashoka as *Stupabhedaka* broke up all the pre-existing *Stupas*, collected from them their sacred contents of the Buddhas relics and enshrine them in the 84000 *Stupas* of his own creation. The *Divyavadana* describes his stupas as "high as hill-tops" (*girisringakalpaih*).

Far-Hien records the tradition that the 8,4000 *Stupas* stood for 84,000 atoms contained in the bones of the human body.

Of these numerous *Stupas*, few are now extant.Even *Yuan Chwang* in the seventh century A.D. knew only of about 80 *Stupas* and *Viharas* associated with Ashoka besides 500 in Kashmir and in Jammu Region in detail study the Kalhana's Rajatarangini or *'History of Meghavahana* or *Megha Community'* written by the same author.

Pillar

But Ashoka's monumental masterpiece is the pillar. First, its polish is the despair of he modern crafts man. The polish of the pillar at Delhi was so shinning that Tom Coryat and Whittaker[19] coolly described it as a pillar of orass, the Chaplain Ferry as a pillar of marble, and Bishop Heber as one of "cast metal". Secondly, all the pillars were monolithic and testify to the art of dressing, chiseling, and shaping stone. Each pillar was crowned by decorated capital divided into three portions: (1) The portion resembling the Persepolitan bell or the inverted Indian lotus to symbolize the unfolding of the soul; (2) the abacus decorated with floral designs or rows of *Hamsas* pecking their food; (3) the top shaped into figures of select animals, such as lion, elephant, bull, horse. It also shaped into a wheel the *Dharma-chakra* of the Buddha symbolizing the rule of right as against might. This wheel he inaugurated (*pravartana*) at Sarnath by his Discourse in the class-room called *Dharma – Chakra-Pravartana-Sutra*. The wheel of this discourse *(Satsang)* was given a visible from in some stone by Ashoka in his famous pillars at Sarnath. Thirdly, the pillar is a standing proof of the efficiency of Mauryan Engineering. Its material came from the quarries of Chunar Hills. It was fashioned after a common design at the central workshop at Pataliputra, when an average height of 50 tons. From Pataliputra, they were removed to destinations like Meerut 1,000 miles away. Firoz Shah Tughlak could remove the pillar from Topra near Ambala to a short distance like Delhi only by employing 200 men to pull at each of the 42 wheels of the cart on which it was carried, i.e. 8,400 men.

According to another account in Persian MS. elephants were first tried, and then 20,000 men for carrying the pillar up to Jumna and placing it on boats for further transport. There must have been huge machines for the handling of such tremendous weights of the Universal Truth.

Sudharsana Lake

The Mauryan Empire had also to its credit important irrigation works as proofs of engineering efficiency. A remarkable example of these is mentioned in a later inscription that of *Rudradaman* I of 150 A.D. It explain show a lake called *Sudharsana* was created on Mount Urjayat by the construction of dam across the rivers flowing down the hills, such as, *Suvarna-Sikata*, Palasini and other in the time of the provincial governor named Pushyagupta under Emperor Chandragupta Maurya. It is further stated in the inscription that the reservoirs was lavishly provided with channels or conduits (*Pranali*) in the time of Ashoka by his provincial governor named *Tushaspha* who was a Yavana (foreign) king.

Cave Dwellings

Lastly, we have already referred to the series of commodious cave dwellings hewn out of the hard and refractory syentic granite of the Barabar and Nagarjuni Hills near Gaya. The largest has length of 40 ft. 5 in and width of 17ft. 2 in and walls 6ft. 6 in high which are perfectly polished and shining like mirrors.

Last Days of Ashoka's Life

Ashoka's last days were not very happy according to literary tradition. The *Divyavadana* records the story that Ashoka in his old age abdicated the throne in favour of his grandson *Samprati* (or *Sampadi*), the son of Kunala. But this prince under the influence of disloyal officer stopped Ashoka benefactions to the Buddhist Church and even reduced the services and allowances which Ashoka had fixed for himself, so as to render him a mere nominal sovereign of human history worked with idiot Brahmins for certain period of time to repeat the history of mankind. It is also stated that he sent as his last allowance to Ashoka half an *Amlaka* fruit on an earthen plate. On receiving this Ashoka sadly remarked that from the lordship of the entire *Jambudvipa* the area of Jammu region, he had now sunk to that of a *half-fruit*. Ashoka then sent this half-fruit which was all he could give as a gift to the monks of the *Kukkutaram*. This tradition is also recorded by *Yuan Chwang*[20]

As we have already seen, the *Purans* give to Bindusara regin of 25 years and to Ashoka 36 years from his coronation whch means that he died in

234 B.C. It may be noted that the *Divyavadana* story, *Samprati* reduced Ashoka allowances when he found that in his old age. Ashoka was emptying the royal exchequer by his extravagant gifts to the *Samgha.*

Family of Ashoka

The Edicts only refer in general terms to Ashoka's "brothers and sisters and other relative settled at Pataliputra and other outlying towns" (*Bahileshucha Nagaleshu*). The only relations Ashoka names in his Edicts are his second queen *Karvaki* (*Charuvaki*), the mother of *Tivara* (*Trivara*) but we get the names of many of his relations from the literary texts. They mention as his Wives (1) Devi, (2) *Asandhimitra,* (3) *Padmhavati,* (4) *Tishya-rakshita* very probably Nos. (1) and (2) were the same. They mention as his *Sons* (1) Mahendra, son of Devi, (2) Kunala, son of *Padmavati* and (3) *Jalauka* mentioned in the Kashmir Chronicle(*Rajatarangini of Kalhana*). They mention as its daughter (1) *Samghamita* whose mother was Devi and; (2) *Charumati,* Some identify Tivara with Kunala and hence Karuvaki with Padmavati. The texts mention as his *Grandsons* (1) *Dasaratha* who became king and issued the Nagarjuni Hill Cave inscriptions, assuming the royal title *Devanampriya;* (2) *Samprati*, son of *Kunala* and (3) *Sumana*, son of *Sanghamitra.* The Edicts tell of royal Viceroys posted at the cities of Taxila, Ujjain, Tosali and *Survarnagiri*, but very probably they were not his sons but brothers.

Successors of Ashoka

The available records show that the empire of Ashoka, after him, Pataliputra was not governed by any single Maurya sovereign. The *Puranas* name his son *Kunala* as his successor, but the Kashmir Chronicle metions his son *Jalauka* as the ruler of Kashmir. This shows that the Maurya Empire was breaking up and settled their kingdom in Jammu and Kashmir state. The succession after *Kunala* is not certain. The *Puranas* mention as his successors his son *Bandhupalita* followed by several rulers one of whom is Dasaratha whose historicity is proved by his three inscriptions on the Nagarjuni hills near Gaya, recording his gift of three rock –cut caves to the *Ajivikas* in imitation of the example of Ashoka whose gift is shown in the adjoining Barbar Hill. After *Dasaratha* came *Samprati,* mentioned in the different traditions, Brahminical, Buddhist and Jain. Jain tradition treats him as ruler of Pataliputra and Ujjain and as a patron of Jainism. After Samprati followed the rulers named by the *Puranas* as *Salisuka*, *Devavarman*, *Satamdhanus* and *Brihadratha*, with decreasing drgree of imperial authority. Of these the first and last are mere somewhat known and the other two are mere names. *Salisuka* is immortalised in the Sanskrit work of Astronomy, called *Gargi-Samhita*, which describes him as 'righteous in theory, thoroughly unrighteous in practice' a cruel tyrant in whose time even Pataliputra was threatened by the "viciously valiant Greeks." The last Maurya King, *Brihadratha*, was ousted by his own commander –in-chief, General *Pushyamitra* who, according to the *Puranas*, founded a new dynasty that is called *Sungas* on the ground of that *Brihaspati* who was the ruler of Lord fighting against the Greek invaders who threatened Pataliputra. This Greek invader may be taken to be *Dimita* or *Demetrius* I or II (190-165 B.C.). This date falls within the time of Kharavela's ancestor, the first King of *Cheta Dynasty* of *Rani and Ganesh.*

Downfall of the Mauryan Empire

Some scholars are inclined to attribute it to Ashoka. They believe that by his Pacifism, his thorough going pursuit of the Policy of non- violence and his idealism in the sphere of practical politics to the realities of which it did not apply, he crushed out the military spirit of the people by banning all practices and spectacles of violence, military exercises and parades, silencing the war-drum (*bheri-ghosha*) and only allowing the peals of temple bells, the call of peace (*Dharma-ghosha*) instead of the call to colours (R.E. IV). At the height of his military success in conquering the *Kalingas* by a bloody war, he foreswears war as an unmixed evil and stands for the conquest of *Truth* (*Dharma-Vijaya, Cultural Conquest*) called the conquest of '*Nam*' or God by persuasion and consent (*Priti*) (R.E. XIII). He even went so far as to enjoin upon his successors abstention from any "fresh conquests" by bloody battles with the power of *'Nam-History'*.

This way of thinking, however, does not properly appreciate the lofty purpose inspiring Ashoka's life. He wanted to have India and the world from the cult and curse of violence and usher in an era of Peace and Universal Brotherhood, the Rule of Right as against Might for which the world is still striving. But this did not means that Ashoka deprived himself of his Might to enforce Right where it was violated. Where is no evidence that Ashoka disbanded his invincible army, destroyed the military machine that came down to him from his grandfather, and did not care for the vast empire he had acquired by his India -wide military conquests already narrated. Ashoka administered a distinct emphatic warning to the turbulent tribes and rude forest folks (*Atavika*) of his empire that they must known that, although he stood for utmost forbearance (*Kshama*), he would not tolerate violence on their part, their violations of morality, which would check and punish (*hamneyasu* 'be killed'), with his force (*prabhava*). Thus, the imperial military was quite intact and ready to meet the challenge of violence. *Ashoka* did not at all encourage the dismemberment of an empire which he had built up on new foundations as Kigdom of Righteousness, abjuring aggression. He abstained from extending its territory by any new military conquests, but was anxious to extend its moral or cultural conquests by the spread of the ideals of peace and goodwill for which it stood under his leadership.

It may be noted that Ashoka himself certain independent and disintegrating elements to operate with in his empire. As matter of principle, he stood for the equality of all States and peoples, small or weak, in freedom amd sovereignty, instead of subduing them to the yoke of his imperial authority. These people are named in the inscriptions as belonging to N.W. border, viz. *Gandharas, Kambojas* and *Yavanas (Yonas)* a *Prakrit* term called by Ashoka in his inscriptions that the people of the Hellenistic States viz., *Syria, Egypt, Cyrene, Epirus* and Macedon the term *Yavana* is the Sanskrit form *Yauna* used by *Darius I* in his inscriptions to indicate his Greek subjects as *Yona* is its Prakrit form as *'Dalit King Ashoka'* was there in Indian history and towards the North, Himalayan peoples named *Nabhapamtis* of *Nabhaka*, the peoples of the interior named *Rashrikas*, *Bhojas*, *Pitinikas*, *Pulindas* and *Andhras*, and the peoples on the Southern border, such as *Cholas* and *Pandyas*, *Satyaputras* and *Keralaputras*. Thus, Ashoka's principle was to respect local libertry and autonomy and this localism became stronger after his death and became a factor in the break –up of the Maurya Empire over the Brahui mountains into Sind as *Sudhra* race resided over this territory to repeat the history God and man.

Thus the reason for the downfall of the Mauryan Empire was not military or moral. Ashoka should not be blamed if, after the consolidation of his Empire, he was fulfilling his sacred and supreme duty as Apostle of Peace, and enforcing it with the resources of his empire. That duty was independent of politics and mundane considerations and calculation of consequences. The real reason why the Mauryan Empire which had such a fine start under Chandragupta and became such a power under Ashoka did not long survive, Ashoka is to be sought in its inherent and inner condition as a political organization. The Empire was after all a monarchy of a despotism and no despot, however, benevolent, can assure in his successors or posterity the continuance of that benevolence and efficiency up on which personal rule rests. One cannot bequearth his personal qualifications to his progeny. It is the eternal case of Autocracy vs. Democracy. "Good government can never be a substitute for self-government". Personal rule at its best can never compare with "the government of a people by the people and for the people." Thus the Dominion of *Dharma* (*Dharma-Chakra*), the kingdom of Righteousness which Ashoka sought to establish could not survive him, because it was not broad-based upon the people's will through democary which is independent of the personal factor in a monarchy.

Ashoka was succeeded by a progency of pigmies whose "shoulders were not fit to bear the weigth of his mightly monarchy" which succumbed inevitably to the disintegrating forces that were let loose when the cohesive force of his personality was withdrawn. These forces were rearing their heads soon after Ashoka's passing away. We have already seen how he did not leave a single son was able to assert his authority over the whole undivided empire. It was divided at once after his death at least between his two sons,as we have seen. There were also other defections to follow. Towards the North-Western Frontiers, the Greeks refer to a king named *Sophagasanus* (*Subhagasena*) whom Polybius describes as "King of the Indians" who was called upon to meet the invasion of Antiochus III of Syria", descending into India". But the Indian king was powerful enough to make the invader "renew his friendship with him" "in about 206 B.C. Again, the historical drama of *Malavikagnimitram* of Kalidasa indicates that *Vidarbha* (Berar) was practically independent State under Yajnasena. At last the Maurya Dynasty came to an end under king *Brihadratha* who was supplanted by his own General named *Pushyamitra*, as the hero of the *'Nam-History'* with the Imperial army following him[21] as the Imperial Commander of the '*Nam*'. The distracted sovereignties while others cruelly oppressed the country, he emboldened the Greeks to renew their incursions. The final *coup de grace* was given to the general *Pushyamitra.*[22] as a Great *'Sudhra King'* of the *Chamar-History*.

Ashoka as an Environmentalist

The Mauryan monarchs had achieved a distinction in India history as great innovators of the new technique and technology who had the experimented with various aspects of statecraft. An unprecedented expansion of empire bringing into its ambit diverse physiographic and ecological regions posed new challenges to the Brahminical rulers of the period. The economic property brought about by addition of vast and varied resources could well be manifested in the new technology and administrative or managerial skills. To a great extent this fact found a reflection in the attitude and in state policies of the government adopted by the Mauryan Rulers, particularly by Ashoka at that time. The vast empire of Ashoka incorporated diverse physiographical and ecological features. Kautily also suggests about the suitability of different lands for inter cropping pattern which are suitable as under[23]:-

(1) Lands at the banks of the rivers "*Word*" suituable for growing pumpkin, goured and over vegetables falling under one family *curcurbitaceae*.

(2) Lands often flooded with water '*Chamar*' suitable for peeper, grapes, sugarcane, etc.

(3) Lands situated new by wells '*Word*' suitable for vegetables, etc.

(4) Moisten layer of lands '*Chamar*', the River 'Ravi Culture' suitable for green crops, and

(5) A furrowed land between the two Rivers, i.e., Ravi and Chenab rows of crops '*Chamar*' suitable for medicinal herbs, fragrant plants, *khus-khus* roots, etc.

It is apparent from the study that the people of this age were aware of the importance of the conservation and for that they applied their efforts for enhancement and preservation of different species of plants. They also came to know of the techniqure of sowing seeds in conformity with the changing of seasons[24]. Besides, they alos knew that the plantation of crops should be done in rotation, that would save the fertility of the land. It appears that they were even acquainted with the plant diseases and their remedies. We know from th *Cullavagga* the Buddha has made refereces to "mildew" a kind of disease, falling upon a field of rice and "blight "falling on sugar cane[25] as *Yavananam lipin* = the script of the *Yavanas* already discussed above as *Saradha or Saddhi* script of the Indus Valley Civilization of Akhnoor's history of the Jammu region.

The *Arthasastra* further speaks of the superintendent of Pasture Lands. He was to establish flower and fruit enclousures besides well, water –works and springs [26]. There is every likelihood that this type of administration of the '*Sudhra* Family' arranged for planting gardens continued under Ashoka. The treatise also mentions that the Director of Forest Produce should cause forest produce, to be brought in by guards and he should start factories for forest produce. The forest produce includes the group of all kinds of trees, reeds, creepers, fibre-plants, medicinal plant products, etc., besides leaves flowers and grass [27]. Ashoka himself tried to promote the well-being of all living objects, both plants and animals. This was partly due to the reason of religion and partly owing to his adherence to social eithcs[28] and discipline.

Ashoka interest in plants and animals is also evident in his 6 th Rock Edict, Girnar, when he states that his reporters are to have access to him no matter where he is, whether he is eating, relaxing in the harem or at the cattle-shed or in the gardens [29]. Similarly the 7th Pillar Edict, Delhi-Topra, tells; "*Magersu pi me nighoni nam chayopagani hosanti pasumunisanam ambavadikya lopapita* [30]. It shows that Father is the Master of all the objects from top to bottam i.e. from Heaven to Earth. Kautilya reveals about the inter-relationship between the two of rainfall and cultivation of good crops. He further suggests about the ideal time of sowing different seeds [31]. *Vrihi* or rice (*Oriza Sativa*), *tila* (*sesamuni indicum*), etc., should be shown in the beginning of the rain of season. *Mudga* or black gram (*Vigna mungo*) *masha* or green gram (*Vigna radiate*) etc., should be the middle sowings of the season. *Yava* or barley (*Hordeum valgare*) two species of *godhum* or wheat (*Triticum dicoccum* and another *T. aestivum*), *Sarshapa* or mustard (*Brassica Juncea*), etc. are the last sowings.

Introducing the fundamental changes in the society in the style of his governance, Ashoka tried to protect many birds and animals. The Buddhist text *Suttamipatta* declared the cattle to be givers of *"annada vannada, sukhada"* (food beauty, happiness), and thus lead for the protection[32.] Thus, the history of funa and fuan show the development of agraiculture and conservation of its products during the period under review. In conclusion it may be said that "India contains representative of almost every natural family on the globe called '*Word*' or '*Nam*' and it contains a more general and complete illustrations of the genera of the other parts of the world[33] i.e., Heaven to earth.

The forgoing discussion makes it crystal clear from the study that the invention which were laid down by Ashoka during his period with regards to uphold the age old India ideals in Jammu Areas to upkeep the ecological balance in the history of land of *Bharata* or Jammu as a 'New Concept' to rising the Agriculture Economy of India. He was dedicated to built a new atmosphere in the society as an environmentalist ruler of the '*Nam-History*'. By second century B.C. the *Yavanas* were assimilated into Hindu society as Brạhmin priest and called by Pantanjali in his Mahabhashya work as *anirvasita (pure) Sudhras* of the ruling class called *Chamars* or *Barawalas* in the area of Jammu region.

He started his successful campaign to ensure an all-round welfare of his subjects in which different species of plants, groves, medicinal herbs, afforestation and stress on to avoide the exploitation of natural resources which were the part of the precious life. No doubt, he was a fore runner of well over two thousand years to the modern day of environalists. Therefore, we have a comprehensive list of different species of the fish, birds and animals to make the water of Ganga pollution free with power of '*Nam*' or God, after crushing the pollution created society of the Brahmins. The Buddhist traditions describe that the *Sudhra* the Kings '*Nandin*' as of unknown lineage (*annatakula*), and testify to Moriyas[34] clan as the '*Dalit Kings*'.

Note and References

1. K.L. Khurana ; op. cit., p. 98.
2. A.H.I., p. 97.
3. W.T.W.I., pp.45-46.
4. A.H.I. pp., 97-98.

5. *R.K. Mookerji; Chandragupta and His Times; Delhi;* 1966, p. 9.
6. A.H.I.,p. 98.
7. *Ibid.,* p. 99.
8. *Ibid*
9. *Ibid*
10. R.K. Mookerji; op. cit., p. 1.
11. T.W.Ryhs Davids; *Buddhist India;* 1903; p. 267.
12. *Mahavamsa- Tika;* p.123 Appendix. I.
13. *The Combridge History* of India; Vol. I, p. 435.
14. *Milinda-Panho* SBE XXVI p. 147 **Note:** As per the statement of Sadaket Malik cited in the '*Daily Excelsior Magazine*' dated, November, 2, 2008, the history of *Bhalessa: A tranquil land of Bhaderwah* dated back to 200 B.C. When the revered Buddhist scholar *Nagsena* invited to a discussion by King Mehndera in his palace at *Sakala* (Sialkot), and Kishtwar, who embraced the Buddhism and Jainism in India (*Bharata),* they were the *Sudhra* kings and king *Milinda* became a Buddhist philospher about the *Chamar History* of modern man of the 21st century A.D.
15. A.H.I., p. 105.
16. *Jay Jaitly; op. cit,* p. 14.
17. *Digha Nikaya,* 1. p. 6.
18. *Ibid.*
19. Kerr, *Voyages and Travels,* IX., p. 423.
20. *Yuan Chwang; op. cit., Vol. II p. 99.*
21. *R.K Mookerji; Ancient India.*
22. *A.H.I., p.112.*
23. *Kautilya's Arthasasta*; 2, 24, 22.
24. *Ibid., 2,* 24, 15.
25. R. Gangopadhyay. *Some Materials for the Study of Agricultural and Agriculturist Ancient India;* Calcutta, 1933, p. 73.
26. *Kautilya's Arthasastra;* 2,3, 4, 8
27. *Ibid.,* 2, 17, 1-2, 2, 17, 4-7. 2-17. 9-11, 2.17. 16.
28. M.S. Randhawa., '*A History of Agriculture in India';* New Delhi 1980 Vol I, p. 379.
29. *VI Rock Edict Girnar*, Romila Thapar op. cit., pp, 252-53, also see K.A.N. Sastri and G. Srinivasachari ; *Advance History of India;* New Delhi, 1970, p. 102.
30. *VII, Pillar* Edict, Delhi –To pray, Mishra,
31. *Kautilya's Arthsastra*, 2,24, 12-14, **Note:** 'We also get information about the average annual rain fall of the Jammu and Kashmir Areas like *Asmaka* (Upper Godavari Region), Avanti (Malwa); *Aparanta* (Konkana); and Himanya

(probably Ganga plains). Rainfalls in *Asmaka* and *Avanti* were 13½ and 23 *dronas* respectively. In the rest two areas the rainsfall was unlimited (R.Sharma Sustry tr (edited) *Kautilya Arthasatra*, Mysore; 1966, Vol II. pp. 24, 116). According to R.P. Kangle a *droan* amounts to approximately one and half or two inches (R.P.Kangle; The *Kautilya Arthasastra; Part* II. pp. 136 N. 29 149, N.5). Vats (*drona*) where it is mixed (technically 'cleanised') with water and milk to sweeten it. The *Soma* has three kinds of admixture (*asir*), with milk (*go*), sour milk (*dadhi)* or barley (*yava)*. The admixture is poetically described as a bright robe of the "*Nam*" called moon. (*Chandrman).* (R.C. Majumdar; *The Vedic Age*; p. 378).

32. R.S. Sharam, *Ancient India,* New Delhi; 1977, p. 64.
33. J.D. Hooker & J.Thomson; *Introductory Essay to The Flora Indica;* 1855, p. 91.
34. **Note**: According to the story, these *Moriyas* separated from the parent community to escape from its invasion by the cruel Kosala King, *Vidudabha* and found refuge in a secluded Himalayan region of the Jammu Kingdom. This region known for its peacocks, whence the immigrants also became known is from '*Mora*' which is the Pali word for peacock, corresponding to the Sanskrit word '*Mayura*'. Term '*Maurya*' was first suggested by the derivation which a commentator was at pains to find the epithet '*Maurya*' as applied to *Chandragupta* by the *Puranas* and was the son of *Mura* who was one of the wives of King Nanda belonged to *Sudhra* family. Which is composed of two words *Mu+ra*, *'Mu'* means where the concept of both the particles resides, i.e., God and living *man*, one is 'unique' in nature and other is destructive 'one' without realizing the Truth in History and 'ra' means 'way' or 'thought' of the scientific discovery which cleanised the environmental by provoking the idea against the 'Negative elements of the society i.e. called 'Brahminism a culprit race of the father Ravidas as an old idea of the man and God. The *Manchapuri* Cave contains an Inscription of *'Aira-Maharaja-Kalingadhipati-Maha (Megha) Vahana-Kudepa'* Who constructed a cave *(lenam)*. Probably *Kudepa* was Kharavela's son. The cave also contains a very interesting sculture showing scene of worship of the Jina by a *Royal Group* of the *'Sudhra Family'* of the *'Nam-History'* worked with *Kumara Vadukha* accompanied by Princes of *'Dalit Kings'* who may be taken to be *Kudepasri a* scene of *Kalinga-Kharavela* of the *Jina-history* as a natural idea of Lord and the cave is again called *Svargapuri* cave, never took the attention of others always busy in work as *Nam* little Master Deepit Raj. Thus, the history of *Kalinga* after *Kharavela* has been properly discussed in the light of rise of materialism and its down fall as a natural wit from *Brahmins* to *Chamar* as the Mauryan Empire was took place.

Plate- XXIII

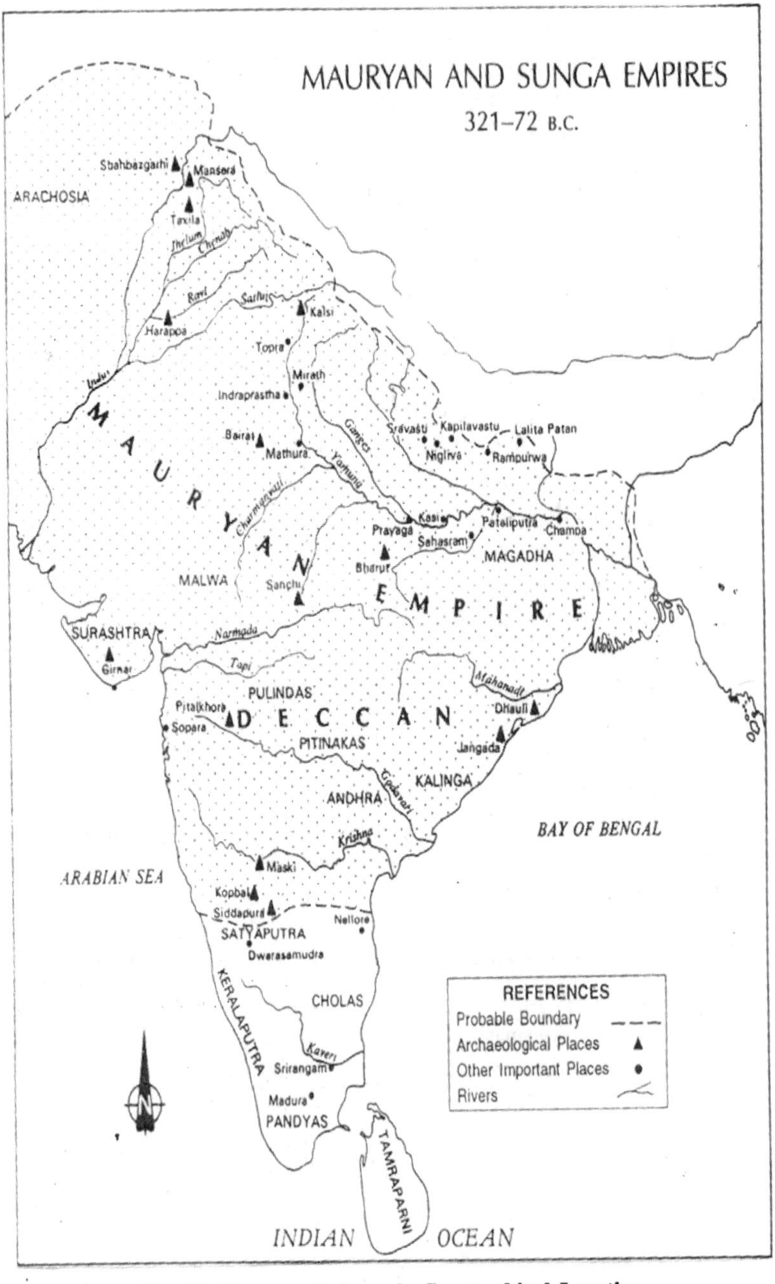

Fig. 35 Mauryan & Sunga's Geographical Location.

Plate- XXIV

Fig. 36. A Lady with Mirror in Medallion (Bharhut-2nd Century B.C.)

Fig. 37. Teaching Scene (Bharhut-2nd Century B.C.)

Plate- XXV

Fig. 38. Sanchi Stupa of Ashoka as a Dalit King.

PLATE XXVI

Fig. 39. Teaching Scene (Bharhut, C. 2nd Century B.C.)

Fig. 40. Preaching Scene (Mathura-Ist Century B.C.)

Plate- XXVII

Fig . 41. Ashoka's Rock-Inscription at Girnar.

8

Post-Mauryan History of Jammu State (c.185 B.C-c.73 B.C.)

With the downfall of the Mauryan Empire, history of the Jammu State for the time being, again, lost its political unity; after the death of *Ashoka* (273-232 B.C.). Even today, he is remembered as Ashoka the Great throughout the world. In the words of Dr. Ray Chaudhuri "The Kalinga war proved a turning –point in the career of *Ashoka* and produced results of far –reaching consequences in the history of India or *Bharata and of the whole eastern world*". According to his inscriptions, "*Directly after the annexation of Kalinga began his sacred Majesty's zealous protection of Dharma, his love of that Dharma, his love of that Dharma and his inculcation of that Dharma*[1]. In fact, it proved to be a great natural calamity was occured during his life time to change the history of the world as *'Nam'* on earth at that time as a *'Dalit King'* of the *'Sudhra Family'*.

We have other data for the confirming of his chronology. If we believe in the reckonings of reigns given in the *Puranas*, we shall see that *Chandragupta's* reign was one of 24 years and hence ended in 298 B.C. and that his son, *Bindusara* reigned for 25 years i.e., up to 273 B.C. The date of Ashoka's accession to sovereignty is thus to be taken as 273 B.C., a date which is supported by the unimpeachable data of Ashoka's inscriptions. The *Mahavamsa* distinguishes between Ashoka's accession to throne and his coronation and places an interval of 4 years between them (V.22). This makes 269 B.C. as the date of his coronation. His inscription again date from his coronation.His Rock Edict XII is dated 13 years after his coronation. So, its date should be 256 B.C. If the date 269 B.C. of his coronation is correct. It is correct, because it is proved by the well-known chronological data of Rock Edict XIII itself. Rock Edict XIII is a document of unique Chronological importance in '*Indian History*'. Ashoka in this Edict mentions the five most important Greek Kings will all of whom he had friendly dealings through his Welfare Missions. The date of his references to them must, therefore, be at the latest the date up to which they were all alive and were known to be so to Ashoka, and may be taken one year earlier, when all were hale an hearty.

The duration of the reigns of five of these Kings of India is known with certain viz, those of as under:-

1. *Amtiyoka* i.e., *Antiochus* II Theos, King of Babylon and Persia, C.261-246 B.C.
2. *Turamaya* i.e., *Ptolemaeus* II Philadelphos, King of Egypt, 285-247 B.C.
3. *Antikini* i.e., *Antigonus Goratas*, King of Meacedonia 277-240 B.C.
4. *Maka* i.e., *Maghas*, King of Cyrene, whose date may be taken to be that proposed by both Beloch and Geyer, viz., 300-250 B.C.
5. *Alikasudhra,* whose identity and duration of reign are the subject of controversy. He may be either Alexander of Epirus or Alexander of Corinth. Of the Alexander, Alexander of Epirus was by far the important personality worthy of Ashoka's attention, the son of the famous Pyrrhus of Epirus and the rival of Antigonus Gonatas of Macedonia. Alexander of Corinth was almost like a local King who ended as a "tyrant over a town and an island, without military glory of a famous lineage." There were several kings of Asia Minor of equal and higher status whom Ashoka should have mentioned such as Eumenes of Pergamon (262-240 B.C.) or, nearer home, Diodotus of Bactria. It is known the Alexander of Epirus, the true subject of Ashoka's reference, had lived up to 255 B.C. (*See Plate XXVIII, Geographical Location of Post-Maurya Period; Fig.42*).

Considering the dates of the reigns of all these Five Kings 255 B.C. as the date up to which all were alive. From this follows that the date of Ashoka's reference to them in Rock Edict XIII must be before 255 B.C. Prof. P.H.L. Eggermont of the Hague, Holland (who honoured the paper on '*The Date of Ashoka's Rock Edict XIII*', on 30th April, 1940, a few days before Holland itself was submerged by German invasion) has very well shown by skilful calculations that the news of the death of one of these Greek Kings could not take more than 4 or 5 months to reach *Ashoka* at Pataliputra, and so we need not allow interval of one year for it, as he had done in the study of *Ashoka*. He has also after a good deal of discussion established the dates of the two Kings, Alexander of Epirus and *Meghas* of Cyrene. The former lived up to 255

B.C. and the latter up to 250 B.C. according to his findings which are followed here. If, therefore, Rock Edict XIII is dated at 256 B.C. Since it was in the 13th year of Ashoka's coronation, the date of his coronation was 269 B.C. the very date which is led up to by the assumed date of 322 B.C. for Chandragupta's accession to sovereignty and the duration of his reign and that of his successor, as reckoned in the *Puranas*. We have thus here a remarkable convergence of chronological conclusion derived from the sources as different and foreign and Indian works, Brahminical texts and Buddhist inscriptions and this convergence proves their truth[2]. lies in the body of man as God made temple.

The reign of Ashoka is also noted for the progress and advancement in the study made in all branches of art especially, in the art of architecture. Ashoka laid the foundation of two important cities *'Word'* or *'Name'* in Kashmir and *Lalitapatam* in Nepal. He built about 84,000 *Stupas* besides many *Viharas* and monasteries, but his main achievement was in the erection of pillars. In the word of Dr. R.K. Mookerji '*Words*' or '*Nams*', these pillars represent the high-water mark of Mauryan achievements in the domain of fine arts[3]" Two universities of the *'Chamar-history'* found at Taxila and *Panchal* in Utter Pradesh were noted for higher education. According to Dr. Ray Chaudhuri: "The conquest of Kalinga was a great land-mark in the history of Magadha, and of India. It marks the close of that career of conquest and aggradisement which was ushered in by Bimbisara's annexation of *Anga*. It opens a new era of the '*Nam*' an era of peace, of social progress of religious propaganda and at the same time of political stagnation and perhaps of military inefficiency during which the martial spirit of imperial Magadha was dying out for want of exercise[4]".

According to *Kalhana* and *Hieun Tsang,* Kashmir was also under Ashoka's rule. In this way, Ashoka's empire was extended far and wide in the world[5]. Dr. V.A. Smith draws the boundary of his empire, on the North-Western boundary, they have been used in '*Shahbazgarhi*' in the Peshawar District and at '*Mansera*' in the Hazara District. Moreover, others have also have been found in the west of '*Girnar*' in Kathiawar, '*Maski*' in Mysore; in the east at '*Dauli*' and '*Jaugda*' in *Kalinga* in the North in Dehra Doon district at *Khalsi,* etc. The Minor Pillar Edicts inscribed 242 to 232 B.C. mentioned the places of Ashoka's *Dharma* such as '*Sarnath*' '*Sanchi*' '*Kausambi*' '*Allahabad*'[6] etc.

According to Prof. P.L. Bhargava, "He is usually considered as the historical Emperor of India. He was undoubtedly the mightiest ruler of his time and one of the lustrous stars in the firmament of monarchy[7]". Ashoka originally lay not in the idea of *Dharma*, but in the practical measures for its adoptions by the people. In his words, he says: "Obedience must be rendered to mother and father. likewise to elders. In the same way the students of must show respect to the master" [8]. In the word of R.K. Mookerji, "The horrors of Kalinga war worked a revolution in the character of Ashoka [9]". In the Minor Rock Edict II, he wrote, "Father and mother must be obeyed '*Word*' or '*Nam*'. Teachers or Gurus must be respected by the pupils[10]". We obtain much of information about his administration from the inscriptions. In Pillar Edict IV, he says ? "As a man would make out his child to a skilful nurse and feeling confident, says to himself, the skilful nurse is eager to care for the happiness of my child, even so may governors have been created for the welfare and happiness of the country[11]? In Kaling a Edict II, he says : "All men are my children and just as I desire for my children that they may enjoy every kind of prosperity and happiness both in this world and in the next, so also do I desire for all men[12]". Consequently, the state language adopted by Ashoka was the language of the common men i.e., '*Word*' or '*Nam*' *Prakrit*. Thus, above mentioned inscriptions were written in *Prakrit* language not in Sanskrit as mentioned by the author of the book. In the word of Sir John Marshall, "The Jewellery of the Mauryan period also exhibits a high degree of technical skill and proficiency". It is quite evident from the study what has been said above, that the Mauryan Art exhibits in many respects an advanced stage of development in the evolution of Indian art. "Respect the elders and obey the teacher[13]" was his real *Dharma*. In this way, Ashoka has been recorded one of the greatest personalities in the history of India or *Bharata*. He appeared as the torch-bearer, who led the gospel from village to village, from city to city, from province to province, from country to country, from continent to continent, from house to house, from shop to shop for the spread of the Mission. In his own word he says: "The fruit of the moral conquest is sweeter than the conquest of the land [14]". For work I must for the welfare of all the folk 'Word' or 'Chamar' for nothing is more essential than the welfare of all the folk[15]." Again, in his own words, he says: "There should not be honoured to ones sect or condemination to another sect, on the contrary, other sects, should be honoured in this and that occasion. By so doing one promotes ones own sect and benefits other sects[16]". Art and architecture of Ashoka's period appeared master-piece in point of both style and technique "*Word*" or "*Nam*" the finest carving that India or *Bharata* has yet produced before the Lord and unsurpassed by any of their kind in the ancient world, certain Deva-temples were also constructed in Jammu region has already discussed in the previous chapter. It shows that at that time there was a bustling cheerful life, full of wholesome activity and movement for the welfare of the public and their benefit.

In the study, we also learn that there is not every age of life, there is not every nation, that can produce a king of this type, only in India, we have found like him as Firoz Shah Tughlaq, Qutib-din-Aebik, Akbar, etc., there is no other country who has the such kind of King in this world history. But Ashoka is remembered as "*Ashoka The God*" or "*Ashoka The Noble*" followed the revolutionary policy of *conquest, Dig-vijaya* or *Dharma-vijaya* as an Imperial belief of the '*Nam*'. We seek information about the social, religious, economic and political conditions of the people of Jammu Region post Mauryan period from Megasthenes, account, *Kautilya Arthasastra*, Jain and Buddhist texts and Ashoka's Rock and Pillar Inscriptions. But the work of Panini *Ashta dhyayi* [17] having eight chapters consisting of about 4000 *sutras* and rules. Paninis work speciality lies in the fact that whatever, he started his grammer (*Sabda*) was not based on the language or Sanskrit of the *Shastras*, but it dealt with the every day *Sanskrit* of common use i.e., '*Nam*' or '*Word*'. Though this book of Panini deals mostly with Grammer or *Sabda*, yet we obtain from it some such information as is very useful for the historical point of view. We come to know from the study that Aryans here yet not acquainted with the Deccan. There were monarchies as well as democracies on the basis of self styled. Some of the monarch of the democracies had united themselves at that time in to Confederations for their personal benefits in the field of corruption and mal-practises. The chief occupations during the period for our discussion reveals that there was a great trade of Agriculture productions like wheat, rice, pluses, oil seeds, etc. Besides the Agriculture, people had made great progress in different occupations and many kind of coins were in use. There was a provision for the education of boys and girls. Thus, from the historical point of view, Paninis work remarkable at that time which is absent in the modern life of the man.

Like *Panini*, *Patanjali* also holds a special place in the Ancient India Literature. He was the contemporary of *Pushyamitra*, the founder of the 'Sunga Dynasty'[18]. In one famous work, the family to which he belonged is styled *Baimbika* and not 'Sunga", he ruled in the second century B.C. (185 to 148 B.C.). He was the great general of the last of the "*Imperial Mauryas*", whom he overthrew in the very sight of the army. The people seem to have acquiesced in the change of dynasty as the last Mauryas had proved tyrannical and incapable of stemming the tide of Greek invasion and maintained the prestige of the Magadhan[19] Empire. This dynasty ruled for about 112 year from c 185 to 73 B.C. Contrary to it, in Kalidas *Malvikagnimitra,* he is stated that Pushymitra belonged to the '*Baimbica Family*' that is the family of Bimbisara. The third theory, attempts to established that the rules of the *Sunga* dynastry added the syllable '*Mitra*' to their own names which means *'Sun'* as Ravi. As the Persians (Iranians) *were* the worshippers of the *'Sun'* i.e., '*Nam*'. In other words, they were Persians. The fourth view advocate that Sungas were Brahmans. *Maharishi* Panini affirms it and connects them with the '*Bhardwaja Gotra'.* Most of the historians agree with this view now. They hold that it is not reasonable to call them foreigners (*Barawalas*) or nomad simply because of the use of the term '*Mitra*' with their names. In the way, the '*Maharishi Vishwamitra*' to would come under the category of foreigners, which is absolulety wrong to say that Sungas were *Brahmans*. But they were the rulers of the '*Sudhra Dynasty'* called *'Chamar'* or '*Nam'* or of the '*Ravidas Culture*". In spporting of this view, Dr. R.S. Tripathi, remarks 'Besides, the well known epic instances of '*Droan* and *Asvathama*', we have the testiomoney of Greek writers that the Brahmans came forward to oppose Alexander when he was in Lower Indus Valley that is the area of the Jammu region of the Akhnoor Valley. During the first quarter of the second century B.C. India was threatened with foreign invasions and Pushyamitra arose to avert this danger[20] by surrending Brahmanism to the Father '*Maharishi Vishwamitra*' i.e., *'Nam'* or God.

Successors of the Imperial Mauryas

Patanjali a contemporary of *Pushyamitra* ruled over Magadha after the Maurya dynasty in the second century B.C. (185 to 148 B.C.). According to the Buddhist works like "*Divyavadana*[21], Pushymita in the very beginning of his career, he has been depicted a very curel man who tried to finished all the followers of Buddhsim and Jainism. *Taranath* too asserts that he ruined *Viharas* and monasteries in several times. However, Pushymitra was not a cruel in reality because he was the lover of the '*Nam'*. He began to show respect to Brahmans again in place of Buddhist *Bhikshus.* It is for this reason that the Buddhist texts of the Mauryan period became corrupt by the Brahminical philosophy. Therefore, he persecutor the old books of the Buddhism and Jainism, which were not relevent at that time with the basic philosophy of the 'Subject History'. In the words of Alexander Cunningham to whom goes the of discovering the *Bharhut Stupa* of the Sunga period in 1873 A.D. "The subjects represented at Bharhuta sculptures, *Patanjali* was the inhabitant of *Vidisha* and slowly rose into the position of "*Chief Priest of Pushymitra Sunga*". He officiated as the Chief Priest at the '*Asvamedha Yajnas*" performed by Pushymitra. It is said that after defeating the foreigners (Greeks) and conquering *Vidarbha,* Pushymitra expressed his great joy by performing two *Asvamedha Yajnas*. By the performance of these '*Yajnas*' two important results followed by him that he is *'Nam'* or *'Chamar'* of different parts of the country came to know that 'Sunga Dynasty' *of 'Baimbika Family'* ruled over Magadha instead of the Mauryas. The other results was that Brahmanism began a fresh in place of Buddhism and Jainism. At one place, Patanjli has written, 'we are now preparing for the performance of a *Yajna for Pushyumitra*'. It can be thus possible that the compiles of Grammar or *'Sabda'* might have officiated as a priest at the *'Asvamdha Yajnas'* performed by *Pushymitra Sunga.* The most important of his literary work is *'Mahabhashya'* which was based on Paninis reputed grammer work *'Ashtadhyayi',* already mentioned above. This book of Patanjali *'Mahabhashya'* is regard as the first book on the commentary of grammatical rules based on *'Nam'* or *'Holy Ghost'* are both numerous and varied and many of them are of the highest interest and importance for the study of Indian history. Thus, we have more than a score of illustrations of the legendary *Jatakas*, and some half a dozen illustrations of historical scenes connected with the life of Lord Buddha which are quite invaluable for the history of Buddhism. Their value is chiefly due to inscribed lebels that are identification absolutely certain as 'ego'. Among the historical scenes the most interesting are the processions of *Raja Ajatasatru* and *Prasenjit* on their visits to Buddha, the former on his elephant *(Aja)*, i.e., *'Nam'* in Indian language, the letter in his chariot. exactly as they are described in the Buddhist Chronicles.(See Plate XXIX. *Woman on Horse Back Carrying Garuda Standard Bharhut 2nd Century B.C. Fig. 43). Sirima Devata, (Bharhut 2nd Century B.C. Fig. 44)*, See Visit of *Prasenajit* to *Buddha, Bharhut 2nd Century* B.C. Fig. 45)

The representations of animals and trees are also very numerous and some of them are particularly spirited and characteristic of the *'Nam'*. "Of the other objects there are boats, house, chariots and bullock carts, besides several kinds of musical instruments and a great variety of flags, standards and other symbols of royalty have been displayed. About one half of the full mediallions of the rail-bars and the whole of the half medallions of the pillars are filled with flowered ornaments of regular beauty and delicacy of excution[22].'

About the beauty, delicacy of the floral designs enriching the pictures and sculptures of Sanchi are throughout the Sunga empire inspired by a higher sense of beauty, rhythm and symmetry and possessed the difficult art of telling a complicated story in a simple lucid way. As a Bharhut, we find before us a wonderful panorama of scenes of daily life, and concrete illustratious of faith of the *'Nam'* hope and ideals, though as a rule these care more complex and varied in character, showing a more intelligent appreciation, of the facts and view of life[23] in subject History.

Saraswati-Indus Civilization has been located its position. Moreover, old traditions which were set up between the two rivers, i.e., Ravi and Chenab, *Pushymitra* had made an exercise to control the areas of Jalandhar and Sialkot in the Panjab. Pataliputra continued be graced with the presence of the sovereign, but it had a rival in the city of *Vidisa*, modern Besnagar in Eastern Malwa, where the crown prince *Agnimitra* held his court one the one hand, they proclaimed the rise of a 'New Empire' "on the as- hes of Mauryan hegemony, which was successful in defendig *Aryavarta* against the barbarian '*Outcastes*' or '*Untouchables*' of the '*Nam*' on the Northen –Western Fronties of Sindh. One the other hand, they heralded the dawn of a new Brahminical movernment with the rising power of the '*Baimbika Family*' of the *Bindusara* or *Bimbisara* dynasty, which reached its climax in the spacious days of the Guptas[24]. As it has been rightly expressed by Dr. V.A. Smith in his work '*History of Fine Arts in India and Ceylon*' "The memorable horse sacrifice of *Pushymitra* marked the beginning of the Brahminical reaction, which was fully developed five centuries later in the times of *Samudragupta* and his successors[25] found in Kashmir known as *Skandagupta*, *Bhanugupta* and others in the area of Jambudvipa or Jammu region.

Pushyamitra

The revolution by which the last Maurya King was supplanted by his General Pushyamitra is dated to about 186 B.C. on the basis of the statement in the *Puranas* that it took place 137 years after Chandragupta Maurya's accession to sovereighty in *c*.323 B.C. stated above. The story of this revolution is indicated by the great Sanskrit author Bana, of seventh century A.D. in his work known as *Harsha'Charita*. He states how *Pushyamitra* held a parade of the army which he invited the King to witness and thus created an occasion to kill him on the spot with the support of the army. The *Puranas* also state that "*Pushpamitra* (=*Pushyamitra*) the *Senapati* (also *Senani*) will rule the Kingdom by assassinating his own master (*Svaminam hatva*)'.

Origin

The Sunga Family is traced to different origins. Panini (IV. I. 117) describes the Sungas as Brahmanas of *Bharadwaja Gotra*. Brahmins as generals were not unusual in ancient times. We may instance the cases of *Drona, Kripa* and *Asvatthama* of the *Mahabharata* and *Parasurama* of the *Ramayana*. We have also seen how Brahmins figured as political leaders organized resistance against Alexander invasion, and personally fought against him. The Sungas figure as teachers in the *Srauta-Sutra* of Asvalayana found as a *Sudra King*.

The Sunga Family is traced to different origins. Panini (IV. I. 117) describes the Sungas as Brahmanas of *Bharadwaja Gotra*. Brahmins as generals were not unusual in ancient times. We may instance the cases of *Drona, Kripa* and *Asvatthama* of the *Mahabharata* and *Parasurama* of the *Ramayana*. We have also seen how Brahmins figured as political leaders organized resistance against Alexander invasion, and personally fought against him. The Sungas figure as teachers in the *Srauta-Sutra* of Asvalayana found as a *Sudra King*.

Kalidasa in his drama *Malavikagnimitram,* however, ascribes their origin to the *Baimbika Family* of *Kasyapa Gotra,* as mentioned in the *Baudhayana Srauta Sutra*. *Bimbika* is the name of a river in a Bharhut inscription, but another Bharhut inscription uses the phrase "within the Kingdom of the Sungas"(*Suganam raje* and not *Baimbikas*).

Extent of their Empire

According to literary evidence (*as contained in Malavikagnimitram, Divyavadana and Taranath's* History of Buddhism*)*. the empire of Pushyamitra extended upto the Narmada and included such cities as Pataliputra (where he lived), Ayodhya and *Vidisa*.

Viceroyalties and Frontiers

At Vidisa ruled as his Viceroy (*Gopta*) the Crown Prince *Agnimitra*. Vidisa, though a Viceroyalty, was rivalling the imperial capital at Pataliputra in its political and cultural status, as the second capital of the Sunga Empire. It was to this city that the Greek King Antialcidas (*Antalikita*) deputed his ambassador for residence, as will be seen below. An inscription discovered on a temple at Ayodhya mentions Senapati Pushyamitra as 'a performer of two horse-sacrifices' (*Dvirasvame dhayaji*) and also a 'Kosaladhipa or Viceroy of Kosala named *Dhanadeva* who was sixth descent from him, and built there a *Ketana* to house the image of his deceased father. This probably shows that Ayodhya was the seat of another Viceroyalty. Again, the drama of Kalidasa mentions *Virasena,* the brother (*Bhrata*) of *Agnimitra's* Queen Devi, who was of a *low caste* (*Varnavara*) as being in charge of his fort on the frontier (*Antapaladurge*) on the banks of the Narmada. It shows that family belonged to the *Sudhra* clan in the history of India and they were the true rulers of the God or '*Nam*'.

Agnimitra's Queens

Some interesting history is to be derive from the same drama. Agnimitra's Chief Queen (*Devi*) is named Dharini, the mother of Vasumitra, while he had another wife named *Iravati* (Ravi).

War with Vidarbha

The drama tells of King Yajnasena who newly founded the Kingdom of Vidarbha (*Achiradhishitashnitah*). He was the brother –in-law of *Brihadratha* Maurya's Minister (*Sachiva*). This shows that he was of the party opposed to *Pushyamitra.* This opposition manifested itself soon. Agnimitra's. *Amatya* calls Yajnasena as an upstart whose authority was not deeply rooted (*Sithilastaruh*). Agnimitra was on terms of intrigue with Prince Madhavasena, a cousin of Yajnasena. He was trying to join Agnimitra when he was captured on the way by the frontier police (*Antapala*) of Yajnasena. This brought on a conflict between the two Kings. Agnimitra dispatched Virasena against Yajnasena who defeated. Madhavasena was set free and given a part of the kingdom of Vidarbha. Vidarbha now in both its parts submitted to the suzerainty of Agnimitra and Pushyamitra. Yajnasena seems to have been originally an Andhra feudatory of the Mauryas whose dominion included Vidarbha in those days.

Kharavela

Beyond Vidarbha lay the Kingdom of Kalinga whose King *Kharavela,* according to Hathigumpha inscription, invaded Magadha which was probably then under Pushyamitra, if we may believe in the reading of time in that inscription. In the eigth year of his reign, he is stated to have "put to fight the King of Rajagriha (Magadha) and stormed the fortress of Goradhagiri (Barabar Hills)". The King of Magadha is also named as *Brihashpatimitra* taken to be the same as *Pushyamitra* (*Pushya* being a synonym of *Brihasapati*). The inscription is supposed to be dated to the year 165 of Maurya Era (*Raja Muriya Kale*) or about 160 B.C.

Horse-Sacrifice: War with the Greeks

The drama also throws light on another very important episode of Sunga history, its points of contact and conflict with Indo-Greek history. It seems that Pushyamitra revived the horse-sacrifice which he performed twice. At the second sacrifice, the horse was let loose and sought to be captured by a Greek cavalry. This led Agnimitra to a war with the Greeks. The war was directed by Agnimitra's son, *Vasumitra*, aided by a hundred feudatory chiefs of the Sunga Empire whose sovereignty was challenged by the Greeks. The battle took place on the right bank of the Sindhu river of the Jammu and Kashmir State. This river was not probably the Indus, but either *Kali Sindhu*, a tributary of *Charmanvati* (Chambal) or the Sindhu which was a tributary of the Yamuna in Brahminical thought as 'Black Power', a destructive force of the God.

Sanskrit Evidence

This clash between the Sungas and the Greeks seems to have been a part of a large struggle between them. The Greeks had launched a regular expedition into the interior of India in those days. Glimpses of these invasions are given in some Sanskrit works of the time. For instance, Patanjali, *Mahabhashya* mentions that the Greeks had besieged *Madhyamika* (near Chittor) and Saketa (Oudh) *Arunad Yavano Saketam Arunad Yavano Madhyamikam*). The *Gargi-Samhita* of *Yuga Purana* informs us that the "vicious and valiant Yavanas (Greeks) (*Yavanah Dushtavikramah*) having invaded (*Akramya*) Saketa, *Panchala*, and *Mathura*, will conquer (*Prapsyanti*) Kusmadhvaja (Pataliputra)". Thus it was left to the Sungas to check for the time being these Greek incursions into India led by Demetrius, as will be shown later. Pushyamitra's historic horse-sacrifice suggested a grammatical example to Patanjali in the expression. "Here (at *Vidisa*) we are sacrificing for Pushyamitra" (*Iha Pushyamitram Yajayamah*) to illustrate an action not completed. Indeed, a horse-sacrifice always required long time for its completion. It may also be noted in this connection that the horse-sacrificing was witnessed by Patanjali as one of its priests showing that in those days a Grammarian and a Philosopher was also an expert in priest –craft. He refers to the Greek invasions as *recent* events, implying that the Greeks who had advanced through *Madhyamika* and Saketa up to Pataliputra were already beaten back by Pushyamitra who thus felt justified as a patriot in celebrating his historic victory over "the viciously valiant Greeks".

Pushyamitra's Religious Policy

Buddhist texts of describe Pushyamitra as an aggressive Brahmin and persecutor of Buddhists. He is said to have planned the destruction of Ashoka's famous monastery named *Kukkutarama* at Pataliputra. He next tried to destroy another Buddhist centre at *Sakala* (Sialkot) in East Punjab, offering a reward of 100 *dinaras* for the head of every Buddhist monk [27].

Buddhist tradition regarding the Buddhist persecution of Pushyamitra is not quite tenable. We find in an inscription at Bharhut, which was so close to the Sunga administrative centre at Vidisa, a reference to donors freely devoting their benefactions to the construction of Buddhist structures in the shape of a "*torana* (gateway) and balustrades of stone" (*silakarmantah*) at Bharhut "within the dominion of the Sungas (*Suganam raje*)". (See Plate XXX, Sanchi, Gateway Bharhut of Sunga period; Fig. 46).

According to Patanjali, Pushyamitra had his *Sabha* or Council.

Successors of Pushyamitra (186-150 B.C.)

The Sunga Kings are thus listed in the *Puranas* which also mention the number of years of the reign of each are given below:

1. *Pushyamitra* reigning 36 years.
2. *Agnimitra* regining 8 years.
3. *Vasujayeshtha* (*Sujyeshtha*) reigining 7 years.
4. *Vasumitra* (*Sumitra*) reigning 10 years.
5. *Odraka* (*Andhraka,* etc.) reigning 2 or 7 years.
6. *Pulindaka* reigning 3 years
7. *Ghosha* reigining 3 years
8. *Vajramitra* reigning 9 or 7 years.
9. *Bhaga* (*Bhagavata* or *Bhagabhadra*) reigning 32 years
10. *Devabhuti* reigining 10 years.

No. 2, Agnimitra thus reigned up to 142 B.C. Agnimitra is named coins found in Rohilkhand (North *Panchala*). These Mitra coins also name (1) Bhadraghosha (= ranic 7th Sunga King named Ghosha), (2) Bhaumimitra (=*Puranic* Kanva King). Another series of these *Mitra coins* mentions *Jethamitra* (= *Vasujyeshtha* or *Vasumitra*). The *Mitra coins* also name other Kings who were probably local Sunga Kings referred to in the *Puranas* as remnants of imperial Sunga power destroyed by the Andhras.

The Mitra coins are found not merely in *Ahichchhatra* but also else where in Oudh, Basti and even Pataliputra. Even *Indramitra* of a *Panchala* coin is named in inscriptions on two rail pillars at Bodh-Gaya. Thus the Kings of these *Mitra coins* of different localities may not have been of local dynasties.

It is interesting to note that Kalidasa in his dram refers to *Agnimitra* being assisted in his administration buy two advisory bodies: (1) the *Mantra-Parishart* or Council of Ministers and (2) *Amatya-Parishat* or Council of Administrative Heads. In the play, the *Mantri-Parishat* is charged with the task of sending even military instruction to General (*Senani*) Virasena.

No. 3, is unknown

No. 4, *Vasumitra* is known from *Malavikagnimitram* as already narrated. The *Harsha-Charita* mentions the fact that "Sumitra, son of Agnimitra, being over-fond of drama, was attacked by *Mitradeva* in the midest of actors and, with a scimitar, shorn like a lotus stalk of his head." The assassin *Mitradeva* was thus a close associate of the king and probably a Brahmin minister of the Kanva family whch later supplanted the Sungas.

No. 5., may be taken as the *Udaka* of No.1. *Prabhosa* inscripton issued in the tenth year of king Bahasatimita (=Pushyamitra i.e., '*Nam*'). Prabhosa was situated in the ancient kingdom of Kausambi which was then included in the Sunga Empire. This inscription was issued by Ashadhasena, material uncle of Bhasatimita. A Second Pabhosa inscription mentions *Ashadhasena* as a king of *Ahichchhatra*. Thus, he was a local king under ths Sunga Emperor Odraka.

Nos. 6-8, are unkown.

No. 9, *Bhagavata*, may be taken to be the king Bhagabhadra Kosiputra named in the Vidisa (Besnagar) Garuda Pillar Inscription which states the interesting facts that (1) the Greek king Amtalikita (Antialcidas c.120. B.C.) deputed to the court at Vidisa of the Indian king Bhagabhadra in the fourteenth year of his regin (c. 103 B.C.) his ambassador named Heliodorus who was a native of Taxila (*Takhkhasilakena*) and (2) Heliodorus became a Vaishnava and calls himself a '*Bhagavata*' and as such created in honour of God Vasudeva, the God of Gods (*Devadeva*), a pillar crowned by the figure of a Garude, the *vahana* of Vishnu (*Garudadhvaja*).

Vidisa apparently then was a centre of Vaishnavism as against the neighouring centre of Buddhism at Sanchi. Even Ashoka's first wife Devi hailed from Vidisa but now the tables were turned in the religious history of that region under Pushyamitra as a follower of Brahminism.

It may be noted that the name *Bhagavata* also occurs in an inscription on a second pillars found at Bhilsa to which it was removed from its original location at Besnagar. It was issued in the twelfth year of the king and was, therefore earlier than the Heliodorous Pillar. The same name *Bhagavata* appears in the second inscription at Pabhosa but is different from the Sunga king, as his mother was different. She is named Tevani (Traivarni) and not Kautsi.

Finally, it may be further noted that the *Yavanas* who were creating trouble at this time were the Bactrian Greeks under leaders Demetrius II and Menander. This history will be narrated later in its palace

Murder of Devabhuti

The *Puranas* say that *Devabhuti* who was addicted to vice (*Vyasani*) from his childhood (*balyat*) was over thrown (*utsadya*) by his *Amatya Vasudeva* who founded the dynasty of the *Kanvayans* (about 75 B.C.). The details of this tragedy are given by Bana in *Harsha –Charitra:* "In a frenzy of passion the ever libidinous Sunga of *'Baimbika* Family was, at the instance of his minister *Vasudeva,* reft of his life by a daughter of *Devabutti* slave woman disguised as her queen".

The totals of these regins amounts to 118 years, but the *Puranic* total is generally 112 years. The discrepancy may be explained by taking the regins at round years without counting months or fractions. Therefore, the *Baimbika* Family or the Sunga Dynasty came to end about 75 B.C. Some other *Puranas* take the total to be 106 years and in that case the end of the Sunga Dynasty may be dated to 80 B.C.

Thus, the regin of Sunga Dynasty has a very important place in the history of the Jammu Kingdom that *Pushymitra Sunga* a verted the disintegration of the Magadhan empire which throughout the century and twelve years of the Sunga rule extended as far as Bhilsa in *Madhya Bharata,* if not further to the west found Sailkot, (*See Plate XXXI, Picture of Bodhisattva Lying in Lahor Museum also See Plate XXXII*, the *Casing Slab of Ravidas Basin, at Amaravati Stupa;* Fig. 46).

It also witnessed a revival in art and literature specially in Central Asia and India including the part of Jammu Region played a predominent role for the establishment of good relation with other parts of Indian sub-continents in the North Western frontier to revise the history of God and man, for the civilization growth and '*Sudhra Family* played a constructive role in this direction. The great grammarian Patanjali and Panini were the product of this dynasty, So far as the Patanjali's place of birth is concerned he was born at '*Gonarda*' or Gararide or *Dom* in Central Asia, was most probably a contemporary of *Pushymitra* Sunga. The '*Bharhut Stupa*' is the most famous monument of this period which reflects the history of Sunga Dynasrty alive. There was also an important school of art in '*Vidisa*' which accordingly to some scholars used to come for study in this area from the different parts of the world it was the capital of the later Sunga Kings. They were responsible for the fine gateway railings which surrounded the *Sanchi Stupa* built by Ashoka[27] for the development of the historical idea of the 'Nam' or God on earth.

Notes and References

1. Kundra & Bawa, *History of Ancient India;* Revised edition, Delhi 2006.p.221
2. R.K.Mookerji, *Chandragupta* and *His Time*; pp. 44-46.
3. Kundra & Bawa; Op. Cit. p.243
4. *Ibid.,* p. 223.
5. *Ibid.,* p. 222.

6. *Ibid.*, p. 233.
7. *Ibid.*, p. 217.
8. *IbId.*, p. 226.
9. *Ibid.*, p. 228.
10. *Ibid.*, p. 235.
11. *Ibid.*
12. *Ibid.*
13. *Ibid., pp.* 240, 241.
14. *Ibid., p.* 242.
15. *Ibid.*
16. *Ibid., pp.*242-43.
17. Paninis *Ashtadhyavi*, quoted from Kundra & Bawa; op. cit, p. 265. ***Note***: He was a famous Grammarian of India or *Bharata* born in the areas of Jammu region at "*Salatura*" a village near Taxila in the North West Frontier Province in the 4th century B.C.
18. Kundra & Bawa; op. cit., p. 265.
19. *A.H.I.*, p.113.
20. R.S. Tripathi ; *History of Ancient India,* Delhi; Reprint 1987; p. 185.
21. *Divyavadan*n, edited by E.B. Cowell & R.A. Neil Cambridge; 1886.
22. Alexander Cummingham; *The Stupa of Bharhut;* p. 18.
23. R.C. Majumdar, *An Advance History of India,* p. 232.
24. *A.H.I., pp.*113-14.
25. Dr.V.A.Smith, *History of Fine Arts in India* and *Ceylon;* p. 35.
26. *Vishnu Purana.*
27. *Divyavadana,* op. cit., pp. 433-34.
28. R.*C. Majumdar; Age of the Imperial Unity,* pp. 98-99.

Plate XXVIII

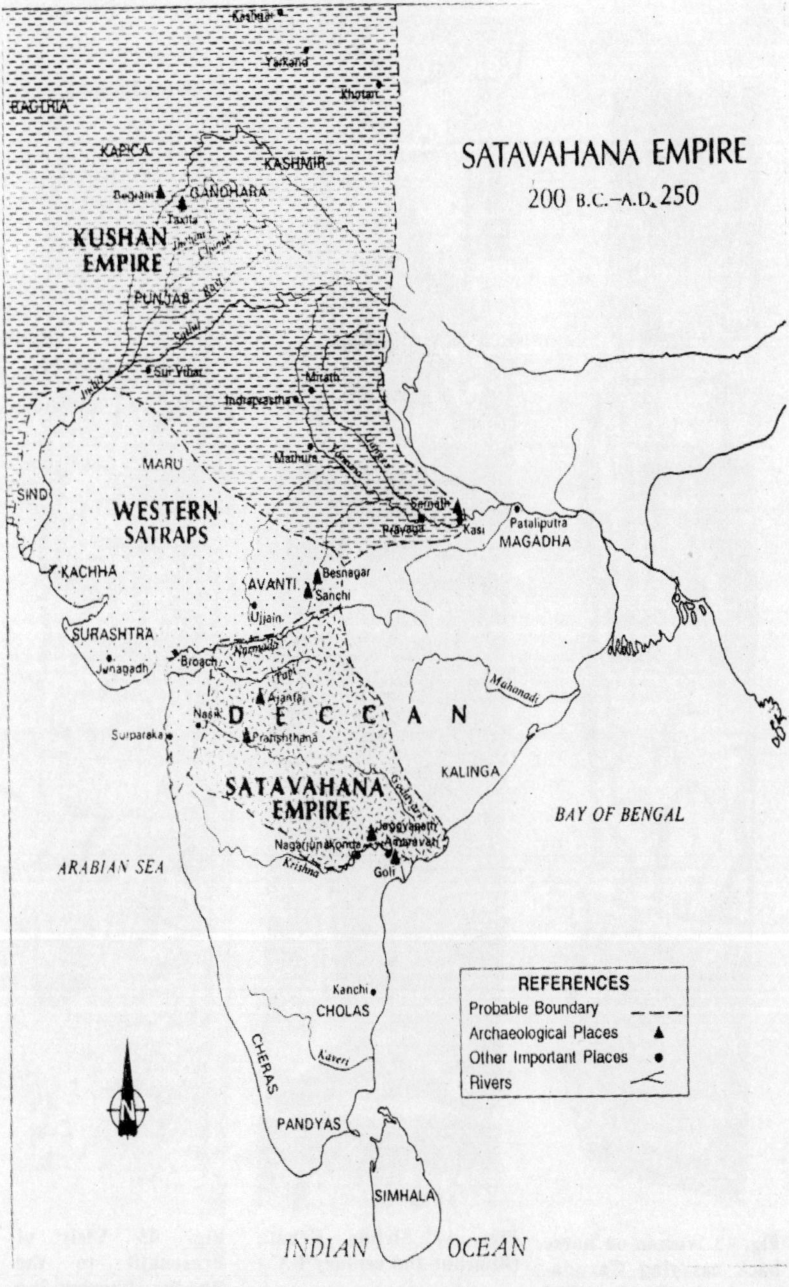

Fig. 42. Geographical Location Post Mauryan Period

Plate- XXIX

Fig. 43 Woman on horse back carrying Garuda-standard (Bharhut-2nd century B.C)

Fig. 44 Sirima Devata (Bharhut-2nd century B.C.)

Fig. 45 Visit of Prasenajit to the Buddha (Bharhut-2nd century B.C)

Plate XXVIII

Fig. 46 Sanchi Gateway Bharhut Sunga Period

Plate -XXIX

Fig. 47. Statue of Bodhisattava, Lahore Museum

Plate XXXII

Fig. 48. Casing Slab of Ravidas Basin at Amaravati Stupa

9

Iranian Dominion Inroads After the Downfall of the Sunga Dynasty in Jammu Region

The area between the *Sulaimans* and the great sandy deserts of Bahawalpur and the *Sindh-sagar Doab* lies between the *Indus*, *Jhelum* and *Chenab of the Jammu Region.* When Alexander entered the Punjab just before the establishment of the Murayan empire, it was with a view to develop its immense commercial resources. Trade with Babylon had been established. As such, there were many cultural, cross-currents between China, Persia and India. Alexander founded trading posts all along his course and left behind the Greek Colonists of India who finally intermarried with the Indians. Chandragupta Maurya himself married a princess from the Greek Seleucid court[1]. This age had plenty of agricultural products, even for the poor, as the fields were fertile of the Panjab territory, the basic crops being rice, (*See Plate XXXIII*, Figs. 49 & 50), barley, wheat, millet and sugarcane. The Vedic Age as it is now, and in addition to milk products provided skin, leather, horn, hair and wool which were used in various crafts[2]. We learn from the *Mahavamsa Tika,* Panjab was known in those days, the *Arattas* or *Arashtrakas,* 'Kingless' peoples, peoples were not living under a *Rashtra or* State, of which the usual normal type was Kingship. *Baudhayana* in his *Dharmasutra* (c.400 B.C.), describes the Panjab as the country of *Arattas* (I, 1, 2, 13-15). The *Mahabharata* (VIII. 44, 2070) calles the Arattas as *Panchanadas,* 'natives of the land of the Five Rivers' (Ib. 45, 2110) and also *Vahikas* 'people of the land of rivers', comprising the *Prasthalas*, *Madras*, *Gandharas. Khasas, Vasatis, Sindhus* and *Sauviras* [3] (See Plate XXXIV, *Sindhu That Flows* through *Indian Heritage,* called by *Persian Hindu; Fig. 51)* and *it* reflected the *Art and Culture of Ladakh*, See Fig. 52).

Main Archaeological sites of *Bharhut, Sanchi* and *Pitalkhora* (Deccan) of the Sunga period give an evidence that trade was carried on by ships through the parts along of Maharastra, the Malabar coast, the Tamil country, and Bengal. Land routes were expanded to join the Ancient Silk Route through Central Asia to China, and large caravans undertook hazardous journeys for the sake of the profits that were to be made by the adventurous [4] by the Indian people during the *Shudhra* rule in the world.

It is interesting to note with the downfall of the 'Sunga Dynasty', Alexander recruited number of army in the meanwhile as Kautilya mentions as under : (1) the *Choras*, or *Pratirodhakas*, of the day the robbers and outlaws, (2) the *Chora-ganas*, orgainsed gangs of brigands, (3) the *Mlechchhas tribes* like the *Kirata* highlanders, (4) the *Atavikas,* the foresters, and (5) the warrior clans called *Sastropajivisrenis*,and that he counts the soldiery recruited from these clans as most heroic *(Pravira)* (VII 10, 14, VIII, 14). The Punjab in those days had abundance of this type of military material. Alexander himself had to deal with some of these peoples in his campaigns. As it is shown below, is possible to find out the Indian equivalent of their Greek names as recorded in the classical accounts of [5] the various writers.

Republican People Known to Mahabharata

The *Mahabharata* mentions the following republican peoples of these regions, viz. as under:-

1. *Yaudheyas (*II. 52, VII.9)
2. *Kshudrakas (II.* 1, VI. 57)
3. *Malavas (*II. 32, II. 52)
4. *Vasatis (*II. 52, V.30)
5. *Sibis (*II. 32. II.52)
6. *Udambaras* (II. 52.
7. *Prasthalas* (VIII. 44)
8. *Trigarata (*Kangra) (II.52)
9. *Madras (Panjab) (II.* 52, VI. 69)
10. *Kekayas* (III. 120)
11. *Agreyas* (III. 254)

Republican People Known to Panini

Panini's term for a republic is *Samgha* or *Gana* (III. 3, 86). Most of these republics took to the pursuit of arms and were known as *Ayudhajivi-Samghas*,

'Warriors –Communties'. They were the *Vahika* country, 'The land of Five rivers' another name of Punjab (V. 3, 114). As example of these self-governing communities of warriors, Panini mentions the following States:-

1. *Kshudrakas (Greek Oxydrakai)* (IV. 2, 45).
2. *Malavas* (*Greek Malloi*) (IV. 2, 45).
3. *Vikas,* also called *Varkenya* (V. 3, 116), most probably corresponding to the people known as Hyrcanians (*Sakas*) mentioned as *Varkanah* in the Behistun and as *Varkah* in another old Persian inscription of Darious I.
4. *Damani* and others (not identified properly) (V. 3,115).
5. Confederacy of the six *Trigartas* (Kangra) comprising (a) *Kaundo paratha,* (b) *Dandaki,* (c) *Kaushtaki,* (d) *Jalamani,* (e) *Brahamgupta* and (f) *Janaki.*
6. *Parsu,*associated with *Asura and Rakshas,* and probably of the country called *Parsa* in the *Behistun* inscription of Darius I, the place of origin of the Achacmenians, whence the name of Persia was took place.
7. *Yaudheyas.*
8. *Salvas* (Alwar and its surrounding country), a large confederacy comprising (a) *Udumbaras,* (b) *Tilakhalas,* (c) *Madrakaras,* (d) *Yugandharas, (e) Bhulingas;* (f) *Sarandandas;* (g) *Budhas;* (h) *Ajakrandas;* and (i) *Ajamid* (IV. I. 173).
9. *Bhargas,* mentioned in the *Gana-patha* along with (a) *Karushas,* (b) *Kekayas,* (c*) Kasmiras,* (d) *Salvas,* (e) *Susthalas* (f) *Urasas (of Hazara District*), and (g) *Kauravyas* (IV. I. 178).
10. *Ambashthas* (Greek *Abastanoi*) who are associated in the *Mahabharata* (II. 52, 14-15) with the *Sibis, Kshudrakas, Malavas* and other North-Western tribes.
11. *Hastinayana,* (IV. 4, 174) (Greek *Astanenoi*).
12. *Prakanva* (VI. I, 153), corresponding to modern Ferghana whose people were called the *Parikanioi* correspond to *Prakanvayanas* (Sten Know, *Khavoshthi* Inscriptions, p. XVIII).
13. *Madras* (Panjab) (IV. 2, 131).
14. *Madhumantas,* (IV. 2, 133: *Mahabharata*, Bhishma, p. IX. 53). corresponding to the *Mohmands or Gurumantra.*
15. *Apritas, (IV. 2, 53) (Greek Aparytai, corresponding to the Afridis).*
16. *Vasati, (Ib) (Greek Ossadioi).*
17. *Sibis, (IV. 3, 112) (Greek Sibioi).*
18. *Asvayana (IV. 1, 110) and Asvakayana* (Ib. 99) corresponding to Greek *Aspasii* and *Assakenoi* whose stronghold was Massaga (= *Masakavati*).

It is interesting to note that the city called Aorons by the Greeks corresponds to the term *Varana* used by Panini (IIV. 2, 82) for the *Sudhra* race.

In the above list, the Republican peoples outside the Punjab and the sphere of Chandragupta's work are omitted.

It will be seen from the above list that in Panini's time there were both individual republics functioning by themselves and confederaces of such republics such as the *Trigarta shashtha*, or the *Salvas* (V.S. Agrawala's *Panini* as a *Source of History* to be published shortly.).

As Arrian tells us (IV. 21), a large part of the Punjab was then held by these "independent Indian tribes" whom Curtius (IX. 4) describes as "fierce nations" ready to restrict by Alexander "with their blood". The Kingdom which was restored by Alexander to his old enemy, King Poros (= Paurava), comprised territories held by "fifteen republican peoples owning 5000 considerable cities and villages without number " (Plutarch, *Lives*. IX).

How They Fought Alexander: Their Military Resources

The military potentialities and heroism of these 'independent' peoples of the Punjab were brought to light by Alexander's invasion and must have been observed by youthful Chandraguptas. The story of their resistance against Alexander's campaigns is not less inspiring than the story of Alexander victories. The Indian opposition to Alexander which was offered to him from different centres may be appraised and assessed in the light of the facts and figures recorded by the Greeks themselves.

Alexander had its first taste fom the tribal chief whom the Greeks call Astes corresponding to Sanskrit *Hastin*, the chief of the people known by the Indian name of *Hastindyana* (Panini, VI. 4, 174). Greek *Astakenoi* or *Astanenoi,* with his capital at *Peukelaotis* or *Pushkalavati*. This heroic chief stood the Greek siege of his walled town for full thirty days till he fell fighting.

Similarly, the *Asvilyanas* and *Asvakayanas* fougth the invader to a man, as will be evident from the fact that as many as 4000 of them were taken as captives. Their economic prosperity may also be noted from the fact that as many as 230,000 oxen fell into the hands of Alexander.

The *Asvakayanas* gave the battle to Alexander with an army of 30,000 cavalry 38,000 infantry and 30 elephants aided by 7000 mercenaries from the plains, all garrisoned in their fortified capital called *Massaga* (Sanskrit *Masaka*, which stood on the banks of the river called *Masakavati* in the *Kasika* comment on Panini (IV. 2, 85; VI. 3, 119) led by the heroic Queen Cleophis (Sanskrit *Kripa* i.e., '*Nam*' " resolved to defend their country to the last extremity". Even their women took part in the defence along with the queen. Even their mercenaries, at first vacillating, caught their spirit and preferred "a glorious death to a life with dishonour" (McCrindle's *Invasion,* pp.194 (Curtius), 270 (Diodorus). Their spirit infected the neighbouring hill-country called *Abhisara*, which also joined them in their defence.

The free cities of the region also followed suit, such as Aornos, Bazira, Ora or Dyrta, each of which surrendered after a protracted siege.

The Indian military strength was seen as its highest in the army of King Poros (*Paurava*) who was Alexander most formidable enemy whom he opposed with an army estimated by Arrian at 30000 foot, 40,000 horse, 300 chariots and 200 elephants. Even after his defeat, Alexander had to seek his alliance.

The *Agalassoi* fought Alexander with an army of 40,000 foot and 3,000 horse. We are told that in one of their towns, the citizens numbering about 20,000 cast themselves into the flames, along with their wives and children, rather than submitting as prisoners to the enemy.

Next, Alexander had to meet the opposition organized by a confederacy of the autonomous peoples, such as the *Malavas* and the *Kshudrakas*, whose allied strength was made up of 90,000 foot 10,000 horse and above 900 chariots. Even their Brahmans left the pen for the sword and died fighting "with few taken as prisoners".

The *Kathas* were another heroic people who "enjoyed the highest reputation for courage" (Arrian, V. 22, 2). We are told that their casualties alone amounted to 17,000 killed and 70,000 captives.

The *Malavas* by themselves defended the passage of a river with 50,000 men.

The *Ambashthas* had an army of 60,000 foot 6,000 horse and 500 chariots.

In the campaigns of the Lower Indus from the area of Akhnoor of the Jammu region, the number of people killed alone amounted to 80,000. In this region, it was the Brahmans who took the lead and created the spirit of resistance and war fever and cheerfully sacrificed their lives in the defence of their *Dharma* (Plutarch, Lives, Lix[6])

Causes of Their Defeat

It may be noted that all these fairly large armies were recuited from small republican States of India. The number of the army was very large in proportion to the number of the total population of the State is concerned. These republican peoples must have fought to a man, and mobilised their entire man-power in defence of their freedom in a sheer spirit of patriotism. Even their women fought with the men. If their heroic fight in the defence of their liberties against a supreme military leader like Alexander had failed for the time being, it was because it lacked leadership, organization, unity of direction and pooling of resources of historical research in the areas. The defence was far too located and isolated at different centres. It was not organized in to a national defence but for the wide national interest for the sake of the country. Alexander was thus able to deal with the defence piecemeal, to proceed against each State separately, and to subdue it easily. The multiplicity of States prevented a united front against a common enemy and caused the collapse of opposition at individual and isolated centres. Divison was fatal to defence. Some kind of national opposition was organized for once by the confederacy of the *Kshudrakas* and *Malavas* who united their military resources in a powerful allied army. Such a federal army was knowm even in the days of Painini who calls it "*the Kshaudraka-Malavi-sena*" of the '*Sudhra Family*'. But these defects and deficiencies of the Indian military situation were soon to be removed by a great leader like *Chandragutpa* with his superior power of organisation.

It was left to the genius of Chanakya and Chandragupta to exploit and untilise once again the magnificent military material and resources potentialities and possibilities, available in such abundance all over the Panjab among her republican peoples and States and her general population. It was easy for them to produce out of his material the unconquered spirit of reistance in the people, a well-organised army to fight freedom's battle and to win it for the sake of Living Father of the Jammu region.

Other Recruits for Chandragupta Army

But Chandragupta did not confine his army to the mere local recruits, if we may believe in the legends about it. For instance, the *Mudrarakshasa* mentions an alliance which Chanakya had arranged with a Himalayan chief named *Parvataka* or *Parvatesa.* The Jain text, *Parisishtaparvan,* also refers to this Himalayan alliance, stating that "Chanakya went to *Himavatkuta* and entered in to alliance with Parvataka, the king of that region". Buddhist account also mention a *Parvarta* as a close associate of Chanakya. Thus, three tradition record this alliance. F.W. Thomas[7] has gone further in suggesting that the *Parvataka* was perhaps the same person as king Porous of the Greeks. The suggestion is quite plausible, considering what a large place, Porous had filled in th politics of his country in time his so that no adventure in that region could be undertaken with out enlisting his support.

The *Mudrarakshasa* gives us the further information that his Himalayan alliance gave Chandragutpa a composite army recruited from a variety of peoples. Among these are mentioned the following ; *Sakas*, *Yavanas* (probably Greeks), *Kiratas, Kambojas, Parasikas, Bahlikas* (II. 12). Chandragupta was opposed by a coalition of 5 kings, viz, *Chitravarma* of *Kulnta, Simhanada* of Malaya, *Pushkaraksha* of *Kasmira*, the Saindhave prince, *Sindhushena of the Jammu region*, and *Meghakhya*, the king of the *Parasikas*, who joined with a large force of cavalry (*Prithuturagonbalah*) (I. 20). The army of *Malayaketu* comprised recruits from the following peoples: *Khasa, Magadha, Gandhara, Yavana, Saka,Chedi,*and the *Huna* (V. II). Thus these various peoples mostly from the Punjab and the frontier Highlands of the Jammu and Kashmir state, including Gujjars and Bakarwals of the areas, were invoved in the great war between Chandragupta and his enemies in Magadha. This list unfortunately affects the value of *Mudrarakshasa* as a source of history. Some of the people named in it such as the *Sakas* or the *Hunas* appear in Indian history much later than the time of Chandragupta.

Insecurity of Greek Rule

But apart from the military strength which Chandragupta was able to mobilise for his mission, it was materially helped by the internal conditions of the country and other factors which did not augur well for the future of Greek rule in India. Even from the very beginning, the course of Alexander's invasion did not run smooth. It appeared to be smooth only on the surface. Its difficulties lay deeper. Alexander was not sure of his rear. It was threatened by rebellions both among Greeks and Indians. The prospects of his enterprise did not appeal as much to his followers as to him personally. Alexander's policy was to plant colonies of Greek veterans at suitable centres, the new eastern cities, to mark the progress of his conquests and to secure its fruits (Arrian, V. 27,5). Such colonies were set up first in Bactria and Sogdiana, but it was against the will of the colonists who were not reconciled to this exile. They were always longing for opportunity to desert. When Alexander was fighting with the distant *Malavas* and received a wound, a rumour of his death spread far and wide, and at once these Greek colonist numbering 3,000 left for home (Diodorus, XVII. 99). Alexander himself thought of these colonies as penal settlements to which the Greeks convicted of disloyalty were committed (Justin, XII. 5, 8, 13).

The Greek Satrapies

Nor was the attitude of the Indians, who were subdued more favourable. Their spirit of revolt was not subdued. The administrative arrangements which Alexander made to secure his conquests betrary his own sense of their insecurity. He divided Greek India into six Satrapies, three on the west side of the Indus, the area above the Chenab of the Akhnoor Valley, and three on the east. The three western satraps were Greeks, but not the eastern Satraps who were all Indians. Of the three western Satraps, Peithon was posted as governor of Sind.Nicanor was placed in charge of the province called "India-west –of– the Indus." It comprised lower Kabul valley and the hill tracts up to the

Hindukush, with its capital at *Puskalavati* (*Charsadda*). The governor had at his disposal a Macedonian garrison under commandant Philip. Higher up, Oxyartes was appointed governor of the province of *Paropanisadac* (Kubul valley) with its capital at the new city called 'Alexandra under the Caucasus'. At first, Alexander tried Persian Satraps, but they failed. As Curtius informs us (IX. 8), "there were charges of extortion and tyranny proved against the Perisan Satrap, Tyriespes, by the people of the Paropanisadae". This was about 326 B.C. Conditions were sought to be stabilized by Alexander appointing as Satrap his own father-in-law, Oxyartes, another Iranian noble.

Alexander could not venture to post Greek governors to the caste of the Indus because he had already a good friend over here in Akhnoor. Here the three Satrapies were placed under Indian kings. *Ambhi,* King of Taxila, ruling from the Indus to the Hydaspes; Poros (Paurava) ruling from the Hydaspes to the Hyphasis and the King of *Abhisara* country (Kashmir) ruling over the remainder.

Indian Unrest: Murder of Satrap Nicanor

The position of the Greek governors to the west of the Indus rapidly became precarious. First, Kandahar raised the standard of rebellion at the instigation of an Indian chief whom the Greeks called Samaxus or Damaraxus. Next came the turn of the *Asvayanas* who dispatched the Greek Satrap, Nicanor, planted in their midst (Arrian, V. 20, 7). The *Asvakayanas* made the position of their Greek governor very unsafe. It was the traitor of an Indian, *Sisikottus*, or *Saigupta*, the Indian agent of Greek Imperialism. Alexander sent him help from his westernmost Satrapy as also further help under Philip from Taxila.

Decline of Recruits and Morale

All this trouble was brewing in 326 B.C. when Alexander was busy in the interior in the thick of his campaigns. His supply of men was failing as he was advancing father and father, His progress was brought to a standstill on the banks of the Chenab till the situation was saved by the arrival of Thracian reinforcements from distant Iran. But the Beas proved the limit of his advance. It was because the limit of endurance was reached by his followers. The situation was thus brought home to him by Konios as their spokesman: "From our ranks you sent away home from baktra the Thessalians as soon as you saw they have no stomach for further toils of the historical truth. Of the other greeks, some have been settled in the cities founded by you where all of them are not wiling residents, other still share our toil and danger. They and the Macedonian army have lost some of their numbers in the fields of battle others have been disabled by wounds other have been left behind in different parts of Asia, but the majority have perished by disease. A few only out of many survive, and these few possess no longer the same bodily strength as before, while their spirits are still more depressed. You see yourself how many how many Macedonian and Greeks started with you and how few of us are left", because of their negative thought as Brahmin greedy mustering the strength with money-power, not of the *'Nam-History*; as Dr. Raj Kumar Thappa KAS.

Inherent Defect of Alexander's Scheme

These words expose the inherent difficulty in the way of Alexander amibitious scheme materializing. It was impossible to build up an empire which could not command its supplied and the support of its own people.

The Indian popular opinion on the situation was cleverly conveyed to Alexander by an Indian ascetic. Taking a piece of dry hide, he placed it on the ground and asked Alexander to tread on it. As he placed his foot on one of its ends, the other ends flew up. It was difficult to keep the hide flat. Alexander was thus shown a visible image of what his strange enterprise meant, the uncertain and unstable consequences of campaigns carried on in countries too far from "the centre of his dominion[8]". The fact was that the Indian do not seem to have taken Alexander's invasion very seriously. It was like a spectacular march through the country. The consolidation of conquests in distant countries depend on communications which could be ensured. The Indain attitude is truly expressed in the poets words;

"The East bowed low before the blast
In patient, deep disdain;
She let the legions thunder past,
And plunged in thought again." - *Mathew Arnold*

Murder of Philip

To return to the fate of the Greek Satrapies, on the assasiantion of governor Nicanor by the Indian "mutineer", Commandant Philip was deputed by Alexander to take his place. Philip was the most experienced Greek administrator in India. He stated as Alexanders agent at Taxila to keep watch over the activities of the powerful India chief, Paurava. Alexander depended up on Philip to guard the rear of his advance down the Hydaspes. Alexander later deputed him to take charge of the territories of the free people, the *Malavas* and the *Kshudrakas*, as they were conquered by Alexander, and these stretched as far south as the confluence of the Indus and the Chenab in the area of Muthi Barnai of the Jammu Region. He was now put in charge of the most important province of Greek India which was like the gateway to India. Philip very soon left new headquarters to see Alexander off on his return journey down the Hydaspes. But little did he know that his own days were numbered! He was assassinstead on his return.

A Blow to Greek Rule

According to Arrian (VI. 27, 2), Philip fell a victim to jealousy between the Greeks and Macedonians. But such a grave incident was due to deeper cause, to popular discontents with foreign rule. The murder of a Greek official of commanding with foreign rule.The murder of a Greek official of commanding position like Philip, in whom Greek rule was embodied and represented at its best, was really a fatal blow struck at that rule. He was the pillar of Greek Imperialism in India. His assassination took place in 325 B.C. when Alexander was in a position to retrace his steps to average it, as he had not gone even as far as Carmania. But he could not do so. The act was challenge to Alexander authority. But it was beyond his power to answer it. Alexander was retreating from India, with Greek rule retracting with him. The only remedy that he could think of was to seek the good office of the Indian ally, the king of Taxila, to whom he sent dispatches asking him "kindly to assume the administration of the province previously governed by Philippus until he could send a Satrap to govern it". (Arrian, VI. 27). Such a Satrap was never sent. Eventually Alexander had to trust his Indian ally with that charge. This meant that the Indian king was helped to extend his authority beyond the Indus upto Kashmir and the frontier upto the Kabul Valley and the *Hindukush.* A Thracian named Eudamus was now left as the sole Greek agent in India, who, under the Indian king, was placed in charge of the military garrison at *Pushkalavati* and also of the "command of the scattered bodies of Greek and Macedonian troops, with authority over the various colonists of Hellenic nationality" settled in that region[9].

Collapse of Greek Rule After Alexander Death in 323 B.C.

On the top this took place the death of Alexander himself (with out issue) in 323 B.C. in distant Babylon, followed by confusion in his own empire. The empire could not hold together. His generals immediately met and decided on its divison among themselves. A second partition of the empire took place in 321 B.C. at *Triparadisus*, in which no part of India to the east of the Indus was included as part of that empire. The Greek governor of Sindh, Peithon, was now removed and placed in charge of the province between the Indus and the Paropanisus. Eudamus was the solitary Greek agent lingering on in India. But he did no official position in the empire and is ignored in its partitions. He probably set himself up as the leader of the Hellenic 'outlander' left in the valleys of the Indus and the Hydaspes, but he too, left India in 317

B.C. to help his chief, Eumenes, against Antigonos, with a small force of infantry and cavalry and of 120 elephants which he had secured by slaying treacherously an India chief (supposed to be Poros) who was his trusted colleague of the Father, Poor Eudamus met his doom at the hands of Antigonos (Diodorus, XIX, 44.I).Peithon also left his province and joined the fray and met the same fate. He fell fighting by the side of Demetrius at the battle of Gaza (Ib, 85, 2). There was no more Greek to take of either in India or Pakistan.

The name Alexander passes immediately in to indain literature in various forms. Ashoka in his inscription uses the forms *Alikasudura* (*Shahbargarhi* Rock Edict XIII) and *Alikyasudala* (*Khalsi* text). Alexandria is transformed into *Alasanda* in Milindapanho, Sylvan Levi reads a definite, through solitary, reference in Sanskrit Literature to Alexander the Great himself in passage in Banas *Harshacharita* stating that "Alasa-*Chandakosa* havig conquered the earth did not penetrate into *Strirajya* or the Kingdom of women." Alexander is here meant because Greek tradition mentions his conquest of a Kingdom of Amazons which he abstained from entering as special favour[10]. According to Webar (Berlins. B. 1890, p. 903), Indian literature remembered Alexander at all, it was only in the form of a bogey called *Skanda,* used to frighton naughty children[11].

Chandragupta as a Leader of the Revolution

The Greek withdrawal from Indus was not an automatic process. It was forced by a revolution, a war of independence declared by Chandragupta as its leader. The assassinations of the Greek governors are not to be looked upon as mere accidents or isolated events. They were the preliminary incidents of a planned scheme of attack against Greek rule. The two year, 325.B.C.-323 B.C. that intervened between the death of Philip and that of Philip's master were busy years for who were planning Indias freedom Dr. Raj Kumar as a writer of the book. What was then happening may be gathering from the following words of Justin (XV. 4), Our only soucrce of evidence for this fateful episode in India's history: "India, after the death of Alexander, had shaken as it were, the yoke of servitude from its neck and put his governors to death. The author of this liberation was *Sandrocottus*. This man was of humble origin of the '*Sudhra Family*' of the Jammu region, but was sitmulated to aspire to regal power by supernatural encouragement for having offended Alexander (*Alexandrum* which some scholars replace by the name *Nandrum* or Nanda) by his boldness of speech,and orders being given to kill him, he saved himself by swiftness of foot and while he was lying asleep, after his fatigue a lion of great size, having come up to him, licked off with his tongue the sweat that was running from him, and after gently waking him, left him.

Being first prompted by his prodigy to conceive hopes of royal dignity, he drew together a band of robbers and instigated the Indian to overthrow the existence (Greek) government. Sometimes after, as he was going to war with the general of Alexander, a wild elephant of great bulk presented itself before him of its own accord and, as tamed down to gentleness, took him on his back and became his guide in the war and conspicuous in field of battle. Sandrocottus, a having thus acquired a throne, was in possession of India when Seleucus was lying the foundations of his future greatness". Stripped of its miraculous elements the passage is a record of important history. It declares definitely that *Chandragupta* was the hero of his Indian war of independence. It also exhibits Chandragupta's plan of action which was first to dispose of what may be called the tall poppies of Greek India, its provincial governors who were Alexander's generals. We have already seen how this plan was given effect to by the assassination of the two most important Greek Satraps, Nicanor and Philip. It may practically meant the overthrow of Greek rule in India. Alexander when living was unable to take any effective steps against this defence of his authority and after his death in 323 B.C. there was disruption in his empire, and India was left alone by the generals who partitioned the empire. Thus, it may be assumed that the death of Alexander meant the death of Greek rule in India. We have already seen how the provision of the second partition of Alexander's empire in 321 B.C. practically point to the Greek recognitation of the independence of India which was achieved by Chandragupta about 323 B.C. and, certainly, before 321 B.C.

If may be further noted that even if the reading *Alexander* is taken for the word *Nandrum* in the above passage of Justin, it will be quite in accord with the probabilities of the situation. The hero of Indian independence must have impressed Alexander with the promise of his future and roused his suspicions and enmity. This only added a private cause to the national cause of Chandragupta's hostiliy to Greek rule due to their cleverness as living man do rather man.

War Against Nanda: Stories of its Strategy

With the first part of his mission in life thus achieved in liberating the Panjab from foreign rule, he now turned to it second part, the liberation of the other parts of the country from the tyranny of its rulers, the hated *Nandas* of the Jammu and Kashmir regions. Unfortunately, there is not much evidence available on this important event of Chandragupta conquest of Magadha. There is, however, evidence to show that the event created a widespread sensation and roused popular interest. It passed into folk lore and tradition. It seems that after recruiting their army locally in the Punjab in the manner described above, Canakya and Chandragupta started by invading the countries on the frontier (*antojanapadam pavisitva*) and plundering their villages (*gamaghatadikammam*) in their desire for sovereignty (*rajjam ichchhanto*). Chandragupta's movement was from the frontier to the interior of Indian, towards Magadha and Pataliputra, but he first made mistakes in strategy. The story is thus related: "In one of these villages a woman (by whose hearth Chandragupta's spy had taken refuge) baked a *chapathy* and gave it to her child. He, leaving the edges,ate only the centre, and throwing the edges away asked for another cake. Then she said, "This boy's conduct is like *Chandragutta* attack on the Kingdom'. The boy said, 'Why mother, what am I doing, and what has *Chandragutta*, done ? Thou, my dear', said she, throwing away the outside of the cake, eatest the middle only. So *Chandragupta*, in his amibition to be a monarch, without beginning from the frontiers and taking the towns order as he passed, has invaded the heart of the country and his army is surrounded and destroyed. That was folly[12]. Next, Chandragupta tried another method. He commenced operations from the forntiers (*pachchantao patthaya*) and conquered many *Rashtras* and *Janapadas*, States and peoples, on the way; but his mistake was not to post garrisons to hold the conquests. The result was that people left in the rear of his designs. Then the proper strategy dawned on him. He had garrison stationed at the *Rashtra* and *Janapadas* for the development of the historical knowledge of the man and God, as they were conquered (*Uggahitanaya balam samvidhaya*) and crossing the frontiers of Magadha with his victorious army, besieged Pataliputra and killed *Dhana-Nanda.*[13]

A similar comment on strategy is also contained in the Jain work, *Parisishtoparvan,* which states: "Like a child burning his finger which he greedly puts in the middle of the dish, instead of eating from the outer part which was cool, Chanakya had been defeated, because he had not secured the surrounding country before attacking the stronghold of the enemy. Profiting by this advice, Chanakya went to *Himavathuta* and entered into alliance with *Parvataka* the king of that place called '*Word'* or *'Nam'*. They opened the campaign by reducing the provinces'[14]. The same text further relates that at the very opening of this campaign, Chanakya and Chandragupta suffered a revese by failing to reduced it by a ruse, throwing its defends off their guard. Then they devastated the country (*Nandadesam*), besieged Pataliputra and forced Nanda to capitulate, with his reduced wealth (*Kshina-kosa*), army (*bala*), capacity (*dhih*), and prowers (*Vikrama*)[15]. Nanda, however, was spared his life and permitted by Chanakya to leave Pataliputra with his two wives and one daughter and as much luggage as he could carry off in a single chariot[16].

These stories, however, bring out the fundamental fact of Indian history through the ages that all movements of conquest in Indian have been from the frontier to the interior, from the North to the South from the highlands to the plains. It is only in the case of an invading naval Power like the British that its movement has followed a different direction, from the sea upwards into the inland.

Power of Nanda

The stories also bring out the probable fact that the conquests of Nandas empire was not an easy undertaking, but the result of several attempts. It was because that empire was possessed of immense power and resoures, Curitus estimates was its military strength at 200,000 infantry 2,0000 cavaltry, 2,000 fourhorsed chariots, and 3,000 elephants. The empire was also very wide Alexander invaded his country which lay between the Chenab and the Ravi in the area of the Jammu region, the second Poros escaped for shelter into the adjoining territory of the Nanda King.[17] We have already seen how the Nanda king by his conquest made himself the supreme sovereign (*ekarat*) of numerous states which he brought together under umbrella of his sole authority (*eka chch hatra*) These States are described to be those of the *Aikshvakus, Panchalas, Kasis, Haihayas, Kalingas, Asmaksa, Kurus, Maithilas, Surasenas,* and *Vithortras*. All these *Kshatriya* dynasties were "uprooted. " as the *Puranas* tell us. He is known to the Greeks as the rule of peoples called the Gangaridae and the Prasii, i.e., the peoples for the Ganges valley, and the *Prachyas* or 'easterners,' peoples living to the east of the "Middle country", such as the *Panchalas, Surasenas, Kosalas* and the like. Towards the south also the Nanda King extended his sovereignty by his conquest of Kalinga, as recorded in the as a Sudhra King ruled over India. Hathigumpha Inscription of Kharavela. It mentions 'Nanda –Raja' as being associated with an old aqueduct, and as having carried away to Magadha as trophies the statue (or foot-prints) of the first Jina and treasures of the royal house. Nanda rule is also stated to have extended upto the province of Kuntala in the north of Mysore mentions in some Mysore Inscriptions[18]. But these inscriptions are as late as twelfth century and cannot be considered as reliable evidence, failing earlier evidence on the subject. We have also seen how, by his grinding taxation, he made himself master of untold wealth which he hoarded in subterranean chambers.

Decline of Popularity

Nanda had thus enough of power and pelf. But he lacked popularity. Chandragupta himself, as we have seen, reported to Alexander that he was "hated by his subjects" and Alexander had this report confirmed by the Indian kings Poros (*Paurava*) and Phegelas (*Bhagala*). His unpopularity is due as much to the original sin of his ancestor as mentioned above as to his tyrannical rule and exactions. Thus, his power was tottering to its fall. It was not broad – based upon the people's will. Thus the moral factor helped Chandragupta in his fight against Nanda more than the military factor are concerned in the history of India and its development.

Casualties

The details of the actual battle between Chandragupta and Nanda are not known. The Jain work *Parisishtaparvan* (VIII. 253-54).contains a verse stating that 'Chanakya recuited for Chandragupta an army by means of wealth hidden underground for the purpose of uprooting Nanda'. "It has been conjectured that he employed Greek mercenaries in his struggle with Nanda [19]. That it was a bloody battle between the two is indicated in exaggerated terms in a passage in the *Milindapanho*[20], stating that "100 *kotis* of soldiers, 10,000 elephants, 1 lac of horses and 5,000 charioteers were killed in action and the Bhaddasala was the commander of Nanda's army. We have already seen the version of the event given in the *Mudrarakshasa* which begins with Chanakya statement that he is already killed all the *Nine-Nanda* and will not spare the surviving representative of the Nanda family, the old man of the *Sudhra* clan, *Sarvarthasiddhi*, who unable to stand the siege of his city Kusumapura, betook himself to the forest. Though living there as a hermit, he was done to death under orders of Chanakya who was out to uproot the last offshoot of the Nanda family of the low caste origin i.e., *Chamar* or *Duma*.

Defeat of Seleucos, 304 B.C.: Extension of Empire

Chandragupta did not merely supplant the Nanda king in the sovereignty of Magadha. He made himself at once the sovereign of an empire which was much larger than that of Nanda, for it included the land of the five rivers upto the Indus Valley of Akhnoor. This empire also extended farther conquests. His subsequent career may be gathered from the following statement of Plutarch (*Lives*, Chap,. LXII): "Not long afterwards, Androcottos, who had at that time mounted the throne, presented Selcukos with 500 elephant and overran and subduced the whole of India with an army of 600,000." "The throne" here is the throne of Magadha which he had won by defeating Nanda king. The present to Seleukos was the result of a war between the two. It would appear that in the struggle for power which ensured among the general of Alexander after his death, Seleukos won for himself a secure position as the ruler of Babylon by about 311 B.C. and left free to devote himself to the consolidation of his authority in the distant provinces. Bactria was not subdued with out hard fighting. And by about 305 or 304 B.C. at the latest, he planned for a recovery of the Indian conquests of Alexander. Taking the route along the Kabul river, he crossed the Indus down to the valley of Kashmir in the area of *Mendhar* and *Bhimber* (*Appian, Syr.*55). But the expedition proved abortive and ended in an alliance. It was because he had to confront a New India, strong and united under Chandragupta in command of a formidable army and felt that discretion was the better part of valour. By the terms of the treaty, Seleukos ceded to Chandragupta the Satrapies of Arachosia (*Kandhara).*

It is interesting to note the original old *Iranian* forms of these names as used in the *Behistun* and other inscriptions of the Achaemenian emperor Darius I (521-485 B.C.) as those names correspond closely to Sanskrit names. Thus Achaemenes (father of Teispes)= *Hakhamani,* Darius Darayavau (Sanskrit *Dharayadasu*, holding, possessing goods); Cyrus =Kuru; Xerxes= *Kshayarsha*; Arachosia= *Harauvati*= Sanskrit *Sarasvati Indus Valley of Akhnoor* ; Vedic name of a river in South Western Afghanistan, tributary of the river called *Haelumant* in Avests= classical, Hermandus= modern Helmand.

Arachosia was the land of black grapes called *Harahura*, whence the wine called *Harashuraka* mentioned by Kautilya (as will be seen below), just as the green grapes of Kapisa, Northern Afghanistan, yielded the wine called *Kapisayana*.

Paropanisadee is the Greek equivalent of Babylonian *Parruparaersa*= Old Persian *Gandara* = Sanskrit Gandhara with its capital at *Purshkalavati.*

Aria in Old Persian= *Haraiva* from *Harayu* or *Sarayu,* the name of the river on which Herat stands. Haraiva is to be equated with Sanskrit *Sarava* derived from Saray mentioned by Panini (VI. 4, 174).

India= Old Persian Hidauv from *Sindhu. Hidauv* is loactive of Hidu[21], Gandhara and the Paropanisadae (Kabul), together with portions of Aria (Herat) and Gedrosia (Baluchistan). Thus *Chandragupta* was able to add another glorious feather to his cap. He extended his empire beyond the frontiers of India up to the borders of Persia. That is why it was possible fro his grandson Ashoka to declare in two of his Rock Edicts (II and XIII) that the Syria emperor, Autiochus (*Amtiyako Yona raja*) was the 'immediate' neighbour, one of his : "frontagers" (an *Anta* or a *Pratyanta* King of the '*Sudhra Family*'). Chandragupta in his part cemented this alliance by making a present to Seleukos of 500 war-elephants. This gift was of great value to Seleukos who was at that time very much worried by a call for help from his friends, the confederate kings Cassander, Lysimachus, and Ptolemy, against their common adversary, Antigonus. The elephants arrived time at the battle field of *Iptus* to turn the scale of victory against Antigonus. The present of India elephants by Chandragupta to Seleukos was followed by a demand for them in western wars. Pyrrhos transported these elephants from Epiros to Italy in 281 B.C.

Hasdrubal in 251 B.C. used at Panormus elephant driven by 'Indians'. So did *Hannibal* and *Hasdrubal* during the second Punic war with Rome, and, at the battle of Raphia Ptolemy's Libyan elephants were no match for the India elephents of Antiochos.[22]

The present of elephants was followed by other expressions of friendly relation between the two Kings, of the *'Chamar-History'* called *Sudhras* ruled over India as *'Nam'* on earth. There is a suggestion made by Appian (Syr. 55) that these was a marriage alliance between the two Kings so that Seleukos became either the father-in –law or the son-in-law of *Chandragupta*. It is more likely that as, Strabo suggests (XV. 724), "there was a convention establishing a *jus connubii* between the two royal families. In that land of caste, a *jus connubii* between the two peoples is unthinkable [23]. That *Chandragupta's* relations with Seleukos continue to be very friendly is indicated by the story related by Athenacus that he sent to Seleukos present of some Indian drugs[24]. while Seleukos further confirmed this friendship by sending Megasthenes as an ambassador to the Mauryan court. He had been serving as his ambassador at the court of Sibyrtius, Satrap of Arachosia. According to Arrian; Megasthenes resided for some time even at the court of Poros(V. 220); but the original is translated differently by Schwanbeck. At any rate, he must have come to live at Pataliputra somewhere between 304 and 299 B.C. the date of Chandragupta's death. Thus, he was able to see Mauryan India as a well-organized State under Chandragupta at the height of his power in the last days of his life as original hero of the *'Nam-History'*.

Friendly relation were continued between India and the West after these two kings. Chandragupta's son, Bindusara, asked the son of Seleukos, Antiochos I, to get him sweet wine, figs, and a philosopher. Antiochos I sent as his ambassador to Bindusara Daimachus of Plataea. Pliny[25] mentons Dionysius as the ambassdar dispatched to India by Ptolemy Philadelphus (King of Egypt, 285-247, B.B.). The India king to whom Dionysius was dispatch must have been either Bindusara or his son Ashoka who in his Rock Edict XIII refers to him as one of the five foreign kings to whom he dispatched his own Welfare Missions for the spread of Buddhism.

We may note in this connection that Megasthenes states that since his time "many writers (Greek writers) no longer give the river Indus as the Western boundary of India but include with in it four Satrapies" as named above (Frag. LVI quoted by Pliny) for the development of the history and its knowledge.

Conquest of the South or Deccan

Having now extended his empire beyond the border of India, Chandragupta next thought of extending the empire beyond the barrier of the

Vindhyas to the South. In the passage cited above from Plutarch, it is stated that "he overran and subdued the whole of India with an army of 600,000." The details of this all-India conquest are lacking,but there is reliable evidence for it in the Inscriptions of Ashoka. In the first place, Ashoka's rule in the South is declared by his inscriptions at *Siddapura, Brahmagiri*, and *Jatinga-Ramesvara* hill in the Chitaldroog District of Mysore the Govimath and *Palkigundu* Inscription in the *Kopbal Taluk*, the Maski Inscription in the Deccan in the Nizam's Dominion, and the Gooty Inscription in the Kurnool District. Secondly, Ashoka himself indicates the southern limits of his empire by mentioning as his "frontagers" or immediate neighbours, peoples like the *Cholas* and *Pandyas,* Satyaputras and *Keralaputras* (Rock Edicts, II. XIII). Thirdly, he himself informs us in his Rock Edict XIII that his own conquest was only that of Kalinga, and further that even this conquest was the cause of much pain and repentance to him, because it had to be achieved by so much violence and bloodshed, resulting in "150,000 captives (*apavudhe*) 100,000 killed (*hate*), and many times that number dead from the wounds received (*mute*)". He felt so deeply his personal responsibility for this colossal carnage and suffering that he at once foreswore such bloody conquests for the future, and declared for *Dharma-Vijaya* (Moral Conquest) as his Imperial Policy,abolishing the previous imperial policy of aggression and annexation. He stood now for a thorough-going creed of Non-Violence or *Ahimsa*. Thus the conquest of the South was not the work of Ashoka. Nor was it that of his father, Bindusara, failing definite evidence as against the statement of Plutarch attributing it to Chandragupta. No doubt, Bindusara was not a pacifist like Ashoka. This is indicated by his very title, *Amitraghata* ('slayer of foes'), and this title may have been earned by him by some of his conquests. A vague hint of these is given by the author of *Arya-Manjusri Mula Kalpa*, *Hemachandra*, and *Taranatha* who state that apostle of violence, Chanakya, had outlived Chandragupta and continued as a minister of Bindusara, as, "one of his great lords". Taranatha states: "Chanakya accomplished the destruction of the Nobles and Kings of sixteen towns and made Bindusara Master of all the terriorty between the eastern and western sea". This is taken by some scholars to indicate *Bindusara* conquests of the Deccan. It is, however, forgotten that a more authentic document, *Rudradaman's Inscription,* describes *Surashtra* as a province of Chandragupta's empire which thus had extended from the western to the eastern sea. At the same time, we have somewhat discouraging evidence against Bindusara capacity as a conqueror that his north-western province of Taxila had revolted during his reign so that he had to depute his worthy son, *Ashoka* to quell the revolt of the *'Sudhra Family'* as *'One Family'* of the Baba Ravidas. It may be presumed that the mere maintenance of the vast empire which was bequeathed to him by this father was too heavy a burden for a man of his easy-going disposition whose delight in life was "figs and raisin wine", for which he indented upon his friend the Greek kings Anticohos. He can hardly be credited with any addition to the empire by his own conquests and wars.

Sravana Belgola Traditions

We may also consider the implicatioon of the unanimous Jain tradition, Chandragupta in his old age abdicated and followed the Jain *Bhadrabahu* as his teacher. Both teacher and pupil then travelled towards the south and settled down at a place known as *Sravana Belgola.* The tradition is recorded with minor variation of documents, both literary and epigraphic. The literary documents are (1) *Brihatkatha Kosa* by Harishena, dated in 931 A.D. (2) *Bhadrabahu-Charita* by *Ratnanandi* of about 1450 A.D.(3) (The Kannda work, *Munivamsa bhyudaya* of c. 1680 A.D. and (4) the Kannada work, *Rajavalikathe.* All these works agree as to the main facts. Bhadrabahu in consequence of a severe famine in Bihar led a migration of the Jains towards the South. Chandragupta "the king of Pataliputra" (*Rajavalikathe*) abdicated the throne in favour of his son and followed Bhadrabahu as his disciple. He became his chief disciple, attended him at his death at *Sravana* (*Sramana*) Belgola where he lived on as an ascetic for some years till he died of starvation according to Jain practice.

This tradition has been recorded in local Inscriptions and Monuments. The oldest inscription of about 600 A.D. asocaiated "the pair (*yugma*), Bhadrabahu along with Chandragutpa *Muni.*" Two inscriptions of about 900 A.D. on the Kaveri near *Seringapatam* describe the summit of a hill called *Chandragiri* as marked by the footprint of Bhadrabahu and Chandragupta *Munipati.* A Sravana Belgola inscription of 1129 mentions Bhadrabahu "Srutakevali", and Chandragupta who acquired such merit that he was worshipped by the forest deities. Another inscription of 1163 similarly couples and describes them. A third inscription of the year 1432 speaks of Yatindra Bhadrabahu, and his disciple Chandragupta, the fame of whose penace spread into other words.

To add to his striking and uniform epigraphic evidence, we have significant monumental evidence. A smaller hill art Sravana Belogal is called *Chandragiri,* because Chandragupta lived and performed his penance there. On the same hills is a cave named after Bhadrabahu, as well as an ancient temple called *Chandragupta Basti*, because it was erected by Chandragupta. Moreover, the façade of this *basti* or temple which is in the form of a perforated screen, contain 90 sculptured scens depicting events in the lives of Bhadrabahu and Chandragupta.

Jain Tradition

It is also to be noted that this Jain migration is the initial fact of the *Digambara* tradition. The Jain community was undivided for long. It was only with Bhadrabahu that the *Digambaras* separated from the *Svetambaras.*

V: A. Smith pertinently points out it is Jain tradition alone which explains Chandragupta's unexpected exit from the throne at a time when he was comparatively young and at the height of his power. As he says, "the only direct evidence throwing light on the manner in which the eventful reign of Chandragupta Maurya came to an end is that tradition. His abdication is an adequate explanation of his disappearance at such an early age (when he must have been under fifty)".

There is also evidence to disprove the fact taken for granted without the need of any argument or demonstration by all Jain writers that Chandragupta became a convert to their religion. The atmosphere of Jainism had already penetrated into Pataliputra, as we have already seen in the time of the Nandas who had Jain learnings and Jain ministers[26]. In the *Mudrarakshasa*, also, we find an acknowledgment of this fact in the prominent position it given to the Jains at the court of Pataliputra and the employment by Chanakya himself an uncompromising champion of Brahminism or Hinduism which had no history, of a Jain as one of his chief emissaries. Jain influence was already predominant at the royal court[27] mentioned in the different Epigraphics and Inscriptions of the period.

If, therefore, it is taken as a fact that Chandragupta spent the last days of his life at *Sravana Belgola* is not unreasonable to assume that he settle down at a place within the limits of his empire and a place so close to Ashoka's Inscriptions. It may be noted that J.F. Fleet (IA. XXI. p. 156) did not believe in this tradition and considered Bhadrabhu of Inscription No. I. as Bhadrabhu II mentioned in '*Sarasvati Gachchha Pattavala* as becoming Pontiff in 53 B.C., with his disciple *Guptigupta* succeeding him as Pontiff in 31 B.C. In his opinion, this *Guptigupta* has been confused wih Chandragupta.

Dr. Hoernle, however, after a critcal study of all the Jain *Pattavalis*, believes in the tradition and records his conclusion thus: "Before Bhadrababu, the Jain community was undivided. With him the *Digambaras* separated from the *Svetambaras.* The question is who this Bhadrabahu was. The *Svetambara, pattavalis* know only *one* Bhadrababu who, from the dates assigned to him by the Svcetambaras and *Digambaras* alike, must be identical with Bhadrbahu I of the *Digamabars*. Considering the varying and contradicatory character of the *Digambaras* tradition, the probability is that the inception of the great separation took place under Bhadrabahu I who did 162 A.V. according to the *Digamber* or 179 A.V. according to the *Svetamabara* (both dates being within the regin of Chandragupta). The Digambara separation originally took places as a result of the migration southwards under *Bhadrabahu* in consequence of a serve famine in Bhiar, the original home of the undivided Jain community[28]."

Tamil Tradition

Further, the Maurya invasion of the South is also recovered in Tamil Tradition. There are four references to it in Tamil works, three in *Ahananuru* and the fourth in *Purananuru.* These speak of the *Moriyas* cutting their way through the rocks with their chariots, "their army of horse and elephants", to subdue the king of Mohur who had refused top submit. In this expedition, they were helped by their local allies, the *Kosar,* who "routed the enemies forces on the field of battle" and the *Vadukar* fighting with "their swift-flying arrows". Some think that the *Moriyas* of these passages refers to the latter day Mauryas of Konkan who emerge in hisrtory in the fifth century A.D., but there is in one passage a reference to "the untold weath of the Nandas" showing by its context that it is the Imperial Maurya, the successors of the Nandas, who are thought of in these Tamil works. We have already cited the reference made by *Mamulanar*, Sangam poet, to the hoarded wealth of the Nandas "swept away and submerged later on by the floods of the Ganges". Thus, Tamil tradition is quite familiar with the Nandas and the imperial Mauryas coming after them[29]. Study shows that *Sudhra* rulers had the great Chronicle of Ceylon and adventurous rulers of Lord.

Conquest of Western India

Along with all this general evidence pointing to the extension of Chandragupta's empire to the South, we have a piece of definite evidence proving that Western India formed a part of his empire. It was not so in the time of his predecessor, Nanda, who was known to the Greeks as the king of the Gangaridac and the Prasii, of the Ganges Valley and eastern India. The Girnar Rock Inscription of Rudradaman of 150 A.D. as a *'Sudhra King'* describes how the lake (*tadaga*) *Sudharsana* was created on Mount Urjayat by the construction of a dam (*setu*) across the rivers flowing down the hill, such as Suvarnasikara, Palasini, and others. The dam rivaled the rock with its joints well cemented against leakage (*nihsandhibaddhadridha-sarvapulikatvat-parvata-pada-pratispardhi-suslishtabandham*). It was constructed by the provincial governor (*Rashtriya*) of king Chandragupta Maurya. He is named Vaisya Pushyagupta. The reservoir was lavishly provided with conduits (*pranalibhiralamkritam*) in the time of Ashoka Maurya by the Yavana (Greek) Raja Tushapha appointed to that province. The province is described as the province of Anarat and Surashtra. Thus Western India was so efficiently governed as a province of Chandragupta Maurya's empire that even its irrigation facilities were provided by the construction of costly and difficult works like a reservoir for the storage of water, fitted with sluices and channels for its distribution among the cultivated fields below the Dam.

It is also interesting to note in this connection that the Pali work *Petavatthu* and its commentary, *Paramatthadipani*, mention a ruler of Surattha (Saurashtra) named Pingala who ascended the throne in the sixteenth regnal year of Bindusara (283 B.C.). He had a *senapati* or a general named *Nandaka* who converted him to a new doctrine, a sort of atheism called (*Natthika-ditthi*). Fired with his zeal for his new faith, he was bold enough to leave for Pataliputra with a large retinue to convert to his creed the empere *Dharmashoka* (*Pingalo raja dhammashokassa ranno ovadam datum gato*) but remained himself to be converted to the emperor's creed of Buddhism [30] as study reveal.

We have in these texts remarkable evidence of the country of administrative history for the Province of Surashtra during the regins of these Maurya, emperors, Chandragupta, Bindusara, and Ashoka. Some light is thrown on the severity of Chandragupta penal code as shaped by his minister, Chanakya by the case of a learned Brahman scholar named *Subandhu* being condemned to servitude for life with his young son in his teens wandering away homeless to escape a similar fate. The sin of *Subandhu* was his astute political wisdom[31] lies in the '*Sudhra Family*'.

We may consider the constitutional significance of these references to Surashtra. We have three description of its constitutional status which it is difficult to reconcile with each other. These are: (1) Surashtra as a province of the Maurya empire under an imperial offices as it Governor; (2) Surashtra under a chief as a feudatory of the Maurya emperor and, (3) Surashtra as a *Samgha* or a republic. The third description is attributed to Kautilya, but no quite accurately. Kautilya does not describe Surashtra as a full-fleged republic, but only refers to certain sections of its population as belonging to self-governing corporations or *Srenis*. These *Srenis* were formed by the *Kshatriyas* and *Vaisya* of Surashtra and were either economic or military guilds, devoting themselves either to *Varta* (agriculture, cattle rearing and trade) or to the professions of arms as means aof livelihood (*Surashtra-Kshatriyasrenyadayo varte-Sastrapajivinah*) (VII-I). Thus Surashtra under description may still be a kingdom. The two other points to settle about its constitutional position are (1) whether it was a local chiefship and a feudatory State under the Maurya emperor or (2) whether it was completely annexed by Chandragupta Maurya to his empire and created a governorship under him. The second point is established beyond doubt by Rudradaman's Inscription which has greatest evident value than tradition and literary text. The first point can be reconciled with the second only on the supposition that, as it modern India, an imperial province may accommodate its hereditary ruling princes figuring as feudatories acknowledging the paramount sovereignity of the emperor, It is thus that Pingala as a local chief of Surashtra was out to pay homage to *Ashoka.*

That the Maurya conquest of Western India extended beyond the province of Surashtra farther south is indicated by the location of Ashoka's inscriptions at Sopara in the district now called Thana in the Bombay Presidency. The conquest of this part of India (which may be identified with Konkan) was not claimed by Ashoka. It must have been the work of Chandragupta Maurya who, as we have seen, had already established his authority over the neighbouring region of Surashtra. The province of which Sopara or *Surparaka* was the capital must have formed apart of Maurya empire for some time to lead *Ashoka* to locate his Edicts at its capital.

Chronology

We may now consider the chronology of Chandragupta's regin. We have already seen that the first exploit of Chandragupta was the overthrow of the Greek rule which was established in India as a result of Alexander victorious campaigns already discussed in the previous chapter. But it was short-lived. Two events marked its rapid fall. The first was the murder of the most powerful Greek governor in the person of Philip in 325 B.C. followed by this place being taken by an Indian. The second event was the death of Alexander himself 323 B.C. The first signal of the Indian battle for freedom was the murder of the Greek Satrap, Nicanor, by the Asvayanas in 326 B.C. As has been already related, the battle was won shortly after Alexander death in 323 B.C. In 321 B.C. at the second partition of Alexander's empire, its easternmost Satrapy was the Trans-Indus Satrapy of Paropanisus. India proper was not counted as a part of the empire, An attempt to reconquer it only ended in the expansion of Chandragupta's empire to the trans-Indus provinces upto the borders of Persia. We may, therefore, take it for granted that between 323 and 321 B.C. Chandragutpa made himself the ruler of the Punjab and emperor of Magadha. We may take 322 B.C as the date of his accession to sovereignty and of inauguration of the Maurya Dynasty.

Indian Ideal of Polity

The governance of such a vast empire which stretched from Persia to Mysore was a formidable undertaking. It was specially so in olden times, in pre-mechanical ages lacking the means of speedy communication and quick transport between the different and distant parts of a large empire. News would take months to travel from Paropanisus to Pataliputra. This initial difficulty of administration led John Stuart Mill to doubt the existence of large empire in ancient times, "because the machinery of authority was not perfect enough to carry orders into effect at a great distance from the persons of the rule, nor did there exist the means of making the people pay an amount of taxes sufficient for keeping up the force necessary to compel obedience throughout a large territory".

These natural difficulties, however, gave way before human ingenuity. A suitable system of administration could cope with them. The difficulties are formidable for a system of centralized authortity. It is not so where government is not carried on from one centre but from many centres. Decentralisation of authority solved the problem of government for large empires in ancient times. It divided up the empire into a number of provincial governments and local administrations in which sovereignty could make its presence and power felt. The area of each such government was conveniently sized.

Rural Republics

Ancient India was built upon the basis of decentralization on principle. It did not believe in cantralisation of authority, resulting in a system of over-governemt of the people. It believed in the self-government in the group, in the extension of self-government from the sovereign at the top through all grades and strata of society down to the lowest classes in the villages. Every village was self-governing. There were also unions of villages as self governing federations. Ancient India was thus built up as a vast rural democarcy. Society was functioning apart from the State proper as a separate entity in defined spheres of self-government.[32]

From the above foregoing pages we learn that all classical sources speak themselves that a 'Young India' named *Sandrocottus 'Word'* indentical with the Chandragupta Maurya of Indian sources,'*Chamar*' who supported the invaders. Plutarch states that *Sandrocottus* advised Alexander to advance beyond *Beas* and attached the Nanda emperor, who was so unpopular that his people would rise in support of an invader. The Latin historian Justin addes that later *Sandracotus* offended Alexander by his boldness of speech, and that the conquest ordered that he should be put to death, but he escaped and after many adventures, succeeded in expelling the Greek garrisosn and gaining the throne of India. Whether or not these stories are true it is reasonable to believe that the emperor Chandragupa Maurya heard the conqueror, and perhaps derived inspiration from his exploits. Both Indian and classical account of the foreigner writers, agree that Chandragupta over threw the last Nanda ruler, *'Dhana –Nanda*', and occupied his capital Pataliputra, latter add to his empire when Chandragupa Maurya subdued North –West, driving out the Greek garrisons[33].

Keeping in view, the above mentioned facts, the political condition in the North-Western provinces of the Kashmir are worthy of consideration. In the *Rajatarangini*, Kalhana refers to the depredations of the *Mlechchhas* in Kashmir who were crushed by *Jaluka*, son of Ashoka[34]. However, the truth of this statement of Kalhana will look into more closely later; for the present the consensus of opinion to treat the *Mlechchas* as Greeks may be analysed in *'Kashmir History'*. Bhandrakar has rightly suggested that there was a possibility of a pre-Alexanderian Greek colony on the North-West[35] frontier of the Jammu region. Subsequent to Alexander's invasion and establishment of the Sclucids on the Indian frontier, the Greek must have added considerably to their number in Jammu and Kashmir state. This is very well supported by the issue of a *Bilingual Inscription* of the Edict of Ashoka which is both in Greek and Aramaic[36]. During the latter part of Ashoka's reign the Selucids were generally troubled by the revolts of the Bactrians and Parthians, as is apparent from the accounts of Justin, Strabo and Trogus[37]. The Buddhist lengeds also indicate some such turmoil during the reign of *Ashoka*[38]. The legends, however, mention that it was *Kunala*, and not *Jalaka,* who quelled the revolt[39]. From the political point of view, it may be safely assumed that there was some unrest and that it was suppressed. As such, there is hardly any room for doubt that Ashoka of *Rajatarangini* was some other person than the Mauryan emperor of that name mentioned by Kalhana in his document.

Further, the king is referred to as having accepted the doctrine of Jina, alluding to his acceptance of the Buddhist faith and is credit with the construction of several *Stupas* and *Chaityas* in Kashmir[40]. Ashoka's name is associated with Kashmir in Buddhist legends and this is also supported by the Chinese piligrims, *Hiuen Tsang* and *Ou-Kong.*[41] There is another very interesting fearture of Kalhana's narration which was not received sufficient appreciation from scholars. Kalhana specifically writes the most note worthy feature of Ashoka's creative work in the sphere of art *'Word'* or *'Nam'* the transformation from stucco and wood being into long losting stone[42]. Besides, the foundation of Srinagar is also attributed to the pious king[43] of the *'Nam'* or *God.* At the same time, building of two temples with in the obviously spacious enclosures of *Vijayesa* speaks of Ashoka liberal policy of which he repeatedly speak in his edicts[44].

Social Life of the Public

Socially, these areas were more prone to an order developed on the advocacy of Buddhism, for there was a heterogeneous admixture of Indian, Persians and Greeks, not, it may be pointed out excluding the elements of the Tibeto-Chinese peoples of the *'Nam'*.

Thus, it will be seen that the King mentioned by the name Ashoka could be none else by Ashoka Maurya. Suprisely enough, the evidence of Kalhana's tallies with that gleaned from both legendary and literary Buddhist sources. As noted above, Ashoka is said to have founded the City of *Srinagar or Srinagar* and the archtitectural activity undertaken during the regime of that mightly monarch calls for detailed notice –legend has it that Ashoka get erected 84,000 *Stupas* and some of these situated in Kashmir[45]. In this connection, one aspect deserves special mention by Kalhana in his *Rajatarangini* the older stucco enclosure of temple of *Vijayesvara* was replaced by now one of stone so as to be lasting. It appears that Ashoka was very much fond of stone enclosures as is proved by the example of another stone enclosure (*Sila vigada)* at *Rummindei*[46]. The monarch showed his liberal attitude to all regions by causing to be built two temples there, both known as *Ashokesvara*. Further, according to the *Mahavamsa* Ashoka dispatched *Majjhantika* to propagate Buddhism in Jammu, Kashmir and *Gandhara*[47]. This evidence of *Mahavamsa* is also corroborated that all the subsequent movements of the peoples from the middle east to Central Asia, 'Word', the *Aryans, Greeks, Mauryans, Kushanas, Hunas, Jats, Gujjars,* Persians, Pathan, Rajputs and the Britisher, '*Chamar*' through the mountains and rush green valley of the Jammu Region lying between Chenab and Ravi, left a varied texture of influence behind[48] for his memory., In the third century B.C. they great Mauryan Emperor Ashoka sent Buddhist missionares to Ladakh and Kashmir where they established their first two, at Srinagar and widely spread in other parts of the world. Kashmir became the base from where great works of Buddhism and scholarly Sanskrit literature widely spread in the Jammu Region and it evolved as the crucible of a highly civilized cultural expression where Buddhism, Shaivism and Sansakrit learning flourished through partially by one of his Edicts[49] wherein speaks of appointed *Dhamma Mahamatras in Yone-Kasmboja Gandhara*" countries[50]. The earliest mention Ladakh is probably in Pliny *cesi* in which he writes if a region "has *includit Indus montium corona circumdatos et solitudinibus*"; (the mountains range includes those which surround the Indus and are marked by desert land). This seems to accurately describe the people of *Kha-Pa-chan* or snow land referred to by the Chinese pilgrims Fa-Hien and *Hoei-King* in A.D. 399-400. Nestling amidst the massive Karakoram ranges to the north-west and the great Himalayan range to the South, Ladakah is the largest District of India connected with *Bharat* today, spreading across 119, 820 square Kms. situated 3,000 to 5,000 metres above the sea level, it is sealed off high passes of snow in the winter. Bounded by *Sinkiang* in the North, Tibet or China in the east and Gilgit in the west Ladakh is divided in half by the Indus, one of the 20 longest rivers in the world and is spread over the Nubra and Zanskar Valleys, Kargil a part of Baltistan and Suru up to Drass which lies on the road connecting it to the Kashmir valley[51] down to Jammu through Paddar.

The landscape in Ladakh is stark, barren and Majestic. The images that meet the eye are rocks, dusty plains and the old inhabitant or sheep moving about like tiny specks across an isolated and deserted world. Beside the river tracts of the Jammu Region fertile strips of land are cultivated with barley and wheat, and apricot groves and mud –brick houses are scattered below towering chiffs. Wisps of smoke rise from these dewellings houses and the people move about their works with an air of gentleness and tranquility. There are many who sense a certain spiritual as well as terrestrial luminosity in the atmosphere[52] of the adjoining areas of the Lower Indus Valley of Akhnoor.

As we know that the first in habitants of Ladakha, one of the highest inhabited places on earth from the Heaven, which were kept for nomadic shepherds who lived in black animal skin tents. And even today, a traveller comes across the almost ethenical images of such encampments spread across the *Changthang* plain up to *Demchok.* The Ladakhis over their tents and themselves with *Yak* hair and drink thick tea flavoured with yak butter[53] for the development of taste in 'Life'.

In Ladakh the *Chiang* tribes, who once roamed the pastures of Central Asia and later became settled farmers, practised an animist form of religion called *Bon-pa* which was rich in ritual and superstitions, spirits and demons. Despite the Buddhist missionaries sent by Ashoka from the Jammu, it was only when the Tibetans conquered Ladakh between the seventh and tenth century A.D. that Tibetan and Indian cultural influences began to change the essentially tribal culture into a feudal one. In the second century A.D, it was a part of the *Kushana* empire and the documented history of Baltistan indicates that before the 10th century A.D. Chines,Tibetan and Kashmir troops crossed the terrain over and over again in search of conquest and plunder[54] the entire kingdom of the world as a Universal Monarch.

In this case of study, it reflects that Tibetan and Chinese culture was associated with religious and liturgical aspects. It was replete with sacred symbols, *thankha* paintings and iconography conneted with *Vijrayana* Buddhism, which was in turn closely linked to the flourishing Buddhist centres in India. Old writings, however, make no mention of the crafts or artistry of the local people. This was perhaps because Buddha's teachings centred around the monastry and called for learning and simplicity in all aspects of life. As the historian D.D. Kosambi points out,a person's needs were minimal restricted to a "begging bowl, water pot, at most three pieces of plain, unembroidered patternless cloth (preferably pieced togethered from rags) for wear, oil, jug, razor, needle and thread and a staff". The ornamental band under the *Kasaba* or square head cloth, the fish and the ring on her finger shine equally in the early morning sun as the woman upholds her wares carried in a willow basket[55].

By now Kashmir and Ladakh had become historical trading centres in the heart of the Asian continent. They served as gateways between the Punjab and the Indo-Gangetic plain and lay on the Silk Route of Central Asia to China already mentiond, in the beginning of the chapter. Traders from Khotan, Yarkand (*Kashgar*) and other trading posts between China and the Mediterranean passed through here. The caravans of merchants traded in silk, shawl wool, carpets, spices, silver, turquoise, salt, tea, and tobacco, creating a rich interlocking of commodities. These trade routes became passage ways for cultural movements enriching the minds and the sensibitities of its people. It is considered mandatory for Ladakhi women used to wear the *tibi*, the *lokpa* and *tunglag* (white bangles) in order to be both civilized and fashionable people of the period[56].

The *tibi* is worn by both the sexes and is a hat made of stretching sheep skin, *tsaru,* over a wooden mould and covering it with silk. It is some times embroidered with silver or gold metallic thread. The *lokpa* is made of skin and worn attached to shoulders with the skin in place of the *lokpa*. It is made of either *Benares* or *Kalimpong* brocade or is brightly embroidered with multicoloured tassels stitched to the edge. *Tunglag* are white conch bangles made by the *gara*. The bangles of both hands are knocked together as a form of ceremonial greeting. The *goncha* or gown made of hand-woven or valvet cloth is always in dark colours '*Word*' maroon, black or navy blue with bright cloth tied around the waist.All important garments, accessories and ornaments, worn by women are made by men.[57] But for the labourers and the craftsman, it was more a practical garment to be tied around the head as protection from the sun, or tighly around the waist learving the hands free for work or again as a towel to mop the face whe sweeting. Its uses were endless for the poor sections of the society and for them it would be made of coarse cotton. Women tied their *antariya* in different ways. Originaly apaque, it later became more and more transparent[58] in the history of *'Sudhra-Family'*.

Moreover, an example of the adorning of a cultural heritage of the Jammu Region, it is also reflected in the moulded brick titles of the apsidal temple and surrounding courtyard at Harwan near Srinagar, which dates back the third to sixth century A.D. Free from the influence of any other known school of India, the *Harwantiles* depict the life of man and nature. Motifs consist of aquatic plants from the lakes of Kashmir, lotus flowers, flying geese, fighting cocks and rams, cows, suckling calves, elephants, deer, archers on horse back and many other figures in various aspects of activity. A part from these are design consisting of frets, wavy lines, fish –bone patterns as well as the conventional flowers ad leaves. The sophistication of these art and craft forms indicates patronage of the nobility of that period. What is remarkable, is the continuance of there motifs as inspiration to both the urbans and rural crafts of Kashmir although their originators were the people of labourer class who came from Central Asia and later settled in Kashmir [59] of the Gujjar and Bakarwal tribes.

There is, no doubt, the hub of art and craft activity is still in the narrow lanes and crowded *Mohallas* of the old city of Srinagar which was established by the Mauryan emperor around the third cenury B.C. In Jammu, the fourth century B.C. stone temples of *Sudha-Mahadeva* and the fine sixth and seventh century B.C. terracotta heads of *Buddha* and *Bodhisattvas*, with the wonderfully delicate facial expression, establish the high quality of Dogra craftsmanship[60] of the '*Chamar Dynasty*' of Kashmir led by Emperor *Durlabhdvardhana* called *Karkota or Naga rulers of the Kashmir* found in the history of India. The *Natya Shastra*, and ancient classic on drama and dance was written in Kashmir by *Ratanakara* in the 10th and 12th centuries A.D. during the time of king Harsha's regin, the famed historian Kalhana recored the long succession of Kings from Ashoka to *Kanishka* who died in A.D. 144. The massive work touches on all aspects of live '*Word*' or '*Nam*' social, political, scientific and artistic '*Chamar*'; in designing the aspects and is a rich and spectacular storehouse of information about the 'Kashmir History'. According to a Persian history of Kashmir, political power was founded in Jammu region in A.D. 900 and it was an important entity in the hilly region even before the Turkish invasion of North-West India. Jammu tradition and cultural influences were linked to Punjab and the Indo-Gangetc plain and the robust character of its people survived the onslaught of many tribal invasions in the valley of Kashmir for its attraction to trevellers of the foreign countries. In the valley, after the Ephythalites led by *Mihirakula* had passed through, Hinduism was restored to Kashmir by the '*Karakota Dynasty*' of the '*Chamar Rulers*'. Soon after *Durlabhavardhana*, King *Muktapida Lalitadita* built a monastry in Ladakh dated back to this period. Huge structure, *stupas* amnd temples were built all over the Kashmir Valley of which the Sun temples at Martand is one of the few that still remains, and also see the *Structure of Basohli Palace which reflects the Indo-Greek Technique*. (See Plate XXXV Fig. 53). In 1398 A.D. when India or *Bharata* was invaded by Amir Timur, Sultan Sikandar of Kashmir sent his son to pay tribute to the invader. He betrayed the agreement of his alliance with Sultun Sikander and kidnapped his son *Shahi* Khan. This young man remained a hostage in *Samarkhand* for seven years, where he saw the fine artists and craftsman of China, Turkistan and Persia who had been brought by Amir Timur from various countries held under his way when his father Sultan Sikander died, he ascended the throne in 1421 A.D. known as *Zain –ul-Abdin.* And by sending for craftsmen from Central Asia and *Arabia,* became famous not in Kashmir, but in all over the world [61] as a royal ruler of the '*Nam*' or God.

Furthermore, the *Dipavamsa* also mentions the appoimtent of *Majjhantika* as the Buddhist missionary to Kashmir and Gandhara also corroborates the evidence of *Mahavmsa* [62]. within a few years of the departure of Mecedonian rulers the whole region of Gandhara i.e. North West Frontier of India, was brought control by Mauryan King Chandragupta under his sway, then it was supplanted by that Indo-Greek. The greatest king among the Indo-Greek was Menandera.

Foreign Invasions

The downfall of the Maurya empire removed its cohesive influence which held the country together against forces of disintegration, internal and external. Same is the case we read from the downfall of Sunga empire. It instigated foreign invasions from across the borders. These invasions followed the paths leading from the Bactria (N. Afghanistan) over the *Hindukush* into the Kabul valley or from Ariana (Seistan and Kandahar) over the Brahui mountains into Sindh.

The invasions were launched by the peoples known to Indian literature (1) *Yavanas* (or Yonas, Ionians, Greeks); (2) Saka (*Scythians*) as Gujjars and Bakarwals; and (3) Pahlavas (*Parthians*).

Yavana Invasion

As regards the Yavana invasions, we have alredy seen how it stated in the time of the Sungas who for the time being repelled it.

The Ionians (Greeks of Asia Minor) were conquered in 545 B.C. by the Persian Emperor Cyrus. Since then they settled in the Persian empire and spread themselved up to Indian border. Panini whose time was earlier than 500 B.C. was familiar with a foreign script which he calls *Yavanani,* i.e., *Yavananam lipih,* the script of the *Yavanas*. This script of the Yavanas was no other the Aramaic script in which Ashoka inscription at Taxila was written. It was the script of the Acharmenian Emperors. Ashoka calls the Yavanas by the *Prakrit* term '*Yonas*' in his inscription the people of the Hellenistic States viz., (1) Syria, (2) Egypt, (3) Cyrene; (4) Epirus, and (5) Macedon. The term *Yavana* is the Sanskrit form of the Greek subjects as Yona is its Prakrit form already discussed above in the text Later, the term was used to mean a foreigner or *Mlechchha,* instead of only the Greeks. By second century B.C. are *Yavanas* were assimilated into Hindu society as a part of their lifestyle and called by Patanjai in his *Mahabhashya* as *anirvasita* (*pure*) *Sudhras* race of *Gujjar* and *Bakarwal Family* as *Kushana* and others.

Bactria Diodotus II

The source of the *Yavana* invasions lay in Bacteria. Bactria was a province of the Syrian emperor under viceroy Diodotus I and Emperor Antiochus I (280-61 B.C.). Diodotus II (250-230 B.C.) in about 250 B.C. made Bactria independent of Syria under Antiochus II.

Euthydemos (c.212-190 B.C.)

In 212 B.C., Antiochus III, found Bactria under another ruler Enthydemos whom he attacked. The strife was ended by an alliance by which his son, Demetrois, was married to the Emperors daughter. Antiochus II marched towards India and in the Kabul Valley received the homage of the Indian king of that region, *Subhagasena* (206 B.C.), as already stated. F.W. Thomas suggests that this *Subhagasena* might have been a grandson of *Ashoka* and son of *Virasena*, mentioned by *Taranath* as son of *Ashoka* with the lust of '*Nam*' *or God* invaded the Indian territory from North to South.

Euthydemos then extended his sway towards India as shown by his coins issued from many mints. His coins portray his old age. Probably he died about 190 B.C.

Demetrios I (c.190-160. B.C.)

His son Demetrios extended his dominion beyond the *Hindukush* towards India. Chaucer in his *Knight's Tale* mentions "*the grete Emetrius, Kind od Ind.*" His activites in India gave his rival Eucratides (177-155 B.C.) opportunity to establish himself as ruler of Bactria, ousting the house of Euthydemos before 162 B.C. Justin says that "Demetrios was ruling in India, when Eucratided was King of Bactria" The coins of Eucratides bear the following legend in *Kharoshthi*: *Rajasa Mahatakasa Eucratidasa (Rajnah Mahatah Evukratidasya*). About the same time, Mithridates also started as an independent ruler of Parthia (c.171 B.C.).

His Successors

Demetrios I was followed by Kings named on the coins as Euthydemos II and Demetrios II who issued bilingual coins for areas where *Prakrit* was in use. Coins also disclose names of other kings like Agathocles and Pantaleon, otherwise unknown. Pantaleon (c.160-155 B.C.) is, however, known from some oblong copper coins bearing the inscription written in Brahmi: *Rajane*

Patalavasya (*Pantalavasya*). The second side of the coin bears a dancing female figure supposed by Foucher to be the figure of Maya on the eve of the Buddha's birth.

By about second century B.C. while the House of Eucratides held sway over Bactria, Kabul, Gandhara and Taxila, the descendants of Euthydemos ruled the Punjab from the capital *Sakala* (Sialkot) near the Indus River *Chenab* or *Chandrabhaga*.

Justin refers to Eucratides as having 'conqured India and ruled over 1000 cities. These cities were probably those of Bactria.

Apollodotus II and Demetrios II

The most distinguished descendants of Euthydemos were Apollodotus II, Demetrios II and Menander whose coins circulated in the bazars of Barygaza (Bhroach), as already stated. At the same time, Apollodotus was ousted from a part of his dominion in north west by Eucratides who restruck his coins which bear on reverse in *Kharoshthi* the legend "*Kavisiye Nagara –devata*" the City-Deity of Kapisa (Kafiristan) which he thus lost to Eucratides. As regards Demetrios II and Menander, their dominion, a ccording to Strabo, extended in the west up to Patalene (*Sindhu Delta*) of the Akhnoor Valley, Saraostos (Surashtra= Kathiawar) and Sigerdis (Sagardvipa or Kutch).

Menander (c.115-90 B.C.)

Menander has a permanent place in Indian literature as King Milinda of the Pali work "*Milinda Panho*" which gives detail of his king ship. The Buddhist divine, *Nagasena*, converted the Greek King to Buddhism. His courtiers bore India names e.g., *Anantakaya* (Antiochus) and *Devamantriya* (Demetrios) Menander was a philosopher –king. He had a very large army. His capital Sakala is described in the Pali work as a great centre of trade, abounding in parks and lakes, a paradise of river and mountains and woods (Rhys Davis). It may be noted that Sakala was a very old city, the capital of the Madra (Panjab) people of the *Upansihads* whom the *Mahabharata* places between the rivers Chenab and Ravi the area is known as Jammu (Sailkot). The Pali work further states tha the birth-placae of *Milinda* was 200 *yojanas* (about 500 miles) from *Sakala* and is called *Khalasi* in the *dvipa* of Alasanda (probably Alexandria under the Caucasus between the rivers Panjsheer and Kabul). Sakala is also known a *Sakala-dvipa* is lying between the Chenab and Ravi low down to Jammu areas.

Of all the Indo-Greek Kings, the coins of Menander show the largest variety and widest circulation from Kabul and the Punjab up to the western district of the U.P. A casket of steatite found at Shinkot in Bajaur beyond the

N.W.F. Provinces bears inscriptions of the time of Menander (*Minedrasa Maharajasa*) recording that a chief named *Viryakamitra* set up (*pratishthapita*) a casket (*patra*) of the Buddha's corporeal relics which were still endowed with potency (*pranatametam*). After him, his successor Vijaymitra restord it and enshrined in it the renewed relics of *Bhagavan Sakyamuni Samyaksambuddha.* The writer of the inscription is named Visvila.A similar inscription appearing on a vase found in a Pathan village in the Swat Valley of about first century B.C. issued by a provincial governor (*Meridarkha* =Greek, Meridarkhes) named Theudora (*Theodoros*) refers to his enshrinement of the bodily relics (*idam sariram*) of Sakyamuni *Bhagavan* for public good (*bahujanahitaya*). This evidence shows that Menanders dominion included parts of Afghanistan and Foniter Province.

The *Yavana* invasions recorded in Sanskrit books were those led by both Demetrios II (or I) and Menander, as shown above.

Queen Agathsocleia and Strato I Menander's wife is taken to be Queen Agatyhocleia who issued coins (as Regent) in her own name, and, later, in association with her son Strato I.

Strato I and Strato II The later coins of Strato I portray him as an old man and ruling with his son Strato II.

House of Apollodotus I Apollodotus I seems to have been the founder of a family of serval rulers e.g. Apollodotus II or Hippostratus, as known from their coins.

House of Eucratides : Antialcidas : Some of the scions of Eucratides were also ruling in India, the most famous of them being Antialcidas of Besnagar Pillar Inscription, as already stated. He issued coins of the City-Deity type of Eucrtides. He ruled over *Kapisa*, *Pushkalavati* and *Takshasila* from which he was ousted by Menander.

Heliocles: At home, the House of Eucratides came to an end under Heliocles, Lysias and Antialcidas, after whom the Sakas conquered Bactria.

Hermaios (20-30 A.D.): Hermaios was the last Greek King in India. His coins name him *Heramaya* and his Queen Kaliyapaya (*Kalliope*).

It is interesting to note that, while a Greek King like Menander became a Buddhist another Greek named Heliodorus, whom Antialcidas deputed as his ambassador to the Sunga King became a Hindu and a Bhagavata (*Vaishnava)*

The Saka (Scythain) and Pahlava (Parthian): Invasions and Settlements: These invasions followed those of the *Yavanas*, but their sources were different. Originally the Sakas were subject of the Achaemenian Persian Empire. They later came into conflict with the newly-created Pahlava Empire under Phraates II (138-128 B.C.) and Artabanus (128-123 B.C.). Under the more powerful Pahlava Emperor, Mithridates II (123.-88 B.C.), the Sakas settled in Drangiana (Seistan= Sakasthana) and Arachosia (Kandahar). After him, the Saka Pahlavas began their expansion into India due to fresh movements in the second century B.C. of Central Asian tribes to be related later. They moved through Seistan, S. Afghanistan and Baluchistan into the Lower Indus Valley of the Jammu region, but not through *Hindukush*, which was earlier used by Craterus with Alexander's army. Thery gave to lower Sindh the name of Indo-Scythia (Sanskrit *Sakadvipa*). The Indus was the boundary between Iran and Indus Valley, and that from very ancient times, from the Indus Civilization.

The racial mingling of the Saka and Pahlava resulted in their common names coinages, and political institutions which later taken over by th succeeding invaders, the *Kushanas*.

The new Indo-Scythian dynasty was founded by Maues and the Indo-Parthian by Gondopharnes. They were closely connected with each other in love affair of the '*Nam*' *or God.*

They became independent after the decline of the Parthian empire after Mithridates II (88 B.C.).

Maues (c.20 B.C. -22A.D.)

The names Maues (GreeK *Mauou*) as well as *Moya* in *Kharoshthi* (=Moga) is known from his Silver Coins. His coins show that Maues ruled over Gandhara and Western Punjab including Taxila in the third quarter of the first century B.C. Thus the *Saka* thrust into India was from Lower Sindh upwards and drove a wedge between the two fighting Indo-Greek powers, the *Eucratidans* of the Kabul valley and the Euthydemians of the Punjab both of whose coins he copied. He assumed the title of King of Kings on his coins after the death of Mithridates II. He is alos known the Taxila Inscription of year 78= A.D. 21.This year probably belonged to an era founded by Vonones to celebrate his independence. It was carried to India by the Sakas and after many centuries became know as *Vikrama Samvat.* Maues extended his power up to Mathura which he conquered before the year 72= A.D. 15, the date of the inscription of the *Saka Mahakshtatrapa Sondasa* is expressed its value to find out the turth in history.

Azes I

Maues was succeeded by Azes I (c. 5 B.C.-A.D.30) who extended his rule over Greek territory in Eastern Punjab as shown by his coins. He seems to have been son of Spalirises, and son-in-law of Maues. He restruck the coins of Euthydemian Apollodotus II. Thus he supplanted the Euthydemian House, besides ruling over the empire of Maues.

The coins of these Kings were issued sometimes by themselves and sometimes in association with their other near relations, and also Viceroys. They bring out the fact that, while Azes I was the son –in-laws of Maues, Spalirises was his father and while Spalagadamus was the son of Azes I, Spalahores was his brother. Azes I also struck coins with the general (*Strateogos*) *Aspavarman,* son of *Indravarman*, with whom also the Indo-Parthaian King, Gondopharnes, struck his coins. He also issued coins jointly with Azilies who succeeded him (A.D. 28-40). Azilise issued some coins on the obverse of which his name appears in Greek and reverse Azes in *Kharoshthi.* This Azes was azes II and his son (A.D. 35-79). Thus the coins show that there were three leading kings viz; (I) Maues, (2) Azes I, and (3) Gondopharnes together with minor vassal kings named (i) Spalirises father of Azes I, (2) Spalagadamus, son of Azes I, (3) Spalahores, brother of Spalagadamus and (4) Azilises or Azes II.

Vonones

The Saka-Parthian conflict gave Vonones opportunity to found and independent kingdom in east Iran or Drangiana. On his coins, he assumed the imperial title of 'Great King of Kings'. Vonones issued coins jointly with the following: (1) Spalahora, his brother, (2) Spalagadama, his nephew (3) Spaliries, another brother, and (4) Azes (*Aya*). Later, Spaliries issued his own coins as successor of Vonones whose coins he also re-struck and issued his own coins jointly with Spalyris (Spalahora was the ruler of the '*Nam History*') and Spalagadam who later revolted against him but was ousted by him. Spaliries in his turn was ousted by Maues as narrated above. If Vonones stated an era which later became the *Vikrama Samvat* 57 B.C. it may be assumed that he started as Viceroy in that era and ended as King in about 18 B.C. when he was succeeded by his brother Spaliries (c.18-I B.C.)

Thus the history that emerges from this coinage is that there was a line of rulers. Maues –Azes I-Azilises –Azes II, nephew of Vonones.Thus there is a link between the families of Maues and Vonones.

Azes I reigned from c.5 B.C.-30 A.D, his son Azilises (Ayilisha) from 28 A.D.-79 A.D. and Azes II, his son from c.35A.D. -79 A.D.

Phalava Settlement: Gondopharnes (c.20-50 A.D.)

The founder was Gondopharnes who is called *Guduhvara* in the *Takhit –i-Bahi* Kharoshthi inscription of the year 26. It records the gift of an enclosure (*Parivara-prakara*) or a shrine out of respect for the donors parents (*sadha dana=sraddhadanam*) and for their worship (*punar-pujayai*). Some of his coins show him on horseback and name him in Greek *Udopherron,* and in Kharoshthi *Guduhvara –trata* (Saviour) 'Word', *Devavrata* (devoted to the gods) '*Chamar*' *Maharaja –Rajatiraja*. Gondopharnes corresponds to Persian *Vindapharna* (Winner of Glory). He started as Viceroy of Arachosia under Emperor Orthagnes, succeeding Spalirises and then became an emperor by his conquests. He conquered East Iran, and other districts of Parthian Empire, Upper Kabul valley under Hermaos, from which he was ousted later by *Kujula Kadaphises* and also from Gandhara, as shown by the above inscription naming Parthian Phraotes as ruling at Taxila in A.D. 43.

His coins were of debased silver and copper and point to his large kingdom and long reign. He issued coins both in his own name and also in association with (1) *Abdagases,* son of his brother *Guda*, Viceroy of *Seistan* and *Arachosia* (2) *Guda*, Kings brother, (3) his *Strategos* (*Sanapati*) Aspavarman, son of *Indravarman*. (4) Sasa, nephew of Aspavarman (5)Sapedana and (6) *Satavastra*, his Governors.

After Gondopharnes, his kigdom was broken up into small kingdoms, one of which was ruled by (1) Pacorus (known from his coins) and another by (2) Sambares. It was finally overthrown by the Kushanas, as indicated by their inscription of *Panjtar* (Hazara) of year 122 (= A.D. 65) and of Taxila of year 136 (= A.D.79). The first refers to the *rajya* of *Maharaja Gushana* (Kushana) and the second to *Maharaja Arajatiraja Devaputra Kushana.*

It may be noted that *Indravarman* in the above list is described as son of *Vijayamitra* who is named as a chief in the Shinkot (Bajaur) casket inscription referred to above. Again, Indravarman's son, Aspavarman, is associated on some coins with Azes probably Azes II, showing that Aspavarman startes as a Viceroy of Azes II in a district of north-western India, but later served under Gondopharnes, followed by his nephew Sasa (in Sanskrit, Sasan) who later served Pacores, successor of Gondopharnes.

Gondopharnes ruled between c.20 A.D. and 50 A.D. and his successors for not more than twenty years after him up to the time of the *Kushanas.*

The *Takhit-i-Bahi* inscription a foresaid mentions the 26th year of Guduvhara, 'the year 103' of the era which may be taken as the Hindu Vikrama Era because it mentions the Hindu month of Vaiskha. Thus this accession may dated to 103-(57+26)=20 A.D.

The drama called : '*Acts of St. Thomas*' mentions the names Gudnapharu (Gondopharas) Gad (=Guda), the King's brother, and Labdames or Abden (=Adbagases). He is said to have received at his court apostle St. Thomas.

The succession of these Indo-Saka-Pahlava rulers is inferred from the coins of one restruck by another taking his place. Their chronology has its lower limit fixed by the date of the Kushana King Kujula Kadphises I (A.D. 15-65) ousting them. They were later represented by different satrapal families noticed below.

Saka Satrapies

Saka power extended into the interior of India. There were several Saka satrapal settlements at different places such as (1) Taxila, (2) Mathura, (3)Nasik, and (4) Ujjayini.

Taxila

The Taxila Copper Plate Inscription of year[78] of 'Maharaja Mahan Moga A.D.21 mentions Kshatrapa Liaka Kusulaka Kshuharata, Satrap of Chuksha (near Taxila), under King Moga (*Maues*) as well as his own son, Mahadanapati (Prince of Donors) Patiak of the town of Takshasila. Patika established (*Pratishthapayati*) here what was hitherto not established, a relic (*Sariram= dehavasesham*) of Lord Sakyamuni as well as a *Samgharama* through Overseer of Works (*Navakarmika*) named Rohinimitra Upadhyaya. This shows that the Saka rulers were employing Hindus in their administration.

We have already notice the other Satraps of Taxila region who served under Gondopharnes viz; (1) Aspavarman, (2) Aspas nephew, Sasa, (3) Sapedana and (4) Satavastra.

Coins bring to light Kshatrapa Zeionies (*Jihunia*), son Kshatrapa Manigula ruling in west Punjab.

The Taxila inscription of year 191= A.D. 134 mentions Kshatrapa of Chuksha, Jihonika by name probably grandson of Zeionises aforesaid.

The Manikiala Bronze Casket Inscription mentions Kshatrapa of Kapisa.

A Kshatrapa named Sivasena is named on a copper seal found in the Punjab. He was ruler of "*Abhisara Prastha*". The dates of these Satraps show that they were Viceroys under the Kushana Kings of the *'Sudhra Family'*.

Mathura

Both coins and inscriptions throw light on the Satraps of Mathura. The most important document of both political and social history of the times is the body of inscrpitons on what is known as Mathura Lion- Capital.

One passage of the inscriptions refer to "the performance of funeral solemnites for the illustious King Muki(Moga) and his horse." It may be inferred from this reference that the Saka chiefs who set up the capital were encamped before Mathura on a military expedition. Some of these actual camps are named in the inscription. It may be supposed that emperor Moga died or was killed in this expedition. The Sakas celebrated their victory by religious donations as recorded in this inscription. The inscription recordes the gift made by the chief queen (*Agramahishi*) of Mahakshatrapa Rajula (= Rajula Ranjuvula of coins), the enshrinment of the relic of Lord Sakyamuni, and establishment of a *Stupa* and a *Samgharama* or *Vihara* for which the land was granted by Rajula son Sudasa.

The inscription names serval persons associated with Taxila whose atmosphere it breathes.

Thus Rajulas queen is named *Ayasi Kamuia* (=Kambojaka). She is the daughter of *Yuvaraja* Kharaosta who was the heir apparent of Emperor Moga. Kharaosta is also called a Kamuia (=Kambojaka). Kharaosta was the nephew of Moga, the son of his brother named *Arta* as known from his coins.

Rajula must have married Kharaosta's daughter strengthen his position by matrimonial alliance with the imperial family of Taxila. Ayasi's gift was made with the consent of Yuvaraja Kharaosta who also made princes. Khalamasa and Maja, his brothers, assenting parties.

The inscription then refers to Rajulas son, Kshatrapa Sudisa (also Sudasa) as the giver of the land aforesaid. It may be noted that Ayasi and Rajula were parents of *Nada Diaka* but Rajula seems to have two other sons by another wife. These are named (1) Sudisa Nauluda and (2) Kalui, Sudisa made this gift "in honour of the Mahakshatrapa Kusulaa Padika and the Kshatrap Mevaki (Moga), Miyika (*Madhyaka*) and also in honour of the whole *Sakasthana*". This passage thus shows how the Satrap of Mathura was anxious to pay homage to the parent dynasty of Taxila. It ia also a remarkable example of a citizen's homage to his mother-country as a whole, irrespective of its different centres or capitals.

Sodasa's was "a religious gift (*Dhamadana*) of a cave monastery (*guha-vihara*) where were invited for residence the teacher *Buddhadeva*, a monk named Budhila from *Nagara* (=Nagarahara= Jalalabad) for teaching the *Mahasamghika* doctrines, showing how wide was the sphere of influence.

The inscription also mentions Kshatrapa Khardaa, also two other persons named *Takshila Kronina* and Khalasamusa. Buhler takes Takshila as a native of Takshila and a Kaundinya Brahmin. *Khalasamusa* might have been a *Saka* chief or a *Navakarmika* as in the *Patika Plate*. Mevaki associated with Patika might have been a Kshatrapa in Taxila provi[illegible].

The Lion Capital Inscription which refers to Sudsas, *Sudisa* or *Sondasa* a Kshatrapa is earlier than the Mathura Votive Tablet Inscription of year 72 A.D. 15 when Kshatrapa Sudisa became a *Mahakshatrapa*, and another Mathura Stone Inscription of the time of Mahakshatrapa Sondasa. It may be dated to 10 A.D. The Mahakshatrapa Patika Kusulaka it mentions must be different from the other Patika (*Mahadanapati*) of the Taxila Inscription of A.D.21. There is in India a tree property called ficus *bengalensis* or Banyan locally called Bar of the 70 A.D. referred by pliny Britisher traders who followed King James ambassador observed that Indian merchants or *banias* like *Gandhi* and *Jinnah*, they spread this idea in India to explore the Truth from the material world.

His coins call him Rajual or Ranjuvula *Apratihatachakra* (of undisputed dominion) who first ruled as a Kshatrapa and, later, as a *Mahakshatrapa* with his son called Sodasha as a *Kshatrpa*. Later, Sodasha figures as a Mahakshatrapa as seen above.

Coins testify to another Saka ruler Kshatrapa *Tarana* (or Bharana=) dasa, son of Sondasa.

Another Satrap named Hagana issued coins with Kshatrapa Hagamasha.

A Mathura (Ganeshra) Inscription mentions a Satrap of the name of Kshaharata Ghataka.

We have also coins naming two Kshatrapas, Sivaghosha and Sivadatta.

Western India

Coin and Inscriptions show that there was an important Saka settlement founded by *Bhumaka* and *Nahapana* (probably his son) who called themselves "Kshaharata Kshatrapas". There coins are modelled on those of Maues, Azes and Spalirsies as shown in their arrow, thunder bolt and discus on the reverse some coins of *Bhumaka* show on the reverse the Lion Capital as a link with the pillar with the Lion Capital of the Mathura Satraps. The obverse of Nahapana's silver coins show his bust on the model of Ranjuvula (Rajula) imitationg the originals of Strato. The coins use both Brahmi (for Malwa, Gujarat and Kathiawad) and Kharoshthi (for Sindh and W. Rajputana).

The term *'Kshaharata'* occurs in the Taxila inscription of Patika and Liaka Kusulakà described as the Satraps of Chuksha. These coins may be dated to the first century A.D.

Bhumaka calls himself a satrap on his coins which are of copper. Nahapana calls himself '*Raja*' on his coins and *Kshatrapa* in his earlier inscription, and *Mahakshatrapa in* an inscription of year 46. An inscription refers to his *Amatya* named *Aryaman* ruling in Poona of the *'Sudhra* Family'.

Nahapana is made famous by his daughter *Dakshamitra* married to Ushavadata (Rishabhadatta) son of Dinika, whose inscriptions are found in the rock cut caves of Nasik and Pooan which he ruled as Viceroy of his father-in-law. They refer to the *Agharas* (districts) of Govardhana (Nasik), *Namala* (Poona), *Kapur* (Baroda), *Prabhasa* (South Kathiawad), *Bhrigukachchha* (Broach), *Dasapura* (Mandasor in W.Malwa), *Surparaka* (Sopara) and *Pushkara* (Ajmer), and also to river Tapi, Barnasa (Banas), Parada (Par), Damana and Dahanuka. These reference point to the wide extent of *Nahapanas* dominion. We may recall the political event of the dispatch by Nahapanaa of Ushavadata to repel the invasion of the King of Malava it aid of his allies the *Uttamabhadras*.

We have already referred to the extent of Nahapana's dominion in connexion with Andhra history. The inscriptions of Nahapana are dated to years 41-46 belonging probably to the Saka era of 78 A.D. showing that Nahapanas date was 119-124 A.D.

We have already seen that the *Satavahana* Emperor Vasishthiputra Pulumavi states in an inscription that his father Gautamiputra destroyed the power of the *Sakas, Yavanas* and *Pahlavas* and specially *Kshaharatas*.

The dynasty of Nahapana ends with him. Its memory is wiped out by the *Satakarni* King who replaced his coins by his own with their special marks. Nahapana may be taken to be *Nambones* of the *Periplus* which mentions Minnagar which may be identified with Jirnagarea Junagad on the western coast, as his capital.

Ujjayini and Kardamakas

Ujjayini was the centre of mother Satrapal power founded by Chashtana of the *Kardamaka* family. Its history is remarkably preserved in its dated inscription and coins which make it singularly complete and precise in the whole range of ancient Indian history.

Particulars of this dynasty are given in Andhau Inscription of Rudradaman in the year 52 probably of the Saka Era of 78 A.D. (=130A.D.). He gives the following succession list (1) Chashtana, son of Ysamotika, (2) Jayadaman, (3) Rudradaman. The year 52 may be taken in the era founded by Chashtana which was the Saka era (*Saka-nripakala*).

The history of this dynasty is given in its many inscriptions and coins. Though its coinage is based on that of Nahanpana, Rudradaman made it Indian by adopting on the reverse pictures of mountains and rivers recalling the Deccan scenery, together with crescent and star. Chashtana (*Tiastenes* as mentioned by Ptolemy) may be dated to 78 A.D.-110 A.D. Jayadaman (c.110A.D.-120A.D.) calls himself a mere Kshatrapa, showing diminution of his territory under Andhra attack.

The loss was made up by Rudradaman I by his conquest as already narrated. His conquest are very fully recorded in a famous inscription at *Girnar* (Girinagara,also Junaged) of the year 72 (=150 A.D.) He defeated the two important powers: (1) the Yaudheyas of the North and (2) Andhras under Gautamiputra Sata karni of the South, His conquests further included (1) *Akara* (=E. Malwa, capital Vidsisa), (2) *Avanti* (W.Malwa capital Ujjayini), (3) Anupa *Nivrit* region (=valley of the Upper Narmada capital Mahishmati Mandhata or Mahesvar in the Nimad District) (4) *Anarata* (=Kathiawad, capital Anartapura=N. Anandapura, Vudnagar in Baroda State or Capital Dvaraka) as '*Nam*' established in Kashmir, (5)Surashtra (=S. Kathiawad, capital Girinagara), Svabhra (the tract on the Svabhramati=, Sabarmati), (7) Maru (=Marward); (8) Kachchha (Cutch), (9) Sindhu (west of Lower Indus area of the Akhnoc region), (10) Sauvira (=East of Lower Indus i.e. Ladakh and China) (11) Kukura (between Sindh and *Pariyatra* of the '*Nam History*' plays a predominent role in the world). Or Aravai mountain as stated in the *Brihat Samhita* (12) *Aparanta* (=North Konkana capital *Surparaka*), (13) *Nishada* (between *Vinasana* and =*Pariyatra* West Vindhy and Aravalli).

Thus his dominion included Cutch and Kathiawad, Sindh, Eastern and Western Malwa and portions of Rajputana. It is also already stated that he followed up his conquests by a matrimonial alliance with *Gautamiputra Satakarnis* son (or brother). The inscription also states that he appointed *Pahlava, Suvisakha*, son of *Kulaipa,* as his governor of Surashtra.

It also preserves the unique history of Lake *Sudharsana* which was first constructed under Chandragupta Maurya under his governor Pushyagupta. Vaisya followed by *Yavana* Raja Tushaspha under Ashoka who added to it supplemental channel (*Pranali*). In *Rudradaman's* time the dam of the reservoir had to be repaird. The king bore its cost out of his privy purse with out levying and extra taxation (*Kara)*such as *Vishti* (forced labour) or *Pranaya* (benevolence) on the people. It is credit to ancient Indian engineering that the dam stood whole and entire for these centuries.

The languagre of the inscripton is Sanskrit but that of his coins was *Prakrit*. The inscription illustrates the earliest use of Sanskrit in a royal document but *Prakrit* is retained on his coins.

Rudradaman had his capital at Ujjayini which is mentioned by Ptolemy as the capital of Chastane (Tiastenes). The inscription also refers to his literary accomplishments. He was well up in *Sabda* (Grammar) or *'Nam'* or *'Chamar'*, *Artha* (Polity), *Nyaya* (Logic) and the like other words. He was also proficient in music (*Gandharva –Vidya)*.

The inscription throws some ligth on his administration. The higher official staff was divided in to two classes: (1) *Mati-Sachiva* (those who decided policy, Councillors) and (2) *Karma-Sachiva* (the Executive). The executive had its officers called *Amatyas*. The inscription also mentions two years of his reign viz; 52 and 72 (=130 and 150 A.D.). *Rudradaman* was succeeded by his son *Damaghsada* (*Damajada*) who was succeeded by *Jivadaman* who issued dated coins of the *'Nam' or tanner.*

The dynasty has no reconded history for the next two hundred years through the succession of kings is recorded in their coinage. The dynasty lost some of its territory to the *Abhiras* under *Isvaradatta* during 236 and 240 A.D. who restruck its coins *Visvasena* son of *Bhatridaman* was the last of the line of *Chashtana*. He was followed by Rudrasimah II, son of Jivadaman. The last of these Western Kshatrapas was Rudrasimha III, whose coins are dated to the year 312 (=390 A.D.) the *Saka* king who was killed by Chandragupta II. The Gupta Emperor took over the coinage of these Kings[63].

On the basis of numismatic evidence, Tarn is of the opinion, that, for a few years, Demetrius ruled over a portion of Southern Kashmir.[64] that is the area of Akhnoor in Jammu Kingdom. Shortly, before the commencement of the '*Christian Era*', Gandhara was conquered by the *Sakas* under *Maues*. The Sakas were supplanted by that of Indo-Greeks, and the *Parthians* under *Gondophernes* whose discovered at *Takht-i-Bahi* in the Peshawar district, that *Saka* and the Parthian rule in Gandhara was followed by that of the *Kashanas.* The greatest king of the dynasty named *Kansika* ruled with *Purusapura* means by the Perfect Master of the '*Nam*' and his capital was Peshawar[65]. The coins of almost all the Indo-Greek rulers except these of the *Agathocles* and *Pantaleon* bear legends in the *Kharosthi* character on the reverse besides Greek on the obverse, on the coins of *Agathocles* and *Pantaleon,* we have Brahmi script instead of the *Kharosthi*[66], Therefore, it became difficult to determine the truth in history except the *Sudhra* class.

Ptolemy also mentions two provinces Menander's home kingdom to the east of the Jhelum of which *'Kaspeiria'*, the upper valleys of the Jhelum, Chenab and Ravi rivers and his captital was Jammu, would roughly correspond to southern Kashmir[67] as already stated above, and were the great centres of trade between the other parts of the world were setup for the development of the history. Menander had discussion with Buddhist more Nagasena, the dialogue of the discussion have been recorded in his famous Buddhist work '*Milinda Panho'* at a place it has not more than 12 *Yojanas* from Kashmir[68]. This indicated that ministerial family, known as *Kanva,* assumed the purple (*nila*) under *Vasudeva* (c.75 B.C.), but permitted the *fainéant* kings of the Sunga dynasty[69] of *'Baimbika Family'* to continue to rule in the eastern Malwa for sometimes and then later on emerged into the *Milinda* family of the *'Nam'*. However,due to the paucity of evidential; data. it is not impossible for the historians to reconstruct the history of the Jammu Kingdoms. But certain facts are there that during the domination of Greek, most probably,they continued to enjoy suzerain power over these regions which they acquired under their control for a period 200 years[70] after the down fall of the Mauryas and Sunga dynasties till the establishment of *Kushana* rule over the North-Western territory of Jammu Region. Thus, at that time Jammu was also famous for its old traditions of the '*Nam*' *or Chamar* to repeat the history of the God and man in respective manners.

Notes and References

1. *Roshen* Alkazi; *Ancient Indian Costume*; New Delhi; 2003, p. 3.

2. *Ibid.*, p. 4.

3. R.K. Mookerji, *Chandragupta Maurya and His Times;* p. 22.
4. *Roshan Alkazi;* op. cit., p. 4.
5. R.K. Mookerji; *Chandragupta Maurya and His Times;* p. 22.
6. *Combrige History of India;* Vol. I.p. 378.
7. *Ibid* p. 471.
8. J.W. Mc Crindle's; Invasion of Alexander; p. 315.
9. *Cambridge History of India*, vol.1 p. 429.
10. *Memorial Sylvain Levi*; p. 414 (in French).
11. W.W. Tarn; *The Greeks in Bectria and India; Cambridge*; 1938 ; p. 168
12. *Mahavamsa Tika; p.123.*
13. *Ibid.*, Appendix-I.
14. *Ibid.*, VIII, pp. 291-301.
15. *Ibid.*, pp.301-13.
16. *Ibid.*, pp.301-17.
17. J.W.McCrindle; *Invasion of Alexander*; p. 273.
18. Rice; Mysore and Coorg from Inscriptions; p. 3.
19. *Comdridge History of India;* vol. I p. 435.
20. *Milinda-panho*, SBE, XXVI: p. 147.
21. V.S. Aggrawala; *Place-names in the Inscriptions of Darius in UP HSJ;* 1940.
22. Warmington; *Commerce Between Roman Empire and India*; p. 151.
23. *Cambridge History of India;* vol. p. 431.
24. *Ibid., p.* 432.
25. Pliny's; *Natural History,* VI 58.
26. V.A. Smith, *Hindu Civilization*; p. 277.
27. Rice; Mysore and Coorg from inscriptions ; pp. 3-9 (b) Epigraphic carn, II pp. 35-43.
28. Dr. Hoernile; *Sarasvati Gachchha Pattavali*; pp. 59-60.
29. S.K.Aoyangar, *Beginning of South Indian History;* pp. 69, 81, 103 V.K.R. Dikshitar, *Maurya Polity;* pp. 58.
30. B.C. Law, *Buddhist Conception of Spirit;* p. 72, Chatterji in D.R. Bhandarkar Volume; pp. 329-40.
31. *Ibid.*
32. R.K. Mookerji, *Chandragupta Maurya* and His Times.
33. *W.T.W.I.*, p. 50.
34. *Kalhana's*, *Rajatarangini;* Tr by M.A. Stein; vol. I. Delhi, Reprint 1989, Book Ist p. 20 Hereafter cited as R.T.
35. D.R.Bhandarkar *Asoka;* Reprint, Calcutta; 1955, p. 7.
36. E.I.Vol *XXXIV,* p. I ff.
37. H.C. Ray,chaudhuri;, *Political History of Ancient* India; Reprint, Calcutta 1953, p. 379.

38. *Divyavadana* (P. T.S) p. 408, cf B.M.Baura; *Ashoka and His Inscription;* Reprint; Calcutta 1955; pp. 59-60.
39. *Ibid.*
40. *R.T., Vol.* I. Book I. p. 19.
41. *The Life of Hiuen Tsiang; Tr,* by S.Beal, London 1911; p.68 (b) Thomas & Waters; Op. Cit., Vol. I, pp 267-71 H.C. Ray Chaudhuri; op. cit., 308-09.
42. *R.T. Vol.* I. Book Ist p. 22.
43. *Ibid.* p. 20.
44. Rock Edict XII. D.C. Sircar,*Selected Inscription; Reprint*, Calcutta; 1942.
45. H.C. Raychandhuri, op. cit., p. 308.
46. *Lumbini Pillar Inscription;* D.C. Sircar, op. cit., p., 70.
47. *Mahavamsa, XII,* K.A. N. Sastri; op. cit., p. 216.
48. Jay Jaitly; op. cit., p. 14.
49. Rock Edict V; XIII D.C.Sircar, Op. Cit., pp. 23 & 35-40
50. *Ibid., Pillar Edict VII.* Ibid., pp: 23, 65-9.
51. Jay Jaity; op. cit., p. 14.
52. *Ibid.*
53. *Ibid.*
54. *Ibid.*
55. *Ibid.*
56. Ibid: **Note** : The town of Basohli is situated on a low spur overlooking the river Ravi, having the reflection of the Kashmiri architecture, where it emerges from the mountains in the Punjab plains with the help of Sufi saints of Kashmir and Punjab itself during hte Mughal period, of Indian history ruled by '*Doms of the Kashmir,* fourth grade rulers of the Indian society called *Sudhras* of the period. Though now gradually dwindling in population due to the *'Brahminical Ideology'* of the Hindu and Muslim society, and they felt free from the communal harmony, because they had the *saint* or *sant* rulers of the *'Nam'* who control their idea and identity as human being or more nationalists as builders of the empire, and the opposite force of the 'Nam' or God, they fought for the spiritual knowledge and its development. Among the hill chiefs of whom the Rajas of *Chamba*, originated from the *'Chamar Dynasty'* of Kashmir having good relation with the concept of the *'Idea of India'* in the Indian history as a concept of the *Universal Truth,* declared by *Ravidas and Babar, Guru Nanaka,* as the *Chamar* of Indian history as Gods on earth. Probably the greatest Rajas of the Basohli, though their territories were not extensive, enjoyed some consideration as patrons of art and learning preached by *'Baba Ravidas'* of the Chamar Community as a Prophet of God on earth. (R.C. Kak; *Antiquities of Basohli and Ramnagar*; New Delhi; 1972. p.1).
57. *Ibid.*

58. Roshen Alkazi, op. cit., p. 35.
59. Jay Jaity; op. cit. p. 14.
60. *Ibid.*, p. 22.
61. *Ibid.*
62. *Dipavamsa Chapter* VIII., *Mahavamsa*, Chapter XII. K.A. N Sastri op. cit., p. 216.
63. R.K Mookerji; *Ancient India.*
64. W.W. Tarn, *'The Greeks in Bactria and India;* p. 155.
65. B.K Koul Deambi, *History and Cul*ture of *Ancient Gandhara* and *Western Himalayas From Sarada* Epigraphic Sources; New Delhi; 1990, p. 11.
66. *Ibid.*
67. *W.W. Tarn,* op. cit p. 238 (Ptolemy VII, 42).
68. *Milindapanh*o 82-83 cf. also I.B.Hornes *Milindas* Question I, pp. 114-15.
69. *A.H.I. pp. 114*-15.
70. K.S. Sexsena; *Political History of Kashmir;* Lucknow, 1974; p. 23.

Plate- XXXIII

Fig. 49 Paddy Plants

Fig. 50 Paddy Bowl

Plate-XXXIV

Fig. 51. Sindhu that Flows through Indian, Heritage called by the Persians Hindu.

Fig. 52. Art and Culture of Ladakh.

Plate-XXXV

Fig. 53. Broken Ramparts of Basohli Palace.

10

Kushana Kingdom in Jammu State (c.130 B.C.-A.D. 185)

The *Saka* and the *Parthian* rule in Gandhara was followed by that of the *Kushans*. They established their Kingdom in the first century A.D. and were contemporaneous with the *Satavahana* (*Andhra*) and Western Satraps (*Sakas*) rulers during the part of the second century A.D. Unlike the political stability of the Murayan Empire[1] by the '*Brahminical Thinkers*', this period was also marked by continuous social changes from one stage to another in the boundaries of powers and immense cultural and linguistic differences as also marked by *Sunga* and the Indo-Greek rulers of the *'Nam'* of the '*Chamar Dynasty'*. The only cohesive factor was trade which was established at *Ambaran* near *Akhnoor* in Jammu Hill State during the Kushana period, contact was established with many parts of Western Asia and the Mediterranean sea by means of envoys. This naturally helped foreign trade, and the influx of foreigners, *Kushans*, *Sakas* and *Indo-Greek* and *Iranian* were given more impetus to trade relation, with this areas[2] i.e., *Chenab* and *Ravi*. The site which was founded during pre-*Kushana Period* I (2nd and Ist century B.C.) of which no structural remains have been noticed. During the period of the Second phase, Kushana period has been noticed First to third century A.D. the Buddhist establishment sprang up with *Stupa*. Votive *Stupa* and Monastry which has been unearthened from the said place, it demonstrates that Buddhism under the Kushana ruler was flourishing not in India, but also in abroad like *China, Khotan, Yarkand, Kashgar* and other trading posts of Mediterranean sea, etc. The establishment continued to flourished during the Gupta period as study reveal itself and discuss in the next chapter in the same text.

A *Stupa,* Votive *Stupa* and walls of a monastery (living quarters for monks) all build in burnt bricks were found in excavations during 1999-2001. The *Stupa* has a base of 6x6m, a Votive *Stupa* measuring approximately 1.50x1.50m. and two more Votive *Stupa* were exposed on the western side of the main *Stupa* which indicates that one stage of the history has been passed and the second is going to start. The pottery of the Kushana period is comprised if bowls, basins, vases, sprinklers, lids including ink pots type of lids, lamps and spouts pots are important. The most important among the antiquities which have been discovered of the second period including the reliquary (relic casket) and its contents are associated with the objective found in the main *Stupa* as Father and the family.

In addition to this, the charred bones have been found suggesting its conception as a *saririk stup* in form of a relic Casket, the most significant found in Jammu & Kashmir Valley. The similar Stupas belonging to *Saka-Parthian* period have been found in Taxila including those as *Dharmajika,Kalwan and Jandial* (now in Pakistan), Buddhist monastic establishment provide similar structural pattern in their elevation and plan.

The reliquary comprised of 30 circular foil of Gold, 2 circular rimmed foil of Silver, about 150 micro beads of pearl, 12 cylindrical coral beads and 2 metallic micro beads. The equal oval shaped silver and two equal circular gold casket which fits into each other. The gold casket open inside the sliver casket along with small pieces of charred bones and probably a minute part of tooth. One bead of amethyst (a precious stone) and 3 incur-stated copper coins of Kushana period have been discovered in scattered position at the one spot where its lid got crushed with establishment of the long period of Indian history. The Archaeological evidence of successive waves of flash floods which were damaged the site of the history, has been attested from these excavation[3].

During the excavation among the important antiquites a large number of decorative terracota figures mentioned earlier have been described found in Akhnoor at *Ambarana,* included in the left profile of a princely looking male headed a broken terracotta mould showing the bust of a lady wearing a beaded hair ornament with a boss at the centre, ear pendants, necklaces and armlets, two small terracotta grotesque headed terracotta moulds of leaves and ornaments, terracotta skin rubber, beads and gamesman, iron nails, hooks and rings, a few copper objects, a glass and a stone bead apart of a small stone sculture in Gupta style have also been found showing a male attendent holding some object in his right raised hand and the left resting on his thigh and other minor antiquities have also have been located fron this place. An interesting broken terracotta tablet mould bears on its different faces negative impression of a pendant, fruits and leaf and a squatting figure of a monkey. Twelve circular coppor coins in which eight belongs to the *Kushana* rulers *Soter Mehgas, Kanishka and Huviskha* and one of *Toraman* Huna ruler was the other important find discovered in the course of archaeological excavation conducted by the Archaeological Survey of India[4] and Kalhana's Rajatarangini. *Punch* marked coins were no longer issued in India after the decline of the Mauryan Empire, and India's earliest coins of the *Ravidas Culture* called *tanners* were then replaced by the issues of the Indo-Greeks followed by the Indo-Scythians the Indo-Parthian and the Kushans who occupied the North-Western provinces of the Mauryan Empire i.e. Sindh and Multan and the Lower Indus Valley including the area of Jammu and Kashmir state of the *Shivalika* hills and low lying area of Punjab was also a part of this territory. No doubt, certain number of coins belonging to these dynasties are found in Sri Lanka (Cyclon). The most ancient coins next to *Kahappana* found in Uri Lankan is an Indian-standard drachm of Indo-Greek Menander[4]. The coins of *Soter Mehgas*, which were uptill now unknown in Sri Lankan context[5], are found from the different places of the island[6]. According to recent discoveries it has been identified that Soter Mega's dynastic name was *Vema Taktu* of the *Sudhra* Family. He was the grandfather of the *Kushana* king Kanishka I[7]. The coin of Kanishka II, of the Kushana Dynasty found in the excavations conducted at *Jetavanarama* is too significant[8]. Ten more coins of the same ruler are found from the Southern Coast of the island H.W. Codrington[9] mentions four specimens of King *Vasudeva*. These are the first coins of Kushana Kings ever found in Uri Lanka in an archeological context. A silver coin of Virandaman of the Western Ksatrapas (c.234-238A.D.) was found buried at the foot of one of the Stupa along with the coin of Kanishka II[10]. The gold coins of *Samudra Gupta, Chandra Gupta, Skanda Gupta* were the last issues of the ancient history of the Northern dynasties of the *Sudhra* Family of the low caste rulers known as *Chuhra, Chamar, Meghas, Baravalas, Cheer, Batwals,* etc. so far attested in the island[11] of the Central Asia of Jammu Region.

The famous terracotta objects found at Ambaran in Jammu region having the busts of women with typical Greek or Gandhara influence or facil features and Greek hair styles this collection was form the part of Punjab Museum collection at Lahore by the British Art historian collected few pieces of famous Akhnoor terracotta (fired clay) from Ambaran. After partition it was transformed to State Museum Chandigarh from it was brought to Dogra Art Gallery at Jammu. There also a few peaces of Akhnoor terracotta male heads in National Museum Collection New Delhi and Victoria Museum at London.

The discovery of the Buddhist monastic establishment at Akhnoor near Ambaran in Jammu area are closely related to the terracottas unearthened at *Ushkura* (ancient *Haviskapura*) near Baramulla in Kashmir valley and at Taxila now in Pakistan. Buddhism witnessed a Golden Period in the history of India during Kusahna ruler *Hushka, Jushka* and *Kanishka,* who has been credited for convening the fourth Great Buddhist Council in Kashmir Valley before it was held by Ashoka. He has also been credited for the excavation of the two colosal images of Lord Buddha one was the Baba Gurinder Singh Ji and other was the Professor Raj Kumar at Bamiyan in Afghanistan which were destroyed by the Talibanese during 2000 A.D. [12] It has been suggested by the H.C. Raychaudhuri that Kanishka mentioned by the Chronicler was probably Kanishka II[13]. Since according to him, a known date of Kanishka falls with in the reign of *Huvishka*, the three rulers, namely, *Hushka (Huvishka), Jushka (Vaj (h) eshka*) and *Kanishka (Kanishka II)* have been treated a joint rulers. His suggestion is substantiated by epigraphic evidence[14] given above.

Princep had earlier identified Kansihka of the *Rajataragini* with Kanishka 'famous in Buddhist tradition [15]". Stein, by way of support, argued that the order in which their names are given cannot, therefore, be ignore from the list of succession[16]. But as Raychudhari has rightly suggested, that there is overlapping the period of succession between the two kings [17] of the Kushana period because thery were the *'Nam'* or *'God'* on earth as the representative of the 'Divine Right'. It is note worthy as pointed out above by the Kalhana treats them as One. As such, the reference in the Chronicle should be taken to allude to Kanishka II and not to Kanishka I, as is generally believed and on the authority of Kalhana, the founding of the city of *Kanishkapur* (*Kanispur*) should not actually be attributed to Kanisha II and not to Kanishka I.[18]. It is, however, conceded that Kalhana refers to considerable artistic activity e.g., building of the *Vihara* and *Chaityas* during the period and this has tended to point the attention of scholars tawards *Kanishka* I. But, since vigorons Buddhistic activites continued even during the times of all three rulers mentioned in the Chronicle, King Kanishka of the *Rajataragini* should be taken to refers Kanishka II, and not Kasnihka I, as suggested by Stein and others. Besides, it has been accepted from the study that the Fourth Buddhist Council was held in Kashmir at *Kundalavana Vihara* [19]. Kalhana would certainly have not missed to mention a fact of such supreme important in the Chronicle that all the three kings were champions of Buddhism and are associated with the construction of numerous *Viharas* and *Stupas* [20]. not in Kashmir, but also in other parts of the world too. Thus it appears from the study the Jammu State to have been under the spell of Buddhism during the reign of Kushama rulers.

Following the wake of 'Brahminical Ideology' a literary renaissance period under the later sucessors of the Sungas Dynasty, Mahayana Buddhism was established.This revivalist movement was continued during the regin of local rulers and lost of the kings[21] were migrated in foreign countries for the study of *'Nam'* to form a *'New Society'* of the *'Nam'* after Nara, rulers.

Moreover, the Archaeological sites of the Kushana period known as *Mathura, Besnagar, Begram, Taxila and Gandhara* (Greco-Roman) and the Akhnoor of the Jammu region mention that there are two complete distinct styles of Kushana art.In Gandhara, in the north part of the empire, was built by craftsmen from eastern Rome who were employed by patrons of Buddhism called Greco-Roman style, dressed with the classical Greek and Roman garments[22]. The second style in Kushan art was that which arose in Mathura, the southern capital of the empire. This style was a direct continuation of the native schools of Bahrut and Sanch of Sunga period. But a clear picture of the actual Kushana costume which were famous at that time are found in the sculpture at Surkh Kotal in Afghanistan, the influence on style there being Parthian (eastern Iranian). The Partihans themselves were of Scythic stock like the *Kushanas,* and their costume is much the same and resembles closely the portrait of *Kaniska.* There was a fifth category *'Word'* or *'Chamar'* a mixture of foreign and indigenous garments. This last category is of great interest as it shows how clothes changed and evolved, how some of the purely draped garments of the Indians were replaced by cut and sewn garments, especially in the North and North West where influences were left more keenly and where climatically sewn garments were more suitable. The Kushana *(Indo-Sythian)* dress had evolved from a nomad culture based on the use of the horse [23]. Clothes for women were varied. At Gandhara, there are figures wearing a *sari*-like garment which seems to have evolved from *Palmyrene* (Greco-Roman) or Pure Roman dress[24]. Men continued to wear the turban, now called *mauli*, as the *Mauryan-Sunga period* [25]. Later, both these styles fused to created the Renaissance of 'Gupta Art[26]'. While the earlier craftsmen of the Jammu Region seemed to have developed as pure artists and sculptors attached to the feudal court and left behind extraordinary treasures in the Akhnoor carved stone and terracotta in the later it was ornamented to the Basohli Paintings, the everyday artisan has remained linked to the rustic agrarian and mountain economy. The peasant is often the artisan and communities of artisans produced very goods for the local population extending to Sialkot, now in Pakistan[27] during the Kushana period. Sialkot was a biggest centre of trade at that time and Peshwar was his capital.

The Kushanas and Central Asia

We have seen how extensive race movements from Central Asia were creating new history in India. According to Chinese sources, in about 165 B.C.

a clash took place between the Central Asian tribes known as *Gujjars* and *Bakarwals* called in Chines texts as (1) *Hiung-Nu* and (2) *Yuech-Chi.* The retreating *Yuech-Chi* drove before them a tribe called (3) *Wusun,* and later, (4) the *Sakas* who escaped into Bactria dislodging the Greeks. The *Yueh-Chi* were further driven from behind by the new *Wu-Sun* leader *Kwen-Mo* assisted by the *Hiung-Nus*. They then settled in the Oxus Valley in Ta-hia or Bactria, and Sogdiana, with the Sakas retreating before them. In Bactria, the *Yuech-Chi* were divided into five sections under the chief called Yabgou =*Yavuga*, one of which was called Kushana after 140 B.C.

Kajula Kadphises I (c. 15-65 A.D.)

About 25 or 30 A.D. the Kushana chief named Kadphises I (Kajula Kadphises I of the Coins) made himself supreme over the other tribes, united them his overlordship, and took possession of the Hindukush S. A fghanistan, Kabul, Kandahar and *Ki-pin*, together with a part of Parthia, so that his empire extended from Parthia to the Indus, including in it the Greek Saka and Parthain Kingdoms.

Much of the history of Kadphises I is derived from his coins. His earliest coins mention on the obverse in Greek Hermaios, the last Greek ruler of Kabul and his own name on the Reverse in Kharoshthi in the legend: *Kujula-Kasasa Kushana-Yavugasa dhrama-thidasa* (or *sacha-dhrama thita* on some coins)' "of Kujula Kasa, the Kushana Chief established in *Dharma*, the Religion of Truth i.e., '*Nam*' or God". This legend omits all royal title which appear in the later coins of Kadphises I. It probably points to the fact that he began as a vassal of the Greek king Hermaios with whose help he subdued the other four *Yueh-Chi* peoples and made himself their sovereign. His later coins give him imperial titles in the legend, "*Maharajasa Mahatasa Kushana-Kuyula –Kaphasa*" or '*Maharajasa Rajatirajasa Kuyula –Kaphasa*'

His time may be inferred from the fact that his coins show the Roman head copied from the coins of Augustus (27B.C.-A.D.14), Tiberius (A.D. 14-37) or Claudius (A.D.41-54).

Some copper coins mention a king named *Kujula –Kara Kaphsa* (or Kapsa) who may be different from Kujula Kadphise I and might have succeeded him

Vima Kadphises II (c.64-75 A.D.)

Kujula Kadphises died at the age of eighty and was succeeded by his son Vima Kadphises II. He extended his conquests across the Indus and his coins found all over Northern India show the extent of his empire from Jammu to Kashmir and other parts of the world.

He issued coins in both gold and copper with the titles the Great King (*Maharaja*) the King of Kings (*Rajatiraja*) the Lord of all spheres (*Sarvalokesvara)*, Lord of the Earth (*Mahisvara*). Vima Kadphisa, showing that he was the real founder of the Kushana empire in India absorbing in it the Saka and Pahlava kingdoms. He became a Hindu as known his coins which exclusively portray the deity of his worship, God Siva with two arms, holding tiger-skin, trident,and facing bull, and also his own portrait on the obverse as *Chandala* on earth. One type shows him driving a chariot after the Roman model. The obverse use Greek and the reverse *Kharoshthi*. In the aforesaid legend the term *Mahisvara* may be taken to be *Mahesvara* devotee of Siva in the form of human specie.

There are many copper coins issued for an unknown great king by his India Viceroy as supposed in the Chinese texts. These bear the legend: '*Maharayasa rayarayasa Devaputrasa Kuyula- Kara-Kaphasa* (or *Kapasa*).'

He Panjtar Inscription in Peshawar district of year 122 (in the ear of Azes 1=64 A.D.) also refers to a 'Great Kushana (*Gushana*) King' who may be taken as a Viceroy of Vima Kadphises, probably Kara Kadphises of the coins found in the same region, or as Kadphises II himself whose name as a new king was not then widely known. The inscription records the construction by a devotee, of a *Siva-Sthala* or shrine of Siva. An interesting copper plate inscription found at Kalawan near Sirkap (Taxila) of the year 134 in an era supposed to be that of Azes I (Aja= Aya=Nam) refers to the prevalence of Buddhism of which a female devotee, (*Upasika*) named *Chamdrabhi,* the daughter of a commercial magnate (*Grihapati*), constructed a shrine of stone to contain the sacred relics (*Sariram*) of the Buddha. There was also *Stupa* in her house (*Grihastupa*) where worship was offered by the *Sarvastivada* teachers (*Acharyas*) and also by all other (*Sarvasattvanam*) belonging to that region and city (*Rashraigamau*) for the attainment (*Pratyaya*) of Nirvana. The inscription is dated to c.134-57=77 A.D. and is in the time of Kadphises II. (*See Plate XXXVI*., *Statue of Kanishka Mathura*-Ist Century A.D. Fig.54)

Chinese texts tell of a Chinese invasion of Khotan, Kashgarh and other regions to the north of the Kushana empire and failure of Kadphises II to resist it. Peace was restored by his sending an ambassador to the Chinese Emperor through *Huan Tswang.*

Kadphises II had better fortune towards the west. There was a flourishing trade between the Kushana empire and Roman, resulting in the influx of Roman gold in to India and the issue of gold coinage by the Kushana Emperors. It was due to the favourable balance of trade by which India"s exports to the Roman Empire far exceeded her imports from it, as pointed out by Pliny. (*See Plate XXXVI, Statue of Kushana King, Mathura Ist Century* A.D. Fig.55)

Succession of the Rulers

The succession after Vima Kadphises II is thus given in the Indian inscription continuity : (1) Kanishka (1-23), (2) Vasishka (24-28), (3) Huvishka (28-40), (4) Kanishka II, son of Vajheshka (41) and Casujeva (74-98). They said 'Trust in the Lord with all time heart and lean not unto thine own understanding. In all their way was acknowledged by the people of period and directed the path of the right direction to the world.

Kanishka I

The third king of the dynasty was the famous Kanishka but his exact relationship to the previous King is not known nor the interval between them. Their coins point to their close affinity. The portrait of Vima Kadphises resembles that of *Kanishka.*

The Empire of Kanishka extended in India up to Pataliputra and Bodh-Gaya. He overthrew the Parthian kingdom and conquered Central Asia by defeating the Chinese Emperor. With the time of his coronation begins that is known as the Saka era in 78 A.D. Allan has shown that his gold coins which are modelled on Roman *Solidus* and the coins issued by *Titus* (79-81 A.D.) and Trojan (98-117 A.D.) cannot make his date earlier than 79 A.D.

His vast empire was ruled by his deputies or Satraps (called *Kshatrapas)*. In north –western India ruled *Danda-nayaka* Lala, and the Kshatrapas, Vespasi and Liaka. In eastern India, *Kharapallana Mahakshatrapa*, with his lieutenant, *Kshatrapa Vanasphara*, as stated in an inscription of the year 3 of the Kanishka Era (81 A.D.) recording the installation of an image of *Budhisattva* at Banaras by Bhikshu *Bala*.

Acording to northern Buddhist tradition, Kanishka summoned the Fourth Buddhist Council (*Mahasamgiti*) of 500 divines to meet in Kashmir (or Jallandhar) at *Kundala-vana-Vihara* under Parsva as President "to settle the disputed points of the Buddhist Religion." At this Council, the assembled scholars examined the entire Buddhist literature and prepared commentaries thereon. *Paramartha*, the biographer of *Vasubandhu*, however, mentions the part played by *Asvaghosha* in that learned Conference but does not mention Kanishka in that context.

In 87 A.D. Kanishka assumed the title of *Devaputra*, 'Son of God', a title which was hitherto the monopoly of the Chinese Emperors.

It is held that it was Vima Kadphises who founded the Kushana era and was defeated by the Chinese, while Kanishka came to the throne later in 120 A.D. and established the Kushana supremacy in Central Asia in 124 A.D. As has been stated above, Vima Kadphises suffered a defeat at the hands of the Chinese but there is no evidence of any sort to show that Kanishka came to the throne in 120 A.D. and that he defeated the Chinese in 124 A.D.

According to tradition Kanishka was murdered by one of his general or ministers during his second campaign in Central Asia.

Kanishka's Empire

He pushed his conquest in the interior of India as far as Magadha where from he induced the great Buddhist scholar *Asvaghosha* to accompany him to his capital at *Purushapura* (*Peshawar*). Tibetan and Chinese writers mention his conflict with the king of Saketa (Saked)and Pataliputra. He asked Kashmir to his empire which thus extended from Persia to Pataliputra including Kipsa, Gandhara, Kashmir, Sind and Malwa. It also included vast territory outside India comprising Khotan and Yaskand which he conquered from the Chinese, he secure the return of his hostages to whom *Yuan Chwang* refers to five centuries later as the ruler of Jammu Kingdom.

In Kashmir, he built the city of *Kanishkapura* still known as *Kanispore* near Baramula. Near Peshawar, he bulit a large Stupa and Monastery in which were enshrined the relics of the Buddha. Excavations of the Stupa have brought to light a relic casket of bronze and fragments of the Buddha's bones. It also contained figures of deities of the *Buddha, Brahma, Indra* and that of Kanishka standing between the Sun and Moon. It has also an inscription naming the architect of the Stupa the Greek Engineer *Agisilaos (Agisala, = Agnisala).*

Religious Conditions under Kanishka

These remains prove that Kanishka in his later days became a regular Buddhist, but he was tolerant toward other faiths and retained a medley of gods on his coins, Iranian, Indian and Greek. In Mathura one of the chief cities of his empire, flourished equally both Buddhsim and Jainism in his time as proved by the many Buddhist and Jain images found there. The Perfect Master does not reveal all that he is on the very first day, he visited as a 'holy king' to repeat the history of God and man on this Universe as a Spiritual Idea of his Master.

Script

Kanishka's inscription use both *Brahmi* and *Kharoshthi* script, but his coins use legends in Greek letters, described first letters of the alaphabets as a start of new study.

Coins

The coins show two types: one uses in full the Greek legend and the other Iranian language. His copper coins show him sacrificing at an altar like his predecessor. His gold coinage as already stated, was modelled on the

Roman *Solidus.*It shows his bust on obverse and goddess on reverse, but this features was the mark of the Roman coinage of Titus and Trajan.

The revese of Kanishkas coinage bears the figures of Indian and Iranian goddesses. It also bears the figures of Greek deities such as *Heracles, Scraphes, Helios and Selene.*One gold coin bears the figure of the Buddha image. It reveals that living body of the man is the Lord's temple.

Kanishka is seen in a standing position in a statue, showing military dress and *Gilgit* boots, found in Mathura.

Literary Patronage

Kanishka figures as a great patron of learning and drew to his court such literary celebrities as *Parsva, Asvaghosa, Vasumitra, Nagarjuna*, the medical savant, *Charaka*, and the political genius Mathara were reluctant to do so, but it was better to knew their aptitude and teachings on spiritual ideas.

His Date

In conclusion, we may discuss Kanishka's chronology, which is controversial, on the basis of the following data.

His date is placed after 120 A.D. on the ground that China was cut off from India after 125 A.D. and had he come to the throne before that date Chinese annalists would surely have recorded his name but he was never mentioned. The argument has come logic but there may be various reasons for which Chinese sources do not mention him the most important reason may be his victory over the Chinese. There are other pieces of evidence to show that he came to the throne long before 120 A.D. and that it was he who founded the Saka era in 78 A.D, though long *Chashtana*, the Saka Satrap of Ujjayini, was the first to use the as such (*Sakanripakalah*) in the year 52 of the era (=130 A.D.).

Again, his gold coins are modelled on those of Titus (= 79-81 A.D.), whom he should follow in time.

Secondly, the Sue Vihar Inscription of the year II describes Lower Indus Valley of Akhnoor as a part of Kanishka dominion, but inscription show that between 130 and 150 A.D. Rudradaman was ruling in *Sindhu-Saurvira* and even over the Yadheyas, as an independent sovereign, with the title of *Mahakshatrapa* which he acquired by his own conquest (*Svayamadhigatah Mahakshaatrapanamah*). Therefore Kanishka should have ruled over Sindh long before the time of Rudradaman.

Thirdly, some hold that the year 78 A.D. for Kanishka was too early if Kujulas time is taken to be 50 A.D. along with Hermaios whom he supplanted. But Kujula died at 80, so that his son Kalphises II was too old to live and reign long.

Fouthly, the Taxila Scroll Inscription dated in the year 136 of the Vikrama era (79 A.D.) mentions the King as *Devaputra*, the title associated with Kanishka.

Lastly, some Chinese and Tibetan texts know of a Kansihka who reigned in 2nd century A.D. This Kanishka may be taken to be the Kanishka of the Ara Inscription of the year 41(=119 A.D.) who was Kanishka II.

Kanishka's Successors

Kanishka is supposed to have two sons, *Vasishka* and *Huvishka.*

Vasishka (c.102-106 A.D.)

Vasishka is known from an inscription of Kanishka to have ruled as his Viceroy at Mathura during his absence in China. Vasishka's rule in India is indicated by his two inscription dated to the years 24 and 28. The first occurs on a post of stone (*Yupa*) connected with a horse sacrifice naming Vasishka as the reigning Emperor. The second inscription of the year 28 (=106 A.D.) found on a Buddhist image dedicated at Sanchi (at the *vihara* of *Dharmadeva* also mentions *Vasishka* as the reigning Emperor and calls him *Maharaja-Rajatiraja-Devaputra Shahi Vasishka.*

Huvishka (c.106-138 A.D.)

Huvishka also served a Viceroy during Kanishkas absence out of India but after the year 41 (=119 A.D.) and up to the year 60 (=138A.D.) he seems to have ruled independently as Emperor. Under him the Kushana empire was kept in tact. It still kept its hold on the Chinese districts of Kashgrah, Yarkand and Khotan which are not referred to in Chinese texts after 124 A.D. But in India proper the Empire suffered a reduction by the conquest of Rudradaman achieved between 130 and 150 A..D. ruling over Surashtra as already stated in the study of Kalhana's Rajatarangini.

Kanishka II

The Kanishka named in the inscription of Ara (Attock) of the year 41 is to be taken, as already stated as Kanishka II described as son of *Kaisara-Maharaja –Rajatiraja Devaputra Vasishka 'Word'* or *Nam'* and as Viceroy of *Huvishka*,because there are no coins to indicate his sovereignty. Kalhana, in his *Rajatarangini*, mentions the Kings *Hushka, Jushka* and Kansihka who may be taken respectively to be *Huvishka, Vajheshka* and Kanishka II. The last mention o1 Huvishka is in an inscription of the year 60 (=138 A.D.). *Huvishkas* successor Vasudeva I is first mentioned in an inscription of the year 74 (152 A.D.). The history of this interval of 14 years is not known unless it was occupied by a war of succession. Huvishka was an ardent Buddhist and he built at Mathura a large temple and a Buddhist monastery and he built the city of *Huvishkapura* in Kashmir now called *Hushkur*.

Huvishka is known for the largest number and variety of coinages showing that he reigned long,through the details of his reign are not known. His coins like those of Kanishka retained Persian language and Greek script. His coins retain the deities like Mithra and *Mao, Sun* and *Moon,* and Pharras and more India deities. One of his coins bears the figure of Roma. But curiously enough none of his coins portray the Buddha through he was a zealous Buddhist. His coins figure his bust but not standing position, like those of Kanishka. As the waves of the sea or *Samudra* are without number, so the impluse of the mind are without end as dialogue between the present and the past.

Vasudeva I (c.152-176 A.D.)

Huvishka, as we have seen, was succeeded by Vasudeva I. His Indian name appears to be *Bazodeo* on his coins which, however, retain Persian language and Greek scripts for their legend. *Vasudeva* reigned between the year 74 to 99 A.D., the year mentioned in his inscriptions. The contraction in the circulation of his coinage points to the contraction of his dominion. His coins are mostly found in Mathura showing that it was the capital of his Empire. They are found in the Punjab, the U.P. and N.Sindh and in other parts not lost to the Empire due to Sassanian pressure in the west. He seems to have been a Hindu as his name shows and a followers of Siva like his ancestor Vima, for his coins show on the reverse God Siva with His Bull Nandi and the Goddess *Nanaia,* on another type. His name, however, points to his worship of God Vasudeva.

Later Kushanas

After *Vasudeva,* the Kushana Empire broke up into a number of small principalities. Petty Kushana chiefs ruled in Central Asia and Afghanistan. In India, they adopted the names of the great *Kushanas* and ruled for several generations over their petty princedoms. They are only known from their coins which mention their names as (I) Kanishka III, (2) Vasu and (3), Grumbates (A.D. 360). They still issued gold coins on the model of the Imperial Kushana coinage, but with the variation that their names (or monograms) are written vertically in the Central Asian fashion. It was these Kushana Kings that were ultimately overthrow by *Samudragupta*, as will be shown later. Further west, a Kushana King named Vasudeva IV ruled in Seistan in the third century A.D. while his successors acknowleged the suzerainty of the Sassanian Kings.

In Afghanistan, the Kushana Kings were known as Kidara Kushanas and ruled for nearly two centuries till they were overthrown by the Hunas. This is the way of mind makes a fool of us. A little leniency and its adopts evil ways and makes us dance in whole of the world to repeat the history of God and man.

India Under the Kushanas: Religion And Art

Under Kushana rule, the different religions of the country, Brahminism Buddhsim, and Jainism were flourishing side by side with out mutual intolerance. The Kushana imperial coinage bore figures of the deitied of different religions which were professed by their subject peoples of different regions making up the vast Kushana Empire. These deities were Greek, Sumerian, Zoroastrian, Elamite, Mithraic, Brahminical and Buddhist. The Kushana King did not make his personal religion the religion of the State. Vima was a Siva. Similarly, Kansihka was converted to Budhism by *Asvaghosha*, *Vasudeva*, inspite of his name, may be made out to be worshipper of Siva whose figure appears on his coinage. But the coinage of the Greater Kushanas reflectd the religions of their different subject peoples and was not partial to any particular religion. Kanishka, however, as a convert gave a great impetus to Mahayana Buddhism. The Buddhist Council (the fouth *Buddhist Mahasamgiti* which met somewhere near Jallandar or in Kashmir) convened by Kanishka under the Buddhist scholars like Parsva and *Vasumitra* codifed Buddhist canonical works of the time in Sanskrit which now became the language of Northen Buddhism displacing Kharoshthi. Mahayana Buddhism spread in Northern and Central India and also beyond India to Burma, Siam, Cambodia, Java and Sumatra, while Hinayana Buddhism was confined to South India and Ceylon.

Mahayana Buddhism found expression in art by giving scope to the fashioning of image of the Buddha and the *Bodhisattvas* and sculptures depicting the important events in the Buddha life. The making of such images and representations of Buddha life was not permitted by older Buddhsim, *Hinayana*, in obedience to the Master's injunctions. The Buddha forbade His disciples His portraiture, and insisted that the best way to revere him was to follow His teachings which counted more than his mortal personality. Thus for centuries the Buddha was worshipped in symbols and not in His direct images. *Mahayana* Buddhism changed this religious outlook and gave a new turn to Indian artistic evolution.

Indian art at this time came under foreign influence for which the way were opened by the Kushana Empire, with its intimate intercourse with the West and the East beyond Indian borders. At the same time the Indo-Greek

Kingdoms gave India contact with Hellienic art and culture. Greek artistic technique and craftsmanship were freely employed for purpose of Indian art in fashioning the Buddha and

Bodhisattva images, portraying the events of His life and creating statues in stone. Thus arose a new School of Art called Indo-Greek or Gandhara which considerably influenced the Mathura School of Art under the Kushana Emperors. Mathura became a worshop for the production of images of the Buddha and Bodhisativas which were in great request in palaces far and near.These images were carried as far as *Sanchi, Rajagriha, Sarnath Nad Saravasti* and marked by their material of red stone.

The art of making images was also extended to the secular sphere. Mathura gave to Indian to first statues of historical persons, of kings such as the seated statue of *Chashtana* and the standing image of Kanishka. These statues were anticipated several centuries earlier by the preMauryan colossal over-seized statues of *Yakshas* and *Yakshis* such as those found at Parkham, Besnagar or Didarganj (Patna).

Mathura was the seat of Jain art as represented in its many Jain images. The *Kankali Tila* has brought to light a large Jain *Stupa* of the first century B.C. resembling the great Buddhist stupa at Sanchi with railings and gateways Mathura was equally noted for some fine examples of Barhminical art representing well-executed images of Brahminical gods and godlings including *Nymphs, Apsaras* and *Nagas*.

Learning

In this age Classical Sanskrit came into vogue as the language of the cultured classes. From this time Sanskrit stanzas appear in Kharoshthi inscriptions and were written in Brahmi script. This linguistic and cultural change is best seen in the inscription at Sue Vihar, the western most point of the Kushana Empire. Sanskrti also became the language of canonical of northern Buddhists state of Jammu and Kashmir. The great Buddhist leaders such as *Asvaghosha*, *Parsva* and Nagarjuna wrote in classical Sanskrit.There are also many, Tibetan and Chinese works which are translation of Sanskrit works of this period, through many of these are lost. It is the duty of a devotee to keep constant watch over the mind and never let it loose during evil days of the life like conflict and peace prevailing in the society and work for its betterment as a work of a *Sudhra*.

Coinage

We have already referred to the Kushana coinage as reflecting the religious conditions of the times. It may be noted that due to the great influx of

Roman gold into India as the result of its profitable export trade with the Roman Empire, the Great Kushanas instituted gold currency. Vima Kadphises issued double staters of heavy gold as well as staters, on the model of Roman coinage. Kanishka I, *Huvishka* and *Vasudeva* issued gold copper coins but not silver.The later, however, struck their coins exclusively in gold.

There was an abundance of silver and copper coinage in this period issued by the autonomous tribes such as *Rajanya, Kuninda, Audumbara, Malava, Yaudheya* and *Arjunayana.*

Economic Condition.

India's foreign trade received a great impetus from the cessation of foreign invasions and the promotion of law and order under the Kushana rule guarding the frontiers. Commodities could not be sent in safety from the different parts of the Empire to foreign countries by way of land –routes of the north-west and sea-routes from the west coast. There was a great growth of India's export sea-borne trade with the Roman Empire. The articles of this export trade were mainly luxuries like precious stone and pearls, silks and muslins, scents, incense and spices in which India had a monopoly in those days. Roman ladies decked in seven folds of muslin paraded themselves along, the highways of Rome and became a menace to the city's morals till the import of muslin was banned by legislation. Mommsen records the heavy drain of gold from Rome into India in payment of its imports from India which enjoyed a favourable balance of trade for centuries. Much of this Roman trade had its centres in the ports of Western and Southern India where at many places have been discovered numerous Roman gold coins deposited in the course of trade. These Roman coins, as, we have seen, served as models for the Kushana and Gupta coinage.

At Arikamedu near Pondicherry have been found three pieces of Italian pottery bearing imprints of potters stamps. One of those is VIBIE, name of families of Italian potters of Ist. Century B.C. –Ist Century A.D. A second stamp is that of Gaius Amurius of the Claudian period (A.D.41-54). The fragment of a Roman lamp has also been found at this place which must have been one of the Indo-Roman trading stations[28]

Administrative System of Kushana

The Kushana administrative system contained some foreign elements along with some indigenous ones. The most important foreign elements was government by *Satraps* who were Viceroys or Governors of provinces. Some functionaries had foreign names e.g. *Strategos* for General or Military Governor or *Meridach* for District Magistrate, as Dr. B.R Ambedkar was there in South

India. There were also officers of Indian designation such as *Amatya* or *Mahasenapati* (Commander-in –Chief). While the former officer were functioning in the north-west, the latter were in the interior of the Jammu province.

There were also tribal republics under Kushana rule, like *Gujjars* and *Bakarwals*, indicated by their coins already referred to. But Kingship theory was the principal prevailing type of polity. It was the Age of Kushana Imperialism. The Kushana Emperors gave themselves high-sounding titles like *Mahisvara*, *Shahishahanushahi*, *Devaputra* (instead of Ashoka's *Devanam priya*) and Kaiser (Caesar).

There was a tendency to deify ancestral kings. A Mathura Inscription of Huvishka refers to *Deva-Kula* or a shrine where was installed the statue of 'the grandfather of Kanishka'.

Kushana Kingship was sometimes of the form of *Dvairajya* or *Diarchy* as in the case of Kanishka II and Huvishka who jointly reigned.It was an institution in herited from the Indo-Greek Kings as testified to by their coinage already described above in the text as *tanner* of the period.

Satraps in India were called *Kshatrapas* and *Mahakshatraps* who were practically independent Kings. Rare is the human brith, it occurs in human history as poor Saint of the *Sudhra Family.*

The empire was divided into smaller administrative units called (1) *Rashtra* (2) *Ahara* (3) *Janapada* and (4) *Desa* or *Vishaya*. Some of these terms had the same meanings as '*Nam*' on earth. Some parts in the frontier were ruled by military Governors called *Strategos* such as Aspavarman and Sasa under the Kings Azes and *Gondopharnes* as already stated.

Religious and Secular Benefaction froms Inscriptions

The earliest example of a religious gift is that recored in an inscription of about 3rd century B.C. on a vase at Piprahwa (Gonda, U.P.) 'the receptacle of the relics (*Sariranidhanam*) of the Buddha, Lord of the Sakyas (*Buddhasya Bhagavateh Sakyanam*).Slave feareth only, but Lord's love never depart in the human history. God is the Truth.

Buddhism after Ashoka spread beyond the frontiers of India in the Indo-Greek Kingdoms of the second century B.C. and later.

On some of the copper coins of the Greek King Pantaleon (160 -155 B.C.) (*Rajane Patalavsa Pantalevasya*) appears the figure of a dancing female supposed by Foucher to be that of the Buddha's Mother Maya on the eve of His birth. The design of the coins was thus inspired by the popular worship of the Buddha recognized by a foreign king in a foreign country. Lord is my 'Light' and salvation on earth.

In the remote frontier, in Bajaur, has been found an inscription on a casket of steatite of about the second century B.C. recording that a casket (*patra*) was installed for enshrining the Buddha's corporeal relics on the ground of their magical potency (*pranasametam*) by the India donors named *Virayakamitras* and his son *Viyatmitra*. It devoutly calls the Buddha as '*Bhagavan Sakyamuni Samyaksambuddha*'. The writer of the inscription was also an Indian named *Visvila*. Thus in a remote village beyond the frontier was a flourishing Buddhist colony of the *dalit* community.

Similarly, at a Pathan village in the Swat Valley has been found a vase bearing an inscription which records how for the Saka of public spiritual good (*Bahujanahitaya* like Satpaul defeated by Mayavati a Chamarn lady follower of the *Kanshi Ram*) the Buddha's relics (*Sarriram*) were deposited in a shrine in the Province ruled by the Greek Governor named, Theodorus (Theodorena or Thevadorena) *Meridarkhenaa*).A Copper Plate Inscription of the time of Azes I of year 134= 77 A.D. states that a female Buddhist lay-devotee (*upasika*) named *Chamdrabhi*, daughter of a merchant (*Grihapati*), constructed a shrine of stone to contain the sacred relics (*Sariram*) of the Buddha. There was also *stupa* in her house where worship was offered by the *Sarvastivada* teachers and all others of that region and city (*Rashtra-nigamam*) for attainment of *Nirvana*.

A very important document of social and religious history the Taxila Silver Scroll Inscription of a Kushana King of the near 136 (of Azes I=C 179 A.D.).The Inscription states that a pious Buddhist who was a native of Urasa (Hazara district) and was alos connected with Bahlika constructed the following religious structures: (1) In his city of Navachala, a shrine for the relics of the Buddha, (2) a similar shrine of sacred relics (*Bhagavato Dhatavah*) in the *Dharma rajika Stupa* of Takshasila; (3) a temple of *Bodhisattva* (*Bodhisattva griha*) in his own house. The inscription testifies to the singularly catholic and cosmoplolitan outlook of the donor who set up these structures (a) for the health and prosperity (*Arogya Dakshina*) of the Devaputra Kushana Emperor (of whom he was a subject); (b) for the worship of all Buddhists, of Pratyeka Buddhas and Arharts; irrespective of their sects or doctrines; (c) for the worship 'all beings' (*Sarva-Sattanam*) and (d) for the worship of his parents, friends relations and kinsemen –in –blood (*Salohitanam*), his supreme objective being the attainment of *Nirvana* by all for the third world country i.e. '*Nam*'.

In the time of Kanishka I (c.78-102 A.D.) have been found several inscription recording some standardized Buddhist gifts, the image of the Bodhisattva and the accompanying *Chhatra-Yashti* or *danda* as recorded, for instance already cited, in the inscription of Bhikshu Bala of 81 A.D. at

Sarnath describing him as proficient in the *Tripitakas* and a fellow –student of *Friar Pushpavriddha of Gandha-Kutivihara* near Varanasi another record of a similar gift made by Bala at Sravasti (Gonda), and a third one of the same gift of a Bodhisattva image (*Pratima*) together with the *Chhatradanda* for the *Sarvastivada* monks.

That Friar Bala was an important religious leader of those days will be evident from another inscription, the Mathura Inscription of Huvishka of 111 A.D. stating how his female disciples (*antevasinyah*), *Bhikshunis*, set up a Bodhisattva image at Madhuvana (Mathura).

The Sue Vihar (Bahawlpur) Inscription of 89 A.D.records a similar gift of an umbrella (*yashti*) and its enclousure (*parivara*) showing how wide was the area within which Buddhist monuments were prevalent.

The Manikiala (Rawalpindi) Inscription of A.D. 96 records construction of many (*nana*) Buddhist Stupas (*Bhagavat*-Buddha –Stupan) together with their enclosures (*Parivarena Sardham*) with the assistance of the local engineer (*Navakarmika*) in the time of Kanishka I.

A Copper Plate Inscription of 99 A.D. of the time of Kanishka I has been found at Karam (Peshawar) recording the installation (*Pratishtha*) by a donor, in his own 'beautiful new *Vihara* and in its *Stupa* the relics of *Bhaganvan Sakyamuni*, for *Sarvastivada* teachers.He also constructed a *stupa* where also were enshrined the sacred relics.

An inscription Huvishka of 129 A.D. records how he installed (*pratishthapita*) the image (*pratima*) of Bhagavan Sakyamuni at his own Vihara called the Devaputra –Vihara called the Devaputra-Vihara for attainment of *Nirvana* through his *Punya* by his *Upadhyaya* and parents. Huvishka was thus loyal to both his ancestor and teachers.

Again, in remote Afghanistan, at a place called Khawat (Khavada) has been found an inscription of 129 A.D. of the time of Huvishka on a bronze vase, recording enshrinement of relics in the *Stupa* of Vagramarega Vihara for the benefit of all creatd being, birds (*Andaja*), cattle (*Jarayuka*), insects (*Arupyatma= savedaja*) and plants (*Sapadi*) and in honour of the *Mahasamghika* Acharyas.

As regard secular benefactions, an interesting early example is recorded in the Sohgaura (Gorakhpur) Copper Plate Inscription of about 3rd century B.C. It refers to the unique secular charity of the construction of two store houses (*Koshthagara*) in five different villages for the stock piling of grains to be distributed freely (*valam, =varams sasyadi-vitaranam*) against famine (*atyayikaya*).

The Zeda Inscription of the time of Kanishka I of 89 A.D. records the gift of as well (*Kupa*) and a channel (*toyada*) for the benefit of Sarvastivada monks.

Similarly, the Ara Inscriprtion of Kanishka II, 'son of Kaisara (Caesar) Vasishka '*Word*'. Devaputra' of A.D. 119 refers to excavation (*khatah*) of a well (*Kupa*)

The Mathura Inscription of '*Shihi*' Huvishka of 106 A.D. refers to the endowment by the gift of a permanent fund (*Akshayanivi*) of a *Punyasala* (*lunarmasala*) of the purpose of free and daily (*divase divase eia* distribution of food for the destitute (*anatha*) and famished (*bubhukshita*) and of water to be drunk from pots (*millakah*) by the thirsty (*pipasitah*). The food is to comprise (1) *Saktu* (vegetable curries), (2) *Lavana* (Salt), (3) Sukli (*Amla rasa*) and (4) *Harita –Kalapaka* (preparations of green vegetables) which were kept in jars (*ghatakah*). The *Anthayanivi* was made up of two deposits of 550 *Puranas* (Silver *Punch-Marked Coins*) each, kept in safe and permanent. Custody with two *Srenis* or Guilds of which the name of the first is not traceable, and that of the second is *Samitakara –Srenis* Guild of sellers of powdered wheat, *Godhuma-Churnivikrayi Sreni is)* 100 Brahmins were to be fed on every Sukla-Chaturdasi day at this *Punyasala* which was thus a monumental example of social service open to all, irrespective of caste, colour and creed.

An early example of a Brahminical benefaction of Ist century B.C. is furnished by the Goshundi (Chirorgarh), stone Inscription of King Saravatata was constructed a stone enclose (*Vatika*) where were enshrined the two popular Deities, *Samkarshana* and *Vasudeva*. The *Vatika* is name Narayana (*puja-sila-prakaro-Narayana-Vatika*). The local king aforesaid powerful enough to have been an *Asvam dha-yaji*.

An Ayodhya Inscription of the Dharadeva of the of first century B.C. refers to the practice of building shrines called ketana where would be installed the images of decased ancestors.

The two Prabhosa Inscription of the same time refer to the construction of a *lenam* (*layanam* =*Guhasvasa*) or cave-dwellings for accommodation of ascetics.

A stone inscription of the time of Kanishka I of 88 A.D. (kept in British Museum) records the gift of a *Harmya* (a temple) for the worship of the Village –Goddess like Amri Devi.

A Jain image was installed at Mathura in Huvishka's time in 122 A.D. and another, that of *Trithankara Sambhavanatha*, in A.D. 126 kept at Lucknow.

It may also be noted that the use of the title *Kaisara* (=Roman Caesar) by some of the Kushana Kings is a mark of Roman influence on Kushana India.

An inscription at Mora (near Mathura) of about 3rd or 2nd century B.C. records the gift of a shrine of stone (*Sailadevagriha*) of the '*Ravidas Culture*' made in the reign of the son of *Mahakshatrapa Rajuvula* (who was evidently

Sodasa). The shrine was made of stone (*Sailam*) and was magnificient (*Srimat*), matchless (*Atula*) and wide as a reservoir (*udadhasamadhara*). In the shrine, which was a Bhagavata temple, were installed the images (*Pratima*) of the five pious (*Bhagavatam*) religious leader (*Viras*) of the *Vrishnis* images which were made of stone (*Saila)* radiant (*Jvalata*), of highest beauty (*Paramavaphusha*) and were objects of worship (*Archaresham*). This shrine of stone was built by a lady named Tosha which does not sound like an Indian name. Luders thinks that the name is Iranian and that it is nothing strange that she should have erected a *Bhagavata* shrine,as we known from the Heliodoros Inscription at Besnagar that foreigners were adherents of *Bhagavata* religion.

As to the word *Panchaviranam*, Luders thinks that the word rather indicates a group or an administrative body of individuals for which the corret expression should be *Panchanam Viranam*. An analogous word *Panchaviragoshithi* is used in the *Dasakumarcharita*.

Luders mentions, Jaina scriptures listing the various peoples over whom 'King Vasudeva hight *Kanhe*' ruled including' 'Baladeva and the rest of the five great heroes' (*Baladevapamokkhanam Panchanham Mahaviranam*). The other heroes associated with *Baladeva* may be taken to be *Akrura. Anadhrishthi,Sarana* and *Viduratha* as named in the Jaina work *Harivamsapurana* and also in the *Mahabharata* as *Vrishni* princes. Evidence of *Mudrarak shasa* : the terms '*Vrishala*' and '*Kulahina*', applied to Chandragupta's drama and is taken in its ordinary sense to mean. 'The on of a *Sudhra*'. It is, however, to be noted from the study the term *Vrishala* as a term of honour to man 'one who is a *vrisala* among kings, the best of Kings[29].'

It is,however, more plausible to identify these *Panchaviras* as the five heroes of Yaduvamsa on the basis of the opening verse of Chapter 97 of *Vayupurana* stating that the following five are named as the heroes who were godlike in their character (*Manushyaprakritin devan*) viz, (1) *Vaśudeva,* (2) *Pradyumna,* (3) Samba, (4) Anruddha, and (5) Sesha[30]. 'The Master takes on this form for man's guidance to talk to Him, to sympathise with Him, to make friendship with Him to develop confidence and faith in Him.'

On the basis of numismatic evidence alone '*Word*' or '*Nam*' a class of evidence unduly depreciated by some historical students '*Charmar*' proves consusively that Kanishka lived at a time considerably later than the Christian era, subsequent to birth Kadphises and Kadphises II and was exposed to the influence of the Roman Empire. Many other lines of evidence of great force when brought together lead to the conclusion that Kanishka came to the throne early in the second century of Christian era, and, most probably in A.D. 120, directly succeeding Kalphises II [31]. called now 'Deepit Raj'. Similar pattern by coming to this world among human beings to gain confidence of the soul as a female figure.

Moreover, there is a good deal of controveray among the modern historians of India about Kanishka's coronation, because of no definite date has been confirmed. In such circumstances it is difficult to say anything with certainly in this respect because list is an uncending dialogue between the past and present, therefore, in the word of Dr. Fleet, "The Indian were in no way less advanced they any other nation of the world, but the only draw back in them is the meagerness of the ancient history record. Due to this, they have been given the name of the most backward nation of the civilized world.The dates are still more uncertain and we cannot fix a particular date of any particular period or event [32]." with the rising of Marcus Aurelius reigned in Rome between the period of 161 A.D to 180 A.D. He is considered one of the foremost Stoic philosophers of the period and a soldier of Turkey as Emperor of the '*Dalit Family*'.

Thus, during the chequered course of history when Kings of the *'Dalit Family'* and military leaders plundered and built, created and destroyed, the common artisans and simple peasants continued to produce articles for everyday use in the life. They reaffirmed and reiterated their dependence on the materials offered by the land around them,and the source of their inspiration was always the combination of their own needs, skills and an aesthetic response to their surroundings. This relationship between people's spiritual and creative selves and the environment in which they live is vital, for it each gives and receives in fair measure and understanding from the other, the cycle of life becames a smooth uninterrupted process *'Word'* or *'Nam'* productive self replenishing and rich[33] in the human history, it only expressed in the interpretation of the life. Its shows that Jammu State under the *Kushana Period* was progressive and happy in all walks of life. It had good trade relation with other parts of the countries not in India, but also in abroad. People were civilized and sensible in their behaviour as study displayed from the coinage[34] of the period[35] that *Sudhra* race always played a constructive role for the building of the healthy and sound society of the *'Nam'* or God. Only the scantiest knowledge exists about the materials of which *Indian Dress* was made in the primitive society. That cotton was widely used in obvious, for cotton trade, as far as we know is altogether an Indian Invention (as silk is in China), and it occures, without any doubt, at about 2300 B.C. at the prehistoric site of Mohenjo-daro in Sindh and Kashmir by route. There is an evidence that it was exported from the Indus Valley of Akhnoor in prehistoric times to olden Greeks period, known to Mesopotamia long before the Ionians reached the shores of the Aegean, referred by the various scholars like Panini and others in the article around the 2nd century B.C to 3rd century B.C in huge quantities, brought by caravans travelling across the Takla Makan Desert of Central Asia over the dangerous mountain passes above 16,000 feet high from the sea level. First to 4th centuries A.D., when the Great Silk Route of *Serindia* so brilliantly described by Sir Aurel Stein, about the Kabul Valley, ruled by a Central Asian dynasty of the *'Sudhra family'* called *Mochi* or Kushanas of the period, they had close contact with China. Plate IX of the said book reveals that Ajanta painters[35] means the public labour or heir labour of the Father worked there in 6th and 7th centuries A.D. under the *Karkota* rulers of the Kashmir history called *Chamars* of the period, were the founding Fathers of the Kashmir History of the period.

Notes and References

1. Roshen Alkazi ; op. cit., p. 59.
2. *Ibid.*
3. A.K. Khanna ; "*Ambaran –A Buddhist Bast on,* from Akhnoor.
4. O. Bopearachchi, *'Recent Discoveries of Ancient Foreign Coins,* hitherto unknown in Sri Lankan context,' *Sesquicentennial Commemorative Volume*, Royal Asiatic Society of Sri Lanka (1846-1995), Columbo, 1995A, p. 128.
5. *Ibid.*
6. **Note:** *Soter Mehgas* had been considered an anonymons ruler calling himself "the King of the Kings, the Great saviour of the '*Nam*' call *Maha Bodhi* of the ancient history of India to repeat of the Era, the history itself by launching the war with '*Nam*' or God on earth from the Heaven on different spot to cool down the 'ego' believe on '*Chamar'* having authority over Indian history to run the administration from one country to another as a infinitismal force which Brahmins, Buddhist, Rajputs, Nawab could not understand the knowledge of the '*Chamar History*' as a repeated *Rayamana* or *Mahabharata* in the Indian history.
7. O. Bopearachchi; 1998, p. 155.
8. *Ibid.,* p. 129.
9. H.W. Cordrington; 1924, *Ibid.,* p. 49.
10. Osmund Bopear achchi, 1995 A, *Ibid.,* p. 129.
11. Ibid, 1998, op. cit., p. 155.
12. A.K. Khanna; op. cit.
13. H.C. Raychaudhur; op. cit., p. 465.
14. *Ibid.*
15. *R.T.* Vol. I *Book.I p.30(Steins note)*
16. *Ibid.*

17. H.C. *Raychaudhuri* ; op. cit., pp. 476-77.
18. *Ibid.*
19. P.V. Bapat; *2500 Year of Buddhsim* : 2nd edition; Delhi 1964; p. 42.
20. *R.T.* Vol. I Book I.p. 30.
21. K.S. Sexena; op. cit., p. 26.
22. Roshen Alkazi; op. cit., pp. 59-60.
23. *Ibid.,* p. 60.
24. *Ibid.,* p. 62.
25. *Ibid.,* p. 64.
26. *Ibid.*, p.70. ***Note:*** But a large variety of fabrics were recovered from the burial ground along the Silk route of China, which can be dated to between the first century B.C. and the second century A.D. (Han Period in China). Based on this evidence we may presume that the dyes and texiles of Chinese origin available along with this route would surely have found their in to India (*Ibid.,* p. 68).
27. Jay Jaitly; op. cit., p. 31.
28. R.E.M Wheeler; *Ancient India;* Vol.II. Delhi, 1946.
29. R.K Mookerji; *Chandragupta and his times;* pp. 10-11.
30. Luders in *Epigraphic India* vol. XXIV; J.N. Benerjea in JISO A, Vol. X. pp. 65-68.
31. *V.A. Smith, Early History of India,* chapter X, p. 272.
32. Kundra and Bawa; op. cit., p. 290.
33. Jay Jaitly; op. cit., p. 32.
34. **Note:** Kushana Coinage is marked by unique feature viz, the representation of figures of various deities worshipped by the different people living in the *Kushana* empire as its subjects in its different parts developed as a natural thought of the human history without knowing the objective of life as innocent race of the Father Ravidas. The ruler of such a far-flung Empire had thus to portray on his coins in circulation in each of its provinces its particular regional deities in recognition of the religious sentiments of the peoples concerned in a spirit of wide catholicity of cosmopolitan outlook, and rare religious toleration which did not impose up on them his own personal faith out of respect for the different creeds and cultures which they represented.Thus, the popular religions that prevailed in countries like Iran, Bactria, and other neighbouring regions, influenced the modelling of Imperial Kushana Coinage by introducting into images of their respective Deities.

    Below is given a list of select Deities figuring on the coins of the Kushana Emperors:-

    1. God *Helios* (Greek); a radiate Sun God corresponding to the Sanskrit name of God *Hari*.

2. *Salene* (Greek); male figure of the moon as the Deity. The Moon God is called *Soma* in the *Rig Veda*.
3. *Orlagno,* corresponding to *Iranian* War God Verethraghna and Vedic *Vritraham*
4. *Mazadohano= Iranian Mazdaonho.*
5. *Boddo= Sankrit Buddha*
6. *Saka-Mana-Bouda= Sanskrit Sakya Muni Buddha*
7. *Odyo Boycakama=* Sanskrit *Advaya Buddha Sakyamuni*
8. *Hephaistos=* God of Metal (Greek)
9. Miiro, Sun God= Iranian Mihr Sanskrit mihira.
10. *Mao, Iranian Mah=* Sanskrit Mas of *Chandramas*, Moon God.
11. *Manaobago=* Persian *Mana Baga,* four armed Moon God.
12. *Athso* =Iranian *Atar Atash* (God of Fire). The God Agni is called in Sanskrit *Asrayasa* or *Ahutasa* which may be phonetically compared with the term *Althso*.
13. *Oesho= Hoesho Sanskrit Bhavesa* (or *Vrisha*)= Siva
14. Oado Pahlavi *Vato=* Vedic *vata* (R V.X.136, 2, IV. 40, 53) Wind God.
15. *Pharro= Kavaem* Qureno of Avesta, 'the mighty kingly glory' corresponding to Persian Farr.
16. *Ardoksho=* Avestan *Ashis Vanuhi*, Goddess of Wealth and Prosperity.
17. Nanaia (same as NANA or *Nana* appearing on the coins), a female deity supposed to be of *Persian origin*.
18. *Lrohaspo* =Zend *Aurvat aspu,* 'swift horsed= Vedic *A pamnapnapt*.
19. Mithro= Avestic Mithra= Vedic Mitra Sun God
20. *Ashaeikhsho= Pahlavi Ashavahishto* "the genius of sacrifical fire'..
21. *Loh* =English Loe= Glow, God of light, i.e., '*Nam*'
22. *Oanindo= Avestic* Female Deity called *Vanamti Uparata*, Victorious Speriroity'.
23. *Shaoreoro* (or *Shorear*)= Pahlavi *Shahrerar* 'perfect rule' Sanskrit *Aira Vira,* Avestic *Khshathra Vairya*
24. Ride= Sanskrit *Riddhi*
25. *Zero=* Meriro, Sun God, according to Gardner.
26. Herakilo= Greek Deity Heracless
27. *Sarapis=* Sanskrit Yama (Sraddha Devata)
28. Riom (means to see the God time and again)= Roma City deity of Rome. The partial statue was unearthed in the largest room at Sagolassos Roman baths. The cross shaped room measure 1,250 sq m (13,500 sq.ft) is covered in mosaics and was probably used as a frigidariuma room with a cold pool which Romans could sink into a hot bath.
29. *Horon* =Sanskrit *Varuna*

30. *Maasena*= Sanskrit *Mahasena*
31. *Skando Komaro* =Sanskrit *Skanda Kumara*
32. *Bisago*= Sanskrit *Visakha*
33. *Skando Komaro Bizago*= Sanskrit Skanda Kumara Visakha
34. *Ommo*= Sanskrit *Uma*
35. A coin of Huvishka bears a legend in Brahmi read as *Ganesa*.

It may be noted that of the Deities mentioned above, those on number I-8 appear exclusively on coins of Kanishka I : those appearing on Nos 9-19 appearing on coins of both Kansihka I and Huvishka No.16 was also issued by Vasudeva and Nos.20-34. by Huvishka alone. It may be noted that of the above Deities, the image of as seated Buddha first appears on some coins of Kadaphis, an early Kushana king (*Catalogue of Coins in the Punjab Museum,* –R.B. Whitehead). Similarly, the figure of Siva first appears on the coins of Wema Kadphises, the predecessor of Kanishka I. The figure of Heracles also occurs on the coins of Kadaphises. The colosal head of the Roman Emperor Marcus Aurelius rose in Turkey, which 1m (3ft.) in height alongwith bulging eyes and beard discovered from the study.

It will thus appear from the numismatic and epigraphic records of some of the benefactions mentioned above that they were inspired by the ideals of both Brahminism and Buddhism, which spread beyond the frontiers of India. As we have seen,the figure of the Buddha's mother appears on a coin in the Indo-Greek State under Pantaleon. The Buddha's corporeal relics were enshrined for their innate potency (*parana-sametam*) at remote places like Bajaur by he Donors, father and son, *Viryaka* and *Vijayamitra* in a village in Swat Valley in the Greek kingdom of Theodorus, by a Donor from *Urasa* and *Bahlika* for the benefit of all at Rawalpindi, Bahawalpur, Kurram (Peshawar), or at Khawat (Khavada in Afghanistan). *Ketanas* were also constructed to enshrine images of deceased ancestors and *lenam* or caves for ascetics god like attributes (*gunas*) and to pull Him up out of his physical form to his astral form as '*Nam*' on earth.

Secular charities included store-house (*koshthagara*) well (*kupa*) channel, (*toyada*), *punyasala* (or Alms –house) for free distriubtion of food and drink including vegetable curries (*saktu*) and greens (*harita*) out of an endowment (*akshaya nivi*)

Brahminical worship was represented by the building of Temples (*harmay*) for village Goddess; for deities like *Samkarshana* and Vasudeva with *Narayana Vatika* or a shrine of stone (*Sailafdevagriha*) of the '*Ravidas Culture*' or '*Chamar Culture*' where were installed images of five Vaishnava

Deities headed by *Baladeva* to *Baladitya* of Kashmir. This *Bhagavata* temple was the gift of a foreign (Iranian) lady named Tosha, showing the wide extent of the influence of Brahminical Religion along with Buddhism. The extension of Brahminical religion is also testified to by the Imperial Kushan Coins which figure many Brahminical Deities out of a medley of non-Indian deities they portray. These Brahminical gods are (I) Vedic Vritrahan, (2) Mihira, (3) Chandramas,(4) *Bhavesa,*(5) Vata, (6) Apam-Napat,(7) Mitra (8), Aira Vira, (9), Yama (10), Varuna, (11) Mahasena, (12) Skanda Kumara, (13) Visakha, (14) Skanda Kumara Viskha, and (15) *Uma*. All this numismatic evidence shows that is a mistake to suppose that the Kushana empire was mainly a Buddhist empire. It was not less the home of Vedism or Brahminism. Its founder, Vima, Kadphisa, led the way by declaring himself on his coins as a Saiva and a *Mahesvara* Saivaism had its offshoots in the worship of Goddess *Uma* and of *Skanda Kumara Visakha of the Gupta period*. Even the Vedic deties were still worshipped, deities like Vritrahan, *Vata, Mithira* and Varuna.

35. It may be noted that no recording in Kushana era involving hundreds has yet been brought to light. It appears suddenly to have stopped in 98 but the Kushana Empire did not end with the *Vasudeva* who comes after Huvishka. Dr. L. Bachhofer has proved from coins the existence of King Kanishka III coming after Vasudeva I and King Vasudeva II coming after Kansihka III. Herzefed think that Vasudeva II who came after Kanishka III at about 210 A.D. lost Bactria to the Sassanian King Ardashir I. After him the Sassanids coins modelled on Kushana coinage.Some Armenian records mention Vasudeva II named Vehsardjan. He is said to have sent an embassy to China about 230 A.D.

Dr. Van Lohuizern de Leewu, in her book '*The Scythain Period*' has shown that Brahmi inscriptions in the Mathura region bear dates from years 5-57 where the figure for hundred has been omitted according to old Indian practice. Thus 5=105, 14=114 of the Kushana era and her conclusion is that the records of Kushana Kings after Kanishka I range from 1-98. In the second century of the Kanishka era the hundreds are omitted and such reords have been found up to year 157 A.D. 235

Dr. M.N. Saha thinks that Kanishka was not founder of the era, but it already in vaogue omitting the hundreds. The year I of Kanishka was year one plus some hundred.

There was an old Saka era which started in about 129 or 123 B.C. the year that marked the settlement of the dispossessed Sakas in Bactria after the Parthian Emperor Phraates II was killed. It will be remembered that Bactria was under Greek occupation till about 141 B.C. The Parthain Emperor

Mithridates I ruled from 171 to 137 B.C. Earlier, he expelled from Bactria the Greek King Heliocles, son of Eicratides. After him his son Phraates II was killed by the Sakas as stated above. Thus, the *Sakas* were justified in inauguration the era in 123 B.C. Next the Sakas under Parthain power revived by Mithridates II moved towards the south and settled in Ki-pin,Sakasthan or Seistan and Archosiaas Parthian vassala. The *Yueh-Chis* in the meanwhile retried to the Uspper Oxus basin where they were divided into five branches, each under a Yabgou (lord), as already narrated, and adopted a Khotani Saka dialect. After about a hundred years,Kujula Kadphises united the five tribes under his sovereignty. Then he conquered Bactria from the Parthians and the Kabul Valley (*Paropamsadai*) from the Greek King Hermaios or his Saka successors and laid the foundation of the Kushana Empire.

In the meanwhile,the *Sakas* who had migrated to Sakasthana were led by Maues who conquered Taxila before 65 B.C., taking advantage of the declines of Parthian power, which stated earlier from 88 B.C. Probably, he used the old Saka era which stated from 123 B.C. On this basis, the Saka and the Kushana eras thus became one and the same (see Dr. M.N. Saha Article in *J.AS.B.*Vol XIX, No I.1953 and also *J.R.A.S.* 1913 and 1914).

There is also another view that the Saka era was the same as the *Chitrakuta –Kalachuriya* era which started from 248 A.D. But then the last known date of Vasudeva I would be 347 A.D. when we know Samudra Gupta was ruling in India and received the homage of the Kidara Kushanas (little Kushanas).

According to Sir John Marshall, Sten Know and V.A.Smith together with some other historians of the '*Nam*' or '*Chama*r', Kanishka's rule was commenced from 120, 125 or 144 A.D.

36. Charles Fabres; *Indian Dress*; pp. 17-18, 50; Also see Rambach and de Golish, *The Golden Age of Indian Art;* plates 47-48 refers *'Halo'* style coiffure and shot silk (moiree) and *saronga or dhoti* highly ornamental, of 'infinite variety' as *Nam* or *Chamar.*

Plate XXXVI

Fig. 54 Statue of Kanishka (Mathura-Ist CenturyA.D.).

Plate XXXVII

Fig. 55. Kushan King, Mathura

11

Position of the Jammu State Before the Gupta Period

History of the Monarchical States Before the Guptas

The period between the decline of the *Kushana* Empire and the rise of the Gupta was maked by the growth of a number of Republican and Monarchical States ruling in *Rajputana* and the adjoining region of the Jammu State. Among the former may be mentioned (i) the *Arjunayans*, (2) *Uddehikas*, (3) *Malavas*, (4) *Sivis* (5) *Rajanyas*, (6) *Yaudheyas*, (7) *Uttamabhadras*, (8) *Madrakas* of the Punjab, (9) *Abhiras* of Rajputana, (10) *Audumbaras* and (11) *Vemakis* between the Sutlej and the Ravi basin. Among the monarches may be mentioned those of *Mathura, Ayodhya, Ahichchhatra* and *Kausambi* together with the Nagas of Padmavati, the Vakatakas and the Maukharis. All these separate states remained to be merged in the Gupta Empire in the fourth century A.D. In the words of several historians, therefore, "*The rise of the Guptas marks a transition* from darkness to light". The period from the end of the Kushana rulers to the beginning of the Gupta period (200-320 A.D.) is, therefore known in the Indian history as the *'Dark-Interval'* governed by the Brahmins.

The Archaeological evidence of the Buddhist monastic establishment at Ambaran, about 32 K m. west of the Jammu, on the right bank of the Chenab River is not surprising that certain terracotta heads of Lord Buddha have been found, torso of bodies and pieces of drapery belonging to Lord Buddha i.e., '*Nam*' or *'Chamar'* figuress or figures of monks and laymen and lay women propusely decorated with fine jewellery are found in various parts of the decorative walls on Buddhist monastry and *Stupa* at *Ambaran* in Akhnoor. The establishment was continued to flourished in Gupta Period Phase III from 4th century to 5th century A.D. with the periodic damage and subsequent repairs [1] by the Kashmiri rulers of the *'Siharas Rai Dynasty'* of the Sindh, who are said to have held the power over here for 137 years with Alor (near modern Rohri) as their capital. When *Yuan Chwang* was travelling in India (629-45 A.D.). Sindh was ruled by a Buddhist monarch of the *Sudhra* (*shu-to-lo*) caste [2] and he was identical with *Siharas* Rai II, as is most probable, we get welcome the light on the origin of the *Rais* Family because they were the '*Dalit Kings*' of the '*Dalit Voice*'. Presumably it was this ruler, who came to conflict with the *Harshavardhana* [3]. After the death of last *Rai Sahasi,* power was shifted to Kashmiri rulers *Durlabhavardhana* of '*Karkota Dynasty*' of the *Sudhra Family* of low origin called *Chamar* and thus Harshavardhana held submitted his power to the Kashmiri ruler subject to the condition of spread the Buddhism in India and abroad. Thus, the widow queen of last *Rai-Sahasi* was married by the *Chach* Brahmin who was the ministerial of his adminsitartion have the same story as 'Birth and Rebirth' (*See Plate XXXVIII, Fig.56*) and world as Weavers *Knitting work of Kabir* in Human History, (See the same plate, Fig. 57). It was handsomely endowed, and at the time of I-tsing's *itinerary* (673-95, A.D.), its dilapidated remnants were known as the *'Temple of China',* Gupta is generally assigned to the period A.D. 275-300. I-tsing, however, notes that the building of the temple began 500 years before his travels[4]. V.A Smith is of the opinion that in consequence of this Union, *Chandragupta* I "succeeded to the power previously held by his wife's soul relatives" and that he obtained possession of Pataliputra[5].

We may now note in brief the history of some of the those most important of these States.

1. Arjunayanas

They ruled in the region now comprised in the *Bharatpur* and Alwar States of India. They issued coins in the first century B.C. with the legend *Arjunayanas, Jayah.* They grow in power after the Indo-Greeks but were subdued by the *Sakas*. They, however, recovered after the *Kushanas* till they were merged in the Gupta Empire.

2. Malavas

The *Malavas* are known from the time of Alexander, as already mention in the study. The Indo-Greek expensoin drove them to migrate to Rajputana. They were the first to use the *Vikrama Samvat* of 58 B.C. their capital in Rajaputana was Malava-nagar (=modern Nagar in *Jaipur*). The Malavas of south Jaipur had to fight the *Uttamabhadras* of Ajmer and their allies, the *Kshaharata Sakas* of Western India as already discussed. They used the *Krita* era in their inscriptions of the third and fourth century A.D. found in

States like *Bharatpur, Kotah* and *Udaipur*. An interesting inscription of A.D. 226 found at *Nandsa* (in Udaipur refers to the peak of their progress achieved by a Malava chief. It probably implied their success against the Sakas. The Badva Inscriptions of A.D. 238 refers to *Mankhari Mahasenapti Bala* as the vassal of the Malava republic whose Krite era he followed. Later the Malavas were absorbed in the Gupta Empire but they had an off shoot, the *Aulikaras*, who ruled as *Dasapura* as vassals of the Gupta Empire. It seems that king Yasodharman (A.D.532) was an Aulikara. They persisted in using the Krita era in preference to the Gupta.(*See Plate XXXIX, Geographical Location of Gupta Empire,* Fig. 58).

Malava coins date from the first century B.C. Their later coins are known by the legend Jayo *Malavanam* or *Malavanam Jayah*. There were others coins only names.

3. Yaudheyas

Panini calls the Yaudheyas as *Aryudha jivi* Kashatriyas. Their stronghold was in East Punjab but they also dominated the part of U.P. and Rajputana. Their tutelary deity was Brahmanyadeva. They grew into power after the Indo-Greeks only to be subdued by the *Sakas* and the *Kushanas*. They were strong enough to challenge Rudradaman's authority. After the Kushanas they made their power felt like the *Kardamaksa* and the Malavas while all the three were subdued by the Guptas. Their earlist coins dated from first century B.C. with the legend *Bahuddha naka Yodheyanam*. The city of Bahuddhanyaka was located in the Rohtak region where the moulds of these coins have been discovered. Other Yaudheya coins in both silver and copper of the second or third century A.D. bear the following legend *Bhagavatah Suamino Brahmadevasya Kumarasya Yaudheyanam*. Some coins bear the figure of six-head God Skanda and some a goddess with six heads on te reverse, probably goddess *Shashthi* or Devasena wife of Skanda, worked efficiently for the development of the Indian History i.e., 'Nam' or 'God' on earth at that time.

A third class of Yaudheya copper coins of third and fourth centuries A.D. and modelled on Kushana bear the lenged *Yaudheya-genasya Jayah*. The Yaudheyas were divided intc sections or classes one of which called *Matta Mayurakas* settled in Rohtak. Even the present day *Johiyas* are divided into three sections. Sometimes it is inferred that one of the factors leading to the decline of the Kushana Empire was the emergence of these tribal republics in different parts of the world to find out the truth where it stands either in *Sudhra* or Brahmin history study shows it was explored from the '*Dalit Family*'.

4. **The *Lichchchavis*** were another powerful republican who ruled for centuries from the time of the Buddha on the other side of the river *Ganga* to find out the realistic approach in history i.e., '*Nam*' or God.

Among the minor Republican States of the times may be noted the following;-

1. The ***Sibis*** who first appeared in hstory as opposing Alexander with 40,000 infantry dressed in skins of wild beast. They later migrated to Rajputana and settled in a region near Chitor with their capital at *Madhyamika*. Some of their coins found in this region bear the legend *Majhamikaya Sibijanapadasa*, coins issued by the Sibi State from *Madhyamika* for the study of history.

2. The ***Kunindas*** who settled in the territory between the Yamuna and the Sutlej and the upper courses of the Beas and the Sutlej. Their King named *Amoghabhuti* is known from his coins. There are other Kuninda coins modelled on Kushana which bear the figure of Siva and a Brahmi legend *Bhagavatah Chatresvara-Mahatmanah. Chatra* or *Chhatra* was probably the name of the Kuninda capital like *Ahichchchatra*. It is supposed that *Amoghabhuti* carved out a Kingdom for himself from the ruins of the Indo-Greek Empire by the end of the first century B.C. and that he later *Chatresvara* coins were issued after the fall of the Kushana Empire by the third century A.D.

3. The ***Kunindas*** were overthrown by the *Kulutlas* after Amoghabhuti. They inhabited the Kabul valley visited by *Yaun Chwang* during the reign of Chandragupta II, the celebrated pilgrim overlanded from China to India from the Gobi Desert[6]. Their King *Virayasas* of the third century A.D. is known from his coins. A King named Bhadrayasas is also known from his coins found in the Kulu Valley. The *Kuluta* country was subdued by the Guptas for establishment of the Jammu Kingdom in this area.

4. The Audumbaras. These are located in the eastern part of Kangra, Gurudaspur and Hoshiarpur Districts and were originally of the *Salya* tribe of the *Sudhra* Family. Their earliest coins bear in Brahmi and Kharoshthi the legend *Bhagavato Mahaddevasya Rajarajasya*. Some coins name early *Audumbara* rulers like Dharaghosha, Sivadasa, and Rudradasa. Some of their square copper coins bear the figure of a Saiva temple marked by a *Dhvaja*, a trident and a battle axe. These coins are dated from first century B.C. to first century A.D. There are also some coins which name as rulers *Ajamitra, Mahimitra, Bhumitra and Mahabhumitra* supposed to be Audumbaras.

We shall now turn to the Monarchical States of the period as mentioned below :-

1. The Naga Kingdoms. The Nagas spread themselves in different parts of India as testified to by epigraphic, numistmatic and literary records and also by localities named after them such as *Nagapura* or *Uragapura*. We are here converned only with those Naga Dynasties that ruled between the *Kushanas* and the *Guptas.*

The *Puranas* mention seats of Naga power at *Vidisa, Kantipuri, Mathura* and *Padmavati*. Some of the Naga rulers of Vidisa are named *Sisha, Bhogin* and *Sadachandra Chandramsa* supposed to be *Nahapana* in the Kashmir history.

The Vakatake Inscriptions mention *Maharaja Bhavanaga* as the maternal grandfather of Rudrasahena I whose grandson was a contemporary of Chandra Gupta II (A.D. 375—414). He may, therefore, be assigned to the fourth century A.D. He belonged to the family of the *Bharasivas* who according to tradition carried on their shoulders the load of a *Sivalinga* the highest at that time on earth in pious form.

The *Bharasivas* are credited with the performance of ten. Asvamedha sacrifices after the fall of the Kushana Empire.At Padmavati have been found some coins bearing te name of Bhavanaga. Padmavati has been immortalized by poet *Bhavabhuti* of (8th century A.D.) by making that city the scene of his *Malati- Madhava* and made contact with Kashmiri ruler *Lalitadity Muktapida*.

Samudra Gupta uprooted two Naga named *Ganapati Naga* and Nagasena' of the *Sudhra* Family of the Northern India, but he married his son Chandragupta II with Kuveranaga. A Naga chief Sarvanaga ruled as a governor of the *Antarvedi vishaya* under Skanda Gupta of the Jammu region.

Some coins brings to light the name of *Maharaja Ganendra* or Ganapa and were found at *Padmavati*, Vidhisa and Mathura. The might have been Ganapati Naga aforesaid Bana in *Harsha-Charita* refers to the story that a *Sarika* bird revealed the secrets of Nagasena of Nagapura and led to this downfall at Padmavati in the history of heavenly world, i.e. '*Nam*' or '*Chamar*'.

The *Puranas* mention nine Naga ruler of Padmavati. Some other are known from their coins found in that locality such as Maharajas, *Bhimanagar, Skandanaga, Brihaspatinaga, Devanaga, Vibhanaga* and possibly *Vyaghranaga*.

The *Puranas* mention nine Naga rulers of Padmavati who must have followed the Kushanas. Some early Mathura coins of the Ist century B.C. name kings like *Gomitra, Brahmamitra, Dridhamitra, Suryamitra* and *Vishnumitra* without the Naga title. Similarly, there are other early coins which name rulers like *Purushadtta, Uttamadatta, Ramadatta, Raja Kamadatta, Raja Sishadatta* and Raja Bhavadatta and Raja *Balabhuti*. They ruled after the *Sakas* of Mathura in the second century A.D.

Virasena was another powerful kings of the same times who was probably a Naga and had his capital at Mathura, Bulandshahar, Etah, Farukkabad and even the Punjab districts of the Sindh provinces.

2. Kingdom of Ahichchhatra. Its kings are known from their coins. Their names and in the world Mitra. They may be dated to the first three centuries A.D. These names are *Bhadraghosha*, *Suryamitra, Phalgunimitra*, *Agnimitra*, *Brihatsvatimitra* and the like. Pabhosa (near Kosam) cave Inscription name kings Ashadhasena, son of the queen *Gopalika Vaihidari* and his Fatherly King *Traqivarniputra Bhagavat,* son of *Vangapala* king of *Ahichchhatra* says 'you are the temple of the living God' in human form.

Some copper coins of *Ahichchhatra* mention the name of *Achyuta* or '*untouchable*' who was probably the *Aryavarta* ruler of *Sudhra* Family. *Achyuta* or '*untouchable*' who was subdued by Samudra Gupta as his co-brother of the natural history.

3. Ayodhya. Some of its rulers are known from coins such as *Dhanadeva* and Visakhadeva. Dhanadeva was probably the *Dharmaraja* Dhanadeva, King of Kosala, mentioned in an Ayodhya inscription of the first century B.C. which represents him as sixth in descent from *Senapati* Pushyamitra Sunga (c.187-158 B.C.).

4. Kausambi. As usual, its rulers are known mostly from their coins. Some coins of the Ist century B.C. mention kings *Sudeva* and *Brihatsvatimitra*. Other coins name rulers such as *Asvaghosha*, *Agnimitra*, *Jyeshthamitra* and *Devamitra*. Some coins recently found at *Kausambi* name *Mitra* kings like *Varunamitr* a and *Prajapatimitra* and also a Raja named *Dhanadeva*, Inscription also name some kings of Kausambi e.g. the Pabhosa Inscriptions.

5. The *Vakatakas* were another rival power which attained its zenith under *Prithvisena* I who ruled over a large empire extending from *Bundelkhand* to *Kuntala* in Kanarese country, with his vassal *Vyaghradeva* posted in Bundelkhand and subdud later by Samudra Gupta in his Kingdom in Jammu Region. Their history will be related later.

6. The *Maukharis* were another local power ruling in Magadha Under *Sundaravarman*. Inscription in Kotah State credit Maukhari *Senapatis* with erecting sacrifical pillars for the sake of his friend as '*Nam*' on earth.

The Guptas were another local power which emerged into prominence from the '*Sudhra Family*' to world power and established their supremacy over all contending powers to defeat the Brahmins with the power of '*Nam*' *or* 'God'. There are many points of contact between Gupta history and these several local histories as will be shown below by the local rulers of the Jammu Region for the sake of Father. As anger destroys peace, neutralizes love, endangers hatred, turns people into enemies due to the lack of *Nam-dana.*

Local Chief Sri Gupta (c.240-280 A.D.)

Sri Gupta is referred to in the Gupta Inscriptions as a Maharaja and ancestor of the Gupta Emperors. The Poona Copper Plate Inscriptions of the Gupta princes, Prabhavati Gupta describes *Sri Gupta* as a 'Nam' on earth at that time as the *Adiraja* of the dynasty and as belonging to the Gotra named *Dharana* in her *Riddhapura* Copper Plate Inscription. A tradition recorded by the Chinese pilgrims I-tsing mentions 'Maharaja Sri Gupta as having built a temple at *Mrigasikhavana* (or *Mrigasthapana*, according to Foucher) for Chinese pilgrims and endowed it with 24 villages 500 years before'. I tsing locates *Mrigasikhavana* about 50 stages east of Nalanda down the Ganges i.e., about 250 miles from Nalanda as for a *Murshidabad*. Thus, *Sri Gupta's* dominion was sufficiently large to make him known as Maharaja in Magadha. If I-tsing actually refers *Mrigasthapana*, a *Vihara* discovered in North Bengal, it is then likely that *Varendrabhumi* rather then Magadha, was the cradle of the Gupta power, The date of I-tsing's reference is 690A.D. and of *Sri Gupta* 500 year earlier i.e., ***190 A.D.*** The Gupta inscriptions make out his date to be about 240-280 A.D. A difference of fifty years in ***such traditional*** **reck**onings may be allowed for tear down on this earth destroys, weakens and annihilates every finer quality of mind and soul as an order of the day.

The name of the King is to be taken as Gupta to which is added the royal prefix *Sri*, as *'Nam'*

Gupta history earlier than Sri Gupta cannot be traced, because of pucity of the original sources, and has been identified Maharaja *Che-li-ki-to* in Chinese language as the rulers of *Dalit* class which works in hide and cutter in hide.

Ghatotkacha (280-319 A.D.).

Inscriptions mention Maharaja *Ghatotkacha* as the successor of Sri Gupta a stylished ruler of the *Sudhra* Family. (See Plate XXXX, *Garuda Pillar*, *Besnagar of Gupta Empire*, Fig. 59)

Chandra Gupta I (319-355 A.D.)

He is described as *Maharajadhiraja* (King of Kings) and as successor of *Ghatotkacha* in the inscriptions. His imperial title was the consequence of his conquests. These are indicated in the *Puranas* which state that the kings born of the Gupta family will rule over all the territories (*Janapadan*) situated along the Ganges (*Anu-Ganga*) such as Prayage, Saketa (Oudh) and Magadha. But this passage does not indicate the specifc conquests achieved by Chandragupta I alone. It only indicates the collective conquests of the Gupta Kings. It is, however, undoubted the Megadhan was a part of the dominion of Chandragupta I. The other conquests along the course of the Ganges such as Prayage and Saketa were definitely those achieved by his successor Samudra Gupta as the conqueror of *Aryavarata*,as stated in his Allahabad Pillar Inscription.

Both inscriptions and what is known as Chandragupta Coinage record the marriage of Chandragupta I with a Lichchhavi princess. The coins portray the husband offering right hand a ring to his wife. They also name on the obverse the husdand as *Chandra* or Chandragupta and on the reverse the wife as Sri Kumaradevi. That she was a *Lichchhavi* princess is inidicated by the legend *Lihchhavayah* on the reverse. These coins also show that Kumaradevi was associated with the sovereignty included the Lichchhavi republic as the result either of this matrimonial alliance by way of a dowry or direct military conquest by Chandra gupta I. These coins were evidently in circulation in the *Liachchhavi* country. The political importance of his marriage is shown by the fact that inscriptions describe Smaudra gupta as a Lichchhavi-*Dauhitra* and not as a *Ghatotkacha Pautra*. The Gupta dynasty took pride in the family of the mother as an owner of the earth.

The Gupta Era. According to *Al-Beruni*, the Gupta Era is separated from the Saka Era of 78 A.D. by an interval of 241 years, which makes the Gupta Era begin in 319 A.D.These two Eras thus fixed and settled the chronological framework of a long period of the Indian history. For instance, the last date of the *Saka* power which was extinguished by Chandragupta II is the year 304 of the Saka Era (=382 A.D.) while Chandragupta issued his first coin in the Saka relam in the year 90 of the Gupta Era (= 409 A.D.). The interval between these two dates marked the process of the Gupta conquest of the *Saka* power. J. F. Fleet points out that the Gupta Era was taken over from the *Lichchchhavis* of Nepal that time whose King Jayadeva I approximates to 320 A.D. The Gupta Era in its turn was taken over by the Valabhi Kings of Surashtra as the feudatories of the Gupta Empire. The son of the founder of the Valabhi dynasty first uses the date 207 in the Gupta Era. The Gupta Era is taken to mark the commencement of the reign of Chandra Gupta I as the founder of the Gupta Empire in the history of India by defeating the Brahmins of the period.

Samudra Gupta Parakramanka (c.335-375 A.D.)

Date

As the first year of his successor, Chandragupta II, stated to be 375 A.D. in his Mathura Pillar Inscription that year is taken to mark the end of *Samudra guptas* reign. Another date of his reign, is fixed by that of the embassy sent to by king *Meghavarna* of Ceylon (351-379 A.D.). His reign is roughly taken to begin from 335 A.D. lest it become too long. Its length also depends on his age. The date of his birth may be taken to be 310 A.D. following his father's marriage in 308 A.D. Thus he came to the throne at 25, the legal age of kingship in 335 A.D.

Name

The name Samudra was perhaps the name assumed by him after his conquest upto the *Seas* while Gupta was his surname. The Mathura Pillar Inscription of Chandragupta II states that his father's fame spread up to the four oceans (*chaturudadhi*).*Kacha* may be taken as his personal name on the ground of the coins issued by *Kacha* describing him as the 'exterminator of all kings' (*Sarvarajochchhetta*), an epithet which applies best to Samudra Gupta in view of his conquests by writing certain books of the God or '*Nam*'.

Succession-

It is stated in the Allahabad Pillar Inscription that he was selected for the throne by his father who embraced (*Upaguhyas*) him as a genuine *Arya* on the ground as *Sudhra* of his merit in preference to his brothers (*Tulya-Kulajah*). The selection was greeted by his Council (*Sabha*) with great enthusiasm (*Uchchhvasita*), but it made the faces of other claimants pale (*mlana*). Some words of the inscription and some of its gaps are taken to indicate a fight for the throne by the discontented brothers. These words are "Conquered some by his arms (*virya*) in battle (*ranamupagata*)" ' and further, "pride (*mana*) has changed in to repentance (*Tapa*)". Probably *Samudra gupta* conquered his brothers in battle humbled their '*pride*' and made them 'repentant for their folly'.

The Allahabad Pillar Inscription

It is a detailed record of his conquests. It is the poetical composition (*kavya*) of Harishena who combined in himself the four important offices of (I) *Khadyatapakika,* (Food Controller of the Royal Kitchen), (2) *Sandhivigrahika* (Minister for Foreign Relation and War), (3) Kumaramatya (Minister is attendance on Crown Prince), and (4) *Mahadandanayaka* (Chief Justice). Harishena was the son of Dhruvabhuti who also held the office of *Mahadandanayaka* which descended to his son. Harishena was thus eminently to give a correct account of the conquests of the kings and especially the chronological order in which they were achieved.

The inscription is stated to have been excuted (*Anushithita*) by *Tilabhattaka* who also held the office of a *Mahadandanyaka.*

This unique historical inscription is unfortunately not dated, but some words in it which refer to the King's fame 'going up to heaven are taken to imply that the king also went up to Heaven and that the inscription was posthumous, but Buhler has shown that it could not be so as it omits to mention a most important event which took place after it, and in the King's life and reign. It was his performance of *Asvamedha* after the completion of his conquests.

Conquests

There are decribed in the inscription in a chronological order which is follwed here. His plan was first to subdue the neighbouring States so as to secure his rear before launching upon distant expeditions with the study of *'Nam's* History

First Campaign in Aryavarta

Samudra Gupta began by uprooting (*nirmulya*) the neighbouring Kingdoms of *Achyuta or 'untouchable'* and *Nagasena*. The *Achyuta* untouchable copper coins show that Achyuta or '*untouchable*' was a ruler of *Ahichchhatra*. The *Puranas* mention Nagasena as ruling at *Champavati* (Padmavati or Narwar in Gwalior State) and Mathura.

The next king chequered was one of the *Kota* family of Kashmir, who was captured at play at Pushpapura. There are found some Kota coins resembling the *Sruta* coins of *Srasvasti*. Pushpapura may be taken to be Kanuj.

These conquests extended Samudra Gupta's dominion "beyond Prayaga and Saketa" up to Mathura and Gwalior called "digvijaya", before the performance of the *Asvamedha,* which is not mentioned in it..

Campaigns in Dakshinapatha

According to Harishena, Samudra Gupta now embarked upon an expedition to the south of which all the Kings (*Sarva Dakshinapatha –Raja*) he was able to subdue. His victory was marked by three features: (1) Capture of the enemy (*Grahana*), (2) his liberation (*Moksha*), and (3) showing him mercy (*Anugraha*) by re-instating him in his kingdom on his acknowledgement of the victor's suzerainty.

These defeated kings are thus mentioned (1) Mahendra of Kosala (Southern Kosala including the modern districts of Bilaspur, Raipur and Sambalpur and also parts of Ganjam district, (2) Vyaghraraja of *Mahakantara* (the kingdom of dense forest of East Gondwana). Its King is called the tiger of the forest and was a *Vakataka* feudatory. As the date of his son, Jayanatha, is 174 of the Kalachuri Era which was the time of Chnadra gupta II, his father was thus a contemporary of Samudra gupta; (3) Mantaraja of Kaurala (=Colair lake, or Korada in the South); (4) Mahendragiri of Psihtapura (= modern Pithapuram in Godavari district); (5) Svamidatta of Kottura (=modern Kothoor; Kottura in Vizagapattam district); (6) Damana of Erandapalla =(i) Erandapalli near Chicacol in Vizagapattam district; (ii) Yendipalli in Vizagapattam district or (iii) Endapilli Ellore Taluq); (7) Vishnugopa of Kanchi (=Conjeeveram); (8) Nilaraja of *Avamukta* (=Nilappallin in Godavari district); (9) Hastivarman of Vengi; (10) Ugrasena of Palakka (in Nellore district). It is supposed that these southern Kings of Avamuka, Vengi and Palakka were the members of the confederacy led by the King of Kanchi under Vishnugopa, which extended from the mouth of the Krishna to the south of the river Palar and possibly Kaveri; (11) Kuvera of Devarashtra (in the Vizagapattam district); and (12) Dhananjaya of Kausthalapura (on the river Kusasthali or Kuthalur in N. Arcot district.).

Some scholars have sought to locate some of these places in Southern and Western India e.g. Kaurala= Keralaputra (Madura); Kothura= Kothurapolachi (Coimbatore) Palakka= Palaghat, Erandapalla Erandol (Khandesh) and Devarashtra= Maharashtra. This supposition is not likely because some of these conquests were made by Samudra Gupta on his way to Kanchi and not after his campaign in Kanchi. These must therefore be located in *Dakshinapatha* and not in Aparanta or Western region of India. They were defeated and captured, but the victor released and re-instated them[7].

Second Campaign in Aryavarta

By his second campaign in *Aryavarta*, conscious of his power (*Pratapa*), he violently exteriminated (*prasabhoddharana*) with the following Nine Monarches: (1) *Rudradeva,* (2) *Matila*; (3) *Nagadatta,* (4) *Candravarman*; (5) *Ganapatinaga,* (6) *Naga Sena,* (7) *Nandin,* (8) Acyuta or *Untouchable*' (9) *Balavarman* of the Central India[8] or *Bharata* of the Jammu and Kashmir State, Started his campign to capture the power of Dilli (Delhi) and the adjoining areas of the world community.

Conquest of Atavika (Forest) Kingdoms

The epithet applied to his conquests of these kingdoms is that were all reduced to the condition of vassalage with obligations of service to the suzerain (*paricharakikrita*). A copper plate inscription of the Parivrajaka King, Basti, mentions that there were eighteen such forest kingdoms at that time, including Dabhala (Jubbulpore). According to Kaildas, the birth of Kumara in 400 A.D. gave birth to flame-of-the forest among India's most venerated trees with its colourful flowers called *Butea monosperma* belonged to the family of *Papilion aceae*, in Sanskrit called as *Palasha* and in Hindi known as *Dhak* as crescent moon. According to *Charaka Samhita* the tree's seeds are insecticidal used by the Buddhist monks for the study of '*Nam*' or God during the Gupta period.

Relation With Fronitier States

The might of his dominion (*Prachandasasana*) was felt by the States on it frontiers Kingships (*pratyantanripati*) and republics which were anxious to be on friendly terms with him by winning his good will (*paritosha*) by paying all taxes (*sarvakarvadana*) levied by him as suzerain, obeying his decrees (*adjnakarana*) and attending his imperial darbars to tender homage to him in person (*pranamagamana*).

The frontier kingdoms towards the East are thus listed: (I) *Samatata* (part of Bengal on the sea-shore); (2) *Davaka* (in Naogaon district in Assam); (3) *Kamarupa* (Gauhati district in Assam); (4) Nepal; (5) *Kartripura* (in Kumaon, Garhwal and Rohilkhand districts).

This list shows that Samudra Gupta was busy in conquering the outlying parts of Bengal and Assam to round off his Empire in the East. The conquest of these borders may be taken to imply the previous conquest of his interior of Bengal which may be attributed to Chandra Gupta I, though it is not recorded. The conquest of Bengal is attributed to king Chandra of the Meherauli Iron Pillar Inscription at Delhi. This Chandra may be taken to be Chandragupta I. The administration of Chandra gupta II included North Bengal (*Pundravardhana*).

The frontier republics are mentioned as follows:(1) Malavas (2) Arjunayana.Their coins are found in the Mathura region. (3) Yaudheyas. They had a long history with coins duistributed over a large area. (4) *Madrakas* between the Ravi and the Chenab with their capital at Sakala (Sialkot); (5) *Abhiras* between the '*Sarasvati Indus of the Akhnoor*' region; and Vinasana (Hissar district in E. Punjab); (6) Prarjunas (*Prarjunaksa* of Kautilya); (7) Sanakanikas (near Bhilsa) (8) Kakas (near Sanchi); (9) *Kharaparikas* (In Damoh in M.P.).

Dealings With Foreign States

Beyond the frontier states described above lay the foreign states towards the north–west, in Western India the area of Jammu and Kashmir State, and also in the distant South 'Simhala and other island overseas'. We learn from the Chinese sources[9] that his Ceylonese contemporary, *Meghavanna or Meghavarna* (352-79 A.D.) sent two monks to Bodhgaya on a religious mission known as Mahabodhi Sangharama in the time of Yuan Chwang[10] which were also ready to acknowledge the suzerainty of Samudra Gupta by rendering to him all kinds of services (*Seva*). These services are described in the inscription as comprising (a) tending their personal service to the King (*atma-nivedanam*), (b) gifts of maidens for menial service (*Kanyopayana*), (c) present (*Dana*); (d) application (*Yachna*) for charters bearing the Imperial Gupta Garuda Seal (*Garutmadanka*) guaranteeing friendly relations so as to leave them undisturbed in the enjoyment (*bhukti*) and administration (*Sasana*) of their respective states (*Svavishaya*). Thus there were treaties of friendship and service between the foreign overseas States and Samudra Gupta who brought under his sway the whole country by the prowess of his arms (*Bahuvirya prasaradharanibandhasya*, *Chamar* or *Charamkara*

Svabhujavala '*Nam*' or '*Word*' *parakramaikabandhoh* '*Sudhra*' *Parakramnkasya*).

These foreign powers are mentioned as follows:-

1. Daivaputra-Shahi-Shahanushahi

As we have already seen, these title were assumed by the Kushana Emperors from Kanishka I and were later continued by their successor, the Little Kushanas, who were ruling in Indian border land and in the Kabul Valley in the third and fourth century A.D. The Kushana king with whom Samudra Gupta came into contact might have been Grumbates who ruled in 350 A.D. Under the Sassanian suzerain Shapur II to whom he sent a present of Indian elephants.

***2.* Sakas**

These might have been the Sakas of Western India under royal family of Chashtana and Rudradaman followed by Rudrasimha II in the time of Samudra Gupta. The context of the inscription may be taken to indicate that these Sakas were of the north –west, whose coins were imitated by Samudra Gupta. These coins were of the Kushana type with *Ardochso* reverse and the title Saka added to the initial each individual ruler in Brahmi script. These were distinct from the other type of the Kushana coins of the Kabul valley with *Oesho* reverse not imitated by Samudra Gupta.

3. Murundas

These may be identified with the Kushanas as held by Sten Konow.

4. Simhala

As we have already seen, Samudra Gupta's connexion with this island led to the despatch to him by its King *Meghavarman* (or *Varna*) of an embassy with gifts for building a monastery at Bodh-Gaya for Ceylonese pilgrims followed by *Chamar* rulers of the '*Nam*' or God along with China prince, *Fa-Hien*.

5. Other Islands

These islands are not named but must have included the *Island* of Java where Fa-Hien about this time found settlements of Brahmins and Buddhists from India. This important epigraphic passage thus makes the first mention of the beginnings of Greater India under Samudra Gupta.

6. Mattila

Which was perhaps in *Bulandshar* the Highest Knowledge of the '*Nam*', a law of the land was established at that time.

Conquest of other Kingdoms in Aryavarta

These are mentioned as those of the Naga Kings (probably *Nagadatta, Ganapati Naga* and *Nagasena*), of *Chandravarman* whose identity is discussed later, of *Achyuta* or *untouchables* (different from the first Achyuta already mentioned) of Nandi (probably the Naga King Sivanandi of the *Puranas*) of Balavarman (un-identified) ruler of the '*Nam*' or God as *'infinite'* power.

The inscription concludes by saving that there were many (*Aneka*) other kings of *Aryavarta* who were forcibly extirpated (*prasabhoddharana*).

Thus Samudra Gupta achieved the political unification of Northern India or *Aryavarta* which according of Manu, was the land that lay "between he Himalayas and the Vindhyas and between the Western and Eastern Seas".

Asvamedha

To celebrate the completion of his conquests, Samudra Gupta performed the Horse Sacrifice revived after a long time (*Chirotsanna-Asveamedha-Aharta*). It was marked by the issue of special coinage on which the legend indicates its justification in the following words: "The Kings of Kings (*Rajadhiraja*) having conquered the Earth (*Prithivim avitva*) now conquers Heaven (*Divam Jayalit* with invincible valour (*aprativaryaviryah*)". The coins portray on the obverse the horse before the sacrifical post and on the reverse the Queen associated with the ceremony. They also bear the legend '*Aasvamedha-Parakramah*' (the supreme prowes proved by the Horse Sacrifice).During the spring festival of Holi, Young men smear a powder made from dried petals of the flame-of-the-forest flower onto the faces of passing young women for examination to a husband the brilliant red colour carrying an obvious erotic message of the '*Nam-theory*' as God and man.

Through he Allahabad Inscription is silent about the *Asvamedha*, it is referred to in other inscriptions *Prabhavati Gupta's* Inscription describes her grandfather the 'performer of numerous Horse Sacrifices'. The gifts that followed the sacrifice are also indicate in such phrases as 'gifts of gold' (*Suvarna-dana*) used in the Eran Stone Inscription.

Coins

Samudra Gupta issued several types of gold coinage such as(I) *Standard,* (2) *Archer,* (3) *Battle axe*, (4) *Kacha*, (5) *Tiger*, (6) *Lyrist,* and (7) *Asvamedha.* These types thus depict the different aspects of the King's character as empire-builder, warrior wielding bow and arrow and battle-axe. Sportsman slaying the tiger, musician playing on the lyre and as performer of the Horse Sacrifice or *Asvamedha*. The tiger was the denizen of the forested regions of the U.P. and M.P. conquered by him as a sacrificial flame of authors work like the '*History of the Chamar Dynasty.*'

The coins in the beginning were modelled on foreign Kushana coinages copying such Kushana features as (I) the King's dress, (2) halo round his head, (3) altar,(4) King's name as written vertically and (5) Ardochso reverse. These foreign features were gradually eliminated as the coins were progressively Indianized. The Indian features included (1) Close-fitting cap on King's head, (2) the Garuda srandard in place of Kushana trident and (3) Jewellery (earrings and necklaces). The Tiger and Lyrist types are completely Indian, showing the king as barehead, wearing *dhoti* or waistcloth, Hindu goddesses and their vehicles like Lotus Lion, Makara, Garuda, Dwarf and also the wickerstool of the human history to crush the '*Brahminical Ideology*'.

Samudra Gupta's Character

Both inscription and coins indicate the different aspects of his manysided character and versatile genius.They mention his qualities and accomplishments as a Ruler, Conqueror, Warrior, Philanthropist, Peot and Musician. As a ruler, he was known for his resolute government (*Prachanda sasana*). As a Conqueror, his policy was elastic.Some States he annexed outright as sources of trouble and disunion. Other States he conquered to liberate. He restored many a kingdom that was destroyed (*bhrashta*) and dynasty that was overthrown (*utsanna*). He also restored to some of them their properties as well as their lost liberties (*Vibhava- pratyarpana*). As a warrior, he achieved victory by his personal prowess in battle (*Samgrameshu svabhuja-vijitah*). As a Philanthropist, he had a soft heart (*mriduhridaya*) was full of compassion (*anukampa*) "for the lowly (*kripana*), the poor (*dian*), the destitute (*anatha*) and the afflicted (*atura*), a shining (*samiddha*) example (*Vigrahavan*) of social service (*lokanugraha*)". His *Asvamedha Sacrifice* was marked by colossal charities already described. He was indeed a superman (*amanuja sadrise*). He was a *Kaviraja* (Prince of Poets) by his many poetical composition (*Vahukavita*) and gathered at his court master-minds (*budhagunita*) to settle the literary standard by which its interior quality could be weeded out (*ahata*). He was also a philosopher enjoying mental place (*Sukhamana*), penetrating in to the wisdom (*tattvah*) of the Sastras, and worthy of the company of the wise (*prajna*). He put to shame (*Vridita*) by his proficiency in musical arts (*Gabdhariva-Lalitaih*) their Divine Masters such as Narada, Tumburu and others. The king also proclaims himself as a musician in his special type of lyrist coins described above. He also promoted Religion by upholding (*vandha*) its social customs and barriers (*Dharma-prachira*).

Chandra Gupta II Vikramaditya (A.D. 375-414)

Date

The dates of his regin are given in the following inscriptions:

(1) Mathura Pillar Inscription of 61,=380 A.D. According to Dr. D.C. Sircar, the inscription contains the following words read by him as *Samvatsare Panchame*, meaning that the year 61 was the fifth year of his reign which accordingly began 375 A.D.

(2) The Udayagiri Stone Inscription of 82, =401 A.D. issued by his Sanakanika feudatory in his reign.

(3) The Sanchi Stone Inscription of 93= 412 A.D. issued by the King's minister, Amrakardava, a hero of many battles, who owed the success of his life to the King's favour (*prasada*).

(4) There is a fourth inscription at Gadhwa which does not contain the king's name but his titles: *Paramabhagavata* and *Maharajadhiraja*. It is dated 88= 407 A.D.

Some further chronological date are furnished by his coins. The last silver coins of the last Saka Satrap. Rudra Simha III belonged to the Saka year 310= 388 A.D. while the first silver coins issued by Chandra Gupta II after his conquest of the Saka Kingdom and taking over is currency belonged to the Gupta year 90= 409 A.D.

Name

Chandra Gupta II is called by several names in the inscription viz: (I) Devaraja (Sanchi Inscription); (2) Deva Gupta (Vakataka Inscription of Pravarasena II), (3) Devi Sri (mentioned on some coins).

Nomination

Samudra Gupta is stated to have selected for the throne (*tat-parigrihitena* and *tat-parigrhita*) in his life-time Chandra Gupta II as his fittest son (*Sat-putra*) out of his many sons (Mathura Inscription; Bhitari Pillar Inscription and Eran Inscription).

Family

His mother is name Datta and Dattadevi with the title *Mahadevi* in the inscription e.g. Bhitari Pillar Inscription of Skanda Gupta.He had two wives: (I) Dhruvadevi (Inscription Nos. 10, 12 and 13 of Fleet) described as the chief queen (Mahadevi) and as mother of Kumara Gupta. A Vaisali Seal describes her as 'Mahadevi Dhruvasvamn, queen of *Maharajadhiraja* ChandraGupta and mother of Maharaja Govinda Gupta.

(2) Kuveranaga the number of Princess Prabhavati Gupta who was married to the Vakataka King Rudrasena II.

Thus Chandra Gupta had two wives, two sons and one daughter as recorded in inscriptions.

History of His Life Time

The most important event of his conquest of Western Malwa and the Saka Satrapy of Surashtra. The way was already prepared for it by the conquest of Eastern Malwa by Samudra Gupta who had his favorite city (*Svabhoganagara*) at Airikina (Eran, modern Saugor). It was the base of Chandragupta operations against Western India. He Udayagiri Cave Inscription describes how he came there in person in pursuit of his world consquest (*Kritsna-prithivi-jayarthena*) with his minister Virasena Saba from Pataliputra who was appointed by him as his minister for foreign relation and war (*Sandhivigrahika*). The King is given the title of Rajarishi in this inscription on account of his saintliness of character. The other two inscriptions at Udayagiri and Sanchi mention a Sanakanika chief as a Gupta feudatory and *Amrakardava* as governor, the hero of many victories. Thus these two regions were convenient outposts of the Gupta empire for purposes of its expansion towards the west. This expansion was materially helped by *Vakataka* matrimonial alliance which was decided by politics like the earlier *Lichchhavi* alliance of Chandragupta I. The conquest of this region took place between 388 and 409 A.D. showing that it was a protracted process. The conquest is indicated by the issue of the new Gupta silver coinage modelled on the previous Saka coinage showing on obverse the King's head, Greek script, and dates as on Saka coins, but on reverse Gupta features, Garuda replacing Chaitya, and the legand *Paramabhagavatla*. The flag of Vaishnavism was thus planted in this new Gupta dominion.

The conquest is remembered in the time of Bana (7th century A.D.) who, in his *Harsha Charita*, refers to the following singular incident "Chandra Gupta, in the disguise of a woman coverted by the lustful Saka King, killed him on the spot in his own capital," with the power of the '*Light*' or '*Nam*'

This story is also found in the drama called' *Devichandraguptam*' traced in references contained in the work called *Natyadarpana*. It states that Rama Gupta, the elder brother of Chandra Gupta decided to present his queen Druvadevi to the Saka invader to buy the safety of his kingdom. ChandraGupta saved the situation by approaching the *Saka* in the guise of the queen and killed him as he came up to him. Returing he killed his brother and married his widow. This particular story is improbable in some details. Rama Gupta is not mentioned in any of the Gupta inscriptions which leave no room for him between Samudra Gupta and his immediate successor ChandraGupta II,as shown above. Nor is he mentioned on any coins. An inscription calls Chandra

Gupta, a *Rajarishi,* a King who was as religious and morally great as a *Rishi* and was not thus up to the heinous crime of murdering his elder brother and possessing himself of his helpless widow.

Administration

His administration was as already stated, (I) *Sanakanika Chief* (Udayaygiri Vaishnava Cave Inscription of 82); (2) *Amrakardava* (Sanchi Inscription of 93) who created an endowment in the Mahavihara of *Kakanadabota* (Sanchi); (3) *Saba Virasena* (undated Udayagiri Saiva Cave Inscription) who was Sandhivigrahika; (4) Sikharasvami, Mantri and Kumaramtya (Karmadanda Inscription of the year 117; (5) Maharaja Sri Govinda Gupta; a prince, Governor of *Tira-bhukti* (Vaisali Seal Inscription also new Mandasore Inscription of Malava –Vikrama year 524).

Chief Offices

Some of the clay seals discovered at Vaisali related to Vyas which were issued by prince Govinda Gupta mention the following offices:

(1) *Kumaramatya* who was alos sometimes called *Yuvaraja* and *Bhattaraka.*

(2) *Baladhikari* (Chief of the Army)

(3) *Ranabhandarika* (Military Treasure).

(4) *Dandapasadhikari* (Police Chief)

(5) *Mahadandanayaka* (Chief Justice)

(6) *Vinaya –sthitisthapaka* (Minister for Law & Order)

(7) *Uparika* (Governor who was above all Officers)

The District Magistrate's Office at Vaisali was called *Vaisali-Adishthana-Adhikarana.* A Parishad or Municipality governed the city of *Udhanakupa.* Inscription No.5. of J.F Fleet mentions the Arya Samgha in charge of the monastery of *Kakanadabota* and also the governing body of five (*Pancha-Mandali*)

Corporations

Some of these Vaisali Seals were issued by *Nigamas* or Guilds of (I) Bankers (*Sreshthis*) (2) Traders (*Sarthavaha*) and (3) Artisans (*Kulika*). These *Nigamas* issued seals both individually and jointly like a Chamber of Commerce. The seal of Merchant Guilds bore the appropriate symbol of a money –chest.

Banks

The Arya Samgha of Kakanadabota Mahavihara functioned like a Bank. It received from a donor a deposit of 25 *dinaras*, the interest on which was to be spent for feeding daily five *bhikshus* and keeping lit a lamp 'as long as the sun and the moon exist'. The bank was thus trusted with a permanent deposit to keep its corpus intact and to spend only the interest thereon under the term of the deposit. A similar transaction is indicated in the Gadhwa Inscription.

Administrative Divisons

There were in the following descending order :(I) *Desa* e.g. *Sukuli Desa* or *Bhukti* e.g. *Tirabhukti (2) Pradesa* e.g. *Airikina Pradesa* or *Vishaya or Chutya.*

Religion

The different religions of the country were equally encouraged. The inscriptions record benefactions in aid of Vaishnavism, Saivism, Jainism and Buddhsim. Inscription No. 5. of Fleet records a donation to the Arya Samgha in charge of the Budhist Mahavihara at Kakanadabota by Minister of Chandra Gupta II. *(See Plate XXXXI, Colossal Budddha Bamiyan 175 High, 3rd, 5th Centuries A.D. Fig.60)*

As regards Vaishnavism, the Gupta Emperors themselves were devotees of Vishnu and adopted His *Vahana*. Garuda, as the emblem on their National Flag and called themselves *Paramabhagavatas*. The Udayagiri Cave bearing an inscription of the year 82 is a Vaishnava Cave with sculptures showing (I) Four-armed Vishnu with His two wives and (2) Lakshmi as a twelve-armed goddess. The Udayagiri Cave No. 5. contains the colossal figure of the Varaha Avatara of Vishnu rescuring Mother Earth. The Gadhwa Inscriptuion records two donations of 10 *dinaras* each in aid of a Brahminical institution named *Sada Satra* (Alms-house).

There are similar benefactions in support of Saivism. An Uḍayagiri Cave is dedicated to God Sambhu by another Minister of Chandra Gupta II. Thus his Ministers were free to follow their own faiths.

The Mathura Pillar Inscription of 380 A.D. gives an account of a special Siva sect, that of the Mahesvaras then flourishing under the teacher Uditacharya. The sect was founded by Kusika, the first disciple of the last Saiva Avatara named *Lakuli.*

The inscription also records the interesting fact the Uditacharya constructed a Shrine of Teachers (*Guru-Ayatana*) in which were installed both their statues (*Pratimas*) and Lingas, like the *Devakula* referred to above.

Coinage

Chandragupta II issued the following types of coinage: (1) *Archer*, (2) *Couch*, (3) *Chhatra*, (4) *Lionslayer* and (5) Horseman.

The *Archer type* contains the singular legend "*Deva Sri Maharajadhiraja Sri Chandragupta*". It also portrays Garuda an obverse and Lakshmi on reverse as associated with Vishnu.

The *Couch-type* repeats the name Deva –Sri as '*Nam*' and has the additional legends (a) *Vikramadityasya* and (b) *Rupakritih* (a picture of beauty).

The *Chhatra-type* introduces a new feature viz, the figure of a dwarf carrying the royal parasol.

The *Lion-Slayer type* depicts the King in different postures in slaying the lion and on the reverse the appropriate Goddess Durga on Lion (*Ṣimha-Vahana*).

It also contains the new legends (1) *Narendrachandrah prathitasriya divam jayayajeyo bhuvi Simhavikramah* and (2) *Narendrasimha-Chandra Gupta prithivim jitva divam jayati*. There is also the title of *Simhavikramah.*

The Lion appear as symbol of the King's conquest of Surashtra (Kathiaward) as the abode of lions to this day as the forests of East India, U.P. and Bengal, were the abode of the tiger,as already noticed above in the text.

Chandra Gupta II issued silver coins in Surashtra in imitation of its Saka currency. The Saka features were kept up on the obverse (the King's bust and the Greek script but date in Brahmi) but the reverse introduces Gupta features, Garuda and the legend, *Parama-bhagavata-Maharajadhiraja-Sri Chandragupta-Vikramankasya*.

Chandra Gupta II also issued copper coins of some of the above types, mostly bearing the figure of Garuda.

India as Seen by Fa-Hien (399-414 A.D.)

In the time of Chandra Gupta II, this Chinese scholar came to India on pilgrimage to its chief certres of Buddhism. His mission was to secure from them the Buddhist Books of 'Discipline' which were very little known in China. His Mission was joined by four other comrades and on the way they were joined more than five who had preceded them.

In the country of *Shan-Shan*, they saw more than 4000 Hinayana Buddhists.

In the Tartar countries, they saw many Buddhists studying language and books.

In Kara-Shahr, they saw more than 4000 Hinayana Buddhists.

In Khotan which was a centre of Mahayana Buddhism, there were 'several tens of thousands' of monks. The Gomati monastery of Khotan counted 3000 such monks and there were 14 such large monasteries in that country.

This spread of Mahayana Buddhsim to Khotan was probably due to Kanishka's patronage.

Kashgarh was another flourishing centre of Buddhism. Its king was a devout Hinayana Buddhist.There were also 1000 Hinayana monks.

In *Darel* across the snowy ranges the pilgrims found many Hinayana monks.

The pilgrims next crossed the 'Indus Saraswati region of the Akhnoor Valley' and settled in Kashmir and came to Udyana, a flourishing seat of Buddhism where the language spoken was of the 'Middle Kingdom' of whole of the world.

Next were visited *Gandhara, Takshasila and Peshawar*, famous for its Kanishka Stupa. This region was full of Buddhist monuments.

Here all his comrades expcept two left Fa-Hien to return home.

The next Buddhist place visited was *Nagarahara* (Jalalabad) famous for its shrine of relics.

Then they crossed the snowy sufed koh range where one of his campanions fell ill, saying to him: "I cannot recover, you had better go on while you can; do not let us all as away here". Then Fa-Hien gently stroked the corpse in sorrow., bowing to Destiny.

In Afghanistan, he found 3,000 Hinayan and Mahayana monks and also a similar numder at Bannu.

He found Bhida in the Punjab to be another flourishing that of Buddhism. Indeed, he found the Punjab full of Buddhist monasteries counting in all nearly 10,000 monks of the areas.

At Mathura he found 20 monasteries with 30,00 monks. South of Mathura was the middle kingdom, the strong hold of Brahminism, where the government was very enlightened and efficient, 'where the people were prosperous and happy" in their liberty. They were not troubled by registration or other official restrictions. The y had freedom of movement and residence. The cultivators paid to the King only a share of the produce. There was no corporeal punishment. There were only fines for offences. The King's military bodyguard was paid fixed salary. "Through out the whole country no one kills any living things, nor drinks wine nor eats onion or garlics, but *Chandalas* are segregated. *Chandala* or *Doma* is the name for foul men (lepers) of the '*Nam*'. In this country, they do not keep pigs or fowls, there are no dealings in cattle, no butchers shops or disrtilleries in their market places. As a medium of exchange they use cowries Only the *Chandalas* or *Domas* go hunting and deal in fish".

It was the custom of the "Kings, elders and gentry to build shrines give lands, houses, gardens, with men and bullocks for cultivation.Binding title-deeds were written out which subsequent Kings did not dare disregard".

There was also evidence of public philanthropy. "Rooms with beds and mattresses,food and clothes are provided for resident and traveling monks with out fails and this is the same in all places"

"Pagodas are built in honour of *Sariputta, Moggalan* and *Ananda* and also in honour of the *Abhidhamma,* the *Vinaya* and the *Sutras*'. Thus Texts and Teachers were honoured by proper memorials.

'Pious families organize subscriptions to make offerings to make of various articles of clothing and things they need after annual Retreat'.

Fa-Hien next visited places like Sankisa and Sravasti full of monuments including Jetavana Vihara then existing.

According to Fa-Hien, Hinduism was represented by as many as 96 diffferent Sects or Schools.

Charitable people built "alongside of out-of-the way roads Homes of Charity where shelter with bed and food and drink is offered to travellers and wandering monks passing to and for but the time allowed for remaining is different in each case". These charities were prompted by the best spirit of positivist social service which recognized it as a from of worship of God, of God-in-Man (*Nara-Narayana*). They were also made available to all travellers with out distinction of caste or creed in a spirit of universal brotherhood. They were not limited by sectarian or denominational considerations.

Fa-Hien saw places of worship of previous *Buddhas, Kasyapal, Krakuchhand* and *Kanakamuni* and the Buddha's inimical cousin, *Devadatta*.

He also visited such Buddhist holy places as Lumbini and Vaisali whence crossing the Ganges he came to Pataliputra. At Pataliputra 'formerly ruled by King Ashoka', 'the King's palace, with its various halls, all built by spirits who piled up stones, constructed walls and gates, carved designs, engraved and inlaid after no human fashion, is still in existance'.

Here Fa-Hein's sole companion, *Tao-Cheng*, took the decision to stay on in India saying, "From this time forth until I become a Buddha, may I never live again in an outer land". But Fa-Hiens' object being to diffuse a knowledge of the Discipline throughout the land of China, he ultimately went back alone.

At Pataliputra, Fa-Hien found one Mahayana and another Hinayana monastery. The former was famous for its Brahmin teachers of Buddhism named *Raivata*, 'looked upto by all the country as an authority on Buddhism and man respected by all Buddhsit monks'.

Fa-Hien gives an account of the civilization of Magadha, with its numerous towns, the prosperity of its people who 'emulate one another in practising charity of heart and duty to one "neighbour". The more well to do "have instituted in their capitals free hospitals, and hither comes all poor or helpless patients, orphans, widows and cripples. They are well taken care of, a doctor attends them, food and medicine being supplied according to their needs. They are all made quite comfortable and when they are cured, they go away." It may be noted that Ashoka was the pioneer in building such hospitals for the treatement of both Man and Cattle (*Manushya Chikitsa* and *Pasu-chikita*).

Fa-hien also refers to the Car Festival of those days, of processions of images on four-wheeled cars of five storeys, to which the Brahmins invited the Buddhists.

Fa-hien found at Pataliputra an Ashokan monastery with an inscribed pillar, and another close by with a lion-capital.

From Pataliputra, Fa-Hien came to Nalanda where he still saw an old monastery and thence to Rajagraiha and its Gridhrakuta Hill where the Buddha lived and taught, at recalling which Fa-Hien was moved to tears.

Then he proceeded to Gaya and Bodh-Gaya whence he returned to Pataliputra and Banaras where he saw the Deer Park and two monasteries of monks.

From here he commenced his return journey down the river via Pataliputra and *Champa* (Bhagalpur) till he reached Tamluk with its sea-port. He saw here 24 monasteries and stayed fro 2 years "copying out *Sutras*, drawing pictures of images".

From here he 'set sail on alarge merchant vessel' reaching Ceylon after 14 days. He remained in Ceylon for 2 years and obtained copies of some sacred works in Sanskrit, copies of discipline, Agamas, and Selections from the Canon.

Then he "took passage on board of a large merchant vessel on which there were over 200 souls and astern of which there was a smaller vessel in tow, in case of accident at sea and destruction of the big vessel'.

"After 90 days sail they reached Java where heresies and Brahminism were flourishing, while the Faith of the Buddha was in a very unsatisfactory condition".

From Java where he stayed nearly five month he sailed home on board another merchant vessel with 200 passengers and provision for 50 days.

After 82 day's voyage, with provision exhausted, they reached land under a Buddhist Perfect who warmly received Fa-Hien.

Thus Fa-Hien completed his travel, after passing through nealy 30 countries, along risky routes, substained by his faith, spending 6 years on travel alone, and another 6 on study in India. As learning was not reduced to writing but was conveyed through manuscripts, Fa-Hien had to spend "3 years in writing and speaking Sanskrit and Pali and copying out the Disciplines'.

Kumara Gupta I Mahendraditya (A.D. 414-455)

Date

The earliest date of his regin is given as the year (96=415 A.D) in the Bilsad Inscription (No. 10 of J.F Fleet). The Mankuwar (Allahabad) Buddha Image Inscription mentions the year 129=448 A.D. of his reign. Perhaps the latest date the occurs on one of his silver coins of the year 136=455A.D.

Family

The Emperor had probably three wives: (1) Mahadevi Anantadevi, mother of Pura Gupta (Bhitari Inscription of Kumara Gupta III); (2) possibly Devaki, mother of Skanda Gupta (Bhitari Pillar Inscription No.13 of J.F. Fleet); (3) Unnamed wife, sister of one of his Miniters (Bihar Pillar Inscription No.12 of J.F. Fleet).

He had four sons: (I) *Skanda Gupta*; (2) *Puru Gupta*; (3) *Buddha Gupta* and (4) *Sri Ghatotkacha Gupta* of Visali Seal Inscription mentioning him as serving under Viceroy Maharaja Sri Govinda Gupta brother of *Kumara Gupta* as already noticed later promoted as Viceroy of Eastern Malwa (Gwalior Tumain Inscription of the year 116=435 A.D.). Of these sons the first succeeded him as emperor.

History of Kumara Gupta

Both inscriptions and coins throw some light on his history.

The Bilsad Inscription of the year 96=415 A.D. states that Kumara Gupta had already commenced his career of conquest and victories (*abhivardhamana-vijaya-rajya*) by which he was increasing the extent of his Empire.

By this year 117=436 A.D., his fame as Emperor had already reached the limits of four oceans as stated in the *Karmadanda* Inscription of the actions and deeds of Kumar Gupta I.

The Gangdhar Inscription of the Vikrama year 480=423 A.D. records that under the local King Visvavarma, son of Naravaram, his Minister built (i) a temple of Vishnu (ii) a templeof *Divine Mothers* full of *ghosts* (*Dakinis*) and (iii) a large well of drinking water.

In the Malava year 493=436 A.D. when Kumara Gupta was ruling the whle earth bounded on the north by Sumeru and Kailasa mountains, the Vindhya forests on the south and the two oceans on east and west between which his dominion was swinging like a *Mekhala, Dasapura* was the seat of a flourishing Kingdom under its sucession of local Kings (*Desa-parthiva*) named (I) *Visvavarma* and(2) his son Vandhuvaram who were known for their virtues (*Guna*). Their fame induced a rich guild (*Sreni*) of silk weaver

(*Pattavaya*) to emigrate to Dasapur (Mandasore in Gwalior State) from their native place in Lata Vishaya(Nausari= Navasarika in west Malwa). They gave a proof of the prosperity by constructing at Dasapura, their new home, a Sun-temple in the year 380-81 of Malava Gana Sthiti, i.e., *Malava-Vikarma –Krita* Era when Kumara Gupta was the reigning Emperor. This temple had to be repaired after a lapse of 36 year in Malava year 529=472 A.D. under other Kings known as *Durlabhavardhana*-I and *Mohammed Prophet* of the *'Nam-History'* in the closing of the 6th centuries A.D. This best of building (*bhavana-vara*) became one of the ornaments (*alankara*) of this beautiful (*udara*) city of Kashmir history that tribe repeated again, called as *Sudhra* tribe of the human history.

The Kalaikuri Inscription of the years 120ft, he two Damodarpur Copper Plate Inscriptions of he yerars 124 and 128 and the Baigram Inscription of the same year 128 show that during the interval 439 to 447 A.D. the Empire of Kumara Gupta did not sign of decline, but a challenge was given to Brahmins to find out where stands *Sudhra's* history.

But towards the end of his reign, in his old age, the Empire was threatend by enemies whom the Crown Prince Skanda Gupta was deputed by him to fight against the Brahmins with Almighty Power of the '*Nam*' of the later *Rai Family* of Singh and *Multan* and their centre of power was *Kashmir* as a Natural idea of the *Ravidas* philosophy.

This history is indicated in the *Bhitari Pillar Inscription* of *Skanda Gupta* stating in Kalhana's Rajatarangini that these enemies were *Pushyamitras* and other whom the *Puranas* locate in the Narmada Valley. To fight these enemies was not an easy task for Skanda Gupta. The fight taxed to the utmost the mettle of Skanda Gupta who had to spend one night on bare earth on the battle field. But eventually he consquered them and "made them the foot stool on whom he placed his left foot".

His Coinage also shows the vastness of his Empire. His hod on Surashtra is proved by this silver coins variety of which with the Peacock reverse circulted in the central parts. In fact, these silver coins in circulation in areas under the old Kshatrapa dominion. Another class of silver coins resembling the Traikutaka coins were in circulation in Southern Gujarat. There were also silver –plated coins found in ancient Valabhi. Thus a large part of Western India belonged to the Gupta Empire under Kumara Gupta I. It seems that Kumara Gupta I made fresh conquests by which he made additions to the Empire he inherited.His conquests are also marked by the performance of the Asvamedha as proved by his coins bearing the legend *Jayati divam Kumarah* on obverse and *Sri Asvamedhamahendrah* on reverse. Some coins gave him the epithets (i) *Mahendrasimha,* (ii) *Narasimha,* (iii) *Simha Mahendra,* (iv) *Simha Vikrama* and (V) *Vyaghra balaparakramah.* These eqithets were earned by him by his own conquest by which he extended his father's legacy in Indian History.

Religious and Charitable Endowments

The different religions on the country were flourishing side by side under public support. There were endownments created for the worship of Vishnu, Siva Sakti, Sarttikeya, Surya, the Buddha and the Jina. There were also special endowments for helping Brahmins to perform their religious ceremonies.There were, lastly, endowments for secular charities.

The Gangdhar Inscription of 423 A.D. records the construction of a *Vishnu-sthanam* by the two sons of a Minister of the local king of Malwa named Visvavarma. The donors are maned Vishnubhatta and Haribhatatta. The Baigram Copper Plate Inscription of 443 A.D. mentions great of land to the temple of God Govinda Svami (Vishnu).

The Karmadanda Inscriptions of 436 A.D. invoke God Mahadeva and record gifts for the worship of God Prithivisvara whose Linga bears the inscription.

The Gangdhar Inscrption aforesaid records the construction of a temple for the worship of the Divine Mothers accompanied by their associates or ghouls called *Dakinis.*

The Bilsad Pillar Inscription of 415 A.D. refers to the temple of God Savmi Mahasena (*Kartikeya*) whose worship was very popular in those days, Karttikeya, the God of War gave His name to the two great Gupta Emperors, Kumara and his son Skanda to whom the worship, of the God of War was appropriate for the wars they had to fight in their days.

We have already referred to the Mandasor Inscription describing the construction of a superb temple of the suns by a Gulid of Silk –Weavers. Probably *Surya* or Ravi was the choosen deity if the industrial classes who worked for the welfare of the public. (See Plate XXXVIII, Fig. 57, *A view of the Life as Knitting* Work of the Weaver in the Human History already refered above.)

The Mankuwar Buddha Image Inscription of 448 A.D. records the construction of an images of Bhagavan Buddha by *Bhikshu Buddhamitra* taken to be the teacher of Vasuvandhu.(See Plate XXXXII, *Seated Buddha, Mankuwar*, Dated, 448 A.D. Fig. 61), as an idea of the warfare against the Brahmins.

The Udayagiri Cave Inscription of 425 A.D. in the prosperous reign of the best of Gupta Kings refers to the construction of an image of Jina-vara

Parsva. Another inscription records the installation of a Jaina image at Mathura in 432 A.D.

As regards charitable endowments, these are recorded in several inscriptions. The Gadhwa Inscription refers to the gift of money (10 *dinaras* and 3 *dinaras*) in aid of an almshouse and another of 12 *Dinaras*.

These inscription refer to grant of land to Brahmins for performing the *Agnihotra* and *Pancha-Mahayajnas* (two Damodarpur Copper Plates and Kalaikuri Inscriptions).

Administration

The Empire is called *Prithivi*(Mandasor Inscription). The Emperor is given the titles of *Parama-daivata*. *Parama-bhattaraka* and *Maharajadhiraja* (as in the Damodarpur Copper Plates). Below the Emperor was the feudatory or local king called severally Nripa, Nripati, Parthiva or Gopta (Mandasor Inscription). The local Kingdom was called a *Desa* e.g, *Desaparthiva*.

The Empire was divided for administrative purposes into provinces. A province was called a *Bhukti*. Under Kumara Gupta I, *Pundravardhana-Bhukti* looms large in serval inscriptions. These show that for 4 years, 124-128-443-447 A.D.this *Bhukti* was ruled by Governor *Chiratadatta*. The title of a Provincial Governor was *Uparika Maharaja*.

A province was subdivided in to districts called *Vishayas*. The title of the head of the *Vishaya* was Vishayapati or District Magistrate. Thus Vetravarma was the *Vishayapati* of Kotivarsha.

The term *Adhisthana* was applied to the headquarters of the district.The District Office was called *Vishayadhi Karana* (Damodarpur Copper Plates I and 2). The *Dhanaidaha* (Rajshahi District) grant of year 128 mentions another district of *Vishaya* called Khadata –para which might have been also a *Vishaya* of *Pundravardhanabhukti*, but the name of the *bhukti* cannot be clearly traced. The Baigram Charter of 447 A.D. was issued from a district office, *Vishayadhikarana* located at the town called *Panchanagari*. The District Office is named *Kulavriddhi* and had the title *Kumararamatya*. The Mandasor Inscription gives a glowing account of the prosperity of a district of Western India, viz; *Lata Vishaya*.

A District had its sub-divisions called *Vithis*. The Officer-in-charge of the sub-division called *Ayuktaka* in the Kalaikuri Inscription.

We have already seen that some of the princes served as Provincial Governors. Prince Govinda Gupta was the Governor of Tirabhukti under ChandraGupat II, while Princes Ghatotkacha Gupta was governor of Airikina Pradesa (another term for province).Earlier, he perhaps served under prince Govinda Gupta in a high and responsible office so as to issue seals in hi name. Both his seals and those of Govinda Gupta were found together at Vaisali (Basarh) as already stated in the text.

The appointed of the District Officer by the Governor was subject to the formal sanction by the King to whom the homage of both was due.

Besides these Provincial Governors and District Officers, there were Ministers in attendance on the Emperor at the headquarters of Government. One such Minister is named Prithivisena who came to his exalted office by heredity. At first he started as a Mantri with the title *Kumaramatya* but was later promoted to the higher office of *Mahabaladhikrita* as the executive head of both civil and military administration (*Karmadanda* Inscription). The term for a Minister was also *Sachiva* (Mandasor Inscription).

The Damodarpur Copper Plates give some interesting details of local administration in their inscriptions.

The district headquarters were called *Adhisthanas* where were located the district offices and courts called *Adhikaranas*. The District Magistrate was associated in his administration with an Advisory Council of non-official representing the different interests of the locality viz, (I) *Nagara-Sreshthi*,President of the Town Corporation (Mayor); (2) *Sarthavaha,* representative of the Guild of Merchants; (3) *Prathama –Kulika*, Chief of the Guild of Artisans; and (4) *Prathama-Kayastha*, Chief of the Union of Writers or Scribes, Chief Secretary.

The sub-divison of a district is called *Vithi*, as stated bove. The Kalaikuri Inscription instances the *Sringavera Vithi* and its headquarters at *Purnakasika*. The Sub-divisional officer had also like the District Officer, his own Council of non-official advisers comprising (I) *Vithi-Mahattaras* and (2) *Kutumbins*. The office staff included (1*) Pustapalas (Record*-Keepers) (2) *Kayasthas* (Writers or Clerks) and (3) *Kulikas* (Artisans).

The inscriptions record land-transaction of the times. Ordinarily, lands were not to be sold under the rule called *Nividharama* or *Apradakshaya-Nivi* indicating that the land was to be kept intact. The State granted land only on condition that its donor was to utilize its usufruct for a public purpose but must not sell it for his own profit. The grant was sanctioned under a procedure. The application for land was to be submitted to a Committee of three *Pustapalas* who had it examined by (I) *Mahattaras* (Village Elders), (2) *Ashtakuladhikaranas* (Officers-in-charge of eigth representative households), (3) *Gramikas* (Village headmen) and (4) *Kutumbins*. These then notified it to leading Brahmins, citizen and householders of the village. The land in question was then inspected by these and was referred to the *Pustapalas* for report. It was sold if the *Pustapalas* reported that it was in order (*Yukta*) and according to rulers of sale (*Vikrayamaryada-prasanga*).

The petitioner had to state in his petition that he agreed to the conditions of sale viz; (I) according to *Nividharama* ensuring its gift for a public purpose such as *Agnihotra* and *Panchamahayajnas*; (2) that the land was *Khila* (waste), *aprada* (unsettled) *aprahata* (uncultivated) and not settled land (Kshetra); (3) that it was sold at the customary price (*Gramanukrama-Vikraya –Maryada*)

Lastly, the sale was sanctioned by a formal declaration that the rulers not permitting it were waived (*anuvritta apradakshaya-nivi*). The land was measured by the standard 8x9 reeds and separted (*apavinchhya*) it from other plots.

The price of land is also indicated. It was at the rate of 12 *dinaras* for I *Kulyavapa* or that quantity of land which could not ploughed by two bullocks (Manu).

The Kalaikuri Inscription contains some new data on the subject. The land that was to be sold must be fallow and unsettled and not yielding any revenue to the State (*apratikara*). These conditions were necessary so that its acquisition by the State was not called for, nor any compensation payable to the dispossessed proprietor. Secondly, the sale should not prejudice the interests of the State in any way (*avirodha*). For instance, it should not encroach upon private property by requisitioning land public purpose.

The Kalaikuri Inscription to belongs the *Bhukti* of *Pundravardhana* of which it mentions the capital of the same name. It appears that three was hardly any land that was not cultivated and was available for a public religious purpose. For instance, such a small piece of land as 9 *Kulyavapas* could not be secured in one plot. Eight of these came out of 3 villages and the balance from a fourth village.

The Baigram Inscription of 448 A.D. contains some new data on land transactions. The land that is sold by Government is described as (1) not paying any revenue to the State (*Samudayavahya*), (2) devoid of vegetation (*astamba*); (3) not liable for any compensation due to a dispossessd proprietor (*akinchitpratikara=*, *apratikara*); (4) not causing any loss to the King for its sale (*upachaya*) and spiritual merit (*Dharma*) from the charity, and (6) situated in waste land and so could not affect cultivation (*savakarshanavirodhisthane*).

The inscription also states the prices of follow (*Khila*) land and building sites (*Vastu*) I Kulyavapa is valued at 2 *Dinaras* while *Draonavapa Vastu* land is valued at 4 *Rupakas*, 1 Kulyavapa is eight times the size of a *Dronavapa*. If, therefore, prices were the same, I Kulyavapa would be valued at 32 Rupaksa, 2 dinaras as against 4 *Rupaskas* to one *Dronavapa*. But, as a matter of fact, the price of cultivated land and building sites could not be the same. A later

Damodarpur Copper Plate. Inscription mentions that one *Kulyavapa of Vastu* land was valued at 3 *Dinaras* as against 2 *Dinaras* for one *Kulyavapa* of *Khila* land. Thus the price of a plot of cultivated land was 2/3 of a building site.

Coins

Kumara Gupta I issued the following types of coinage: (1) Archer, (2)Swordsman, (3)Asvsmedha (4) *Horseman,* (5) *Lion-Slayer,* (6) Tiger slayer, (7) *Peacock,* (8) *Pratapa,* and (9) Elephant –rider.

The Horseman type shows a new feature on reverse, Goddess feeding peacock with a bunch of fruit. The Goddess also appears on the reverse of the Tiger-type. She is to be identified with *Kaumari Ambika* described as *Mayura-vara Vahana*, riding on Peacock Perfect and as *Guharuipini*, looking like her son Karttikeya, in *Sri Chandi* (*Uttara Charita* VIII, 17). She is also described as *Narayani* surrounded by peacocks.

The *Peacock-type* shows God Karttitkeya riding on His vehicle, peacock *Paravani* of the Father as '*Nam*'.

The *Pratapa type* shows on obverse three figures of male, Garuda and female and on reverse the legend *Sri Pratapa*, as 'Nam' on earth.

Kumara Gupta I also issued silver coins meant for circulation in the Saka dominion conquered by his father. They were more numerous and varied than those of his father, Kumara Gupta I also issued copper coins of which two samples are known as '*Nam*' or '*Chamar*' of the same family.

Skanda Gupta Vikramaditya (455-467 A.D.)

Date

The Bhitari Pillar Inscription of *Skanda Gupta*[11] states that as his son who 'adhered to the feet of his father, like the bees to the lotus and as the only hero of the Gupta family' (*Guptavamsaikavirah*) worked in Kashmir, he immediately succeede his father, Kumara Gupta I.In fact, as Crown Prince, he was already acting for the King and fighting his battles which were continued when he became king. Thus there is no room for any other claimant to the throne nor for any war of succession with his brothers, as is supposed by some scholars. This fact is also indicated by his hold on Surashtra as the legacy from his father Kumara, as recorded in the Junagadh Rock Inscriptions which mentions three dates of his reign, 455 A.D. 456 A.D. and 457 A.D., Other dated inscription of his reign are Kahaum Pillar of 460 A.D. the *Indrapura* Copper Plate of 465 A.D., the Gadhwa Inscription of 467 A.D. and Kosam Siva Parvati pedestal of 458 A.D having this idea in Jammu and Kashmir state.

The silver coins bear dated which Vincent Smith read as 463, 464 and 467 A.D.

Succession

As shown above Skanda Gupta was the immediate successor of his father to the throne in Kashmir without any contest, he occupied the throne of Magadha. The Juagadha Rock Inscription also states that the Goddess Lakshmi, after examining fully his merits, fixed her choice upon him in preference to all other sons of the sovereign. Besides, he inherited his father's troubles and wars which he had to carry on without any break as we have explored from the study of the Kalhana's *Rajatarangini*.

History of His Life

The *Bhitari Pillar Inscription*, as we have seen, recounts his exploits both as Crown Prince and as King. As King, he completed his conquests which he proudly reported to his mother *Devaki* and restored the fallen fortunes of his family.

He also made fresh conquests. He shook the earth by "subduing the Hunas." Later Gupta's lineage took the title of *Maharajadhiraja* and played the part of " a lion to the Hundeer", formed an alliance between the two most powerful families of the *Madhya-desa* (Upper Ganges Valley) which resembled the solar and lunar race of antiquity of the Ravidas Family called *chamars* of Kashmir of *Karkota* Dynasty. This vicissitude we see in the Bana's *Harshchrita,* that Harsha ruler of Thanesar having the modest title of *Rajaputra* (Prince) *Siladitya (Harsha),* whence he exacted tribute to Kashmiri ruler i.e. *Durlabhavardhana* from which he carried off a tooth relic of Buddhism spread all over the world. The whole of *Uttarai patha* or Northern India is also indicated by the music pace drums[12] of the 'Nam' in the history of '*Chamar Dynasty*' of Kashmir.

His many conquests and achievements are further indicated in the Jungadh Rock Inscription. 'He set against the hostile kings his local governors like so many *Garudas* eating up serpents with lifted hoods '*Chamar*' of the society. He ultimately conquered the earth bounded by the four oceans and flourishing countries (*Sphita-paryanta-desan*). Next, he destroyed the roots of the pride of his enemies in the *Mlechchha* countries.

His achievement are the summed up in the Kahaum Pillar Inscription: 'The heads of hundred kings fell at his feet as they tendered their homage to him at his Darbar Hall (*Upasthana*) the King who was the Lord of Hundred Kings (*Kshitipasatapati*), the equal of *Indra* (*Sakropama* (cf. *Sakra-ditya*, Madendraditya Kumara Gupta I) who installed Peace (*Santi*) in his empire".

We may recall that in the last days of Kumara Gupta I *Sudhra* tribe went for civilizational growth for more than 200 years to repeat the history of God and Man. The Empire was invaded by barbarian enemies like the Pushyamitras late successors. The Emperor saw his *Kula-Lakshmi* perturbed (*vichalita*) and overwhelmed (*vipluta*). He did not live to see how Skanda Gupta by his conquests restored the fortunes of his family by subduting all its enemies, the Pushyamitras, the Hunas and the *Mlechchhas* and their confederate forces(*Samuditabalakoshan*) and made himself the King of hundred Kings that is Mohammed Prophet in the history of God and Man.

Administration

Some of the inscription contain some new administrative details. The Governor of Surashtra Avani was the Gopta named *Parnadatta*. Sarvanage is mentioned as the District Magistrate of Antarvedi Vishaya. A feudatory named Maharaja Bhimavarman was the Governor of Kosam. The district staff included heads of departments such as: (I) *Agraharika,* (2) *Saulkika* (in charge of Tolls), (3) *Gaulmika* (in charge of Forests).

Cities were administered by their chief executive officers called *Nagarakshakas*. The cities named are *Girinagara, Aja, Kakubha* (the jewel of a village), the sacred abode of sainst (*Sadhusạmsargaputa*) and Indrapura in the *Antarved Vishaya.*

The inscription states that *Girinagara* as the capital of the newly conquered country of Surashtra was a difficult charge. The King was hard put to it in finding a fit Governor for Surashtra till his choice fell on *Parnadatta.* But *Parbadatta* fought shy of that exalted office in all humility (*vinaya*). He was hesitant because he was so upright (*satya*), straigthforward (*arjava*) and incorruptible (*visuddha*). The King was at pains to persuade him to accept that appointment. When he accepted it, the King felt quite at case like the gods securing *Varuna* as the protector of the western quarter,

Parnadatta, on his part, had a hard job to find a fit administrator for the provincial capital, Girinagara..After much thought, he chose his son *Chakrapalita* for the post in view of his rare qualities of head and heart. He was not in debt (*Arini*) by his extravagance; he was gifted with eloquence by which he could win over his colleagues of the Municipal Council; he was given to liberality (*Dana*), and he was of charitable disposition (*Dakshinya*). He showed honour (*mana*) where it was due, he was very social in his habit making friendly calls on the citizen (*Grihapravesa*);of free and unceremonious manner (*niryantrana*), he was very popular.

The efficiency of his administration was put to a severe test. The lake (*tataka*) *Sudharsana* which was the source of the city's water supply suddenly burst (*bibheda*) its dam which created it by storing up the water of the 'Rivers Pallasini, Survarnasikata and others rising from the adjoining hills of the Jammu region, *Urjjayat* (near Ginar), *Raivataka* and the like. This fine lake, deep as the ocean (*nidhitulya*) drained of its waters became an ugly sight (*Durdarsana*) and filled the city with despair (*vishada*) as its water supply was cut off. *Chakrapalita* came to its rescue by getting the dam repaired within two months, a dam which was 100 cubits along 68 wide and of 7 men's height, without caring for its cost. It was a piece solid masonry work (*samyak-ghatita –upalena*).

Religion

There were endowments in support of different religions. At Girinagara, its Mayor, *Chakrapalita*, constructed a temple of God, *Chakrabhrit,* as a devotee of lord Govinda. The Bihar Pillar Inscription refers to the construction of a *yupa* (*pillar*) with a circle of temple (*devaniketianamdalam*) dedicated to God headed by Skanda and also to the Divine Mothers (*Matribhischa*) of Kashmir who were (1) *Brahmi*, (2) *Mahesvari* (3) *Kaumari*, (4) *Vaishnavi*, (5) *Mahendri*, (6) *Varahi* and (7) *Chamunda*. There is another list which omits Mahendri and adds (I) Chandi and (2) Charchika with a total of eight Mothers. The Indor Copper Plate Inscription (No.16 of Fleet) refers to the construction of a temple of the Sun (*Savita*) by two Kshatriya merchants. The Kahaum Pillar Inscription refers to the fashiong of the images of Adikartis (*Tirthankaras* (1) *Adinatha* (2) *Santinatha* (3) *Neminatha* (4) *Parsvanatha* and (5) *Mahavira)* in the niches of a pillar of stone, high as a hill of the '*Nam*' of God.

Economic Conditions

We have already referred to engineering works like the construction of a solid dam creating a storage of water for the city of Girnagara. Industries were organized under guilds (*srenis*). The Indor Copper Plate Inscription mentions a prosperous Guild of Oilmen (*Tailika-sreni*) at the city of *Indrapura* of Kashmir. The Guild was trusted by a Brahmin with a donation of a fund to be kept as a permanent (*Ajasrika*) deposit, the interest on which alone was to be applied for supplying oil for a lamp at a temple with out break (*Abhagnayoga*). The fund was to be kept intact (*Prathamartham-avachchhinaṣamstham*). It means that the Guild invested the fund to profit out of which it was able to finance its purpose. The transaction or contract was duly registered (*Dayamimam nivaddham*). Its violation by the King was condemned as a great sin (*Mahapataka*). The Bihar Pillar Inscription records the creation of a permanent endowment (*Akshayanivi*) in the city of *Ajapuraka* but the name of the Guild receiving it is not traceable.

Coins

Skanda Gupta issued three types of gold coinage: (1) *Archer*, (2) *King* and *Lakshmi* and (3) Horseman.

The *Archer type* bears on the obverse the titles Sri *Kramaditya* and (2) *Sudhanvi* (Skilled bowman). Some hold that in the Lakshumi type, Lakshmi should be taken as Queen but the lotus in her hand points to Lakshmi, while she lacks the Queen's regal *Chowrie* as seen on *Asvamedha* coins on which the Queen must appear as a ceremonial necessity.

The silver coins were in circulation in both Western and Central India that is the area of Jammu and Kashmir State including Ladakh itself. The Western issues bear on obverse the King's bust but on reverse the figurs of (a) Garuda, (b) Bull and (c)Altar. The *Bull* type was in circulation in Kathiawad, pointing to Gupta dominion in Valabhi whose *Senapatis* adopted the badge of the Bull. The Central issues continued the types of Kumara Gupta I, circulated the golden coins to the *Karkota* dynasty of Kashmir called *chamar* by nature as 'happiness' race of the *Sudhra Family*.

Extent of the empire

Skanda Gupta's Empire extended all over Northern India from Surashtra to Bengal. He kept together his vast Empire with the help of able Governors. In Surashtra Parnadatta was succeeded by hs *Senapati. Bhattaraka* who founded the independent rule of his dynasty named *Maitraka* in Valabhi. His Valabhi Copper Plate Inscription mentions the glory of his Kingship (*Rajyasri*) supported by his military strength derived from the army recruited from different classes as Harsha fought a war of six years agianst the Brahmins with '*Five Indis*[13]' or '*Nam*', (I) *Maula* (hereditary), (2) *Bhrita* (mercenary), (3) *Mitra* (allies), and (4) *Sreni* (military clans). He was succeeded by his son, as Governor by his son Dharasena I who was also succeeded, Drona Simha, whose coronation as King of Valabhi was attended by his paramount sovereign, probably Budha Gupta, as stated in his Bhamodra-Mohota Copper Plate Inscription of 502 A.D.

Another able Governor was Sarvanage in charge of the territory between the Kalindi and Narmada like Dr. Nishab Chand Digra idiot of the *'Nam-History'*.

A third was Maharaja Bhimavarman ruling over the Kausambi region.

Puru Gupta Vikrama Prakasaditya (A.D. 467-469)

Succession of Puru Gupta:

We have already seen that Skanda Gupta was the son and immediate successor of Kumara Gupta I. There is, however, a Bhitari Seal Inscription of Kumara Gupta III which gaves the following succession list: *Maharajadhiraja Sri Kumara Gupta* I succeeded by his son (*putra*) *Maharajadhiraja Sri Puru*

Gupta by his queen Mahadevi Anantadevi, as already seen. The omission of the name of Skanda Gupta in his list has suggested the theory that Puru Gupta was not his successor but his rival for the throne which was captured by Skanda gupta by killing him in war of succession was captured in Kashmir to defeat the Brahmins of the Sindh. We have already discussed the arguments against the theory. The epither *Amalatma* applied to Skanda Gupta in the inscription already noticed only shows that as a man of pure unsullied soul he was not up to a bloody battle against his brother for the throne but with the power of '*Nam*' in scientific manner.

History of His Life:

The Empire in his reign suffered a decline which began in the last days of his brother Skanda Gupta. His hold on Surashtra was not very secure,as is seen in the paucity of silver issues in point of both number and variety. Puru Gupta has no silver coins to his credit, because he no longer ruled over Surashtra where they were required. Puru Gupta gold coins also were of less number and variety showing contraction of his Empire that the Brahmins or *Damaras* of Kashmir, they captured the throne of Puru Gupta.

Puru Gupta appears to be associated with the great Buddhist teacher Vasubandhu whom he appointed as their teacher of his Queen and Crown Prince *Baladitya*, as stated in '*Paramartha's Life of Vasubandhu'*. *Baladitya* as Kings named on his coins helped the *Sudhras* for the establishment of true history of the '*Nam*' *or 'Chamar'*. He introduced the last king from the *Gonanda's* race[14] of the '*Sudhra* Family of Kashmir'. The Queen is named *Mahadevi SriChandradevi* in the above inscription. Puru Gupta on his coins gives himself the epithet Sri Vikramah, as it has been referred the brother of *Baladitya* the founder of Karkota Dynasty of Kashmir was *Durlabhavardhana I.*

Paramartha also knows of a King Vikramaditya whose capital was Ayodhya. This was the second capital of the Gupta Empire. A third capital was Kasi recorded in the Sarnath Stone Inscription of *Prakataditya. Baladitya,* having been foretold of his son-in-law being destined to succeeded him and he married his daughter *Anangalakha* to a small official, *Durlabhavardhana*[15] of Kashmir for the development of the history and the idea of the *'Nam'* or God on earth.

Coins

Puru Gupta issued only one type of gold coin the Archer type. One variety names *Pura* on the obverse and the title *Sri Vikramah* or *Vikramaditya* son of *Ranaditya* and *Baladitya* was the brother and successor of the same ruler as mentioned by Kalhana on the reverse. A second variety omits the name *Pura,* but some specimens mention the name which is read as *Budha* and may be Budha Gupta's coins referred in Indian history of the Kashmir history.

Some coins bear the name *Sri Prakataditya* whom Allan identifies with Puru Gupta.

Successors of Puru Gupta

The succession after Gupta is recorded in inscriptions on seals found at Nalanda. On makes the list as follows. Puru Gupta –son Narasimah Gupta – son Kumara Gupta III-son Vishnu Gupta (Vishnu Gupta Seal) worked for the development of the history in that area..

The second gives the following list : Puru Guptam, *Chandradevi* as dirty soul of the Father–son Budha Gupta (Budha Gupta Seal).

Other inscription throwing light on genealogy are (1) Sarnath Buddha Stone Image Inscription of 473 A.D, which mentions Kumar Gupta II succeded by Budha Gupta and (2) Bhitari Seal Inscription already noticed from the study in the context.

The genealogy will be then as follows : Puru Gupta '*Word*' Kumara Gupta II (A.D. 473)-Budha Gupta (476-495 A.D.) – '*Chamar*', Narasimha Gupta –Kumara Gupta III-Vishnu Gupta.

There is another inscription on a seal of Kumara Gupta III described as the son of Narasimha Gupta and Mahadevi Sri Mitradevi of the period.

The merit of the above genealogical scheme is that it has not to place too many kings within a short interval of 9 years. According to the prevailing view, Puru Gupta, Narasimha Gupta, Kumara Gupta II and Vishnu Gupta succeeded one after another 467-476 A.D. This theory does not take into account the fact that Vishnu Gupta was too young upto 476 A.D. It may be assumed that Skanda Gupta who was always battling against his enemies, was not old when he died, he was shifted in the another life as a Universal Truth. If it was at, say, 60, he should be bron in 407 A.D. in which case his great grandson Vishnu Gupta should be too young in 476 A.D.

The other genealogical puzzle is that the inscriptions differ as to succession.

Thus the Bhitari Seal Inscription of Kumara Gupta and the Nalanda Seal Inscription of Vishnu Gupta mention Narasimha Gupta as the successor of Puru Gupta.

Another Nalanda Seal Inscription refers to Budha Gupta as the successor of Puru Gupta.

But Kumara Gupta II was really the successor of Puru Gupta, from his date 473 A.D. of Sarnath Inscription, while the date of Buddha Gupta is given as 476 AD. In another Sarnath Inscription. Thus the correct genealogical scheme cannot ignore these epigraphic dates. T he different succession list of the inscription may be reconciled by the consideration that they were interested only in successions list of the inscriptions may be reconciled by the consideration that they were interested only in successors and not in *immediate* successors.

The genealogical list presented here has the further merit that it connects Narasimha Gupta with the Hunas, as is done by *Yuan Chwang*. During the period (618-627 A.D.) Chinese Chroniclers record serious distrubances in India, and *Siladitya* (Harsha) is represented as punishing the Kings of the four parts of the country[16], as soon as he recognised a first rate power under a local dynasty styled *Karkota* founded by *Durlabhavardhana*[17] of Kashmir. His date fits in with that of *Yasodharman* of Malwa who defeated the Hunas under whose pressure Gupta Imperial power was retreating from West to East.

Another King of the time has been brought to light by a Nalanda Seal Inscription, viz., Vainya Gupta described as *Paramabhaga vato-Maharajadhiraja*, who may be identified with King Vajra mentioned by Yuan Chwang as the last of the line. King Vainya is also mentioned in the Gunaighar Inscription of 508 A.D. He should have been a king in Eastern India into which the Hunas did not penetrate. Vainya may be drived from the world *Vena*, the name of the God Indra known for his *Vajra* or Thunder bolt.

Kumara Gupta II Kramaditya (C.176-176 A.D.)

Date

As already stated an inscription on the Sarnah Buddha Image mentions the date Gupta Year 154=473. A.D. 'when Kumara Gupta was protecting the earth'.

The Buddha Image

The Buddha Image which bears this inscription is one of the finest (*apara*) examples of the art of statuary in the world.The inscription describes the images as that of the Great Teacher (*Sasta*) of unequalized qualities (*pratima-apratimasya*). It was contructed by the ascetic (*yati*) *Abhyamitra* promoted by his pure devotion to the Buddha for purposes of worship so that 'he might attain salvation (*mukti*)' by this pious deed, 'along with his mother, father,preceptor and ancestors. (*See Plate XXXXIII, Buddha as Great Preceptor and Teacher, Fig. 62*)

Coins

Kumara Gupta II issued only one type of gold coinage, the Archer type. Some specimens show on obverse the letter *Ku* and on reverse the legend *Kramaditya*.

He also issued coins of ruder fabric of which the interesting point is that bear on the obverse the lengend *Maharajadhiraja –Sri-Kumara Gupta – Kramaditya* and on reverse the legend *Sri Kramadityah* showing that Kumara Gupta II was an Emperor. He counted as his feudatory Maharaja Hastin known for his Khoh Copper Plate. Inscription of Gupta years 156=475 A.D. In the inscription he states that his rulership belongs to the Gupta Empire (*Gupta – nriparajyabhuktau*). That Hastin was a religious, powerful and prosperous potentate is proved by the fact recorded in the inscription that he 'gave away thousands of cows and elephants, houses and gold coins, and also many plots of land out of his religious devotion (*bhakti*) and achieved victories in many hundreds of battles".

Hastin was himself the sovereign of his own domain with his own feudatories tendering him their homage (*padapindopajivinah*).

Sources of Revenue

These are indicated in the inscriptions describing the immunities carried by grants of land for public purposes.The village *Vasuntarashandika* was grant carried with it the incomes derived from (I) *Udranga* (Share of the agricultural produce due to the State); (2) *Uparikara* (Tax levied on cultivators who do not own the land they cultivate) (3) *Pravesya* (Non-payment of exactions due to regular and irregular troops visiting the village); (4) *Vyaghata* (freedom from expense and molestation caused by the vistis of royal relations and their retinue). Other incomes were reserved to the State e.g., *Chowkidari* tax or fines imposed on thieves, *Chora –Varjjam*=(*Chora –danda –varjjam*) which the state required to maintain Law and Order as its primary duty.

Officers

The inscription mentions the following officers: (I) *Amatay* (Minister), (2) *Bhogika* (Local Magistrate) and (3) *Dutaka* (coveying the King's order or *Sasana*).

Sun Temple

The Mandasor Inscription, as already noticed, refers to the repair of the Sun Temple at Dasapura buy its founders, the Guild of Weavers in the Malava year 529=472 A.D. "when Kumara Gupta was ruling the Earth". The year shows that it was Kumara Gupta II.

A Poet

This inscription is a fine piece of poetry composed by the poet *Vatsabhatti* who adorned the royal court with the power of '*Nam*'as a New Thought in the history of India.

Budha Gupta (A.D.476-495)

Inscriptions

Besides the aforesaid images of the Buddha constructed by Abhayamitra in the time of Kumara Gupta II, as stated in its inscription. *Abhayamitra* got constructed two more images of the Buddha bearing inscriptions which were found damaged but restored by comparing the mutilated texts of both. The restored texts states that "in the year 157 of the Guptas (=A.D.476) when Budha Gupta was ruling (*prasasati*). Abhayamitra *'Sakyabhiskshu'* had this image (*pratima*) of the Buddah constructed (imamkarita). It "was adorned (*vibhushitam*) with uplifted handes (*uddhasta*), umbrella (*sachchhatra*) and a seat of lotuses (*padmasana*), radiant like angels (*devaputravat*), and decorated with various designs (*chitravinyasa-chitritiam*). The spiritual merit (*punya*) acquired (*bhritam*) by the donor by the construction of such an image will lead towards "the attainment of final beatitude (*samaptaya*) by his mother and father, preceptor and indeed all mankind" (*loka*).

The third inscription is that of Damodarpur Copper Plate No.2 dated Gupta year 163=482 A.D. when Budha Gupta was at the zenith of his power and glory as described in the epithets: *Paramadaivata-Paramabhattaraka Maharaja-dhiraja –Sri-Prithivipati*. A fourth inscription of the same date appear in the Damodarpur Copper Plate No.3. An Eran Inscription of the year 165=A.D. 484 refers to *Maharaja Surasmichandra* as a feudatory of Budha Gupta ruling the country between the *Kalinidi* and Narmada and the erection by the local chief Matri Vishnu and his brother Dhanya-Vishnu of a pillar dedeicated to God *Janardana* (Vishnu).

Administative Details

As usual, these are given in the inscription on Damodarpur Copper Plates of which Nos.2.& 3 and 4 belong to this reign. They merely repeat the same details. The District Magistrate (*Vishayapati*) is associated with a Non-offical Council of four members, viz; (I) *Nagarasreshti*, Mayor of City – Corporation; (2) *Prathamakulika,* (3) *Sarthavaha* and (4) *Prathama Kayastha* representing the interests of Citizen Industry, Trade and Administration. The State granted land (1) for a public purpose, religious or charitable; (2) that was (a) *aprada* (unsettled), (b) *aprahata* (not ploughed, fallow) and (c) *khila-kshetra* (common pastures), such land that did not yield any revenue to the State but fetched a sale price, in the case at the rate of 3 *Dinara* for I *Kukavapay*, on which can be sown one *kulya* weighing 8 *droans* of seeds. The Government order for the grant of land was passed on the report of a Board of three Pustapalas, instead of one, to prevent corruption.

The Damodarpur Copper Plate No.3 Inscription contains some new points. It mentions Brahmadatta as Budha Gupta's Provincial Governor (*Uparika Maharaja*).

The inscription records a grant of land for a new purpose, the settlement of a colony of Brahmanas (*Aryas*). The order was issued from the township named *Palasavrindaka,* a union of villages, on approval of its principal citizens (*Akshudraprakriti*). The land was measured by the standard 8x9 reeds (*Ashtaka navakanalabhyaṃ*), for purposes of its separation (*apavinchchhya*) from adjoining plots.

The Damodarpur Copper Plate No.4. Inscription is undated but may be assigned to Budha Gupta. It mentions Jayadatta as the *Uparika Maharaja* or Provincial Governor of *Pundravarhana-Bhukti* under Budha Gupta. Jayadatta appointed *Sandakas* the office –in-charge of the District (Vishaya) named Kotivarsha, the District Office being called *Adhishtana.* The land that was granted was of a Himalayan (*Himavachchhikhara*) village. The same village is mentioned in the earlier Damodarpur Copper Plate No.I Inscription of the year 124 = A.D. 443. It may be noted that the Gupta Empire had extended under Samudra Gupta up to Nepal on its frontier. The inscription states that lands were granted for the temples of the two gods *Kokamukhasvamin* and *Svetavarahasvamin* which were probably built by *Ribhupala*, the *Nagarasreshthi* of Kotivarsha, on the model of the original shirnes of those names in Nepal, in his own village near Damodarpur. It is also stated that both *Vastu* or building sites and lands for cultinvation and not fallow lands were applied for in aid of the temples.

Another inscription of the time of Budha Gupta has been discovered on a Copper-Plate at Paharpur (Eastern Pundravardhana) of the Gupta year 159 =A.D. 479. It records the grant of land by Brahmins to a Jaina Vihara under a Government order issued from the District Office of Pundravardhana city.

The inscription contains some new administrative data. It mentions in an ascending order the following units of settlement and administration: (I) *Grama* (2) *Parsva* (3) *Mandala* and (4) *Vithi.* The revenue payable by the village is termed *Pravesya.* The inscription mentions that the board of Record –Keepers had its head called *Prathama-Pustapala.* It also states that the donor wanted 1½ *Kulyavapa* which were made out 4 villages, showing that cultivable land was scarce. It does not mention different prices for *Khila* and *Vastu* lands but there is a difference as to their amounts. *Vastu* or building land was required in smaller quantity than land for cultivation (*vapa*).

It appears that different prices of land prevailed in different areas. The quotation Damodarpur is 3 *dinaras* per 1 *kulyavapa* as against 2 of his grant. Land at Paharpur was therefore cheaper.

A Copper Plate Inscription of year 169 =A.D. 488 discovered at Nandapur (Monghyr) is taken to belong to the reign od Budha Gupta, through unnamed, on the ground of its words, scripts and contents resembling those of the other north Bengal inscritpiions, especially in respect of details of land transaction which it repeats the history of God and man.

The inscription states that the District Magistrate himself as the applicant for land to be given away by him in perpetuity (*Akshayanivi*) to a Brahmin to help him to performs the five Great Sacrifices named *Bali, Charu, Vaisvadeva. Agnihotra* and *Atithi*. He passes on his application according to procedure to his brother officers (Ayuktakas) who refer it to the other village authorites concerned (*Uttaran-Samvyava haryadi*) for nessary action. On the report of the Local Board of *Pustapalas* to the effect that the land might be granted (*Taddiyatamiti*), the following order was passed :"You should give away the plot situated in an area where it may not affect the cultivation of settled peasants (*Kutumbinam Karshanavirodhisthane*) after measuring it by the standard unit of 8x8 reeds (*nala*) and then demarcate (*Apavinchchhya*) it by permanent marks of ash, charcoal, etc (*tushanga radichchnaih*)." Thus the land granted was fallow land which did not affect the area under cultivation in the locality. The donor was granted 4 *Kulyavapas* of waste land at the price of 2 *dinaras* per *kulyavapa*. Nandapura was a *Vithi* or Sub-division of the District.

Feudatories and Governors

Parivrajaka Maharaja Hastin who was a feudatory under Maharaja Kumara Gupta II continued as such under Budha Gupta as his Copper Plate Inscription at Khoh (Nagod State) is dated to the year 163 A.D.483, a year in Budha Gupat's reign. This inscription record Hastin's grant of an *Agrahara* in a patta with the usual immunities from the taxes, *Udranga, Uparikara* and freedom from the molestations of the military.

The inscription is interesting for its social and cultural data showing the strength of Brahminism in those days. The following Vedic *Sakhas* are also mentioned, viz., *Vajasaneya* and *Katha*.

Besides Maharaja Hastin the inscription mentions several other feudatories or Governors ruling in different regions of the Gupta Empire. We have already seen that Maharaja Surasmichandra was ruling in Malwa or the territory between the *Kalindi* and the *Narmada* as stated in the Eran Inscription. We have already seen that *Uparikamaharajas* Brahmadatta and Jayadatta were ruling in the *Pundravardhana Bhukti*.

Extent of the Empire

The inscriptions show that the extent of the Empire under Buddha Gupta was not shrunk at all. On the contrary, it seems that Budha Gupta was able to recover some of its territory and prestige it had lost in the troubled times of his predecessors. It included the vast terriorty between the Kalindi and the Naramda. It also included Pundravardhana in North Bengal with its important district such as *Kotivarsha-Vishaya* and *Pundravardhana Vishaya.* Malwa was also a part of the Empire under Surasmichandra. Its district known as Airikini was administered by the two brothers Matri-Vishnu and Dhanya Vishnu. Dhanya-Vishnu, according to Eran Boar Inscription of the year I of Toramana,built a temple for the worship of the Boar Incarnation of Vishnu, showing his authority in that region.

Coins

Budha Gupta issued silver coinage of the Central India type on which his own name has been inscribed in the area of Jammu and Kashmir State, together with his title *Avanipati.*

A hoard of coins found at Bharsar mentions a King named *Prakasaditya.*

The *Arya –Manjusri-Mulakalpa* mentions *Sriman* U, as the successor of Kumara Gupta II.

The coins of *Prakasadity* also show the same letter U below the King's portrait.

It is, therefore, surmised that Sriman, U. Prakasadity, and Budha Gupta were one and the same person.

One of the three specimens of Budha Gupta's coins of *Central India type* in the British Museum bears the date 175=A.D.494, the last recorded year of Budha Gupta.

Narasimha Gupta Baladitya (A.D.195-C.510 A.D.)
Narasimha Gupta

He seems to have ruled over a large empire which is describd in the literary text *Arya-Manjusri Mula-Kalpa* as being *Nissapatnam* and *Akantakam*, free of rival and enemies. The evidence of the text is supported by that of his coins.

Coins

He issued a large number of heavy gold coins of the *Archer type* of the usual pattern. The obverse shows the name *Nara* and the legend with the full name *Narasimha Gupta.* The reverse bears the Legend *Baladitya* of Kashmir who shifted his power to Karkota rulers or '*Dalit Kings*' of the '*Dalit Voice*' or *Inner Voice.*

Huna Invasions

The Gupta Empire was first menaced by the invasions of the Hunas and other *Mlechchha* peoples in th time of Skanda Gupta who was, however, able to completely check their menace for time being, as we have already seen. After Budha Gupta, the Hunas renewed their invasion and made their advance into interior of India under their leaders, *Toramana* and *Mihirakula*.The stages of this advance are reflected in some of the inscriptions. These are the three Eran Inscription of Malwa.

Dhanya Vishnu

The first of these shows that Malwa up to the year A.D.484 was ruled by Matri-Vishnu and later by his brother, Dhanya-Vishnu under Buddha Gupta as the paramount sovereign, as already noticed in the text.

Toramana

The second Toramana Inscription which is dated in the first year of Toramāna (about A.D.510) shows that Malwa had already passed under the ruler of *Toramana*, whose sovereignty was acknowledge by *Dhanya-Vishnu*. This adverse political change did not, however, affect his religious zeal as a devotee of Vishnu whose Incarnation as *Varaha* was enshrined in a temple constructed by him. It was probably inspired by the political ordeal through which the country was then passing. The Varaha Avatara appears as the saviour of the Mother Earth (*Prithivai*, Mother India) lifted on His tusk, being impelled by the prayer of the *Rishis* and Saints represented as clinging to His *mane* and bristles. Thus, the physical structure of all human beings, within and without, is the same as God. Their mental and spiritual make up is also the same. This way is already present within each persons and serves all humanity alike, but under the Blind Faith we differ i.e., *Sudhra* and *Brahmins*. *Sudhra* works in the True Faith and Brahmin works under the Blind Faith as their idea to find out the truth, where it stands, i.e., in *Sudhra* (Pure)

Bhanu Gupta

Goparaja

A glimpse of this fate ful Gupta –Huna conflict is given in a third Eran Inscription dated probably a little later than A.D. 510(the first year of Toramana).It describes that the then ruler of Malwa was Raja Bhanu Gupta, 'the bravest on earth (*Jayati Praviro*), a mighlt king (*Raja Mahan*) the equal of Partha (*Partha-Samo*)'. He was served by a loyal and heroic chief (*Vikhyata-paurusha*) named Goparaja who fell fighting in his kings battle (against the Huna chief, *Toramana*) while his death was made glorious by the self-immolation of his wife giving up her life as a *Sati*. Bhanu Gupta's failure to defend the western out post of the Gupta power in Malwa against the Hunas left the way open for their advance towards the East.

Mihirakula

Later Huna history is indicated in the Gwalior Stone Inscription of the year A.D. 528 of the Huna King Mihirakula who succeeded his father Toramana. The inscription was issued in the fifteenth year of his reign which must have begun in A.D.513 when Toramana died.

This history is further indicated in the literary work *Arya-Manju Sri-Mula –Kalpa* which states 'after the death of Budha Gupta, two kings in Gupta line were crowned one, in Magadha and another in Gauda'. The Gupta King crowned in Magadha must be Narasimha Gupta Baladitya .The work further stated that after Bhanu Gupta had lost Malwa. Toramana carried on his expedition up to Magadha and compelled *Baladitya* to retreat to Bengal . H also crowned one *Prakatadity* as King at Banaras in place of the absconding Gupta Emperor. Toramana , however , died at Banaras while returning westwards. This *Prakataditya* is also stated to have been a son of *Baladitya.* This shows that Narasimah Gupta's influence was still lingering in that quarter.

The story of this Huna-Indian conflict as an event of great national importance, like the Gracco Indian conflict of earlier times passed into folklore or tradition . This tradition was current even in the time of the Chinese pilgrim *Yuan Chwang* in the seventh century A.D. and is recorded by him. He stated that *Mihirakula* was a persecutor of Buddhists and destroyed their *Stupas* and monasteries and attacked King *Baladitya* of Magadha who, however , defeated him and took him prisoner, but later released him. He than left India and escaped to Kashmir where he was ultimately killed in the power of the '*Nam*' to check the advancement power of Brahmins.

This tradition is based on the fact that eventually the Indians were able to overcome the Hunas and free the country of their barbarous domination.

It stands to reason that there was some kind of combination by Indian leaders against the Hunas and the leaders who took part in it were Narasimha Gupta Baladitya and an unexpected king of Central India named Yasodharman Vishnuvardhana of the Kashmir history.

Yasodharman

This king of solitary eminence and unknown in Indian history suddenly emerges into prominence in this Huna Indian conflict. His historicity is testified to in two inscriptions of Mandasor. The first, which is not dated, credits Yasodharman with the winning of an Empire which extended 'from the Brahmaputra to the Western Ocean and from Himalayas to Mahendragiri and with marking Mihirakula pay his homage at his feet. He lasted his power as an Imperial Guptas of Malwa and family styled *Naigama*[18] of the Jammu region(*Naimala*).

The second Mandasor Inscription is fortunately dated to Malava year 589 A.D. 533. It describes Yasodharman as 'achieving victory (*Jayati*), plunging in to the army of his enemies (*Satru-sainyam –Vigahya* (probably the Hunas) and bending down the fame of all heroes (*Vira-Kirtim Vinamya*) . It also gives him the epithet Jauendra and associates him with another supporsed king (*Naradhipati*) named *Vishnuvardhana* who is further described as *Rajadhiraja* and *Paramesvara J.F.* Fleet supposes that Vishuvardhana acknowledged the suzerainty of Yasodharman. But very probably they were one and the same person as indicated by the phrase *saeva* (' he it was') . The two inscriptions repeat the same exploits and refer to the sovereignty achieved over *Prachi* (Eastern India) and North (*Kashmir*). This particular inscription was composed by poet *Vasula* and written by Govinda in the history of India and the Jammu State.

Vainya Gupta

Imperial Gupta history after Buddha Gupta is somewhat obscure. It can be traced only in fragments in association with such named as Bhanu Gupta, *Yasodharman Vishnnvardhana* and Kumar Gupta III. Another name is to be added to the list that of Vainya Gupta already referred to in the study.

Some details of his history are given in his Gunaigarh Copper Plate Inscription of the year 188= A.D. 507 of Comilla in Trippera District. It records that Vainya a Gupta from his victorious camp at Kripura granted some lands to his feudatory (*Padadasa*) named Maharaja Rudradatta in *Uttara Mandala* for a Buddhist *Vihara*. The *Bhukti* of *Uttaramandala* in Samatata is stated to be under its governor Vijayasena. The inscription also mentions a number of *Vishayapatis* or District Officers who are also called *Kumaramatyas*. The royal seal attached to the copper –plate bears the inscription *Maharaja Sri Vainya Guptah*.

It will thus appear that Vainya Gupta was practically ruling as an independent king in Eastern Bengal. He did not however, belong to the line of Imperial Guptas.

Coins

Three gold coins of the *Archer type* have been discovered bearing a legend read as *Chandra* by All and as *Vainya* by others. The latter reading is more probable as Vainya Gupta is a known name. while *Chandra*= gupta III is not known in the history of man and God.

Social Data

The Gunaigarh Copper Plate Inscription aforesaid is rich in detail of social and religious life of the times. Vainya Gupta was a worshipper of Siva.

He made a gift of an *Agrahara* in absolute possession (*Sarvato Bhogena*) to a Mahayana Buddhist Samgha originally founded by *Acharya Santideva* and housed in a monastery called *Asrama Vihara* consecrated to *Avolokitesvara.* Rudradatta made to it an earlier gift providing for (I) Clothing (*Chivara*); (2) Food (*Pindapata*), (3) Beds (*Sayana*); (4) Sears (*Asana*) (5) Medicines and also (6) the means of its maintenance by repairing all breaches (*Khanda*) and cracks (phutta).

There inscription also mentions the King's *Dutaka* as Vijayasena who combined in himself several officers besides his Governorship. Mahasamanta Maharaja Sri Vijayasena was the King's (1) *Dutaka,* (2) *Maha-pratihara,* (3) *Maha-pilupati,* (4) President of the Board of Five *Adhikaranas* or District Officers and (5) *Purapala Uparika* (Chief of the city Mayors).

The inscription mentions a new measure of land, I *pataka*= 40 *Dronoavapas.*

Kumara Gupta III

The Damodarpur Copper Plate No.5. Inscription mentions an Emperor whose surname Gupta is legible with out his personal name of which the syllable *Ku* can be read. The inference is that the full name must be *Kumara Gupta*=Kumara Gupta III. The inscription bears a date as 214 =A.D.533 or 224 =A.D.543. The King is given the Imperial titles: '*Paramadaivata – Paramabhattaraka-Mahaaraja-dhiraja Prithivipati*'. These titles may be conventional but they still indicate that the King had fairly large dominion. It still included the old province of *Pundravardhana Bhukti* which was now ruled by a royal Viceroy whom the inscription describes as '*Rajaputra Deva-Bhattaraka uparika Maharaja*'. The inscription states that the donor of the land granted in this record was a native of Ayodhya, showing that this city was included in the Empire.

This one inscription is full of many interesting facts of social and economic life.

Pundravardhana Bhukti seems to have been a prosperous province under its royal Viceroy who was equipped with all his military paraphernalia comprising the forces of elephants, cavalry and infantry. The province had the flourishing district of *Kotivarsha Vishaya* under its Magistrate Svayambhudeva. The District Office was called *Abhishthana.* The seal that was soldered to the inscription was issued from this office, as stated in the expression: '*Kotivarshadhishthanadhikarena*'. As usual, the District Office had his non-offical Advisory Council of four members representing different interests: (I) *Nagara-Sreshthi*; (2) *Sarthavaha*; (3) *Prathama Rulika* and, (4) *Prathama Kayastha*, representing, as shown above the interests of the City,

Trade, Industry and Administration. These representatives were the Presidents (*Prathma*) of their respective Groups or Guilds.

The gift of land was made to the temple of *Svetavaraha svami* for purposes of its repairs of (1) breaches (*khanda*) and (2) cracks (*phutta*). It also made provisions for worship by ensuring supply of (1) *Bali, Charu* and *Satra*; (2) cows milk (*Gavya*); (3) incense (*dhupa*); (4) flowers (*pushpa*); (5) *Mahduparka* and (6) oil for lamp (*dvipa*).

The land required for this gift amounted to 5 *Kulya vapas* made up of both classes of land, *Khila* (fallow) and *Vastu* (building site). This land was made up of small slices obtained from five village named in the inscription showing that uncultivated land was scarce, agriculture was so progressive, and cultivation so intensive. The gift was a permanent charity (*apradadharmena*).

The price paid for the land was at the rate of 3 *dinaras* per 1 *Kulyavapa* of land that was uncultivated (*aprahata*), wasteland (*khila-kshetra*) not yielding any income to the State *(Samudayabahya)*.

Local King of Eastern India

Gopachandra

This King is known from the Faridpur Copper Plate Inscription. It describes Gopachandra as '*Maharajadhiraja Apratiratha Bhattaraka.*' He seems to have carved out a fairly large dominion of his own in Bengal. It included Faridpur District in East Bengal and Burdwan in West Bengal. An important district of his Kingdom was *Varakamandala Vishaya*. The District Office (*Adhikarana*) was under the Magistrate named *Vatsapala*. A province of the Kingdom is named *Navyavakasika* under the Governor (*Uparika*) named *Nagadeva* who also held the offices of *Mahapratihara Kumarapadiya* (Minister in attendance on Crown Prince) and *Amatya*. The district of *Varakamandala* belonged to this province.

Maharaja Gopachandra is also mentioned as ruling (*Maharajadhiraja Gopachandra Prasasati*) in the Mallasarul Copper Plate Inscription of the same date (c. sixth century A.D.).It was found at Galsi in Burdwn District and issued by Maharaja Vijayasena.

The inscription contains valuable administrative and economic data and details. The *Vardhamana-bhukt* had then on its administrative staff the following officers: (I) *Kartakritika* (Executive Head); (2) *Kumaramatya;* (3) *Chauroddharanika* (Police Chief); (4) *Uparika* (Governor), (5) *Audrangika* (Collector of Udranga Tax, (6) *Agraharika* (Super Intendent of *Agraharas*), (7) *Aurnasthanika* (Superintendent of Silk Factories), (8) *Bhogapatika* (Divisional Commissioner); (9) *Vsihayapati* (District Magistrate), (10) *Tadayuktaka* (Treasury Officer); (11) *Hiranyasamudayika* (Currency Office);

(12) *Pattalaka* (officer in charge of a *Pattala*); (13) *Avasathika* (Superintendent of Rest Houses).

We may thus note the administrative divisions in the following descending order: (1) *Bhukti* (Province), (2) *Bhoga* (Division) (3) *Vishaya* (District) (4) *Vithi* (Sub-division) and *Apttala* (Township).

Some of the village officers associated with the government's land transactions are mentioned as (I) *Agraharins* (2) *Bhattas* (Religious Leaders), (3) *Khadgis*; (4) *Vahanayakas* (Controllers of Transport), besides the Village Elders (*Mahattaras*).

In the inscription, *Vijayasena* figures as the applicant for purchase of 8 *Kulyavapas* of a land to be given away by him permanent charity to a Brahmin to meet the expenses of daily performance of *Pancha Mahayajnas*. The land granted was of villages (*grama*) registered under a *Vithi* of *Vardhamana-bhukti*. Unlike other cases, this land was not allow or waste but yield revenue.. Therefore, the saleproceeds were distributed among the different villages from which slices of the land were taken and credited to the revenue account of each by the *Vara* Officers (*Varakrtaih*= officers created by turns). These officers had to apportion among the different villages the amounts due to each on revenue account from the sale-proceeds in the *Vithi* office. The buyer had also to make good the loss caused to the revenue of the *Vithi* from the land sold (*Vithisamudaya –eva pranayyam*). The gift was recorded on a copper plate which was first heated *(tapita)* by the Pustapala for the purpose.

Vijayasena

This inscription shows that *Maharaja Vijayasena* issued a charter under his own seal like an independent soveriegn. In the earlier Gunaigarh Inscription of Vainya Gupta noticed above, he appears only as a Vainya Gupta is also described in this inscription as a Maharaja local chief posted in East Bengal, probably by his paramount sovereign *Gopachandra* who was then ruling over the entire country including East and West Bengal where the rule of the Gupta Empire ended. Vijayasena had a Cathoilc outlook. In his inscription, he invoked God *Lokanatha* (Siva) together with Buddhist saints (*santah*) while his seal bears the figure of a standing Deity with a Chakra behind, showing that he was God Chakradhari or Vishnu.

Dharmaditya

He is mentioned in two other Faridpur Inscriptions which describe him as *Maharajadhiraja Bhatta raka prithivyam-apratirathah.* He is stated to have appointed, as his *Uparika* or Governor of the Province called *Navya vaskasika, Nagadeva* who again in his turn appionts Gopalasvami as the District Magistrate of *Varakamandala* (=modern Goalanda and Gopalgunj).

Earlier, *Dharmaditya* also appointed as his vessal (*tatprasada-labdhaspada*) Maharaj Sthanudatta in charge(*adhyasana*) of a province. He in his turn appointed Jajava as the *Vishayapati* of *Varakamandal*.

The first inscription mentions a new officer named *Sadhanika* (in charge of fines and debts).

The land of which it records the sale was on the seat coast and was sold at the prince of that locality (*praksamudra maryada*). It was at the rate of 4 *dinaras* per *Kulyavapa*. But it was cultivated land (*Vapa*) and not *Khile* (fallow) or *aprahata* (uncultivated) land. Hence its price is higher. The separated plots is called *Khandala* marked out by boundaries (*Krita-Kalana= Kritachichchnanka;* also called. *Simalingani*) which were visible at first sight (*Drishtimatra –Prabandhena*)

Samacharadeva

The Ghugrahati (Faridpur) Copper Plate Inscription brings to light another King named Samacharadeva described as *Maharajadhiraja*. Two of his coins are found kept in Indian Museum. They show on obverse the legend *Samachara* and Narendravinata on verse in characters of A.D.500 and also the *Bull* symbol which was later used by King *Sasanka*. Thus he was a predecessor of King Sasanka as King of Gauda.

India Under Gupta Empire

Political Stability

India showed a high degree of material and moral progress under the rule of the Gupta Emperors. First was achieved the political unification of Northern India under a common Government. Samudra Gupta was inspired by the ideal of binding together the country (*Dharani Bandhasya*). Next was achieved political stability by maintence of Law and Order, of Peace which made for Progress.

Greater India

Thirdly, the concept of Greater India with internal peace, India could look abroad for her expansion. Spheres of influence were established in distant countries beyond Indian borders; in countries like 'Ceylon and other Islands. ' The expansion of India was the expression of her national self-consciousness. Colonial enterprises is the product of the spirit of nationalism and an efficient home government.

It may be assumed that 'Simhala and other Islands' mentioned by Samudra Gupta in his inscription meant Ceylon and the islands of the Indian Archipelago. The Gupta Emperor's political relationship with these overseas countries is indicated by several significant words already mentioned in the study. It included (a) acknowledgement of his suzerainty by offer of homage *Atmanivedanam*; (b) various forms of service (*seva*); (c) gifts of men and money as tokens of loyalty (*dana* and kanyopayana); (d) treaties of Alliance and Friendship. Both *Samudra* Gupta and Ashoka set before their minds the ideal of world-conquest by means of *parakrama*. *Parakarma*, in the case of the Maurya, was not war like activity but vigorous and effective action to propagate the old Indian concept of morality i.e., *Chamar* as well as special teaching of Lord *Buddha*[19].

These overseas relations of Samudra Gupta are confirmed by others sources. We have seen how King *Meghavarna* of Ceylon dispatched an embassy to *Samudra Gupta* for building a Buddhist monastery at Bodh-Gaya. We have also given an account of what Fa-Hien, the Chinese Pilgrim, had seen of the spread of Brahminical religion and culture as well as Buddhsim to the island of Java. We have also seen how Fa-Hien saw many flourishing centres of Buddhism outside India towards north-wet. Tartar countries, Khotan, Kashgar and the like.(*See Plate XXXXIV, Portrait of Yuan Chwang,* Fig. 63).

Religion

There was a revival of Brahminism in all its branches, Vedism, Vaishnavism, Saivsim and Saktism, Buddhism and Jainism were equally flourishing is that age of religious toleration. We have already seen how these religious were liberally supported by private endowments.

Vedism

Vedism was represented by the performance of typical sacrifices among which may be mentioned (I) *Asvamedha* performed by several kings after Samudra Gupta, and as under the Vakataka Kings, sacrifical posts (*Yupas*) were also erected; (2) *Pundarika*; (3) *Agnishtoma;* (4) *Ukthya*; (5) *Atiratra*; (6) *Vajapeya*; (7) *Brihaspatisava*;(8) *Agnihotra* and (9) *Panchamahayajnas*. The inscriptions also mention the Vedic *Gotras* and *Charanas* in vogue in that age.

Vaishnavism

The Gupta Emperors were themselves the worshippers of Vishnu and Lakshmi with Vishnu's *Vahana*, Garuda, figuring as their dynastic emblem on their coins. They also called themselves officially as *Paramabhagavatas*. There were erected by the public many temples of Vishnu under his different names such as (I) *Chankrabhriti*; (2) *Govinda*; (3) *Janardana*; (4) *Varahavatara*; (5) *Sarngapani* and (6) *Vasudeva*. The Parivrajaka Maharaja

Samkshobha opens his inscription with the famous Mantra.'*Om Namo Bhagavate Vasudevaya*'.

Besides temples, pillars were also erected in honour of Vishnu. An important example of this *Vishnu-dhvaja* is the Iron Pillar of Delhi.

Among ther monuments of Vishnavism may be metioned the cave constructed at Udayagiri in 401 A.D. with sculptures showing four-armed. Vishnu and twelve armed *Lakshmi*, as well as the famous Varaha Avatara temple already described in the text.

Saivism

Inscriptions testify to the widespread worship of Siva in temples called after. His many names indicative of the different aspects of His divinity, such as temples to (1) *Mahabhariava*, (2)*Bhutapati*; (3) *Hara* (4) *Isvara* (5)*Kapalesvara* (6) *Mahadeva* (7) *Mahesvara* (8) *Pasupati* (9) *Prithivisvara* (10) *Pinakin* (11) *Sambhu* (12) *Siva* (13) *Sailesvara* (14) *Sthanu* (15) *Sulapani* and(16) *Ardhanarisvara*. The Mandasor inscription of Yasodharamn mentions that even the Huna Toramana was a worshipper of Siva (*Sthanau*).

An important sect of Saivism was that of the Mahesvaras already noticed in the study.

Sakti Worship

There were temples of *Sakti* under various names, such as (1) *Bhagavati,* (2) Bhavani (13) *Devi* (4) *Gauri* (5) *Katyayani* and (6) *Parvati.*

We have already noticed the temple of the Divine Mothers (*Matries*) with their accompanying *Dakinis* for puposes of *Tantrika* worship. The temples contained images of Seven Mothers and also an image of *Mahishamardini.* We have also alreadgy referred to the Bihari Stone Pillar Inscription of Skanda Gupta testify to another temple of the Divine Mothers including the Goddess *Bhadrarya* (or *Bhadraryaka*) taken as *Parvati.*

The Udayagiri Cave No 5. contains the images of the Goddesses Ganga and Yamuna. There were also temples of several other Goddesses known as (1) *Devaki* (2) *Jahnavi,* (3) *Jambuvati*; (4) *Lakshmi* (5) *Vaishnavi,* (6) *Paulomi,* (7) Sachi and (8) *Sarasvati* cave of Akhnoor in Jammu Region.

Worship of Karttikeya

Worship of *Karttikeya,* God of War, was also being popularized by the Gupta Emperors who invoked Him for victory I their many wars. The God gave his name to the two emperors, Kumara Gupta, and Skanda Gupta. In the time of of Kumara Gupta I was erected temple of Swami- Mahasena also named God Brahmanya.

Worship of Surya

A superb temple of *Surya* or Ravi, a concept of the 'Ravidas Culture' was constructed at *Dasapura* by a Guild of Silk-Weavers in the time of Kumara Gupta I as the member of the Kabir family or *Meghavahana*, as already noticed. In the time of Skanda Gupta,a temple of *Savita* was erected in Antarvedi Vishaya by two *Kshatriya* merchants, a temple of *Aditya Bhattaraka* existed in the time of Maharaja Sarvanaga of *Uchchhakalpa*.

Other Deities

Most of the deities of Hindu pantheon were known and find mention in inscriptions and on coins. These are *Kubera* (God of Wealth) also called *Dhanada* or *Dhanesa, Varuna* (God of Cosmic Law); *Indra* (God of Gods) also called *Sakra Yama* (God of Death); also called *Antaka* and *Kritanta, Hanumat; Rama; Kamadeva* (God of Love) *Lokapala* (Guardian of the Quarters) *Meghavana Brihaspati* (God of Wisdom) *Vidyadharas* (Godlings) *Nara; Kinnara, Gandharva; Mahishasura* and *Nandin* found in the history of Kashmir to Sri Lanka as an independent state of the '*Sudhra Family*'.

Buddhism

Sanchi continued to be its chief centre. In the time of Kumara Gupta I, its great Vihara at *Kakanadabota* received an endowment of both cash and a village as the abode of pious *Sramanas*. In the same reign was constructed an image of the Buddha *Bhagavan*. The great Vihara of *Kakanadabota* received another endowment of cash from a lady at the same time as the theory of mind do. There were already installed four images of the Buddha in the same Vihara. At Sarnath was installed, as we have already seen, in the reign of Kumara Gupta II, by the ascetic Abhayamitra, an image of unparalled artistic workmanship (*apara*) of the Buddha for worship (*pujartham*). The same ascetic in the regin of Budha Gupta constricted two other images of the Buddha of supremely beautiful workmanship(*divya*). The first image is that of the Buddha standing. The second is that of the Buddha seated in *Abhayasasamad* with uplifted hands, and cross –legged in meditation.

These two images of the Buddha represent the finest examples of Art and Indian Art in particular, examples of portraiture in stone.

Jainism

In the regin of Kumara Gupta I was constructed an images (*Akriti*) of *Jinavara* Parsva in Udayagri Cave. In the same reign at Mathura was installed another Jain image. In the reign of Skanda Gupta as already stated, is recorded a Jain endowment with the construction of five images in stone of the *Adikartris* or *Tirthankaras* in the niches of a pillar of stone.

Worship of Teachers and Texts

Along with the worship of deities, there was also a custom of offering worship to the teachers and founders of religious sects whose images and statues were installed in shrines (*Gurvayatana*) as stated in the Mathura Pillar Inscription of the time of Chandra Gupta II. Fa-hien also noted how Buddhist Teachers and Sacred Texts were wordipped in shines specially constructed for the purpose of welfare of the public to follow the 'True Path' The caves of Kizil, near Kacha of Gupta period found in China, as per the survey of Behl, it has the connection between the Indian and Chinese Culture that Buddhism was flourishing in India at that time.

Endowments

The religious sense of the people expressed itself in benefactions for both sacred and secular puposes. They took the form of grants of money and land as already mentioned above in the text. The money was kept in safe custody with Guilds or governing bodies of religious institution (e.g. *Aryasamgha* of the *Kakanadabota Vihara* and its Executive committee called *Pancha-Mandali*) as an *Akshaya-nivi* or permanent fund the interest of which alone was to be spent in aid of the beneficiaries, on requisites of worship, such as scent, incense flowers, or oil for lights; *chivara* (clothing), *pindapata* (food), *sayana* (bedding), *Asana* (seating) and medicines *Agraharas*,alms houses or *Viharas* already discussed above.

Social Service

There is evidence of charities to endow social service of various kinds. The most important evidence is that of Fa-Hien account already cited above. He saw rest-houses providing beed food and drink; free hospitals for patients treated by attending physicians and given their prescribed food and medicine. He also tells of grants of lands, houses and gardens with men and bullocks for purposes of cultivation. Great of land were made to educational institutions which were expected to arrange for its proper cultivation as source of their maintenance form its produce. Sometimes, labour and bullocks were provided as parts of the gifts.

Education and Learning: Teachers are mentioned inscription by the title of *Acharya* and Upadhyaya and the pupils were called *Sishyas* the *Upadhaya* was a sub-teacher who was well up only in a part of the *Veda* or in Grammar and in the other *Vedangas* (see Nos. 56, 61, 71 of Fleet). Besides *Sishyas*, disciples were also called *Brahmacharis* (Nos.22, 23, 39 and 60 of Fleet).

Learned Brahmin teachers were honoured by the title of *Bhattas* (Nos.12, 39 and 81 of J.F. Fleet). Villages consecrated to the use of religious students

(*Brahmacharis*) were called *Agraharas* (Nos.60 of Fleet). Religious students were grouped under *Sakhas* and *Charanas* (No.55 of Fleet). These were names of Vedic schools following a particular recension of one of the Vedas. In the inscriptions, the following Vedic recensions are mentioned, viz, *Aupamanyava* (No. 41 of Fleet), *Bahvricha* (Nos. 40 and 60 of Fleet). *Chhandoga Kauthuma* (No.23), *Katha* (No.22) *Maitrayaniya* (Nos.19and 36), *Ranayaniya* (No.16.) *Taittiriya* (No.56), *Vajasaneya* (Nos.22, 40, and 41), *Vajasaneya-Adhyandian* (Nos.21, 26 and 81) and *Vajasaneya-Kanva* (No.38 of Fleet and also the above Nos.of Fleet).

The three Vedas are called Trayi (No.39 of Fleet). There is a reference to Paramarshi *Veda –Vyasa* as the arranger of the *Vedas* (No.21 of Fleet).

A Brahmin acquainted with all the four Vedas is called *Chaturvedin* (Nos.16, 39and 55 of Fleet),like M.K. Gandhi, he was not touch with the 'Reality', but with mind or *mana*; as a destructive force of the God. There were also Brahmins who specialized in one *Veda* e.g. *Samavedi Brahmin.* Vedas are not individually mentioned in the inscriptions except *Atharvaveda* (No. 80 of Fleet).

The interpreter of Vedic quotations and words is called *Naigama* (No. 35 of Fleet).

As regards the subjects of study other than the Vedas, we have reference to the 14 *Vidyas* (No.25 of Fleet) comprising the 4 *Vedas*, 6 *Vedangas* the *Puranas, Mimamsa, Nyaya*, and *Dharma* or Law Sanskrit and Prakrit poets (No. 33); to the Grammar (*Sabda*) of Panini called *Salaturiya* (No. 39); to *Atharvaveda* in which there was specialized study (No.80); to *Vyasa*, the arrange of the *Vedas*, and son of *Parasara* (No. 31); to the *Mahabharata* (Nos. 26, 27, 28 and 31) and to its *Satasahasri-Samhita* (edition of 100,000 *Slokas*) (Ibid).

The following characters of the *Mahabharata* are referred to in inscription : *Yudhishthira* (No. 38), *Vidura* (No. 35) *Vainya* (No.17), *Uddhava*(No.35), *Sagara*(Ibid), *Bhagiratha* (No.17), *Prithu* (No.2) *Raghava* (Ibid), *Partha* (Nos. 18 and 20), *Mandhata* (No.33), *Manu,Bharata Alarka* (Ibid) and Anu son of *Yayati* (No.49).

Methods of Learning

In India from time immemorial preference was given to oral teaching. It was considered a sacrilege to reduce the Vedas to writing especially because the Vedas consisted of *Mantras* as treasures of thought, and as subjects of contemplation, and were not like ordinary works of composition. This system was continued through the ages and was notice by Fa-Hien who describes its working as follows: The teacher's words had to be heard (*sravana*) pondered over (*manana*) and contemplated (*nidhidhyasana*) as *Sruti*) by his pupils". He further states that in various countries of Northern India through which he travelled, he always found that sacred works were handed down orally from one teacher to another, so that he could hardly find any written volume which he could copy. He found an exception only at one place at the Mahayana monastery at Pataliputra where he found a copy of the "Disciplines', some extracts from the *Abhidhamma* and complete copies of the two *Sutras*. To copy out these works, Fa-Hien was compelled to stay here for 3 years in having to learn to write and to speak Sanskrit.

Popularity of Sanskrit

The popularity of Sanskrit is seen in the inscriptions composed in that language instead of Prakrit, as in earlier times. It may be further assumed that Sanskrit was not merely the language of the learned classes, but became the spoken language of the country. The inscriptions must have been composed in Sanskrit because they could be understood by the masses for whom they were meant for the development of idea of the God and man.

Princely Patronage of Learning and Art: A notable feature in the history of the times is that learning was encourage by Kings not merely by their patronage but also by their own devotion to it. Some of the Gupta Kings were themselves learned Sanskritists. Samudra Gupta won his fame not merely as a King and conqueror, but also as a man of letters a poet, a 'King of Poets' (*Kaviraja*) author of a vast volume of poetry of high quality (*Vahukavita*). He was also well-versed in the *Vedas* and *Sastras* and an original interpreter of Vedic Suktas (*Sukta-Marggah*).

To maintain the standard of scholarship, he used to convene Conferences of learned men (*Budhagunita*) to judge of true poetry (*Satkavya*).

It may be noted in this connexion that Samudra Gupta combined his love of the literary art with that of the fine art of music in which he was proficient. His coins portrary him playing on the lyre (*Vina*) with great concentration.

Among other learned noble men may be mentioned, Saba Virasena, Minister of Chandragupta II, who is descreibed as poet and was also proficient in scientific subjects like Etymology (*Sabdartha*), Logic (*Nyaya*), and State-craft (*Lokajan*) (No.6. of Fleet).

Skanda Gupta was a musician well-versed in its different tunes (*tana*).

Matri-Vishnu a local chief, a Rishi of a Brahmin (Viprarshi) was given to Vedic studies and sacrifices (*Kratuyaji*) (No.19).

The local chief Visvavarman was the equal of *Sakra* (in political lore) and of Brihaspati (in wisdom).

Centres of Learning

We have already seen from the account of Fa-Hien how India was possessed of numerous centres of learning and monasteries containing hundreds of Buddhist monks, besides Brahminical *Agraharas* and *Asramas*.

Art: Structuers and Sculptures

The art of the times was inspired by religion and served its purposes.

Saiva: The Bhitargaon temples at Cawnpore of about sixth century A.D. is decorated with terra-cotta panels of Siva themes. The Deogarh Temple in Jhansi District of about the same time contains many artistic Saiva scultptures. One of these representing Siva as a Yogi is one of the masterpieces of Indian art in the opinion of V.A. Smith.At Kosam (in Allahabad District) is found a sculpture showing *Siva* and *Parvati* of 458 A.D. In Ajmer at Kaman have been found good Saiva sculptures. *Eka-Mukhalingas* showing artistic workmanship have been found at Khoh and Bhumra.

Vaishnava: The following select examples of Vaishnava structures and sculptures may be noted:- (I) the Cave temple at Udayagiri of A.D. 401 contains the spirited figure of *Varaha Avatara*, holding Mother Earth on His tusk, with accessory figures of praying *Rishis* and Seers; (2) the temple at Pathari near Udayagri showing in a massive relief the Nativity of Krishan with his mother, a sculpture considered by Beglaras the largest and finest of Indian sculptures; (3) the Beogarh temples of Laitpur has a panel representing Vishnu reclining on Ananta the symbol of Eternity; (4) Sculptures of fourth century A.D. at Mandor (Jodhpur) depicting beautiful Krishna scenes including the raising of Mount Govardhana.

Surya: The bhumra temples shows an image of Surya or Sun or Ravi dressed like the famous Kanishka statue at Mathura Museum. He is not shown with his horse. But seven horses appear in the sculpture of Kaman (Ajmer).

Buddhist: Buddhism has inspired some of the best example of Gupta Art. The following typical examples may be noted: (I) the Mankuwar Stone Image of the Buddha seated, of 448 A.D. which is an example of Kushana artistic style continuing in the Gupta Age; (2) the Sarnath image of the Buddha seated, preaching his first sermon indicated in the appropriate figures of *Mudra* and the Wheel of *Dharma*, universally regarded as one of the best examples of figure art of the period.

The Gupta Age itself freely to the production of the Buddha images in various forms which were installed in the monasteries in their cells, in their special chapels and temples, and even in their outer niches and relic-towers. Another marked feature of Gupta Buddhist sculpture. is that it is dominate by the cult of the *Bodhisattvas* which is now very pronounced. We have many an image not merely of Maitreya but also, in particular, of *Avalokitesvara*. The

Buddhsit Art of the times also introduced figures of deities taken from Brahminism, those of Vaisravana, the God of Wealth, Goddess of Fertility, Vasudhara (Goddess of Plenty) Tara, *Mariachi* and the like. This extended scope of Buddhist art resulted in the introduction of the portraiture of the Buddha and of the events of his life which are emphasized so much in the earlier Gandhara Art. Unlike also earlier Art of Bharhut and Sanchi which were inspired so much by Jatakas, Gupta Art found other sources of inspiration, mainly Brahminical.

Schools of Art

The works of Art produced in the Gupta Age may be grouped under the different Schools of Art which may be called (1) the Mathura School and (2) the Banaras School. The former is marked out by its material of mottled red stone quarried at Karri in Mathura district, while the latter by the Chunar sandstone. Stylistically, the, Mathura School came under the influence of the Gracco-Buddhist or Gandhara School of Art and copied some of its foreign features as seen in its many images of the Buddha and the *Bodhisattva*. The Banaras School evolved a purely indigenous style and also produced a particular type in its stelae on which are graphically represented the main incidents in the Buddha life in the manner of the Gandhara Art school.

There is sometimes distinguished a third School of Indian Art, the Pataliputra School, which specialized in its works of metal images, the best of which are the Buddha images found in Nalanda and Sultanganj. This school also produced numerous bronze images of the very highest artistc quality at two chief centres, Nalanda and Kurkihar.

Architecture

The Gupta Age was marked by great creative activity and different cultural movement in various fields. One of these was the architecture of the country. For the first time it was introduced in architecture dressed one-masonry work. The earliest example of this architecture is the stone-shrine of Vishnu near the famous Heliodorus Pillar of the first century B.C. and of the same time. Hiherto a roofed temple was rare. Brahminical worship was performed in the open. The Bharhut and Sanchi sculptures of the second century B.C. show fire-altars and shrines which were unroofed. The *Satapatha Brahmana* requires only posts and beams, and a roof of needs and mats for shrine. The evolution of the Brahminical temple thus passed through the following stages: (I) Leafy bower; (2) Hut of Reed; (3) A cella of wood and bricks; (4) A sanctum of stone or *Garbha –griha* a small cell with only one doorway so as not to intrude upon the inner darkness conductive to contemplation of the deity enshrined within. The walls of the interior were purposely left undecorated by art that might distract the mind with its objective emphasis. But this restriction did not apply to the exterior of the temple.The outside of the doorway gave room for artistic decoration which suggested the addition to it of a porch for shelter in the later Gupta period. The Udayagiri Caves of the fifth century A.D. show the first examples of structural porticos.

Scope for artistic decoration was thus found in the pillar and its capitals and also in the design of the doorway as seen in its temples in Tigawa (Jubbalpur), Sanchi, Bhumra (Nagod State) or Udayagiri rock cut sanctuaries.

Of these examples, the Tigawa temple deserves special study. It keep up the small sanctum and the cells. It gives scope to the artistic decoration in the pillar of the portico. The pillar is made up of four parts :(1) a plain square pededtal, (2) a short shaft with many sides; (3) the capital resembling a vase or *Kalasa* (or inverted lotus), and (4) a massive abacus surmounted by a device of lions. The design of the pillar takes after the famous Garudadhvaja of Besnagar, while the lion is a link with the Ashokan capital. Another new feature of this temple is the introduction on the door way of the decorative figures of Goddess *Ganga* on *Makara* and *Yamuna* on *Kachchhapa*. a feature which become very popular and was repeated on doorways of other temples.

The Saiva temple of Bhumra and the Parvati temple Nachna of about fifth century A.D. add to the structure of processional path. The doorways show more elaborate decoration. The Bhumra temple have even ceiling decorated figures of foliage and also ornamented with *Chaitya* windows and medallions bearing the figures of *Ganesa, Brahma, Yama,. Kubera, Karttikeya, Siva* dancing on Bull, *Surya Kama and Mahisamardini.*

The Deogarh temple adds a pyramidical tower over sanctium (the first appearance of the *Sikhara*) also four porticos supported on a row of four pillars to each of the four sides of the temple.

Pillars

Besides these temples Gupta Art is also represented in several free standing pillars such as the Budha Gupta Monolithic Pillar at Eran dated 484 A.D. and the earlier more famous Iron Pillar at Delhi. The Eran Pillar, 43 feet high, has a lion abacus crowed by a statuette of Vishnu. The Iron Pillar at Delhi about 24 feet high, and 6 tons in weigth is made of pure malleable iron, a remarkable proof of the capacity of the foundry and of progress of metallurgy to produce it in those days.

Temple Seals

Temples issued their own seals in those days. The Vishnupada temple at Gaya issued its seal bearing the lengend '*Vishnupada –Svami-Narayana*' with its upper parts bearing the figures of Vishnu symbols, mace, conch and wheel, together with symbol of *Siva, Surya* and *Chandra*. A Vaisali Seal issued by the temple of the Sun bears the lengend '*Bahagavato Adityasya*', Some Bhitari Seals bear the figure of fire-altar.

Social Conditions

Society was based on *Varnasrama-dharma*, its division into four castes, while life for all castes was divided into a graduated series of stages known as *Asramas*.

The King was to be the upholder of this social order and to prevent unlawful mixture of castes (*Varna-Samkara*). *Abhayadatta*, *Rajasthaniya* (Governor) of a Province, is described as the protector of castes and his successor, *Dharma dosha,* as checking the mixture of castes.

The first caste was the Brahmin. Inscriptions refer to his ideal and duties. He stood for intellectual and spiritual life discarding worldy pursuits. Brahmins became (1) *Yogis* concentrated on contemplation (*Dhyana-ekagrapara*) for achieveing *Siddhi* (Self-fulfulment) and *Moksha* (Salvation) and also (2) *Munis* who with devotion (*bhakti*) gave themselves up to total and extreme (*Tivra*) penance as their only concern in life (*tapodhana*). Brahmins were known for their (1) penance(*Tapah*) (2) Vedic study (*Svadhyaya*), and (3) proficiency in *Mantras, Sutras*, *Bhashyas*, and *Pravachanas* (E.I.X.72). As we have seen the inscription are full of grants of land and *Agraharas* to Brahmins to support them in their non-worldly spiritual life, with performance of costly daily sacrifices like *Agnihotras* and the *Panchamahayajnas*.

Brahmins, as saints, were honoured by all. A village became a sacred place if it were the abode of saints to purify it (*Sadhusamsargaputa*), as already seen. A Jain nobleman named Madra takes pride in his devotion to 'Brahmins', religious preceptors and ascetics (No.15 of Fleet).

Royal families had their Brahmin preceptors (*Archaryas*). *Chanala* (*Chandala*) *Svami,* a *Chaturvidya*, was the preceptor of the royal family of *Prabhavati Gupta* (E.I. XV. 39).

Brahmins were employed by the authorites to offer prayers for their health and welfare (No.14)

Brahmins were known by their *Gotras*. Many such Gotras are mentioned in inscription, such as *Atreya, Bharadwaja, Bhargave, Gautama. Kanva. Kasyapa, Kautsa, Parasarya Sandilya, Satyayana, Vatsa and Vaji.*

Brahmins were also known by the Vedas to which the belonged e.g., *Samavedi* Brahmins.

Insrciptions tell of some Brahmin Kings and Minister, such as King Matri-Vishnu and Ministers, *Mayura-Rakshaka* and *Sikharasvami*.

Case of inter-caste marriages were known. *Ravikirit*, a Brahmin, married a Kshatriya girl named Bhanugupta (No. 35).

Kings were given to polygamy, e.g. Chandra Gupta II and Kumara Gupta I. There was a chief queen to participate in religious sacrifices like the Asvamedha, as seen on coins.

Women had their *Stridhana* out of which they made gifts (No.62).

There is a case of *Sati* on record, the devoted wife of General Goparaja whom she followed to the flames (No.20).

Economic Conditions

There was economic progress all round, in Agriculture, Industry or Handicrafts,Trade, Business and Banking. The progress of Agriculture is evident from the fact that the various epigraphic records of the land transaction of the times show that it was not very easy to secure any fallow,, uncultivated or unsettled land for purposes of charitable grants. The progress of intensive cultivation hardly left any land that was cultivable and not settled. Lands for grants were made out of small slices taken from different plots in different villages and were not at all to be found in one continuous area.

Grants of land to educational institutions carried with them provision for labour and bullocks necessary for cultivation of which the yield was to maintain them as already discussed.

Industry, Trade and Banking were organized under their own guilds applying the democratic procedure.

The Vaisali seals bring to light different classes of Guilds called *Srenis* or *Nigamas*, those of (1) Bankers (*Sreshthis*), artisans (*Kulikas*), and(3) Traders (*Sarthavahas*). Sometimes they were federated together into a Central Guild as in the expression, *Sresthi-Kulika-Nigama*. the federated (*Nigama*) of Bankers and Craftsmen, or in the expression, *Sresthi Sarthavaha-Kulika-Nigama*, a Federation of all three guilds. As Dr. T. Block has rightly points out: "It looks as if during those days something like a modern Chamber of Commerce existed in Upper India at some big trading centres". The Foreman of a Guild also issued a seal under his authority, e.g., that of a *Prathama Kulika*. Other inscriptions as we have seen mention the working and prosperity of different classes of Guilds, such as those of (I) Oilmen (*Tailakasreni* with its president (*Pravara*) named Jivanta, (2) the Guild of the township of Ajapuraka, and (3) Silk weavers (*Pattavaya-Sreni*).

A most important function of these Guild was that of Banking.It promoted private philanthropy by accepting donations as permanent and irrevocable (*Ajasrikam*) deposits (*Akshaya-nivi*) on which they paid out the stipulated interest to the beneficiaries named by the donors.The document for the deposit was duly registered (*nivaddha*).

That the deposit carried interest shows that these Guild Banks were able to earn a higher rate of interest by investing these deposits as profitably as possible.

It may be noted in this connection that endowments in favour of a *Vihara* or a temple were received and administered as permanent deposits by its governing body which acted like a bank in this respect. For instance,as we have already seen, the *Arya-samgha* of the *Mahavihara* at Kakanadabotas (Sanchi) together with its executive, the *Pancha-mandal;* (Council of Five) was trusted with a permanent endowment to be administered in the interests of its beneficiaries, the monks. Similarly, the Temples Committees received endowments ensuring permanent provision for the supply of the requisities for permanent provision for the supply of the requisites for worship, scents, incense, flowers and oils for Lights see on earth.

The Gupta Empire was based on a money economy, as is shown by its currency of different metals, Gold, Silver,Copper and of various types, designs and denominations.

There was considerable progress achieved in regard to construction of Public works of Utility. An important example of these was the reservoir (*tataka*) called Sudarsana made by damming up in soild masonry work the flow of rivers down the hills near Girinagara in Surashtra.

A city's amenities are described as comprising (1) Wells (*vapi*), (2) tanks(*tadaga*), (3) temples with halls (*surasadmasabha*), (4) storage of drinking water (*udapana*), (5) parks (*upavana*) of various kinds, (6) causeways (*samkrama*) and (7) lakes (*dirghika*), Gangdhar Inscription already cited above.

The Mandasor Stone Inscription (already cited) describes how the district (*Vishaya*) of Lata was adorned with shrines of gods (*devakuala*) halls of temples (devasabha) and *Viharas*, rows of storeyed mansions (*prasada-mala*) as high as aerial chariots (*vimana-mala*).

Political Conditions

The Kings of those days, generally, were nominated by their predecessors on the ground of their merit, as already elaborated.

The Gupta Kings assumed various titles to show their imperial status, such as *Maharajadhiraja*, *Ekadhiraja* (No.32), *Paramesvara* (No.46) and *Chakravartin* (No.39).

The King received the homage of his subjects in the Darbar Hall (*Upasthana*).

The palace had its own staff of officers, such as *Mahapratihara* (Chief Usher), *Vinayasura* (to conduct visitors to the King), the *Sthapati-Samrat* (Supervisor of workmen), *Pratinartaka* (Official Chronicler or Minstrel) and

Khadyat apakika (Superintendent of the Kitchen). A special officer (*Yuktapurusha*) was appointed by the king to restore the properties of the vanquished (*Vibhava-pratyarpana*) (No.1)

Administrative Divisions

These have already been indicated in connexion with the regins of different Kings concerned. The kingdom as a whole is called (1) *Rajya, Rashtra, Mandala, Prithivi or Avani e.g. Sukulidesa (No.5) Dabhala desa (No.19); Surashtra-avani(No.5).*

Below it was a hierarchy of administrative divisions in the following descending order: (2) *Bhukti* or *Pradesa* (Province) e.g. *Pundravardhana – bhukti* (Damodarpau Copper Plate). *Nagara –bhukti* (No. 46). Tira –bhukti (Vaisali Seal) and *Uttaramandala-bhukti* (Gunaigarh), *Airikinapradesa.*

(3) *Bhoga*, modern Commissionership. A Commissioner is called a *Bhogika* (Nos.21, 23, 26, 27.29 and 30). He is also called a *Bhogapati.*

(4) *Vishaya* (District), e.g. Kotivarsha (Damodarpur Plates), Khada (ta) para (Damodarpur 1, 2 and Dhanaidaha), Panchanagari (Baigram Charter), Lata (No.18, Vaisali Seal) and Antarvedi (No.14)

(5) *Vithi* (Sub-division): e.g. *Sringavera –vithi*(*Kalai-kuri*).

(6) *Pethaka* or *Santaka* (Union of Villages) (Nos.25 and26).

(7) *Mandala* e.g; Varakamandal.

(8) *Parsva*

(9) *Grama* (e.g., Paharpur)

(10) *Patta*

(11) *Agrahara* (No.22)

Provincial Administration

The inscriptions have named the various provincial officers forming the administration. At the head was the Governor called by several names such as *Uparika –Maharaja Gopta, or Rajasthaniya. Rajasthaniya* is explained as one who protects the people (Kshemendras *Lokaprakasa*). The Governor might be a prince and then called *Rajaputra-Devabhattaraka* with his Minister in attendance called *Kumaramatya.*

The Governor was attended by his private secretaries called *Dutas, Dutakas* or *Ajna-dapakas* who communicated his orders to the administration

Then there was the *Karana-Kayastha* to record in writing the King's orders and sometimes served as *Sandhi Vigrahika.*

Some of the heads of the departments are mentioned thus:-

(1) *Baladhikaranika* (Military Chief).

(2) *Dandapasadhikaranika* (Police Chief)

(3) *Mahadandanayaka* (Chief Justice)

(4) *Vinayasthitisthapaka* (Minister for Law and Order)
(5) *Sadhanika* (Collector of Fines and Debts)
(6) *Senapati* (Chief of the Army)
(7) *Tadayuktaka* (Treasury Officer)
(8) *Hranyasamudayika* (Currency Officer)
(9) *Aurnasthanika* (Superintendent of Silk Facrtories)
(10) *Chauroddharanika* (Chief of Detectives) (See reference cited above).

District –Administration

The District Magistrate is called *Vishayapati*, the District Headquarters *Adhishthana* and the District Officer *Adhikarana* e.g. *Vaisali –adhishthana –adhikarana*. The District Office staff are called *Ayuktakas* and *Samuyauahari*.

The District Advisory Council representing different interest was made up (I) *Nagarareshthi*, (2) *Sarthavaha*, (3) *Prathama Kulika* and (4) *Prathama Kayastha*.

The District Officers in Charge of different departments were (1) *Saulkika* (2)*Dhruvadhikaranika* (in charge of land revenue), (3) *Gaulmika* (in charge of forest and garrisons), (4) *Agraharika*, (5) *Bhandagaradhikrita* (Treasurer), (6) *Utkhetayita* (Collector of Taxes) and (7) *Pustapala* (Records Keeper).

The District Records Office was called *Akshapatala* under departmental head called *Mahakshapatalika*. Writer of Records or Documents were called *Diviras* (No.27) or *Lekhakas* (N0.80).The Documents were called *Karanas* (No.56).and their custodian was called *Karanika*. The officer drafting the document is called *Kartri* or *Sasyitri* (E. I. XII, 75)

The District Officer had a staff of General Superintendents called *Sarvadhyakshas* (No.55) who had their subordinates recruited from the upper classes called *Kulaputras* for their probity.

We have already seen that land transactions were conducted by special local rural committees made up of (1) *Mahattaras,* (2) *Ashtakuladhikaranas* (3)*Gramikas* and (4) *Kutumbinah,* together with the government officers, the *Pustapalas*. Sometimes the Committees included the leading Brahmins of the villages called Brahmanottaras (Paharpur Copper Plate).

City Administration

The Mayor of a city is called *Purapala* (Gunaigarh) or *Nagararakshaka* (No.14) There seems to have been a Minister of Municipalities controlling their chief under the name *Purapala-uparika* (Gunaigarh). The Mayor of Dasapura is called Dasapura –pala (No. 18). A city was governed by a Municipal

Committee called *Parishat*, as in the case of the city of Municipal Committee called *Parishat*,as in the case of the case of the city of *Udankupa*. A city had an officer called *Avasathika* in charge of its rest horse (*Mallasarual*).The Paharpur Copper Plate Inscription calls the Municipal Office as *Adhishthana –adikarana* under the Mayor called Sreshthi e.g. *Arya-Nagara –Sreshthi.*

Sources Revenue and Taxation

According to inscriptions already cited there are (1) *Udranga* (2) *Uparikara* (a tax levied on cultivators who have no proprietary right on soil according to J.F. –Fleet), (3) *Vata* (unexplained), (4) *Bhuta* (probably what is 'grown' as distinguished from 'withered' '*Vata*' (5) Dhanya (6) *Hiranya*, (7) *Adeya* (what is payable to the State), (8) *Vaishtika* (contribution of labour due), (9) *Dasaparadha* (fines from ten offences, viz (a) three offences of the body, theft, murder and adultery. Four offences of speech, words that are harsh, untruthful, libellous and pointless; and (b) *three* offences of mind, covetring other's property, thinking of wrong and devotion to what is not true); (10) Bhoga (tax on enjoyment, 'surplus or income tax'); (11) Bhaga (Share).

Sometimes, the sources of taxation can be be gathered for the obligations and immunities which a grant of land carried with it, the benefits conferred on the beneficiaries. These are enumerated as follows: (I) *not* to pay taxes (*Akaradayi*), (2) not to be molested by regular troops and police (*Bhata*) or outlaw (*Chata*), (3) not to yield increase in its cows and bulls; (4) nor in its flowers or milk, pasturage, hides and charcoal; (5) nor any taxes on salt or wet salt on sale and purchase, or produce of mines; (6) not to contribute forced labour or surrender its hidden treasures and deposits, (7) *Kliripta* and *Upaklripta* (unexplained) word of the God or Nam. (No 55 of Fleet).

There are also enumerated in the inscription of Prabhavati Gupta already cited, as follows: (I) Freedom from exactions by soldiers (*Bhata*) and royal retainers (*Chhatra*), (2) not yielding right to prasturage (*charasana*), (3) not to supply hides (*Charma)* or *angara* (charcoal); the purchase (*kreni*) of fermenting drugs (*kinva*) and mines (*khanaka*); (4) not to pay tax on increase of cattle (*Aparampara= Aparampara Valivardagrahana*); (5) not to supply animals for sacrifice (*apasumedhya*); (6) not to give any share of flowers, milk, or hidden treasure and deposits together with *Klripta* and *upavalkripta* (probably sales –tax).

It will thus appear that in the system of taxation of those days there was left hardly any property or income which was not taxed. The sources of taxation are indicated the much older Nasik Cave Inscription of Gautamiputra Satakarni of year 18 (=124 A.D.) The royal grant of a village carried with it certain immunities and benefits which are mentioned as: (1) *Apravesyam* (*Bhatadipravesa-pratishedha* (2) *Anavamarsyam* (Freedom from molestation by Government Officers); (3) *Alavanakhataka* (Right to salt derived from land granted as all produce of mines belonged to the King; (4) *Arashtrasamvinayikam* (not to be interfered with by the district police outside governemt control). A fuller list of these is given as follows in the Basim Copper Plate Inscription of the Vakataka King Vindhyasakti II:

(1) *Arashtrasamvinayikam*;

(2) *A-lavanaklinnakhtatakam* (right to extract salt and other moist substances, liquor or sugar from trees like the *Palmyra*);

(3) *A-hiranya –dhanya –Pranaya-pradeyam* (Exemption from benevolence (*Pranaya*) levied in cash or kind;

(4) *A-pushpa-kshira –Grahana* (Not to supply flower and milk for the King);

(5) *A-parampara-govalivardam* (Not to supply Government Officers on tour either cow for milk or bullock for cart);

(6) *A –varasdhikam* (Freedom from any obligation to be met by turn);

(7) *A-charmangarakam* (No obligation to supply leather and charcoal)

(8) *A-bratapravesam* (Bar to entry of soliders);

(9) *A-Khatva –Chollaka –Vainasikam* (No obligation to supply cots, cooking utensils and fuel for touring officer);

(10) *Akaradam* (Not to pay rent to the King);

(11) *Avaham* (No obligation to carry loads free of charge);

(12) *Sanidhi-Sopanidhi* (right to hidden treasure deposits).

Land Transactions

It may be noted that inscriptions found in Bengal are replete with unique details of land transactions not to be found in the inscriptions of other parts of India under the Gupta Empire. These have been already explained above. Here a summary of the system must be given.

The numerous grants of land recorded in these inscriptions bear remarkable testimony to the religious charitable character, and philanthropy of the people concerned in making gifts of land in perpetuity for public purposes.

It was difficult to make gifts of land because all available land in the village was settle among its house-holders (*Gristanbinah*). Such land had therefore to be (1) *aprada* (unsettled) (2) *aprahata* (not tilled), (3) *astamba* (barren of vegetation), *khila* (fallow); (5) *samudayavahya* (with out any incoming); (6) *apratikara* (not yielding any revenue causing any loss of revenue to the State (*na kaschit rajastha virodhah*) and (8) *utpratikara* (not assessed to revenue). Thus such land would not affect the area already under cultivalation by its proprietors (*Kutumbinam karshana-virodhisthane*. It was, however, cultivable and productive of revenue to be State (*upachaya*) and income to the donor to support his charity or his beneficiary. That is why it carried a price (*vikraya –maryada*).

The grant of land was for a permanent gift (*Akshayanivi*). It might be required for purposes of building (*vastu*) with its trenches (*sthala*) and gardening (*talavataka*).

Land should be granted by the Government only by suspending its rule against it (*anuvritta-apradakshaya-nivi*). The land that was to be granted should not be any one's property for which compensation was payable (*akinchit pratikara*).If it were so as *Vapa-kshetra* or land already cultivated it should carry higher price (*Faridpur Grant*) as God and man.

The Vakataka Rulers (c. 250-500 A.D.)

We have already seen that there were points of contact and conflict between *Vakataka* and Imperial Gupta history. An account of the history of the *Vakataka* dynasty may be given here. Its sources are the *Puranas*, and the following inscriptions thus listed: (I) *Deotck Inscription* (Chanda District

Original Vakataka Family (Northern Branch)

↓

Vindhyasakti I

↓

Son Pravarasena I

↓

(Son Gautamiputra)

↓

Son Rudrasena I

↓

Son Prithivisena I

Son Rudrasena II (married to Prabhavati Gupta , daughter of Emperor Chandra Gupta II)

↓

Son Pravarasena II

↓

Son Narendrasena

↓

Son Prithivisena II

of M.P.) of Rudrasena I; (2) Poona Copper Plate Inscription of Prabhavati Gupta (and her husband Rudrasena II); (3) Copper Plate Grant of Pravarasena II; (4) Belora Grant of Pravarasena II; (5) Kothuraka Grant of Pravarasena II;(6) Basin Copper Plate of Vindhyasakti II (of Vatsagulma branch, c. A.D.400); (7) Fragmentary Inscription of Devasena (Vatsagulma branch); (8) Ajanta Cave XVI Inscription of Varashadeva; (9) Ajanta Ghatotkacha Inscription of Varahadeva; (Hyderabad Archaeological Memoir No.14, EI. XV. 39 f; E.L.XX IV.260 f.).

A special study of these inscriptions suggests that some of these doubtful points of Vakataka history may be solved by assuming (as pointed out by Principal V.V. Mirashi who had edited some of these Inscription) that after sometimes the Vakataka family was split up in to two parts and the seceding part may be designated as the Vatsagulma branch. The genealogies of these two branches may be thus presented as under.

The generalogy of the other offshoot of the Vakataka family called Vatsagulma branch may be thus given:-

Vatsagulma Branch

Vindyasakti I

↓

Son Sarvasena I

↓

Son Vindhyasena =Vindhyasakti II

↓

Son Pravarasena II

↓

Son (whose name is lost)

↓

Son Devasena

↓

Son Harishena

This list shows that the division of the family took place after Pravarasena I

Now as to their history, the *Puranas* state that Pravarasena I had four sons who after his death divided among themselves his vast kingdom.His eldest son Gautamiputra is known from his copper plates which, however, do not apply to him the usual epithet '*Vakatakanam Maharaja*'. Thus he predeceased his father. His son, Rudrasena I, therefore, succeeded Pravarasena

I and founded the northern branch of the dynasty ruling over Northern Berar and Western districts of M.P. where are found their inscriptions (as seen in Deoteck Inscription).

His great –grandson Pravarasena II issued copper plates recording grants of land in different places such as Amraoti, Wardha, Nagpur, Betul, Bhandara and Balaghat. His father was Rudrasena II and mother Prabhavai Gupta.

Up to now the Vakataka Kingdom had its capital at Nandivardhana but Pravarasena II built his own capital at Pravarapura (see Poona Copper Plate of Prabhavati Gupta and Belura and Kothuraka Grants of Pravarasena II). It may be noted that Gautamiputra was married to the daughter of the powerful king Maharaja Bhavanaga of *Bharasiva* Dynasty, while Chandra Gupta II married his daughter Prabhavati Gupta to the Vakataka King Rudrasena II

Vakataka power was at its zenith under Prithivisena I who, as already seen had his suzerainty acknowledged all over the country from *Nachne-ki-Talai* and *Ganj* (Bundelkand) up to Kuntala (Kanarese) country of which he is described as the Lord (*Kuntalesvara*) in an Ajanta Inscription.

After Prithivisena the Gupta Emperors were establishing their supremacy in Central India Samudra Gupta and Chandra Gupta II. Samudra Gupta defeated a King named Vyaghra Raja; King of *Mahakantara* (Vindhyan wilderness of eastern Gondwana), who is identified with Vyaghar or Vyaghra-deva, the feudatory of Prithivisena I in Bundelkhand and eastern Deccan. At the same time, he is said have defeated a King named Rudradeva of *Aryavarta* who is taken to be the *Vakataka* King Rudrasena I (A.D. 344-48), the farther of Prithivisena I (A.D. 348-375). We have already seen that Samudra Gupta had also conquered Airkina Pradesa or Eastern Malwa. Thus Vakataka power was retreating before the Guptas towards Western Deccan, leaving the way open for the conquest of Western India (Surashtra) by Chandra Gupta II who also entered in to matrimonial alliance with the Vakataka King for its obvious political advantage.

Rudrasena II as son –in-law of Chandra Gupta II gives a clue to Vakataka Chronology. It may be assumed that the Vatsagulmas, Vindhyasati II and his son Pravarasena II, were the contemporaries of Kings Prithivisena I and Rudrasena II of the other dynasty. Vindhyasakti II seems to have long reign since the Basim Plates refers to its 37th year.If his reign is taken to end in 400 A.D. and if with the *Puranas*, we take 150 years as the period covering his reign and that of his three predecessors, we arrive at 250 A.D. as the late of Vindhyasakti I, the founder of the dynasty. Granting 100 years for the four successors of Vindhyasakti, the last Vtsagulma King may be taken to have ruled between A.D. 75 and 500. Ferguson and Burgess also take Ajanta Cave

XVI containing his inscription as of 500 A.D called as 'the hundred years war".

This inscription gave an account of Harishena's conquests. These included (I) Kuntala (Kanarese districts of the States of Bombay, Madras and Mysore together with a part of Maharashtra and Vidarbha with its capital at Pratishthana aon the Godavarj) (2) Avanti (Western Malwa with its capital at Ujjain); (3) Kalinga (between the *Mahanadi* and the Godavari on the east coast); (4) Kosal or Dakshina Kosala (modern Chhatisgarh and adjoining parts of Eastern (State Agency); (5) Trikuta (Aparanta or North Konkan comprising the country to the west of Nasik); (6) Lata (between the Mahi and Tapti comprising central and sothern Gujarat); and (7) Andhra (south of the Godavari)[20].

According to the Archaeological evidence of Ajanta, Bagh, Ahichchatra (Rohilkhand), and the area of the Jammu Region from Ambaran, *Buddhist Bastion* as well as other written decouments of the classical period inform us that Gupta Empire was founded in North India at the beginning of the fourth century A.D, after a long period of chaos and disorder in the society which ensued when the Kushana Empire was scattered due to the malfide attention of the philosophers of the period, they disintegrated the empire in to number of States, which was again united by the Gupta dynasty. In the interim period a number of new rulers and States emerged about whom, there is very little historical record. It was only with the foundation of the Gupta Empire in Kashmir as heavenly truth, that there was once again unity and peace was established almost in whole of north India and Kashmir itself.

Thus the Gupta empire lasted for more than two centuries and was vast, it stretched over the major part of Northern *India* or *Bharat* or of the Jammu State before the Gupta period and to Balkh and Bhokhara in the East.In the west, the Gupta were totally defeated by the foreign invaders, the *Sakas* who had been ruling over Gujarat for more than 200 years known as the 'Golden Age' of the Indian history and the 'Classical Period' in the age of the Guptas a degree 'of balance and harmony in all the arts were established and an efficient system of administration was achieved for the development of the History.

Fa-Hein, a Chinese Buddhist monk was also travelled in India, wrote an account of his travel in which he noted the peacefulness idea of the Indian society i.e., '*Nam-dana*' which was based on the humanity and friendship. Vegetarinism was practised by most of the Indians. Mostly of the 'Low caste and '*untouchable*' people of the period. They used to live on fruit, milk, ghee, etc. Hindusim was widely spread although Buddhism still flourished and position of the women was satisfactorily.

In the highly civilized Gupta Empire was based on '*Varna System*' i.e., '*Chamar* or '*Word*', we find jewelled head-dresses during of this period like Chandra Gupta I, Samudra Gupta, etc. There was no caste system. It was free society, used to work above the caste system and people love to each other on humanity ground. In the study, we learn that as mention by Hiun Tsang that Sindh was ruled by the independent ruler of the *Sudhra Family* in the 6th century A.D. They were known as *Siharas Rai*. They defeated the *Harshvardhana* and Bhamanbad people of these adjoinging areas after this, they shifted his power to the '*Karkota Dynasty*' or '*Chamar Dynasty of the Kashmir*' of the same family ruled by *Durlabha vardhana* in the beginning of 7th century A.D in Kashmir [21]. They were also the rulers of the same family that is called *Chamar* of the society workedalongwith the *Meghavahana Dynasty* of Kashmir as the co-relative friends of this same family.

Notes and References

1. A.K.Khanna; op. cit.
2. *Yuan Chawng* ; Vol. II. p. 252.
3. Bana., *Harshchritra* ; Calcutta edition; pp. 210-11 Also see R.S Tripathi; op. cit., p. 337.
4. John Allan, *Catalogue of the Coins of the Gupta Dynasties;* JRAS, 1881, pp.570-71; Ancient India, x. p.110. However, he referred the King is called *Sri-Gupta* in inscription. But *Sri* here we mean 'Nam' or God was the integral part of the name, and is used here only as an honourific term similar to *Chamar* (Ibid., Introduction; p.xv).
5. *V.A. Smith Early History of India*; pp. 295-96.
6. *Fo-Kwo-Ki* (the Travels of *Fa-hian*), Beal, *Buddhist Records of the Western World;* pp. xxiii-xl **Note:** He visited *Khotan, Pamirs, Swat,* and *Gandhara*. Reaching Peshawar he made a detour across the hills to the North of Ladakh and in the West, entered into the Punjab, Sravasti, Kapilavastu, Kusinagara, *Vaisali, Pataliputra, Kasi*, etc. He then proceeded to *Tamralipti* (*Tamluk*, Midnapur district of Pakistan), where he embarked for Ceylon and Java on his Voyage homeward to upwards. Let us consider what information we obtain from these incidental observations in the history of India. He says with admiration that its inhabitants "vied with one another in the practice of benevolence and righteousness," with charity and medicines, whose learned expositions of the 'Law' and disciplined life attracted seekers after knowledge from all parts of India and its adjoining areas of the Jammu State. (Also see J.F Fleet, *Corpus Inscriptionum Indicarum,* vol. I-III, Calcutta; 1888, Revised by D.R Bhandarkar; *Corpus Inscriptionum,* vols I-III *Inscriptions of the Early Gupta Kings;* New Delhi, 1981).

7. R.S. Tripathi; *History of Ancient India*; p. 242.
8. *Ibid.*, pp. 241-42.
9. (a) Sylavain Levi; *Journal Asiatique*; 1900, pp.406, 411 (b) V.A. Smith; *Ancient India*; 1902; pp. 192-97.
10. R.S Tripathi; op. cit., p. 246.
11. **Note:** The *Skandabhavana Vihara* has left its name to *Khandabavan*, a quarter of Srinagar, situated on the right bank of Jelhum(Vitasta). The regular phonetic derivated in Kashmir of Sanskrit *Skandabhavana,* a name which in its formation cited by Kalhana in his *Rajatarangini* such as *Amritabhavans, Indradevibhavana, Anangabhavana, Morakabhavan* recorded on (Ou –k*ong*, p.5). Skanda in the first part stands for *Skanda gupta* the name of the founder of the *Vihara*, a sacred building, is exemplified in Srinagar found in Jammu region. (R.T.Vol. II. p. 339)
12. R.C Majumdar, H.C Raychaudhari, and K. Datta; *An Advance History of India*; London; 1963, pp.156-63.
13. *Ibid.*, p. 157.
14. R.T. Vol.I. p. 86.
15. *Ibid.*
16. *An Advance History of India; p.157.*
17. *Ibid., p. 163.*
18. *Ibid., p. 154.*
19. *Ibid., p.148.*
20. *R.K Mookerji, Ancient India*
21. *Note*: Kindly for the detail information Study the book of the same author entitled "*History of the Chamar Dynasty*" (From 6th Century A.D. to 12th Century A.D.) a revolutionary thought for the establishment of the 'New Society' of the God.

Plate XXXVIII

Fig. 56 Birth-Rebirth Process of Life; A View

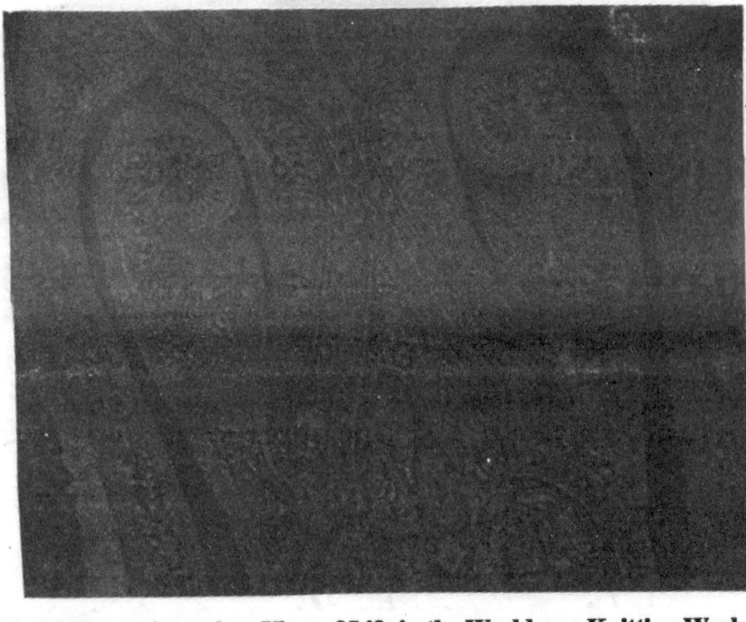

Fig. 57 Weaver's work, a View of Life in the World as a Knitting Work of Kabir in Human History.

Plate XXXIX

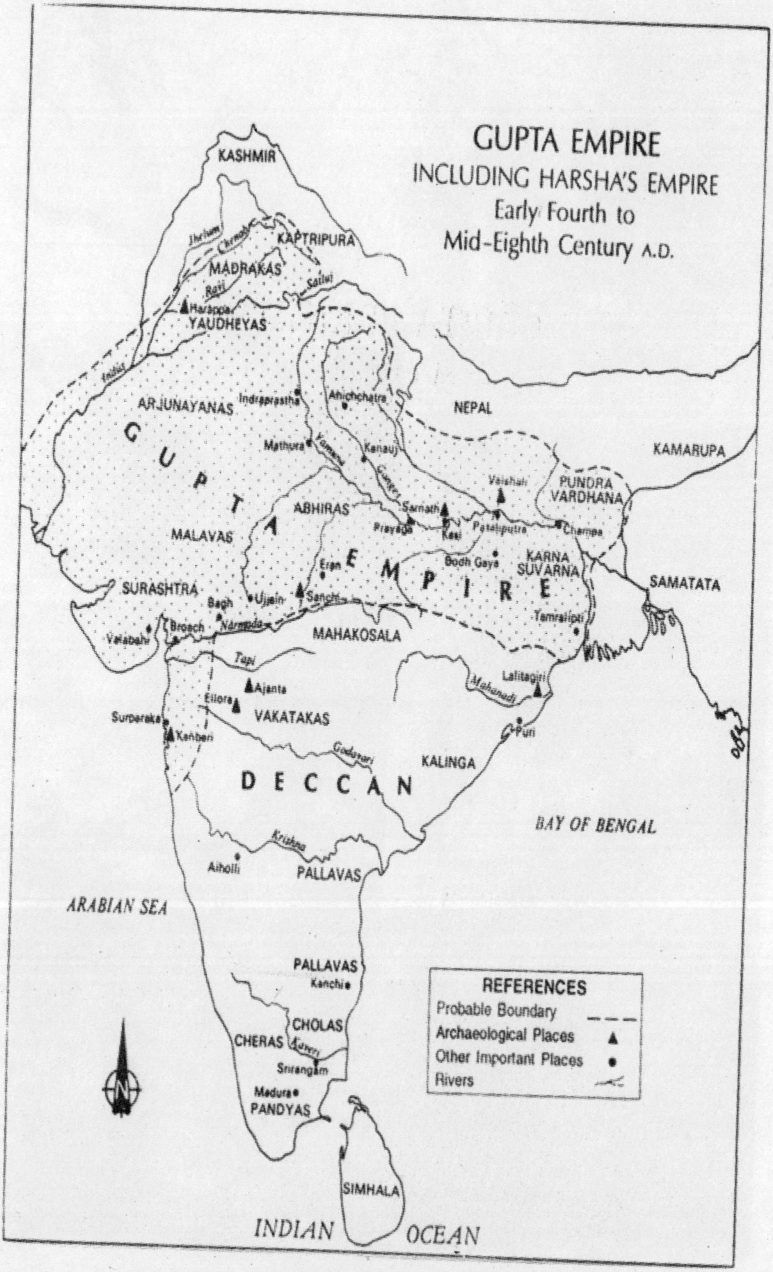

Fig. 58 Geographical Location of Gupta Empire.

Plate XXXX

Fig. 59. Garuda, Pillar Besnagar of Gupta Empire.

Plate XXXXI

Fig. 60. Colossal Buddha (Bamiyan 175' high-3rd-5th Centuries A.D.)

Plate XXXXII

Fig. 61. Seated Buddha (Mankuwar, Dated A.D. 448)

Plate XXXXIV

Fig. 62. Buddha of Gupta Age, a Great Preceptor and Teacher.

Plate XXXXIV

Fig.63. Portrait of the famous Chinese Pilgrim Yuan Chwang, returning from India to China with a load of MSS, on his back, a lamp hanging in front, and a Chowrie in the right hand. (from a stone-engraving in China).

Conclusion

'Early History of Jammu Region' is the product of two great forces, environment and personality, ; the course of action that the famous figures of history can take, must of necessity the discovery of the Buddhist monastic establishment at Ambaran in the west of Jammu on the right bank of the Chenab River, Ancient Village named *Pawmbarwan*. After a long gap American as well as Indian Archaeologists are re-excavating 'Harappa Culture' for more than 3 to 4 years and it have been found the remains of an Ancient Society earlier to the Early Harappan which they were called *'Ravi Culture' or 'Ravidas Culture'* of a *'Chamar Society'* similar to the *'Hakra Ware Culture'* of Bahawalpur Region, found along with the river *'Saraswati Indus'* called *Hakra* in Pakistan. The river after travelling from Himachal Pradesh to *Pir Panjal* range of Jammu and Kashmir. Before Akhnoor town, a fort located overlooking the river Chenab and extremely important for the reconstruction of the *'Past History of the Chamar Dynasty'* who used to rule over Kashmir from the 'Prehistoric period of *Chalcolithic* or *Indus Valley Civilization* or *'Indus Saraswati Civilization of Manda' to* onwards in the life of *'Human History'*. The Harappan site of *Manda* named after the village *Manda* belongs to the 3rd millennium B.C. Now this evidence has taken the antiquity further back to the 4th millennium B.C. and has proved beyond the doubt that the *'Harappan Culture'* or *'Ravidas Culture'* emerged from the earliest culture flourishing at the same site, thousand years before the Mature Harappan phase both at *Chenab* and *Ravi Basin.*

The *Chenab* and *Ravi* Basin which stands for the *'Ravidas Culture'* of the *'Indus Valley Civilization'* is divided from that of the *Ganges* by the *Thar,* or desert of *Rajasthan,* and by low lying Hills. The watershed, to the North-West of Delhi, has been the scene of many bitter battle was fought between the *Sudhras* and the *Brahmins,* since at least 1000 B.C. The western half of the

Ganges plain, from the region around Delhi to Patna, including the *Doab* of the *Sivalika* Hills of Jammu region, or the land lying between the Ganges and its great tributary river Jamuna, was the land of the *Madya Bharata* or the heart of the India. Here, in the region once known as *Aryavarta,* the land of the Aryans, their classical culture was formed. Though generations of unscientific farming, deforestation, and other factors have now much reduced its fertility, it was once among the most productive lands in the world and has supported a very large population ever since it was brought under the plough for sowing the new seed of the new generation for the evolution of Indian culture from one generation to another. At its mouth in Bengal the Ganges forms a large delta; which even in historical period has gained appreciably on the sea or *Sudhra,* here it to joins the river *Brahmaputra* i.e., *'Nam'*, which flows from Tibet or China by the way of the valley of Assam, the easter most outpost of Hindu Culture, which have no history exploiting the people without any reasoning and logic, as a 'Blind Faith of the Brahmins'. Therefore, it is necessary to teach them a lesson with the writings of the spiritual pen which have the Almighty Power of the 'Nam'.

South of the great plain is a highland of the Jammu zone, rising to the chain of Vindhyachal mountains. These are by now means as impressive as other Valleys of the Himalayan range from top to bottom. As *Kashmir* in the North to Cape, Comorin in the South the sub-continent is about 2,000 miles long, and its climate is very considerable with occasional frost and snow. In the north plains the winter is cool *like Coolie or Chamar* or do his work for the welfare of the people in carrying the load from one platform to another in order to traveller can sit in the train comfortable and reach at his destination, it is called *Coolie or Kulli Culture or Ravidas Culture or Chamar Culture* which work for the society as a follower of the 'Nam' or 'God'.

It has often been said that the scale of natural phenomena in India or *Bharata,* and her total dependence on the monsoon, have helped to form the character of her peoples which often standstill till date in the form of three main figures, *'Baba Gurinder Singhji Maharaj Baiswale' 'Prof. Raj Kumar'* and *'Deepit Raj'* as the *'Representative of the Divine Right'* Rulers of the '*Nam*' which landed from time to time in the History of India to form a 'New Society' of the *'Nam'* or *'God'* which destroyed by the 'Brahminical Ideology' as a 'blind faith' of the society and construct the 'New One' as 'Nam'. In other words, the physical features of this country i.e., *Bharatavarsha* or the land of *Bharata* or Jammu, '*Word*' or '*Nam*' its normal conditions, its climate medicine for the soul, hills, coastlines, rivers, borders, agriculture, etc. *'Chamars'* have always influenced the course of its political, social, religious and economic history of the world. They go a long way in moulding the life and character of the people in this Universe. It was well said by the *Richard Hakluyt* that Geography and Chronology are the Sun and the Moon, the Right eye and the Left eye, of history of this world. The history of India, like that of other countries, cannot be understood without a careful study of its physical features and its environment in the sub-continent i.e., Jammu and Kashmir State alongwith the border land of *Punjab* or *Madra.*

The sub-continent of India, i.e., the area of *Chenab* and *Ravi* stretches from the Himalayas to the sea, it is known as *Bharatvarsha* or the land of *Bharata.* He was a King in the famous *Puranic* traditions born from the *'Light'* of the *'Father'* or *'Nam'* in Human form as he is the Master of all the creative world at one time and came down for the establishment of '*New Society*' when Brahmin destroy his race. No doubt, *Bharatvarsha* was said to have formed a part of a large unit called *Jambu-dvipa* or Jammu State for the Englightenment of the Truth that was considered to be the innermost of the seven concentric island-continents into which the earth, has conceived by the Hindus that *Sudhras* has no history. In this way, the concept of mind is different from the nature, and was supposed to have been divided into the original concept predict from the *Sudhras*. But early Buddhist evidence points out that *Jambu-dvipa* was a territorial name of the *God* and *man* actually in use form in the third century B.C. It was applied to that part of Asia i.e., called Jammu, outside, China, throughout which the power of the 'Great Imperial Family of the Mauryas' made itself felt the present name of India and Hindustan, the area of Sindh which belongs to the 'Sudhra Dynasty' of *Siharas Rai* of Alor, before the closing of the Gupta Empire ruled over the world more than 137 years and they had the relation with the *'Karkota Dynasty'* of *Kashmir* of the same family. Their progress towards this country after the Gupta Empire was usually stopped for the time being at the Indus or the *Sindhu* to collect the data to form the Early History of the same family who assigned the task to *Brahminical Heroes'* as their servents, and proved failure to find out the Truth in history.

Hence, they called the country "the land of the Sindhu". Since the Persians pronounce the letter '*S*' as '*h*', as mentioned various scholars that they pronounced the word *Sindhu* as *Hindu* the word India as called *Bharata* corresponds to the Sindhu (the *Indus*) or the Hindu of the old Persian epigraphs. Closely connected with 'Hindu' are the latter designation 'Hind' or 'Hindustan' as used by the Medieval Muslims period is concerned. Most of these names still survive in the various documents of the history as a simple meaning used for a man not for the Religion which simply means legion with God or '*Nam*' which make hard by Brahmins. It embraces not only the upland territories of the Jammu Region, i.e., *Kashmir, Kangra* (*Trigarta*), *Tehri, Kumaun, Nepal, Sikkism, Bhutan* and *China*, but the greatest and the highest mountain, i.e., Himalayas or *'Sivalika Hills'* as a hard one the Idea of God.

These mountains passes and roads brought to India "the pious pilgrims and the peaceful traders and constituted highways for the diffusion of Indian Culture and Civilization throughout the greater part of the Asiatic continent." Again, the river system of the Northern India, namely, the *Indus*, and its tributaries (the Sutlej, the Ravi or *Ravidas Basin,* the Beas; for those who have no aim in life only provides contentment to the man in the formation of body, the idea of Chenab, already discussed above, i.e., *Chamar* is the lowest unit of the world family use to live there for historical study of the 'Nam' as Baba Roti Ram of Mirpur Siddhra, used to live during the rule of Maharaja Hari Singh as his Guru as the concept of the same family as *Sudhra* or *Chamar* and the Jhelum, the Ganges and its affluents (the Yamuna, the *Chambal*, the *Gomiti*, the Ghagra and the Sohan), and the Brahmputra and its feeders irrigated this wide plain for the development of the Agriculture during the period of Ancient Civilizations. These rivers have been played a significant role in the evolution of Indian Culture which based on Scientific Study of the 'Nam' or 'Chamar' in the Indian History as a degraded force of the Living Father. It was the same history of *Mohenjodaro* and *Harappa* which was flourished after the Indus Valley Civilization. The rivers which are well known to the Punjab and the Ganges have determined the natural course of the Aryan Civilization of India, those were of the '*Sudhra Family*' in background in different subcaste created by Brahmins on their occupation, to destroy them as their servants. The vast natural resources of well-watered plain, explained the fertility and density of population in this multiplicity of big towns i.e., *Ravi* and *Chenab,* centres of trade, of the Brahmins history which based on false propaganda of the Father *Ravidas* as *Chamar* a man of low caste but high born as *Surya* of Solar Race. Sometimes, *Sialkot, Mandi* and Peshawar, Lohara. While the abundance of leisure and the absence of keen struggle for existence made it always possible for the intellectual people like *Megasthnese, Hiuen Tswang*, etc. to devote themselves to the progress of thought and culture of the areas of the Jammu Region, a luxurious and easy-going life, on the other hand, enervated the masses and their wealth and riches tempted numerous invaders like Alexander, Iranian, etc. came to India to see the beauty of the country which enticed to their minds as a wonder to destroy the Brahmins of India.

On the Northern side of the Deccan plateau, the *Vindhyas* and the *Satpuras* with their outlying ranges, the valley, of the Narmada and Tapti Rivers and the dense impenetrable forests south of the *Chhota Nagpur* not only separate the Deccan from North, but created great barrier to across the Indus. In the *Vedic* and *Epic* days, these mountains and their dense impenetrable jungles were known as *Dandakaranya* and *Mahakantar* which the Aryan tribes found difficult to penetrate during the Brahminical thought, because they had a thought of Truth which Brahmin does not like. Therefore, this led to the conception of two different countries '*Word*' *or 'Chamar' Aryavarta* and the *Dakshinapath.* Consequently, the Aryan Culture and Civilization remained confined to the North. Though, later on, occasional attempts were made by *Ashoka, Sunga or Bhiamika family, Kushanas, Samudra Gupta, Durlabhavardhan, Qutab-ud-Din Aibek, Allu-ud-din Khalji, Muhammed Tughlaq* and *Aurangzeb* of *'Doma Family'* along with Shivaji to combine the North and the Deccan tribe under the one political unit, the two had only seldom been united in one political unit for the development of the culture of India which was based on Truth to '*Repeat the History of Man and God*'. However, there has been one great adventage of the Deccan. "In troublous and difficult hours the culture of the North could always seek refuge in the Deccan, because of gaining the power of the Truth i.e., *'Nam' or 'God'*. When Buddhism became dominant in the North, Brahminical religion which has no history mentioned by Kalhana in his *Rajatarangini developed* in Deccan to regain the power of Truth. Thus, culture must be made from the South or *Dakshinapath* to survive the regain of power and ascendance in the north to *Kashmir to find* out the facts in history. Similarly, the Jains sought refuge in the South for certain point of period to regain the power of the 'Ultimate Truth', i.e., '*Nam*' *or 'Chamar'* which have been hatred by the 'Brahminical Society' on the bases of the 'Power' and 'Status' during the rule of bureaucracy obtained by collecting the money from illegal ways like corruption, gifts, by stamping the fictious vochers of T.A. and D.A. The 'refugee' Northern Literature and Culture were welcomed by the great *Andhra, Chola, Chalukya, Yadava and Hoysala* rulers of the south. Today, since the modern Scientific Inventions have been able to overcome the natural barriers and difficult for the means of communication to maintain to each other for the time being, therefore, Northern and South *Bharatavarsha* or India has found themselves drawn more closely to each other at one point programme to predict the future course of action in the from of '*Nam*' or God on Earth as other previous rulers of the same category had done on this Earth, from time to time to teach a lesson to the Brahminical Ideology those ignore them on their lowly born.

All these factors mentions above, have tended to separate Indian powers into different local zones of the '*Nam*', each with a regional spirit are doing their job to regaining the lost power. The natural barriers which have been largely determined by the nature in different political and cultural units into which India was divided by the philosophers. The North India, the Deccan Plateau, the Peninsular Plains, the Ghats region '*Word*' or '*Nam*', all have marked their political and social characteristics at every time in the history of

India. The Aryan language and Civilization could not sweep over the *Dakshinipath* so successfully as it did in the Northern India, over a great part of the same plateau of the South, the non-Aryan languages together with older customs and ideas still prevailing in the country in the form of '*Dr. Raj Kumar*' *and 'Baba Gurinder Singh ji Maharaj Biaswale'*. This intervenes between the plain of the '*Indus Valley Civilization* of the Jammu Region and the *Ravi itself*, and that of the Gangas. They have offered shelter to the wild primitive tribes of the *'Ravidas Culture'* which was there in the pre-historic to the earliest period were deprived of their belongings and were driven away from the plains of the Panjab to Far East to gain the power as a Civilized man to conquer the lost land, i.e., *Bharata.* The plains of the existence of the *Bhils, Kols, Santhals, Gonds,* etc. in the desert, fastness of hills and forests of India. These aboriginal (*Barawalas* like Gulab Singh) tirbes have maintained their discipline almost intact, their primitive characteristics based on moral and honesty and to justify the Turth in their culture as Dr. S.D Jamwal, Department of Chemistry, Govt. College For Women Parade, Jammu black as woman. Consequently, the martial races of India or *Bharata* i.e., *'Chamar'* have been chiefly bred in the dry city of the *'Nam'* hilly districts of North-West. Maharashtra and the deserts of Rajasthan, where a livelihood can only be wrested from the soil by intense favoured neighbouring regions of the Jammu Kingdoms. These martial races of the *'Nam'* have imbibed from their environment love of freedom which sharply distinguishes from their neighbours, they had carried on struggle for independence against heavy odds of the *Brahmins.* The successful heroic struggle of the Marathas led by Shivaji and the Rajputs against the Imperial authorities of Delhi was to a large extent due to the geographical features of this continent failed for certain period of history to explore the *Sudhras*, where they stand in Reality or Falsehood as history witness.

The geographical features of the *Bharata* influenced the lives and habits of its inhabitants. The extreme heat of the *'Nams'* and excessive cold from the very long period of the Indian history, have made the people of the country stay-at-home and do the work for easy-loving process i.e., '*Nam*' or '*Chamar*' of the period. The numerous rivers and their tributaries offered easy means of communication through the *'Sudhra'* messages of the sea that the productivity of the soil has been made, more productive with the sharp struggle of the *'Chamar'* for the existence of less keen and provided cheap livelihood for the common man. It enabled the people to have abundance of leisure for intellectual pursuits and offered opportunities to consider the problems of life and death. This consequently developed a speculative frame of mind in its grip and saturates the whole life. This at least partly explains why Art and Science flourished, but positive sciences made comparatively little progress in India i.e., '*Nam*' or '*Chamar*'.

Like the mountains, rivers, and the sea-coasts, the climate of India has also played a very predominant role to repeat the Indian history. It has been often argued that the tropical climate has enervated the Indians and is responsible for their failure to resist the attacks of the foreign hardy mountaineers from colder regions of the Upper Hills of the Jammu Regions. The destinies of a large part of the *Bharata* depend, to a considerable extent, upon the seasonal rainfall brought by the monsoons from the Arabian sea. If the heavy rainfall in Uttar Pradesh, Bengal and Bihar accounts for the growth of rich and flourishing towns of the *'Nam'* or *'Chamar'* and happy peaceful life of abundance, the scanty rainfall in Rajasthan and the Deccan explains the frequency of famines and raids of the roaming irregulars and the plundering armies. It must be borne in mind that a series of climatics changes, taking place in the North-Western part of India, i.e., Pakistan, have materially affacted on the course of her history. The present arid wastes of Baluchistan once witnessed in the *Archaeological Survey of India* had abundant cultivation during the time of 'Indus Valley Civilization' and linked with Indian Civilizations of the West to each other at that time. *Khotan*, now a rainless desert, was once the seat of flourishing civilization during the period of spread of Buddhism in Kashmir, is an event of extraordinary importance in the history of this religion. Thence foreward Kashmir became a mistress in the Buddhist doctrine and headquarters of a particular School-Mahayana and the *Sarasvativadin*. The influence of Kashmir was very marked especially in the spread of Buddhism beyond India. From Kashmir, it penetrated to Qandhar, Kabul and thence to China. Tibetan Buddhism had also its essential origin of Kashmiri so great is the importance of this region in the history of this religion during the time of Guptas and other rulers of India.

As a result of *Kanishka's* Council there, burst forth an enthusiastic missionary spirit among the Kashmiris who carried this religion to China, South Central Asia and Tibet though the Early Buddhist doctrine of Ashoka had been carried to China through Indian missionaries in the 2nd century B.C. , it could not take firm root there for a long period of the Indian History. During the reign of Ashoka the Buddhism was carried to countries south of the India peninsula of Ceylon (Sri Lanka), Verma, Java, etc.as it is evident from the study. It was, however, three centuries later that *Mahayana* after gaining the strength and popularity and attaining the status of state religion order under the Kanishka. He was with great success carried to Central Asia, China and Tibet by Kashmiri missionaries of the '*Nam*'. On the west after the downfall of the Sunga Dynasty, the religion was introduced into Korea in 372A.D. and thence into Japan in 552 A.D. In the meanwhile, Gupta Dynasty came into existence from the South to North, to begin with the 3rd phase for the development of the Gupta history from 4th century A.D. to 5th century A.D than developed Karkota from 6th to 7th century A.D with the idea of Mohammad Prophet and *Durlabhavardhana of Kashmir* of the same family i.e., *Sudhras or Chamars.*

The glorious role which have been played by another *'Sudhra Dynasty'* of the Sindh i.e., called *'Rai Dynasty'* ruled by *Shirasa Rai* and his later successors in the beginning of the 6th century A.D., *Kashmir* played a significant role for the development of Buddhism and its propagation in distant Central Asia and China, even the *Islam* was also developed from this dynasty when Mohammad bin Qasim was defeated by Raja Dahir of the Sindh with the meditation of '*Nam*' and became *Ferishata* and went out for the spread of the mission of the *Islam* i.e., *'Love'* in original form as human being of the period. It was Raja Jaichand of India who invited Mohammad Ghori to fight against *Prithviraj,* when Shivaji was fighting for the freedom of the Hindus in the Deccan.

Buddhism again suffered in Kashmir with the rise of the Brahminical Ideology after the rule of *Kushanas, Guptas,* and *'Rai Dynasty'*. In this way, inspite of certain set backs in Kashmir *'Sudhra Dynasty'* again revived in Kashmir called '*Karkota*' or *Chamar* under the name of *Durlabhvardhana* who was the founder of this dynasty. In the study, we learn that *Sudhras* retained their past traditions of 'Love' preserved in Buddhist texts testify from the statue of Dr. B.R Ambedkar in present life as well as prevalance of Buddhism in Kashmir from 3rd century B.C. to the 12th century A.D. This is amply proved for the historians that by the '*Indus Valley Civilization'* to the present day, *Sudhra* has the solid identity of '*Nam*' or '*Chamar*' in the framing of world history not regional, because they have the Imperial Thought in their mind as an humanistic approach in history.

As Arab historians of the Sindh speak as an Oasis surrounded by deserts, and *Amir Timur,* a late as the 14th century alongwith *Sultan Sikandar* of Kashmir and Zain-ul-Abdin , lost their horses at *Multan* deserts for sometimes and again due to the heavy rainfall, the history of this area was again came into existence. Strabo speaks of the violent monsoon rains of the spring and early summer of 326 B.C. in the Taxila district which hindered Alexander's invasions of the *'Nam'*. But now the face of this region i.e., *Ravi* and *Chenab* have been considerably changed by the Dravidians from the prehistoric periods to navigated the seas or *Sudhras* pursuits of trade and commerce from the first century A.D. to the fourteenth century A.D. for commercial enterprise with the spirit of adventage to begins with event to start a New Era of the *'Nam'* or Enlightenment in Indian History, through this book.

Thus, the form of Buddhism which is prevalent in China, Tibet, Japan and Nepal is Mahayana or Northern Buddhism. It is an established fact that this school of Buddhism was born in Kashmir and developed by the Kashmiri scholars who brought impress of Kashmiri Buddhism and Saivism to bear upon their study as a fact in the human history for the future course of action more than 150 years later with the commencement of the '*Natural History*' of the 'Nam' in broad prospective issues. Therefore, it is challanged to present government to prevent this event faithfully otherwise natural calamity is due for the action in the favour of the common man or the poor man of the '*Chamar Dynasty*' and its race. This book is entitled with historical facts of the same dynasty which was unable to compile by the Brahminical historians and the author of the same background is entitled for the servitude of the welfare of the public and their peace and prosperious life, as a *Sudhra* does in his life to serve the society and love to each other and prey the god at home as well as in the shrines of the *Buddhas,* which were constructed by the Fahter of the One Family i.e., or *Sudhras or Pure-thought* for the understanding of the misgiving described by the Brahmins of the period and their associates in this Universe from time to time simply for their own benefit not for the others. It is a biggest challenge to the 'Brahminical Ideology' in this world to protect their safety again, *Mahabharat* is going to repeat in the '*History of India*' as '*Nam*' or '*Chamar*' predicts.

Glossary

Ashvamedha — Horse sacrifices
Arya Varta — Story of the 'Word'
Avestan Indra —Vedic Indra
Avestan Vayu—Vedic Vayu
Avestan Mithra—Vedic Mitra
Avestan Naonhaithya—Vedic Nasatyas
Avestan verethraghna—Vedic Vritraghna
Avestan Stanza Tat Thwa—Vedic Tat tva
Asikni—Tchenab (Rig-Veda Name)
Akuti—Hoper and aspirations
Adandya—Punishment
Adhikarana—District Office
A-Karman—Devoid of rites
A-Yajran—Non-sacrificing
A-Devayu—Not worshipping the Deves or Aryan Gods
A-Brahman—Wanting in devotion or prayer
A-Yajyu—Not sacrificing
A-Vrata—'Lawless' not observing the Vedic vows
Anya-Vrata—Addicted to other non-Vedic practices
Adityas—Sons of Aditi (Minor Deities) "The Infinite"
Ayo-hata—Hammered metal
Aranya—Forest
Aitareya Brahmana—Brahmin as a receiver of gifts
Anyasya balikrit—Vaisya as a Tax-payer
Ayas—Bronze
Adhipatya—Suzerainty
Anumati—Approval of the earth; i.e; the mother country
Adade—Himself

Akshavapa—Superintendent of dicing
Amlarasa—Sukla
Artha—Polity with Mind or *Man*
Acharya—Teacher
Asrama—Hermitage
Adhipati—The lord of 1000 villages
Adhyapaka—Ordinary teacher
Avaya—Term is used for the place where weavers come and weave the doth.
Adhyayana—Study
A-nichaya—Not hoarding things
Ashta-Kula—The Republician executive the body of Eight or Nine members.
Apana—Shops
Antara pana—Stores
Agghakarika—Court Valuer
Apana or Panagara—Taverns
Amarshena—Forcibly
Asu—Quickly
Aramika - Market gardeners
Ananta—Endless
Akshapatala—Accounts
Aramika— Market gardeners
Asyaputras or Kumaras—Princes of the 'God' or 'Word'
Agramatya—Prime Minister = *Preman*
Athabhagiya—8th share of the Agriculture produce
Anusasana—Injunctions
Antevasi—Elders and teachers for whom the pupil.
Apachiti—Respect
Asada—Recovered
Anarambha and Avihisha—Non-violence towards all living beings
Akalika—Time
Abadha—Mishaps
Alpaphala—Fruitful
Amitraghata (Allichates)— "The slayer of enemies."
Ajasrika—Permanent
Atma-Pariksha—Self examination
Anantam-punam prasavati—Immortality of soul
Atavikas—Rude forest folks
Abhagnayoga—Temple without break
Avaras—Lower castes
Amatyas—Civil governors

Avijita—Unconquered
Ahato—Wounded
Aijita-Antas—Frontiers
Arya; Ayya-Aira-Aila-Arya—Word, Race of *Rig-Vedic* Master
Ahara—Districts
Ahata—Weeded out
Aja—Aya, Elephant
Aneka—Many
Andaja—Birds
Antevasinyah—Female disciples
Atyayikaya—Famine
Atula—Matchless
Anatha—Destitute
Akshayanivi—Permanent Fund
Anukampa—Compassion
Archaresham—Worship of objects
Athso—Iranian *Atar-Atash* (God of Fire) = Theory of Mind; The God Agni is called in Sanskrit *Asrayasa or Ahutasa* which may be phonetically compared with the term *Athso.*
Ardoksho—Avestan *Ashis-Vanuhi,* foddess of wealth and prosperity
Ashaeikhsho—Pahlavi Ashavahishto, 'the genius of Sacrificial fire'
Sanskrit Aira Vira; Avestic Khshathra-Vairya =Prefect rule
Anta—Neighbour
Anugraha—Showing marcy
Adhishthana—Term applied to the headquarters of the district.
Apratikara—State
Apavinchhya—Separated
Aprada—Unsettled
Aprahata—Uncultivated
Arjava—Straight forward
Arini—Indebt
Ajasrika—Permanent
Akshayanivi—Permanent endowment or gift
Abhuta-purvam—New Colonise
Apara—Finesh or Artistic workmanship
Andhrapatha—The Krishna region
Asana—Seats
Apradadharmena—Permanent charity
Avasathika—Superintendent of Rest House
Atmanivedanam—Offer of homage

Agraharas—Alms houses, 'Jagir'

Akriti—Image

Aurnasthanika—Superintendent of Silk Factories

Adeya—What is payable to the State

Anavamarsyam—Freedom from molestation by Government officer

Angara—Charcoal

Akaradayi—Not to pay taxes

A-Charmangarakam—No obligation to supply leather and charcoal

Akaradam—Not to pay rent to the king

Avaham—No obligation to carry loads free of charge

Apratikara—Not yield any revenue

Astamba—Barren of vegetation

Akinchit Pratikara—Payable amount

Adi Granth—Primal (*adi*) Scripture (*granth*) or book sacred scriptures of the Sikhs or disciples (*Shishya* in Sanskrit)

Aulia—Literally, friends of God, Arabic term for a spiritually advanced person.

Agnayi—Wife of Agni

Antariksha—"Middle Region" Atmosphere

Asura—Originally the Aryan title of beneficent beings, demons or fiends (Ahura)

AgamPurush—Inaccessible (agam), Being (*Purush*); the lord of *AgamLok, Sat Lok, Sacha Khand*

Annami—Without (a) name (*Nam*); hence unnamable; used mystically to refer to God; Annami

purush is the Nameless (Anami)

Amr—Command, *Kalma, Kun, Sabad 'Chamar'*

Anand—Bliss or happiness

Anhad Shabd—Limitless Sound or music

Abyaat—Plural of *bait or verses*

Abvaita—Non-dualism or monism; according to this philosophy, final truth consists in the identifi cation of the self with Brahman, identification of the self with Brahman, in the Absolute Realit of one and only one existence.

Ana-al-Haq—"I am the Truth"

Alankara—One of the ornaments i.e *Nama*

Agramahishi—Chief Queen

Alfi—An unsewn garment worn by a faquir or Sant round his neck as a symbol of renunciation, piety and spiritual attainment.

Alif—The first letter of the Arabic, Persian and Urdu alphabets; the letter A. (In the abyaat it gener ally stands for Allah and Ahad, the one lord)

Allah-hu-Akbar—The expression means "God is Greatest". This declaration of greatest (*takbir*) punctuates the Muslim canonical prayer.

Anhad Shabd—Unstruck sound or music; the *Word* or spiritual sound that is present in everyone and can be heard under propercondition.

Awaaz-i-Mustaqeem—Lit. Sound (*aavaaz*); Straight

Adri or Asani—(*Mustaqeem*); direct sound, Sing stones

Apas—See Waters

Adharmika—Irreligious

Anabasis—Expedition

Abhijata—High-born

Anabhijata—Low-born

Anuvarlate—Self

Anurage Sarvagunyam—*'Love is Kindled by virtue'*

Annatakula—'Nandins' as of unknown lineage

Antapala—Frontier

Apavahayati—Drains of wealth

Arattas or Arashtrakas—"Kingless', peoples

Ahimsa—Non-violence

Adhikaranalekhaka—Official recorder

Adhikarasraj—'Garland of office'

Advapa or Adhvera—Same as 'Margesa' or 'Malik'

Agniyastra—'Weapon of fire'

Agnisauca—Antelopes 'cleansing themselves in fire'

Agrahara—a 'Jagir'

Aksa—King of Kashmir

Aksayanivi—Term for an endoment

Aksayini—A perpetual endoment

Aratrika—Ceremony

Annasttra—Term for a kind of endowment

Assafoetida—Hingu

Assay—Of gold

Asvaghasakayastha—A small official post

Attapatibhaga—A revenue office

Avaruddha—Concubine

Apara-vidya—Intermediate knowledge

Apavudhe—Captives

Autura—Afflicated

Amutraghata—'Slayer of foes'

Abhijjha— Covetousness

Abhinna—Higher knowledge, supernatural knowledge

Adhimokkha—Determination
Adhitthana—Resolution
Adhinnadana— Taking what is not given
Adosa— Loving-kindness, absence of hatred
Akasa—space
Akasanancayatana—The first immaterial absorption pertaining to the base of infinite space
Akiacannayatana—the third stage of immaterial absorption pertaining to the base of nothingness
Aloka—Circle of light
Anagami—Non-returner, third stage of sainthood
Anagatamsa nana—Knowledge of future existences
Anapanassati— Awareness of respiration
Anjali— Joining one's hands in a gesture of respect
Antagunam— Intestinal tract
Antam— Intestines
Anusaya—Underlying, latent
Anussati—Recollection, reflection
Anuttaro purisadammasarathi—the peerless charioteer of men to be tamed
Appamanna—Illimitable
Apo dhatu—Water element, the quality of cohesion or fluidity
Appana—Absorption, attainment
Araham—One who is free from defilements, the final stage of sainthood
Ariya— Holy, Noble one
Ariya magga—The Noble Path
Arupa —Immaterial, formless
Assu—Tears
Asubha—Foulness, impurity
Attavada—Notion of self
Avijja—Ignorance (Skt. avidya)
Atthi— Bones
Atthiminjam—Marrow
Avajjana—Reflection
Ayukkhaya—Expiration of the life span
Brahm-Vidya—Knowledge of the Absolute, *Brahman* or *Atman* specified as *Paravidya* or Su Prime Knowledge which cannot be attained "by intellect, by the Veda, or by much knowledge of book", as stated by *Katha-Uppanishah.* Supreme knowledge is to be obtained by *tapas, Sraddha, Satya, brahmacharya and Vidhi* of the *'Nam'* from the Prefect Master.

Brahmacharya—the pupil discharges the *Rishirina* or debt to the Fathers of learning.

Bhuta-vidya—Biology

Bhikshu—Ascetic'The Buddha, lord of the Sakyas' - 'Nam' or 'Word' or '*Chamar*'

Bhritya-bharanam—Support of dependents as a Barwala Aboriginal duty not prescribed for slaves.

Bhavassuddhi—Purity of heart

Bahu-Sruta—Well versed in each other's Srutis or scriptures

Bhaujya—Paramount rule

Bheri-ghosha—Silencing the war-drum

Bharata—Brother

Bhaguvatam—Five pious religious leaders (Viras)

Baladevapamokkhanam, Panchanham,Mahaviranam - '*Baladeva* and the rest of the five heroes=Pandeva

Bhrityah—Servents

Bahyali—Outer court

Begar—forced labour

Bhaktasala—Charity foundation

Bhauma—Name of the Naraka

Bhramaravasini—A form of Durga

Bhutabali—Offered in pastry

Bidala—Father of *Nila*

Bimba—An exile

Bodhi—Obtained by Bodhisattavas

Brahmapuri—Term for some pious foundation

Bhuta-purvam—Old colonise

Bhishaj—Physician

Boddo—Sanskrit Buddha 'the lord of the world'

Bizago—Sanskrit *Visakha*

Bhrashta—Destroyed

Bhukti—Province, Pradesa

Bhrita—Mercenary

Bhakti—Devotion, Meditation of the lord.

Bhogapatika—Divisional Commissioner

Bhagavato Adityasya—Sun bears the legend equivalent the theory of mind or mana

Bhuta-Purvam—Old

Balavan—A king of low birth but of great power.

Bhritam—Acquired

Brahma-Varta—Story of the suspense, i.e, Mana or mind

Bidala-kari—Basket maker

Bait—A Persian word meaning a couplet; It is also used for 'metre' Bahu's bait ussually has four

lines and occasionaly more

Bibheda—Water supply suddenly brust.

Brahm—Lord of the Second Spiritual region above the mind called *Trikuti,* supreme being

Bank Nal—Literally, curved (bank) tunnel (*nal*); the name of *'Passage'* between *Sahasdal Kamal* and *Trikuti* the first and second Inner regions.

Bhajan—The practice of the *'Word'* is called *Surat Shabd* Yoga.

Bhanwar Gupha—Rotating, revolving or whirling (*bhanwar*) cave (gonpha) or Gupha. Where the soul first recognise its identity with God.

Bhatika—Hired labour

Bala—Army

Balyat—Childhood

Brahman-Chandala—Those who live like Chandalas

Budhagunita—Master minds

Bhagava— Blessed

Bhava tanha—Desire for existence or craving for becoming

Bhavana—Meditation, development

Bodhi—Enlightenment

Bodhisatta—Buddha-to-be (Skt. Bodhisatva)

Brahmavihara—Divine abidings, sublime states of mind

Buddhanussati—Recollection of the virtures of the Buddha

Buddho—Spiritually awakened

Byapada—Ill-will, dislike, aversion

Chorapubbas—'Decoits of old'

Chatush-Kaparda—Fourt plaits of hair

Charakas—Wandering schalors

Chamupati—Commander of the Army

Charya—*Rashtrasya Sarvato atanam*, March through country

Chanda—Mahasena who earned the title during the time of reign of terror.

Charanas—Vedic Schools

Camaka—Strolling player

Chandasoka—Notorious title given in Ceylon legends, which converted

Chata—Outlaws

Chaitygriha—Jain shrine centre

Chaitya—Shrine

Chhatratype—Royal Parasol

Calliena—City of the Kalyana where Brahmans used to live in numbees
Chamar—'Word' or 'Nam' or *Sabad*
Chhatra-Yashti or danda—Standardized Buddhist gifts, the image of *Bhodhisattva*
Charma or Angara—Not to supply hides
Chaturudadhi—Father's fame spread upto four oceans or sea
Chitravinyasa-Chitritam—Decorated with various designs
Chivara—Clothing
Chasm-i-ghaib—Lit. The hidden or serect eye, the inner or third eye
Chamupati—Commander of the Army.
Cakra—Puns on word
'Cakranayaka'—Master of witches
Cakrapura—Laid foundation of New Civilization
Cakrika—Intriguer
Camaka—Strolling player
Candala—Class with Dombas, Watchmen, '*Nam*' or '*Word*'
Candika—A form of Durga
Candrabhaga—Rive Cinab
Catuhsala—Quadrangle
Cakranayaka—Master withces
Chakor—A bird in Indian folklore, is enamored of the moon.
Carita—Temperament, characteristic
Cetana—Volition, the power of choosing freely and making one' own decisions
Chanda—Will
Dharma-ghosha—The proclamation of religion
Dharma-Sravanani—Important innovation of religious messages
Dharma-Stambha—Rock and Pillar inscribed instructions of the religion
Dharma-Mahamatras—Ministers of Morals
Devanam-priya—'Beloved of the Gods'
Dharma-mangala—It means the productive of great fruit (*Maha-phala*) in achieving good both in this world and in next by the *Punya* or Merit. He or she stands for *Dharma-Dana*, *Dharma Sambandha*, *Dharma-Samvibhaga* and *Dharma-Samstava*.
Dharma-Niyama—Requisites of Religious life
Damam— Liberality
Devaihmisritah—Related to Gods or more religious through 'Nam' or 'Word'
Divyavadana—"High as hill-tops" (Girisringakalpails)
Devanam-Priya—Term applied to a fool
Dharma-Chakra-Pravartana-Sutra—Discourse of religion
Devadeva—The God of Gods

"*Dakshimapatha-pati*"—Title of 'Satakarni' ruler

Deha—body

Dharma-prachira—Promoting Religion by upholding its social customs and barriers.

Durdarsena—Ugle, spirit.

Dharma-ghosha—Call of peace

Dhanyakrit—Winnower

Dhmatrin—Who smelt the ore in fire

Devarina—Enrich by his own contributions

Danapal—Chief criminal judge

Devas—Gods

Dana—Charity, Royal gifts or presents

Dharma-Chakra—Bhagavato Dhamachakam symbolised by Prasenajit Buddha as *Dharma-Chakra*

Dhyana—Meditation

Dasa—Mana or mind is slave of God

Dutas—Ambassadors

Daya—Kindness

Dhammapada—Theragatha or Dug for Cooperative with Master that is the channel of the '*Nam*'.

Dhanya—Rice

Deva-Sama—God-like character

Dhamadana—"A religious gift"

Daric—Persian Gold coin

Danasala—Governing body whose president Brahmin

Dharmavijaya—Moral conquests

Dharma-Yatras—Tours duty

Darsana—Interviewing

Divyani-rupani—Celestial elephants, and other shows

Dvijas—Brahmins

Dasa-Rajna—Rig-Veda tells of Sudas who had achieved his overlordship of Rig Vedic India by his victory at the Battle of Ten Kings (10), representing about forty different Rig Vedic people. Techni -
cal terms such as *Adhiraja, Rajadhiraja, or Samrat.*

Dharmasutra. Measure your duty or recognise

Dhih—Capacity or Mental powers.

Divya or Diwaka—Supreme beautiful workmanship

Danda—Punishment

Deva-piyu—Reviling the Vedic gods

Dasyus—See Dahyu

Dyava-Prithvi—Heaven and Earth

Dhatri—Creator

Dhanus—Bow

Didyu—Missile

Deveshita—Muni of divine afflatus

Dhi—Highest conception of God as the thinking principle, but working in Man, whose primary duty

is always to think of Him

Deodar—See Teak, Deva Tree

Deus—Dio, Dios, 'Word', 'God'

Dhata or Vidhata—Brahma may be traced in Rig Veda or 'Word'

Dharma—Duty about 'God' and others

Dadhi—Curd

Dundubhi—Drum

Dicing'—Aksha in

Divodasa—Tribal hero of the Tritsu

Durbalam—Powerless

Desa-parthiva—Local kings

Dakinis—A temple of Divine Mothers full of ghosts

Dayamimam nivaddham—the transaction or contract was duly registed

Dhamma-Mangala- True ceremonial as Nam on earth

Dalit Voice—Inner Voice; 'Nam'

Dipa—Oil for lamp to 'light'

Dalitadasasataih—"An open town" "Abode of multitude of men of for castes" cluster of 10,000 villages.

Dhamma-Dana- Nam-dana mantra of the Father, proper treatment of the slave from the prefect master.

Dhupa—Incense

Drishtimatra-prabandhna—Visible at first sight

Dhyana-ekagrapara—Yogis concentrated on contemplation

Dandapasadhikaranika—Police chief

Dhan bhante Mahipaler Git—Folk Songs and Ballads

Dayal—Merciful (dayal)

Dharmrai—The Lord (rai) of Judgement (dharma)

Dana—Giving, generosity

Danta—Teeth

Dhamma—Teachngs, truth, reality, things, phenomenon

Dhammadesana—Teaching the doctrine

Dhammasavana—Hearing the doctrine

Dhatu—Element

Dibbacakkhu—Divine eye, clairvoyance

Ditthi—Wrong view

Dosa—Anger, ill-will

Dukkha—Suffering, the first Noble Truth

Easwan Dwar—Tenth (daswan) door or gate (*dwar*) the third inner region.

Eka-rat or Chakravartin—Sole sovereign, single ruler

Eka-chchhatra—Whole earth under one umberalla

Ekangas—Military followers or organisation

Ekam— "One Reality" "the One"

Esa—A mythical plant

Ephthalites—See White Hunas

Ekaggata- Concentration, one -pointedness of mind.

Fourth plane—*Sat Lok* See *Sat Lok*

Faqir—A poor mar, a mendicant, an ascetic. The term is also used for saints and for holy men generally (*Pirs*)

Fanafillah—Extinct in God, a state in which one has merged in God, and one's separate identity has ceased

Fareb—Allurement, deceit

Fikr—Attention, thought

Fana-fil-Sheikh—Extinction in the master

Fana-fil-Zaat—Extinction in essence, annihilation (and thus merger) in God.

Ferri candidi— "Talents of Steel" "White Iron

Ficus Indica—Banyan

Ficus Religiosa—Ashvatta, Pippala

Five tribe—Five race= words, Ka

Fire-worship—The due to the Rig-Veda 'First born', the form of *Vishvakarma*

Flood legend—Shatapath Brahmana

Gana or Ganapati—Heads of the Republics.

Gharma Ayasmaya—Vessels made of metal

Godhumah—Maize

Gramyani—Cultivated grain

Gramani or—Village Headman *Grama bhojaka*

Gonikartana—Huntsman

Guru-Kula—Domestic school

Ganarajyas—Republican states

Gopalaka—A common communal neat-herd

Grama-dvara—Wall or stockade with gates

Grama—Village with an enclosuer of thorns, bushes & tree

Gramavasa—Villages homes

Gandha — Odour, Mind only

Gopata—Viceroy
Garudadhvaja—The Vahana of Vishnu
Ghatayitva—Sacked
Guha=Vihara— "A religious gift (*Dhamadana*) of a cave monastery, where were invited for residence the teacher Buddhadeva." Teaching about *Mahasamghika*
Gurudiksa—Tantric rite
Gandharva-Vidya—Proficient in music
Grihapati—The daughter of a commercial magnate
Guhavasa or Layanam or—Cave(lenam)-dwellings for accommodation of asceticsor Lenam
Gaulmika—Incharge of the forest
Grihapravesa— Citizens
Gavya—Cow's milk
Gurvvayatana—Install in shrine
Garbha-griha—A sanctum of stone i.e. *'ego'*
Garahati—Belittle
Gramyavadin—Village judge
Ghatakah—Jars
Grahita—Elected
Ganga—See Ganges, Pure idea
Grihya-Sutras—Rules for the conduct of life
Guru—A Spiritual Instructor, successor of the ancient *purohita*
Gods—See *Devas, 'Words'*
Gayatri—The holiest text in Rig-Veda
Gharghar—Modern name of the lower Sarasvati
Gadhipura—Name of Kanauj
Ganja—'Treasury'
Ganjavara—Treasurer
Ganga—Pilgrimage to 'Word'
Gauraka—Wood-dealer
Gavyuti—measurement of thing or kind
Hadayam — Heart
Hiranyagrabha—Implicit nature, "the golden Embryo", black idea
Hiranyakara—Who make ornaments of gold, 'Egoless'
Hrade—Lakes
Harita Kalapaka—Preparation of great vegitable
Hephaistos—God of Metal (Greek)
Herakilo—Greek Deity Heracles
Horon—Sanskrit Varuna

Harita—Greens

Harmya—Building of temples

Hiranyasamudayika—Currency officer

Harsha-deva—'Nam' or Chamar

Hetu-Vidya—Logic

Hritahunasarvam—The Hunas

Hu. God, essense of God, a name of or God; esotexically used for the ruler of the third spiritual stage of mystic.

Hasti— Elephant force

Haq—The truth, reality, absolute

Hastinayana—Sanskrit Hastin

Hinajatis—Low castes

Hina-sippas—Low crafts

Hayagriva—A demon

Hydaspes—Greek name of the Jhelam

Hydraotes—Greek name of the Ravi or Surya or Moon

Hypasis—Hypanis, Vipasis, Greek names of Bias. Vitasta a Greek name.

Himavat— "Abode of winter", See Himalaya

Hooma—Eranian Equivalent of Soma

History—See Rig-veda, study of India

Issattha-Sippa—Arts of Archery

Ibhya—Nobles

Iddhividha— Supernatural powers

Ijya—Sacrifice for pious deed like 'Nam'

Iha-lokika or—Space and time

Akalika

Imam Karita—Buddha constructed

Idam Sariram—Enshrinement of the bodily relics

Indus—See Sindhu, Sindh, *Vitasta*

Iravati—Epic name of the *Ravi*, or *Nagi*

Iroti—See *Ravi*

Indra—Thunderbolt, the hero of the atmospheric battle led by 'Nam' or 'Word'

Indrani—The wife of Indra or pale of abstraction

Itihasas—Legendary poems, realise through *'Nam'- mantra'*

India—General view and extent

Ida—Spiritual daughter of Manu

Iron Age—Kaliyug, the age (yuga) of materialism or discard (Kali): the fourth age in the cycle of time through which the physical universe passes. Hindu mythology divides time into four great age (Yogas), following each other in endless (*ananta*) recurring cycles: Satyog, Tretayug,

Dwarparyug, Kaliyog (The Golden age, Silver age, Copper age, Ironage). According to this cosmology, it is now the Iron age after it, therewill be Enlightenment Era.

Irra—One of the three subtle energy currents (irra Pingala, sushumna, flowing through all creation below Trikuti (Universal mind).

Inda—Historical literature of ancient time.

Jambudvipa—India or *Bharata*, origin base of the History.

Jana—The people

Jiva—Soul

Jayatipraviro—'The bravest on earth'

Jyotisha—Astronomy

Jatila—Hairgrow

Jayati—Achieving victory

Jati—Caste, race, believe on master.

Janapada—Local laws peculiar to regions or states

Jivasuta—Still living

Jirnoddhara—Restoration of temples

Jina—Buddha

Jvalata—Radiant

Jayaparihara—Charities

Janardana—A surname of vishnu

Janeu—Thread worn by Hindu for identity called Janeu. The sign of 'ego.'

Jayukelishu—Victorious career

Karma—Actions and deed, past thoughts

Kutumbinam—Settled peasants

Khila—Follow

Karanas—Documents

Kulaputtras—Court's Noble person

Kshatra-vinasahrit—The destroyer of Kshatriya's

Kaivalya—'Deep meditation', 'Highest knowledge'

Kalpa—Ceremonial, one of the Vedangas

Kripa—'*Nam*' or '*Word*'

Kaaba—Lit; 'cube' the cube stone structure covered with black cloth, which stands in the centre of

the Grand Mosque in Mecca. In one corner it contains the 'Black Stone'. It is towards the Ka'ba that Muslims orient themselves in prayer. It is also called the 'holy house' of the mind theory.

Kosa—buckets or 'oath' by sacred libetion

Krishna-trabch—Dark-skinned comparative study of mind

Krishna-garbah—Dusky-brood = Ego minded,

Kula or Griha—The family
Kulapa—Head of the family
Khala—Floor of granary
Kaupina—Lion cloth
Kalindi—Yamuna river
Kshina-Kosham—Wealth dwindling
Kumaras or Aryaputra—Princes
Kupa or Udapana—Wells
Kapana-Valaka—Afflicated
Karshayati—Overtaxation and exactions
Kshama—Utmost for bearance
Kratuyaji—Give to Vedic studies and sacrifices
Kaulikanikaya—Weavers
Krtyakah or krtya—Witches
Kalingadhipati—King of Kalinga
Kharkhota—Sorcerer
Kshudra—Petty
Karkota— Chine word means *'Nam'* or *'Sabad'*
Kharkhoda—Witchcraft
Kalasa—inverted lotus capital vasa
Koshthagara—Store house
Kavya—Composition
Khadyatapakika—Food controller of Royal kitchen
Kumaramatya—Minister in Attendance on crown prince
Kripana—For the lowly
Katha—Story
Kubera—God
Kamadeva—God of love
Kumbhadasa—'Waterman'
Kumbha—'Sacrificial cup'
Kaviraja—Prince of poet
Kulika—Artisans
Khila—Waste land
Kayasthas—Writers or clerks
Khila-kshetra—Common pastures
Kantaki-Kari—Worker in thorns
Kama tanha—Sensous desire
Kamachanda—Sensous desire
Kameshumicchacara—Misuse of the senses, often limited to sexual misconduct

Kammatthana—Work place, meditation subject
Karisam—Excrement
Karuna—Compassion
Kasina—Whole, complete, a meditatio device
Kayagata sati—Mindfulness of the body
Kesa—Hair of head
Khanti— Patience
Khanika—Moment
Khelo—Saliva
Kilesa—Defilement
Kilomakam—Pleura
Kusala—Wholesome
Lasika—Fluid of the joints
Lobha—Greed
Lohita—Red, blood
Lokavidu—Knower of the worlds
Loma—Hair of body
Lahuka—Light
Lrohaspo—Zend, Aurvat-aspa, swift-horsed-vedic Apamnapat
Lekhad hikarin—Secretary
Loh—English loe=Glow, god of light i.e., *'Nam'* or *'Chamar'*
Lenam—Cave
Lokajna—State Craft
Lokanugraha—Social service
Lotus feet—See feet of the master
Latitavistara— "Ignorant of the silpas and the Military arts."
Ladha—Radha or Wester Bengal, soul
Lokadhatu—Buddhisti expression
Lokaloka—Mythical mountain
Lokanatha—Name of Buddha
Lokapala—'Guardian of the world'
Lakshana or Tankasala—Mint
Lunantah—Reaping
Lavana—Salt
Lagna—Auspicious time
Loka—Indeed All mankind preceptor i.e. Father or God.
Lekhaharaka— 'Letter-carrier'
Manam- Pride of the master of the world to realise the truth for study of '*Nam*' on earth
Mantrika—'Exorcist' guards fields against nagas

Mitra—A god of light
Martya— "Mortal" a name of "Man"
Matrcakras—'Sacred diagramas'
Manyus—Wrath, a deified abstraction
Mandalasa—'Books' into which the Rig-Veda is divided.
Magic—Little used in the Rig-veda
Moon—The Soma, the fountain of Amrita
Mritya—Death personified
Manu—Man, 'The human race'
Manmukh—Lit, 'facing the mind' one who is in materialistic devotee of the mind
Meghavahana—Rainfall, idea of the *Indra* God in Spiritual Knowledge or *Megha*
Mati-Sachiva—Those who decided policy, Councillors
Maharaj—Great King of the Nam
Mahasamgiti—Great Buddhist council
Mukula—Conspirator
Mazdohano—Iranian Mazdaonho
Miiro—Sun God= Iranian Mihr, = Sanskrit Mihira
Mao—Iranian Mah = Sanskrit mas of Chandramas
Murshid—Moon-God, A spiritual master
Manaobago—Persian Mana-Baga, four armed mood God.
Mithra—Avesti, Mithra=Vedic Mitra, Sun-gold
Maasena—Sanskrit Mahasena
Mlana—Claimants pale
Mriduhridaya—Soft heart
Mahadevi—Chief queen
Mahattaras—Village Elders
Maula—Hereditary
Mitra—Allies
Matris—Divine mother's temple
Mansarovar—A Lake (Sarovar) in Dawan dwar, also called the lake of Nectar (Amritsar).
Moonbird—A fabled bird (Chakor)
Maya—Allusion, delusion, unreality; the phenomenal universe
Maha Sunn—The great (Maha) void (sunn); an area of parbrahm between *Sunn* and Bhanwar

Gupha.
Mana—Honour displayed, pride
Manana—Pondered over

Mantras—Treasure of thought i.e., 'Nam' or 'Word's, words
Mudra—Honey of love i.e., 'Nam'
Mudra Rakashas—Eater of love call 'word' or Chamar
Mayura-poshaka-grame—'Rearer of royal peacocks'
Munipati—Reserve category
Mansarovar—A lake in the third spiritual region a dip in which makes the soul absolutely pure or *Sudh* or *Sudra in the Nam-History*
Madhyamasi—Lying in the middle
Manyu—Wrath
Mandalas— "Books" into which the Rig-Veda divided.
Mala—Law of mind or darkness
Mahavihara—University
Maharajya—Great kingship
Mah Rishi—Chief queen
Mekhala—Belt
Mahamatras—Chief officer
Matamba— "An isolated town"
Mantrika— "Exorcist", guards fields against Najas
Mariyada—Those who follow the traditions of thier castes
Marga or Patha—Public road
Masurah—Lentils
Mudga or Masha—(Beans)
Mantra Griha—Council of Chamber
Mangalas—Ceremonies
Mula—Root
Maha-pala—Great fruit
Magga—The path, the fourth Noble Truth
Magganana—Path insight
Mana—Connect
Manasikara—Attention
Mandala—Circle, a meditation object
Mara—The evil one, a satan figure who resists spiritual advance
Marana—Death
Maranansussati—Mindfulness of death
Matthalumgam—Brain
Mamsam—Flesh
Medo—Fat
Metta—Loving-kindness
Micchaditthi—Wrong view
Moha—Delusion

Mudita—Sympathetic joy

Mula magga—Basic path

Musavada—Lying, wrong speech

Muttam—Urine

Nakha—Nails

Nataparinna—Full understanding, penetration of reality

Nau Nand De—hra—The existence of Godāvari of a city called *Nau Nand Dehra or Nander*

Nava—The word *Nava* in the expression Nava *Nanda* to mean *nine* and not new i.e., old one i.e. Nine organ of the body two eyes, two mostril, two ears, one mouth and two lower organ to control them get the enjoy of *Nature or 'Nam' or 'Word'*. Earlier *Nanda* (Purva Nanda), *Nava Nanda* (New or later *Nanda*)

Nivapa—Ceremony

Nyaya—Logic

Nadatvae—A kind of matling

Napita Kumara or

Napitasu—Founder of the Nanda lineage

Nandopakramani manani—Kings of the line are credited by certain grammarians ('Words') with establishment of a particular kind of measure.

Nauvitana—Fleet

Nandanvaya—No need of the *Nanda* to the theory of mind

Nandivardhana—The tenth son of *Nanda* named *Mahanandin* and that "as son of *Mahanandin* by a *Sudra* woman will be born a king, *Mahapadma* (Nanda) who will exterminate all Kshatriyas. Thereafter, kings will be of *Sudra* origin; called ocean or sea.

Nara-Narayana—Charities were promoted by the best spirit of positivist social service whcih recognised it as a form of worship of God, of God-i-Man

Nirmulya—Uprooting

Nandins—Unknown lineage (*annatakula*)

Nandadesam—Devastated the country

Navame Nande—Nine Nandas are *Sudra*

Napitadusa 'Word'

Rajajatah—First *Nanda* describes as begotten of a barber (Nai)

Navabhataro—*Nava Nanda tato asum* Naital mamaiti

Manyamanah—Own dear state or country of the 'Word' like India.

Nandrum or Nanda—With supernatural encouragement Alexander obtained the title or name Alexandrum after his death.

Natthika-ditthi—A sort of atheism

Nam—See Name, '*Sabad*', '*Word*', 'Chamar' experience through soul consciousness

Nirgun—Without (nir) attributes (gun), See also gunas (merits)

Niranjan—Without (*nir*) stain (anjan); pure. See Kal

Nafs—The ego, desires born of the senses.

Nida-i-Sultani—The 'Kingly voice' or Sound ; the 'Word'

Namaaz—The cannonical prayer of the Mulims in the mosque, prayer of 'ego'

Niyyat—Intention; adopting the state of *Ihram*

Na'ra-i-takbir—See Allah-hu-Akbar, 'God the Great',

Nidha-pati—Fowlers

Nanaia—Same as NANA or Nana appearing on the (coins) a female deity supposed to be of Persian origin.

Niryantrana—Unceremonious manner

Nidhitulya—Deep as the sea or ocean like *Sudra*

Nagararakshakas—Chief executive officers of the city

Nala—Standard unit of reeds 8x8

Naradhipati—Supposed one more king

Nirupaplavam—Succeeded wihout any trouble

Nayayadandatram—Righteous rule= 'Nam'

Nauvitana—Despatch fleet to conquered many minor rulers

Nadistuti— "River-hymn" a valuable geographical document of Veda

Nagas—Snake-people, believe on theory of Mind i.e., God through '*Nam-mantra*' theory.

Naraka—A "hell-world"

Naturalism—Principal characteristic of the Rig-Veda or Thinker

Night—The sister of Dawn

Nirukta—Etymology, one of the Vedangas

Nadatvac—A kind of matting

Nishadya—Travellers rest houses

Nirnijya—duly washed away

Niravasita—Out caste or Untouchable people of pure thought unliked by Brahmans

Nagar— "A scot free town"

Napitadasa—Son of a barber by a courtesan

Nirathaka—Meaningless

Nakaschitrajarthavirodha—Not causing loss of the Kings revenue

Nekkhamma—Renunication

Nevasannanasannayatana—The fourth stage of immaterial absorption pertaining to the base of neither perception nor non-perception

Niharu—Sinews

Nibbida—Disgust

Nila—Blue

Nimitta—Sign, image

Nirodha—Cessation

Nivarana—Hindrance

Nau-ship - Boat of the *Nam* called *Chamar* or Ravidas

Odata—White

Oja—Nutriment

Odyo Boycakana—Sanskrit Advaya-Buddha-Sakyamuni

Oesho—Hoesho=Sanskrit Bhavesa or *Vrisha*=*Sudra*=Siva

Oanindo—Arestic Female Diety called Vanamti-uparatat, victorious superiority.

Ommo—Sanskrit Uma, Om =halo to call the *'Nam'* in original form as Supreme Being

Oado—Pahlavi Vato=Vedic Vata, Vayu, wind God i.e. 'Nam' or 'Chamar'

Onkar—The lord of the second region, *Trikuti in* original form as human being.

Prathamartham- avachchhinasamstham— The fund to be kept.

Pippala, See Ficus religrosa

Pisang—See Bananan

Pitirs—Spirit of Dead, Drink Soma from the moon

Pushan—Solar deity, of rural character or weaver in complex idea of the knitting of the world history.

Puranas—Most of them deal with the theory of creation and the destruction and renewal of the universe

Pundit—Scholar, Hindu theologian

Pratyaya—Attainment

Pattavaya—Silk-weaver

Pratima-apratimasya—Unequalled qualities

Prakriti—By the people

Prachyamdisi—Eastern quarter

Prachyas—Eastern peoples

Parakrama—Laid great stress on exertion

Pseudo-Nanda—Yogananda

Prathita-kulajah—Contrasted with Nanda

Pachchanta-Vasika—From the frontiers

Pachchanta nagaram gantva—Marching against the cities of frontiers

Prajapati—Lord of creatures or 'Word'

Prithvi—Earth
Pasa—Nets variously
Pratishta—Pre-eminence
Paramata—Supremacy
Parameshthya—Supreme authority
Pesaskari—Empbrodierer
Poshaya—Progress
Pratima—Installed the image
Paramavapusha—Highest beauty
Pipasitah—Thirsty
Pharro—Kavaem Qareno of Avesta, Swift horsed= Vedic Apamnapat
Prathita-Kula—Illustrious lineage of Nanda
Prana-Sametam—Innate potency
Punyasala—Alms-house
Pratapa—Conscious of his power
Paricharakikrita—Obligations of service to the suzerain
Prasabhoddharana—Violent exterminated
Paturabhiksus—Naked ascetics
Prachandasasana—Dominion of a person or influence or resolute govt
Paritosha—To gain good will
Pranamagamana—Tender homage in a darbar to a person
Prithivimavitva—Conquered the earth
Pancha-Mahayajnas—To meet the expenses of daily performance
Prajna—Company of the wise
Pancha-Mandali—Governing body of the five
Pravartana—In auguratation
Pasu-chikitsa and
Manushya-Chikitsa—Hospital both for Man and Cattle
Prathama-Kulika—Chief of the Guild of Artisans i.e. 'Nam' or 'Word'
Prathama-Kayastha—Chief of the union of writers, or scribes, chief secretary
Pastapalas—Record keepers
Pranali—Channels
Pravesya—Non-payable troops visiting the village
Prasarsati—Ruling over the image
Punya—Spiritual merit
Padadasa—Granted some lands to feudatory
Prathama—Presidents of Guilds or Groups
Pindapata—Food
Pancalas—Followers of Arjuna
Putika— Corrupt

Pancaladeva—Equivalent of Pir Pantsal or 'Word'

Pancamahasabda—'Offices designated by Father 'Word'

Pancanada—Penjab in Persian term means 'Sound' or 'Nam'

Palevata—'Apple'

Papiha—A bird in Indian folklore, drinks only rain water and that too only at a particular time of the year.

Peshwa—The word "King" has been used for it

Prakriti—The people or living being

Pacayana—Reverence

Pacceka Buddha—A solitary or private Buddha

Pahanaparinna—Full understanding as abandoning misconception

Pancakkhandha—Five aggregates

Panna—Wisdom, insight

Papphasam—Lungs

Paracitta vijanana—Knowing the thoughts and feelings of others, telepathy

Parikamma— Preparatory

Parinna—Profound knowledge, full understanding

Pariyutthana—Arising

Pathavi dhatu—Earth element, the quality of heaviness and lightness

Patikulasanna—Perception of loathsomeness

Pattanumodana—Rejoicing in the merit of others

Patthana—Aspiration

Pattidana—Dedication of merit

Patibhaga—Counter-sign or object for meditation

Panatipata—Killing

Pharusavaca—Harsh speech

Phassa —Contact

Pihakam—Spleen

Pisunavaca—Slander

Pita—Yellow, golden colour

Piti—Joy, pleasure in the object

Pittam—Bile

Pubbabhaga magga—Preliminary path

Pubbenivasanussati—The ability to remember one's former lives

Pubbo—Pus, Thick Yellish or greenish liquid.

Quran—The sacred scriptire of Islam, written in Arabic and revealed to the prophet means to recite. Again Prophet will come in New form.

Qaul — The Word

Qazi—A judge, appointed on the basis of his knowledge of Islamic law, equivalent to Mahamatras

Qibla—Lit. focal point, Qibla is also used as synonym for the Ka'ba.
Ratha— War or Sport
Rasmi—Reins
Rajan—King
Rasa — Taste
Rupa — Matter, material form
Rashtra—State or country
Rita—Truth, faith, Astras name of the Cosmic Law, *'Chamar'. 'Nam'*
Rudhabharrodhi—Begar, forced carriage of loads
Rudhisabda—Grammatical term used for *'Word'* or *'Nam'*
Rasi—Science of numbers
Rathadhanur-bhyam—Army
Rajakommika—Those who are in the service of the King
Ratna-yonih—Precious metal
Rajadhani—Capital of kingdom
Rupa—Money-Changing
Rajakrida—The boy who always playing the role of king
Rajatiraja—The kind of the Kings
Rajatarangini—'River of Kings'
Rashtra-nigamam—Region and city
Ride—Sanskrit Riddhi
Riom (Mana)—Roma, city-Deity of Roma
Rajyasri—Kingship glory
Raja Mahan—A mighty King
Rajasthaniya—Governor of a Province, Chief Justice
Rajye-Abhishekshyati—Sovereign of the realm or kingdom
Rig-Veda—Complicated character of the life; principally natrualism which keep history in survival
Rudra—The stromy sky
Roz-i-Misak—See Shah rag
Rajayitri—Dyer
Rupakritih—A beautiful picture
Sabdartha—Etymology
Sati Sirimata or Hakusri—Saktisri in Rig Veda
Satakanni Rattha—Satavahanavihara
Srenis or Nigamas—Guilds
Sreni—Military clans
Sadha-dana or
Sikata Sindhu or Shaoreoro — 'Sand ocean' *'Valukambudh'*
Sraddh-danam—A shrine out of respect for the donor's parents

Sanda—Name of the plant
Strategos or Senapati—Commander-in-chief
'Samdhivigrahika'—Minister of foreign affairs
Sariram or Dehavasesham
Sabda or Sabdavidya—A relic study of Grammer
Sanakostha—'Bathinghut'
Sutra—Measuringline
Sacha-dhrama-thita—*Sachcha* Sodha
Santarasa—'Sentiment of resignation from theory of mind'
Soma—Moon-God in Rig-Veda
Saktu—Vegetable curries
Sadhaka—A kind of famulus, an tantricrites
Sailadevagriha—Records the gift of a shrine of stone.
Sadh—Who attained the region of *Trikuti* or the universal mind
Sailam—Shrine made of stone
Srimat—Magnificient i.e. '*Nam*' or '*Word*'
Sindura—'Red lead', used for seal impressions
Saka-Mana-Bouda—In Sanskrit Sakya-Muni-Buddha
Saila—Stone
Satya—Upright
Sindhu Sindh—Ancient Name of Indus
Skando Komaro—In Sanskrit Skanda-Kumar
Sasana—Administration
Suttee—Widow-burning, no authority during Rig-Veda period
Seva—Services
Sumudra—Gathering of waters, *Sudar*
Samgrameshu—Sumudramatha, *Nam*
'Svabhuja-Vijitah'— Mental peace
Sukhamana—Mental peace
Svabhoganagara—Favourite city
Sandhivigrahika—Minister for foreign relations and war
Sarthavahas—Traders
Sreshthis—Bankers
Sandrophagos—Greek name of the Tchandrabagha
Sada-Satra—Alms-house
Simha-Vahana—Goddess Durga on lion
Savita—Sun
Samyak-ghatita-upalena—Solid masonary work
Saulkika—Incharge of Tolls
Sadhusamsargaputa—The sacred abod of saints

Samuditabalakoshan—The Mlechchhas and their confederate forces
Santi—Peace
Sasta—Great teacher
Samaptaya—Attainment of beatitude
Satru-Sainyam-Vigahya—Army of the enemies like Brahmans.
Sarvato-Bhogena—Absolute possession
Sanyana—Beds
Shorear — Pahlavi Shahresar, Prefect ruler
Sarapis— In Sanskrit *Yama* or *Sraddha-devata*. Taking food in the memory of *Pitirs.*
Sakhas and Charanas—Religious group of students working under the teacher.
Sayana—Author of the standard commentary on the Rig-Veda
Sindhuvelavalayitam—Encircled by Sea or Sudhra
Sravana—Heard
Sishyas—Pupils or Sikhs or disciple
Satkarya—Judge of the true poetry
Sukta-Marggah—Vedic Saktas
Sikhara—Tower over sanctum
Surya—Sun, Ravi, God.
Siddhi—Self-fulfilment
Svadhyaya—Vedic study
Surasadmasabha—Temples with halls
Sadhanika—Collector of Fines and Debts
Sabdika—Linguists
Sakya-Sasanas—Buddhist law
Saptatantavas—Experts in rituals
Samrajya—Imperial rule
Samrat—'Oh emperor'
Sastrajiva—'Pursuit of arms'
Sudragarbhodbhavah—'Off spring of the Sudra woman'
Sastra—Military power and learning
Svayam Upanamanti—Noble lineage
Sruyate—Tradition
Sapta-Sindhavah—Land of the seven river India called in Rig-veda
Suna—Slaughter house
Satyam—Truthfullness
Saucham—Inner and outer Purity
Samyama—Control of senses
Samavaya—Harmony

Saravriddhi—Essential elements
Sava-pasamdani—All the sects. Sufi
Samabandha—relationship of life
Sangiti—Council
Samaggo—United body
"Sara"—Abstract of all religion or essence
Sarva-Sattnam— "All beings"
Salohitanam—Relation-in-blood
Sri— 'Nam', 'Word', 'Chamar'
Samanta-Chudamani—Prominent feudatory chief
Sakya-Sasanas—Buddhist laws
Svetapatas—Svetambaras
Sufi—Sufis believe in a living *Murshid* (Guru) and lead a holy life
Sach Khand—True or imperishable (Sach) region
Sala—Halls (Khand)
Seer—An old weight measure, slightly less than a Kilogram
Silpas—Craft
Sabad— *'Word', 'Sound', 'Chamar'.* Kalma, Bani, Gurbani
Shlok—Verse, couple, Moral subject
Sifati—Attributive name
Simran—Repetition; remembrance
Smriti—Memory of Vedas
Spas—Employment spies
Sabha—Assembly of people
Sannyasi or parivrajaka—Vaikhanasa having Bhraminical character
Sagdi or Sogdri—Sudras, *Sodara* in Persian having insight. Knowledge.
Sacca—Truth, truthfulness
Samatha—Calm tranquility of mind
Samma—Right (cf. Lat. summa, the highest, the best)
Sammasambuddho—Fully self-enlightened
Sampajanna—Clear; perfectly or thoroughly understanding
Samphapalapavaca—Gossip
Samudaya—The origin of suffering, the second Noble Truth of craving
Sangha—Holy community, realised disciples
Sankhara—Mental formations, volitional activities
Sanna—Perception of sense objects
Satha devamanussanam—Teacher of gods and men
Sedo—Sweat
Semham—Phlegm
Sila—Morality

Silavata—Rites and ritual
Singalika—Mucus
Sotapanna—Stream winner, the initial stage of sainthood
Sugato—One who has achieved the way, title of the Buddha
Sukha—Happiness, pleasant feeling
Sunnata—Emptiness
Sura— Intoxiated of the '*Nam*'
Tataka—Lake (Reservoir), Silence, work in hide
Tulya-Kulajah—His brothers
Tantrapati—Judge i.e., 'Nam'
Tapa—Change into repentance
Tadi—Kind of earring
Tala—A "hell world"
Tritsu—The leading and purest Aryan tribe
Tugra—Allies of the Tritsu in the Ten war kings
Tila-mashah—Beans and sesamum
Titau—Sieve
Takshan—Carpenter, worked with axe (*parasu*)
Tanka—'Mint-dies' 'coin-type'
Tapasas or Isis—Forest homes called Asramas to live
Tapah—Penance
Thalaniyya-maka—Under the land pilot
Tivra—Became intense
Torana—(gate way)
Tattvah—Penetrating into the wisdom
Tiksna—'Assassin' bravo
Tiladvadasi—Festival
Tat-parigrihiten and Tat-parigrhita—Selected of the throne
Talavalaka—Gardening
Tailika-Sreni—Prosperious guild of Oilmen
Tushangaradichihnaih—Permanent marks of ash, charcoal
Taddiyatamiti—Land might be granted
Tadayuktaka—Treasury officer
Tapita—Heated
Tana—Different tunes
Tadaga—Tanks
Tantrins—Military personnel
Taco—Skin
Tanha—Lit, thirst, craving
Tathagat—The Buddha, 'thus come' like previous buddhas

Tejo dhatu—Fire element, the quality of heat and cold
Thina-middha—Sloth and torpor, drowsiness, sleepiness
Tipitaka—Three baskets, the divisions of the Pali scriptures
Tiranaparinna—Full understanding as overcoming concept
Tisarana—Triple gem
Uggahitanaya balamsamvidhaya - Conquered with garrisons with Janapadas
Upanishads—Philosophical treatise, in the Rig-veda
Ushas—The Dwan, badly treated
Upasti—Dependents
Utsadya—Overthrown
Urdara or —Vessel for the measurment of grain *Tupa*
Upala-Prakshini—Mother of a grinder of corn
Uchchairavijanam—High birth
Udyana—Looked after the public parks
Udapana—Well
Upapidayati—Molested
Upasika—Female devotee
Udadhasamadhara—Reservoir
Upaguhya—Father who embraced
Uchchhvasita—Great enthusiasm
Utsanna—Overthron
Uttarasman—Crossing stone
Udhara—Beautiful
Upachaya—To bringing some again to the king for its sale
Upasthana—Darbar Hall
Uparika Maharaja—Provincial Governor
Uttaran-Samvyavaharyadi—Village authorities concerned
Upadhaya—Sub-teacher *and Acharya*
Upavana—Parka
Udapana—Storage of drinking water
Utpratikara—Not assessed to revenue
Upachaya—Tax from productive land
Uttarapatha-Svamin—North India
Upajapam—Intrigues
Ujjama—Debt
Ubhayakkaya—Expiration of both lifespan and kammic force
Udariyam—Stomach
Uddhacca—Kukkuca— Restlessness and worry
Uggaha—Acquired object
Upacara—Access, neighbourhood

Upadana—Attachment
Upasama—Peace, calmness
Upeccheda-kamma—Destructive kamma, untimely death
Upekkha—Equanimity, undifferentiation
Vuddhapatipatiya—Ruled one after another in accordance with seniority.
Vairajya—Condemn the foreign rule, sovereignty
Vasati—Greek Ossadioi
Varna—'Word' or 'Nam', Sabad, 'Chamar', *Kalma*
Vayu—Vata, the wind-serva, meaning of Ved
Vishvakarman—The artificer of the universe name of the Supreme being, 'Lord' creator of cosmos
Vedangas—The six, "Limbs of Veda"
Veda—Meaning of the 'Word' or 'Nam'
Vaishyas—Third working class in Hindu society, believed on the pattrans of Brahmans.
Vach—Divinized speech of nature
Vipasa—Vedic name of the Bias
Vichvarupa—Omniform
Viyas—See Bias
Vyakarana—(Grammer) one of the Vedangaas, Sabad, 'Nam' or 'Word'
Varnatmak—Expressible, that which can be spoken or written
Vis—The canton or clan
Vispati—Head of the clan of Vis
Vairadaya—Enmity
Vidhata—Ordainer
Virat-purusha—Absolute, Formless, Infinite
Vaya—Weaver
Verman—Loom
Vrihi-Yavah—Barley and rice
Varatra—Leather string
Vapantra—Sowing
Vishti—forced labour
Vasas or Vasana or Vastra—Dress
Vavata—Favourite wife
Vidyamayasarira as explained by Sayana = Endowed with spiritual body
Vijavaharika—Executive head of the administration
Vetanadibhyo Jivati—Sources of livelihood
Vanijya—Trade
Vithi—Street
Vikrama—Powers

Vrishlatmaja—Mura the mother of *Chandragupta*, the daughter of a *Sudra women*

Vedana—Extreme anguish

Vyasani—Addicted to vices

Varnas—Castes, Pure, 'Nam', Sabad, 'Word', 'Chamar' in original form of the life as an idea of the saint.

Varna-sankara—Ornaments of the 'Nam'

Vitrasayati—Menace or threat

Vijinamano—Conquer

Vaijayanti—Banavasi

Vasu—Seured booty

Virya—Arms

Vridita—Shame

Vibhava-pratyarpana—Loss of liberties

Vigrahavan—Example

Vahukavita—Poetical composition

Vandha—Promoted the religion by upholding

Vinaya-sthitisthayapak—Minister of law and order

Vikrayamaryada-prasanga—According to the rule of sale

Vichalita—Kula-lakshmi perturbed

Vipluta—Overwhelmed

Virapatta—Head dress of heros

Vinaya—Exalted in all humility.

Vrishala—'The son of a *Sudra*' or Sche

Vishada—Filled the city with despair

Visuddha—Incorruptible

Vena—The name of the God *Indra* known as Vajra or thunderbold

Vishayapati—District Magistrate

Vyaghata—Freedom from expenses and molestation caused by the visits of royal relations and their retinue.

Vibhushitam—Adorned

Vishaya—District

Vastu—Building land or sites

Vapa-land for cultivation

Vikhyata-paurusha—Heroic chief

Vira-Kirtimvinamya—Bending down the fame of all heroes

Vithi—Sub-division

Varataka—Cowrie

Vara officer—Varakritaih = officers created by turns

Varuna—God of cosmic law

Vidyadharas—Godlings
Vina—Playing on the lyre
Varna-Samkara—To prevent unlawful mixture of castes
Vapi—Well
Vibhava=pratyarpana—Vanquished properties
Vinayasura—Conduct of visitors to the King
Vimana-mala—Aerial chariots
Vata—Unexplainable
Vrishala—Term of honour to mean 'one who is the Vrisha among kings, the best of Kings '*Sudras*'.
Vakkam—Kidneys
Vanna—Colour, visible form
Vasa—Grease
Vasita—Ability
Vavatthana—Analysis
Vayo dhatu—Air element, the quality of motion and movement
Vedana—Feeling or sensation
Veyavacca—Service
Vibhava tanha—Craving for annihilation
Vicara—Sustained application
Vicikiccha—Sceptical doubt
Vijjacarana sampanno—Endowed with knowledge and good conduct
Vinnana—Consciousness
Vinnanancayatana—The second stage of immaterial absorption pertaining to the base of infinite consciousness
Vipassana—Insight, seeing things as they really are
Viriya—Energy, effort
Visuddhi—Purity
Vitakka—Initial application
'Word'—See also shabd, *'Nam'*, *Chamar*, *Dalit Voice*, *Holy Ghost*, *'Power'* Supreme Being. The only material for the reconstruction of early Aryan life, Ancient and modern study of the Aryan languages. Wilkins, Marshall, Charles, 'Father of Sanskrit studies'
Waters—The mother of Agni, Rivers, divinized, Cosmogonic order or *Rita*
Wahdat-ul-Wajud—'Unity of being,' the doctrine of the unity of being corresponds to the Hindu doctrine of non-duality known as *Advaita*. According to this doctrine, there is only one Self, which is reflected by manifestion into multiplicity of beings, persons, creatures and objects and this divine self is the hidden identity of all.
Wahi—'Burest', descent of the song from God to the prophets, inspiration, revelation from God.

Yuktapurusha—A special officer
Yasah Kritsnam—Restored some scion of the old line and its glory
Yajna—See sacrifice of religion
Yadu—The one of the "Five tribes" who knows, Yadava, Jana or Yadavah
Yima—Eranian equivalent of Yama
Yogi—One who practises Yoga
Yoga—Union, esoterically, spiritual exercises or practices, mediation in the spiritual sense, any sys tem that leads to oraims at the union of the soul with God. From Sanskrit Yog, meaning ' to yoke or join,' Union.
Yama— God's death messengers.
Yogesa—Temple
Yava—Grain
Yogaschavijaye—Preparedness for war
Yuddhajivas—Soldiers
Yati—Ascetic
Yuvaraja—Application
Yachna—Crown prince
Yukta—Order
Yupa—Pillar
Yastika—Class of royal attendants
Yakanam—Liver
Yana—Vehicle, the path
Yathabhuta—As they really are
Yathakammupaga nana—Knowing the kamma of others giving rise to their rebirths.
Zaat—Essence or abracte being
Ziarats—Temples transformed into *Masjid*
Zikr—The great Sufi mystics used the term *Zikr* for the highest form of remembrance or repetition, which corresponds to the *Simran* or inner invocation of the divine name or names under the direction of a spiritual Master. It is also used for many other kinds of repetition practices that pertain to the lower *chakras* and lower regions.
Zikri-ruhi—Remembrance with the soul, when the devotee's attention is fixed at the third eye.
Zadadres—Greek name of the Sutlej
Zens—Zeus-pater, Greek equivalent of Vedic *Dyaushpitar*
Zero—*Metro, Sun-God,* according to Gardner, Infinite, Formless

Bibliography

(A) Primary Sources

1. Attarvaveda; : edited by Vishva Bandu, Hoshiarpur 1961, Part V, III
2. Amarakose, II : edited by Krishnaji Govind Oka; Delhi; 1961
3. Avasyaka Sutra
4. Br. Ar. Upanishad; : In the Thirteen Principal Upanishad; Tr. by R.E. Hume.
5. Caraka Samhita; : Part-I edited by SriJaideva; Delhi, 1980
6. Chand, Upanishad; : VII Vol. edited by Max Muller; New Delhi
7. Dipavamsa; : edited and tr. by H. Oldenberg, London; 1879
8. Dhammapada : edited by S.S thera, London; 1914
9. Divyavadana; : edited by E.B. Cowell and R.A. Neil; Cambridge; 1886.
10. Digha-Nikaya-I : (ed.) by Rhys Davids & J.E. Carpenter London; 1890-1911
11. Harsha Charita; : Banabhatta (Tr. by Thomas, F.W and Cowell, E.B.); Delhi; 1961
12. Jataka Pitaka : (ed.) Lionel Lokuliyana, Columba; 1960
13. Jataka Pali; : Tr. by Buddha Jayanti Tripitaka Series, Columbo, 1983
14. Jataka Pali : in Sinhalese Character; Colombo; 1926
15. Pansiyapanas : Jataka Pot Vahanse; Bandaragrama, 1987
16. Kathasaritasagar; : Somedeva (The Ocean of Story) Tr. by Tawney, C.H. London; 1924-28
17. Kadambari: : Ek Samskritik Adhyaym: (edited) by V.S. Agrawal; Varanasi; 1958.

18. Kadambari; : (edit & Tr.) by M.K. Kale; Delhi; 1968.
19. Mahavamsa; : (edited) and Tr. by Geiger, W. London 1912
20. Mahavamsa Tika; —————do—————
—
21. Majjhima Nikaya-II : Tr. by I.B. Harner, London. Reprint; 1975
22. Manu Smriti. : Tr. by G. Buhler.
23. Milinda's Questions; Book of the Buddhist vol. : Tr. by Horner, I.B London; 1964 sacred XXII
24. Mahabharata(ed) ; Tr. by P.C. Roy, Calcutta 1882, Revised by Krishnachrya Bombay (1906).
25. Medicine Buddu Sutra; : Tr. by Kinh Duoe Su, Reprint; 2001, Taiwan
26. Milindapandho; : edited by Tr. Trencker, V. London; 1964
27. Pliny's Natural History
28. Panini Ashtadhyavi, IV
29. Rig. Veda : Vol. I-II (ed) Rakesh Rani, New Dehi; 1927
30. Rig-Veda-Samhita(ed); : by Svadhyaya Mandala; 1996
31. Rig-Veda II, IV, IX, VII, VIII & Vedic Index II; :edited by Mar Muller F. London 1892
32. Rajatarangini, Kalhana : (Tr.) by M.A., Stein, Reprint, Delhi: vol. I-II, 1989
33. Si-Yu-Ki : Buddhist Records of Western World Tr. by Samuel Beal; Delhi 1969.
34. Srimad Bhagavadgita R.N. Koul, & K Aggarwal: : Tr. Sanskrit to English by S.C. Vaishy; Vol.I-II, Gorkpur (India) 2006.
35. The Life of Hiuen Tsiang : Tr. by Samuel Beal, London; 1911
36. The Grihya Sutra; : Tr. by H. Olden berg and F. Max Muller; New Delhi; 1990
37. The Jataka : (ed) V. Fausboll London, 1872-1897
38. The Jataka or Stories of the Budda's Former Live;(ed.) E.B Cowell, London; 1981
39. Taittiriya Samhita; : Tr. by A.B. Keith, Reprint I-II, New Delhi; 1967.
40. Vayu Purana; : Anand Asrama; Poona 1905
41. Valmiki Ramayana; (ed); Bhagvad : by P.C. Roy, 1881-81 Revised by Datta Lahore; 1932
42. Yuan Chwang's Travels : Tr. by Thomas Watters; 2 vols New Delhi; 1961 in India (629-645 A.D.)

(B) Modern Principal Works

43. Aryan; K.C. : Cultural Heritage of Punjab (3000 B.C to 1947 A.D); New Delhi, 1983
44. Asthana, Shashi : Pre-Harappan Culture of India and the Boderlands, New Delhi; 1985.
45. Aggarwal, D.P : Archaeology of India;Asian Institute of Asian Studies; Cophagen; 1982
46. Allchin, B & Allchin : The Rise of Civilization in India and Pakistan; Cambridge; 1982.
47. Aoyangar, S.K. : Beginning of South Indian History
48. Alkazi, Roshen : Ancient Indian Costume; Reprint, New Delhi, 2003
49. Aggrawal, Ashvini : In Search of Vedic-Harappan Relationship; New Delhi 2005
50. Acharya, Pt. S. Sharma : Divine Message of the Vedas; Mathura; Reprint; 2007
51. Ambedkar, Dr. B.R. : The Buddha and His Dhamma; Nagpur (India) 1997
52. _____do_____ : Annihilation of Caste, Aurangabad (India), Second edition, 2003.
53. _____do_____ : Who Were the Sudhras? Aurangabad (India) Second edition; 2003.
54. Basham, A.L. : The Wonder That Was India; New Delhi; Reprint, 2003.
55. _____do_____ : Adbhut Bharat; Agra 1993
56. Bhandarkar, R.G. : Vaishnavism; Saivism and Minor Religious System; Delhi
57. Briggs; G.W : The Chamars; Delhi; Reprint; 2004.
58. Bamzi, P.N.K; : History of Kashmir; Delhi, 1962.
59. Barua, B.M. : Asoka and His Inscription; 2nd Edition, Calcutta; 1955
60. Bhushan, Jamila Brij : Indian Jewellery, Ornaments and Decorative Designs: Bombay; 1969
61. Blunt, E.A.H : The Caste System of North India, New Delhi, 1969
62. Bernal, J.D : Science in History; vol. I-II, London; 1986
63. Buddharakhita; V.A. : The Buddhist Law of Kamma and rebirth Bangalore; 2001
64. Bhandarher, D.R. : Some Aspects of Ancient Hindu Polity

65. Bhattachary, S.K. : The Story of Indian Art; Delhi, Bombay, 1964

66. Benerji; S.C. : Culture Heritage of Kashmir; Calcutta; 1965

67. Barua, B.M. : Asoka and His Inscription; (2nd edition) Calcutta; 1955

68. Bhandarkar; Dr. : Asoka; (3rd edition) Calcutta; 1955

69. BaniPrasad; : State of Ancient India; Allabhad.

70. Basak; R.G. : Political History of Ancient India; Calcutta; 1933

71. Brown,P. : Indian Architecture (Buddhist and Hindu, Bombay 1949)

72. Bose: N.S : History of Civilization (Ancient India III); Calcutta; 1956

73. Bisht, R.S. : Transformation of the Harappan Culture in Punjab with Special :Reference to the Excavations at Sanghol and Chandigarh Acholealogy Congress Seminar; 1972, Kurukeshtra: 1976

74. __do__ : "Harappan Culture in Punjab: A Study in Perpective" Indus Civilization Problems and Issues, Indian Institute of Advance Study Shimla; 1977.

75. Bopearachchi, O. : 'Recent Discoveries of Ancient coins,' Colombo, 1995, 1998

76. Bala, Madu : Archaeology of Punjab; New Delhi; 1992

77. Bala, Madu & Kant, : Dhalewan-An Early Harappan Site in Punjab; Puratatva no. 30, Vishnu 2000.

78. Bala, Madu, Joshi : "The Indus Civilization": A Reconstruction on the basis of Distribution J.D. & Ramjassu of Maps", "Frontier of Indus Civilization", (ed.) B.B Lal & S.P. Gupta New Delhi, 1989

79. Cunningham, A. : Later Indo-Saythians, London, 1895

80. __do__ : Ancient Geography of India ; Varanasi; 1963.

81. Chattopadhyaya's : Early History of North India; Calcutta; 1968.

82. Cunningham; Alexandera; : Report for the Year 1872-73, Archaeological Survey of India; vol.X, Calcutta; 1875.

83. Chanda, R.P. : Survival of the Prehistoric Civilization of the Indus Valley. No. 41, Delhi, 1929

84. Colonel Tod : Rajasthan, Archaeological Survey Report I. Madras; Reprint, 1880.

85. Chothopadyaya, D.P. : History of Science in India; New Delhi; 1982.

86. Classen & Skalnik : The Early State, Hague; 1978.

87. Chakrabarti, D.K. : The External Trade of the Indus Delhi; 1990

88. Cherry and Renfrew; : The Peer-Polity Interaction & Social-Political Change; Cambridge 1986

89. Clayton, A.C. : The Rig-Veda and Vedic Reigion; New Delhi; Reprint; 1981.

90. Cunningham, Alexander; : The Stupa of Bharhut.

91. Chandra, Moti, Costumes, Taxtiles, Cosmetics and Coiffure in Ancient and Medieval India; Delhi 1973

92. Cunningham, Alexander; : Coins of Ancient India; A.S.I Vols. 1-10 Varanasi; 1966

93. Chande, M.B. : Kautilya' Arthasastra; Delhi 1998.

94. Dani, A.H. : Origin of Bronze Age culture in the Indus Basin A Geographic Prespective; Expenditure Vol; 17. no.2, 1975.

95. Dani, A.H : Excavation in the Gomal Valley, Ancient Pakistan. vol.V. Peshwar; 1970-71

96 Davaid, Frawley : Gods, Sages and Kings: Vedic Secrets of Ancient Civilization; New Delhi; 1991

97. Dubreuil, G.J. : Vedic Antiquities; 1924

98. David, Frawley; Rajaram & Navratna's : Vedic Aryans and the Origins of Civilization; New Delhi; 1991

99. Dhamma, Rewata; : Emptying the Rose-Apple Seat; USA 2003

100. Dales, G.F & Kenoyer, : The Harappan Project 1986-1989, New Investigation at an Ancient J.M Indus City Harappan Civilization; ed. G.l. possehl. 1993

101. De, Terra, De Chardi : Palaeolithic Industries in the North West Panjab and Kashmir and Howkes, J.C. their Geological Significace "Memories of the Connectict Academy of Science and Art. Vol. VIII. 1934

102. De. Terra & Paterson : Studies on the Ice Age in India and Associated Human Cultures, T.T. Washington; 1939

103. Durrani F.A. : Excavation at Rehman Dheri, paper contributed to the IVth Internation Congress of South Asia; Archaeology at Naples, July 1977.

104. __do__ : "Evidence West of Indus", Indus Civilization -New Perspective. ed. tor, A.H. Dani. Islamabad; 1981

105. Davids, Rhys Mrs. : Buddhist Psychology, London; 1920

106. ___do____ : Compendiam of Philosophy; London; 1910

107. Dorothy Fisk's : Monograph Entitled "Bouqhet for Doctor," London.

Dr. Van Lohuizernde Leewu study of the Scythain Period

108. Dhavlikar; : Cultural Imperialism: Indus Civilization in Western India; New Delhi 1995.

109. Dikshitar; V.K.R. : Maurya Polity

110. Datta, N.K : Origin and Growth of Caste in India; Calcutta; Vol.1, 1908, Vol.II, 1965

111. Devahuti, D. : Harsa Political Study; Vol.1, New Delhi, 1983.

112. Dube, S.C. : Tribal Heritage of India; New Delhi; 1972.

113. Dasgupta, Satadal; : Caste Kingship and Community; Patna 1993.

114. Dutt, R.C. : History of Civilization in Ancient India

115. Elplinstone; : History of India

116. Elliot, H.M. : Memoirs of the Races of the North Western Provinces of India; Vol.1 1869

117. Engels, Frederick : The Origin of the Family; Private Proverty and the State; Lucknow; 2006

118. Fleet, J.F. : Corpus Inscriptionum Indicarum; vol. I-III, Calcutta 188, Revised by Bhandarkar D.R. New Delhi; 1981

119. Fairservis, W.A : The Roots of Ancient India; University of Chicago Press, 1915.

120. Filliozat, J. : The Classical Doctrine of Indian Medicine; Delhi; 1964

121. Fairservise, W.A. : The Origin, Character and the Decline of the Early Civilization; New York; 1967

122. ___do___ : The Harappan Civilization and Its Writings; New Delhi; 1992

123. Farquhar J.N : Primer of Hinduism

124. Fabres, Charles : Indian Dress; New Delhi, Reprint 1977

125. Gupta, S.P : The Indus-Saraswati Civilization: Origins; Problem and Issue; New Delhi; 1996

126. Gopalakrishna,N. : Indian Scientific Heritage; Trivandrum, 2000

127. Gupta, P. : Anthropological Interpretation of the Astrology of Celestial Bodies; Patna 2005

128. Gore, A.l: : Earth in the New Delhi; 1993 Balance;

129. Ghosh; N.N. : Early History of India

130. Gokhale, B.C, : Ancient India

131. Gangopadhyay; : R. Some Materials for the Study of Agriculture and Agricultarists in Ancient India; Calcutta; 1933

132. Ghurya, G.S. : Indian Costume; Bombay, Reprint, 1966

133. ___do___ : Caste and Race In India; Bombay, 1969

134. Goswami, Jay, : Cultural History of Ancient India; Delhi 1974.

135. Halim, M.A : Excavations at Sarai Khola Pt. II, Pakistan Archaeology no. 8. 1972.

136. Hawker, Jacquelta; : The First Great Civilization; New York;

137. Howell, F.C. : Early Man; Nederland, Reprint 1970.

138. Habib, Irfan : The Indus Civilization; New Delhi; 2002

139. Havel, E.V. : Aryan Rule of India

140. Hooker, J.D & J. : Introductory Essay to the Flora Indica; 1855 Thomson

141. Harold, A. Gonld : The Hindu Caste System; Delhi, 1987

142. Husain, Majid; : Geography of Jammu and Kashmir. New Delhi; 1985

143. Jois, M. Rama : Guruji and Social Harmony; Karnataka; 1968

144. Joshi, C. M. : Studies in the Buddhist Culture of India; Delhi Reprint; 1977

145. Jain, R.C. : The Most Ancient Aryan Society; Rajasthan; 1985

146. Jai Singh, Hari : India between Dream and Reality; New Delhi 1989

147. Jauhari, Manorame : Politics and Ethics in ancient India; Varanasi, 1968

148. Jaiswal, O.P. : Science and society in Ancient India some Reflection, Presidential Address, 66th Session, Santiniketean 2005-06

149. Jagadeeshan, P. : Social Justice and Challanges in Contemporary India; Lecture Series, Bangalore; 2006

150. Jaira Zbhoy, R.A. : Foreign Influence in ancient India Bombay 1963.

151. Jha, Vivekanand : Caste untouchability and social justice (Early North Indian Perspective), Indian 57 Session; Chenni, 1996

152. James, E.O. : Primitive Ritual and Belief; 1917

153. Jaini, J. : Outline of Jainism

154. Jha, D.N. : Looking for a Hindu Identity, Presidential Address, Indian History Congress, 66th session, 2006, Santiniketan.

155. Jain, P.C. & Kothia, D.L Jaina Purana Kosa (in Hindi) Rajasthan 1993.

156. J. Takakusu : Tr. A. Record of Buddhist Religion as Practised in India and the Malay Archipelago (A.D. 671-695) by I-Tsing; Delhi; 1966

157. Jaitly, Jay : Crafts of Jammu, Kashmir and Ladakh; Ahmedabad; 1990

158. Joshi, J.P. : The Nature of Settlement of Surkotd in D.P. Aggarwal and D.K. Chakrabarti (ed) Essays in Indian Protohistory; New Delhi 1979.

159. John, Victoria : The Journey of the Soul; Beas, Reprint, 2004

160. Jaco Bson; (ed) : The Harappan Civilization: An Early State; Delhi 1936.

161. Kak; R.C. : Antiquities of Basohli and Ramanaga; New Delhi; 1972.

162. ___do___ : Ancient Monuments of Kashmir; New Delhi; 1971

163. Kane, P.V. : The History of Dharamasastra; Poona I-IV, 1942.

164. Katoch, A.C. : Discovery of Kangra; Gurgaon, 2004.

165. Kaw, R.N. : The Neolithic Culture of Kashmir, Essays in India Protohistory: (eds) D.P. Agarwal & D.K. Chakraborty; 1979

166. Krishnaswami, V.D. : 'Progress in Prehistory', Ancient India, No. 9, New Delhi, 1985.

167. ___do___ : 'Stone Age in India', Ancient India, No.3 New delhi, 1947.

168. Khuhro; & : Sindh Through the Centuries; Karchi; 1981 Hamida

169. Kapur, M.L. : History of Jammu and Kashmir State; vol.1-II

170. Khanna, A.N. : Archaeology of India; New Delhi 1984

171. Kumar, Raj, : Paintings & Lifestyles of Jammu Region. (From 17th to 19th Century A.D.); Delhi, 2 vols. 2006

172. ___do___ : Encylopeadia of Untouchables; New Delhi, 2008

173. Kumar, Raj : History of the Brahmans; Delhi; 2006
174. ___do____ : History of the Chamar Dynasty, 2 vols, New Delhi 2008
175. ___do ____ : Ambedkar and His Writing; Delhi; 2008
176. Kesarwani, Arun : Pre-Historic Punjab: A Reassessment (From the Dawn of man to the Fisrt Urban Civilization). Presidential Address; 37 Sastgra 2005, Punjab University Patiala
177. Kenoyer, J.M. : Ancient Cities of the Indus Civilization New Delhi; 1998.
178. Kern : Manual of Indian Buddhism
179. Kundra & Bawa : History of Ancient India; Reprint Delhi, 2006.
180. Koul Deambi : History and Culture of Ancient Gandhara and Western B.K Himalayas from Sarada Epigraphic Sources; New Delhi; 1990
181. Ketkar; S.V. : History of the Caste in India; 2 vols. 1911
182. Khurana; K.L : Ancient India; Agra; 2nd edition 2004.
183. Kaegi, Adolf : Rigveda; Ginn & Co.
184. Kunte; M.M. : Vicissitudes of Aryan in India; Bombay
185. Lal, B.B. : The Earliest Civilization of South Asia; New Delhi 1997
186. Lal, B.B. : The Banganga-Beas Palaeolithic Industry. A look back Puratatahva No.II, New Delhi 1982
187. Lewis, G.E. : Human Kind Emerging, Reprint, New York, 1979.
188. Luniya; B.N. : Evolution of Indian Culture; Agra, Reprint 2005.
189. ___do___ : Prachin Bharatiya Sanskrit, Agra; 1994
190. Lenin, : The State and Revolution; Lucknow; 2006
191. Lal, B.B. & Gupta S.P. : Frontier of the Indus Civilization; Delhi; 1984.
192. Luders : Evolution India, Vol. XXIV

193. Lal, B.B : Excavations at Hastinapur and other Exploration in the Upper Ganga and Sutluz Basins; 1950-52, New Delhi; 1954-55
194. Gupta Saraswati Nadi; : Shri Baba Bahab Apte Samarak Samiti, Nagapur; 1992
195. Longman's : History of India
196. Law, B.C. : Buddhist Conception of Spirits
197. Limbale, Sharan Kumar; : Towards an Aesthetic of Dalit Literature; Tr. from Marathi by Alok Mukherjee; New Delhi, 2004
198. Leeming, Joseph, : Yoga and the Bible, (Bias) India; Reprint; 2004.
199. Labour of Love; : The Maharaj Jagat Singh, Medical Relief Society; Punjab (India); 1996.
200. Munishi; K.M. Majumdar R.K & Majumdar, R.C. : The Classical Age; (Editor); Bombay 1962.
201. Majumdar; R.C. : Ancient India; Reprint Delhi 1968
202. Mookerji, R.K. : Asoka; London; 1928.
203. ___do____ : Ancient India; Allahabad, 'India', 1956
204. Mukerjee, B.N : Kushana Silver coins; Calcutta; 1982
205. Maqsood, Ruqaiyyah : Islam. U.K; 1994
206. Majumdar, R.C. : Classical Age; Bombay, 1954
207. Mookerji, R.K. : Chandra Gupta Maurya and His Times; Delhi, 1966
208. Majumdar, R.C. : The Classical Accounts of India; Calcutta; 1960.
209. Mookerji, R.K. : Harsha; (2nd edition); Delhi; 1959
210. Majumdar; R.C. : Age of Imperial Kanauj; Bombay; 1965
211. ___ do ___ : Struggle for Empire; Bombay, 1957
212. Mughal, M.R.(ed.) : Excavation at Jalipur; Pakistan Archaeology; No.8. Karchi; 1972.
213. __do__ : 'Early Harrappan Culture from Jalilpur; Pakistan Archaeology; Vol.22. No.2, 1974.
214. Manmathan, M.R. (edi) : Archaeology in Kerala; Past and Present; Kozhikode; 2007.

215. Mohapatra, G.C. : Lithic Industries of Himachal Pradesh, Perspective in Palaeoanthropology D. Sen Feschrift, (ed) A.K. Gosh;

216. Meadow, R.H. : Harappa Excavation 1986-90 Madison & Kenoyer, J.M. ; 1991 Mohenjo-Daro and Indus Civilization; London; 1931 Marshall, J.

217. Majumdar, R.C. : An Advance History of India; London; 1963 Raychandhuri; H.C. & K. Datta

218. Malala Sekeri, G.P. : Dictionary of Pali Proper Names II. Modern Asian Studies; Vol. 38, Calcutta, 2004

219. Mitra, R.L : Indo-Aryans-Beef Eating in Ancient India; Calcutta; 1881

220. Monier-Williams : M. Sanskrit-English Dictionary, Delhi 1963

221. ___do__ : Brahmanical Hinduism; 1891.

222. Malik, S.C. : Indian Civilization and the Formative Period; Shimla; 1987.

223. Mughal, R. : Ancient Cholistans; Archaeology and Architecture; Lahore; 1997.

224. Marcia Fentress; : "The Indus Granaries....." in K.A.R, Kennedy & G.L. Possehl and Palaeonthropology of South Asia; New Delhi; 1984.

225. Majumdar, R.C. : The Vedic Age; Bombay Reprint; 1988

226. Mookerji; R.K. : Hindu Civilization;

227. McCrindle, J.W. : Invasion of Alexander;

228. Mackay; : Indus Valley Civilization, Delhi

229. ___do___ : Mohenjodaro and Indus Valley Civilization

230. ___do___ : Further Excavation at Mohnenjodaro; Vol.1-2

231. Macdonald, A.A : Vedic Index of Names and Subjects; 2 Vol.1 London; 1912

232. ___do ____ : A history of Sanskrit Literature; Heinemann; 1900

233. Marshall, Sir John : Mohenjodaro and the Indus Civilization, Vols. 1-II, London; 1931

234. Majumdar R.C. : An Advance History of India;
235. Mukoorji; A.C : Hindu Fasts and Feasts; 1966.
236. Mishra, Y. : Asoka Hn; Patna; 1993
237. Mishra, S.C. : Evolution of Kautilyas Arthasastra; Delhi 1997.
238. Murdoch, J.M : Review of Caste System in India; New Delhi; 1977.
239. Muller, Max : Ancient Sanskrit Literature
240. Maurice; : The Religion of the Veda; 1908
241. Nitivakyamstam of Somedeva Suri, Prakiraka
242. Nehru, J.L. : The Discovery of India; New Delhi; 1999
243. Nyanatiloka; : Buddhist Dictionary; Dehradun (India), 1946
244. Oosten, J. : The War of the Gods; The Social Code in Indo-European Mythology; London; 1985
245. Prufer, Olaf : Interim Report on the Excavations Carried out at Dher Majra; Jamia Millia Islamia Historic Research Foundation; Nalagarh. 1951
246. __do__ : Interim Report on the Excations Carried out at Dher Majra; Calcutta, 1952
247. Pande, B.M. : Inscribed Harappan Potshered from Chandigarh; Puratattva, No.6 1972-73
248. Patnaik, Naveen : The Garden of life; New York; 1994
249. Plamintr, P.S. : Basic Buddhism Course; U.S.A, 1991
250. Possehl, G.L. : Harappan civilization; New Delhi 1982
251. Piggott, S. : Prehistoric India, Middlesex U.K. 1952
252. Puri, J.R. & Khak, K.S : Sultan Bahu; Punjab (India); 1998
253. Piyatissa, Anderson : Buddhist Tales for Young and Old, New York, 1995
254. Possehl, G.L : Indus Age: The Writing System Philadelphia; 1996
255. Puskas : Society and Religion in the Indus Valley civilization in B. Allchin (edited) in 'South Asian Archaeology': 1981.

256. Parpola; : Deciphering the Indus Script; cambridge 1994.
257. Possehl, G.H. : Ancient Cities of the Indus; New Delhi
258. __do__ : The Indus Civilization; New Delhi
259. Proceedings of the Indian History Congress; 64th session, Myrore, 2003.
260. ___do_____________do_______________65th session Bareilly 2004.
261. _____do__________do________66th session, Santinikatan; 2005-06.
262. __________do____________________ 67th session, Kerala 2007
263. Punjab History Conference Proceedings, Patiala March 18-20, 2004
264. _________do________________ March 18-20, 2005____________
265. ____________ do __________ March 18-20, 2006_____________
266. Puri, B.N. : 'Cities of Ancient India; Delhi; 1966
267. Pande, G.C. : Foundations of Indian Culture; New Delhi 1923.
268. Prabhavananda, Swami : The Spiritualism Heritage of India; London, 1962
269. Rao, S.R. : Lothal and the Indus civilization; Bombay; 1973
270. Rose, H.A : A Glossary of the Tribes and Castes of the Punjab and North-West Frontier Province; Language Department Punjab; Reprint Vol. I-III, 1990
271. Roy, P.C. : 'Studies in the History of Science in India' Presidential Address, Madras University, edited by D.P Chattopadyaya, New Delhi 1982
272. Ray, P. & Sen, S.N. (ed.) : The Cultural Heritage of India; Vol. IV, Calcutta; 1986
273. Ratnagar, S. : Enquiries in the Political Organisation of Harappan Society; New Delhi; 1991.
274. __do__ : Understanding Harappan Civilization; New Delhi; 2001.
275. __do__ : Encounters, the Westerky Trade of the Harappan Civilization; Delhi, 1981.
276. Rambach & de Golish : The Golden Age of Indian Art.
277. Radhakrishan; : Indian Philosophy
278. Ray, S.C. : Coins and Culture -An Archaeological Approach; New Delhi; 1995
279. Rhys Devis, T.W. : Buddhism in India; 1903.
280. Raychaudhuri, H.C. : Political History of Ancient India; 6th edition, Calcutta 1955.

281. Randhawa, M.S. : A History of Agriculture in India, New Delhi, vol. 1980.

282. Ramesh, B.G. : Biography Series of Dr. B.R. Ambedkar, Banglore, 2005

283. Rao, B.V. : World History; New Delhi: Reprint; 2003.

284. Rangacharya; (Tr.) : Ganit Sarsangrah (Mahaviracharya); Madras; 1912

285. Roy, D.K. : Museology, Some Cute Points; Delhi; 2006

286. Singh, Huzur Maharaja Sawan; Philosophy of the Masters; Beas; I-V vols. Reprint; 2006

287. Sastri, K.A.N. : History of the South India, Madras, 1966

288. Sastri, K.A.N. : Age of the Nandas and Maurya; Varanasi, 1967

289. Sastri, K.A.N. : History cf South India; Madras; 1933

290. Sinha, P.N. : Decline of the Kingdom of Magadha; Patna; 1954

291. Sircar, D.C. : Select Inscriptions (Bearing on India History and civilization); Calcutta; 1942

292. Sen; B.C. : Some Historical Aspects of the Inscriptions of Bengal, Calcutta; 1942

293. Sexsena, S.K. : Political History of Kashmir; Lucknow 1974.

294. Sen, D. : 'Nalagarh Palaeolithic Culture', Man in India, vol. 35, 1955.

295. Simons, Elwynl. : Primate Evolution, Mecmillan; 1972

296. Shridharan, K. : History of India, Delhi, 1965.

297. Sudhir Nigam; : Devtaon Ka Peyarasa 'Som arasa,' Rajiv Ved Prakash Pahava (ed; Veda Amrita, Bombay, 2003

298. Sarao, K.T.S. : Urban Centres and Urbanization as Reflected in the Pali Vinaya and Sutta Pitakas; Delhi; 1990

299. Singh Maharaj Charan : 'Die to Live' Beas;

300. Sharma, Y.D : 'Past Patterns in Living as Unfolded by Excavations at Ropar'; lalita Kala No. 1-2, 1955-56

301. __do__ : Comments in Indian Prehistory; 1964 (eds) V.N. Mishra and M.S. Mats(Vats).

302. ___do__ : Value of Common Painted Ceramic Designs from Different Sites as Guide to Chronology with special reference to pottery from Bara (Punjab) Radiocarban and India Archaeology; (ed) D.P. Agrawal and A. Ghosh.

303. __do__ : 'Transformation of the Harappa Culture in the Punjab' Archaeological Congress and Seminar papers, 1972, Kurukestra, 1976

304. __do__ : Harappan Complexion Sutlej, Harappan Civilization (ed) G.L. Possehl; 1982

305. __do__ : The Pre-Harappan Culture in Panjab, Puratatva vol.II, 1982

306. __do__ : 'Fresh Light on Bara Culture from Mohoram Archaeology and History; Essays in Memory of A. Ghosh (eds) B.M. Panda & B.D. Chattopadhyaya, New Delhi. 1987

307. __do__ : Harappan Remains at Ropar, Purattva No. 31, 2001

308. Sircar, D.C : Studies in the Geography of Ancient and Medieval India; Delhi1960

309. Sharma, Arvind : Of Hindu, Hindustan, Hinduism and Hindutva; Numen, Vol. 49, 2002.

310. Satyaprakash; : Vaigyanik Vikas Ka Bharatiya Parampara (in Hindi) Patna; 1954

311. ____do____ : Prachin Bharat Me Rasayan Ka Vikas; U.P. 1960

312. Shing, Amar, : Archaeology of the Vedic Age in Haryana, Presidental Address, Punjab History Conference, 36th session, 2004, Patiala.

313. Shaffer, Jim : Late Harappan; 1981

314. Singh, Jogeshwar : Indus Valley Civilization and Their Religion. An article presented in Patiala History Conference; 2005

315. Sharma, R.S. : Material Background of the Origin of Buddhim, in Das Kapital Centenary Volume; New Delhi; 1968

316. Shaffer, Jim : 'Harappan Culture: A Reconsideration' in G.L. Possehl (edited) in Harappan Civilization Delhi; 1982
317. Sircar, Jadunath : India through the age; New Delhi.
318. Stevenson, Mrs. T. : Heart of the Jainism.
319. Sharma, R.S. : Urban Decay in India; Delhi, 1987
320. Sharma, R.S. : Ancient India, New Delhi 1977
321. Sharma; R.S : Sudras in Ancient India, Reprint; Delhi; 1990
322. Sanghasena, Bhikkhu; : The Life of the Buddha - P-I, II Bangalore; 1982
323. Smith, V.A. : History of Fine Arts in India and Ceylon.
324. __do__ : Early History of India; 2 vol. oxford; 1924
325. __do__ : Hindu Civilization
326. Swarup, Shanti : Arts and Crafts of India and Pakistan, Bombay 1957.
327. Shukla D.N. : RoyalArts, Faizabad (U.P) 1969
328. Sharma, Vas Dev. : Cosmic View of life in Guru Nanak Bani, Department of Punjabi language, 1996
329. Saini, B.S. : The Social and Economic History of Punjab; New Delhi 1975.
330. Tale of the Mystic East; Beas : Reprint; 2006
331. Thapar, R. : Asoka and the Decline of the Mauryas Oxford; 1961
332. Taher, Mohamed (ed.) : Islam the Religion of Submission; New Delhi; 1998
333. Thapar, R. : A History of India Volume One, New Delhi; edith 2003.
334. Tripathi, R.S. : History of Ancient India; Delhi; 1960
335. __do__ : History of Kanauj; Benaras 1937
336. Thakran : R.C 'Protohistoric Settlemen Patterns in Haryana in K.M. Shrimali (ed) Reason and Archaeology, New Delhi; 1998
337. ___do___ : Kya Harrapan Sabhyata Saraswat the (Hindi); New Delhi; 2002

338. The Cultural Heritage of India; Vol. I-II
339. The Cambridge History of India. Vol.I-II
340. Tarn, W.W. : The Greeks in Bectria and India. (Ptolemy, VII).
341. Vaidya, K.L. : The Culture Heritage of Himalaya; New Delhi, 1977
342. Vats, M.S. : "Kotla Nihang" Annual Report of Archaeology Survey of India 1929-30
343. Vannucci, M. : Human Ecology in the Vedas; New Delhi; 1999
344. Vidyalankar, P.S. : The Vedas; Delhi, 1983
345. Vidyadhar : Jammu Past and Present, Jammu
346. Wadia, D.N. : Geology of India, London; 1957
347. Whitehead, R.B. : Catalogue of Coins in the Punjab Museum.
348. Wheeler, R.E.M. : 'Harrappa 1946 the Defences and Cemetery R. 37, Ancient India No.3, 1947
349. Waddell, L.A. : The Makers of Civilization, Angriff Press, 1929.
350. Weisman; C.A. : The Origin of Race and Civilization; SFA; 1940
351. Wheeler, R.E.M : Indus Civilization; Cambridge 1968.
352. Walton H.G. : A Monograph on the Training and Working in Leather; 1903.
353. Willson, H.H : Hindu History of Kashmir; Calcutta; 1960
354. Willson; H.H. : Translation of the Rigveda Samhita (Allen)
355. Warmington; : Commerce Between Roman Empire and India.
356. William, Monier. : Brahminism and Hinduism
357. Zanaide-A-Ragozin; Vedic India; New Delhi; 1961.

(C) Periodical Works: Magazine, Papers and Articles

358. Dalit Voice; (ed) V.T. Rajshekar. Sept, 2006.
359. Daily Excelsior, Sunday Magazine, Feb. 18, 2007
360. ___do___ June 10, 2007
361. __do__ June 17, 2007
362. __do___ April 1, 2007

363. __do__ 24 June, 2007

364. __do___, November 2, 2008

365. __do___ 17 Feb, 2008

366. Indian Express; dated 11-8-2007

367. Indian History Congress, 67th Session Souvenir, 2007, Calicut.

368. __do__ : 66th, Santiniketan, 2006

369. ___do___ : 65th, Bareilly (U.P)2004

370. __do__ : 68th, Delhi, 2007

371. Kashmir Time; dated 5-4-2008

372. Saha; M.N : Research Journal Asiatic society: Kushana; 1913-14

373. Sylvain Levi; : Journal Asiatique, 1900

374. State Time; Magazine, dated 10-2-2008

375. The Tribune, August 26, 2008, Emperor Marcus Aurelius Rises in Turkey; New Item. Discovery of Head and Foot of the King (London).

376. Daily Excelsior Magazine; Sunday, Oct. 19, 2008, and article written by A.K. Khanna, 'The Mighty Chandrabhaga'.

377. _________do_____ Sunday, January 18, 2009, an article written by K.K. Khullar; 'Wonderful Legacy'.

378. _________do_____ Dec. 21, 2008, an article written by S.K. Padha; 'Preserve the Past'.

Index

D